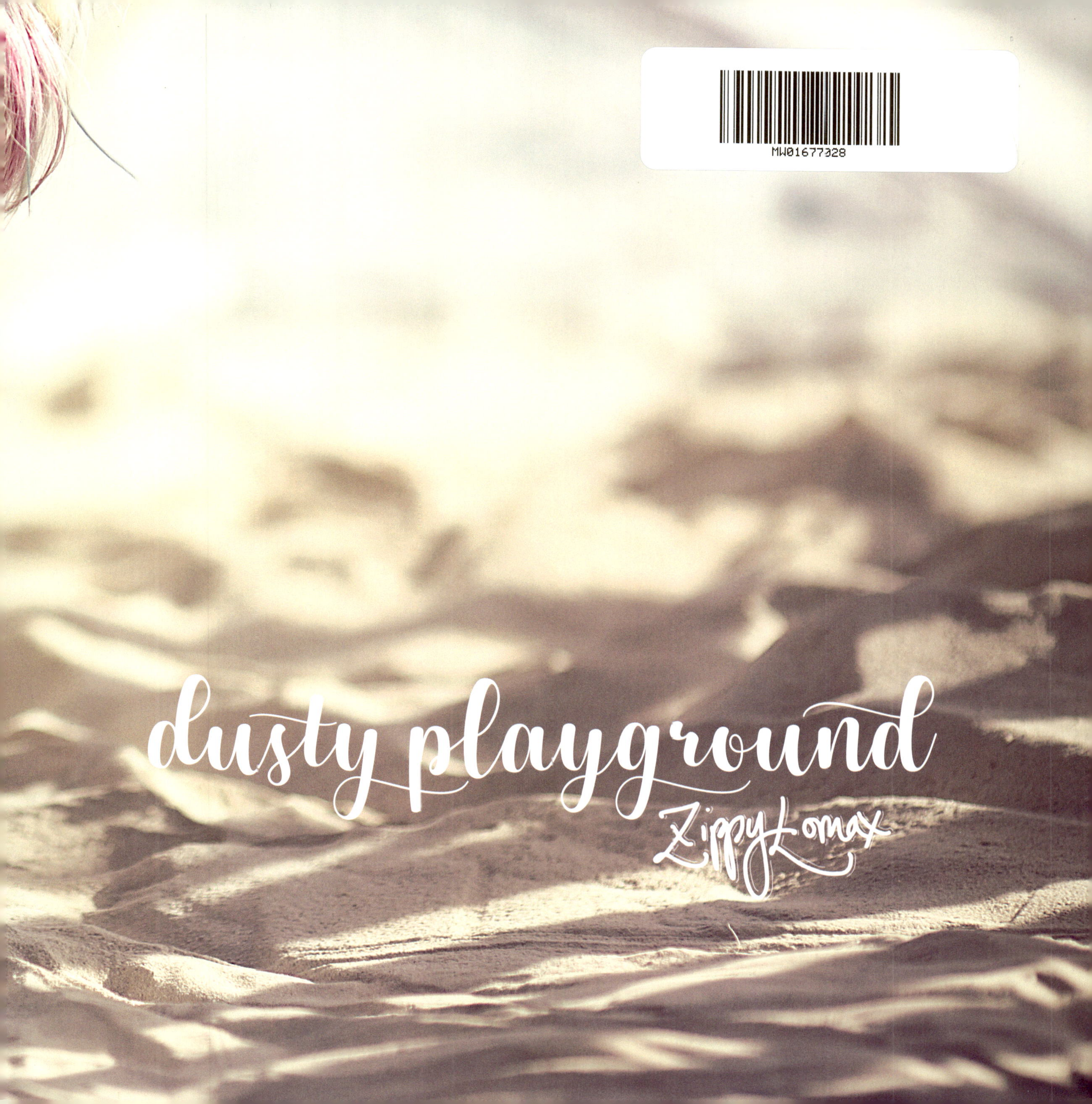
dusty playground
Zippy Lomax

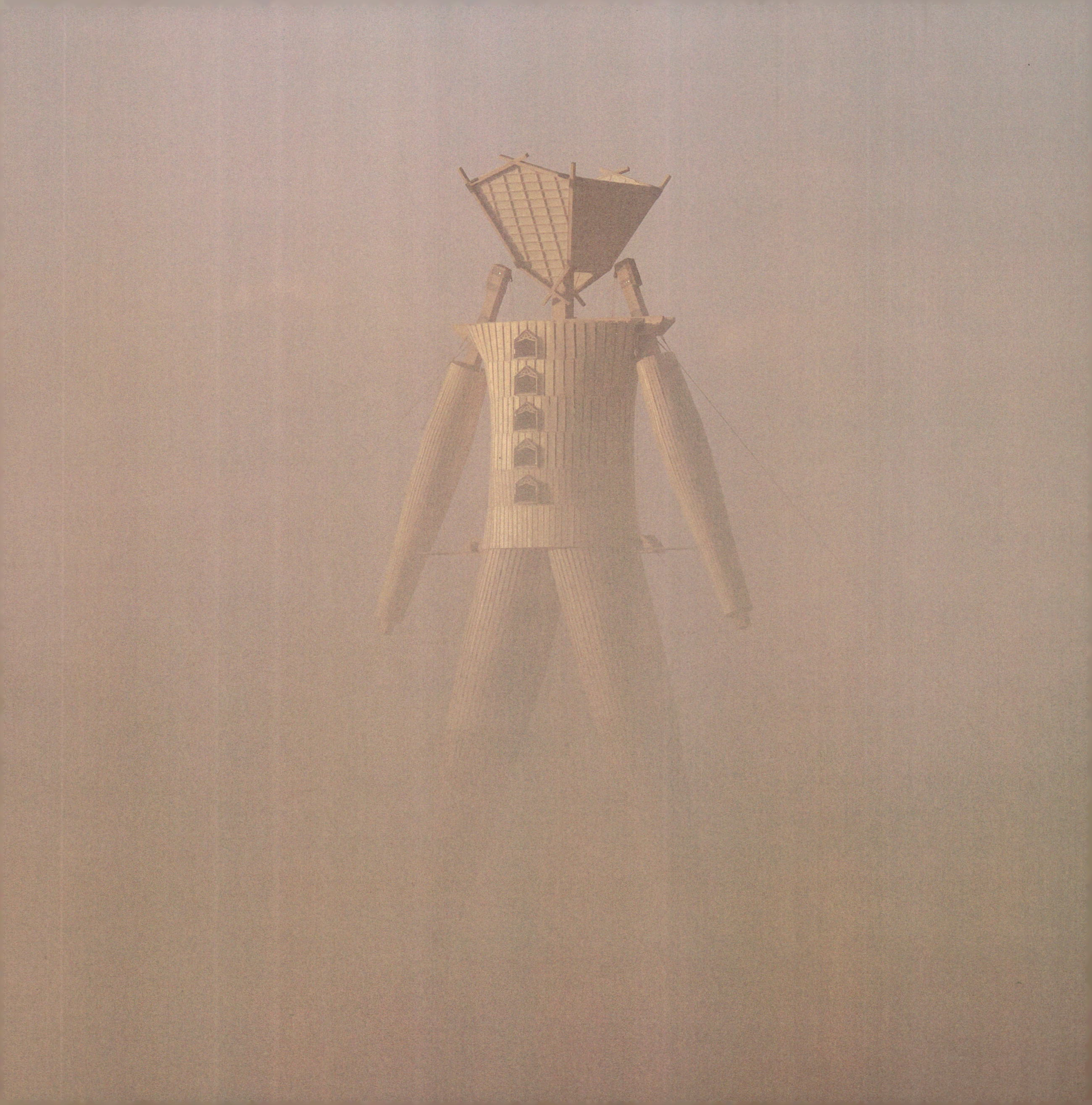

Foreword

By the end of the 90's it was clear to me that Burning Man was on a trajectory to a healthy community of like-minded people. Our desire was to make sure it never became insular or closed; newbies should be welcome, diversity should be embraced, and change should be applauded. It was clear to me then that we should prepare the way for families! Why? In a healthy environment people meet, fall in love, and have families, right?

In 1998 I did what I could. I started a camp for families by creating an email discussion list on the Burning Man Mailman email server, and designated a plot of land in Black Rock City called Kids Camp (before my own family was even a twinkle in my eye). With little more assistance from me it has grown steadily, regrouped into a village, and thrived. Today it is vibrant and bursting at the seams – full of traditions, stories, and people who have grown up at Burning Man. Whether you live at Kidsville or not (and many families don't) the proliferation of children at the event is evidence that we are a healthy ecosystem.

My daughter describes Burning Man as a place where 'adults can play like kids'. I'll take this one step further and remind us that playing is one of the most rewarding forms of experimentation toward learning – *that's why kids do it.* That's what so many adults rediscover at Burning Man – spontaneous, inspired, non-judgmental play. Thank god for the young ones at Burning Man showing us how and why.

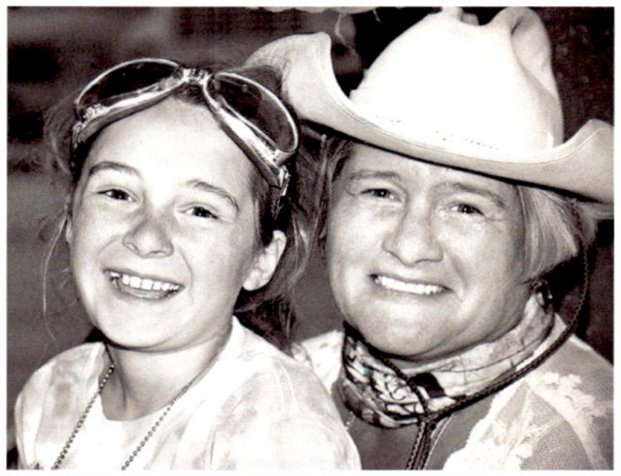

HARLEY K. DUBOIS • CO-FOUNDER, BURNING MAN

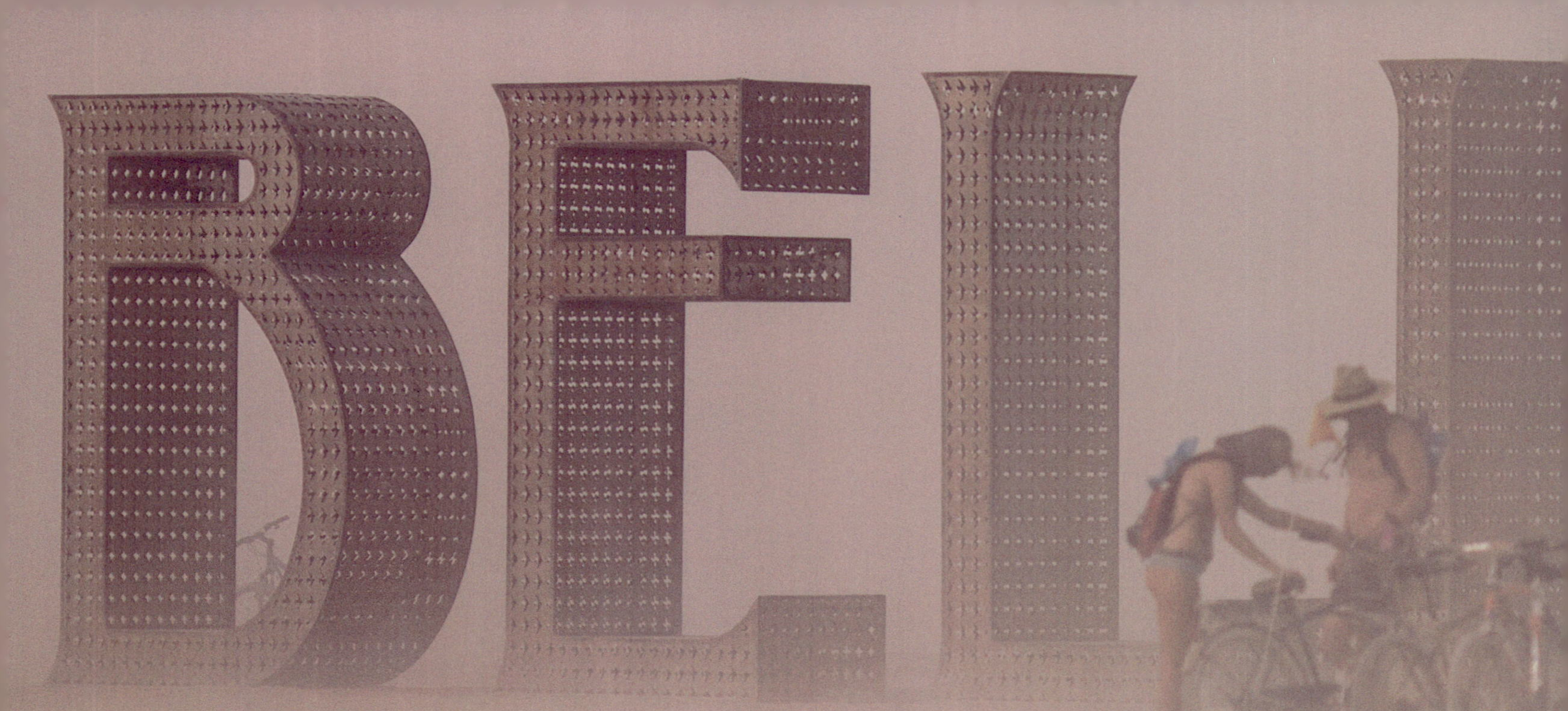

Introduction

In 2002, while meandering through Center Camp, I happened upon an adorable infant sitting on the ground, running her hands through the fine, alkaline dust. She can't have been more than a year or so, not yet toddling. 'Indeed,' I thought as I noticed her plain white onesie with its unapologetic declaration of 'f#@k Bush' written across her chest.

I was instantly enamored, watching how engaged she was in the simple task of repeatedly scooping up fistfuls of dust and letting it spill through her tiny fingers. I was struck by her easy presence, noting how she seemingly had no aversion to this ubiquitous substance that so many find intolerable. To her – as to countless children before and after – the dust was a fascinating plaything unlike any she'd yet encountered.

Though the dream of creating this book was not seeded until many years later, that moment clarified my awareness, drawing my attention to the smallest among us. I recall thinking she would undoubtedly grow up with a broader worldview than her non-Burner peers. I imagined the kind of parents she must have had – unabashed in their bold opinions, clearly not afraid to say the 'wrong' or 'unpopular' thing, tenacious enough to bring an infant into the Black Rock Desert. I thought about how the world needs people like that – adventurous folks who recognize the importance of exposing their children to diverse experiences – to raise kids with the kind of grit required to create meaningful change. Fifteen years later – I believe that more than ever.

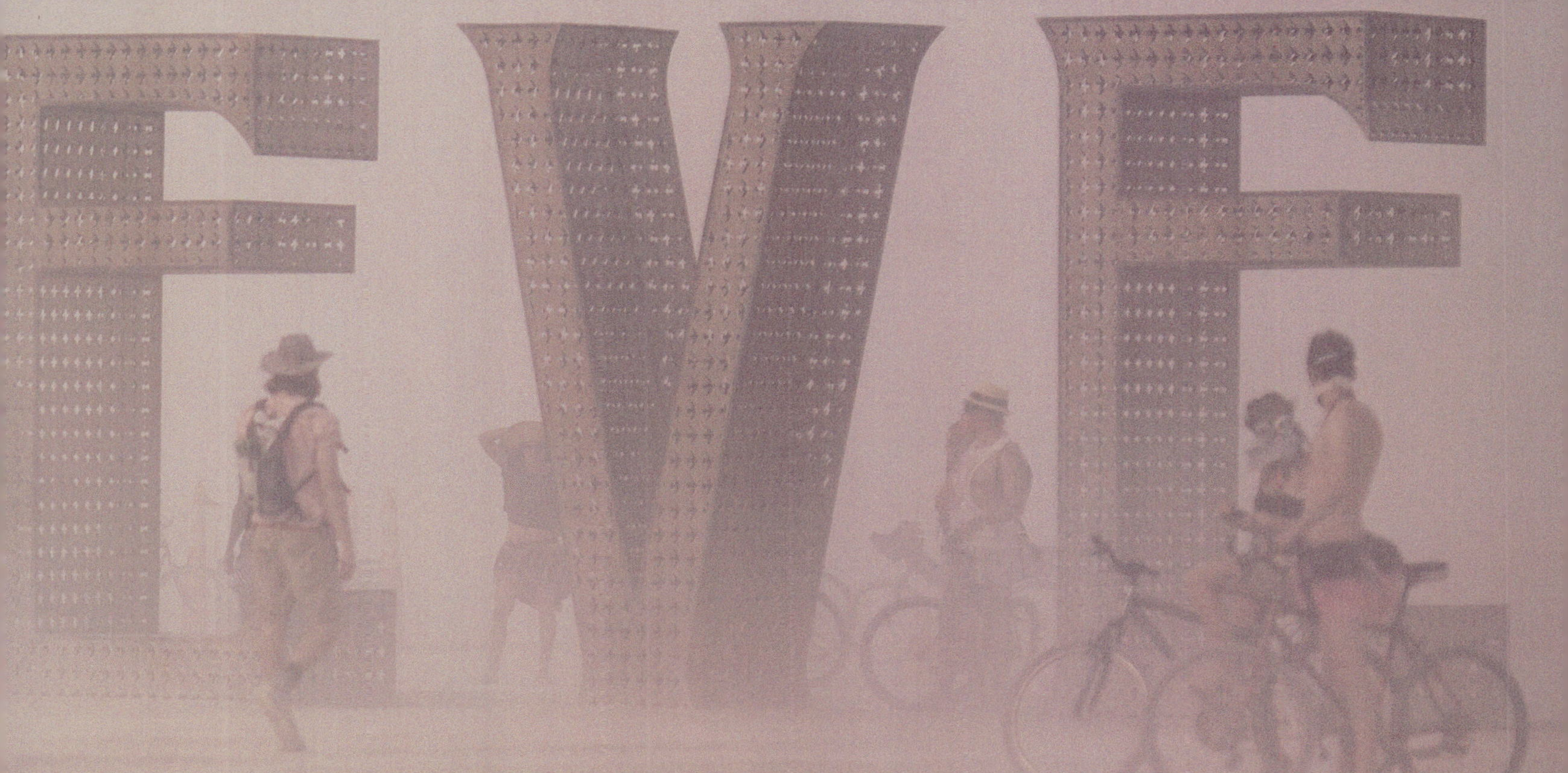

Black Rock City is both a playground and a classroom – learning is an inevitable byproduct of participation in the grand, lively experiment that is Burning Man. Beyond the innumerable, micro-lessons one gleans from individual interactions, there is immeasurable value in being surrounded by thousands of people from across the planet – to be so unified by the shared experience of becoming 'playafied'; covered in dust – momentarily blurring the lines that ordinarily separate. For one, precious week a year, we share the same address, each seeking our own experience yet joined in our mutual vulnerability to the elements – an incredible metaphor for our interconnection as a species, facing global uncertainty, together.

As the population of BRC has grown, the presence of children has blossomed accordingly. I've continued watching – through my own evolution and creative development – deepening my respect and appreciation for the littlest Burners. I suspect they're gaining beneficial insight – an incomparable education in creative innovation, thinking beyond themselves and imagining without limits.

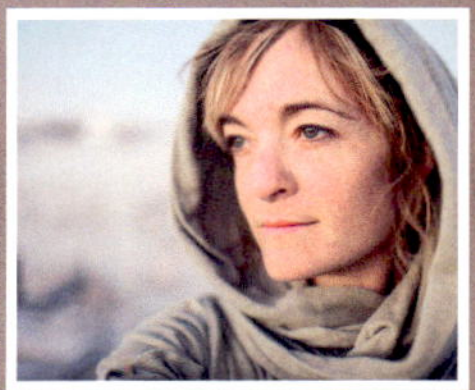

For these dusty little sages who remind me always to be curiously present and light of heart – I offer this book – not as a linear story, but as a grateful record of the bright young ones I've had the honor of meeting in the dust.

With Love, Zippy Lomax

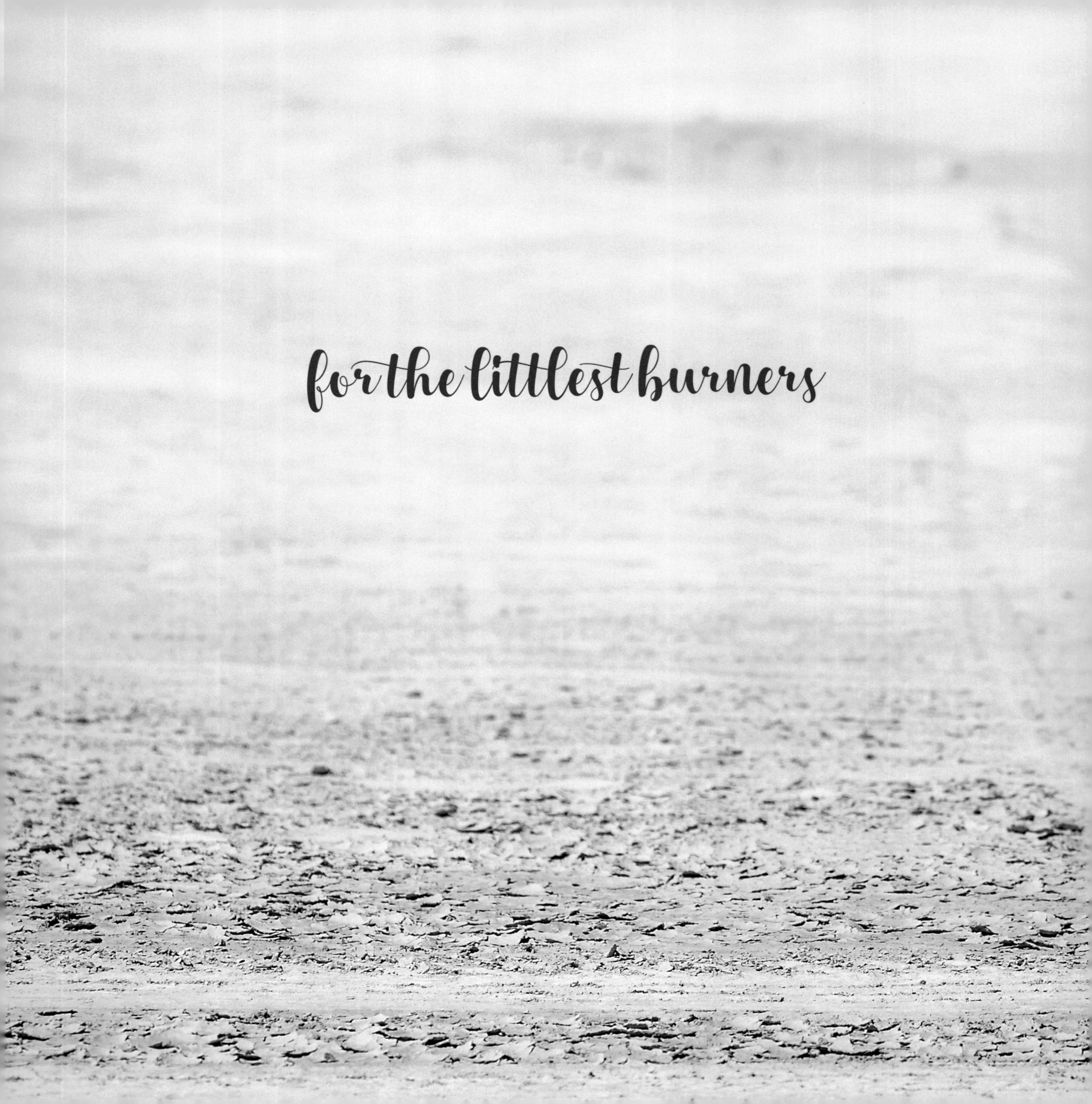

for the littlest burners

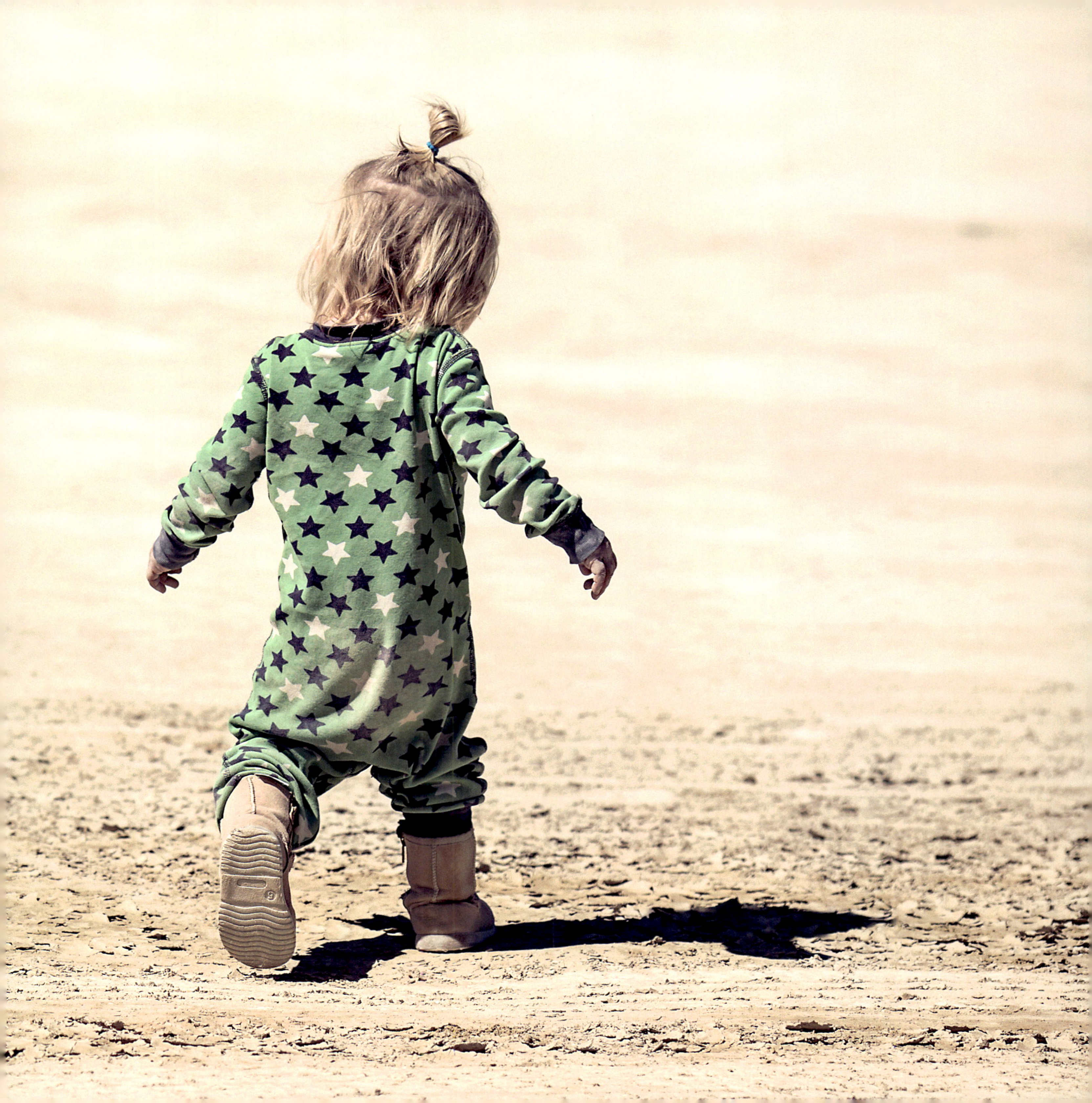

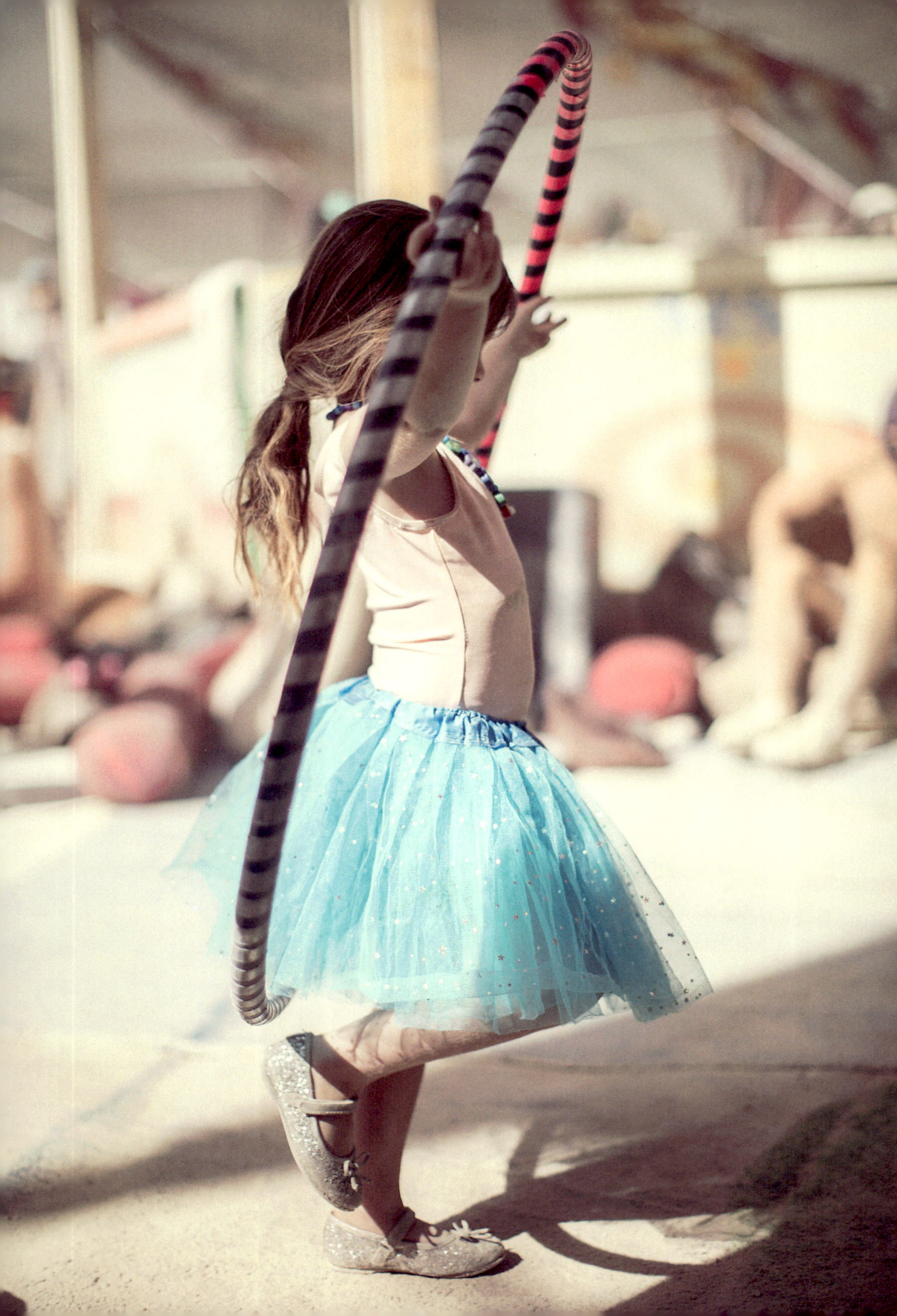

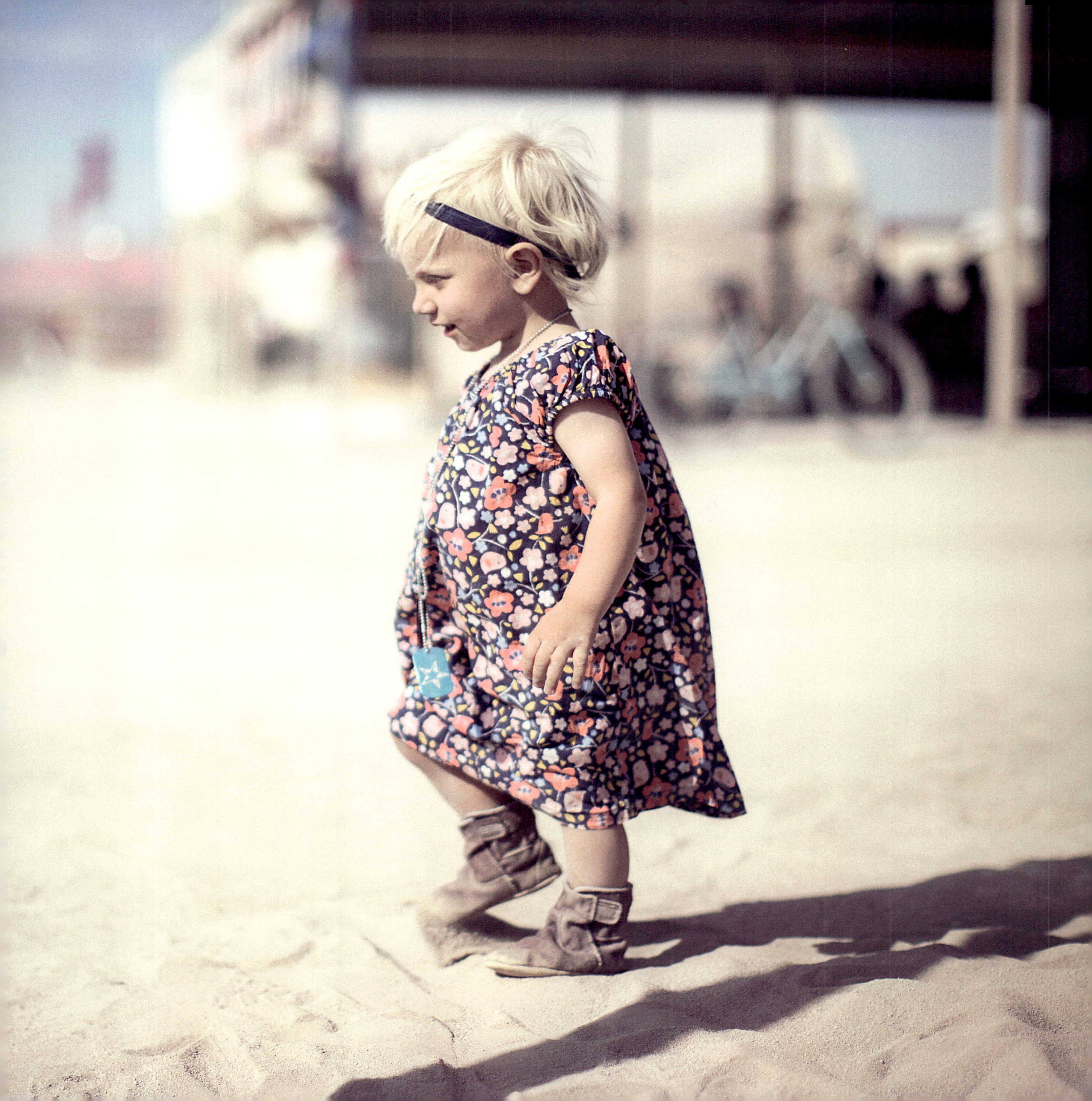

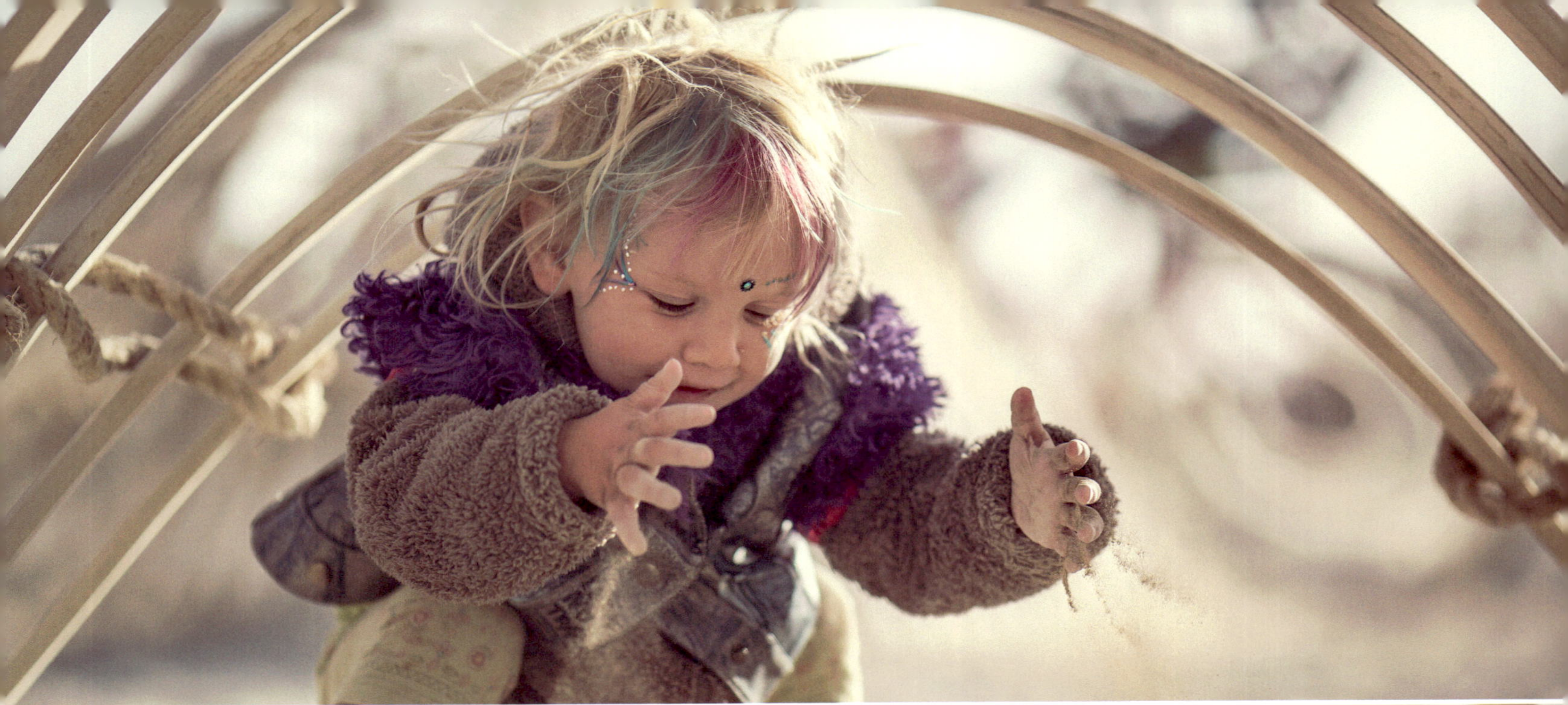
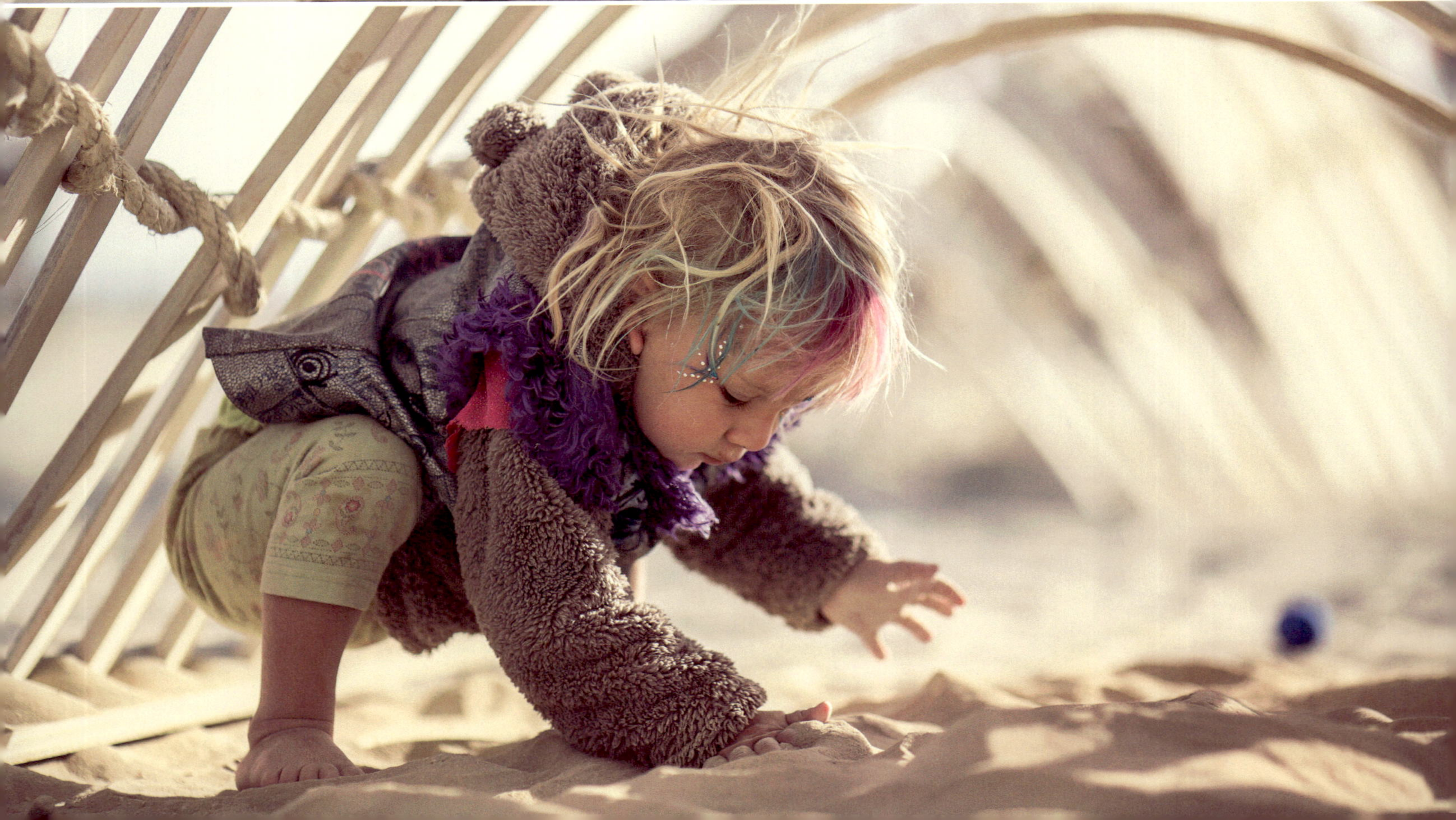

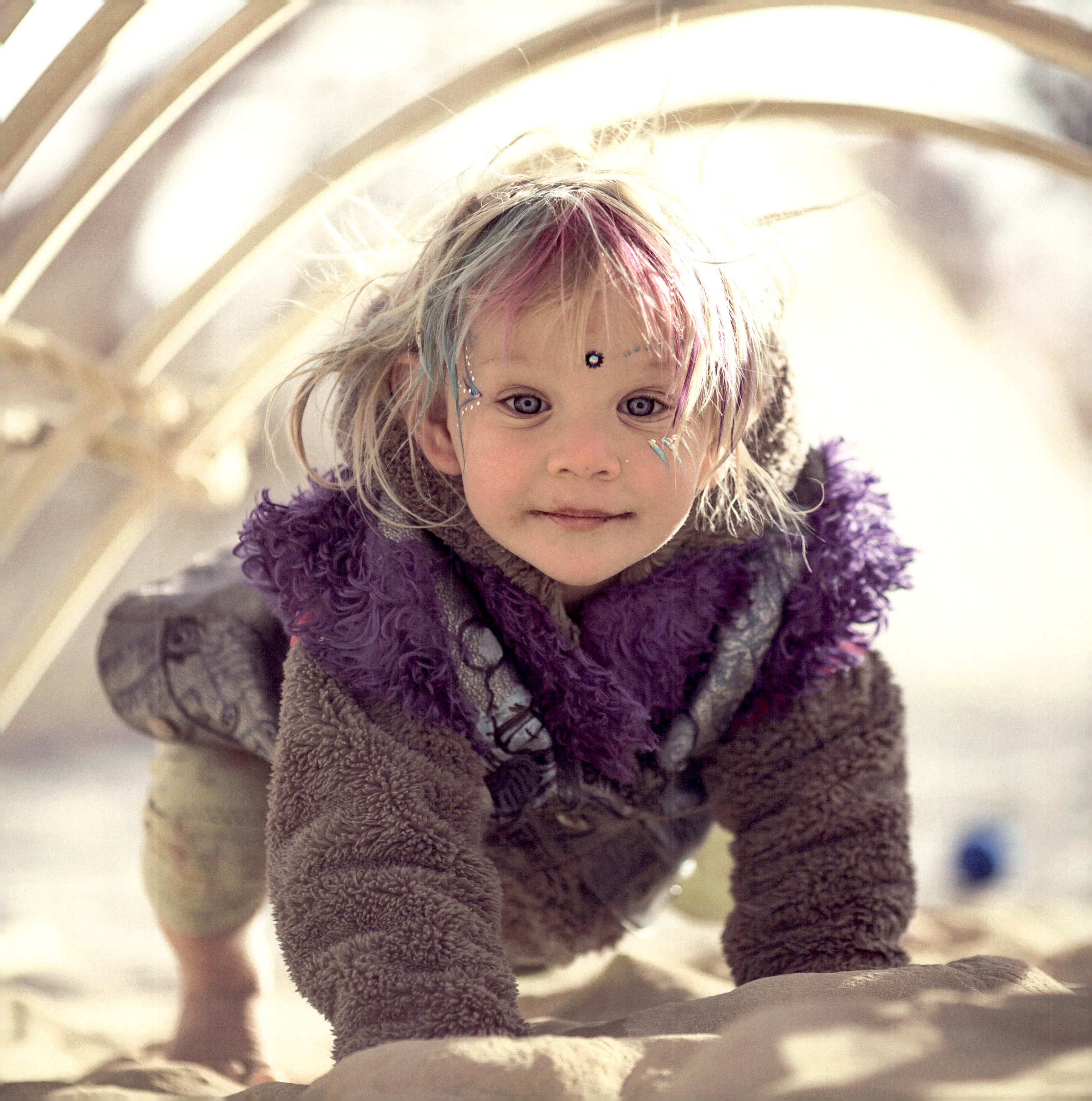

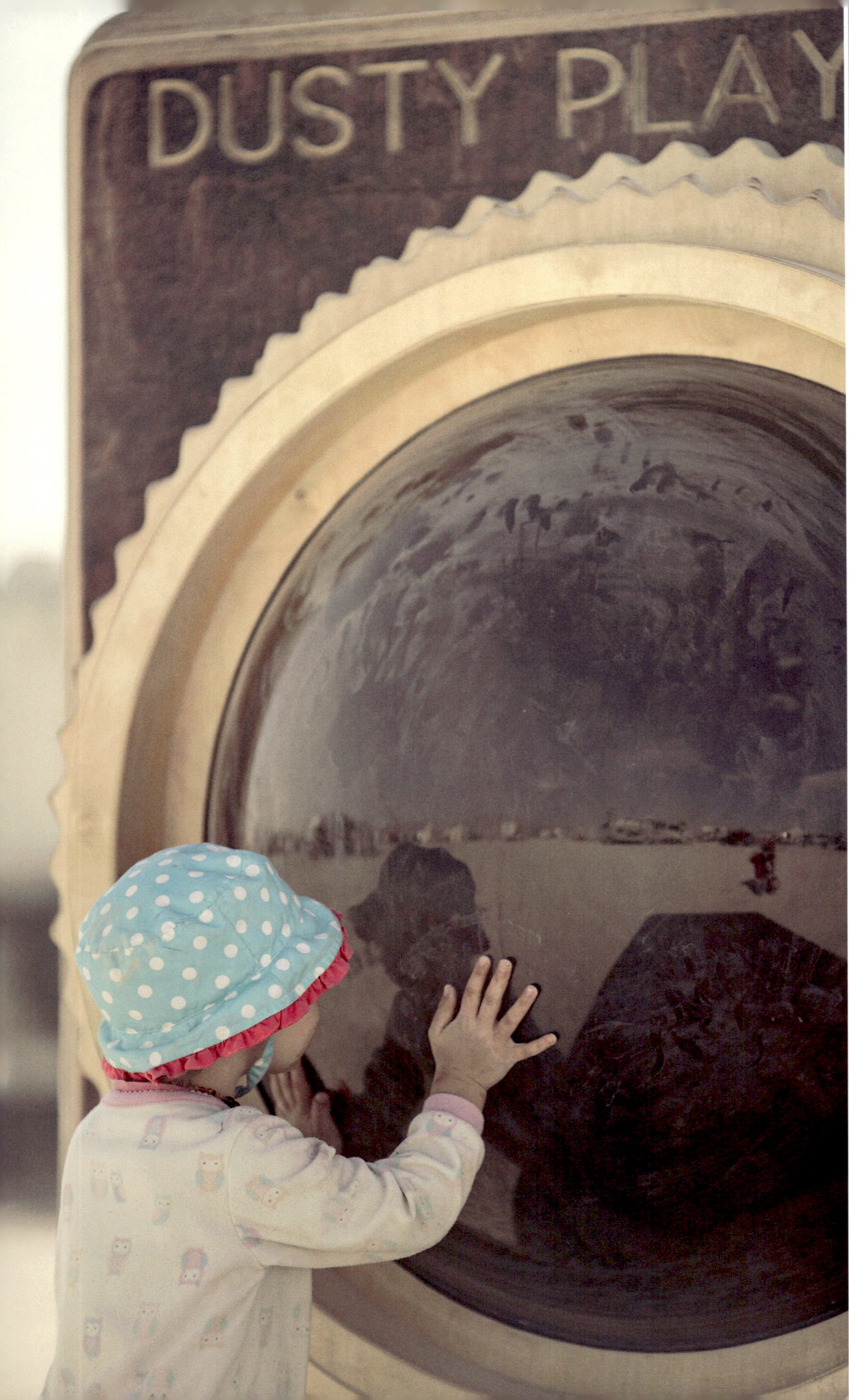
DUSTY PLAY

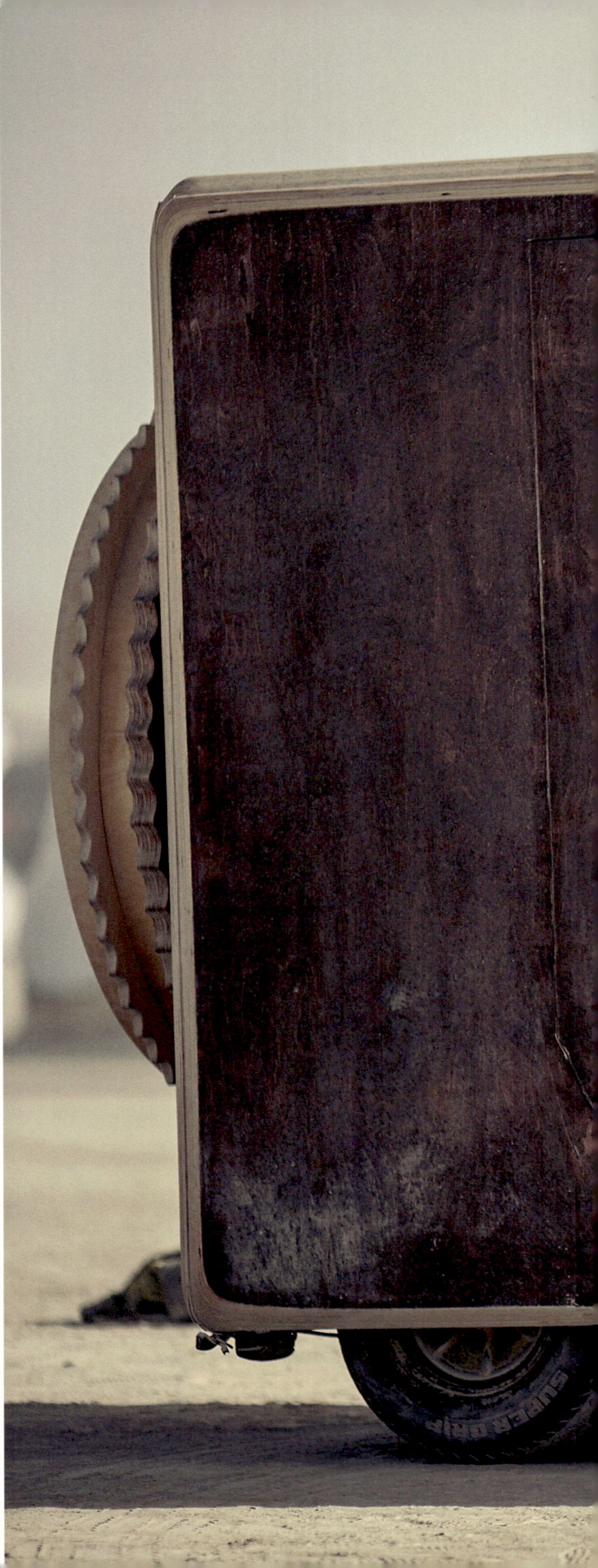

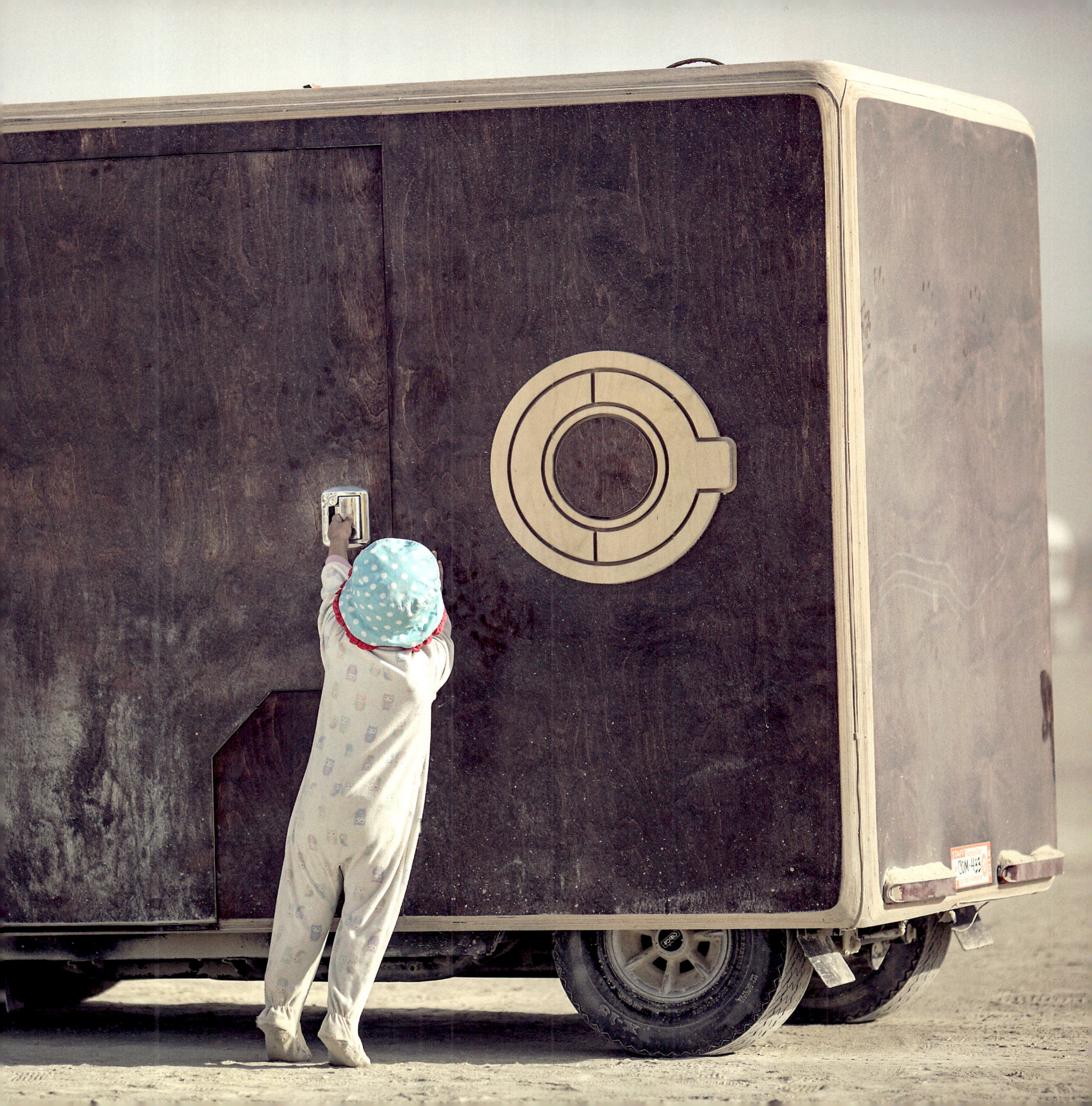
STAFF

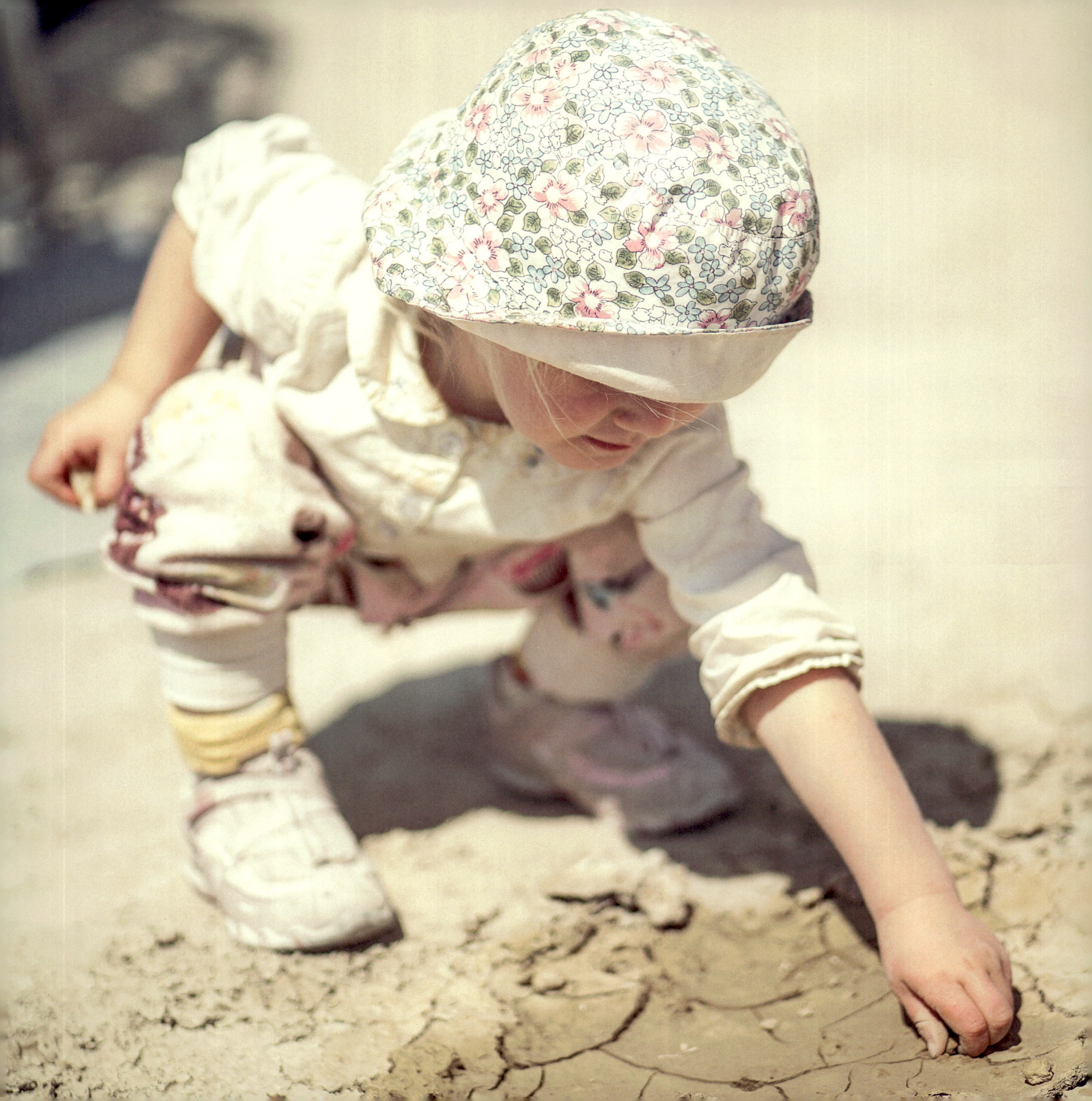

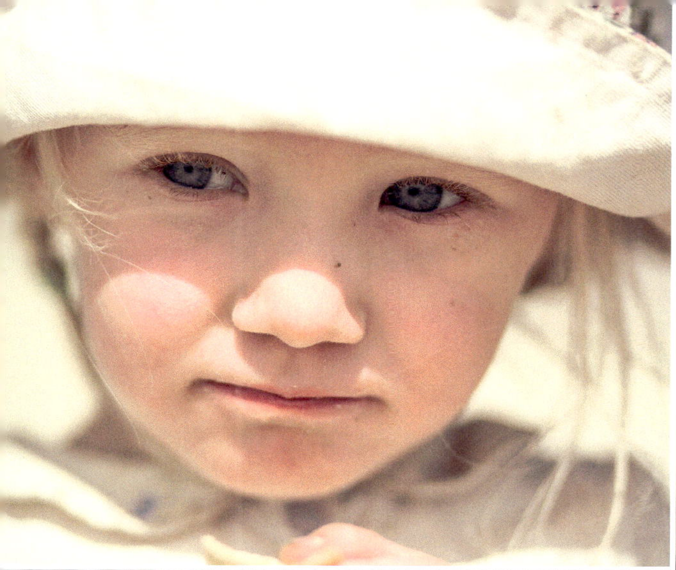
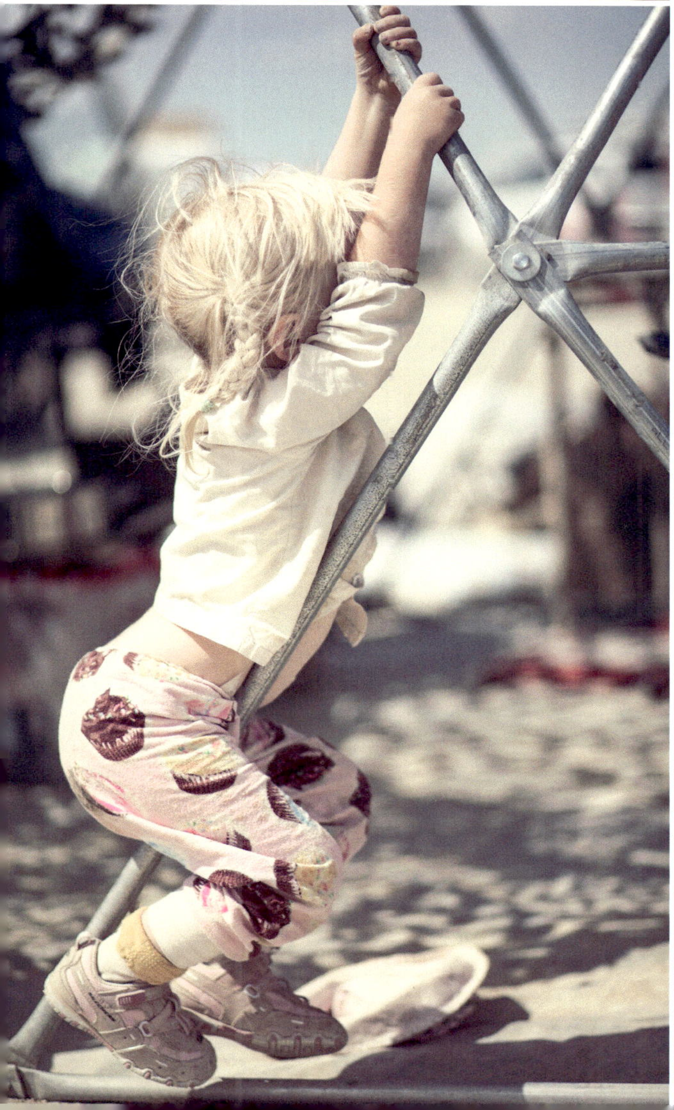
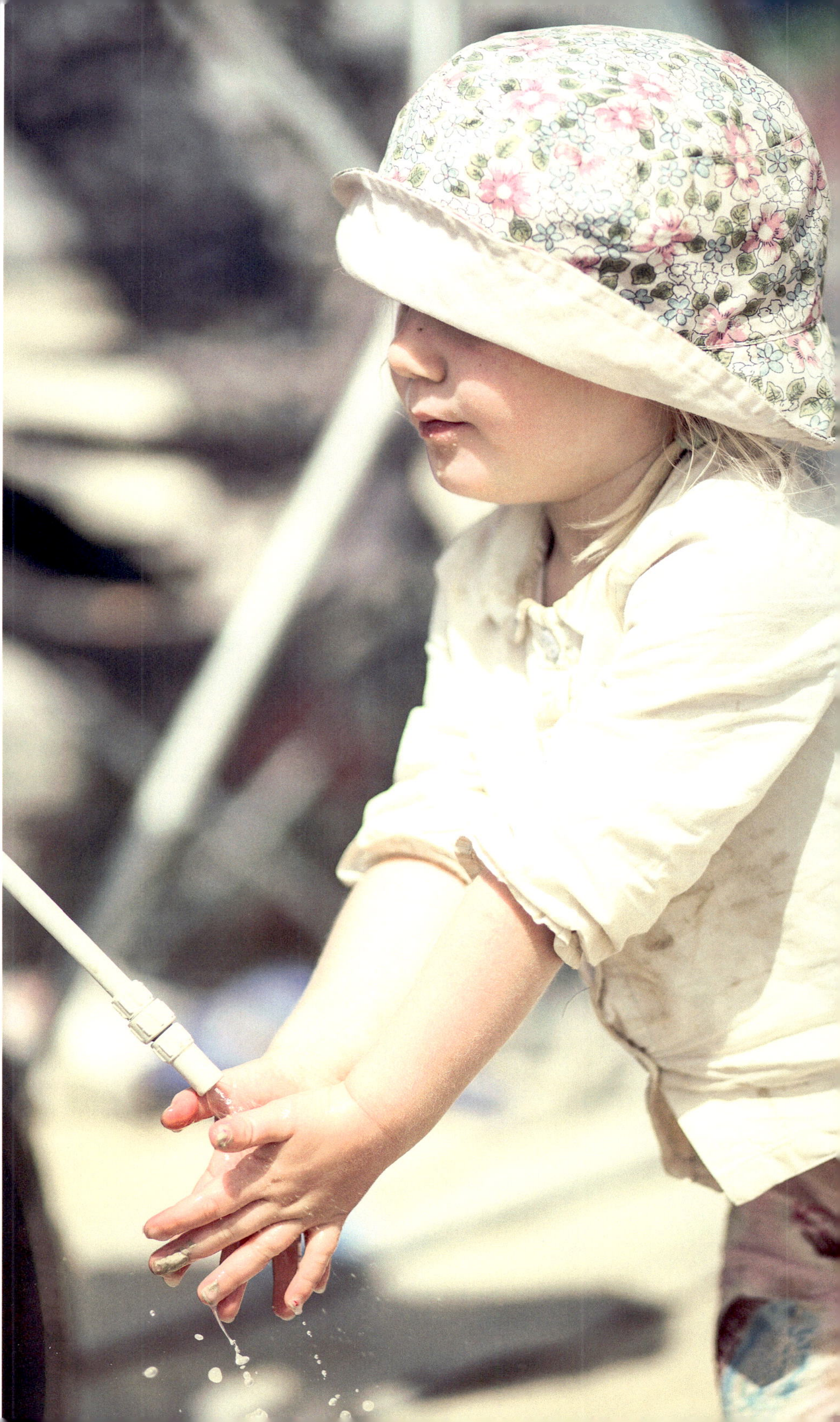

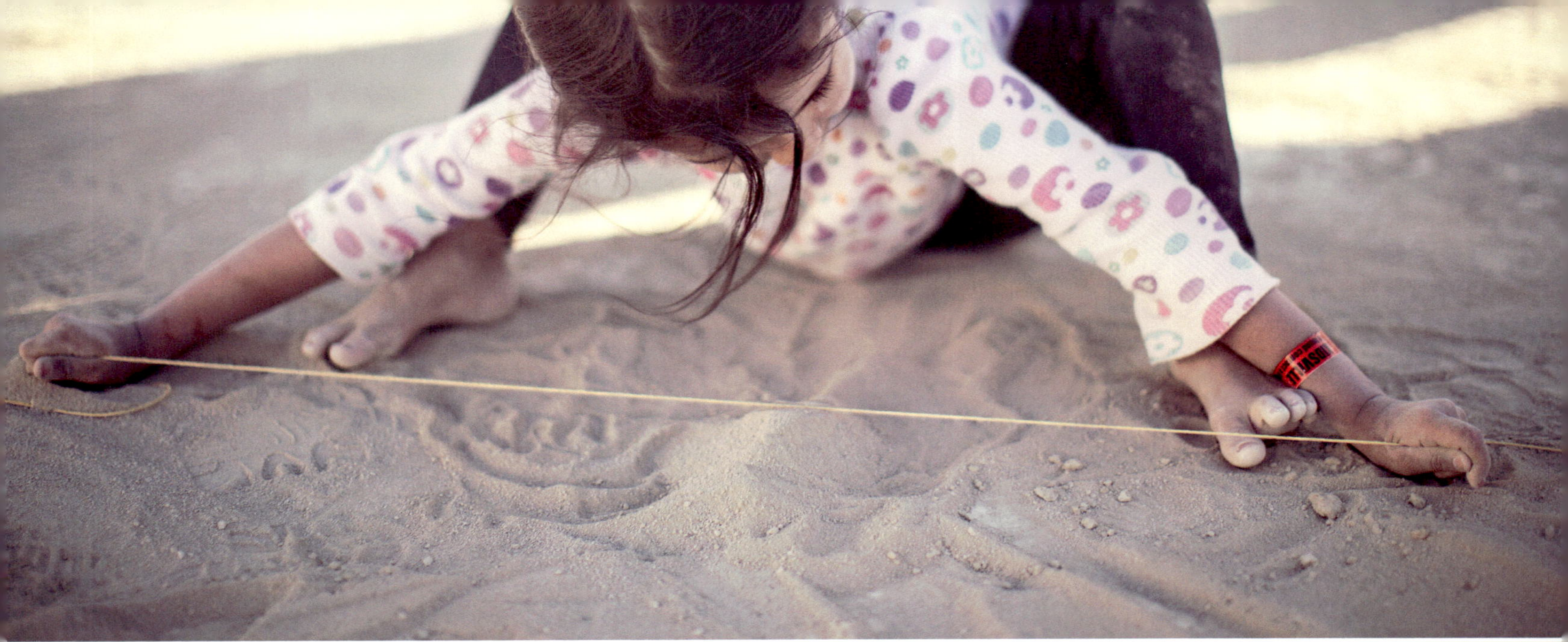

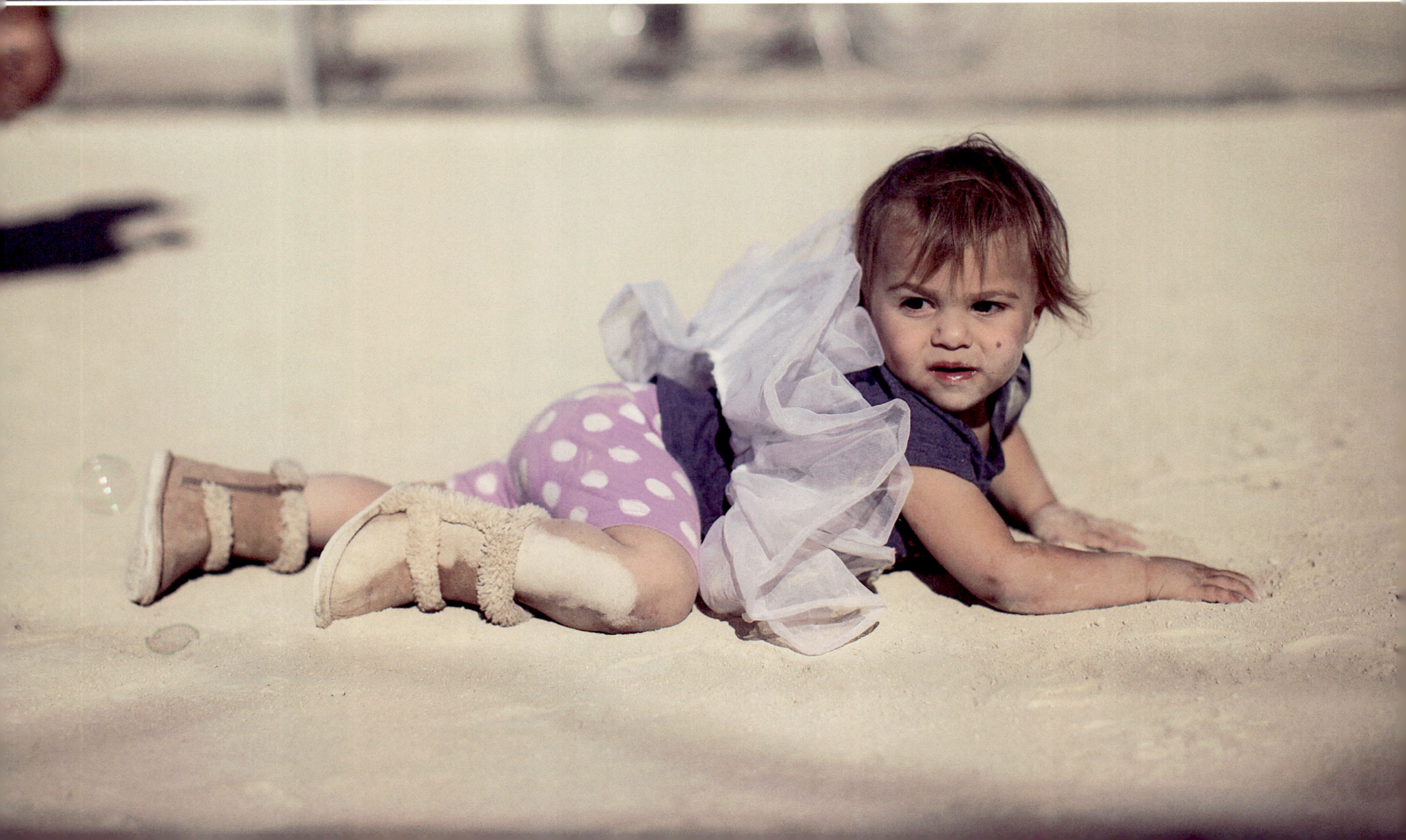

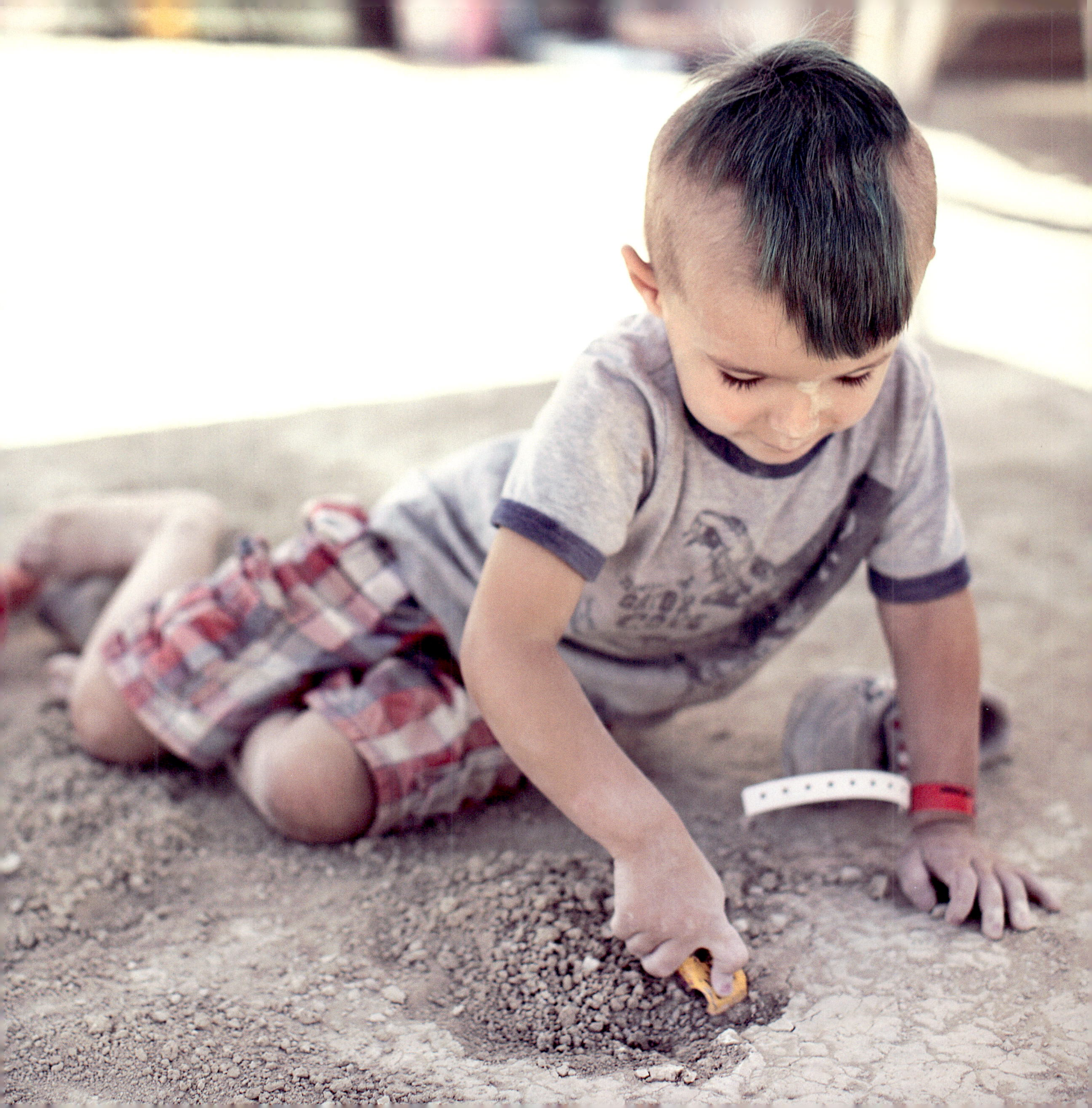

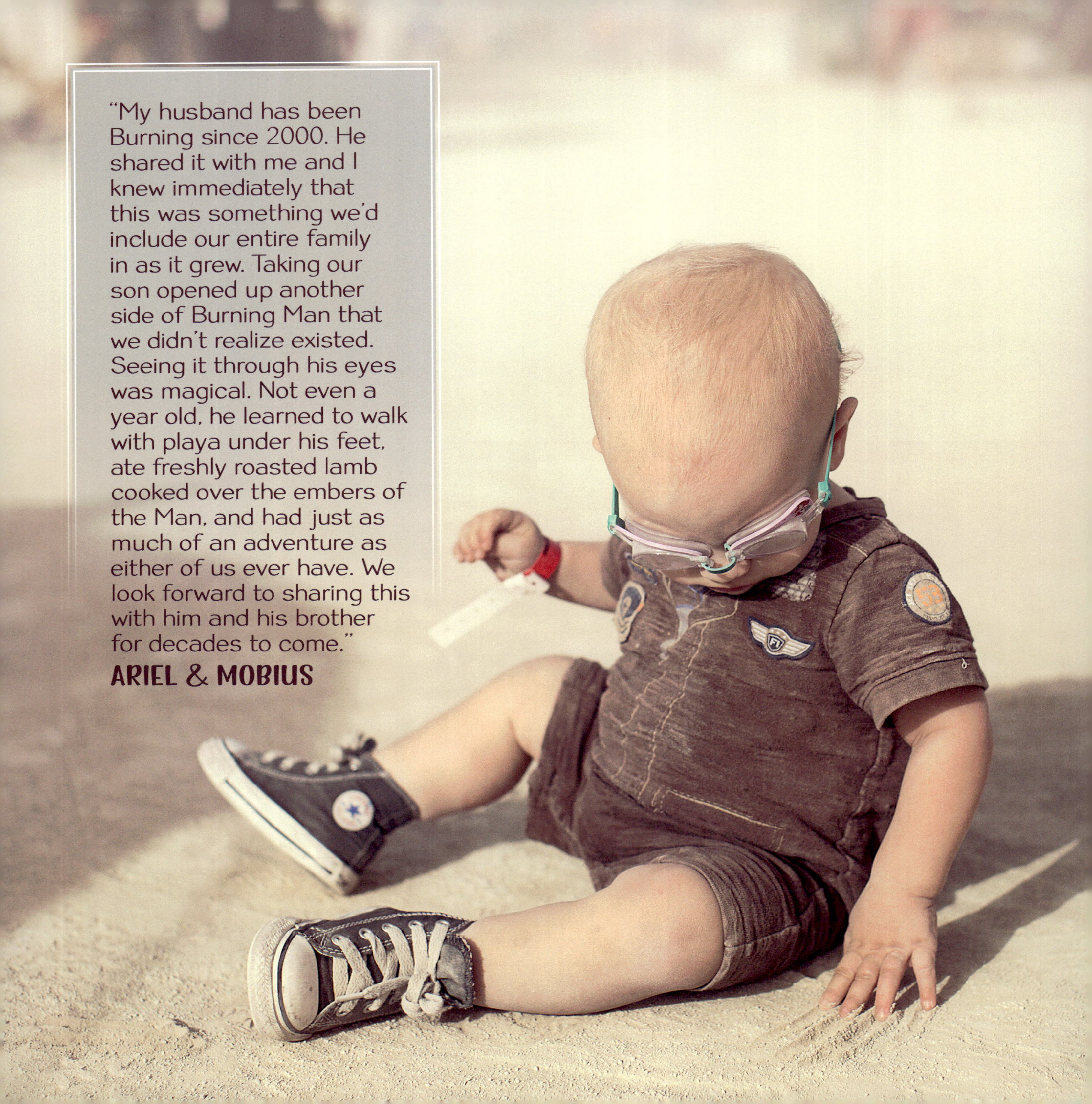

"My husband has been Burning since 2000. He shared it with me and I knew immediately that this was something we'd include our entire family in as it grew. Taking our son opened up another side of Burning Man that we didn't realize existed. Seeing it through his eyes was magical. Not even a year old, he learned to walk with playa under his feet, ate freshly roasted lamb cooked over the embers of the Man, and had just as much of an adventure as either of us ever have. We look forward to sharing this with him and his brother for decades to come."

ARIEL & MOBIUS

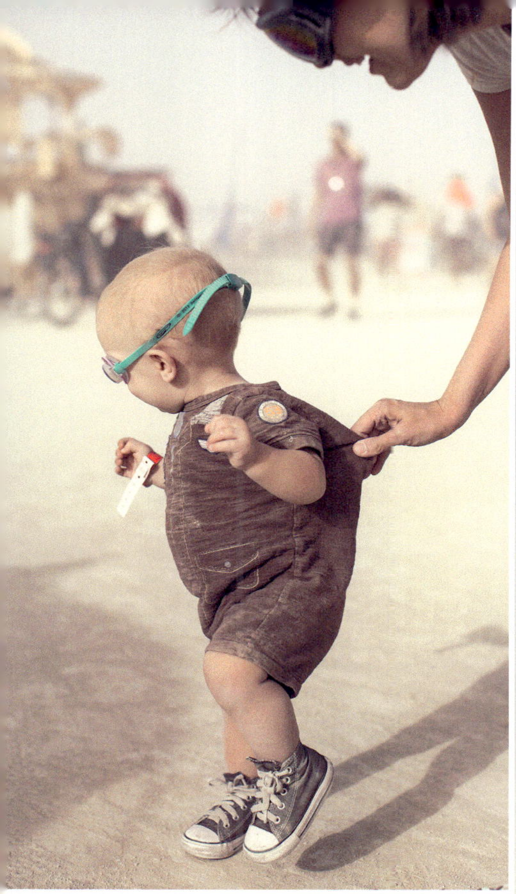

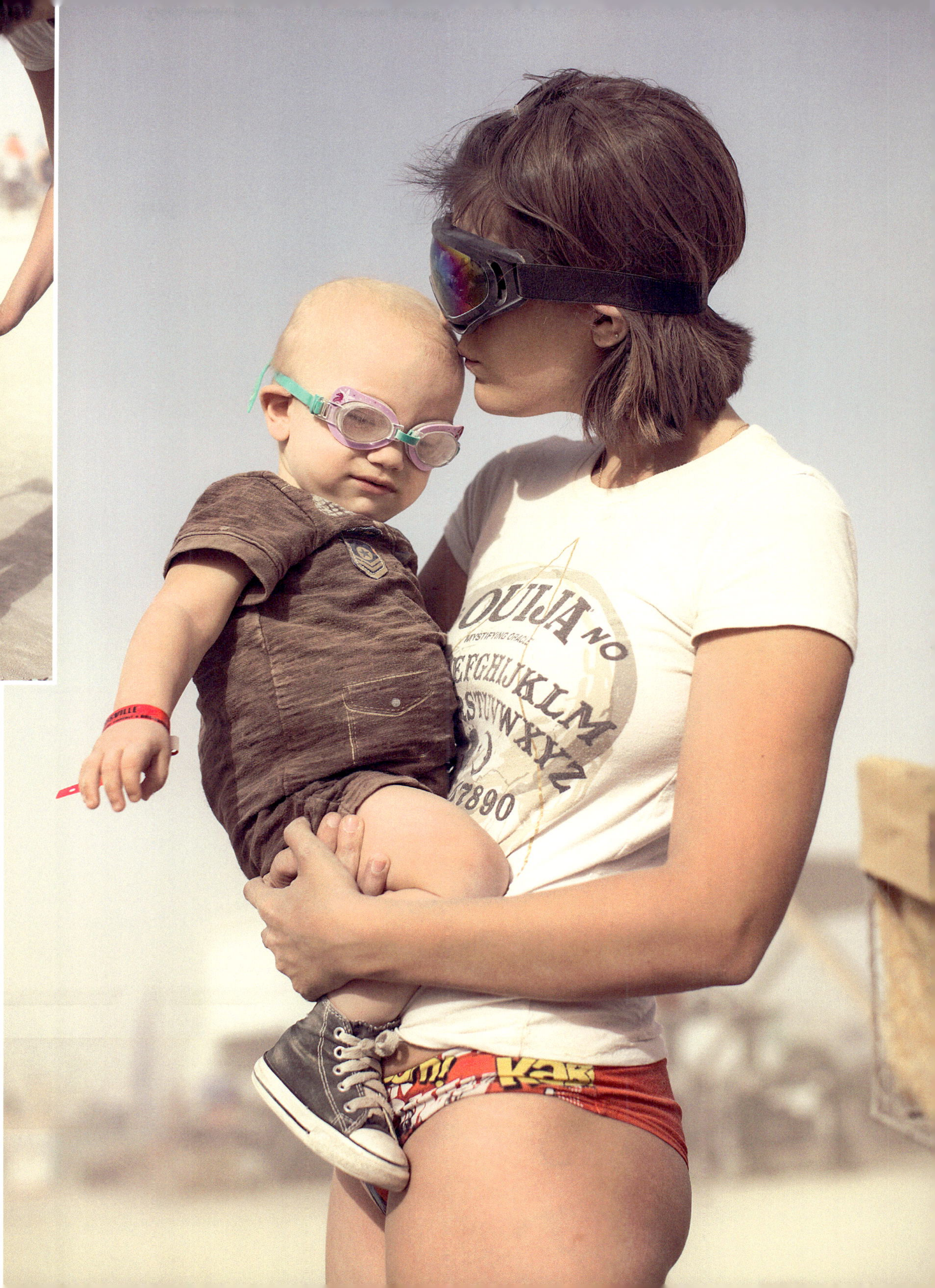
OUIJA
MYSTIFYING ORACLE

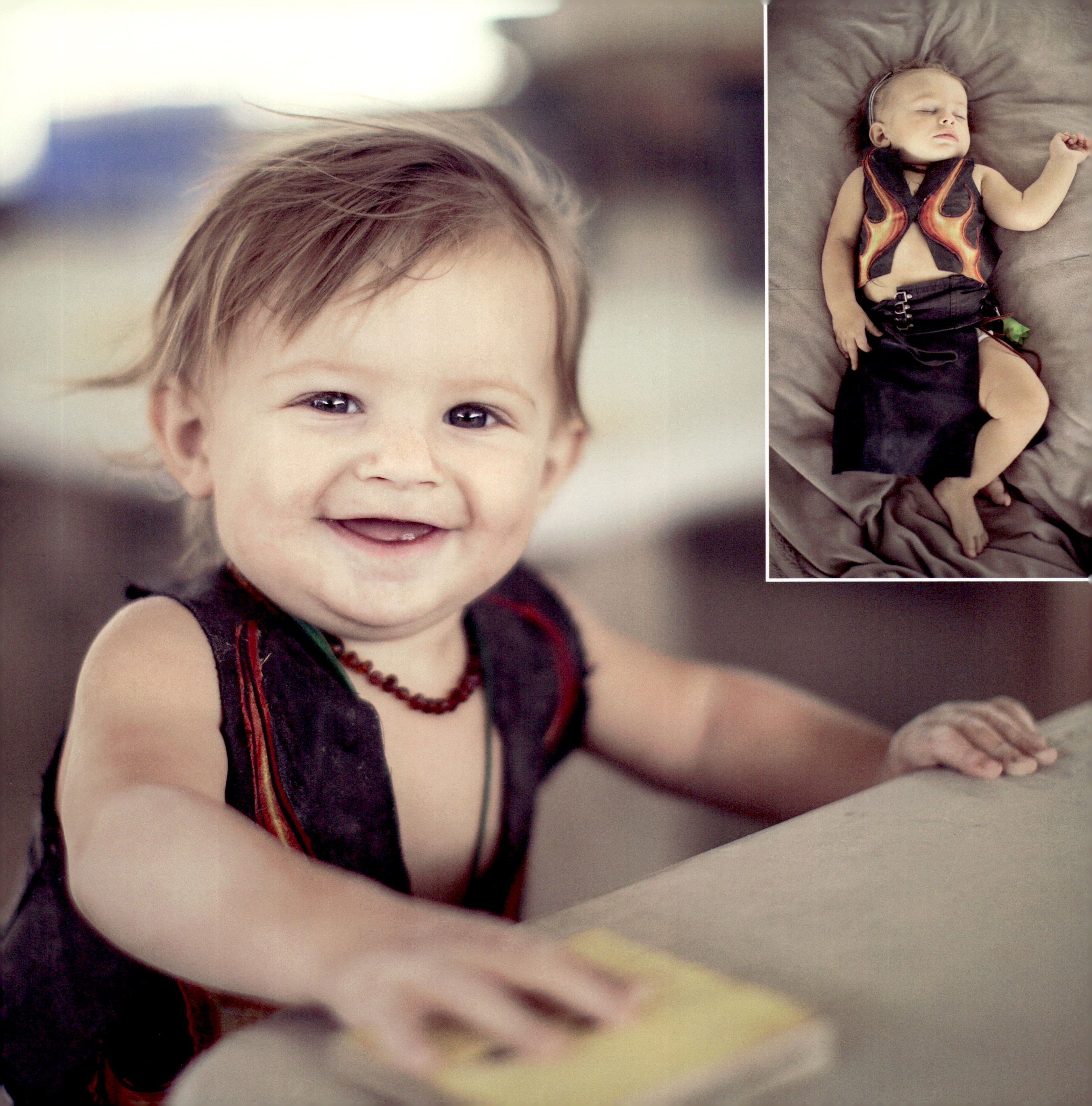

"After 8 years attending Burning Man, it was the most beautiful with my 8 month-old baby. This was 'Hotwheels' second burn as he also attended while I was pregnant. My favorite part was experiencing it through his eyes – he found amazement in things I'd begun to find mundane. Seeing his joy and excitement brought tears to my eyes. I'd been concerned that some Burners might consider kids a 'buzz kill'. However, people took in his spirit with the reverence of a huge art project that touched their hearts. **The community embraced him, enjoyed him and treated him like a superstar.** Although bringing a little one into these conditions is not without challenge and sacrifice, I cannot imagine *not* sharing this amazing community with my child or my child with this community. I couldn't be more proud to have imprinted him with the Burner ethos and intend to continue to bring him up with the Principles that guide this event, its people and my way of life."

KIMAKAZE & HOTWHEELS

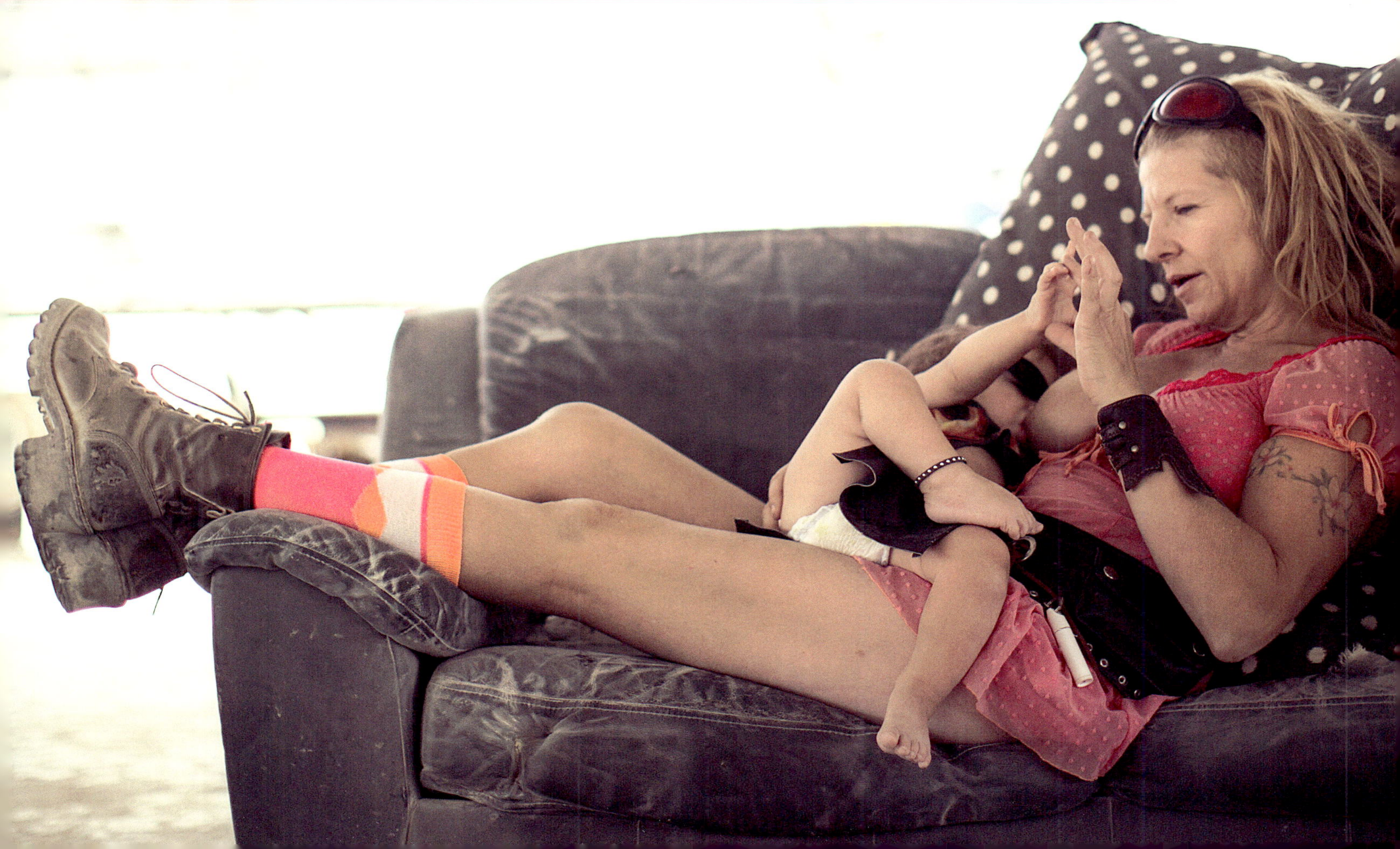

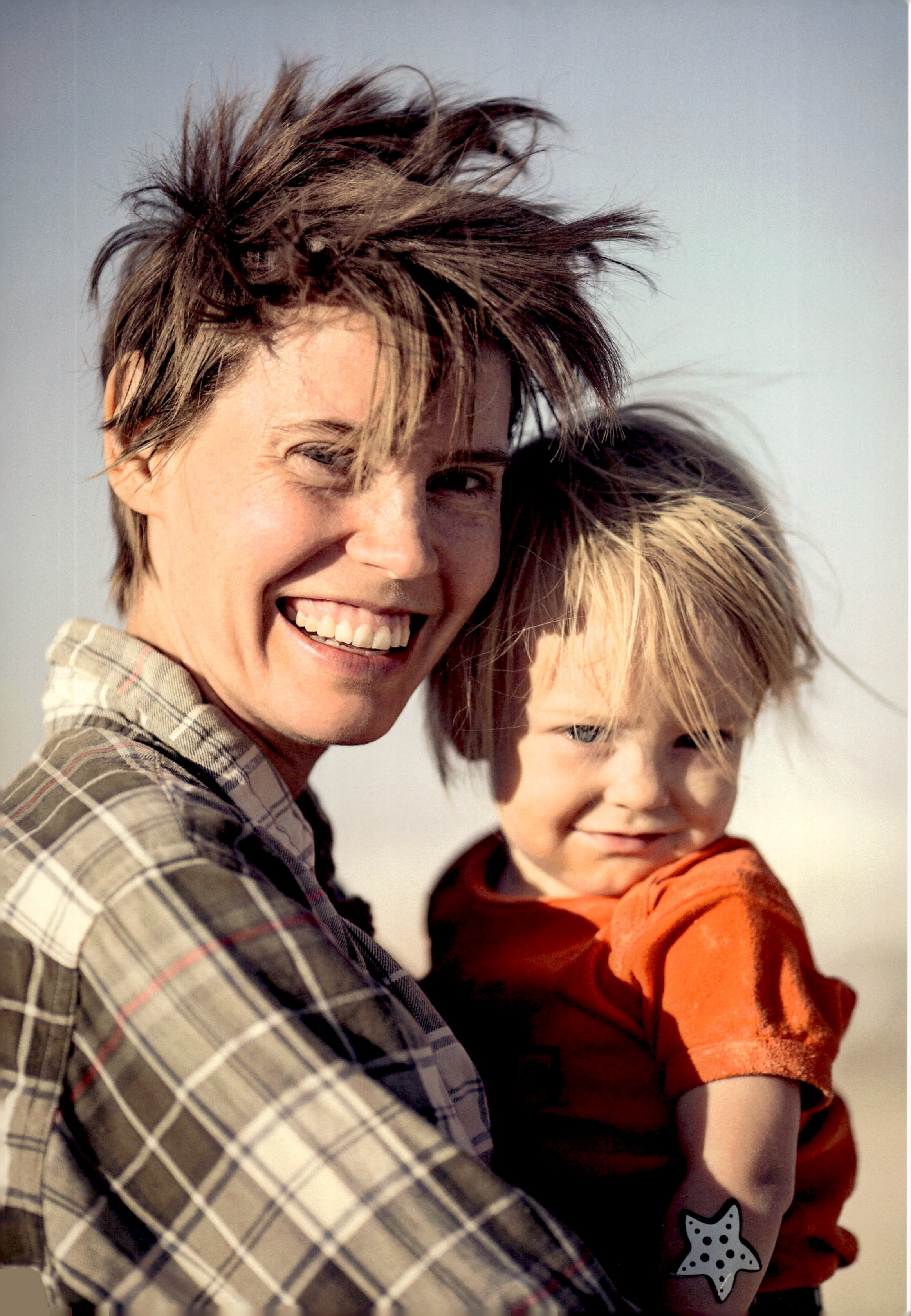

"Bringing my baby to Burning Man made the Burn fun for me again. Having our baby with us forced us to slow down and take good care of ourselves, both physically and emotionally. The biggest experience change for me was how our baby acted as an excellent filter – the people who chose to interact with us were happy, thrilled, and excited. We received more swag and rides on art cars than in all previous years combined, by people who just loved seeing and interacting with a baby."

CHANDRA, JT & INDEPENDENCE SNOW

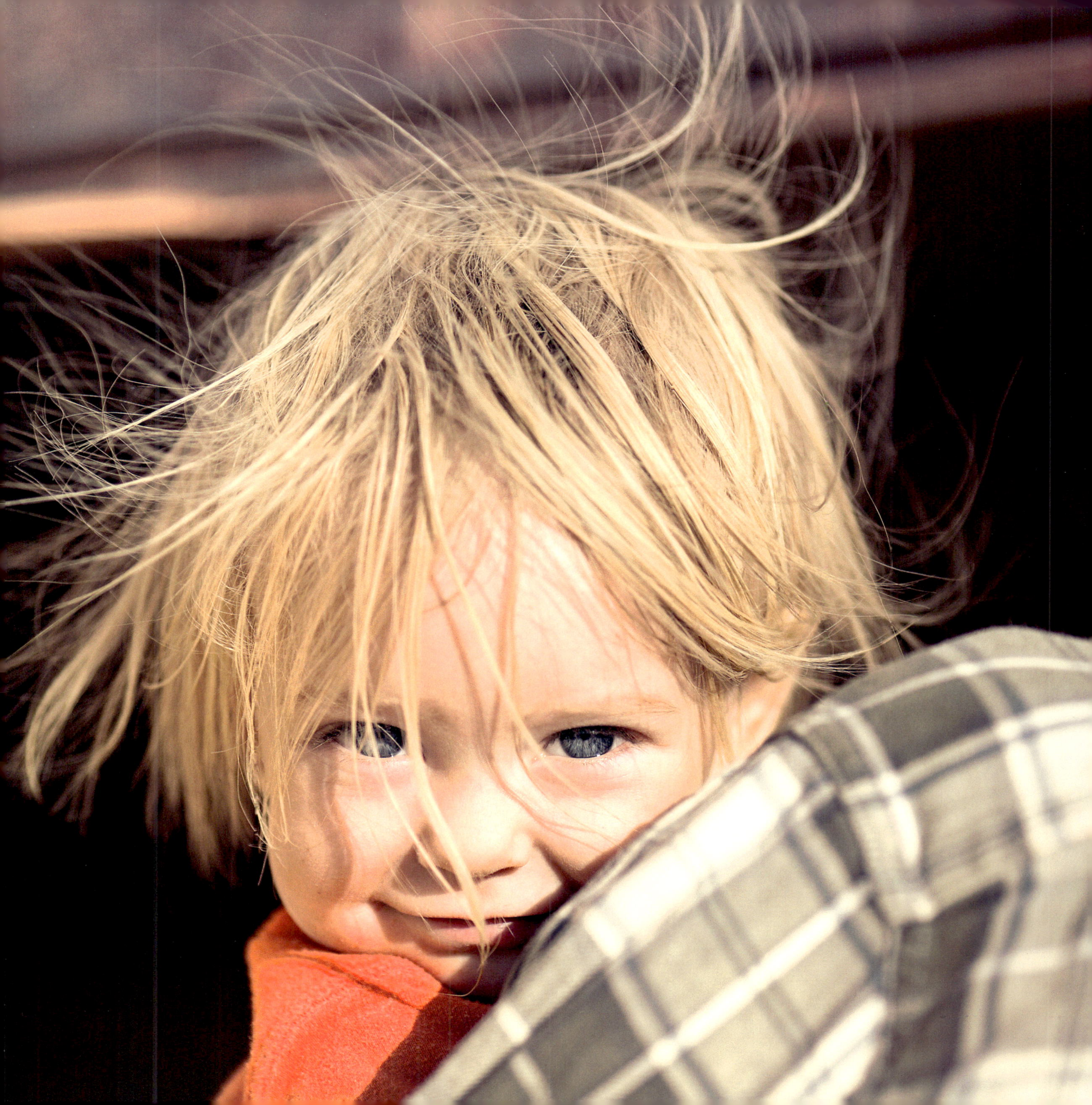

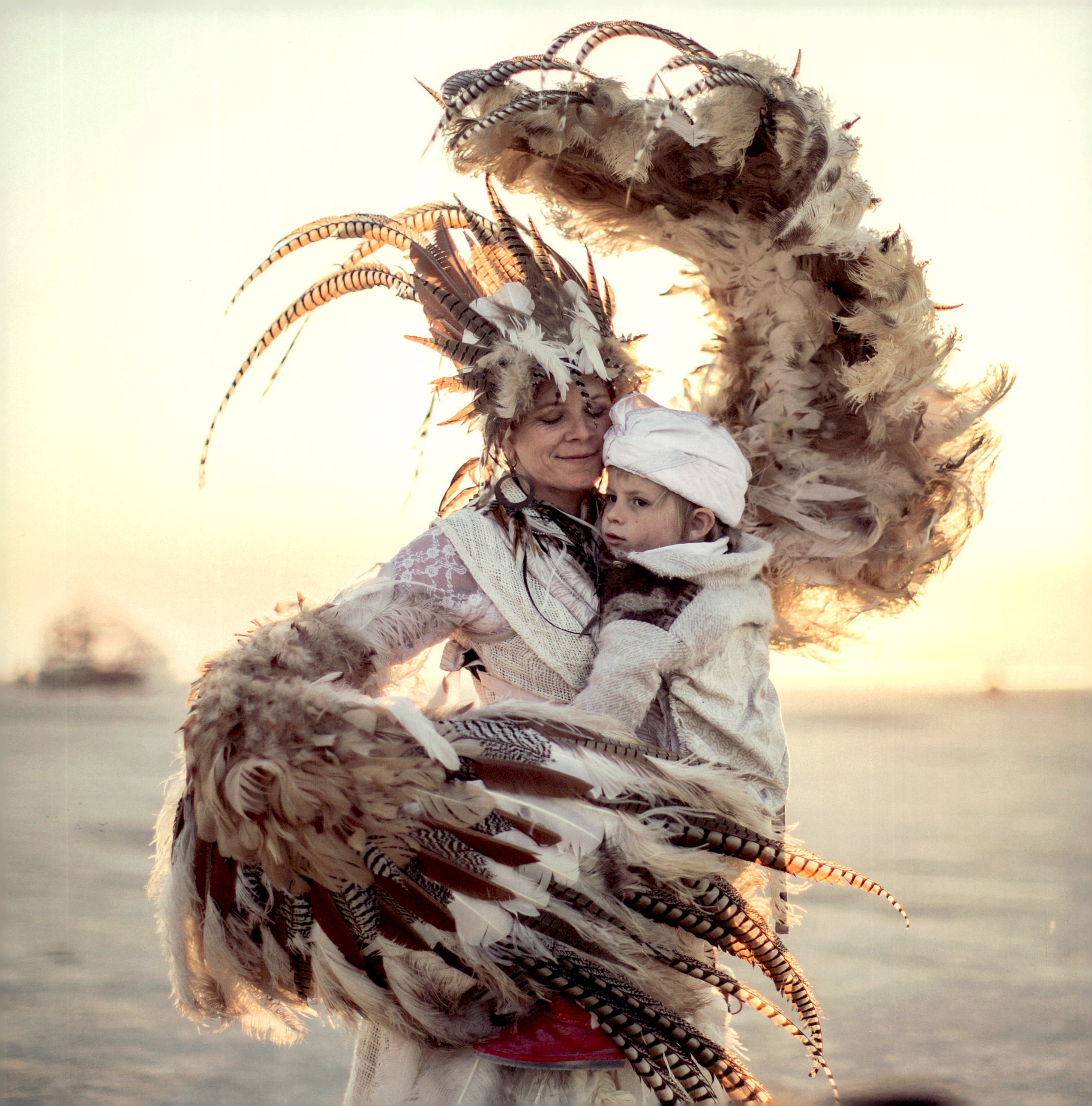

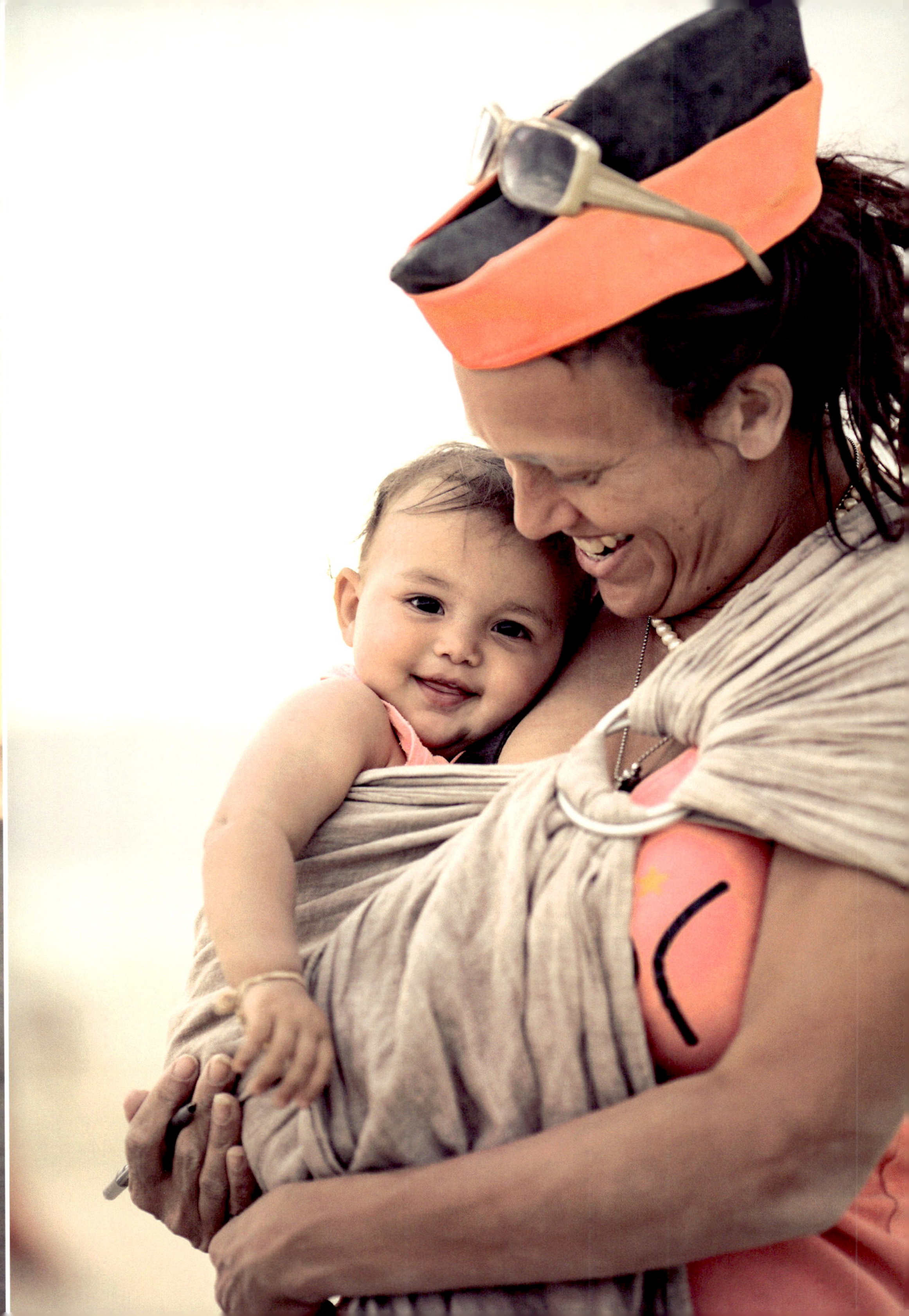

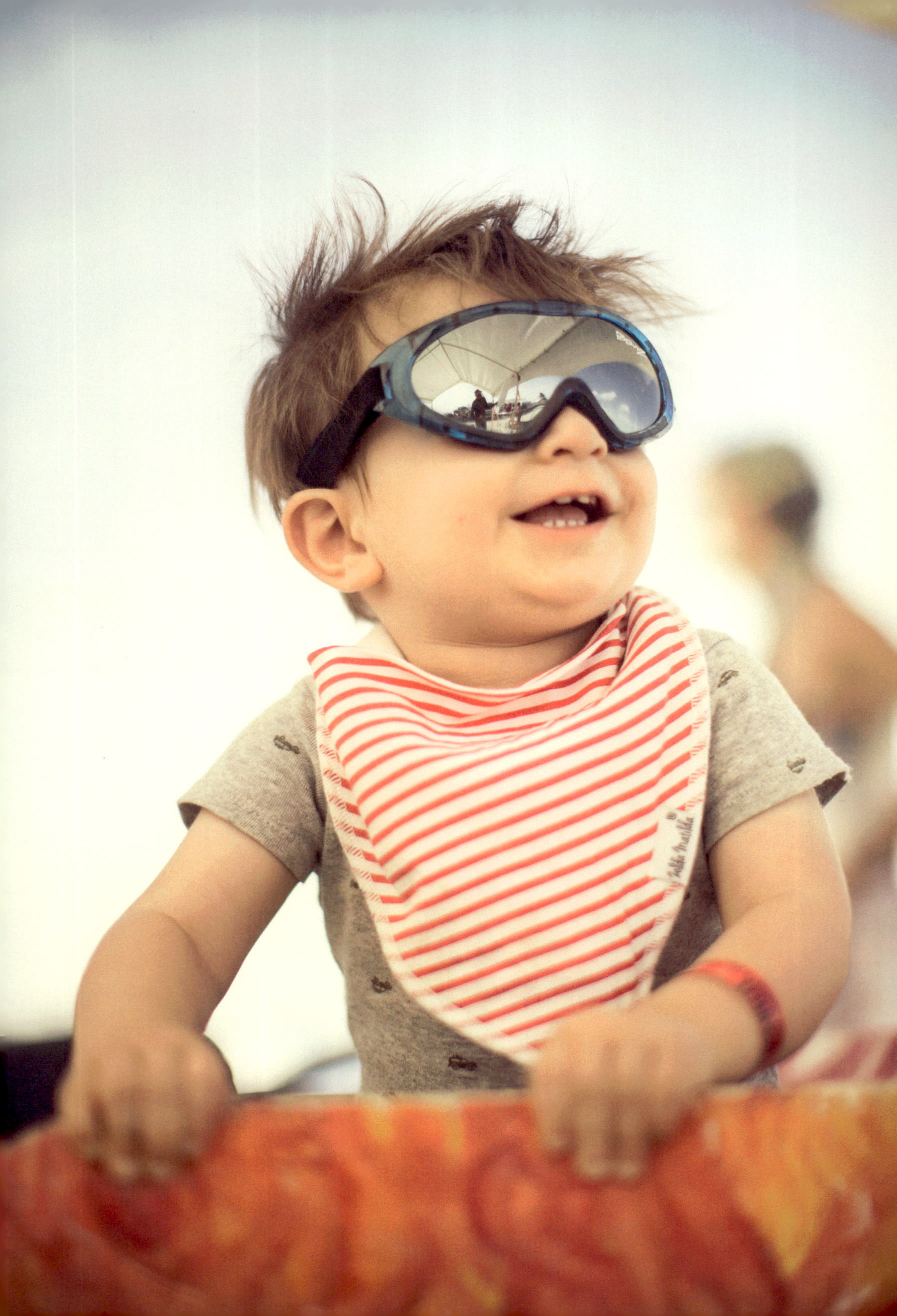
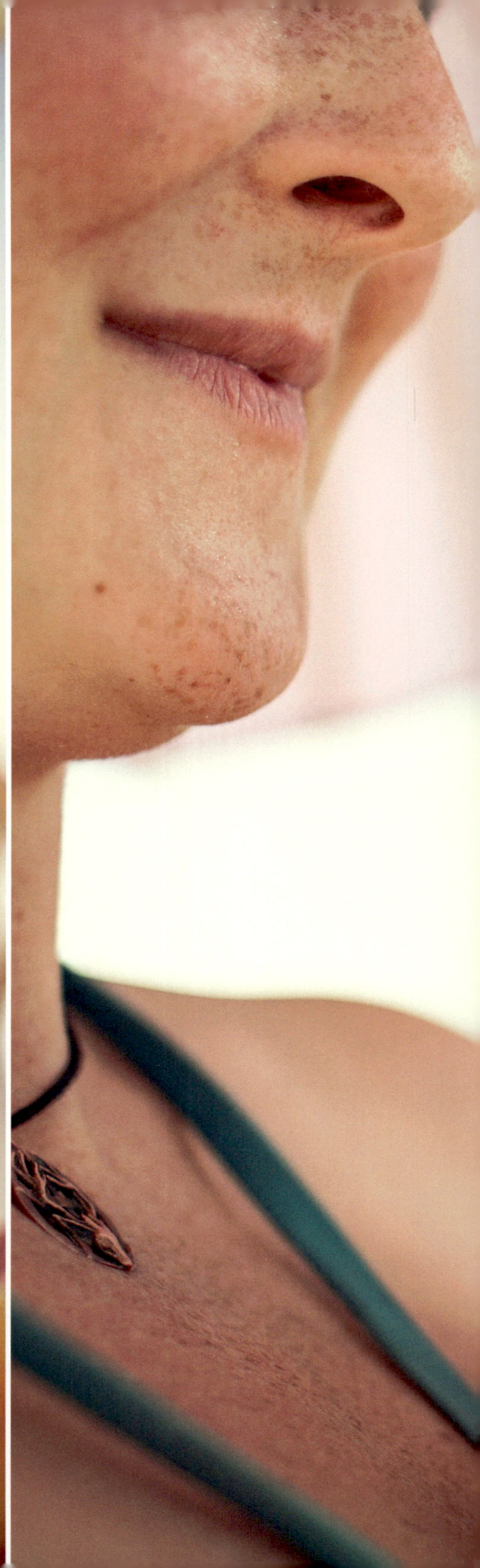

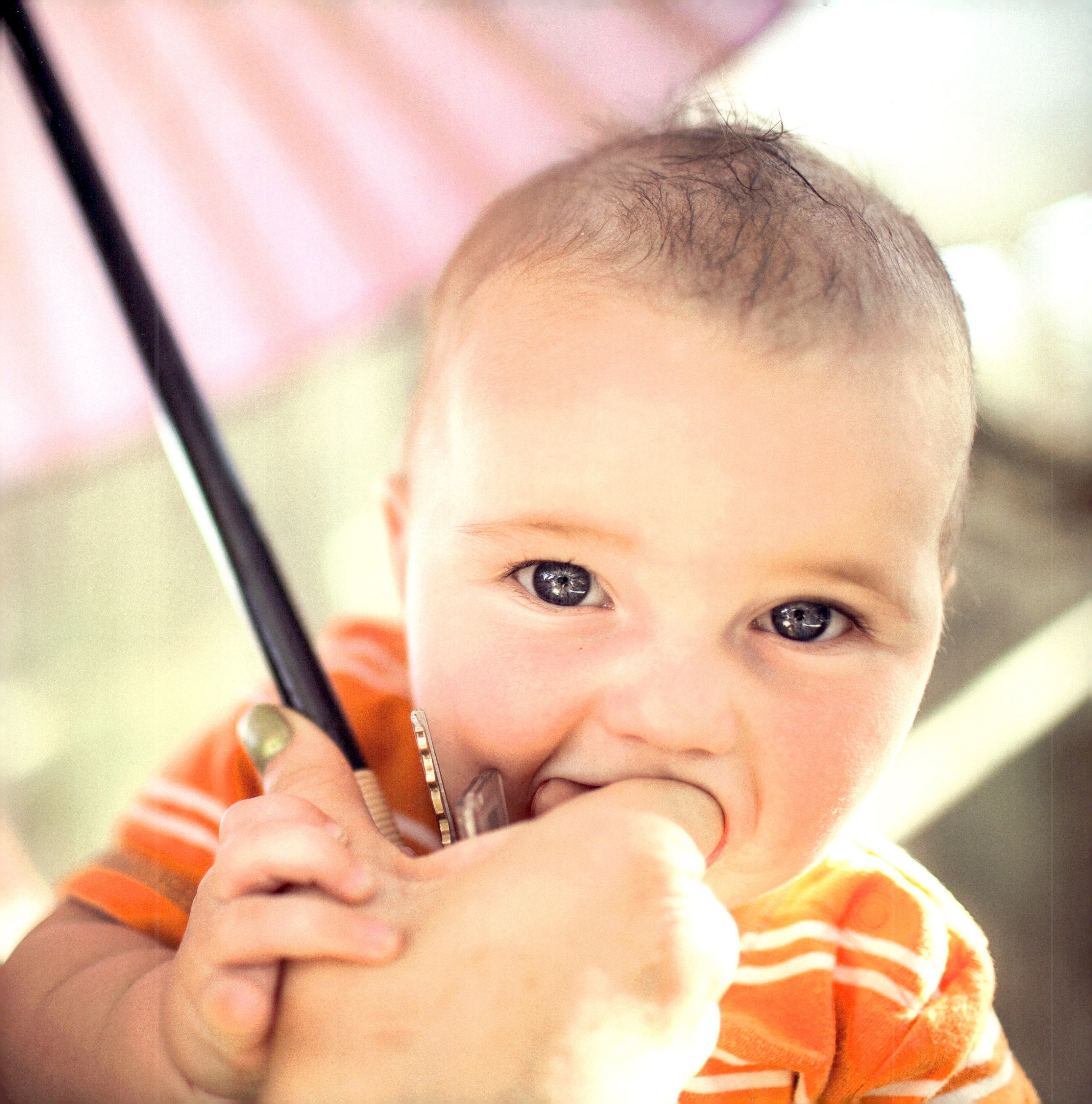

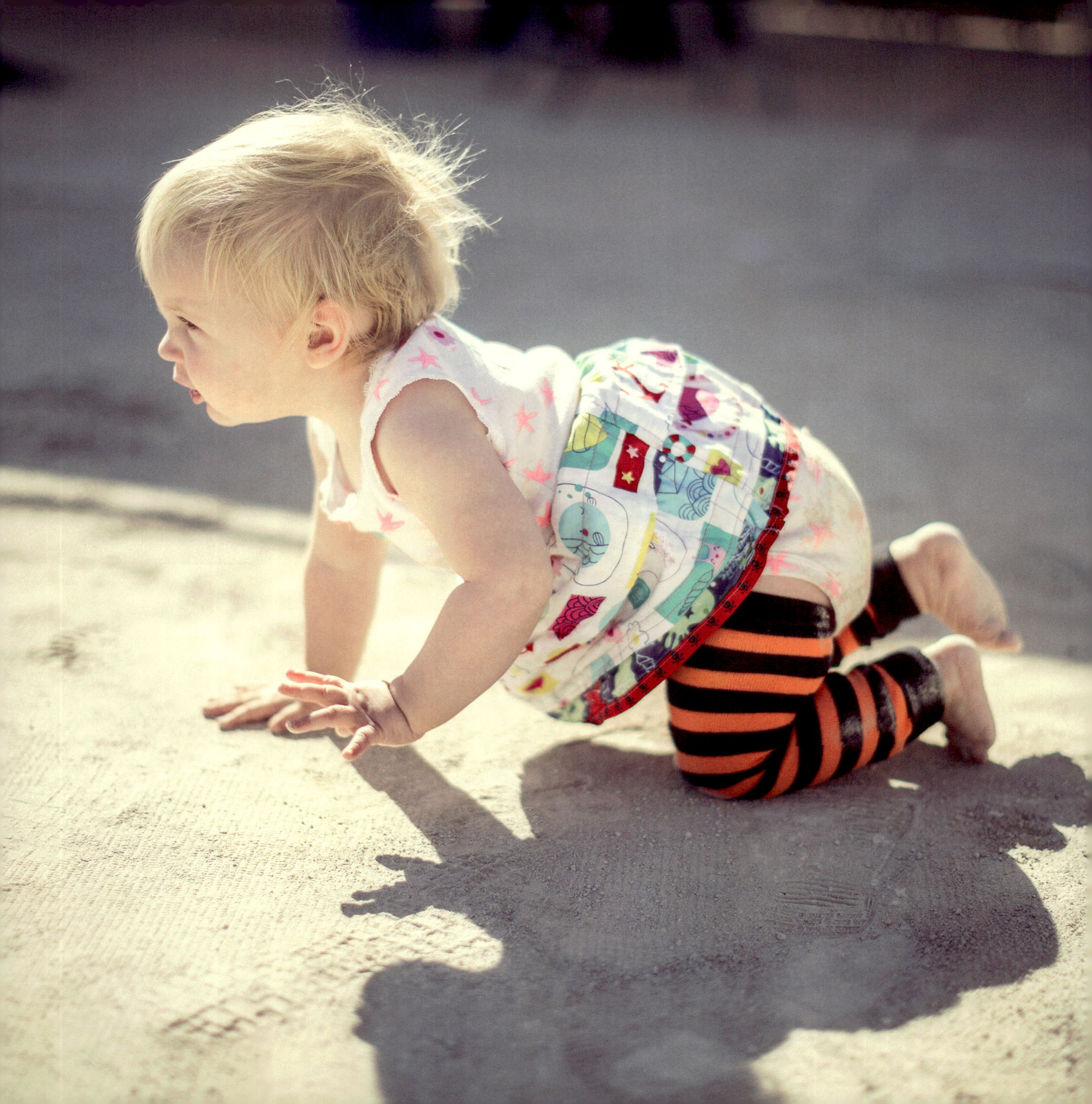

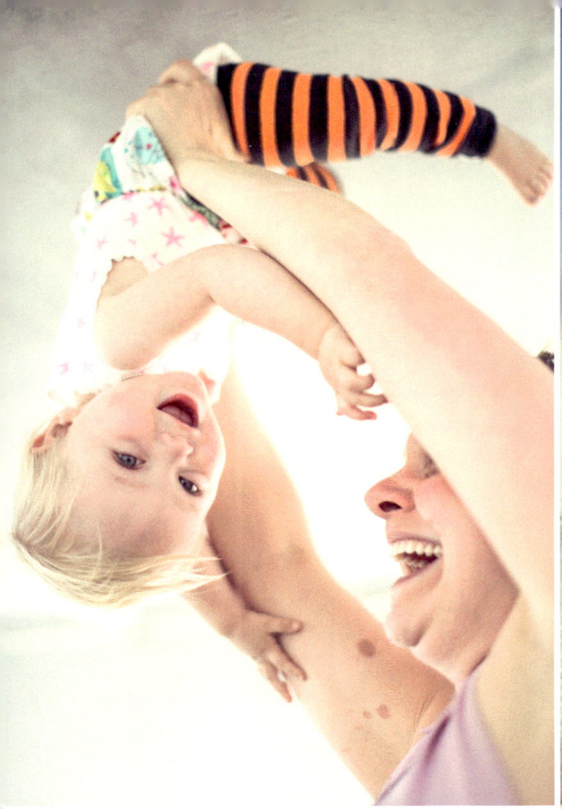

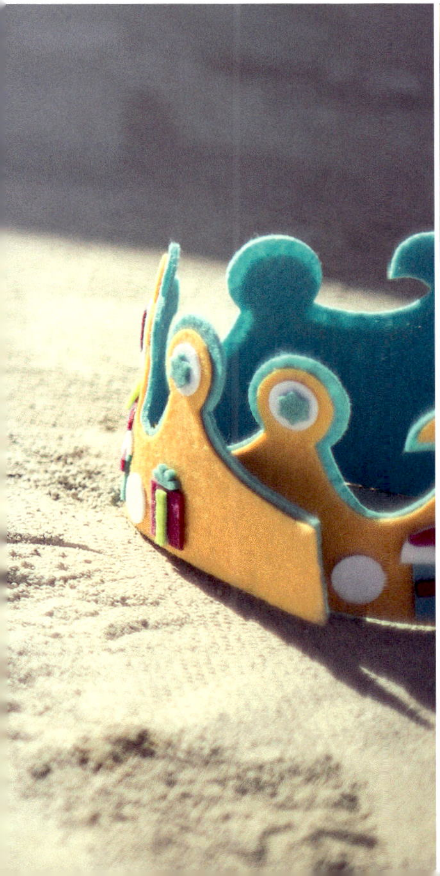

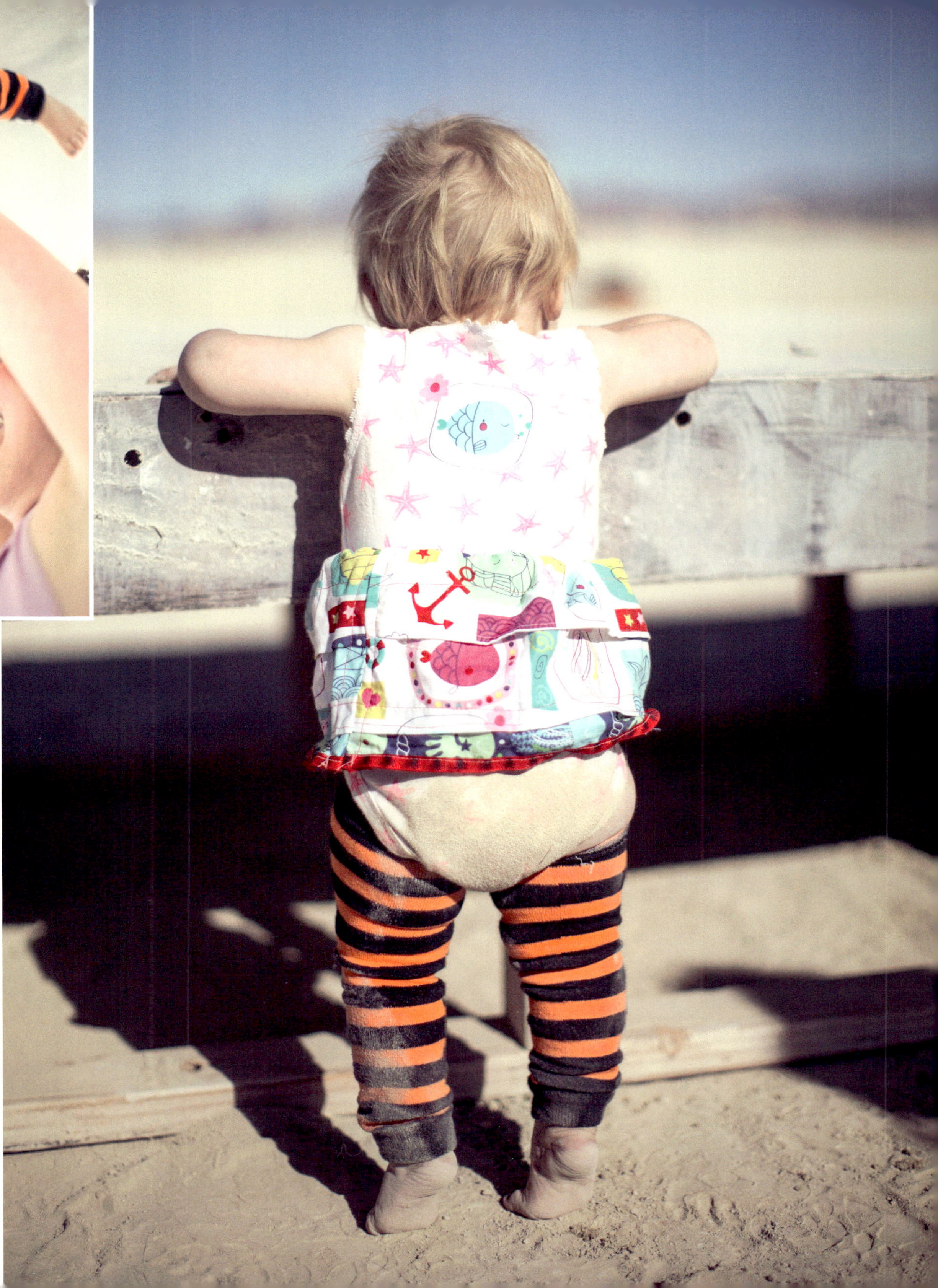

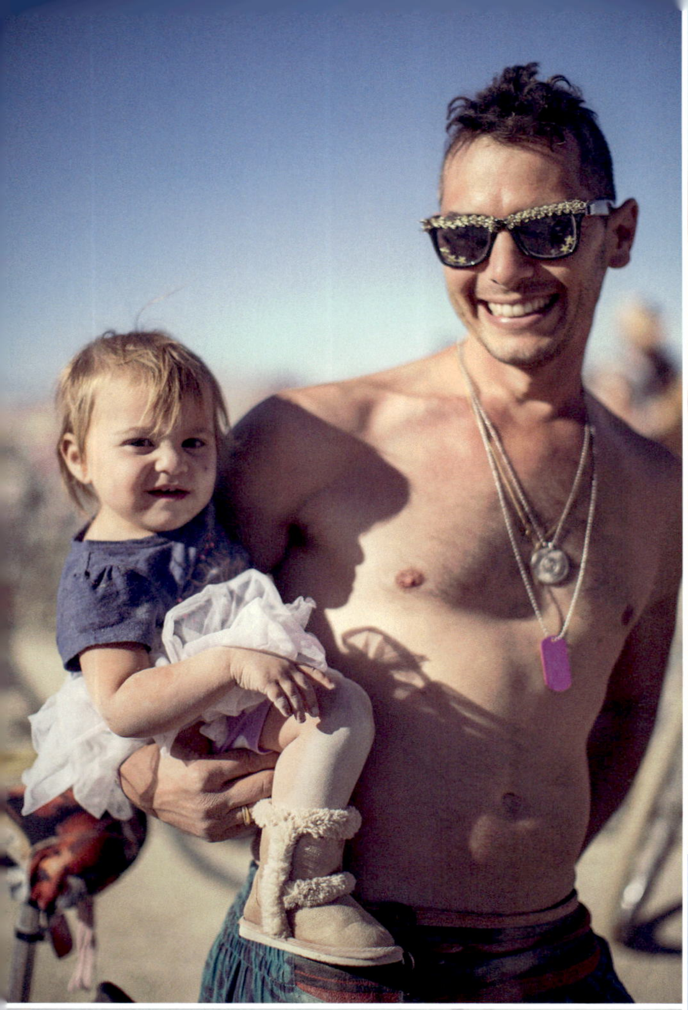

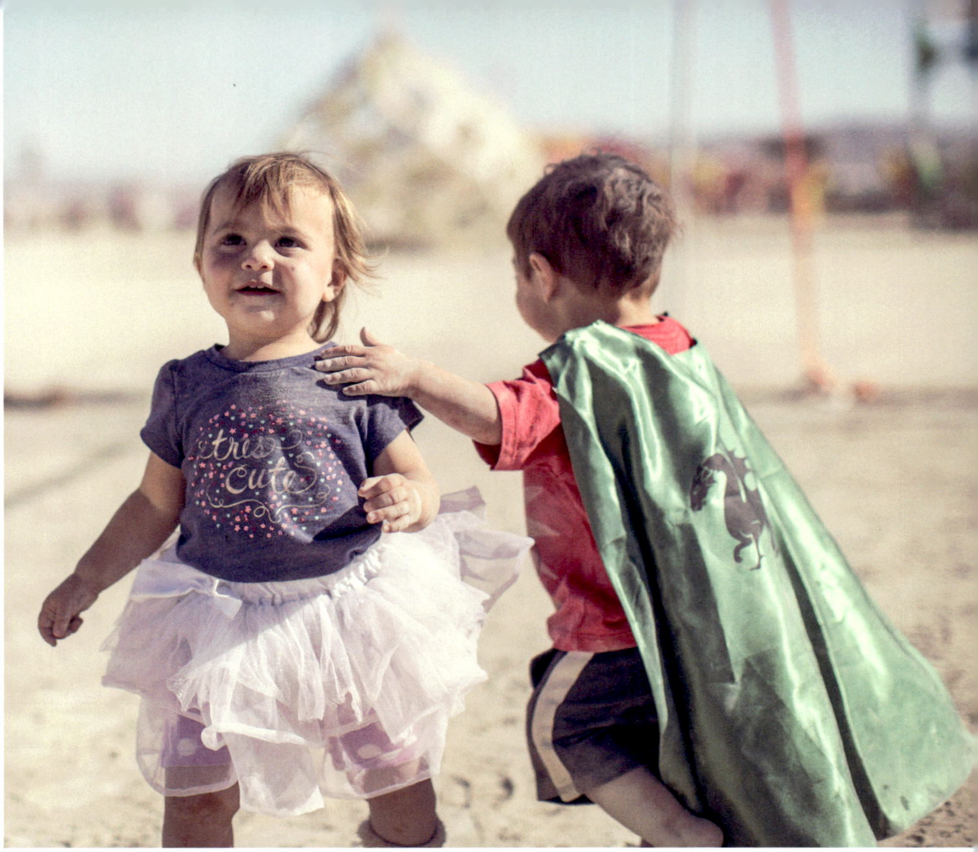
tres cute

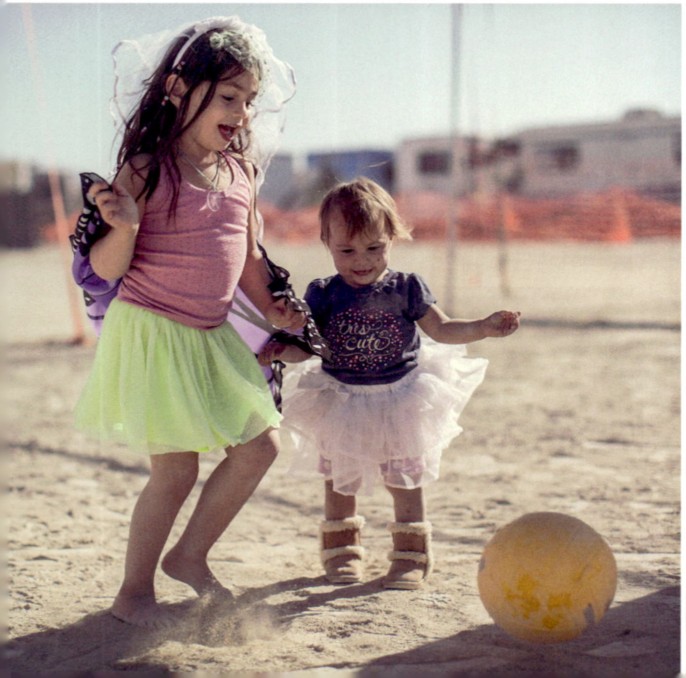

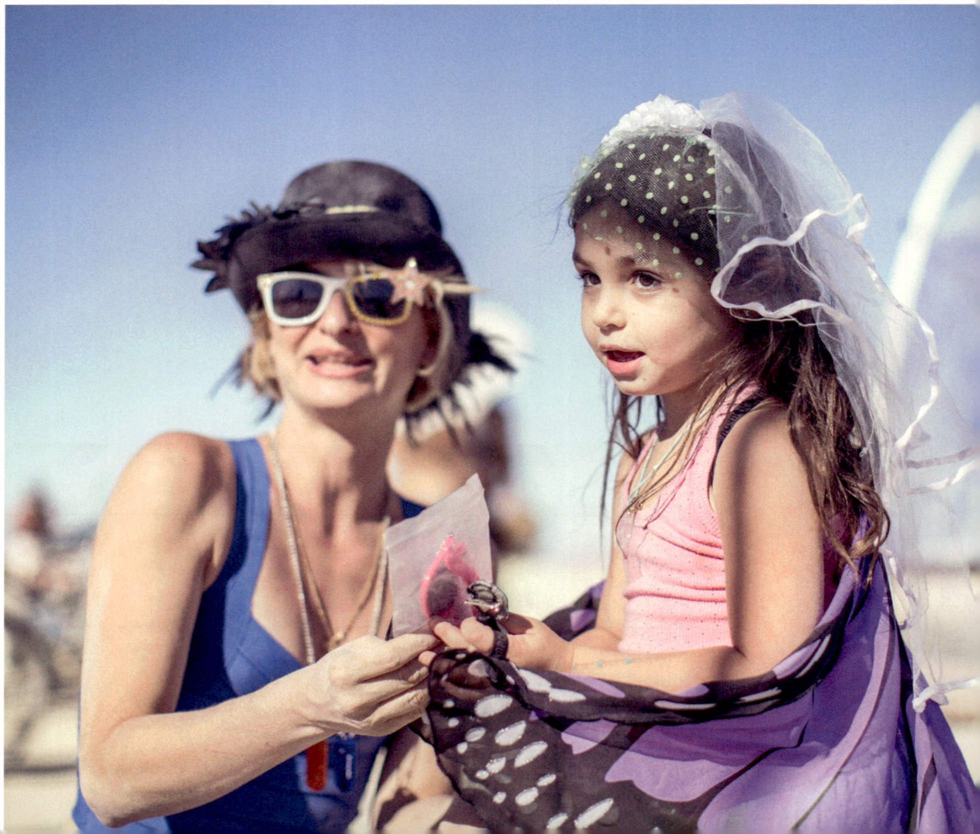

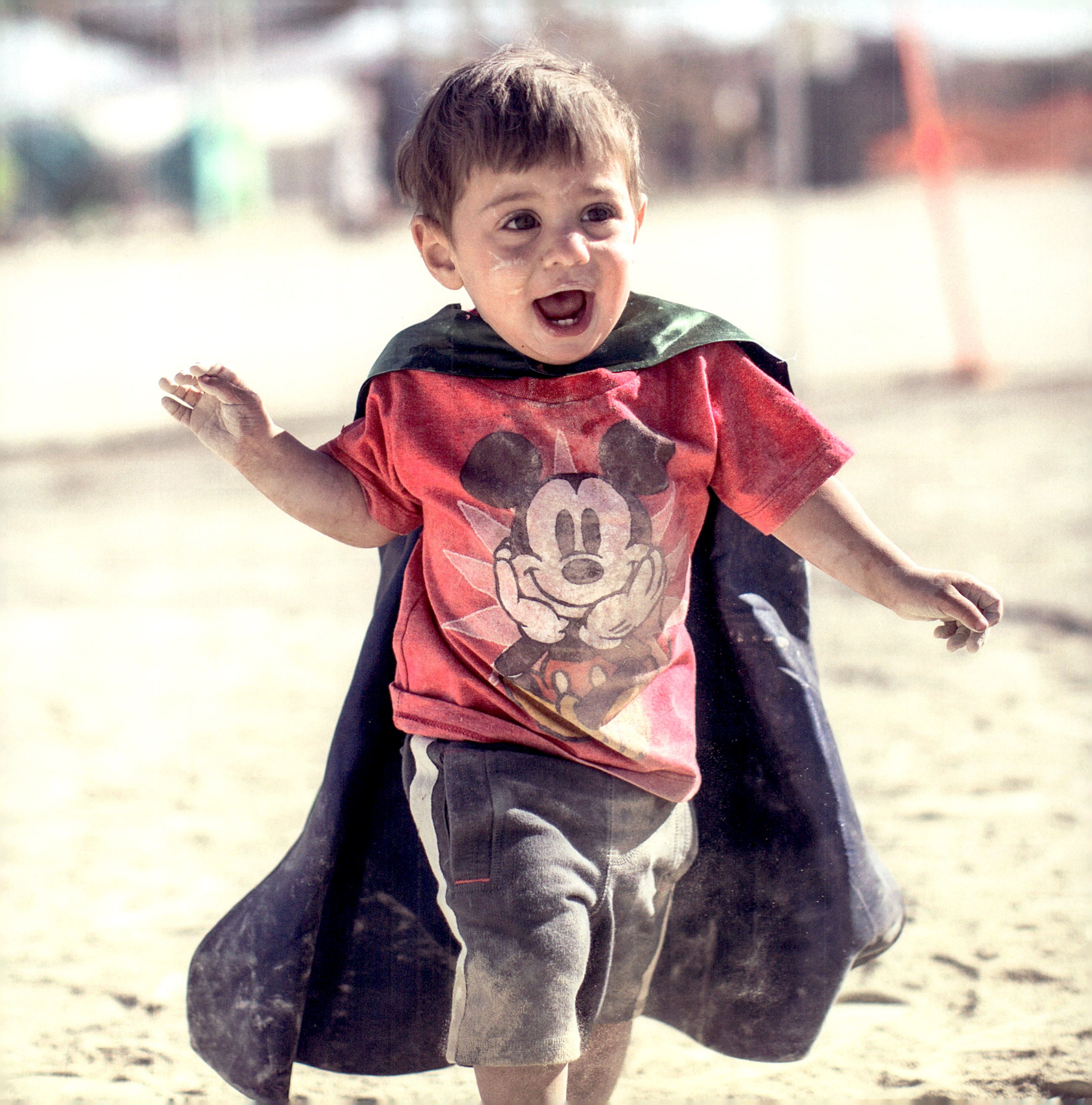

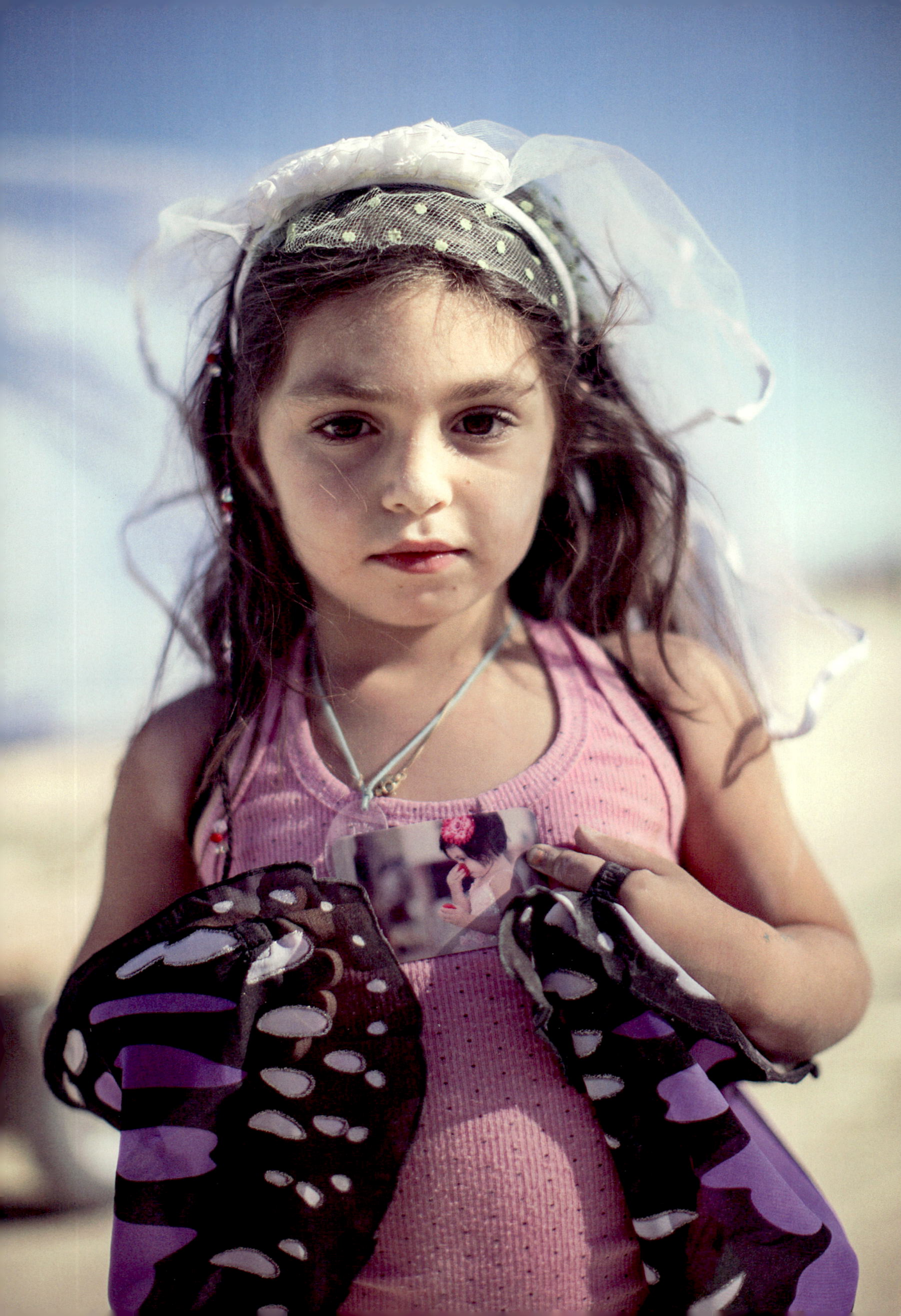

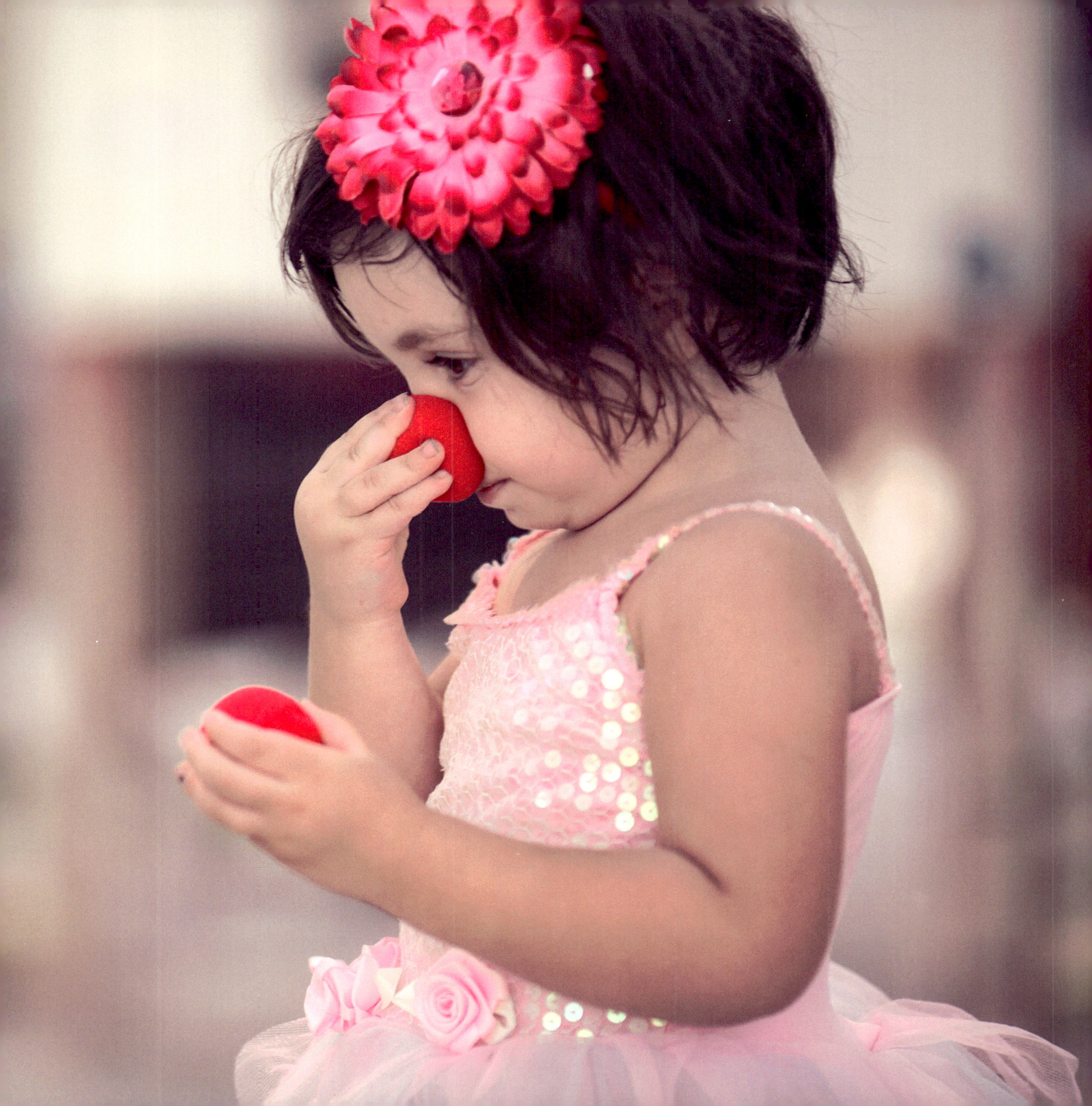

"Burning Man was the first stop on our 8 month trip around the world. We couldn't imagine a better start. It was a life changing experience for us! We'd never experienced so much kindness and support as we did during this week with the Burner families at Kidsville. Stella was the happiest girl in the world playing in the playa dust and running around. While Zippy was taking the pictures she was giggling and shouting in her own baby language: 'Jete! Jete!' which means 'More! More!' – our free and happy little star. It's so much fun to show her the world!"

ELA, ANDREJ & STELLA

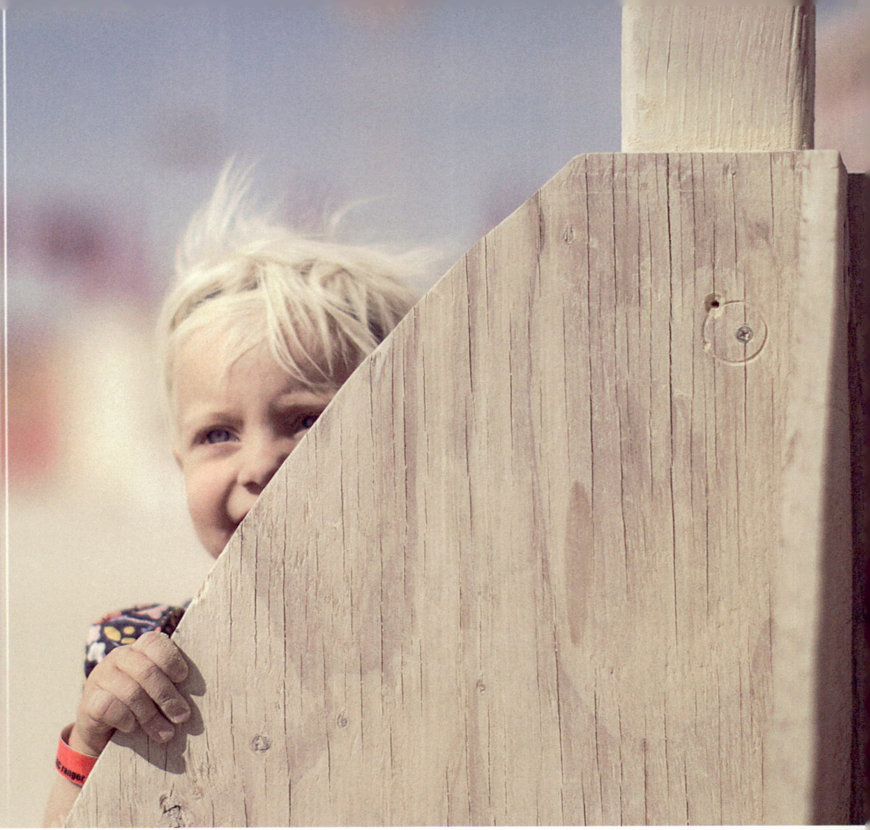

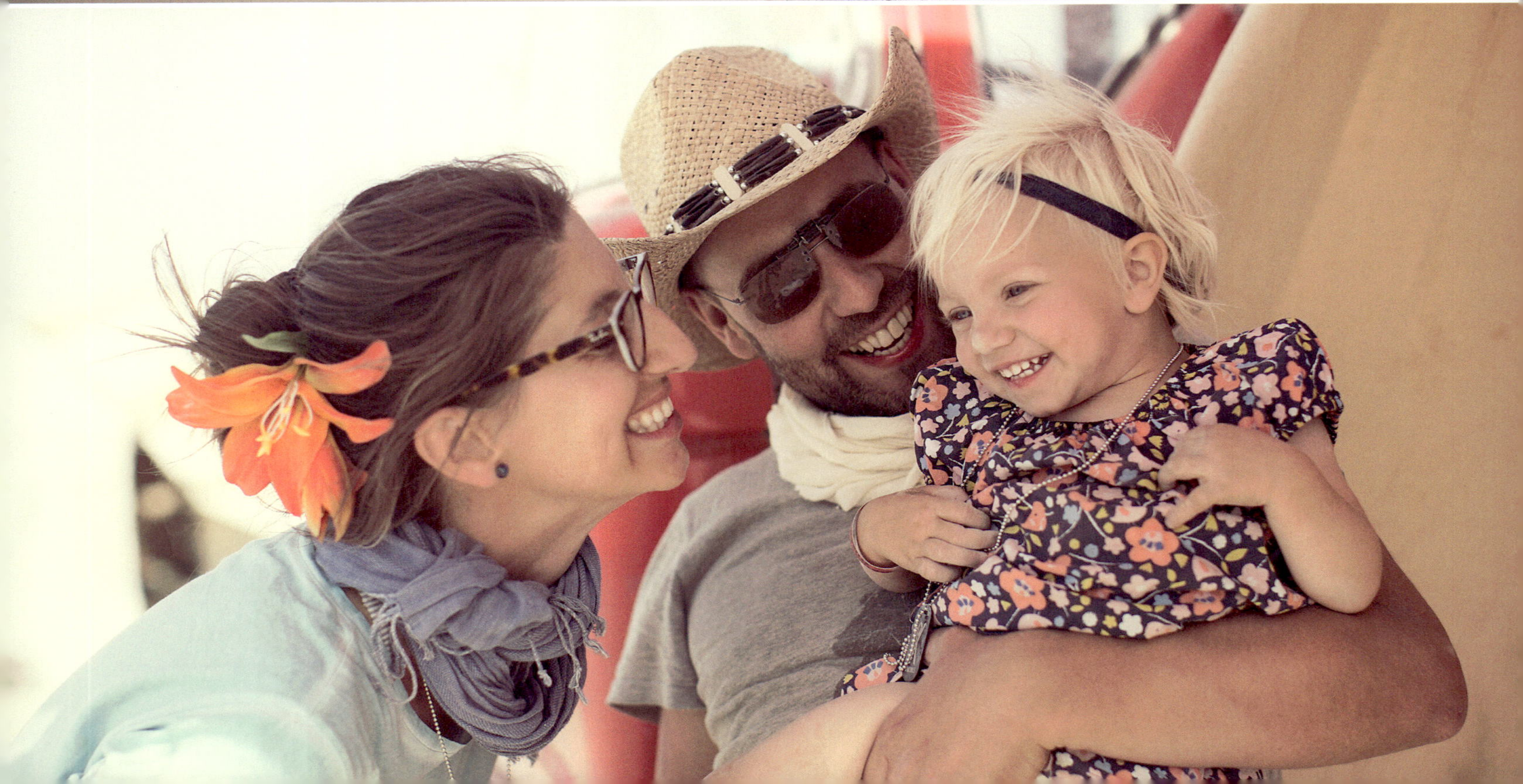

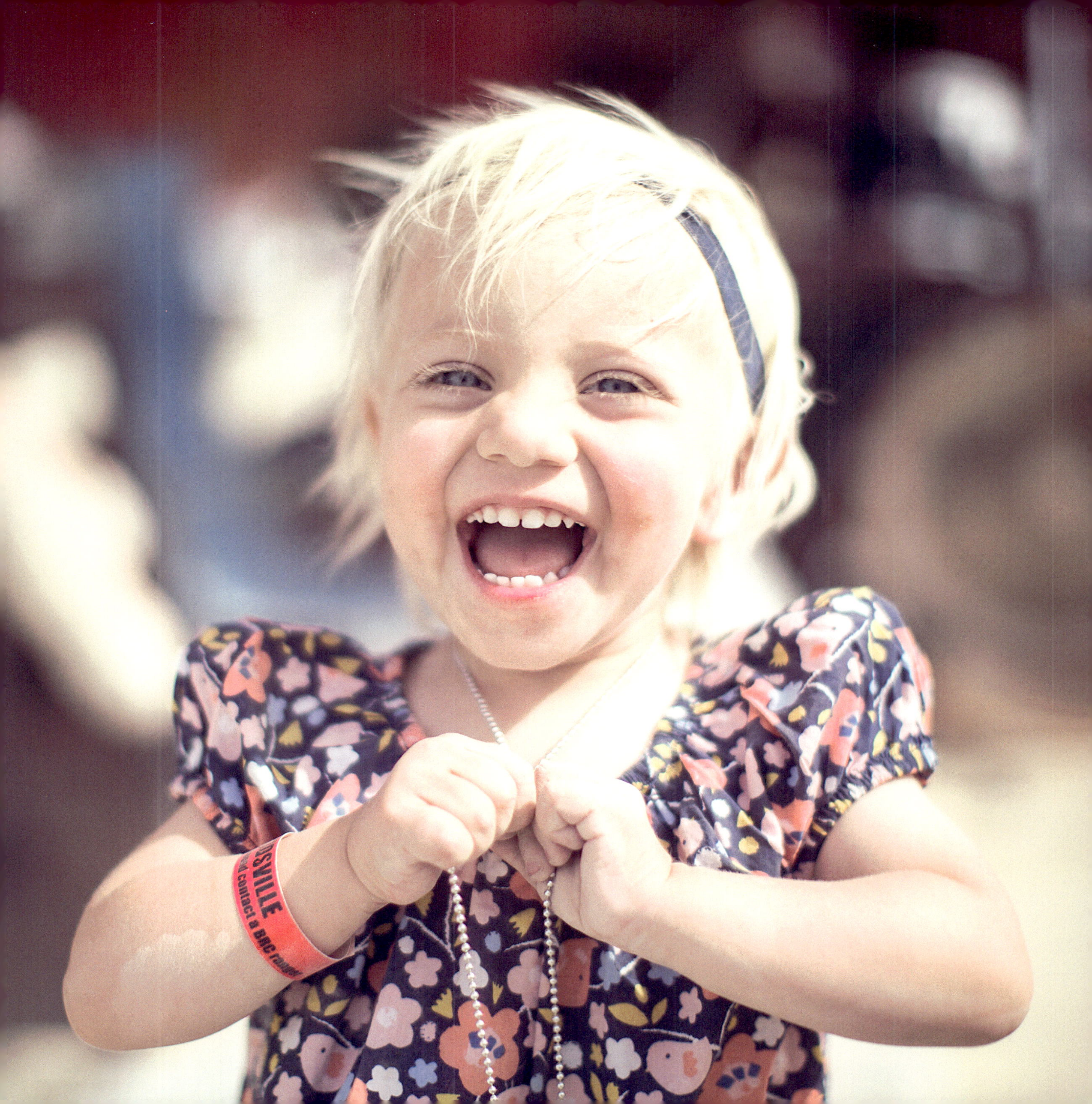
contact a BRC

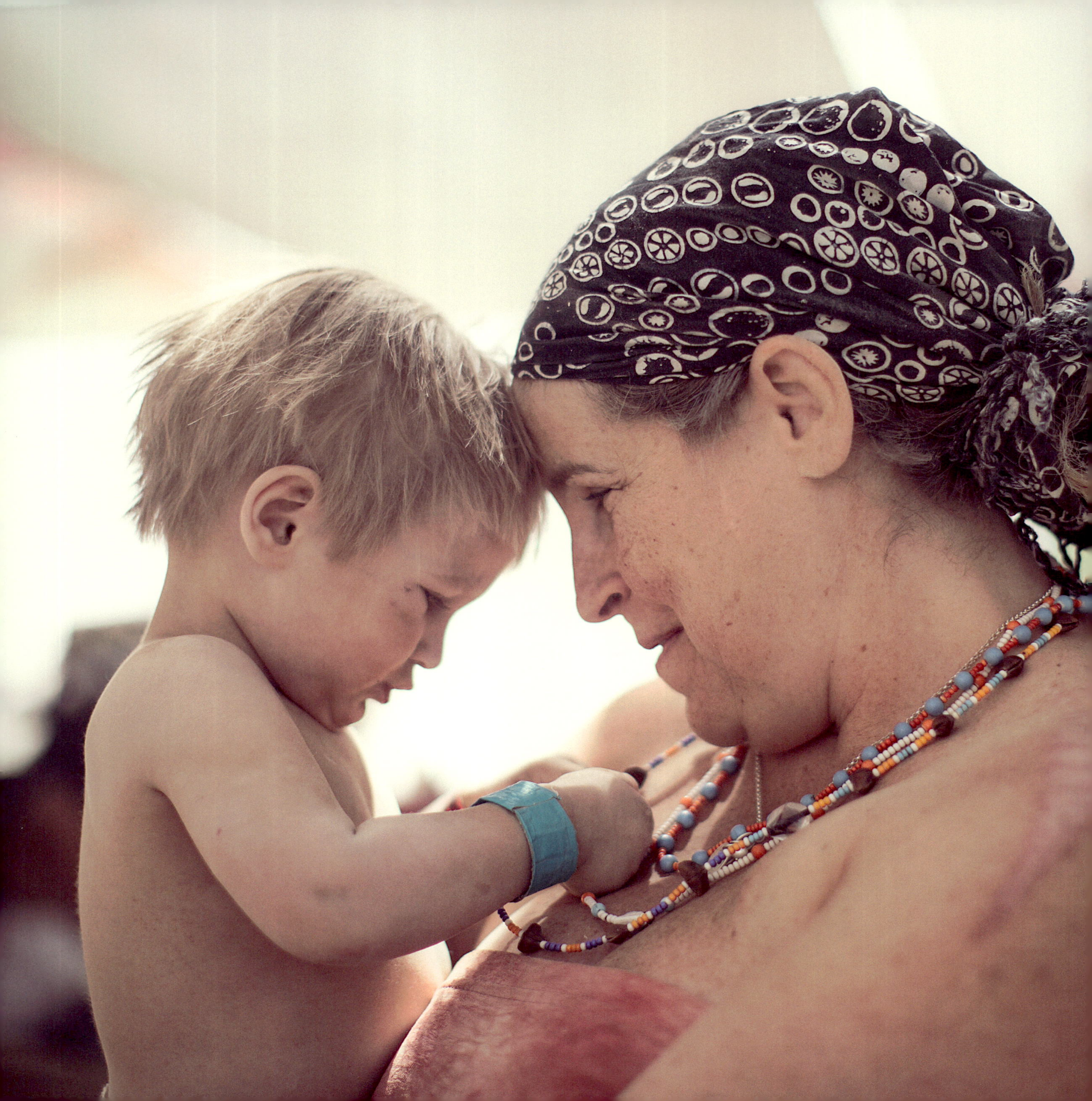

"We've brought our two little ones to the desert since our oldest was in utero. The love they have received has been tremendous. And we've noticed that **as much as the Playa has given them, they are a gift to the Playa as well.** I think it's because children always see you. Before they can communicate with words, they share with their eyes, with their smiles and with their present souls. At Burning Man, they get all of that energy coming right back at them and then some! And they already know how to receive it. It's reminded us that the 10 principles are natural in that we all practice them from birth, before life pulls you in other directions. So we celebrate our own sense of wonder right beside our kids. It's like we've stepped into their world, back to our original selves, and we get to experience the world anew."

LAURIE SALES

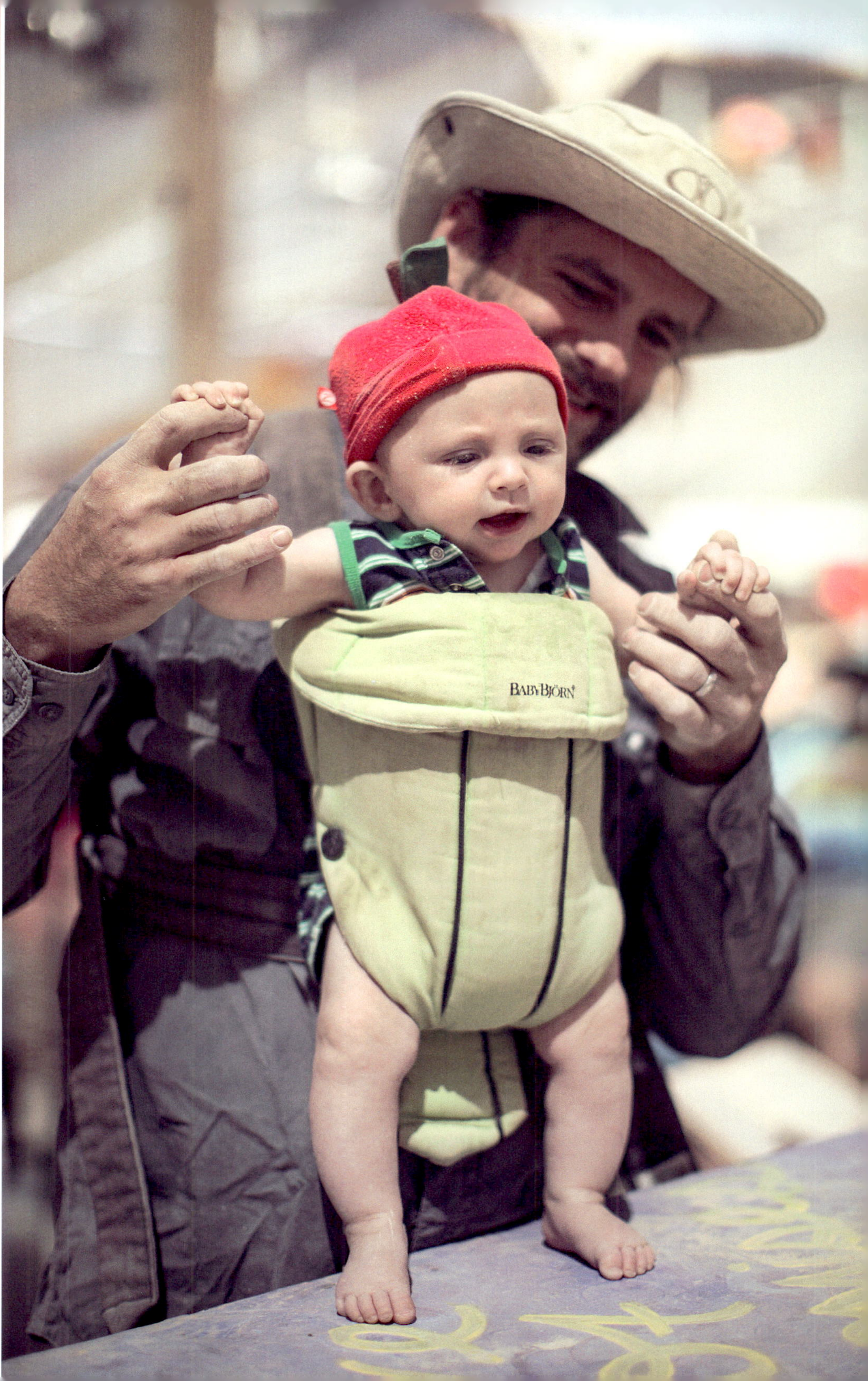

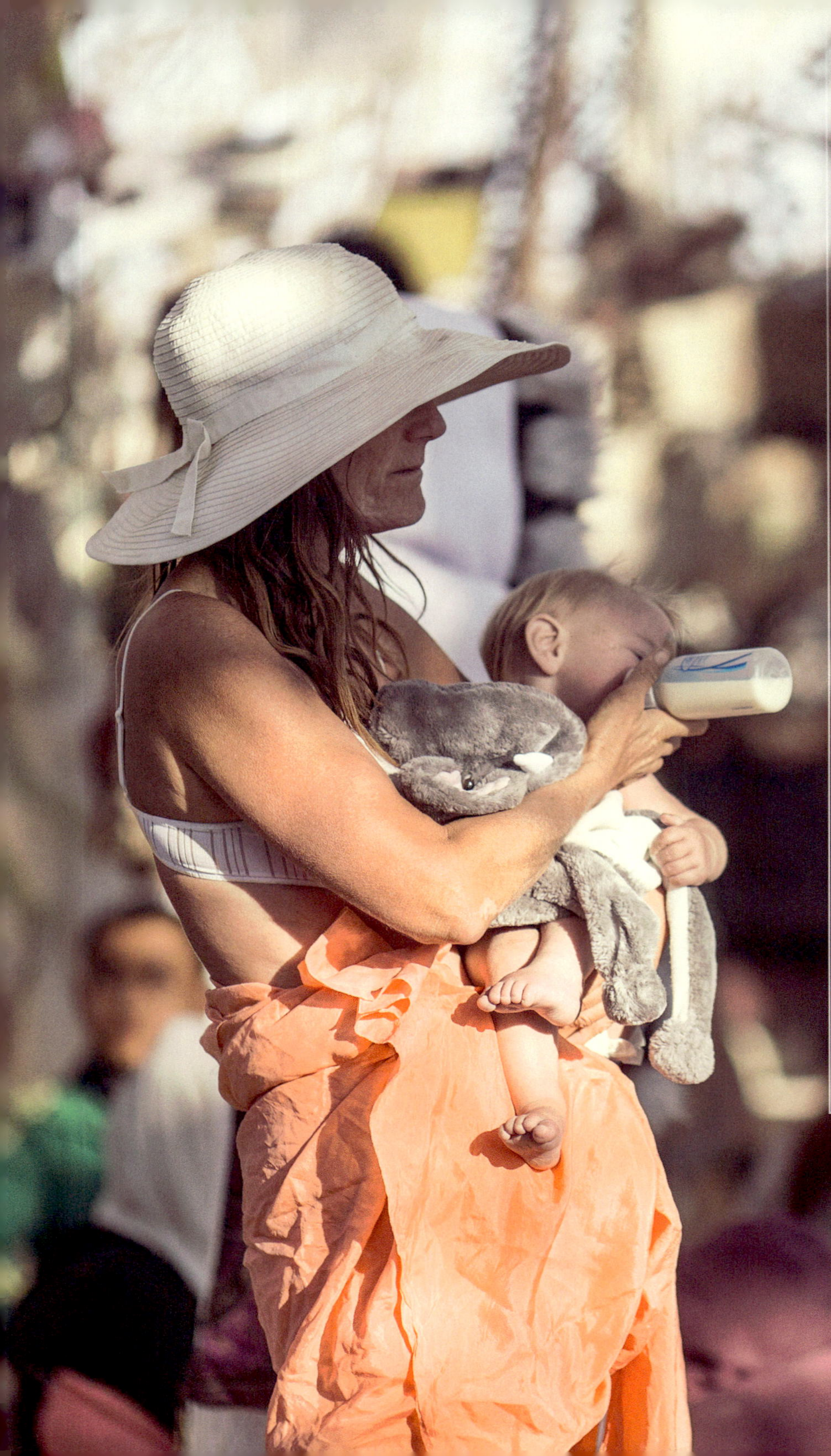

"Having Astara at Burning Man was a mystical experience. Her love radiated and touched so many hearts. The loving connection of all the people felt like family, as she was gifted with hugs and smiles and precious little gifts everywhere we went. It is amazing because it felt like such a natural environment for her. The whole community held a safe container with such love and tenderness and joy. It was my privilege how people would stop to connect with this little infant and hold her or look into her eyes, how they'd look at her in wonder, marvelling that she was out there on the playa – it felt like a dream to some people."

MAURA & ASTARA

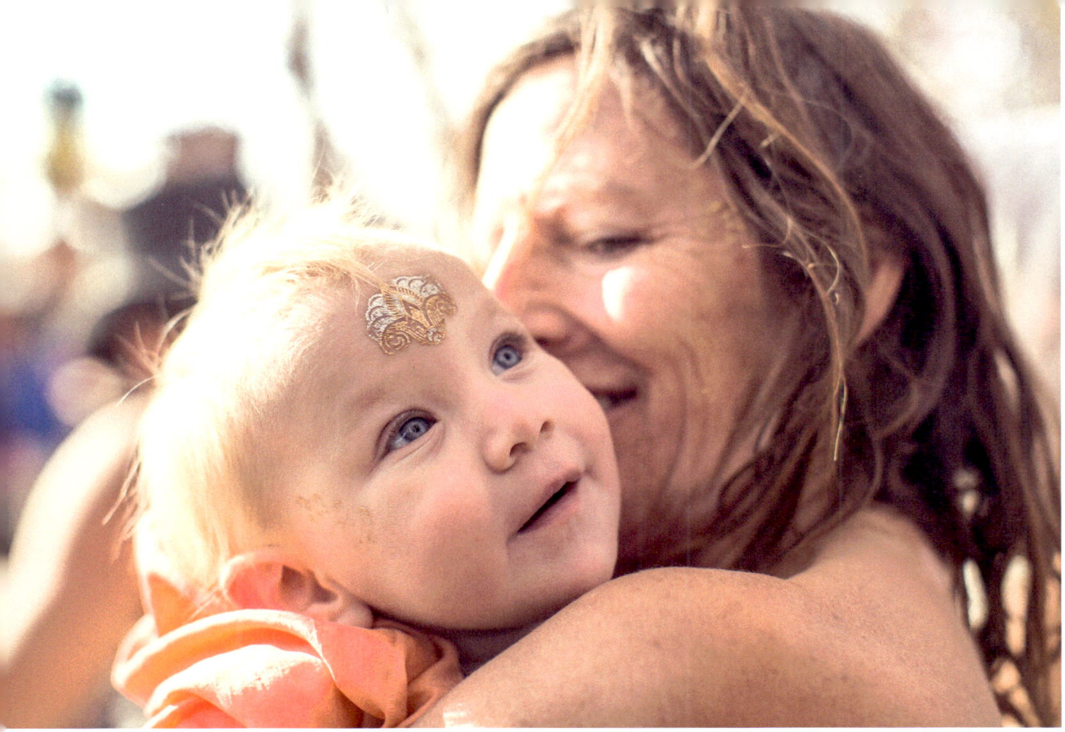

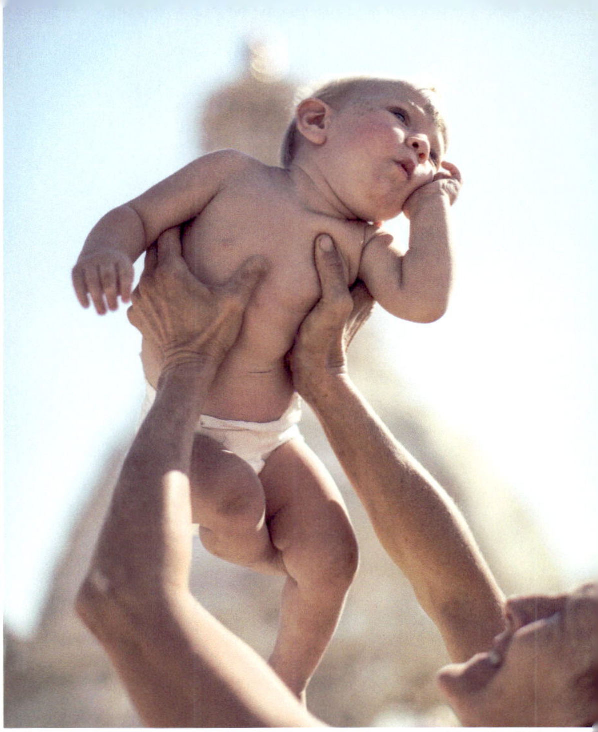

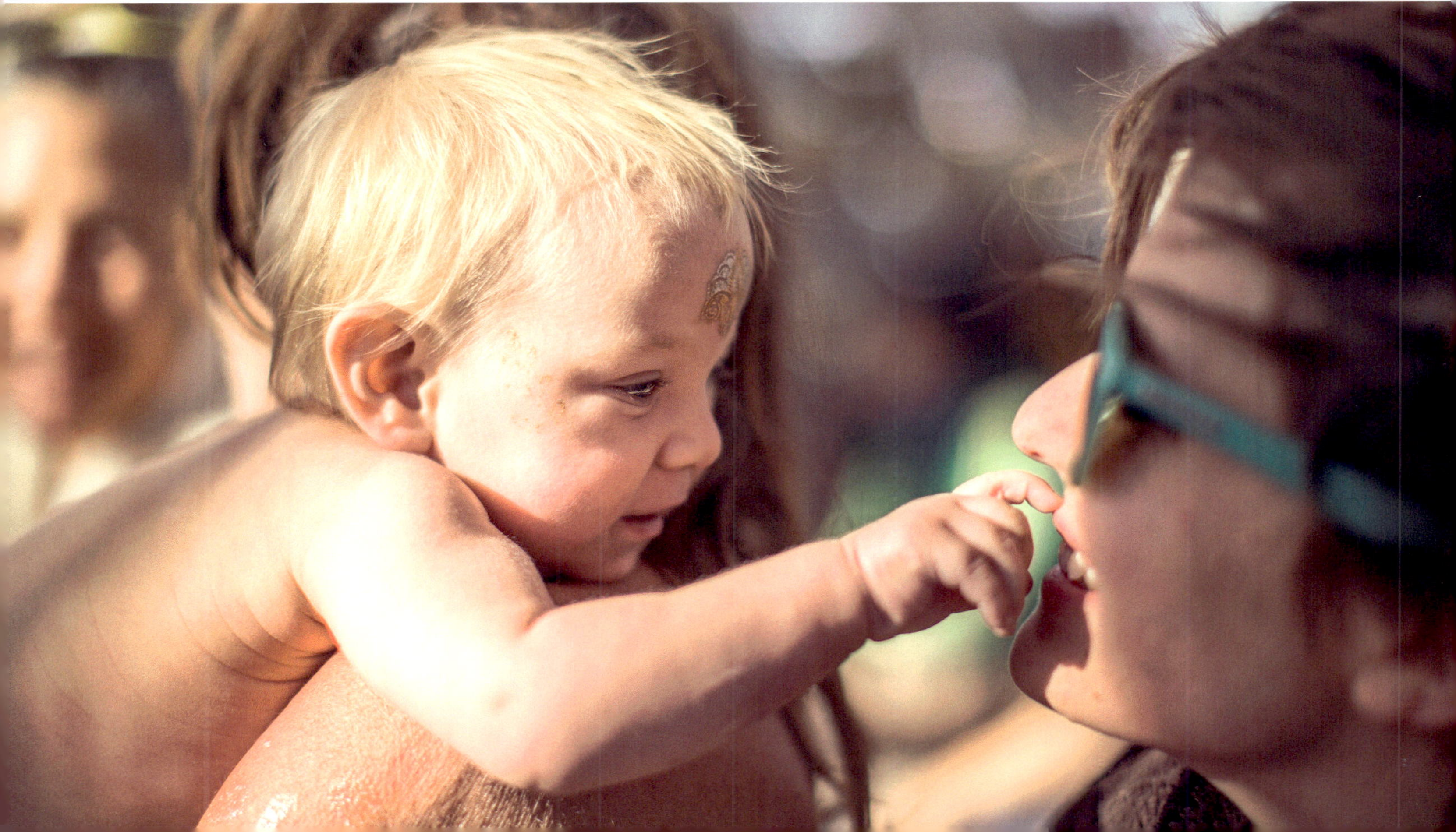

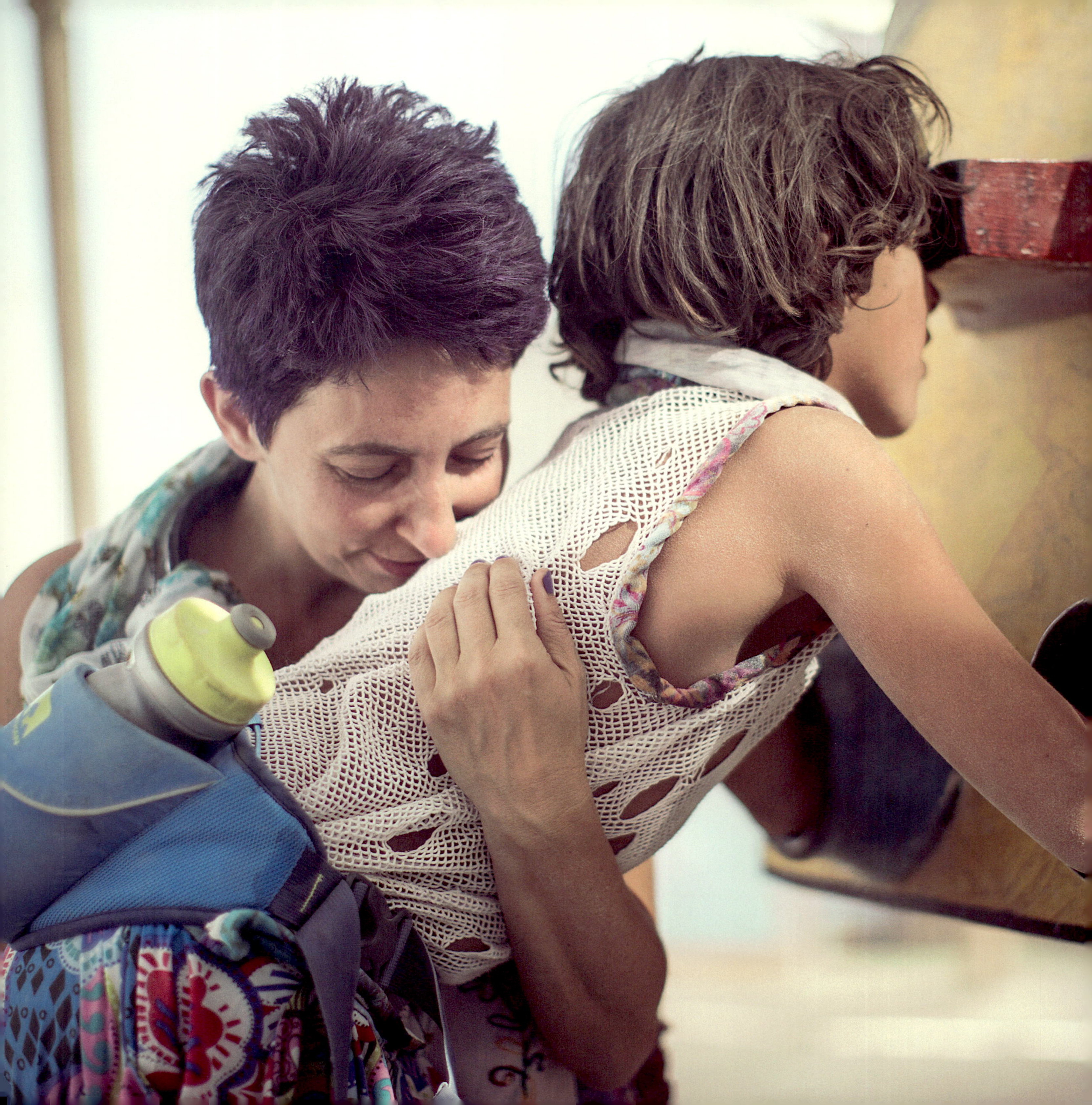

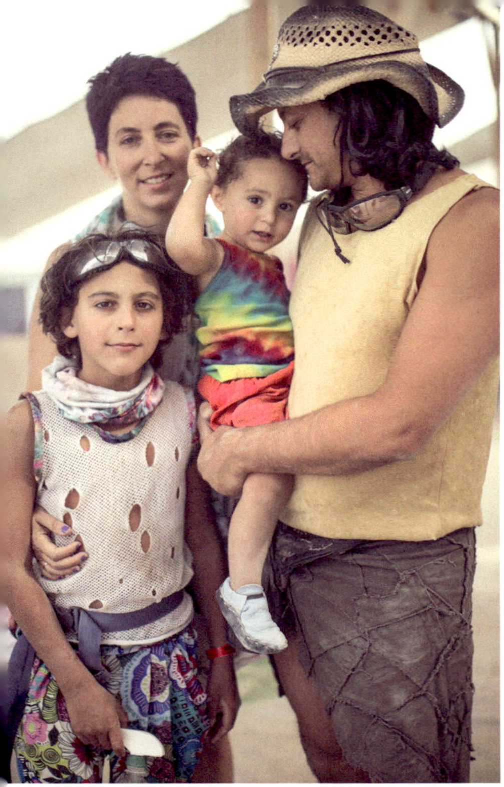

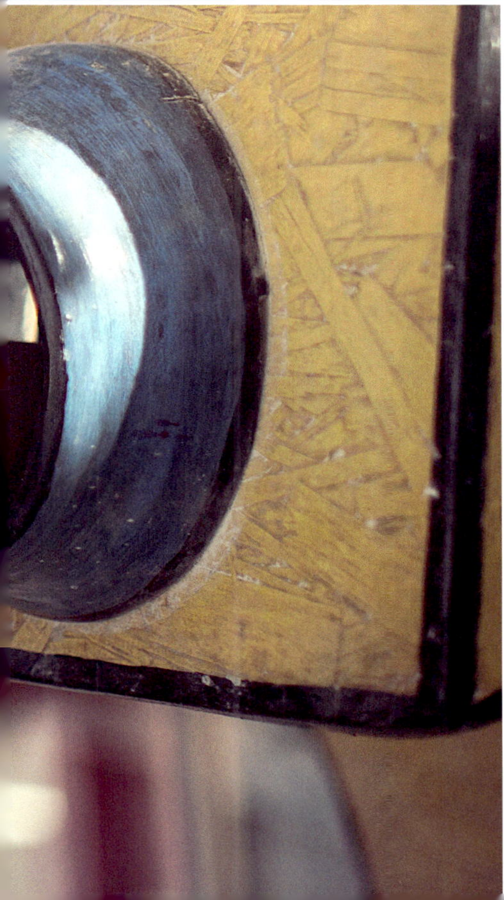

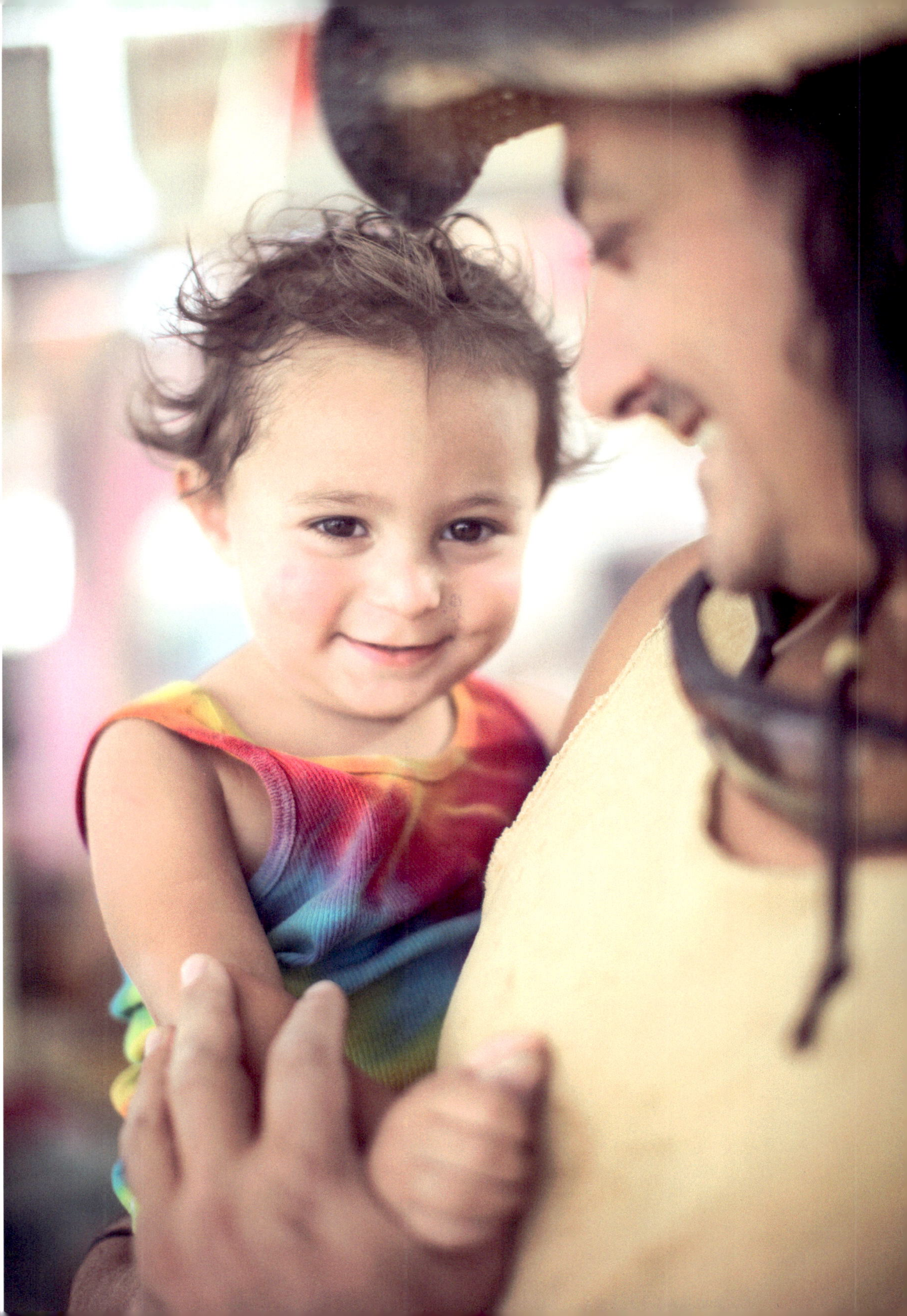

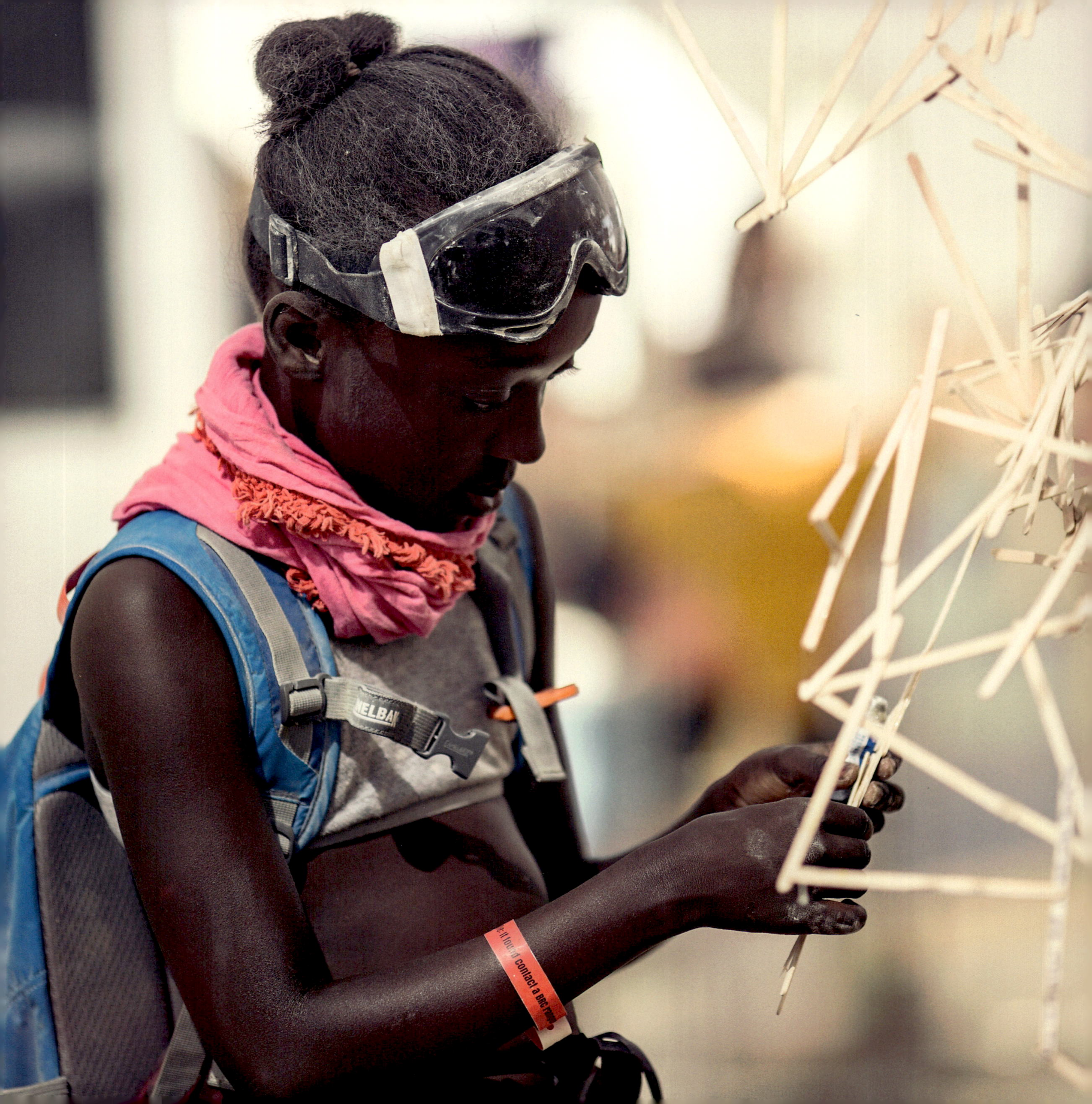

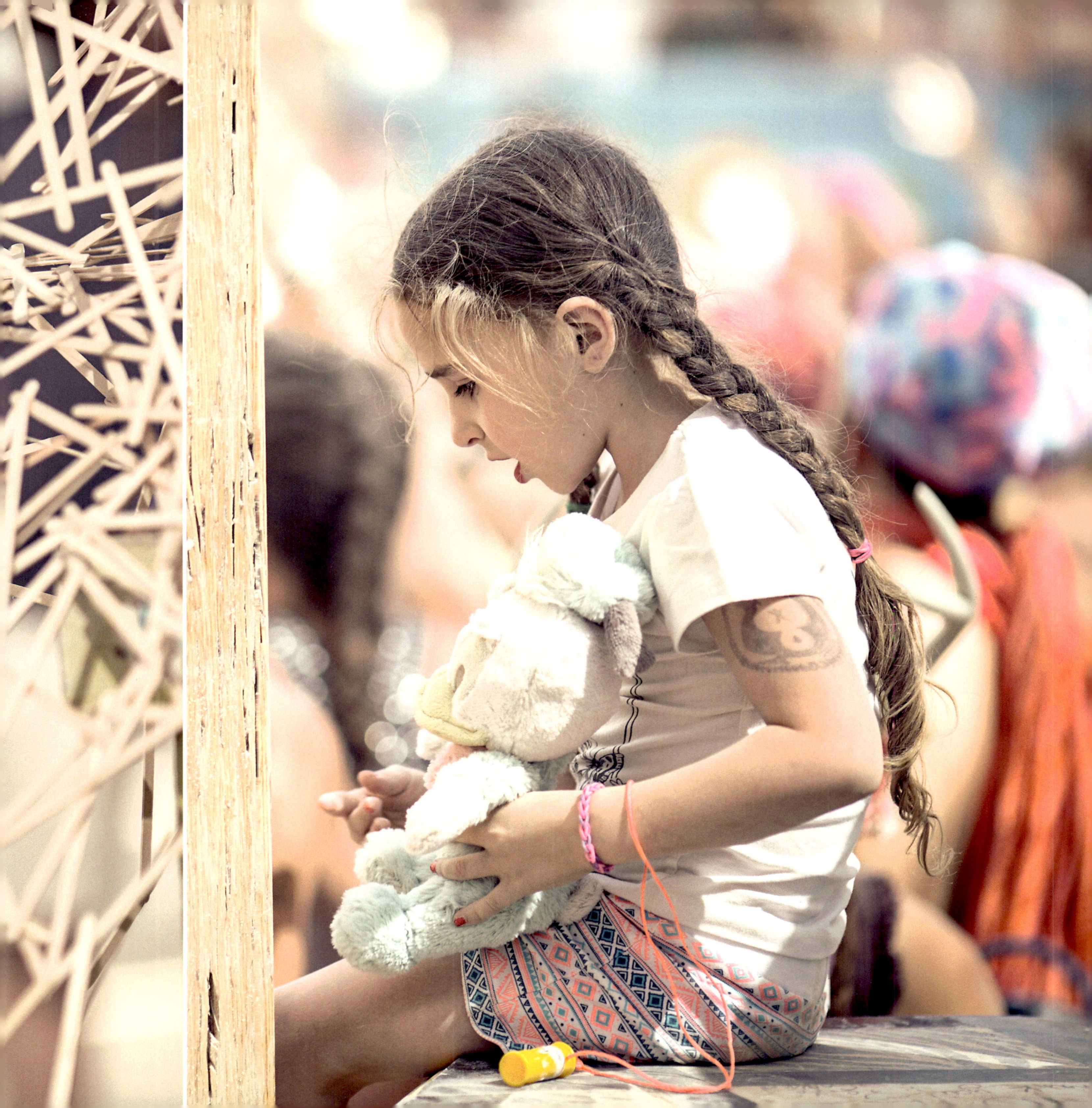

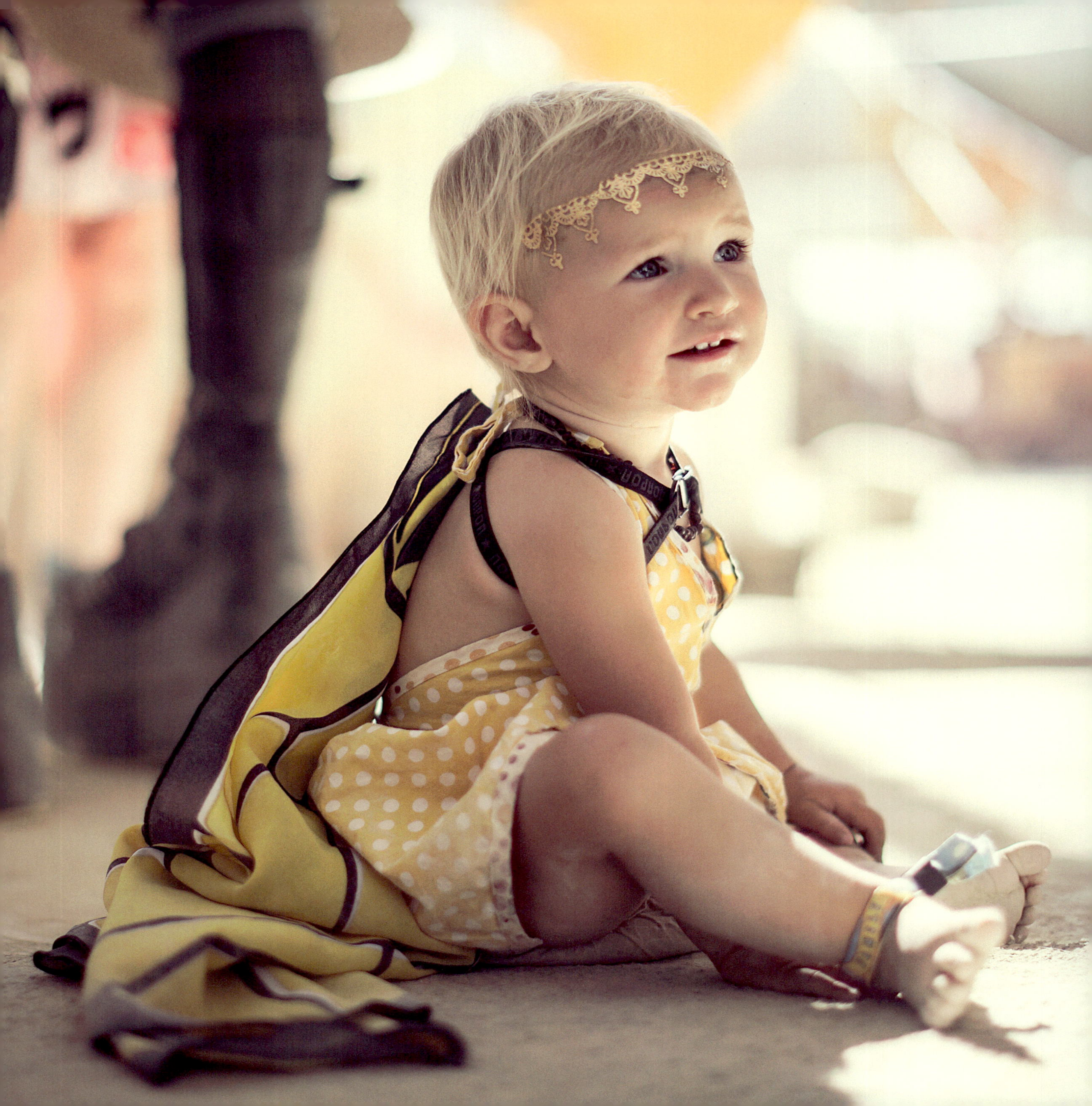

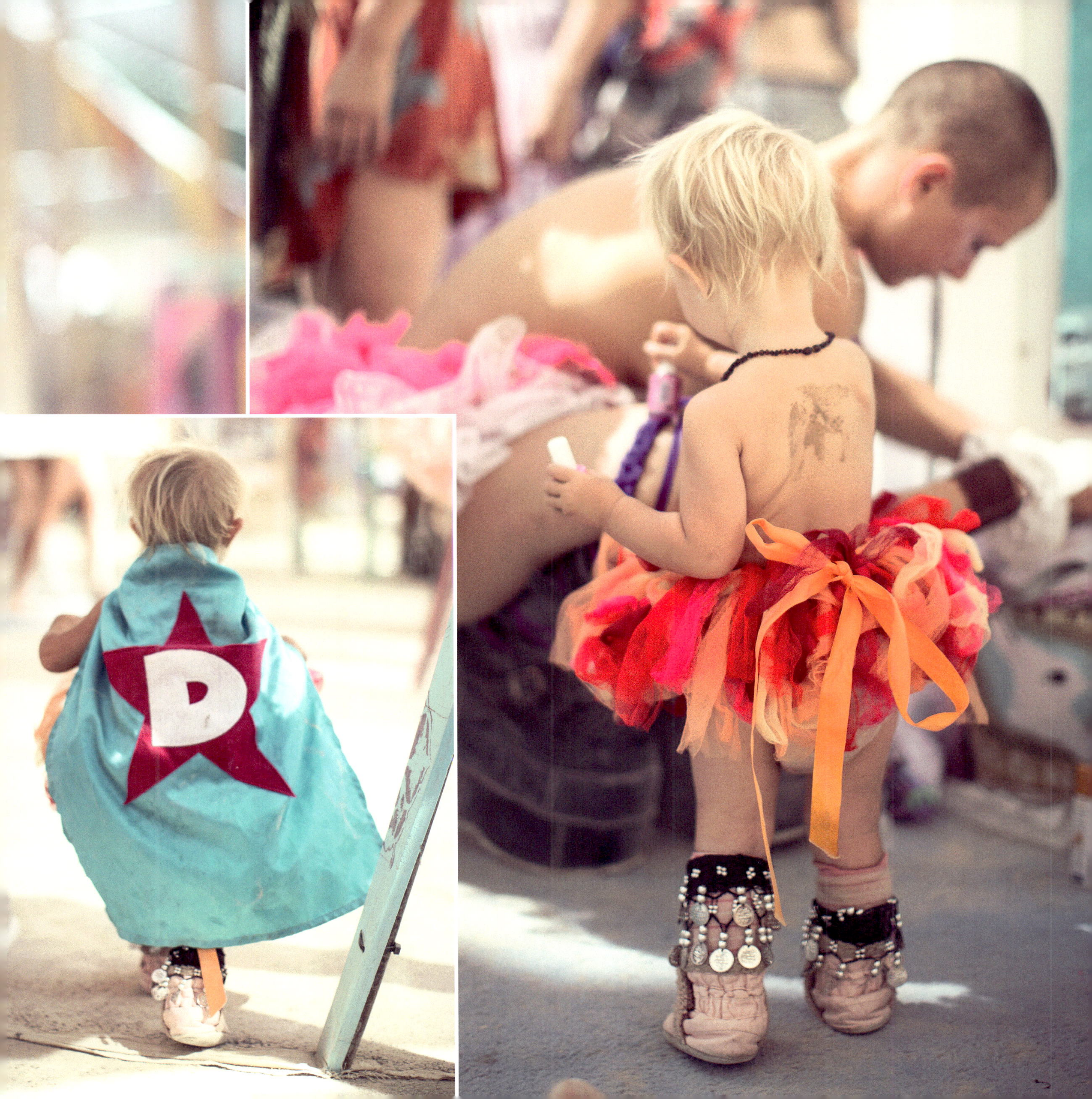
D

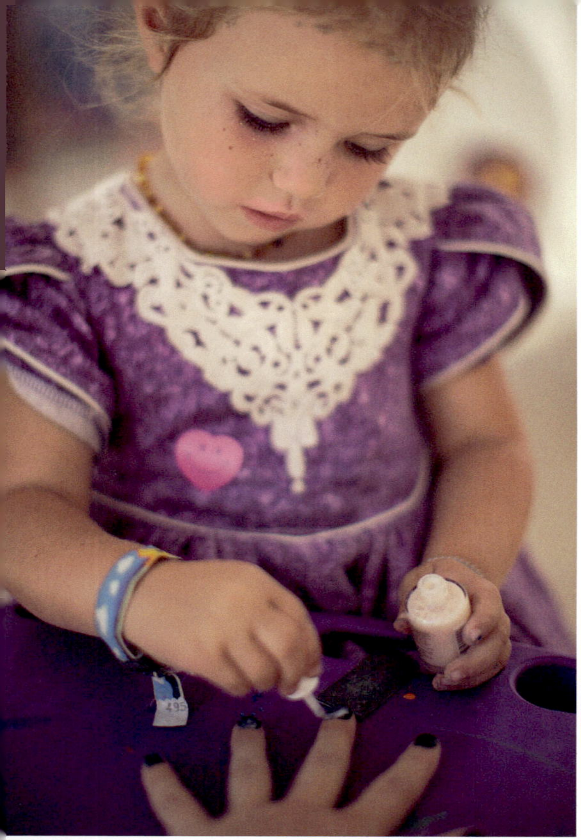
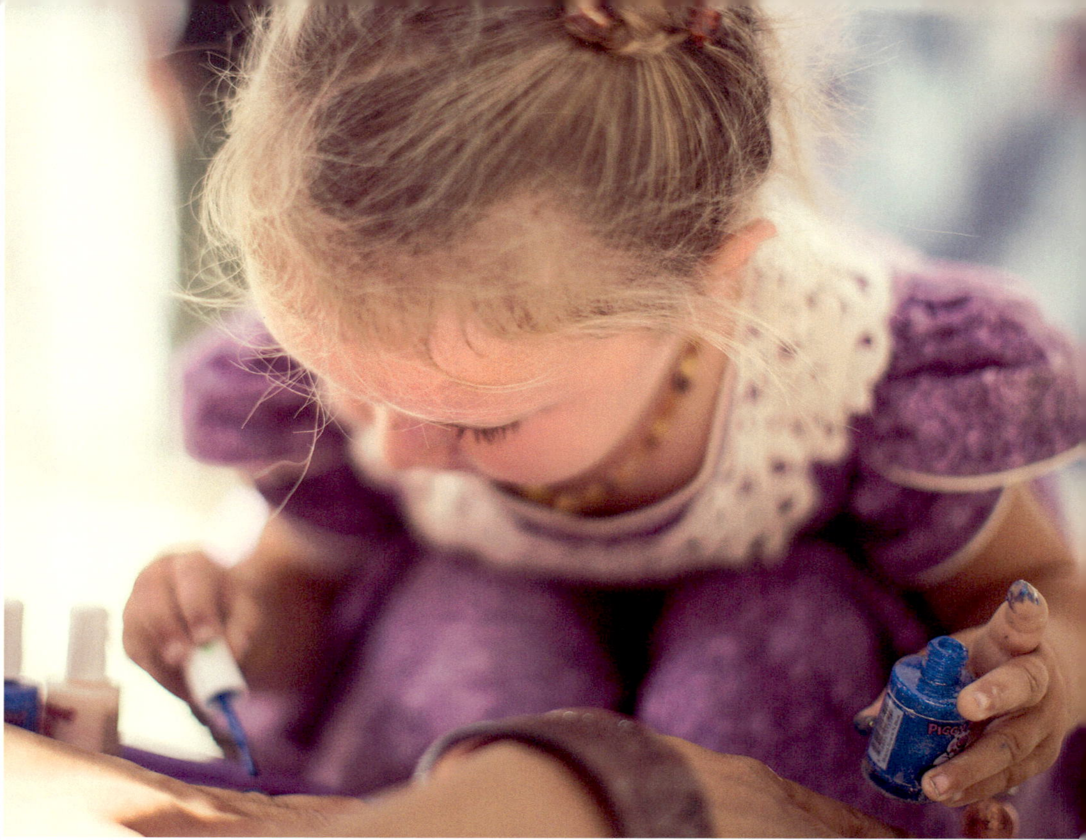
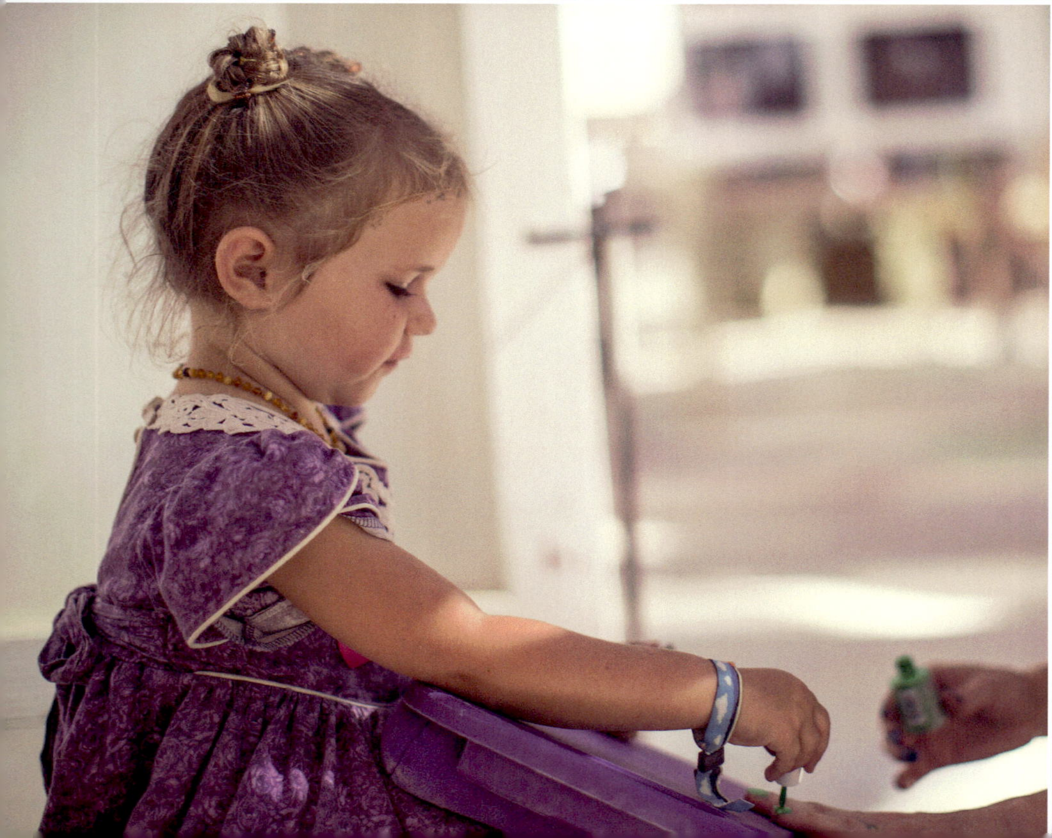
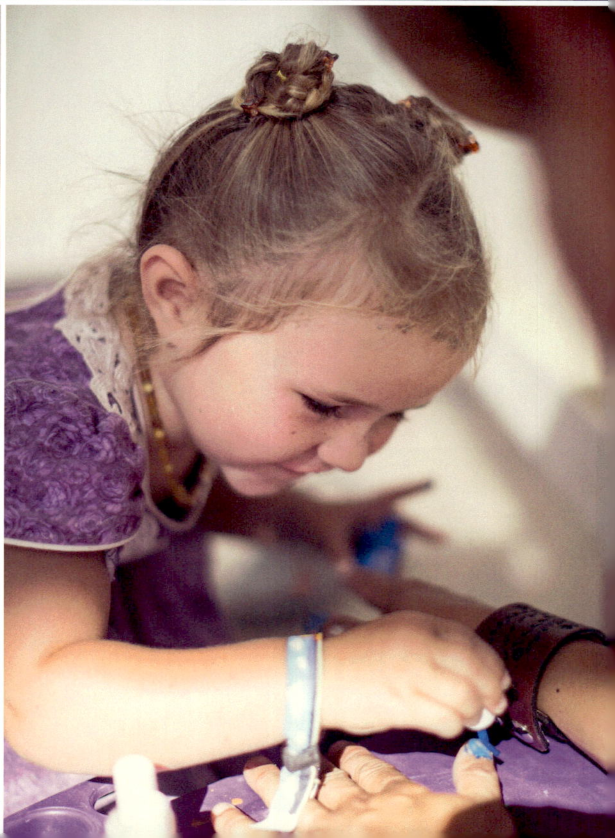

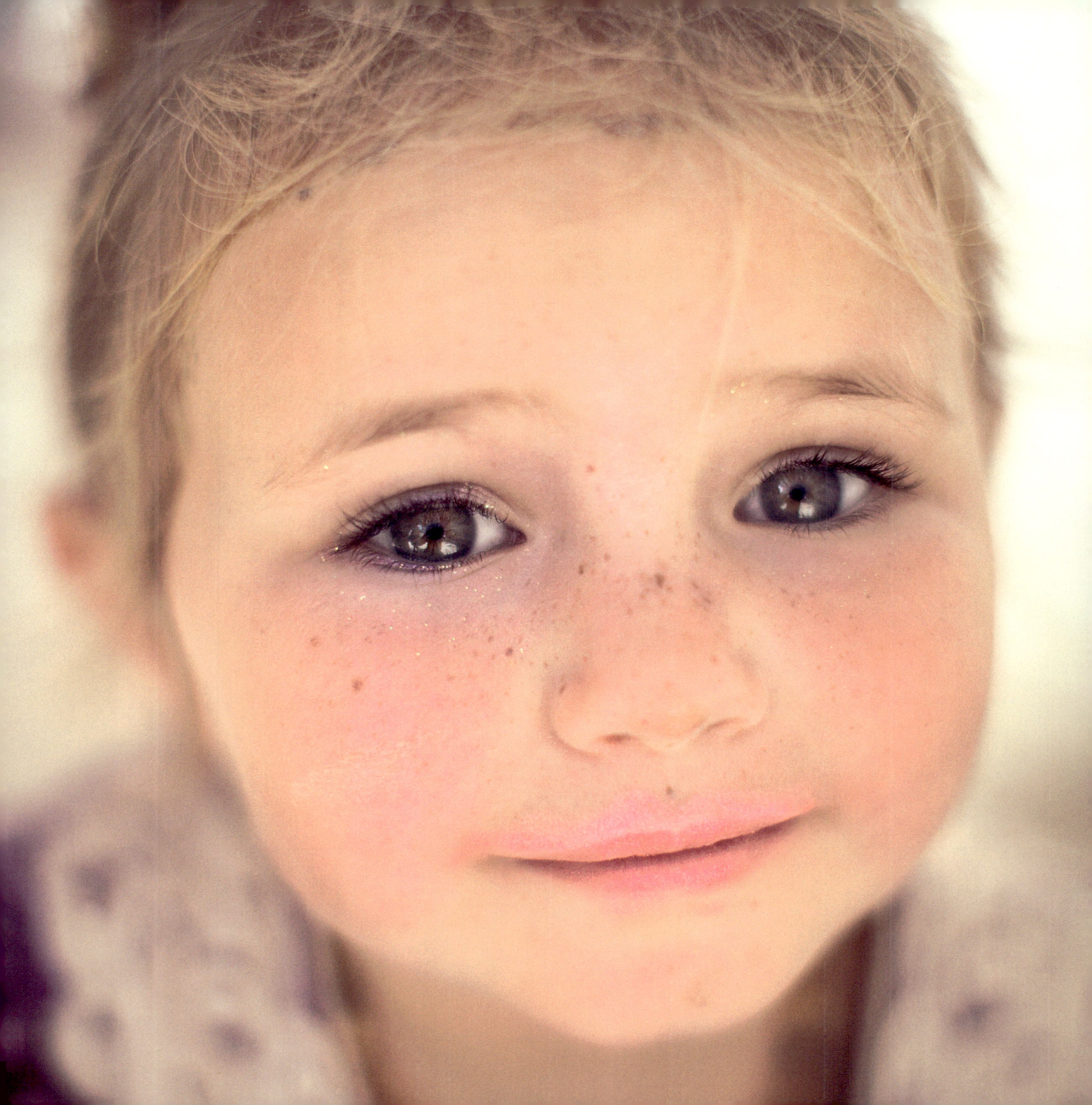

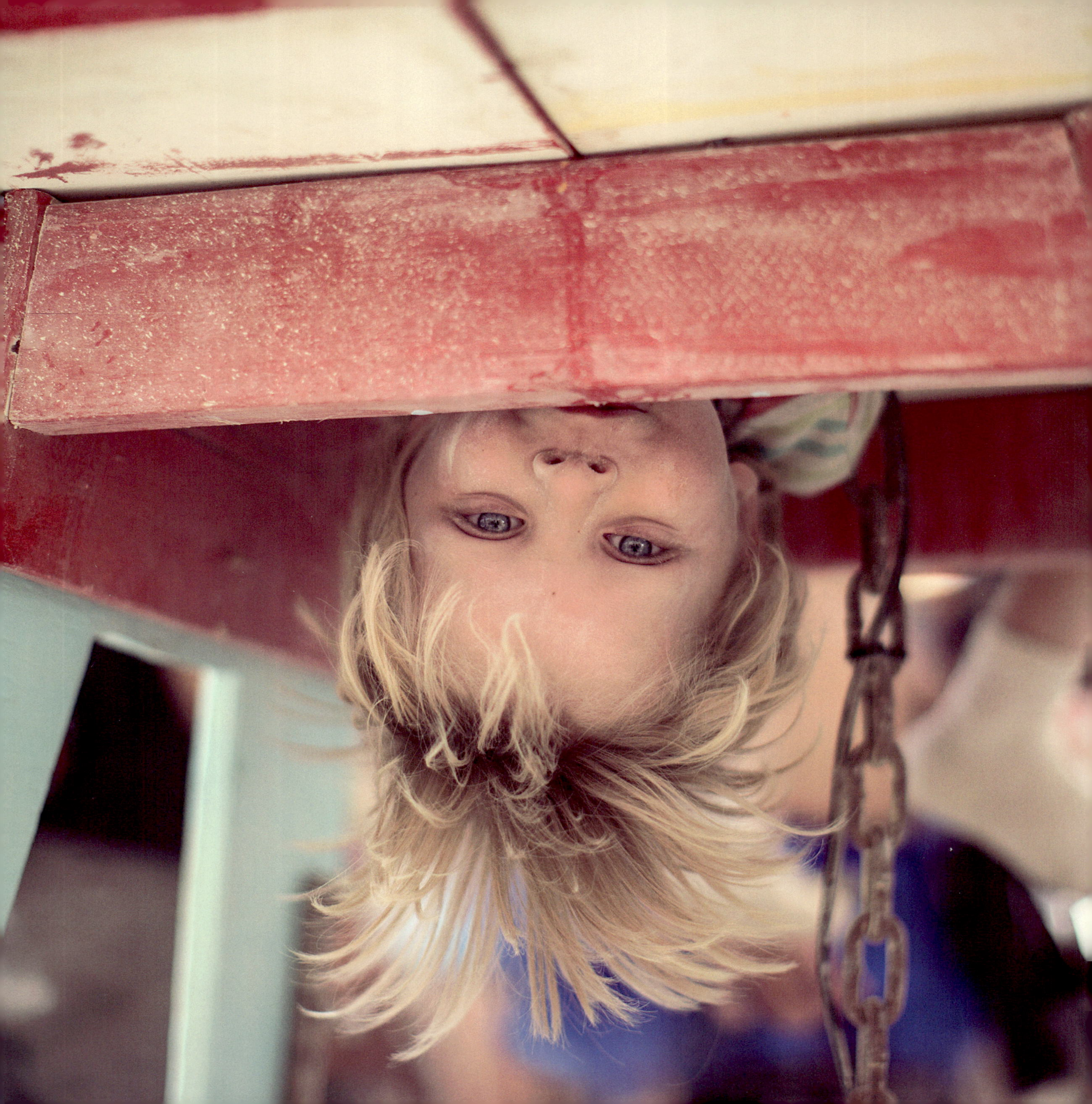

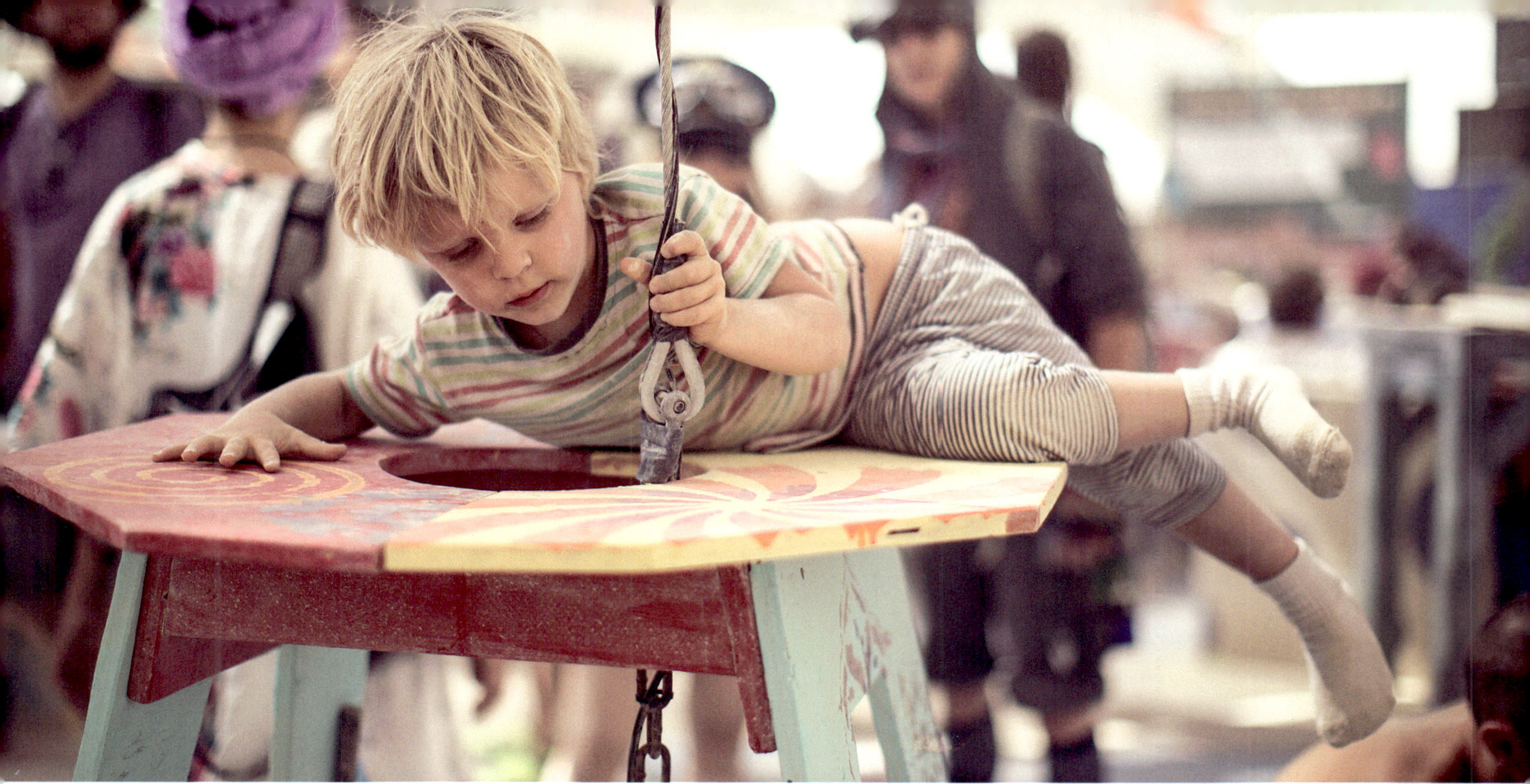
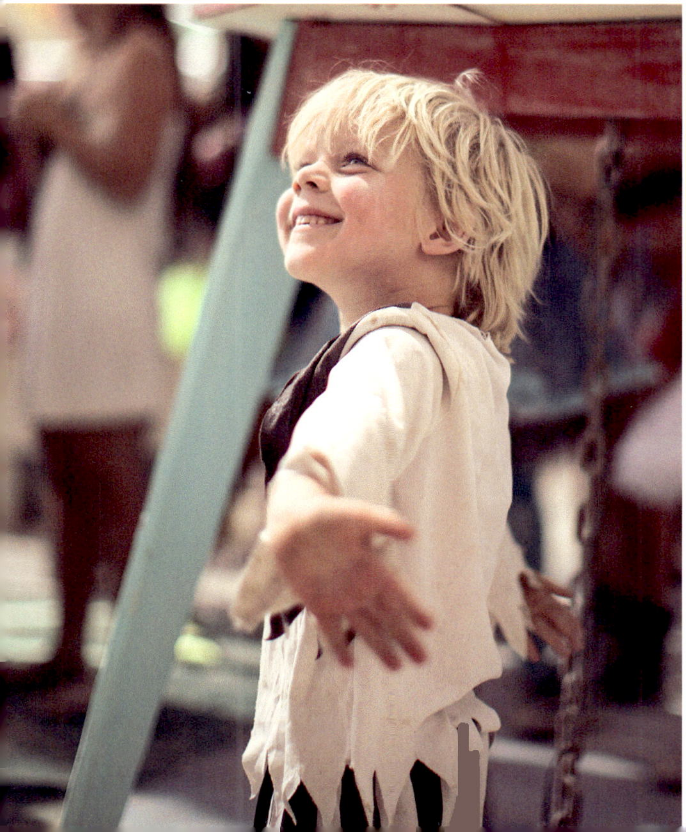
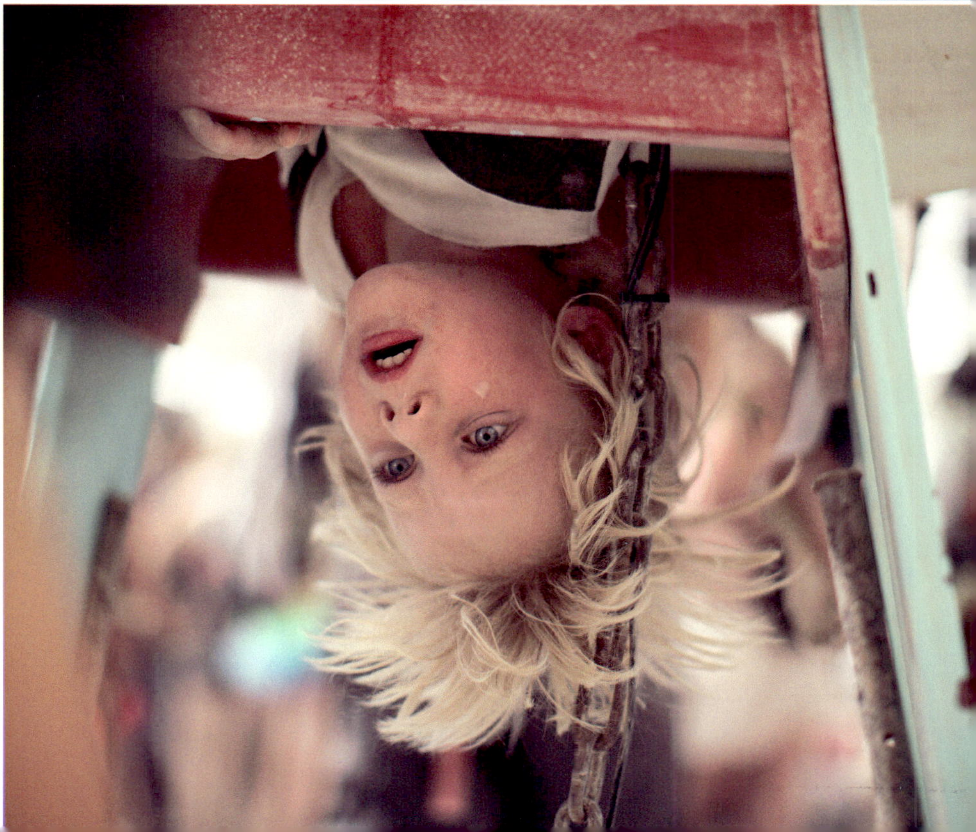

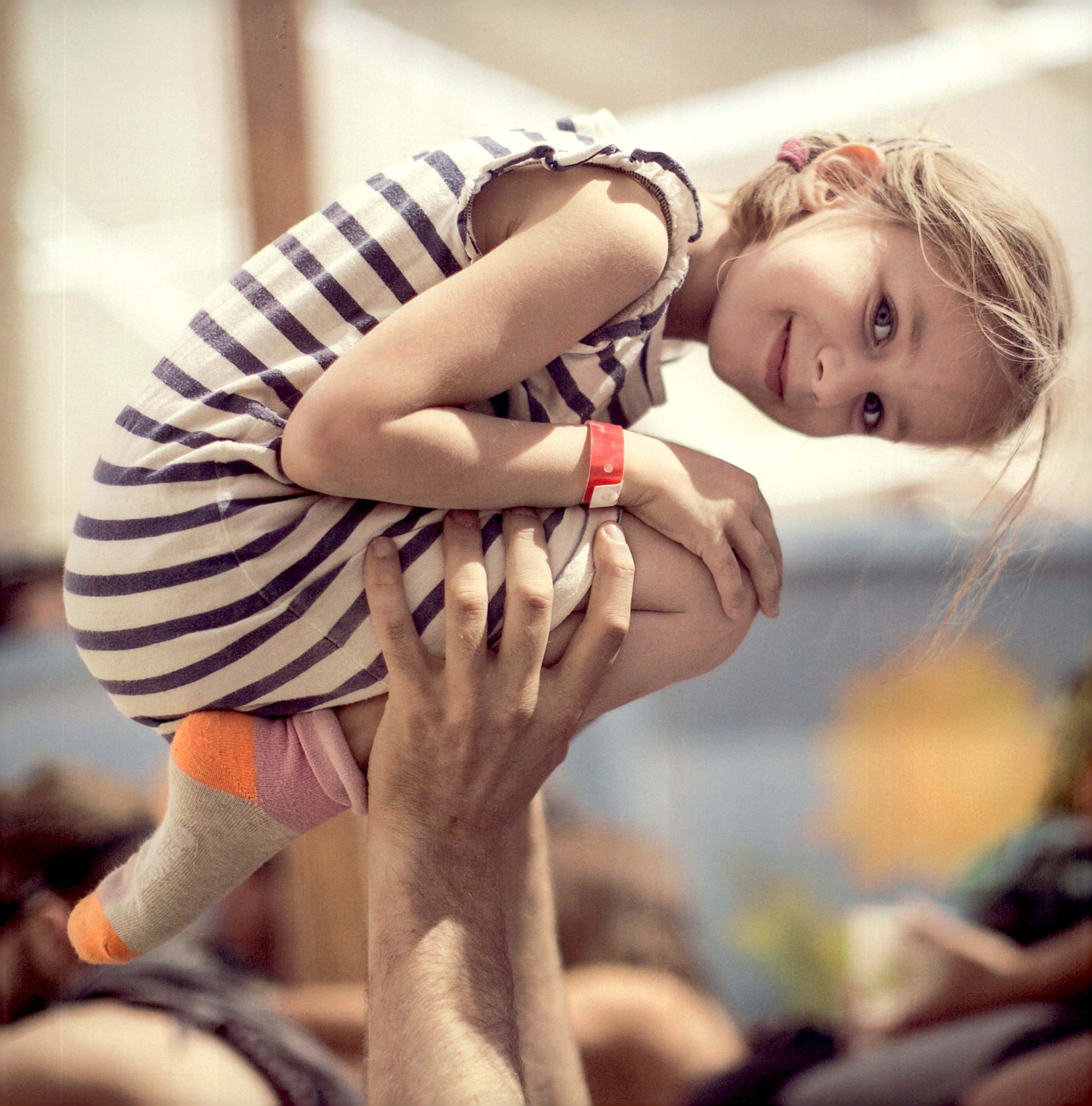

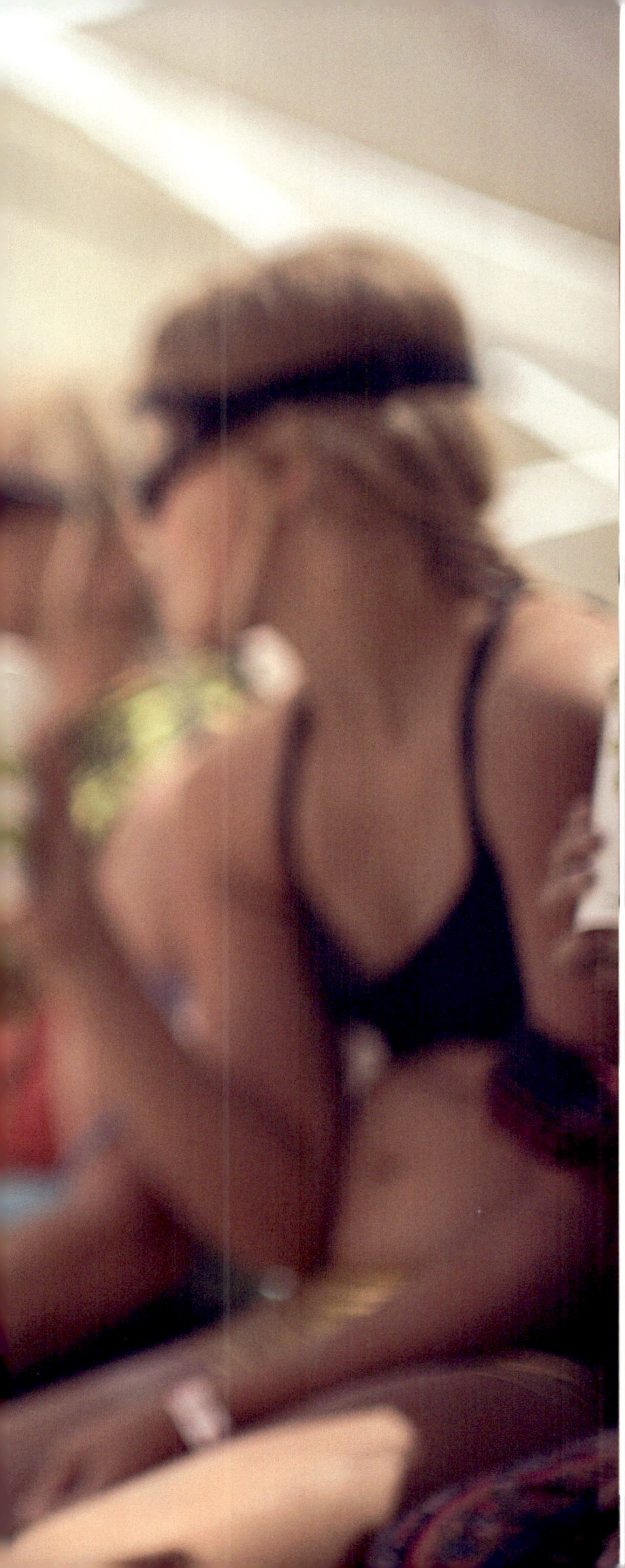
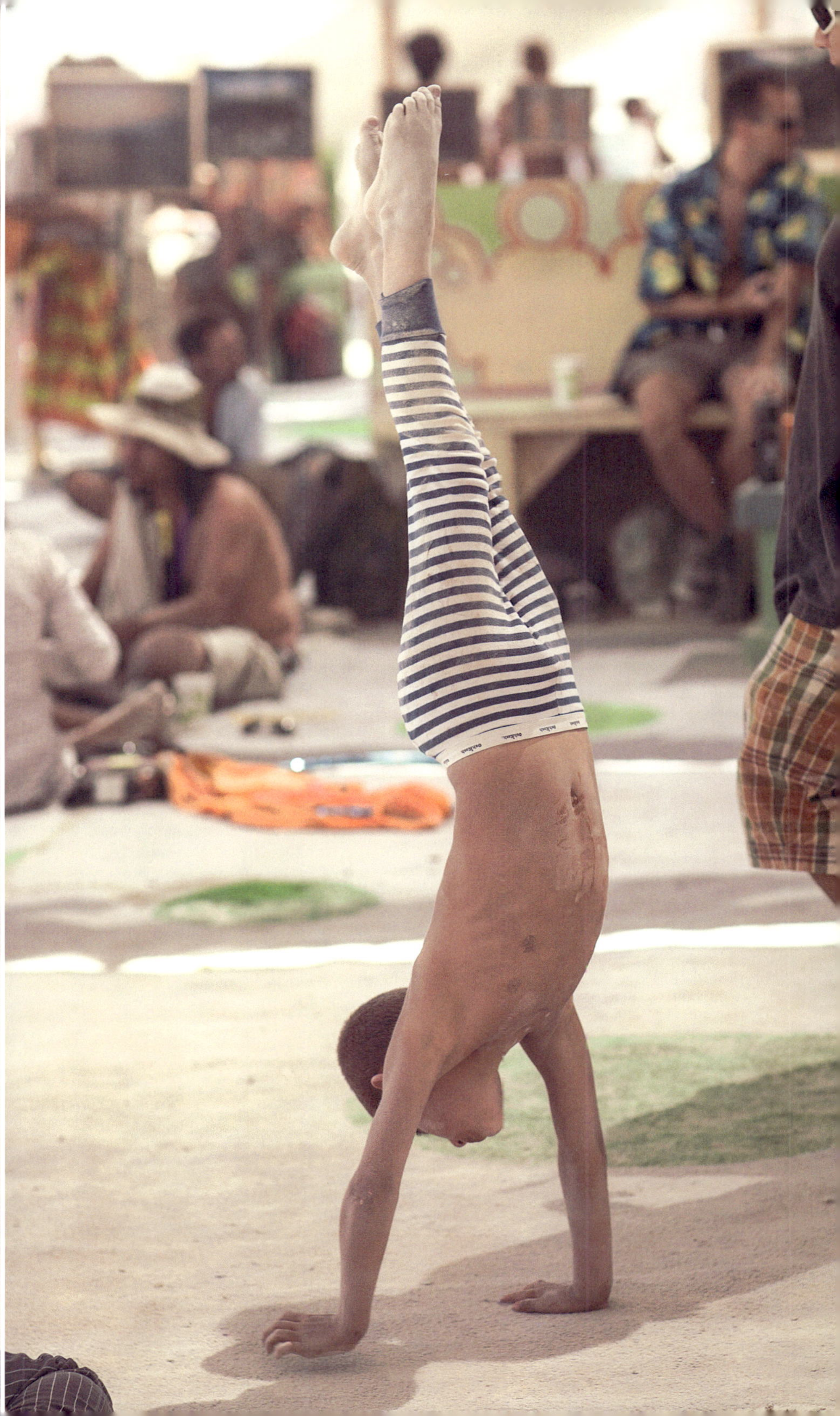

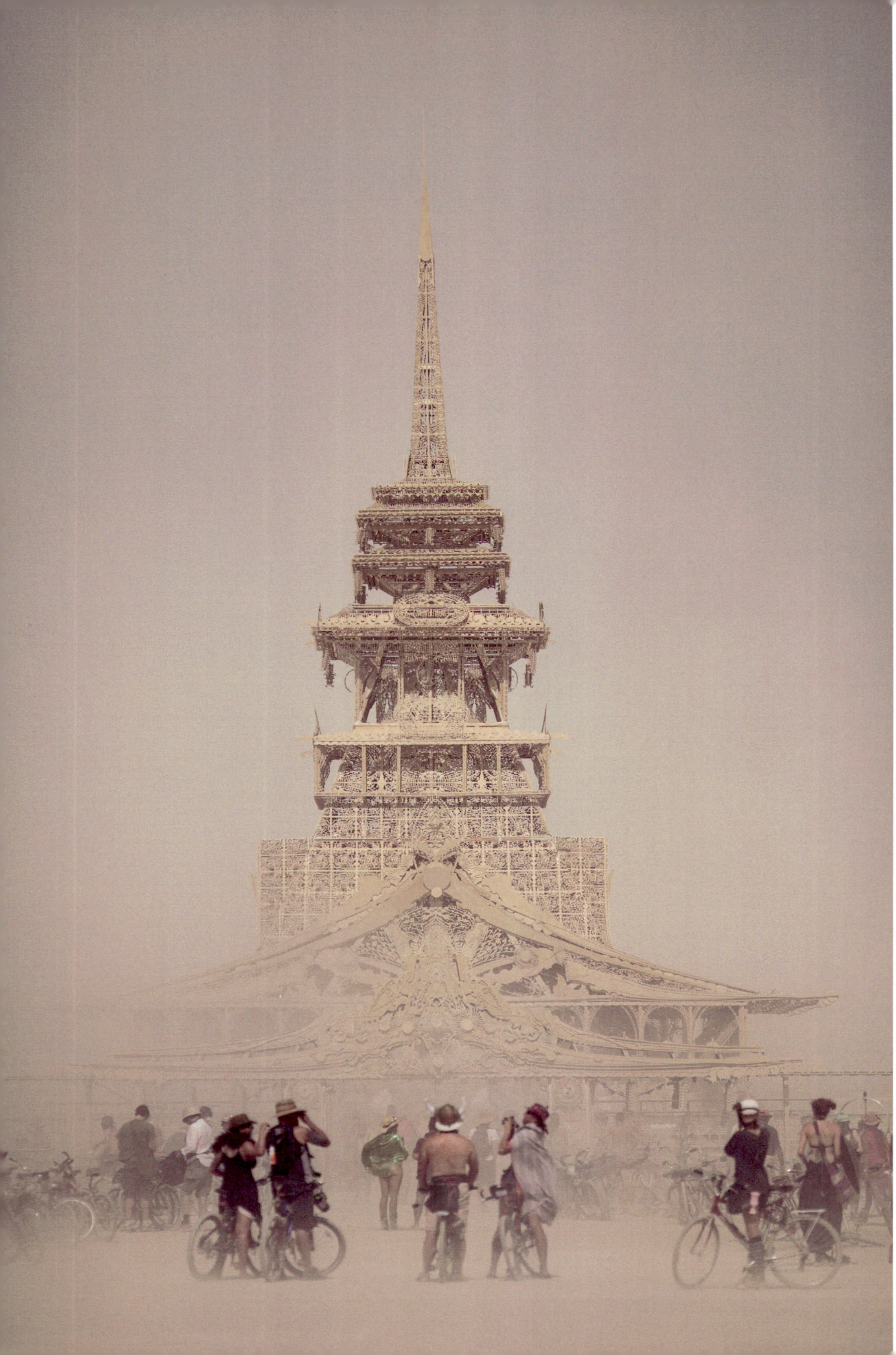

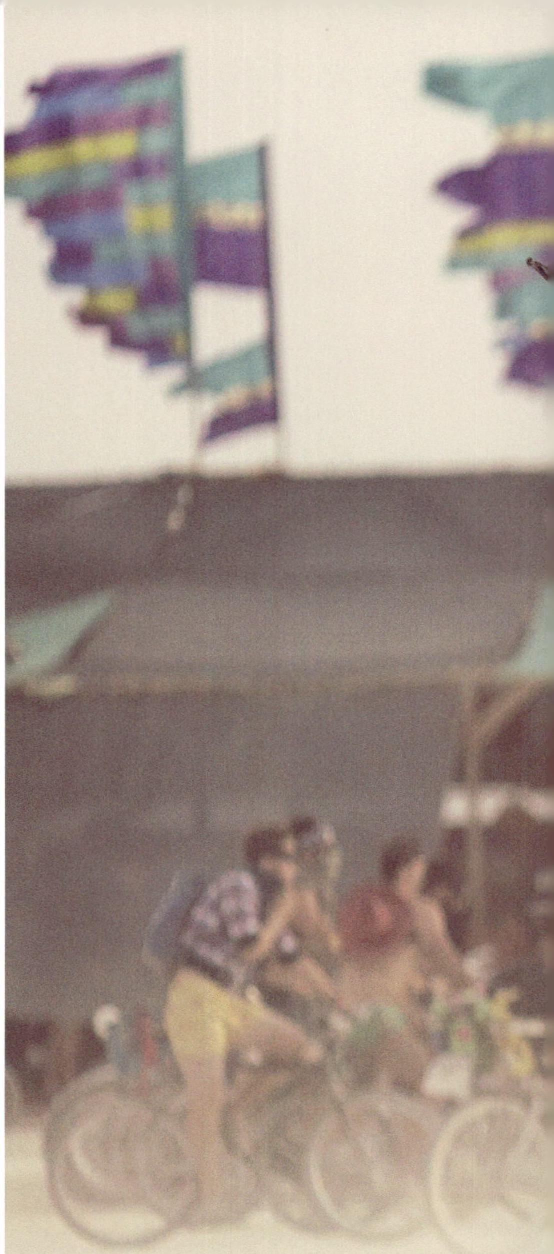

"I like Burning Man because it is a lot of dust and you get dirty with the dust. My favorite piece of art is the Temple and the Lily Pad."

CREED CHILDS

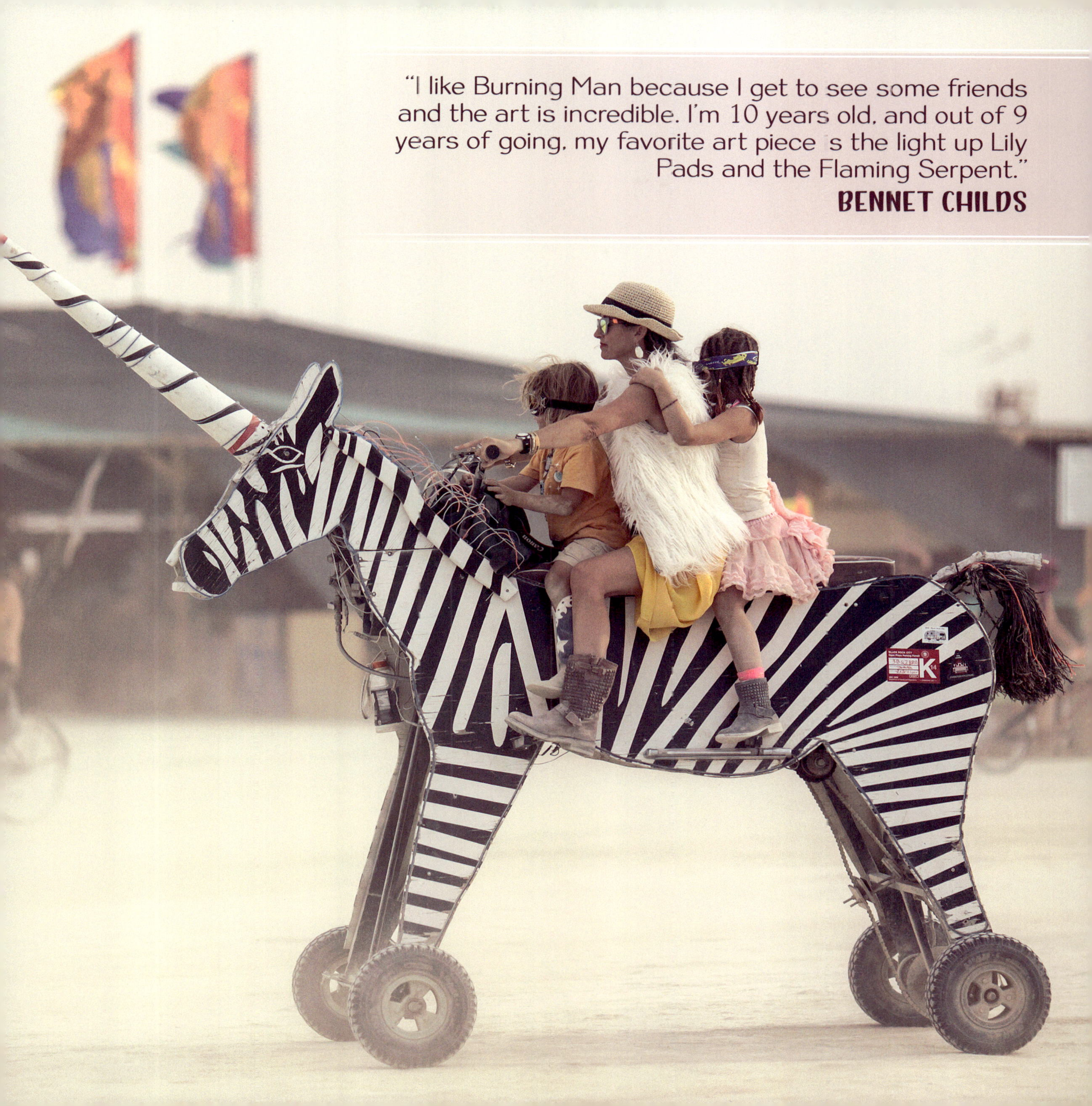

"I like Burning Man because I get to see some friends and the art is incredible. I'm 10 years old, and out of 9 years of going, my favorite art piece is the light up Lily Pads and the Flaming Serpent."

BENNET CHILDS

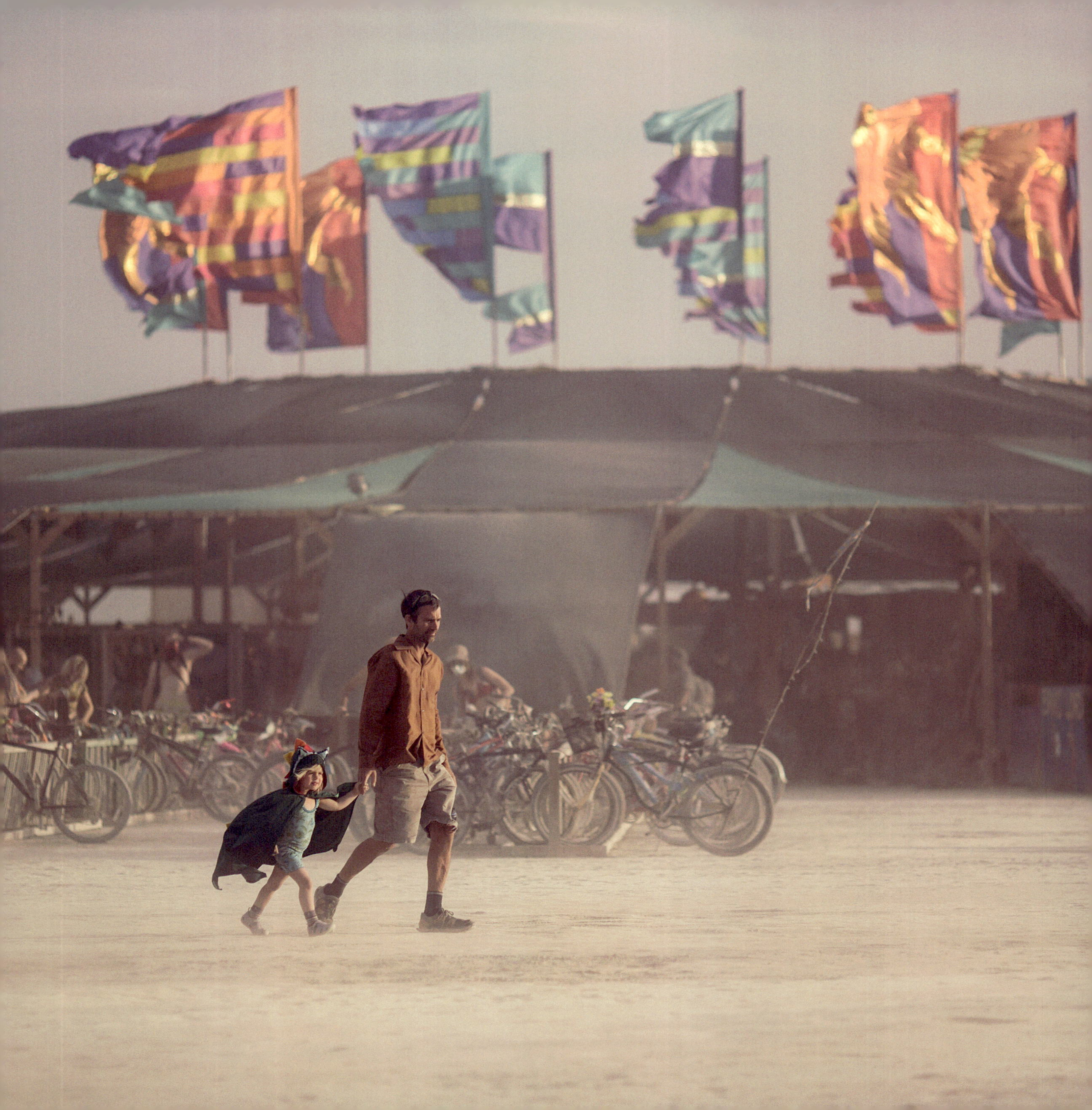

"**We want our children to know that what they imagine can be realized.** On the Playa, not only do they see this as possible, but they also get to experience the imagination of others. We see it as getting to step into a wondrous picture book. Indie still talks about the people she met, the friends she made and the art she encountered. This is an experience that we could not provide on our own. At Burning Man, where people are so generous with their art and imagination, stepping into another world is possible. All this, coupled with the respect of personal space displayed by the community, makes for an unparalleled experience."

TIM, SARAH & INDIE

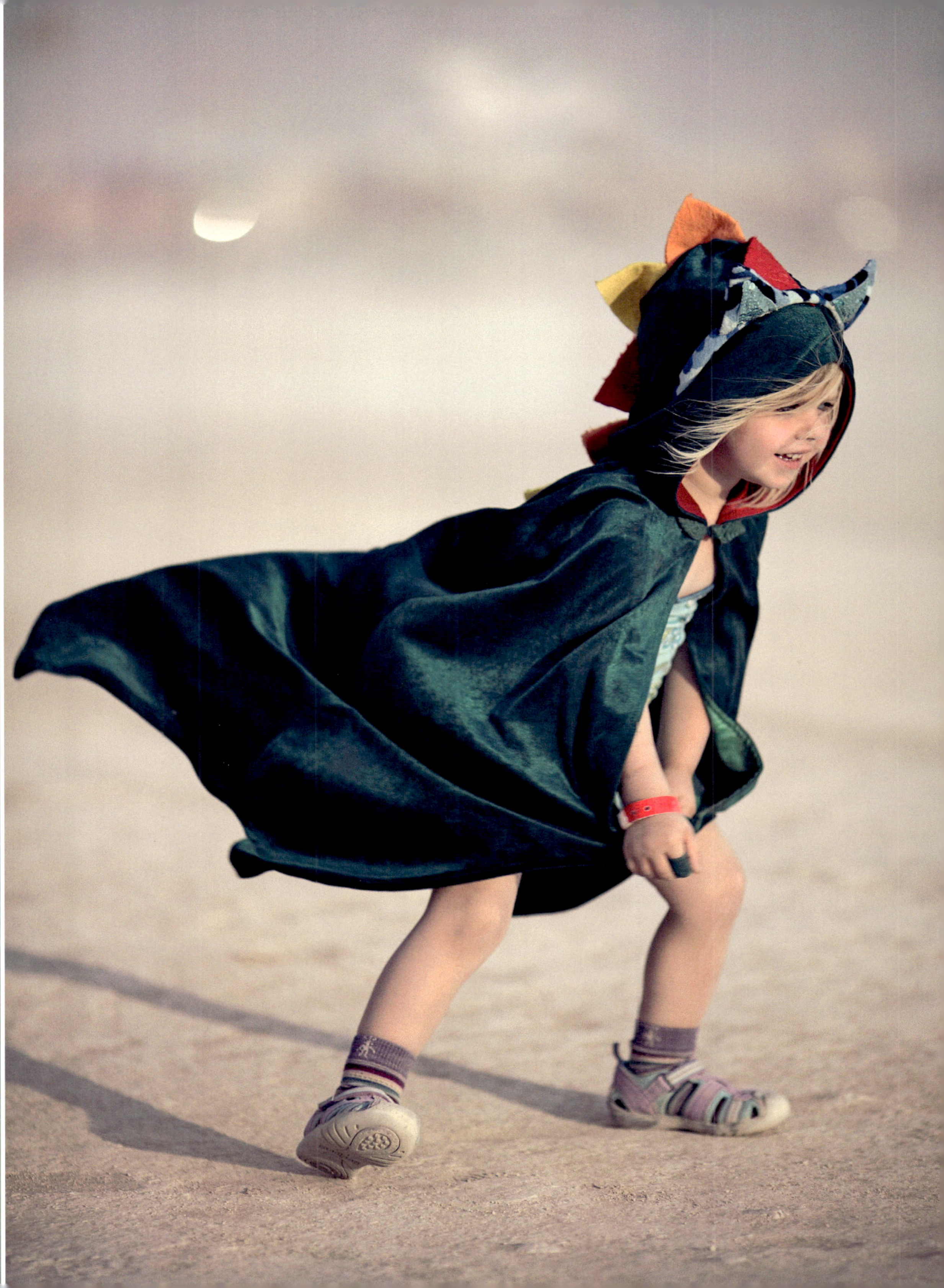

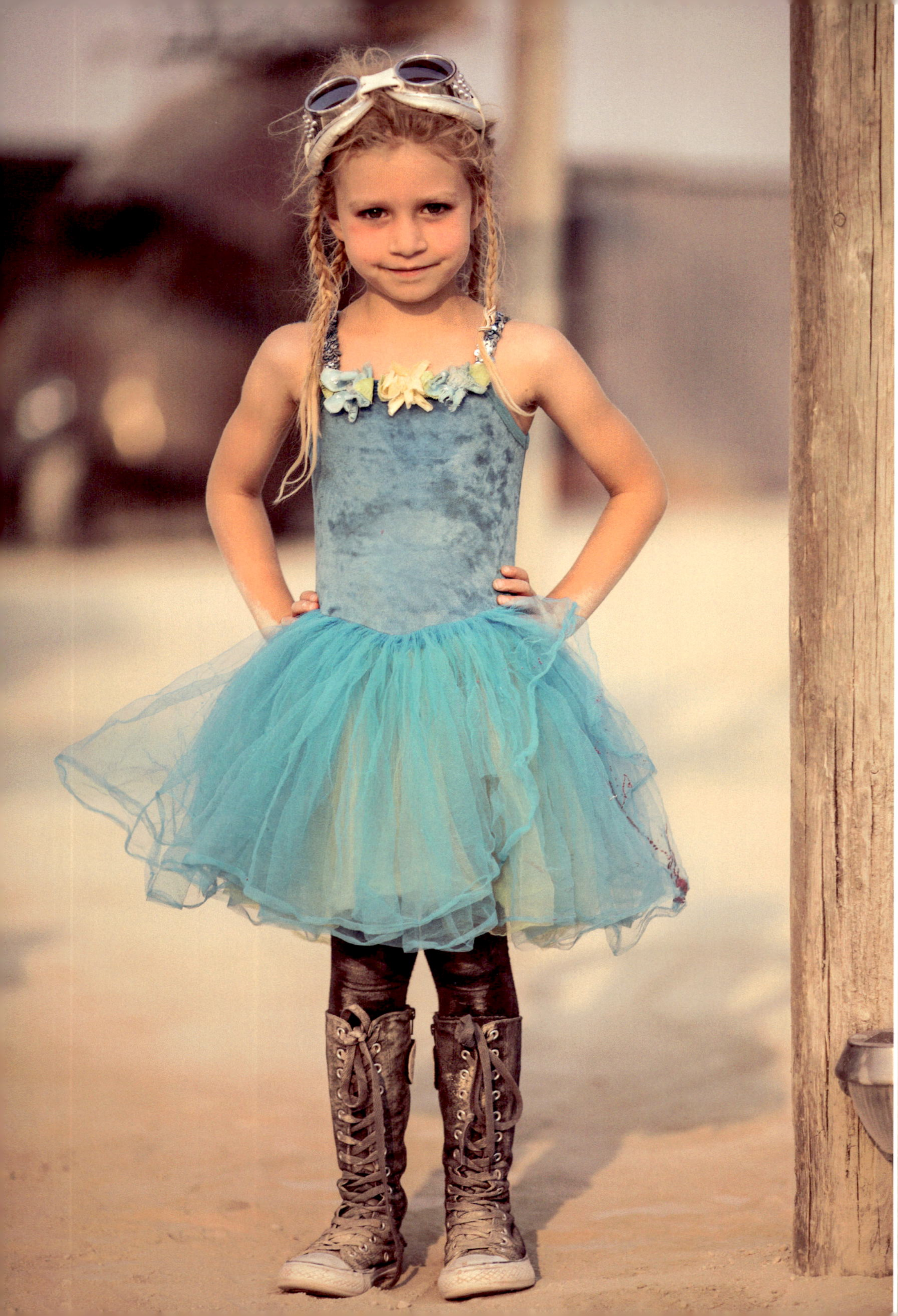

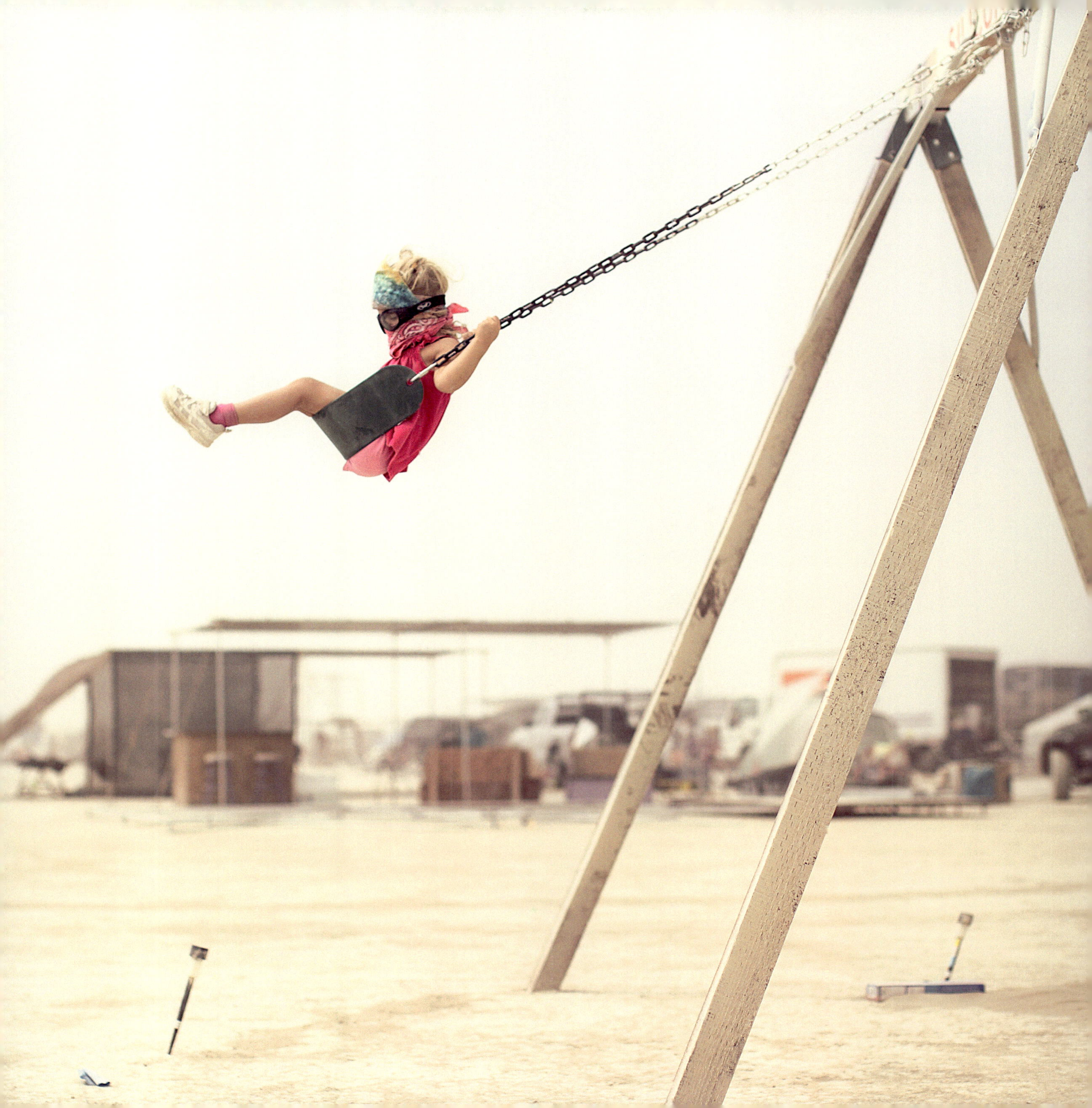

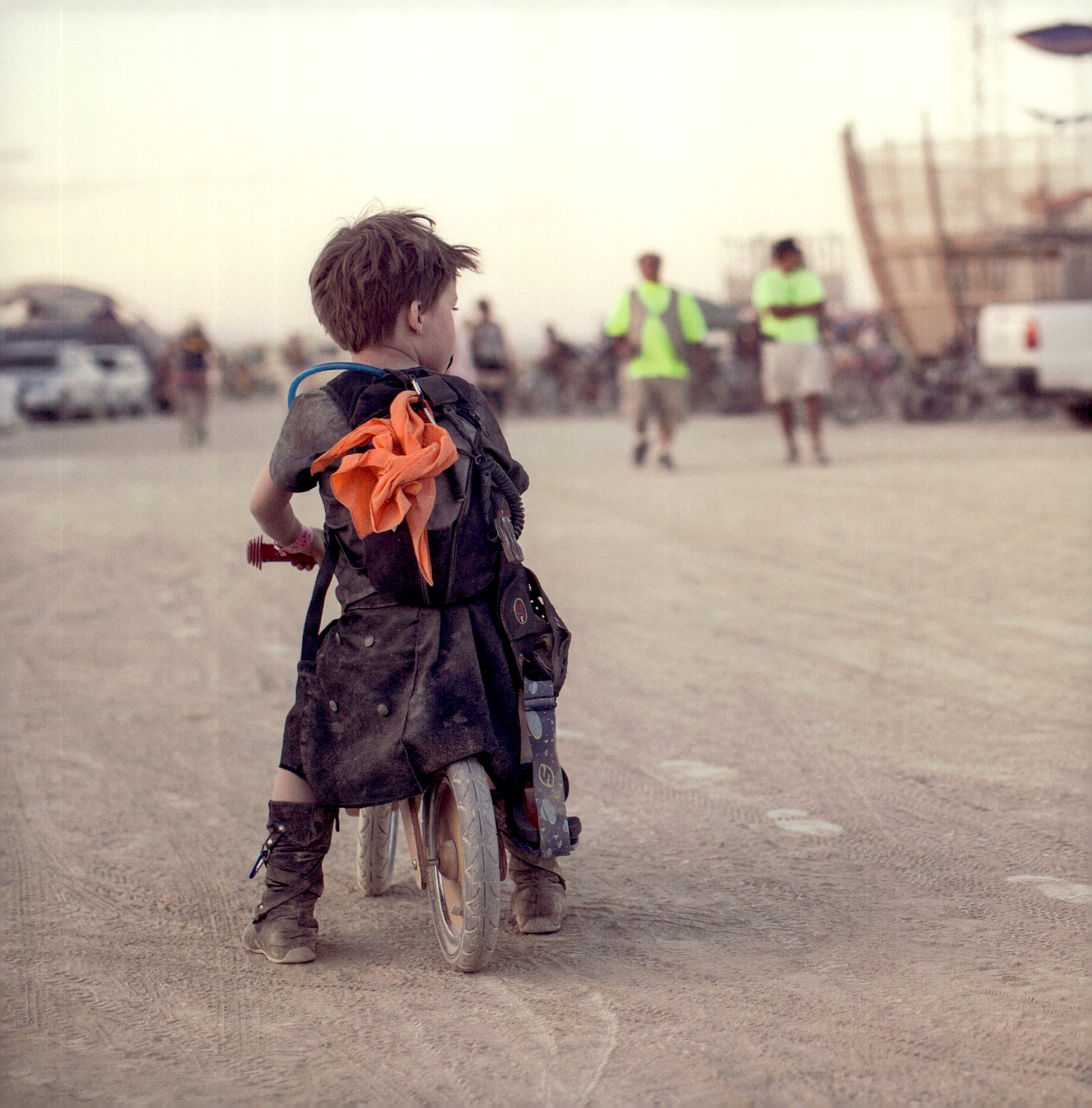

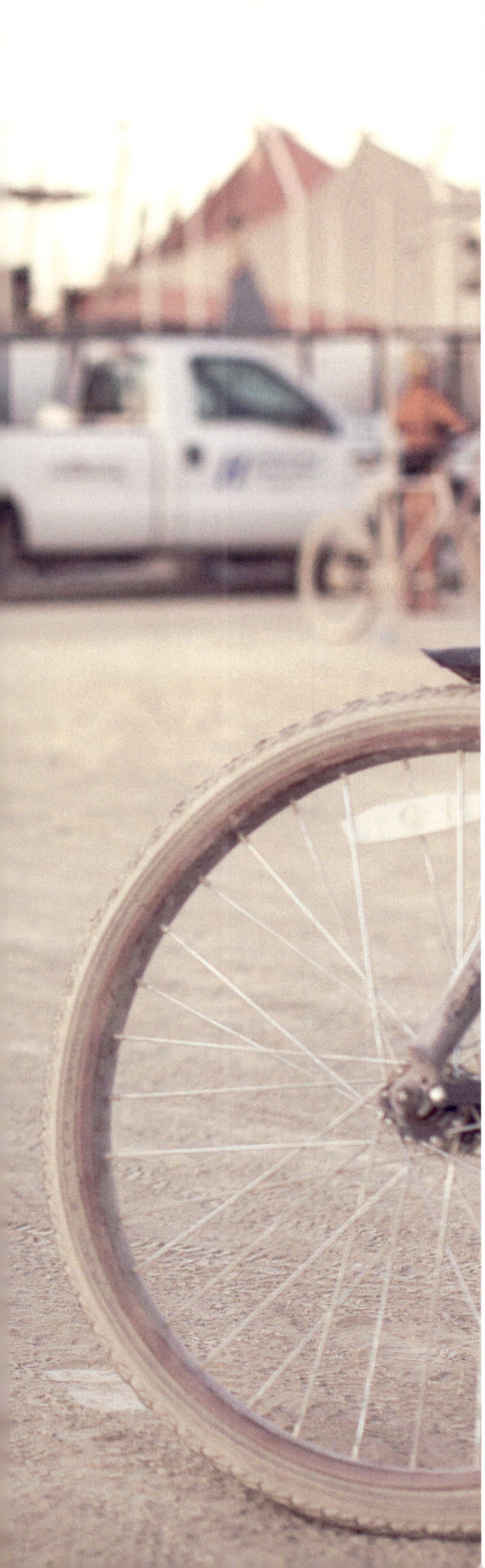
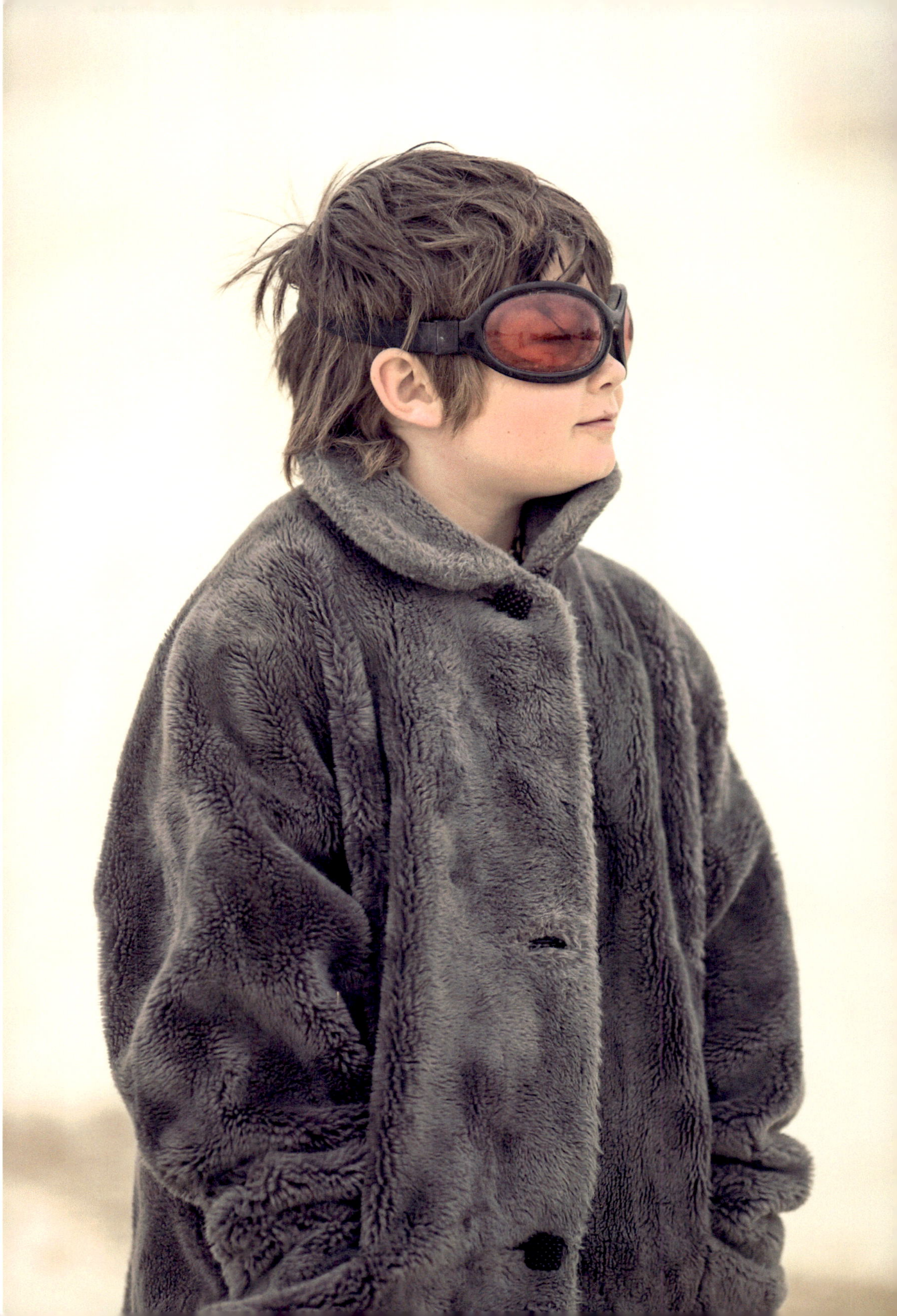

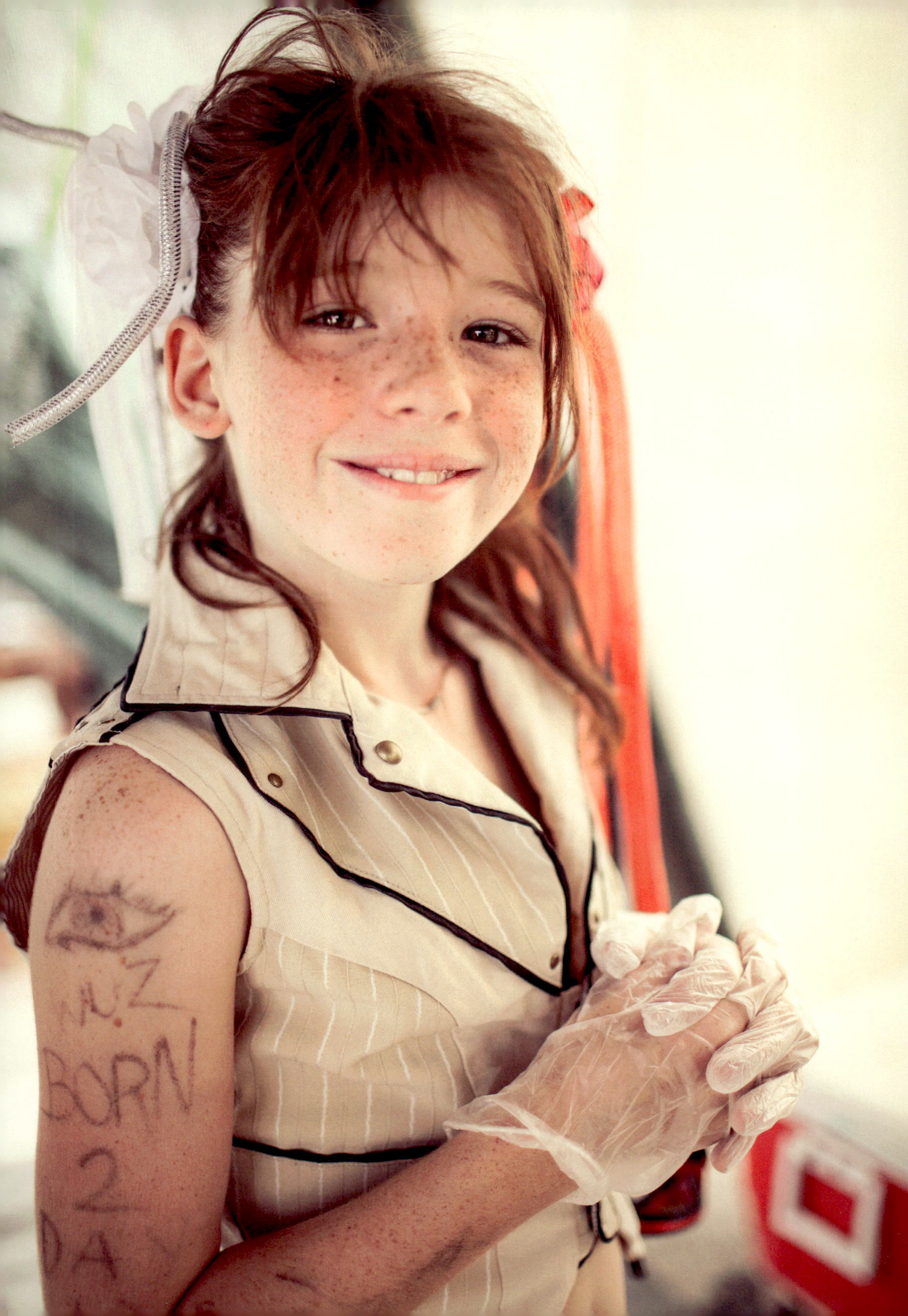
BORN
2
DA

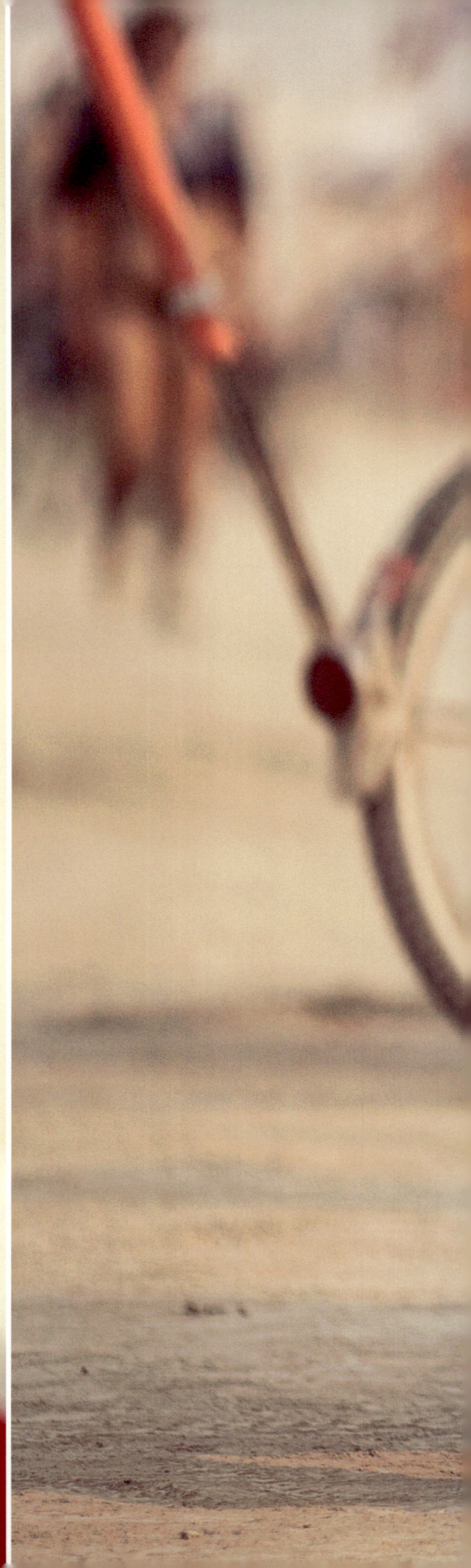

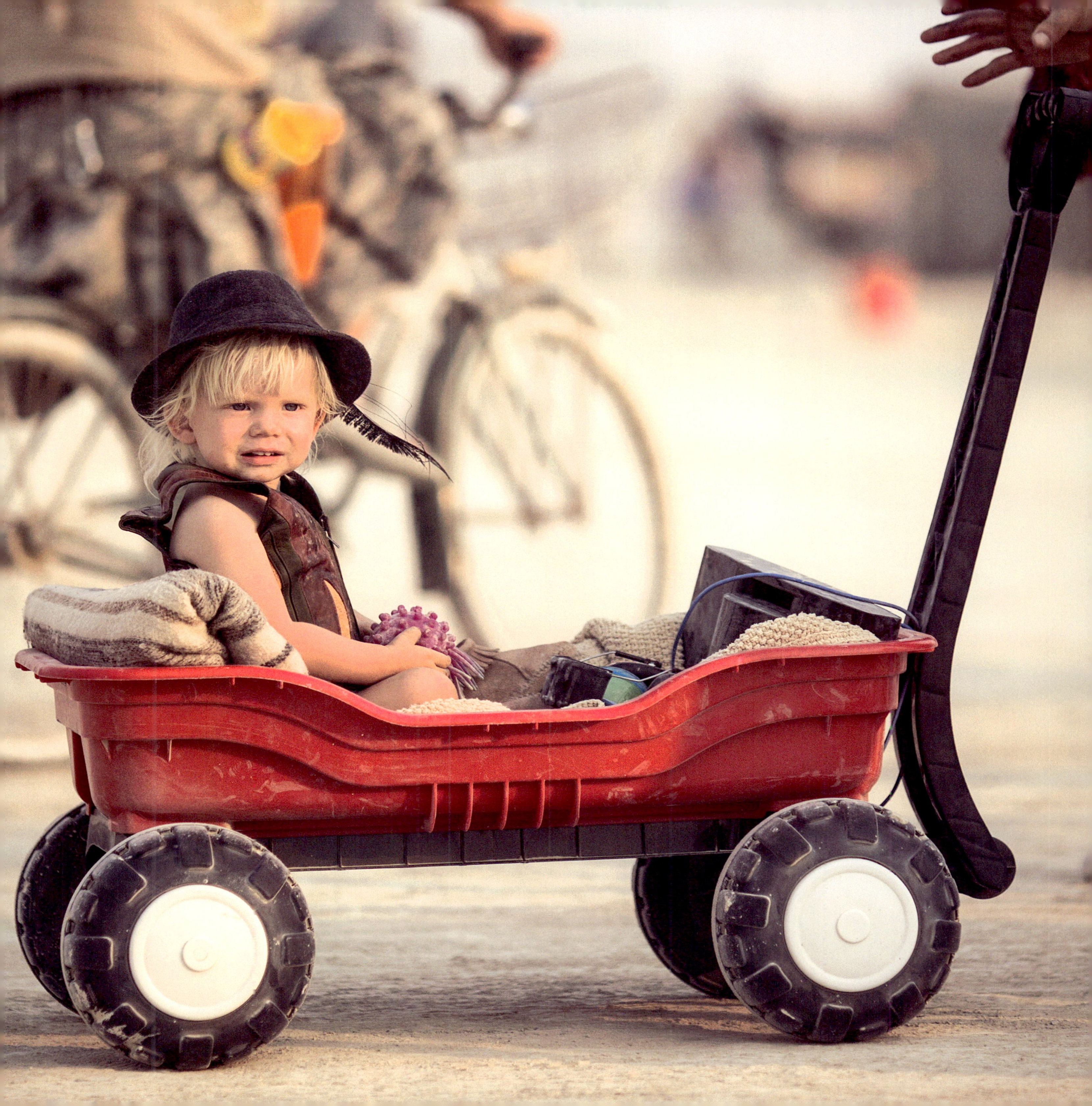

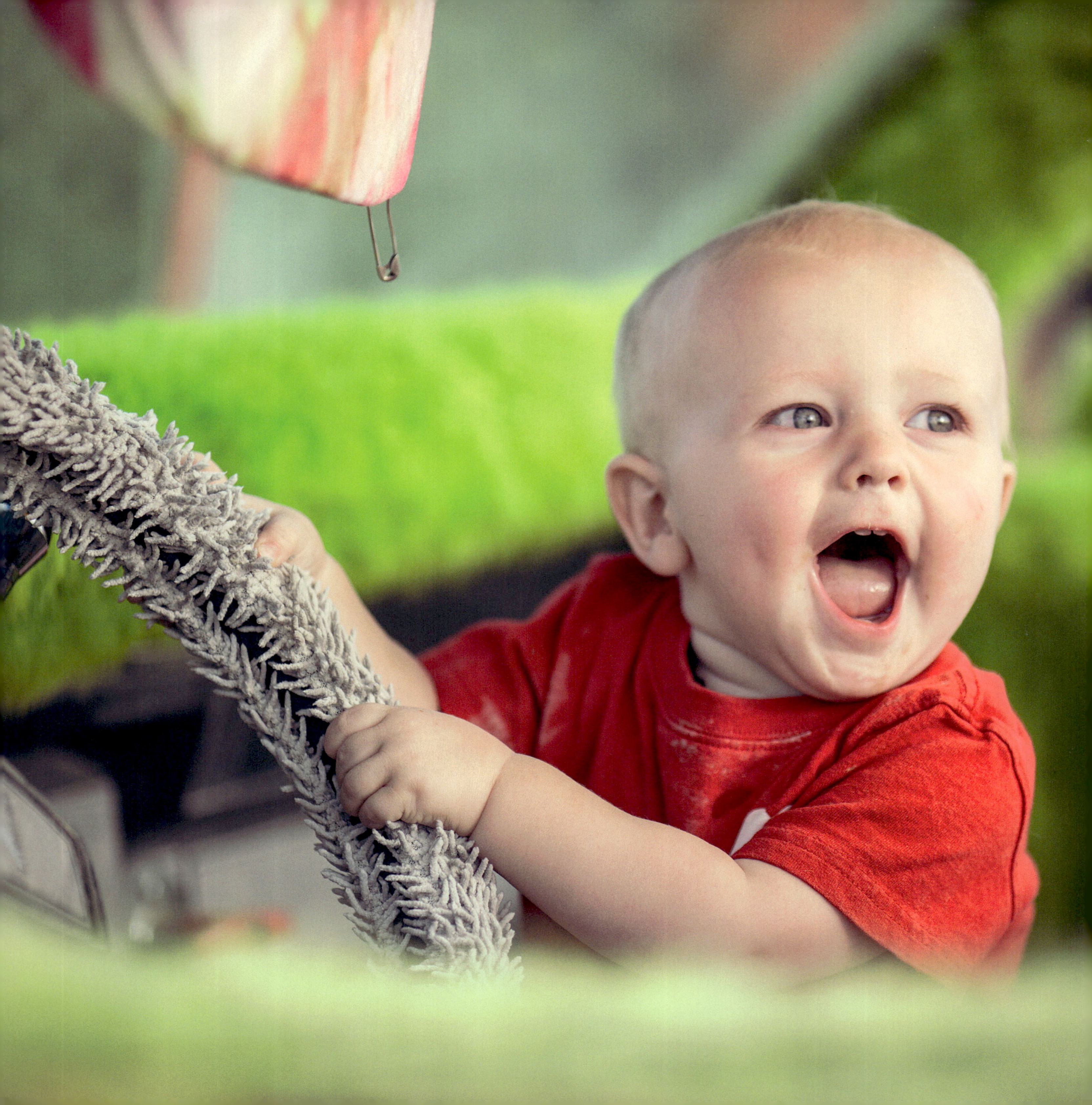

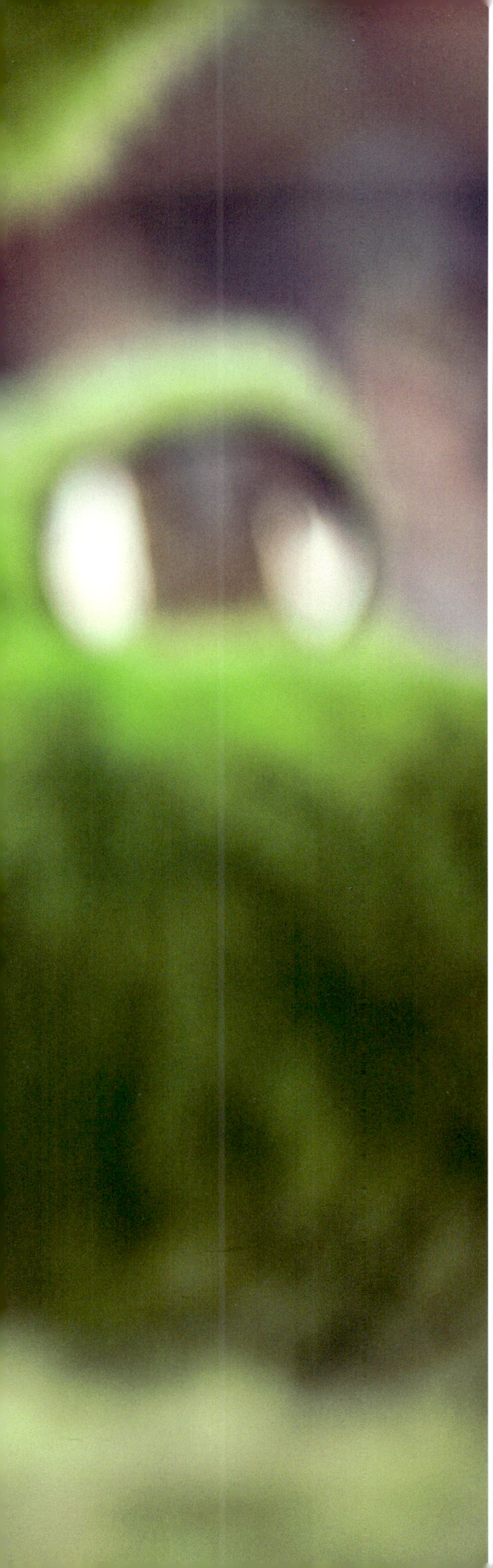
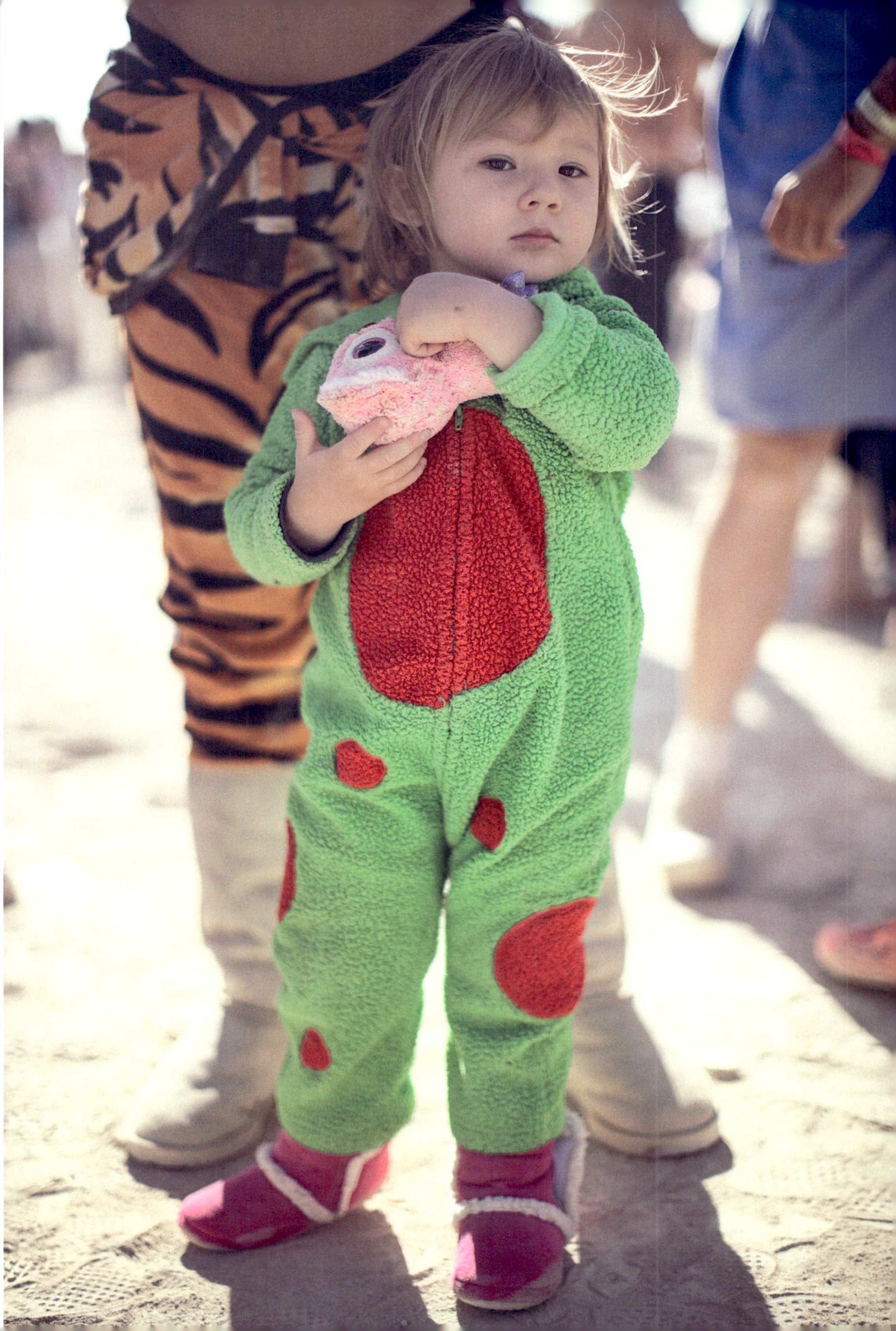

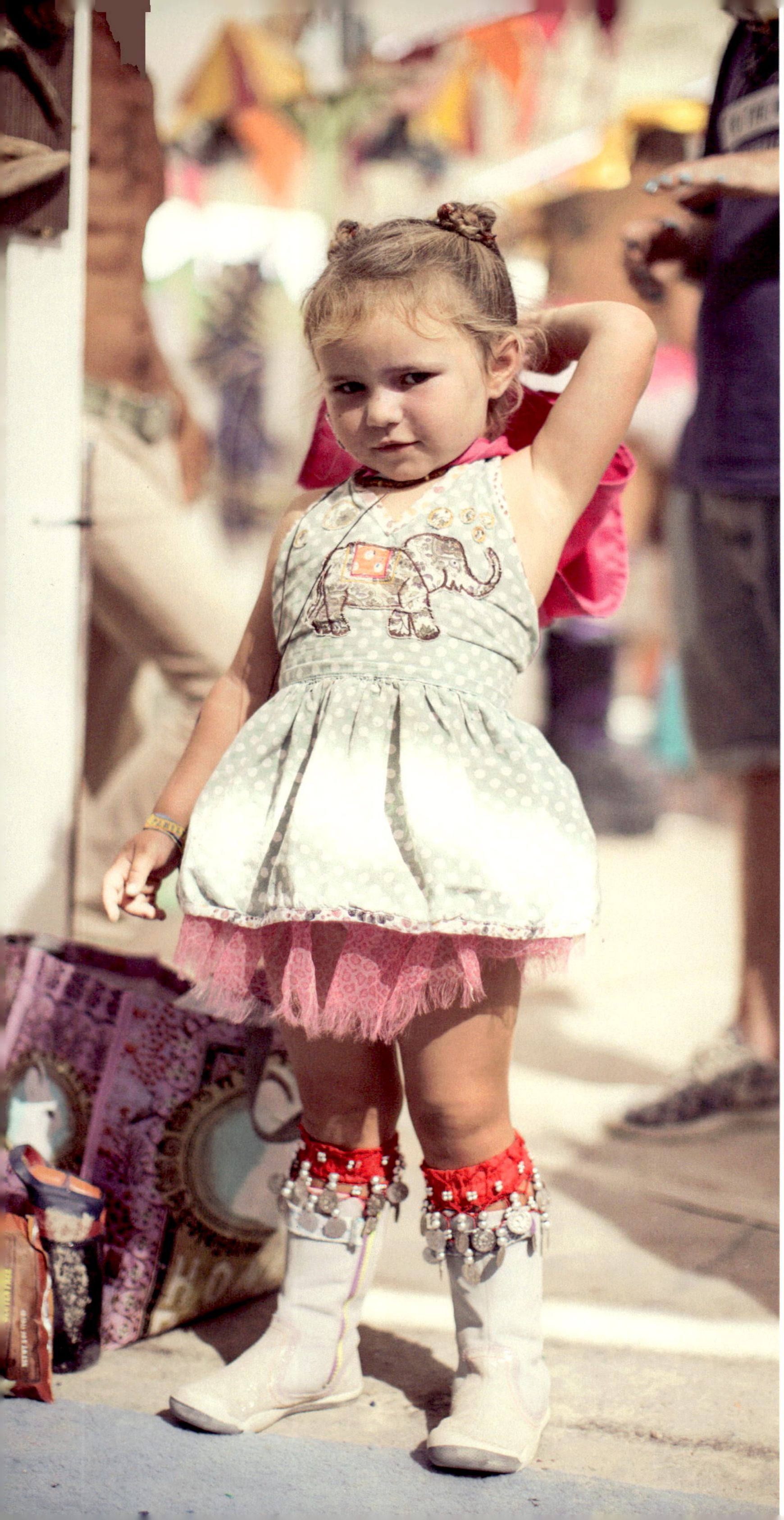

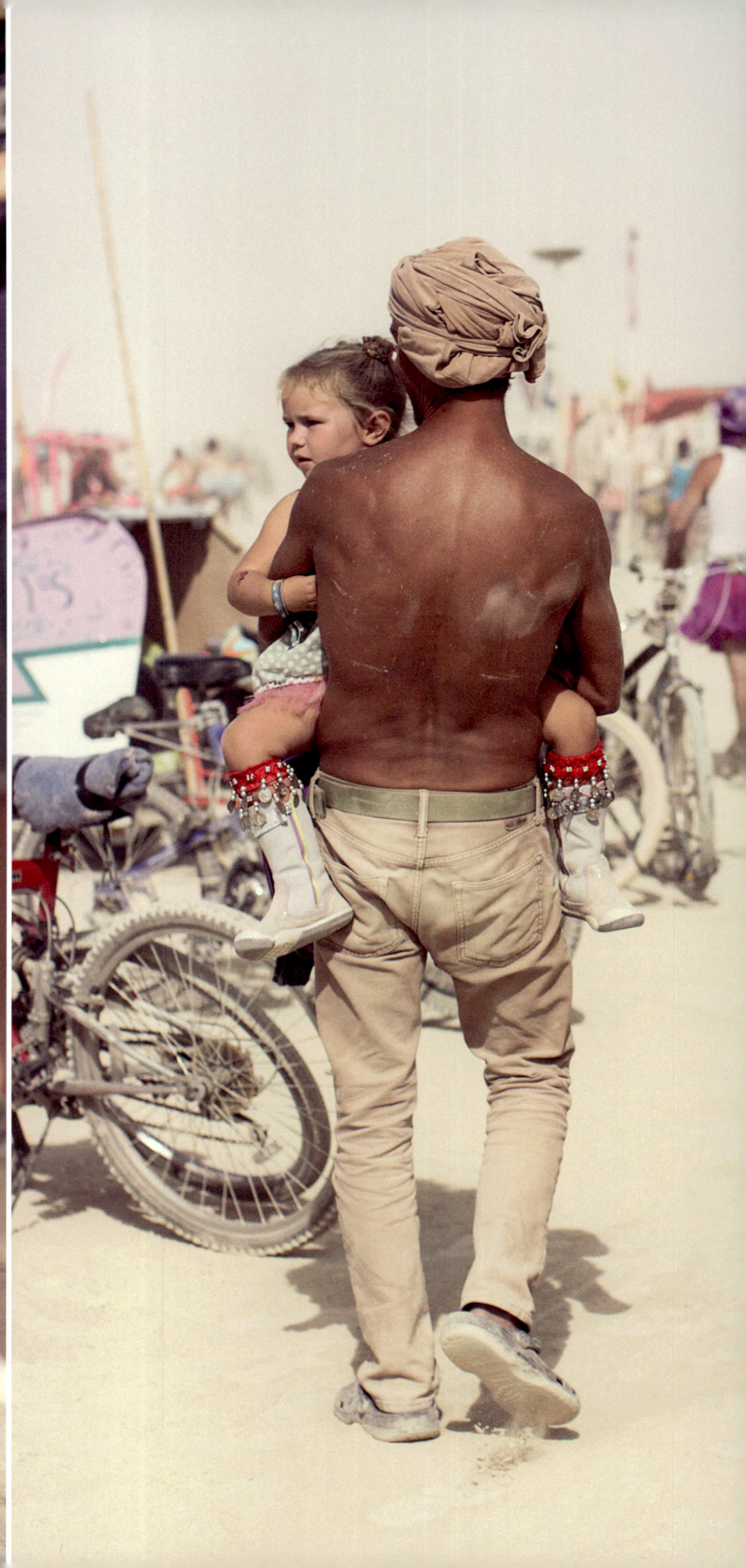

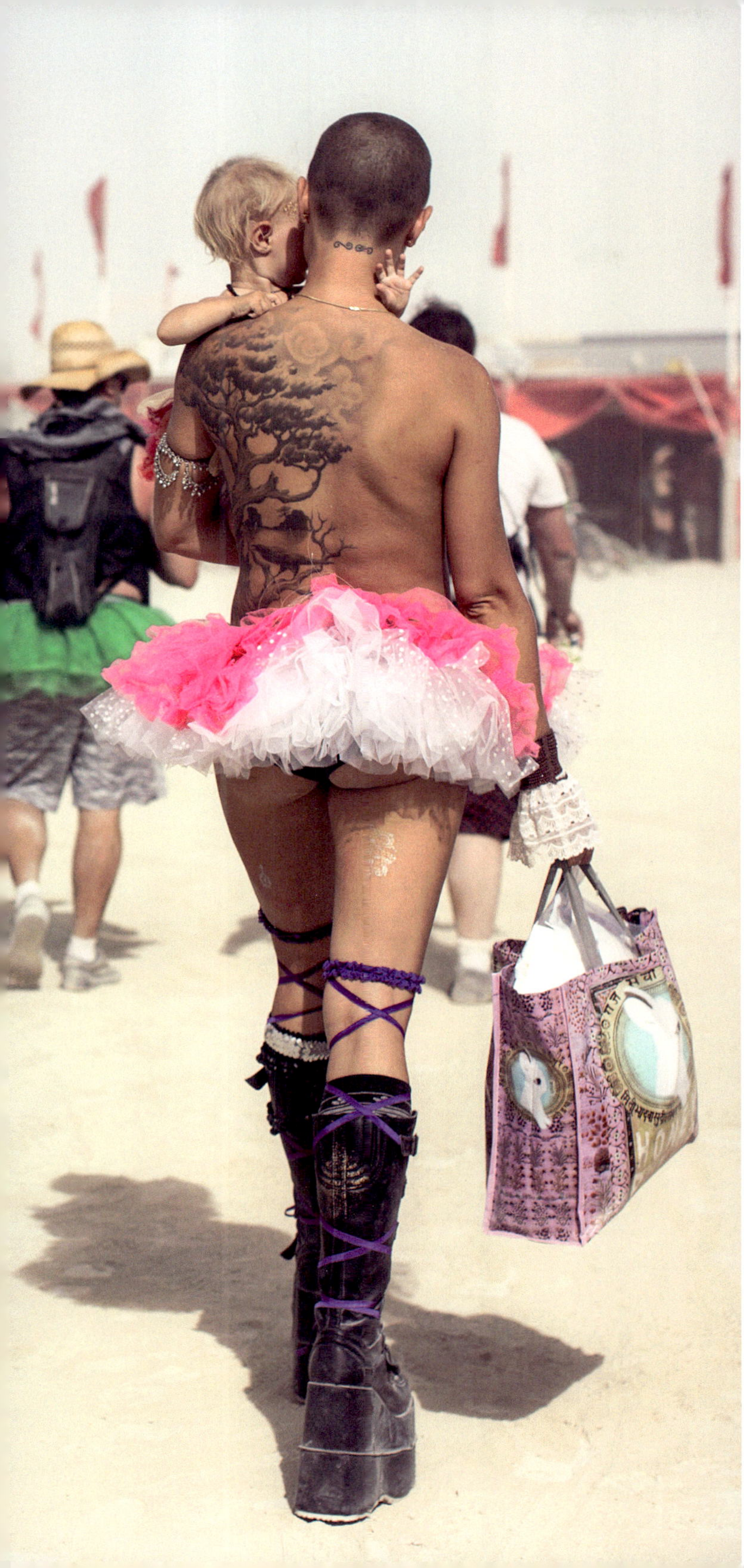

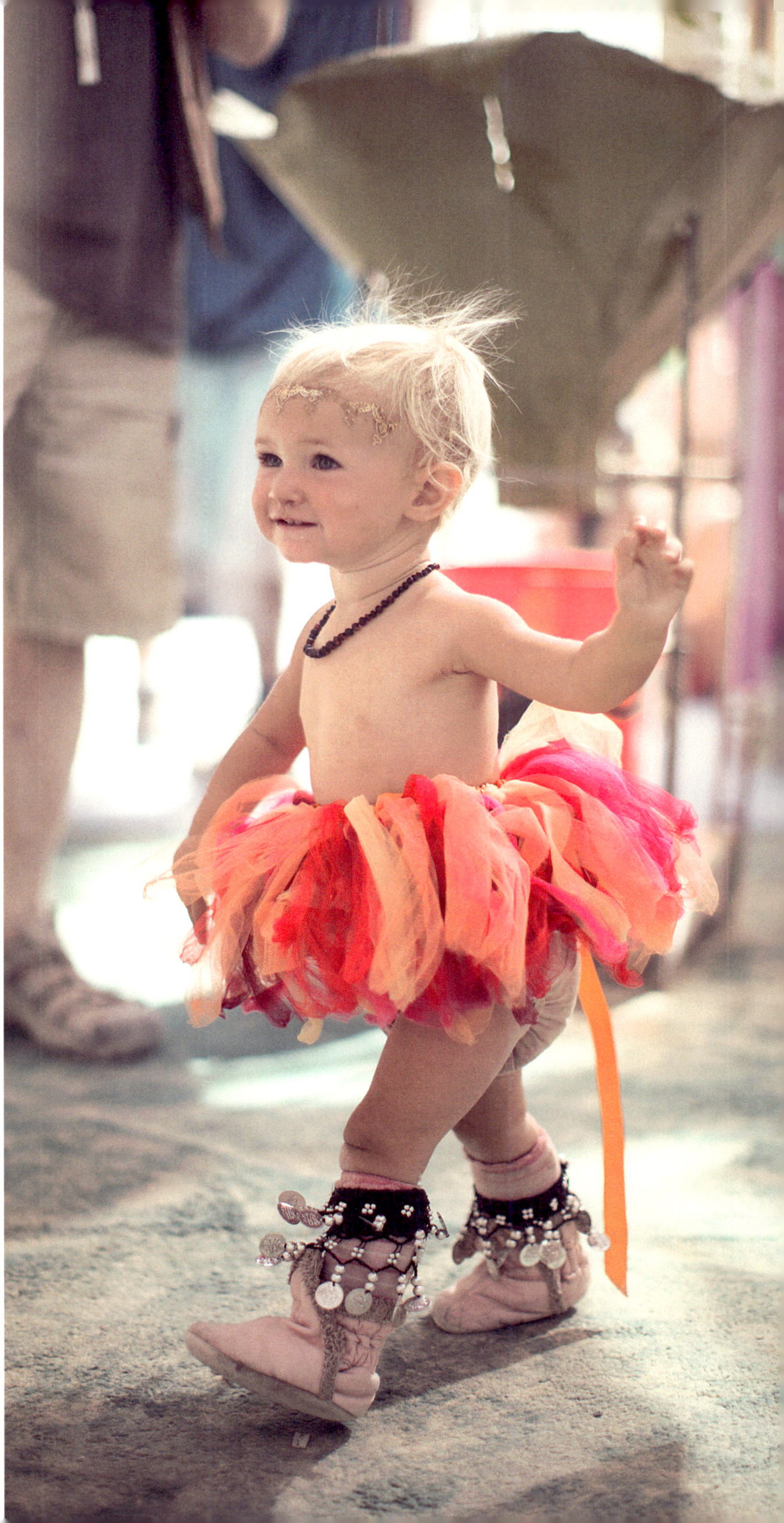

"My favorite art car was the Temple."
LILA URBAN

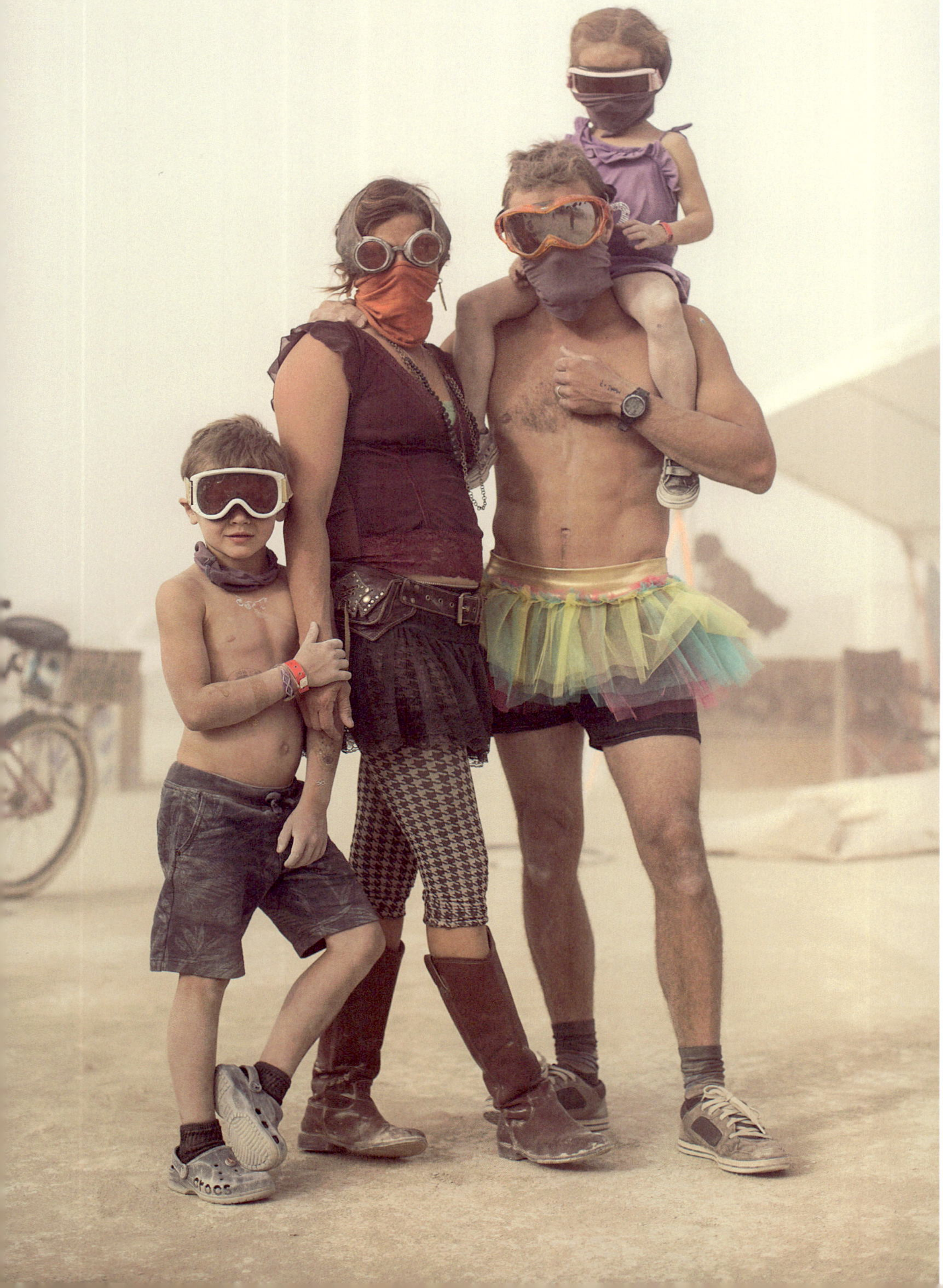

"Taking our kids to Burning Man was an experience we'll never forget – even my youngest who was 4 at the time. As radically different as the Playa is for us adults, it just made sense to our kids. Why shouldn't the day be about having fun, surprising and novel experiences? Why shouldn't we be able to climb on anything we like and play for free, not for pay? Of course it's a rugged experience, whether with the kids or not; if anything we were amazed how resilient the kids were. Katie and I would come home exhausted from a dust storm and crash out in the camper while the kids would just keep jumping on the Kidsville trampoline – masks, goggles and all."
DUSTIN URBAN

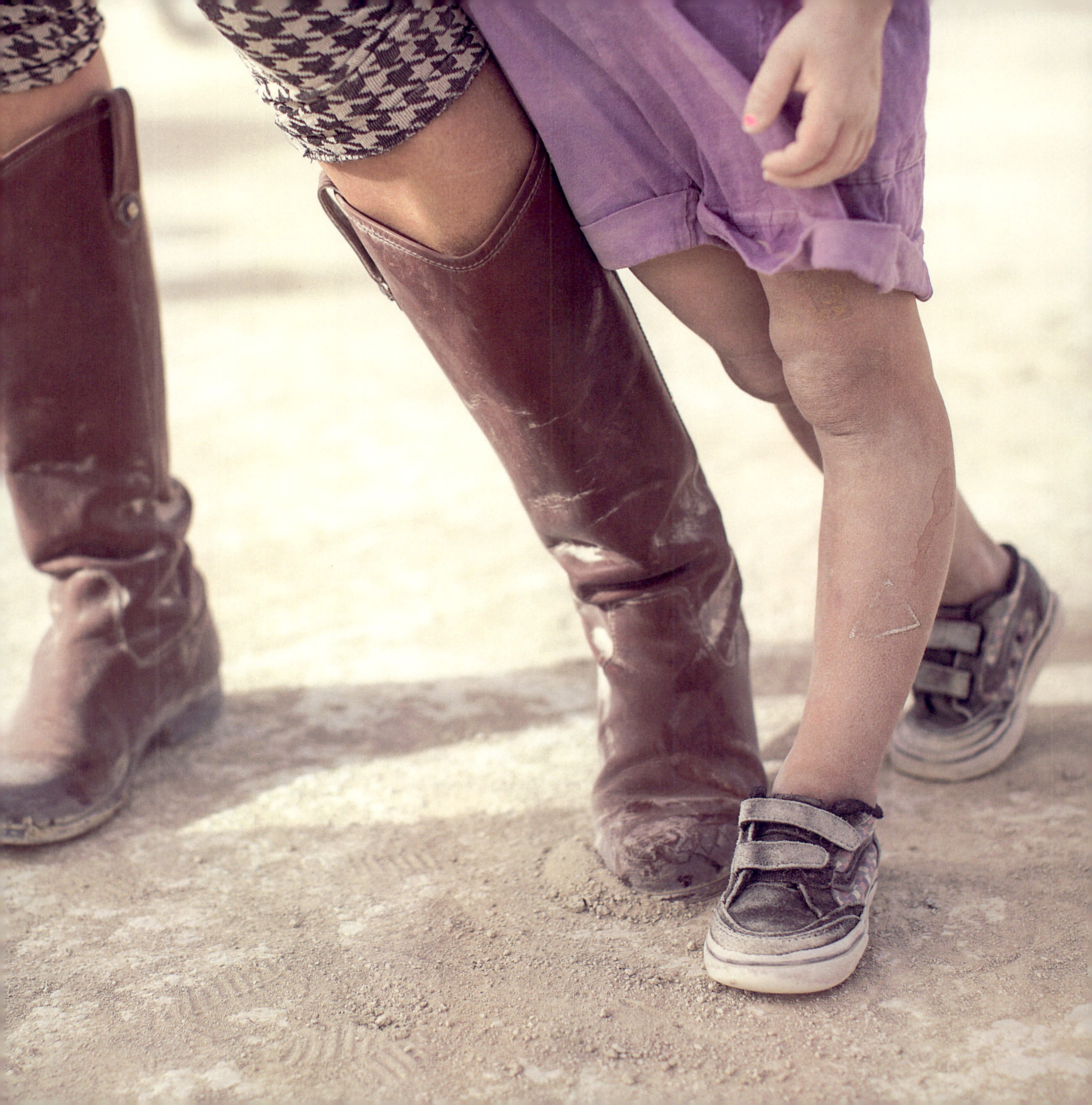

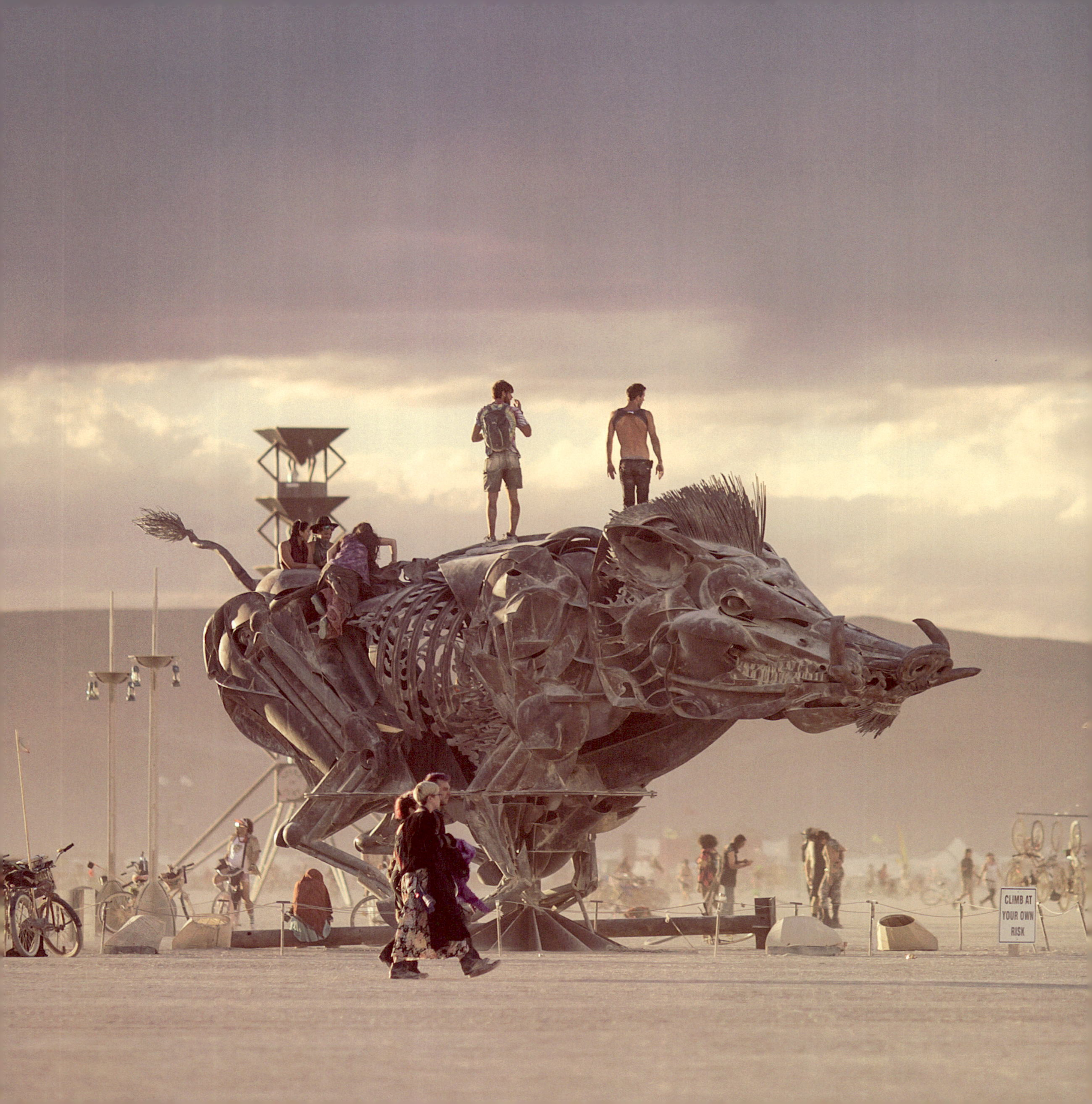
CLIMB AT
YOUR OWN
RISK

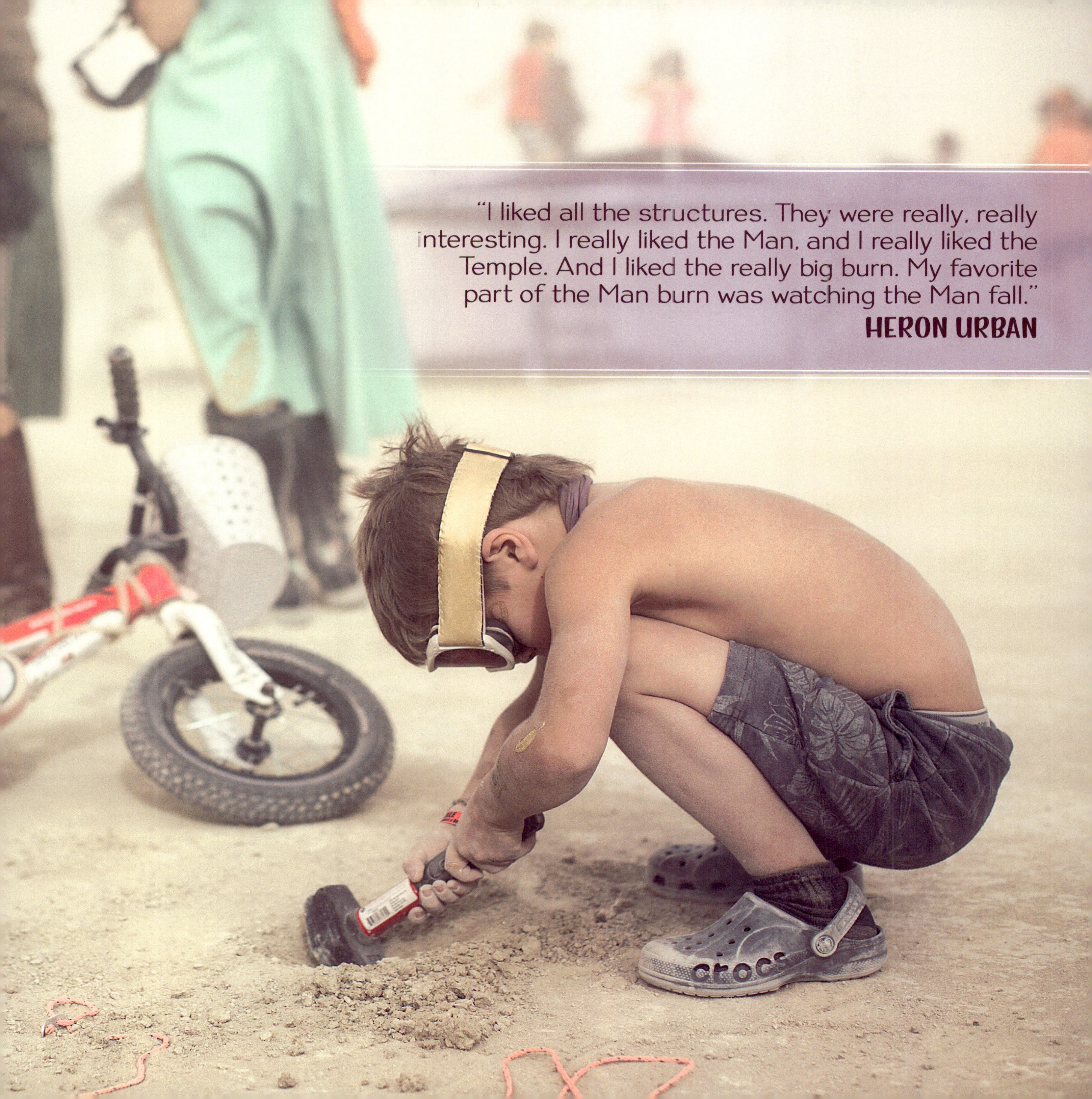

"I liked all the structures. They were really, really interesting. I really liked the Man, and I really liked the Temple. And I liked the really big burn. My favorite part of the Man burn was watching the Man fall."

HERON URBAN

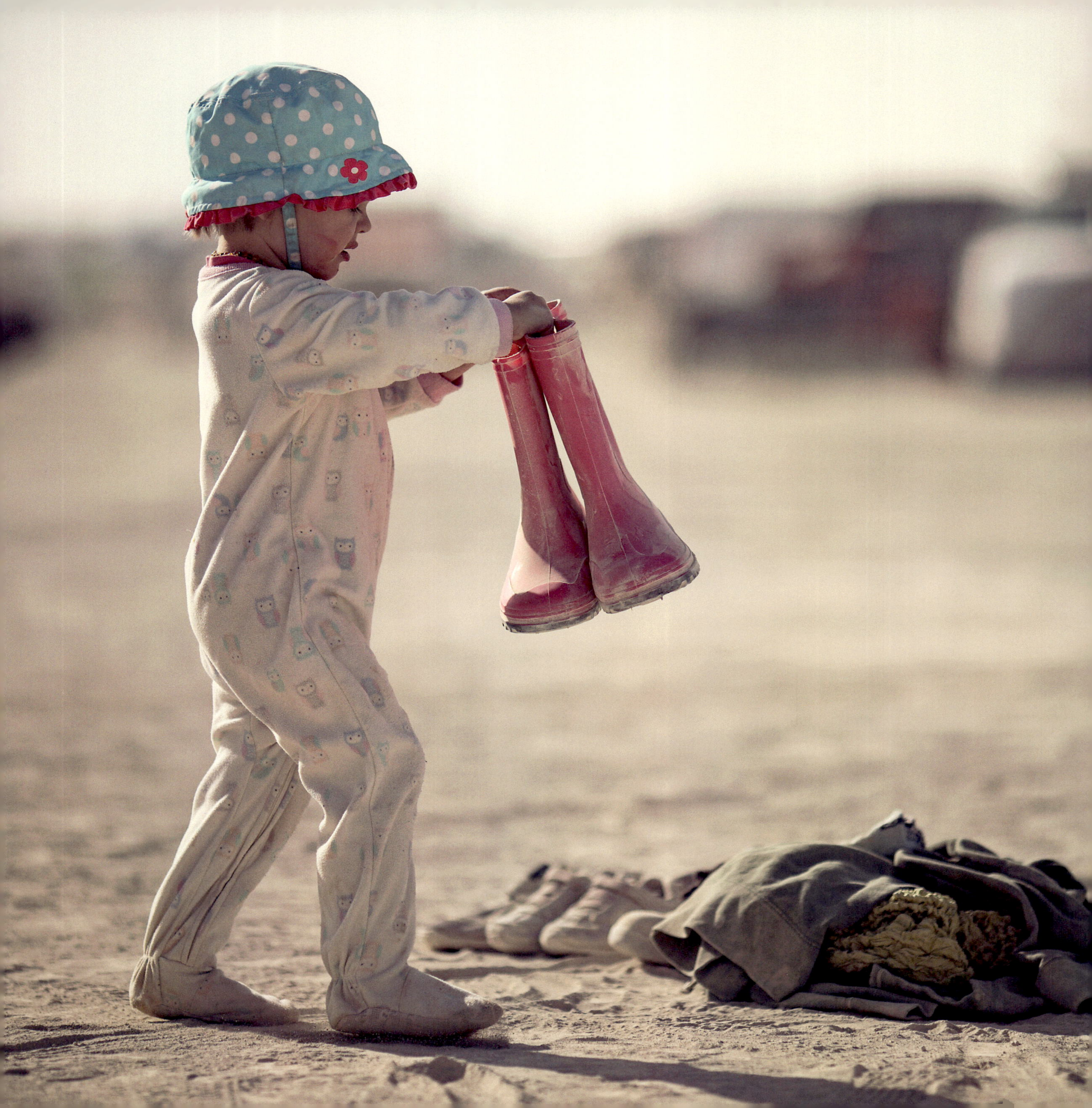

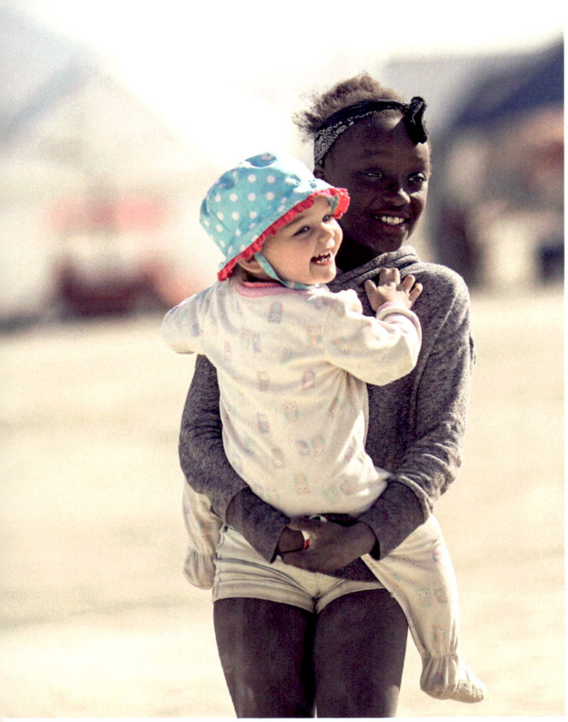

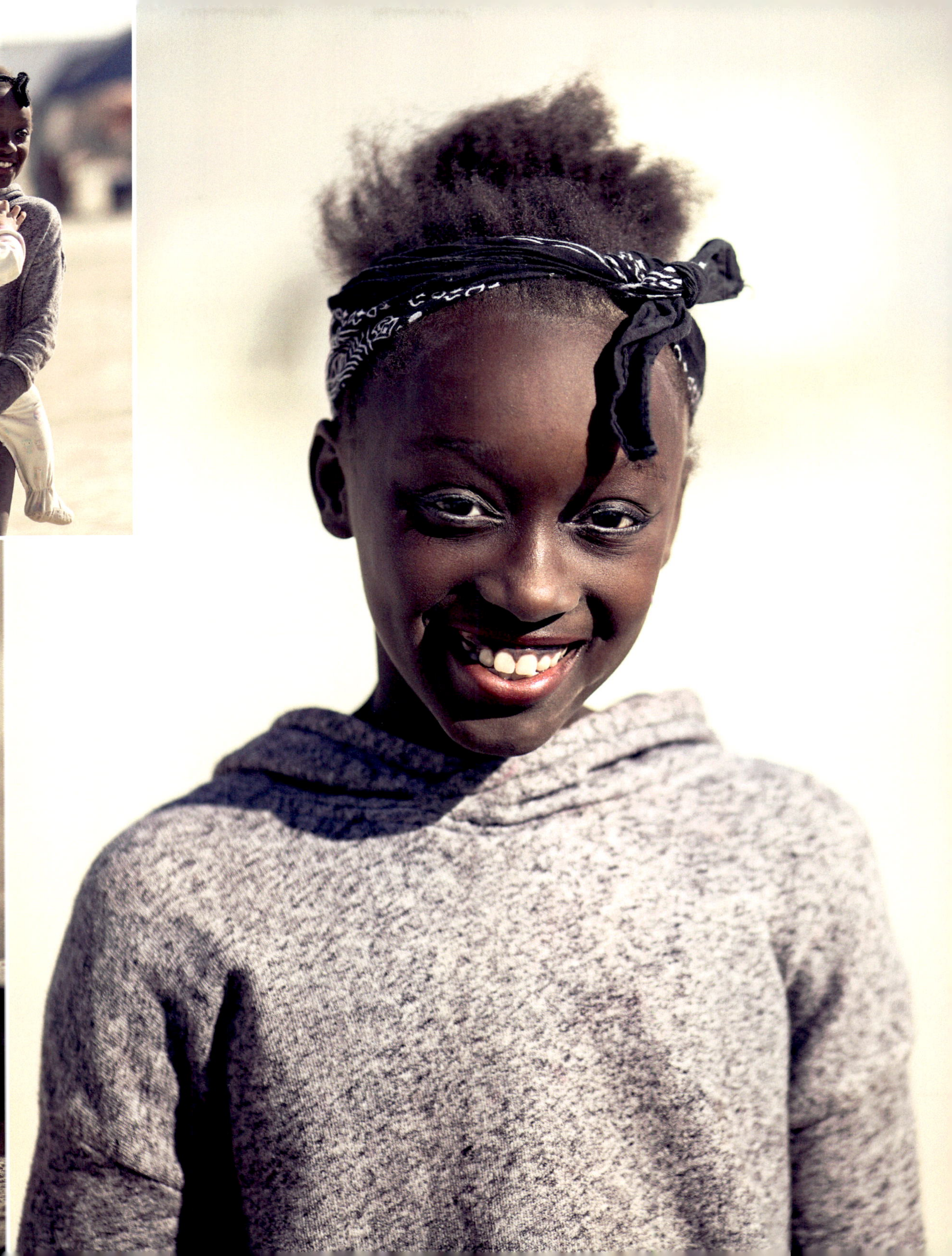

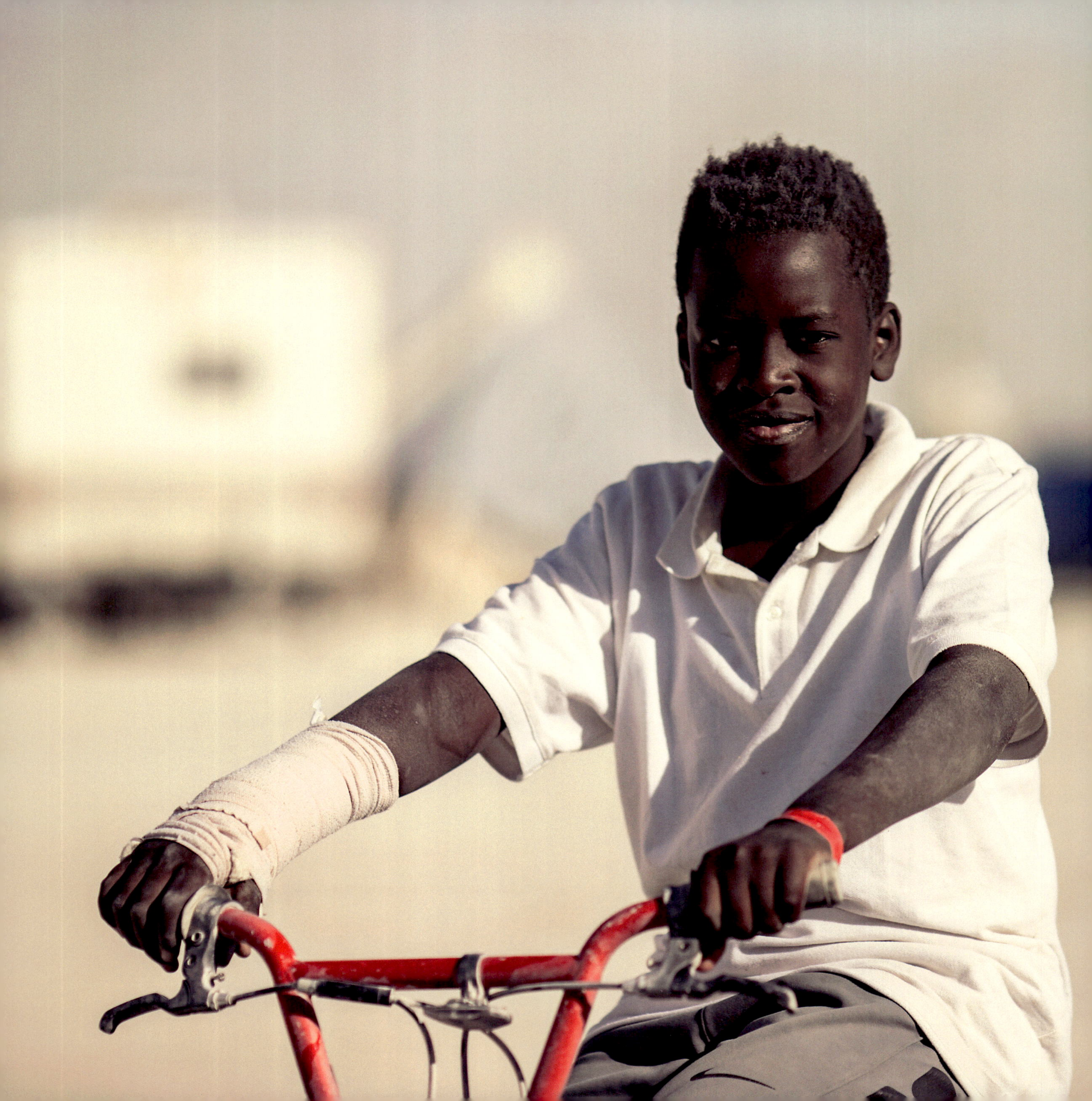

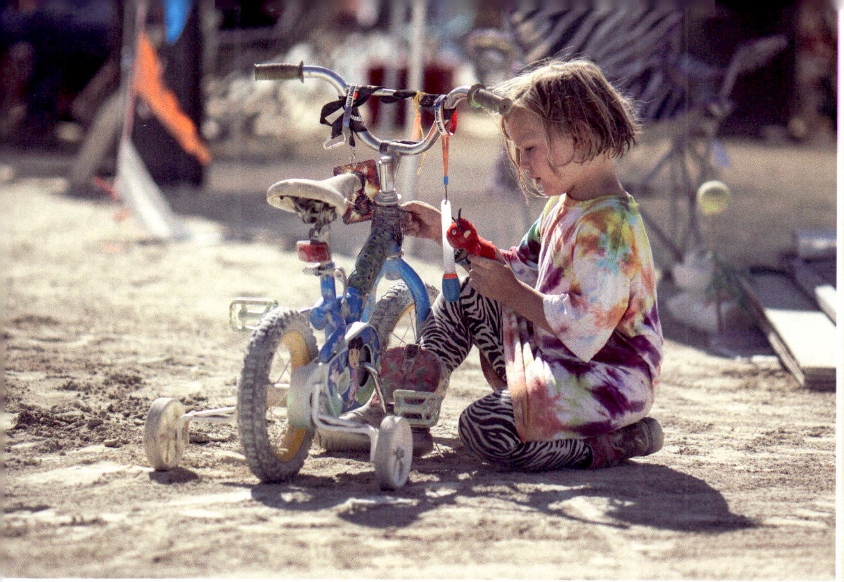

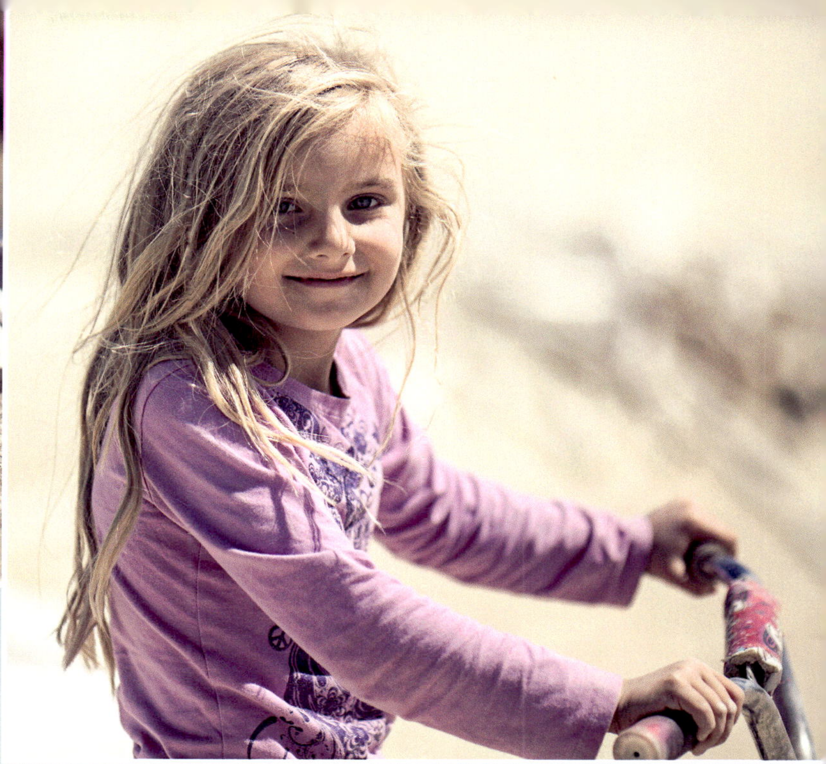

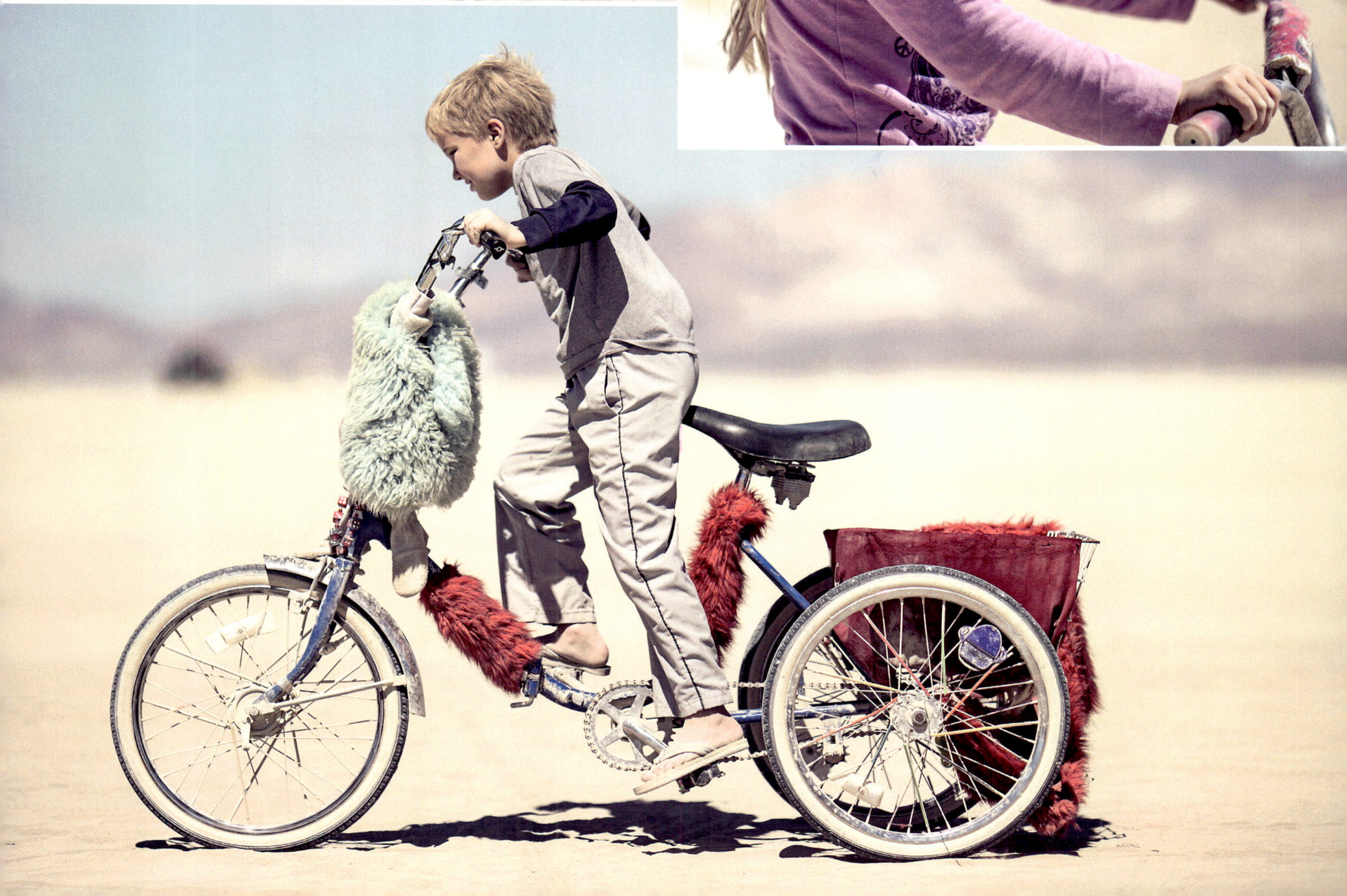

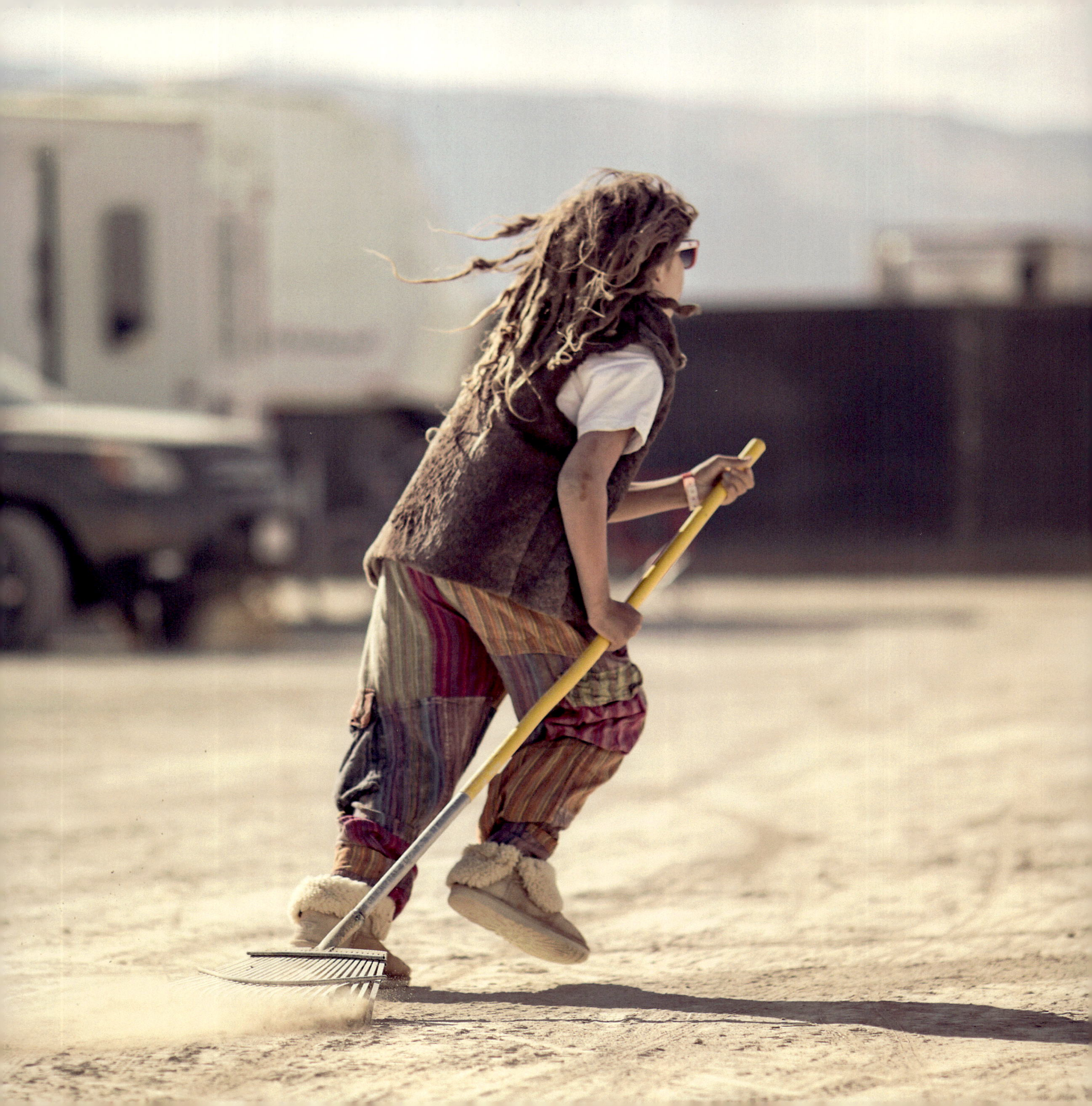

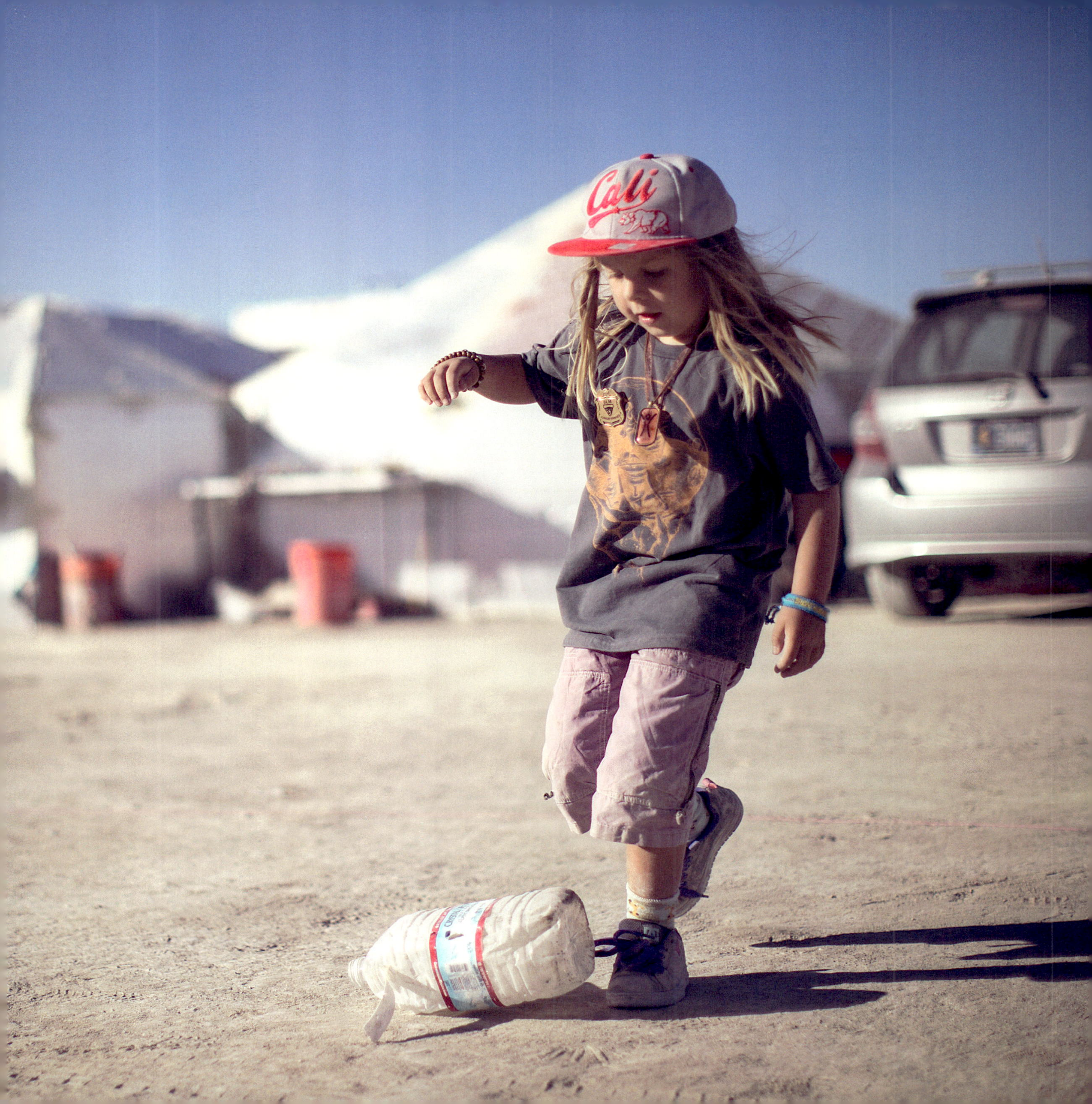
Cali

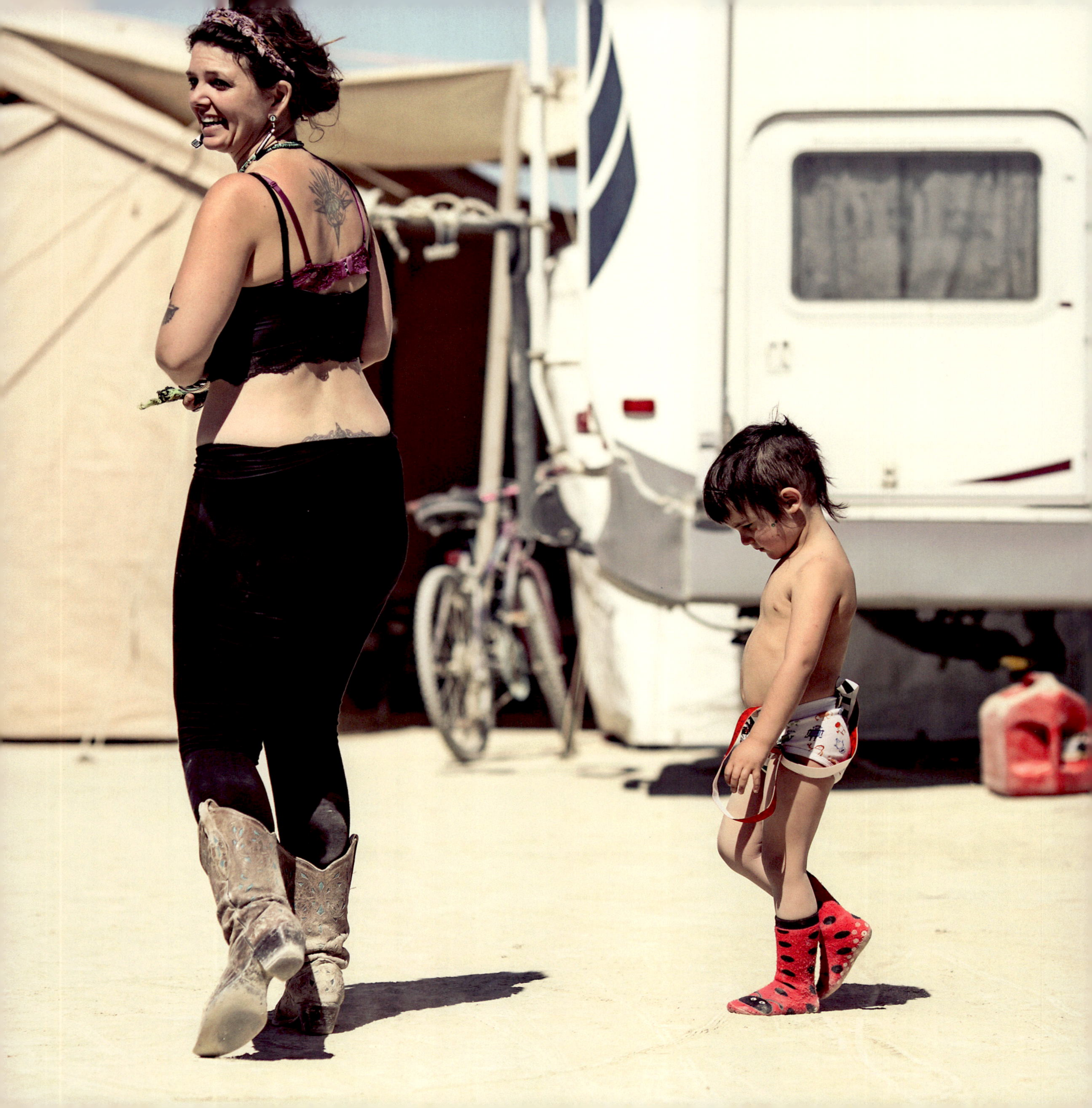

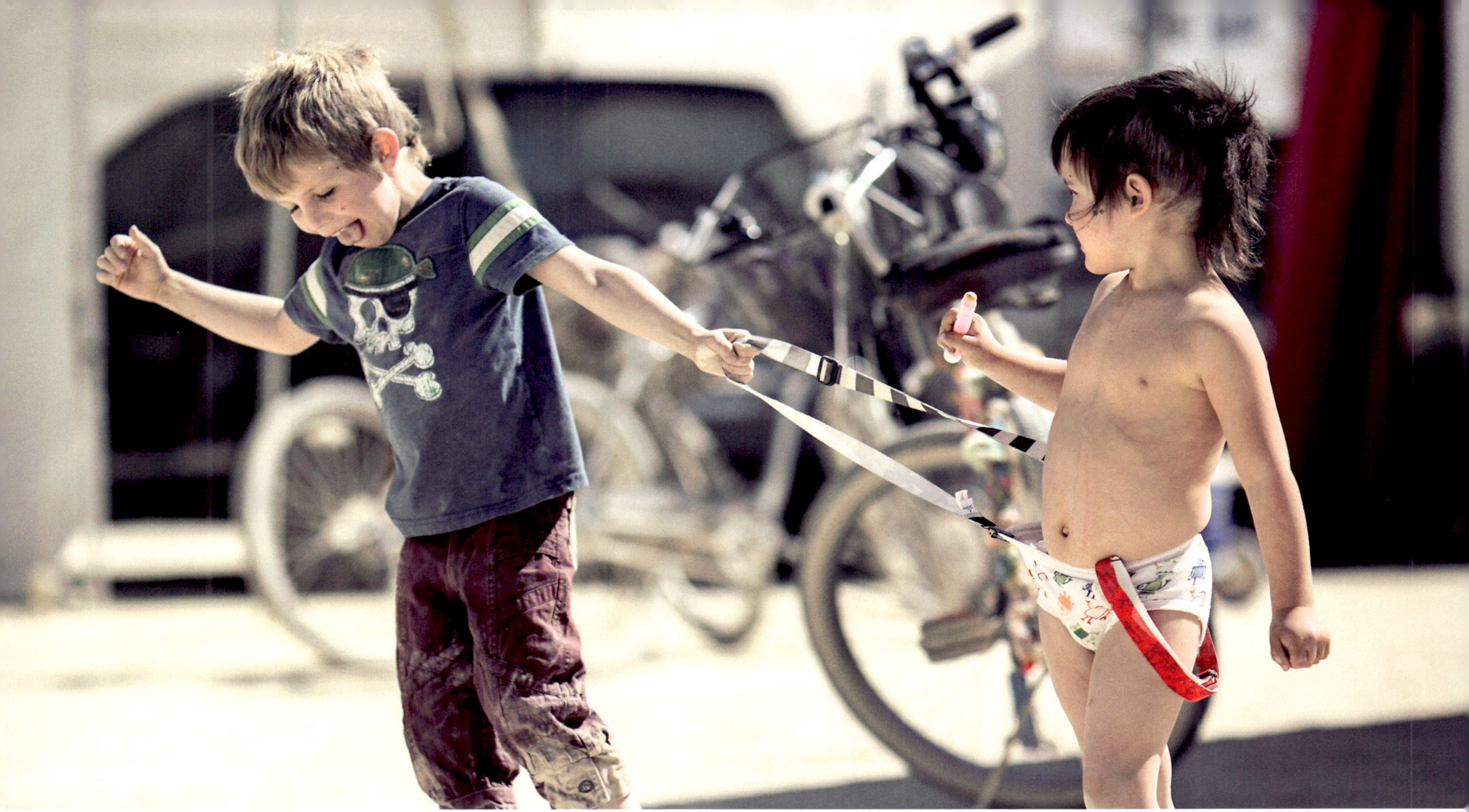
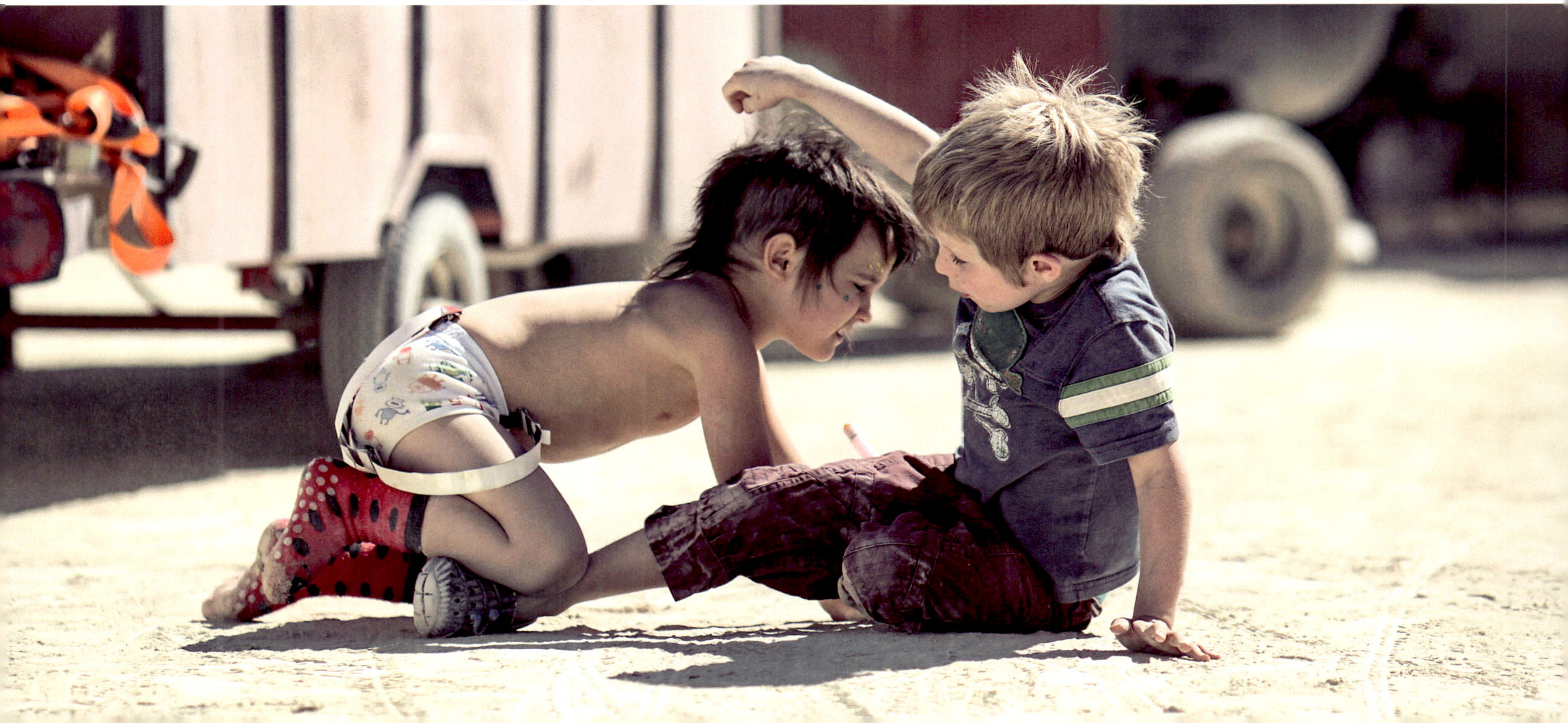

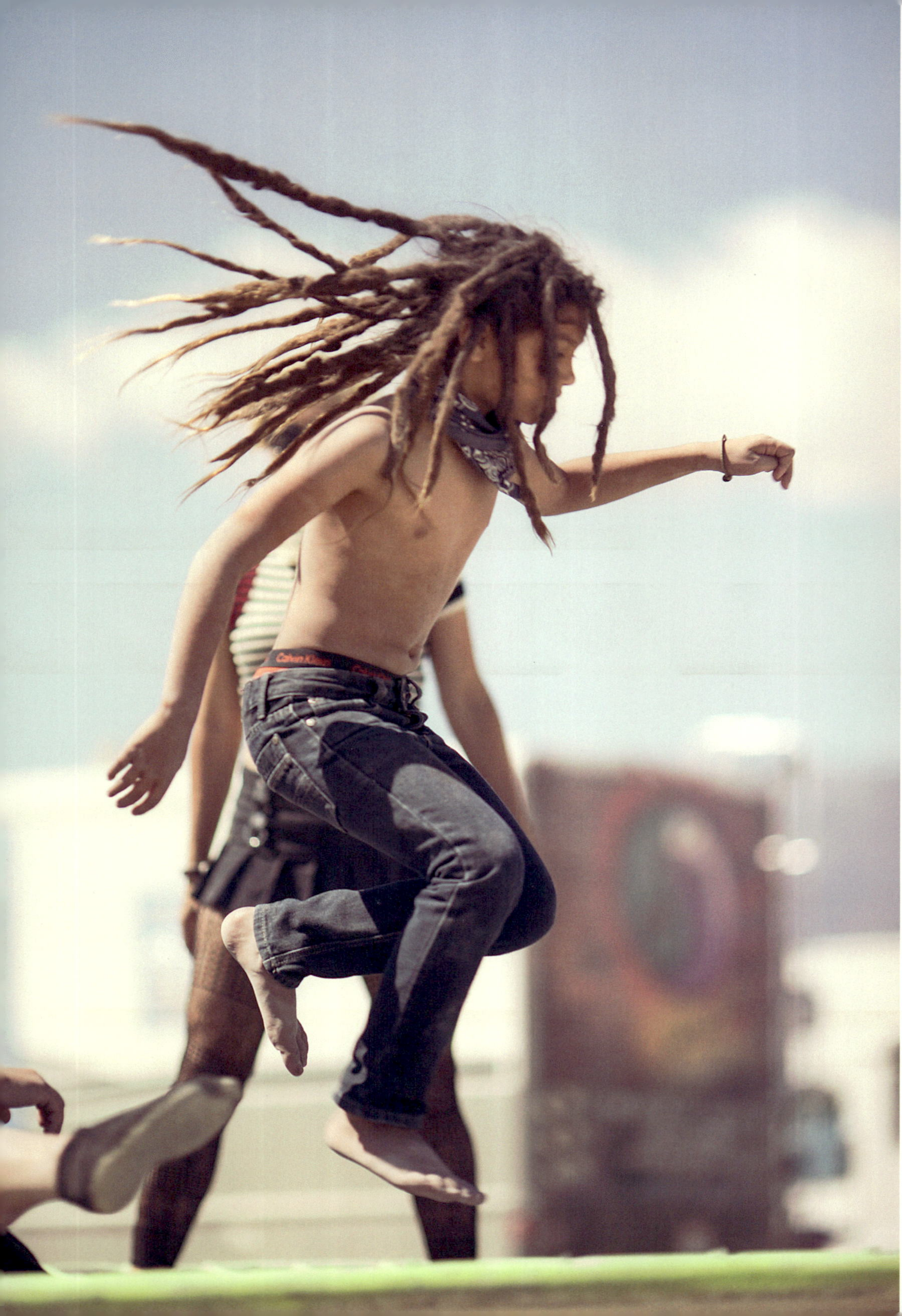

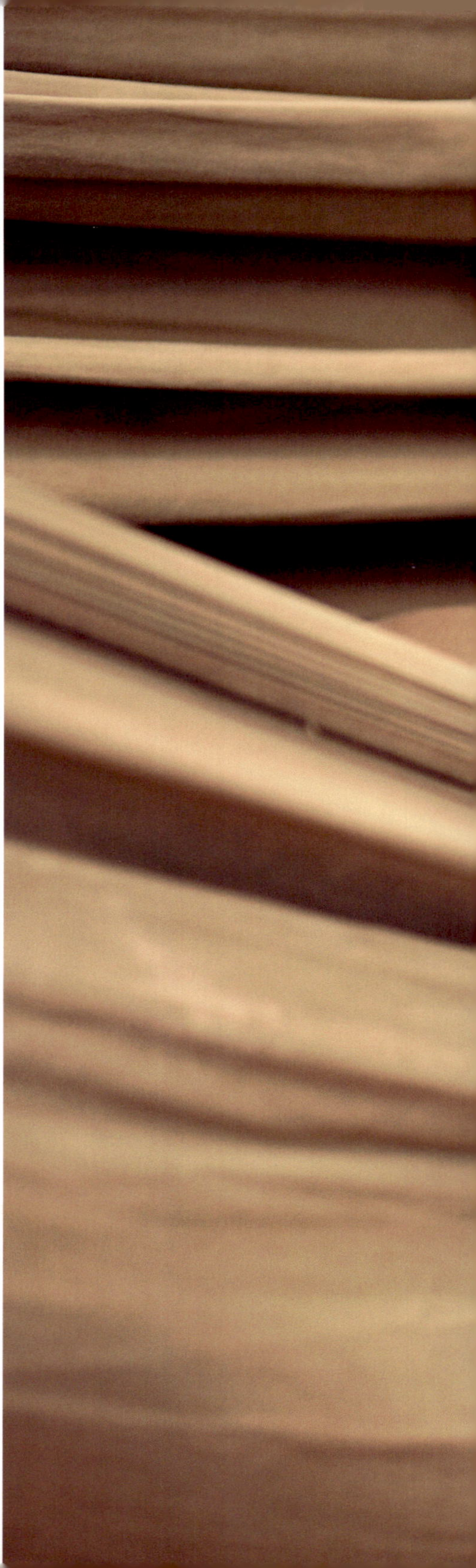

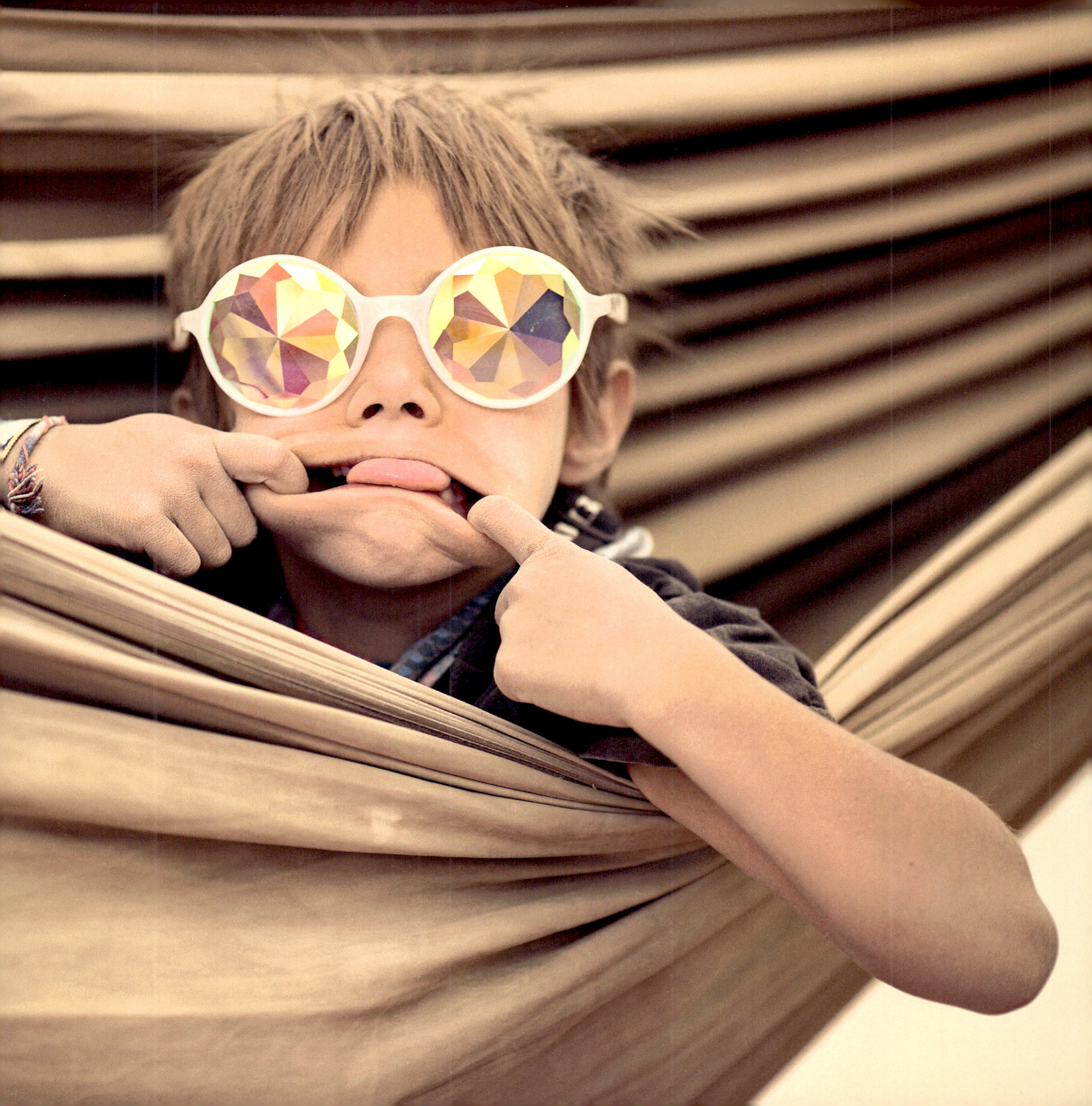

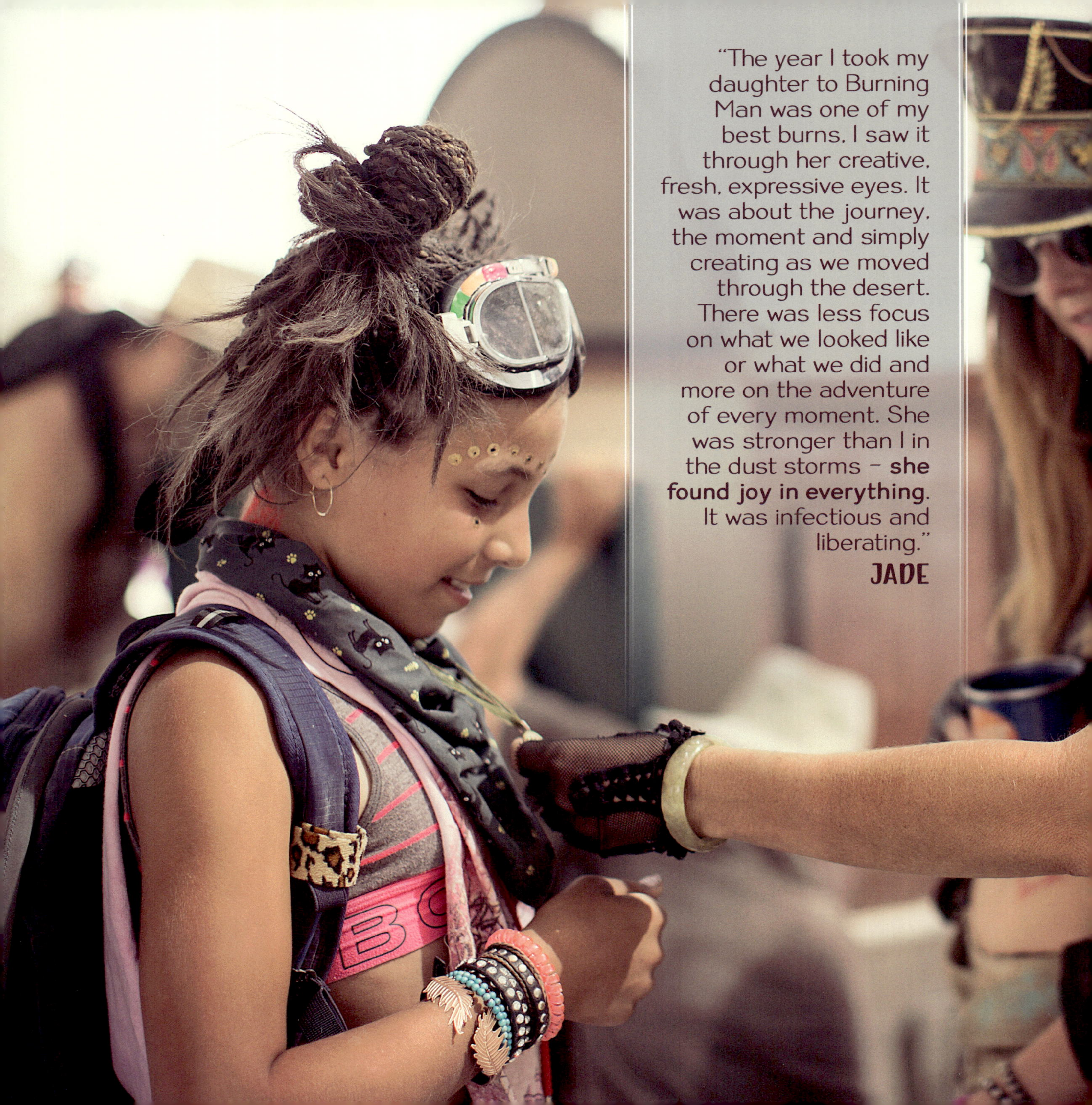

"The year I took my daughter to Burning Man was one of my best burns. I saw it through her creative, fresh, expressive eyes. It was about the journey, the moment and simply creating as we moved through the desert. There was less focus on what we looked like or what we did and more on the adventure of every moment. She was stronger than I in the dust storms – **she found joy in everything**. It was infectious and liberating."

JADE

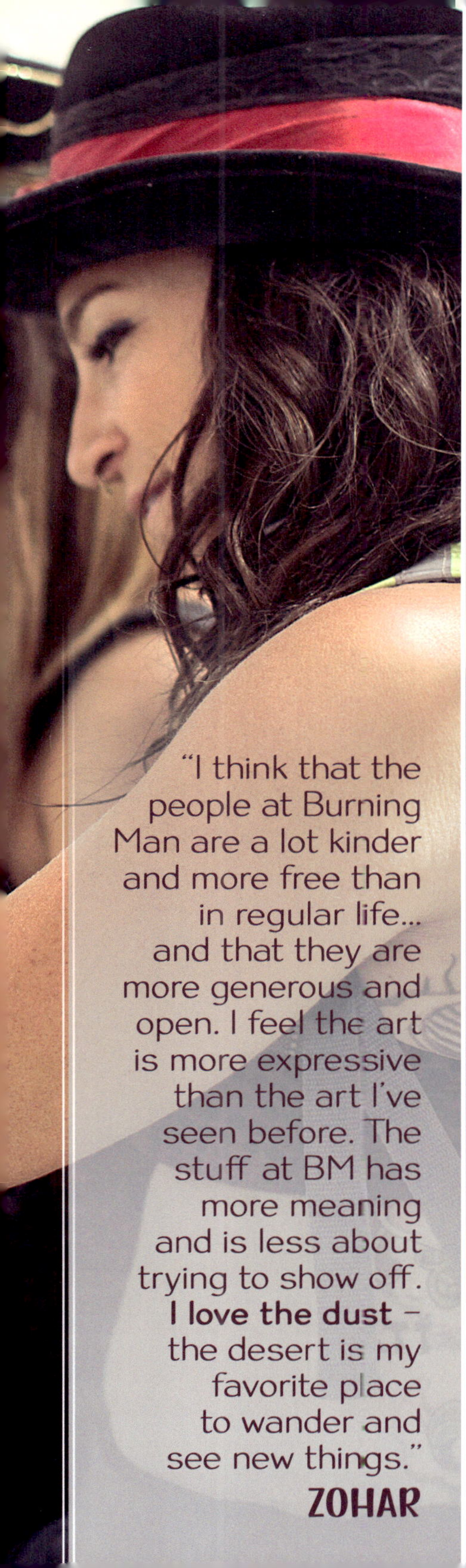

"I think that the people at Burning Man are a lot kinder and more free than in regular life... and that they are more generous and open. I feel the art is more expressive than the art I've seen before. The stuff at BM has more meaning and is less about trying to show off. **I love the dust** – the desert is my favorite place to wander and see new things."

ZOHAR

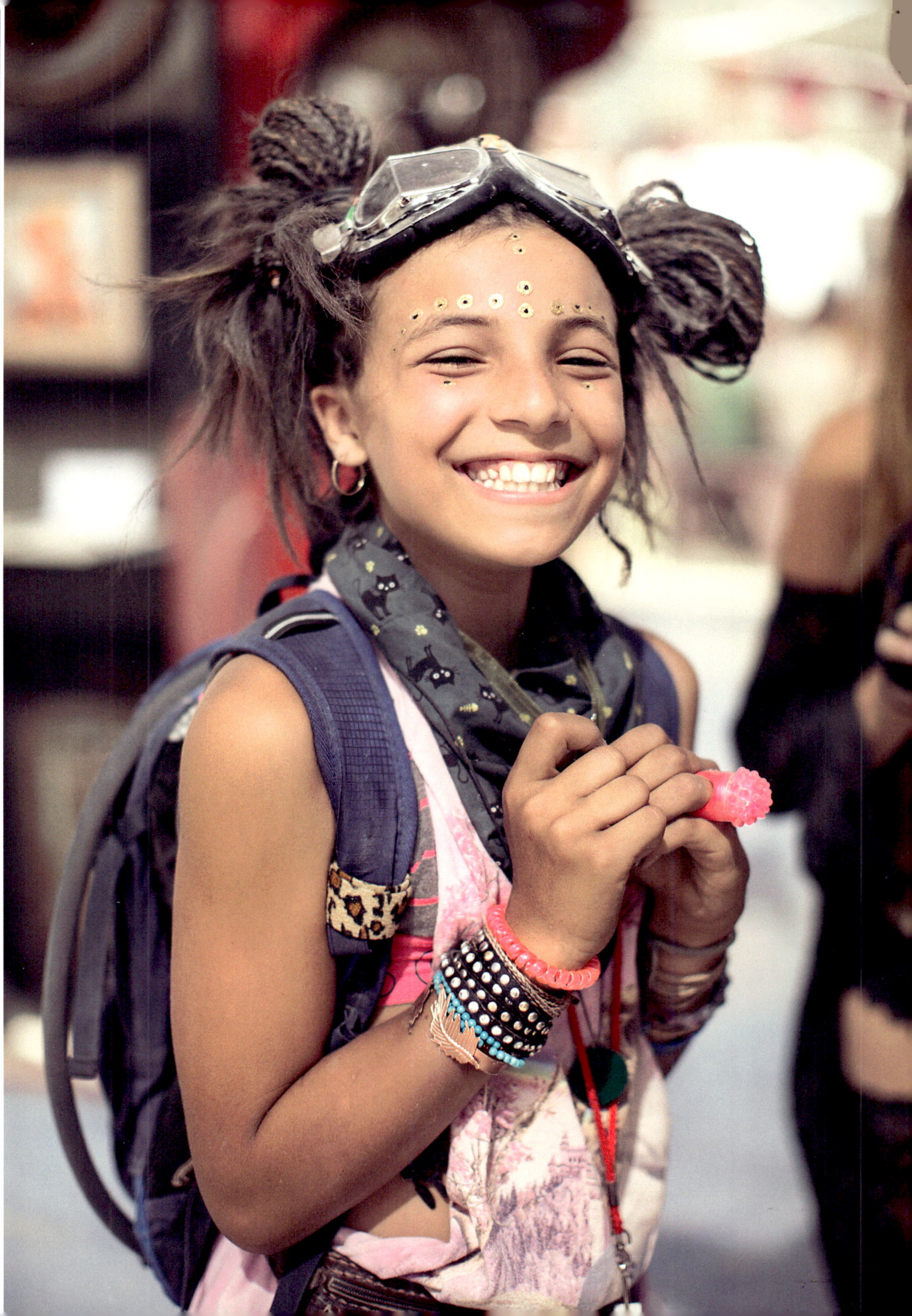

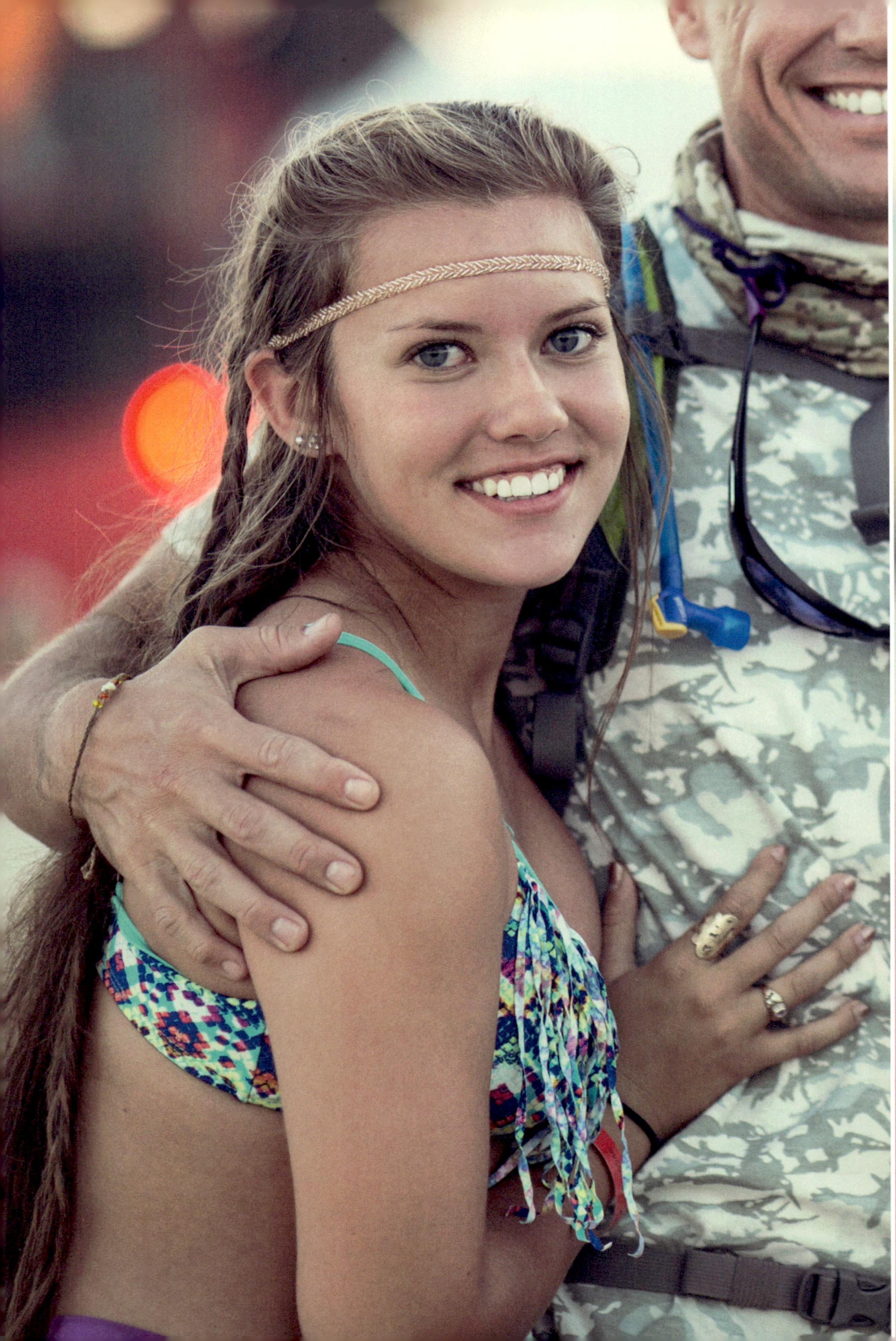

"As parents of two beautiful young ladies, our experience with Burning Man was such an inspiring and bonding time for us as a family. Life is too short and hectic – sometimes you must slow down and appreciate every aspect there is to offer. Focus on the positive in life and teach your children to appreciate this as well. It's the little things that make our life whole."

THE THOMPSONS

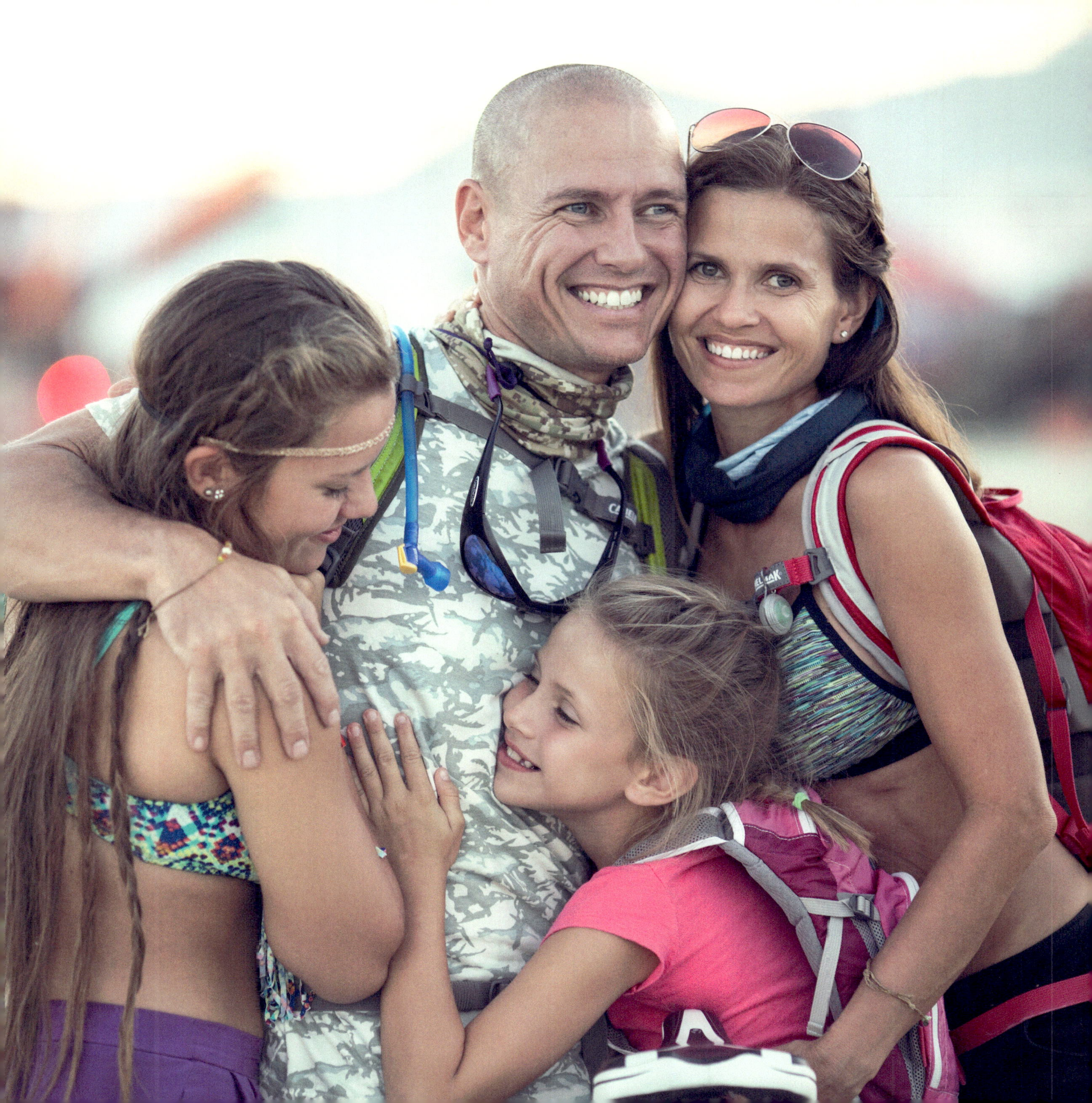

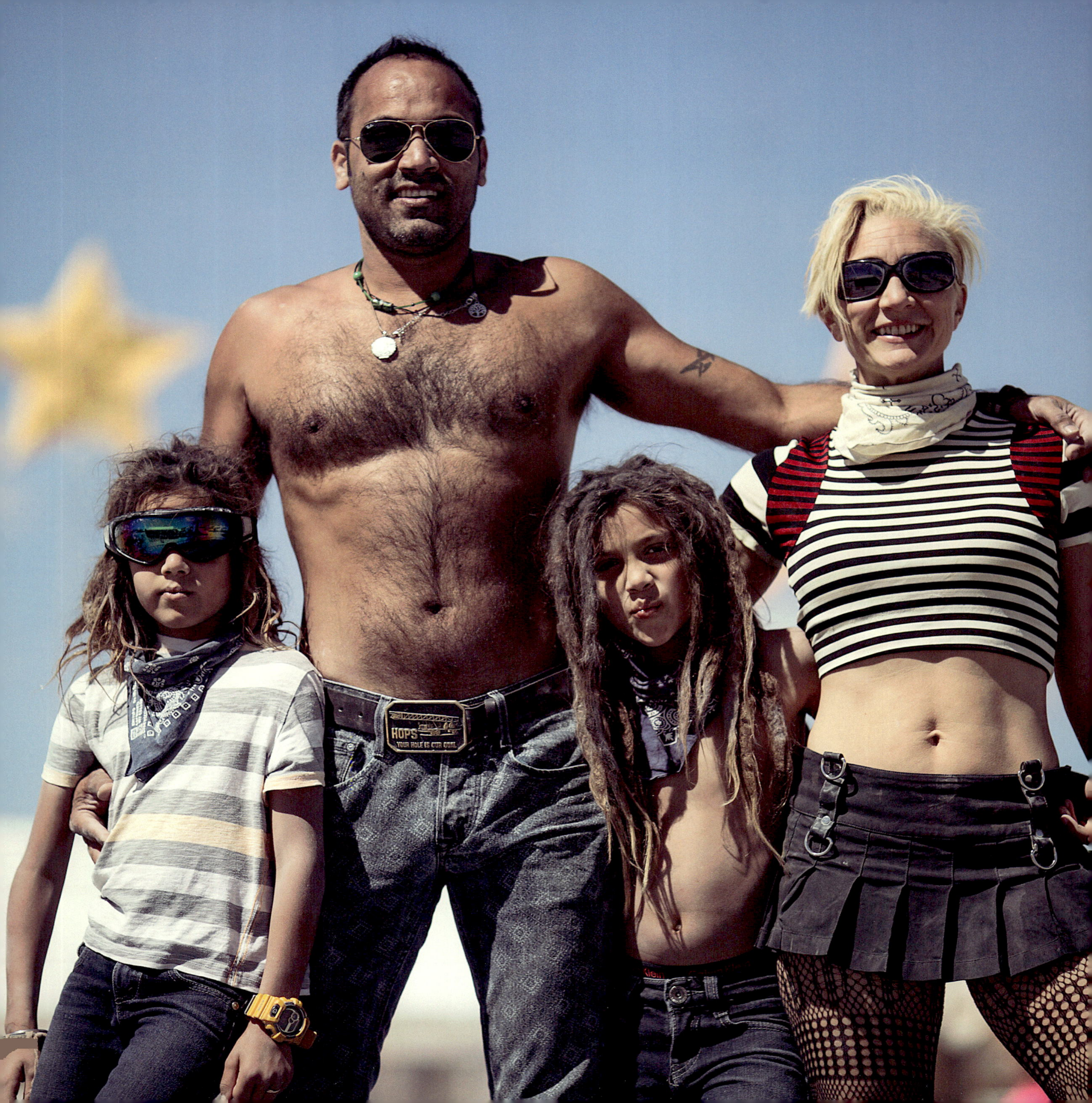
HOPS
YOUR HOLE IS OUR GOAL

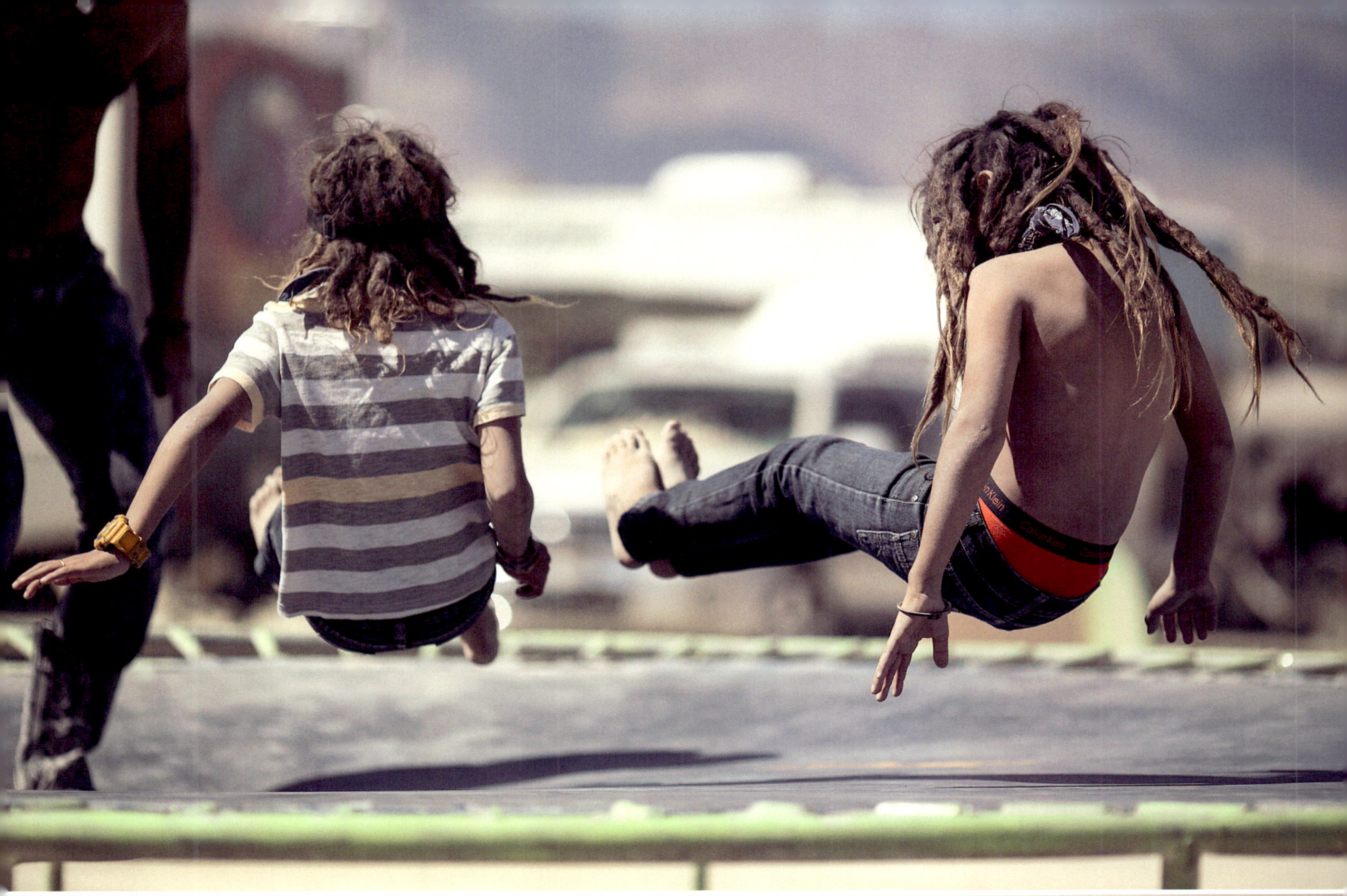

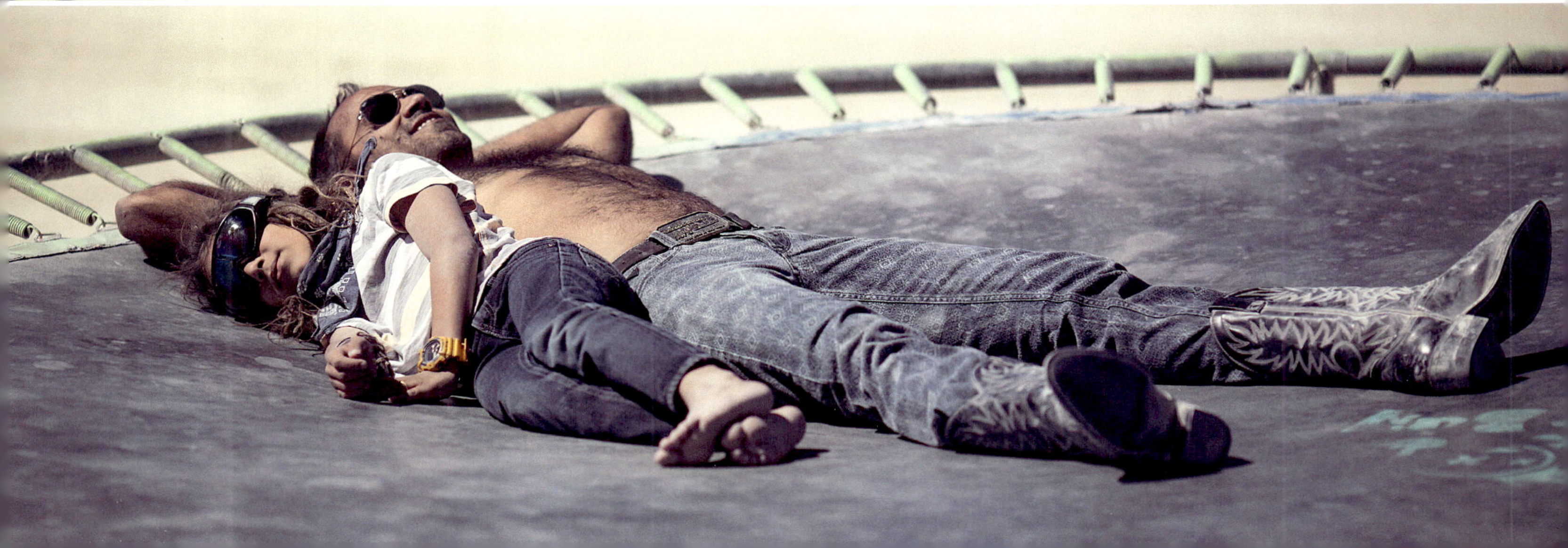

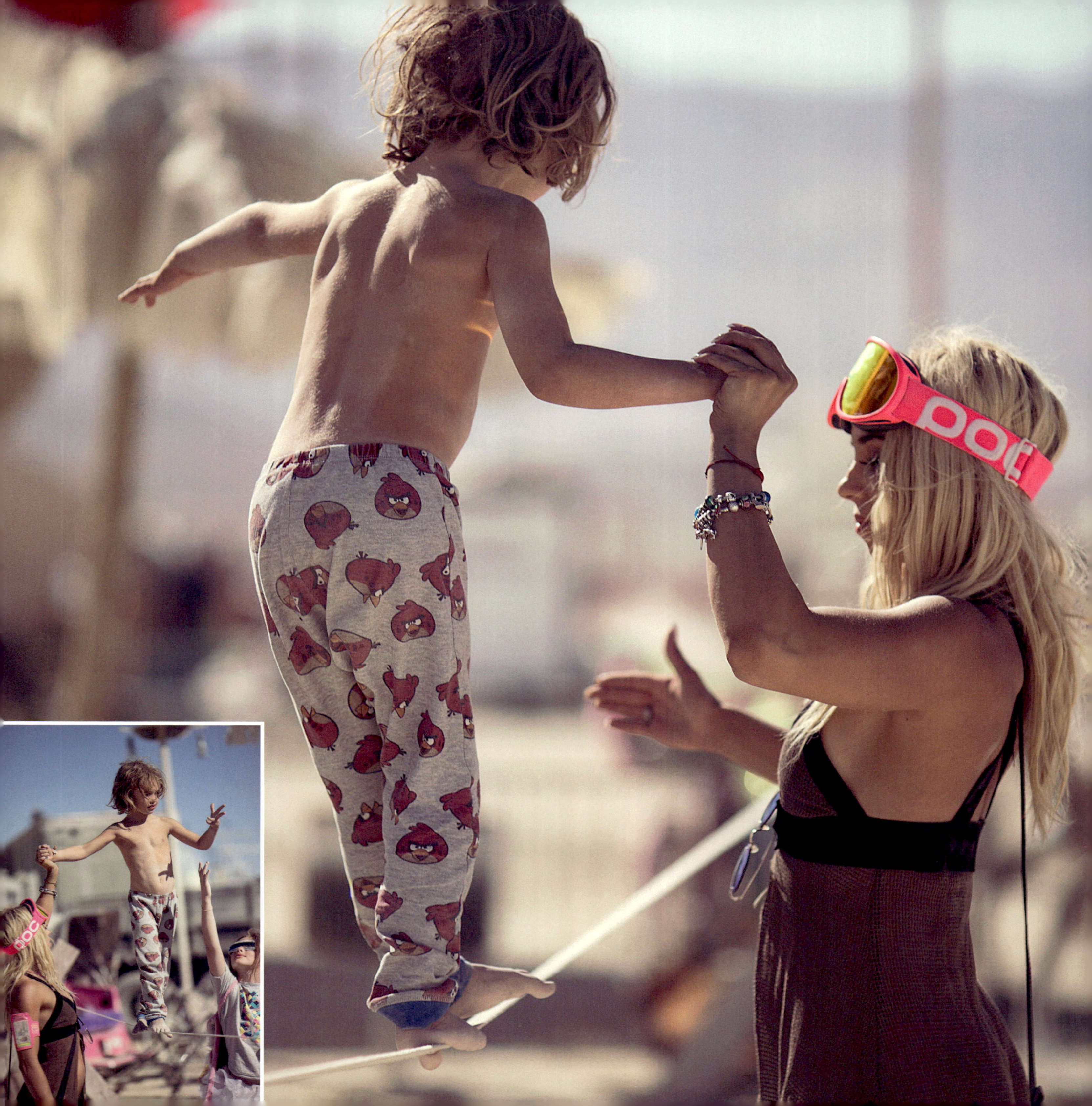
POC

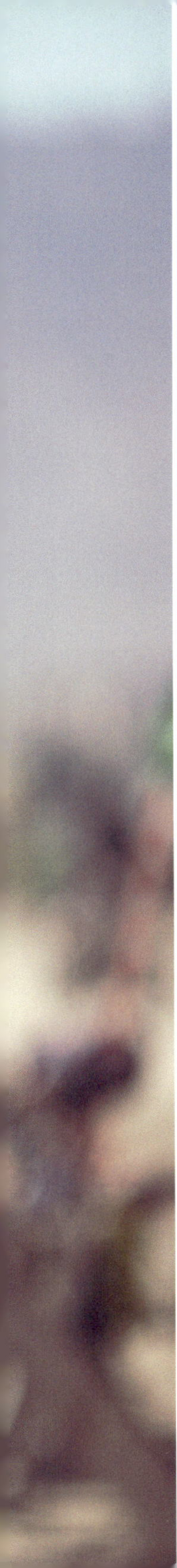
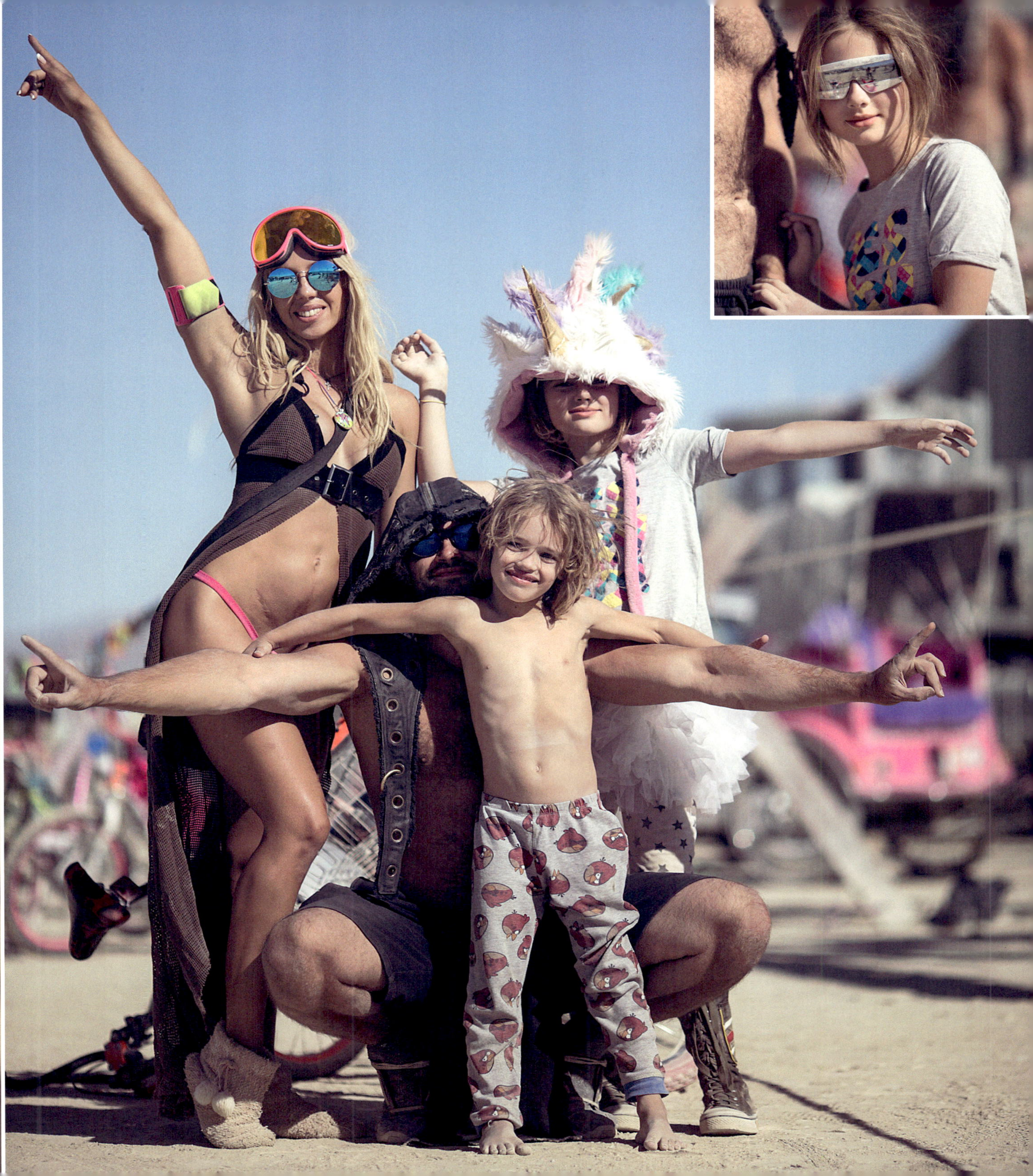

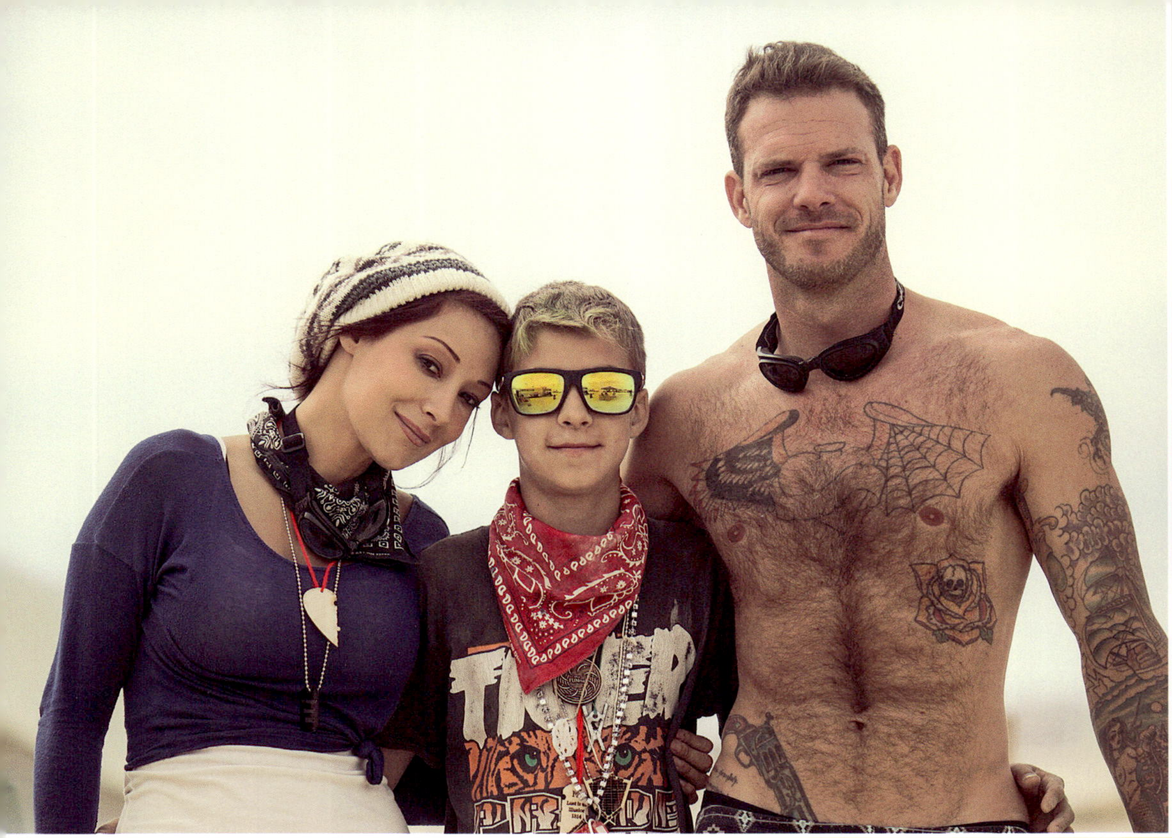

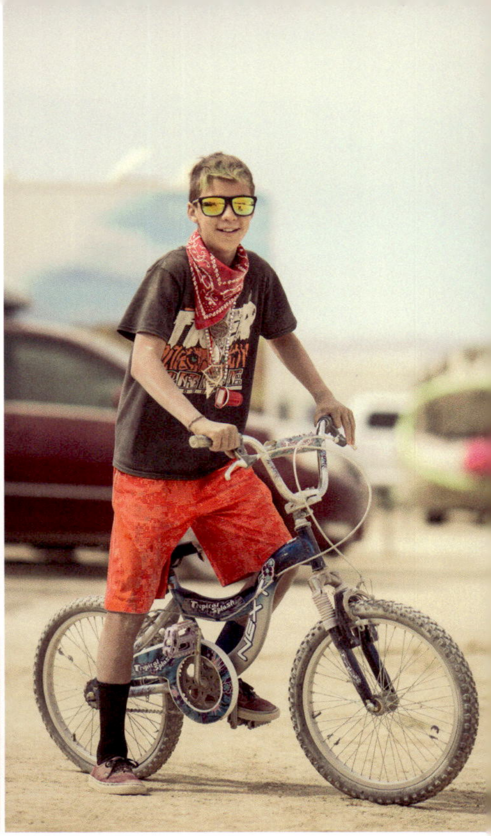

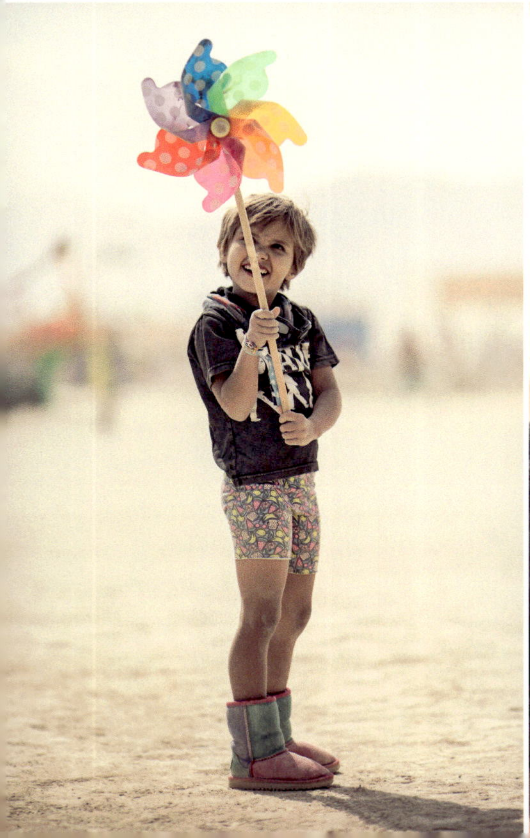

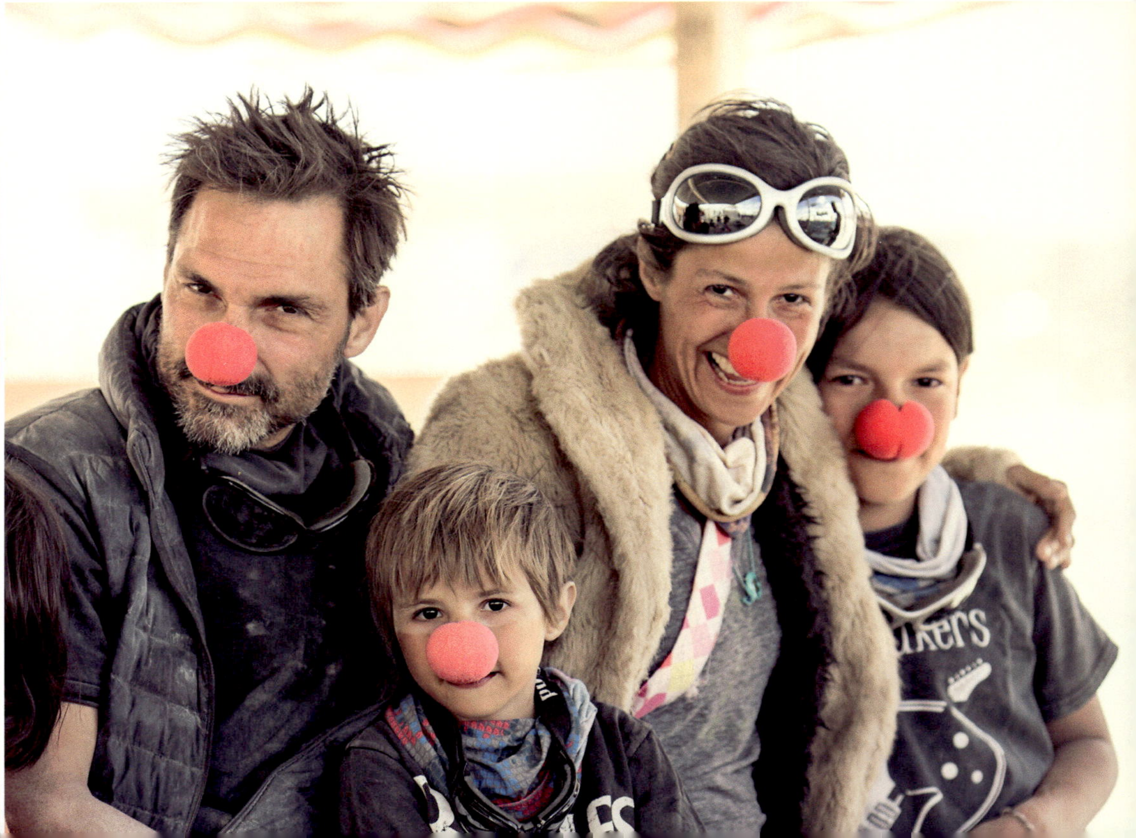

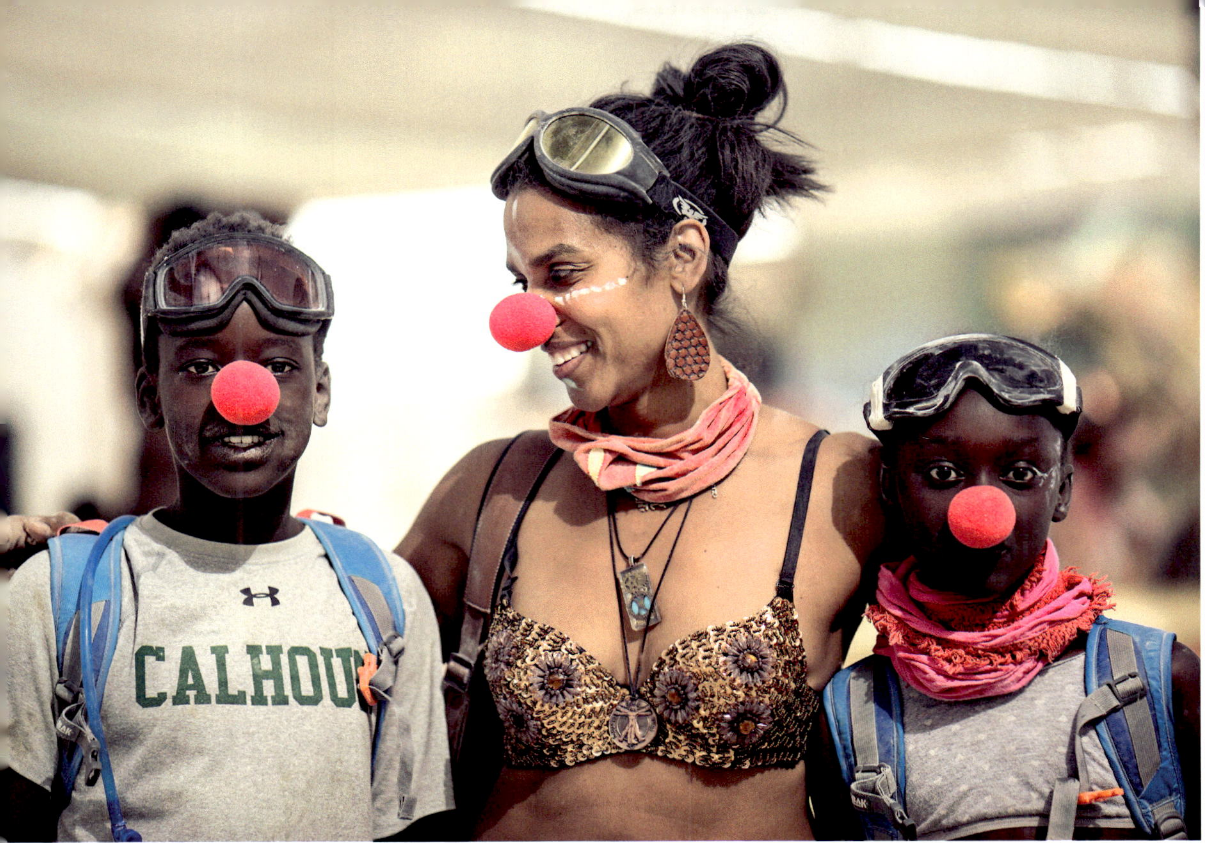
CALHOU

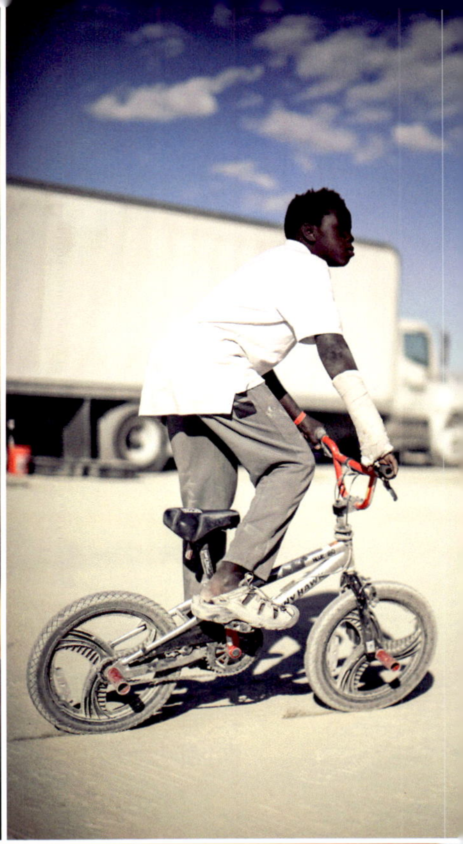

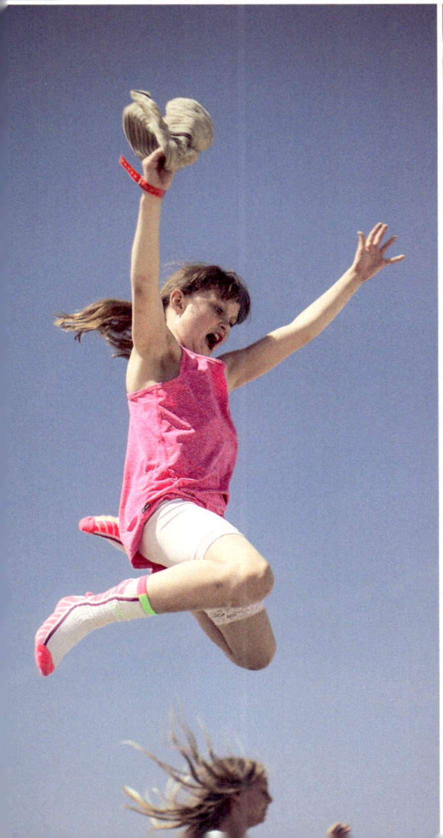

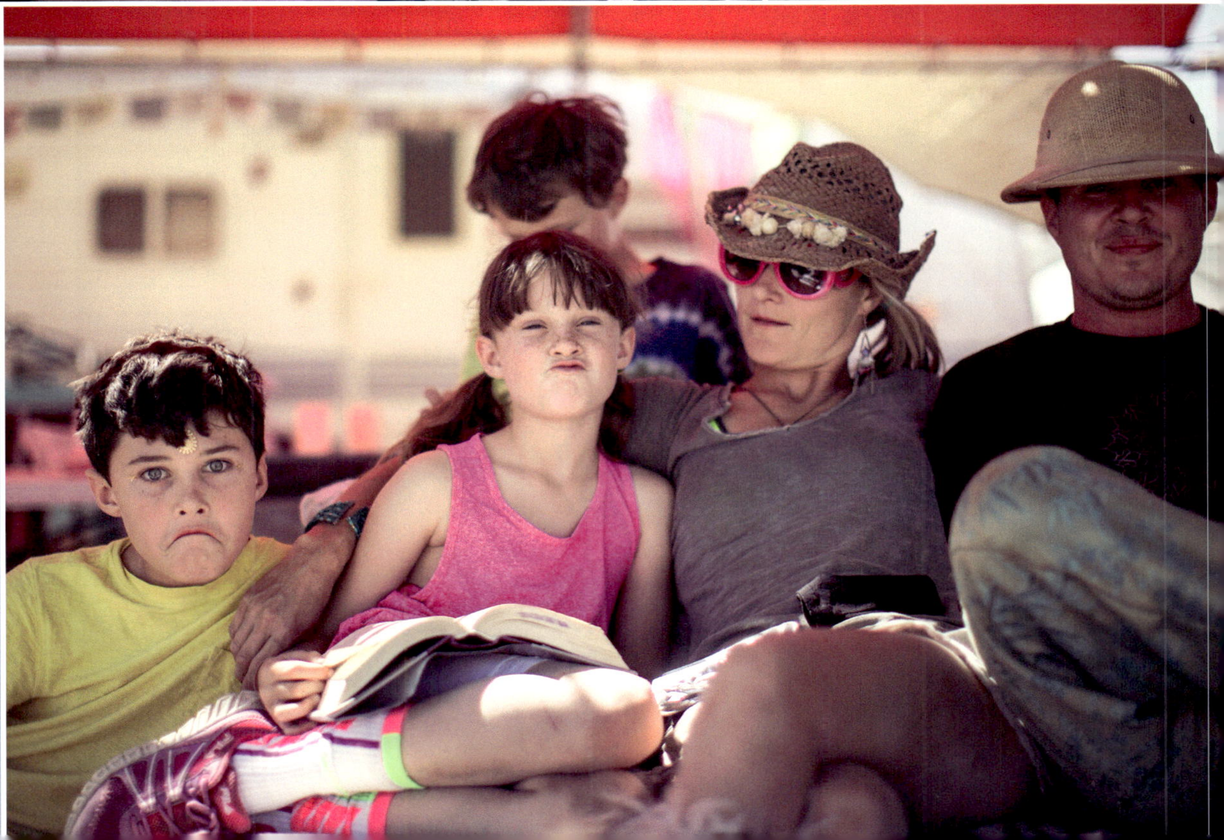

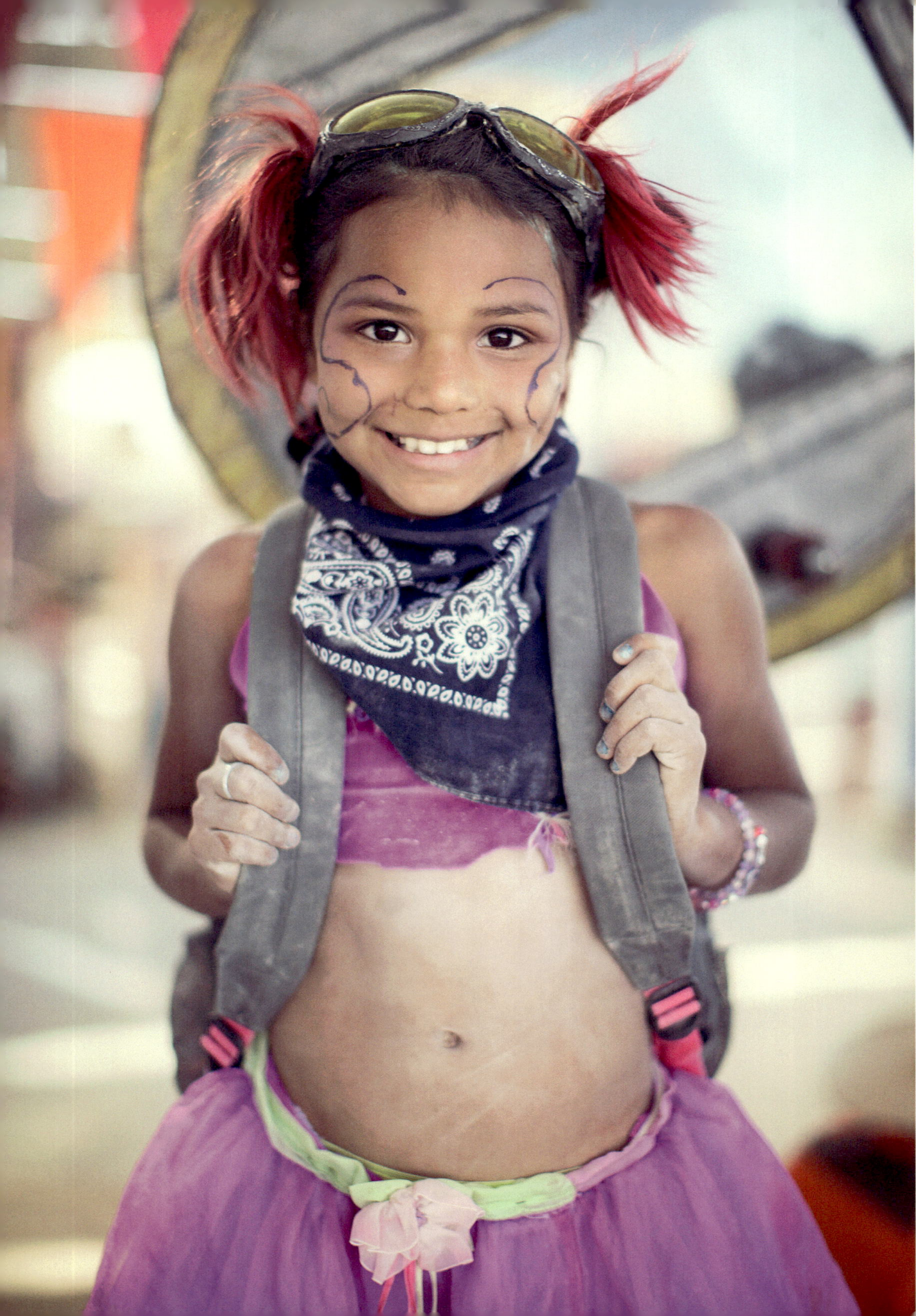
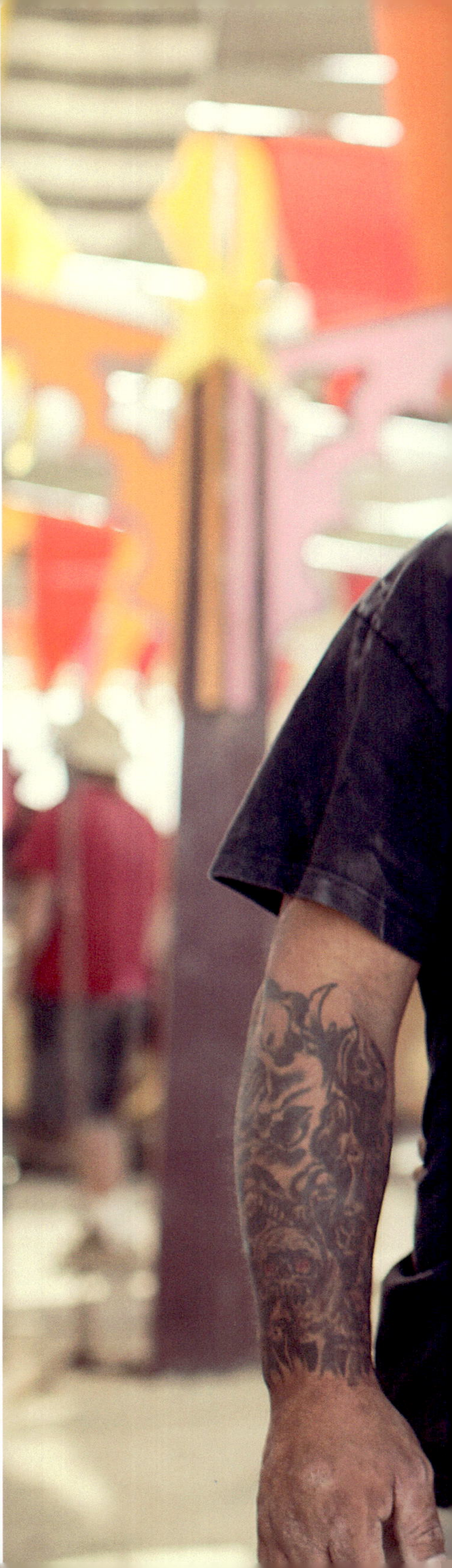

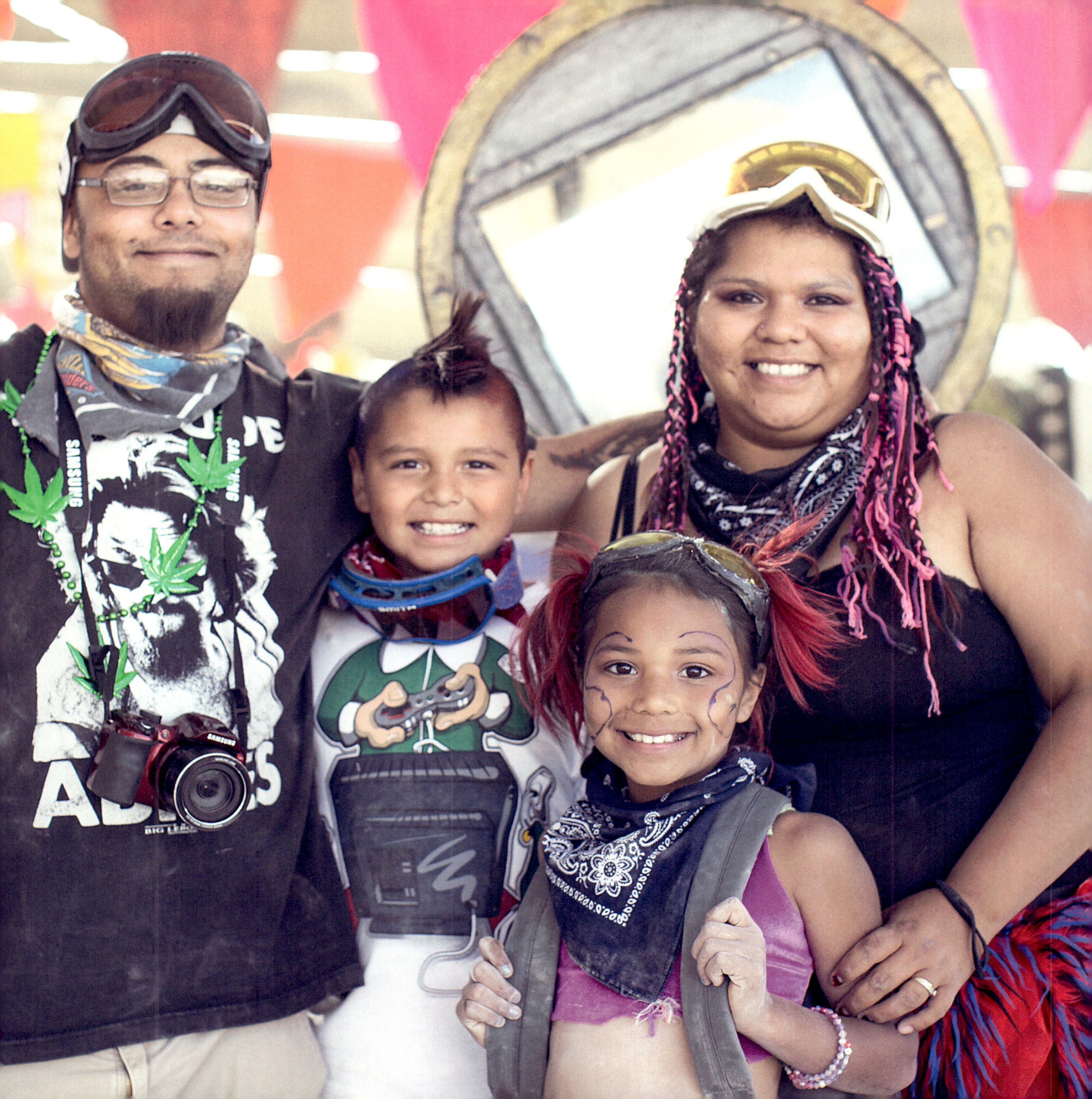
SAMSUNG
SAMSUNG
SAMSUNG

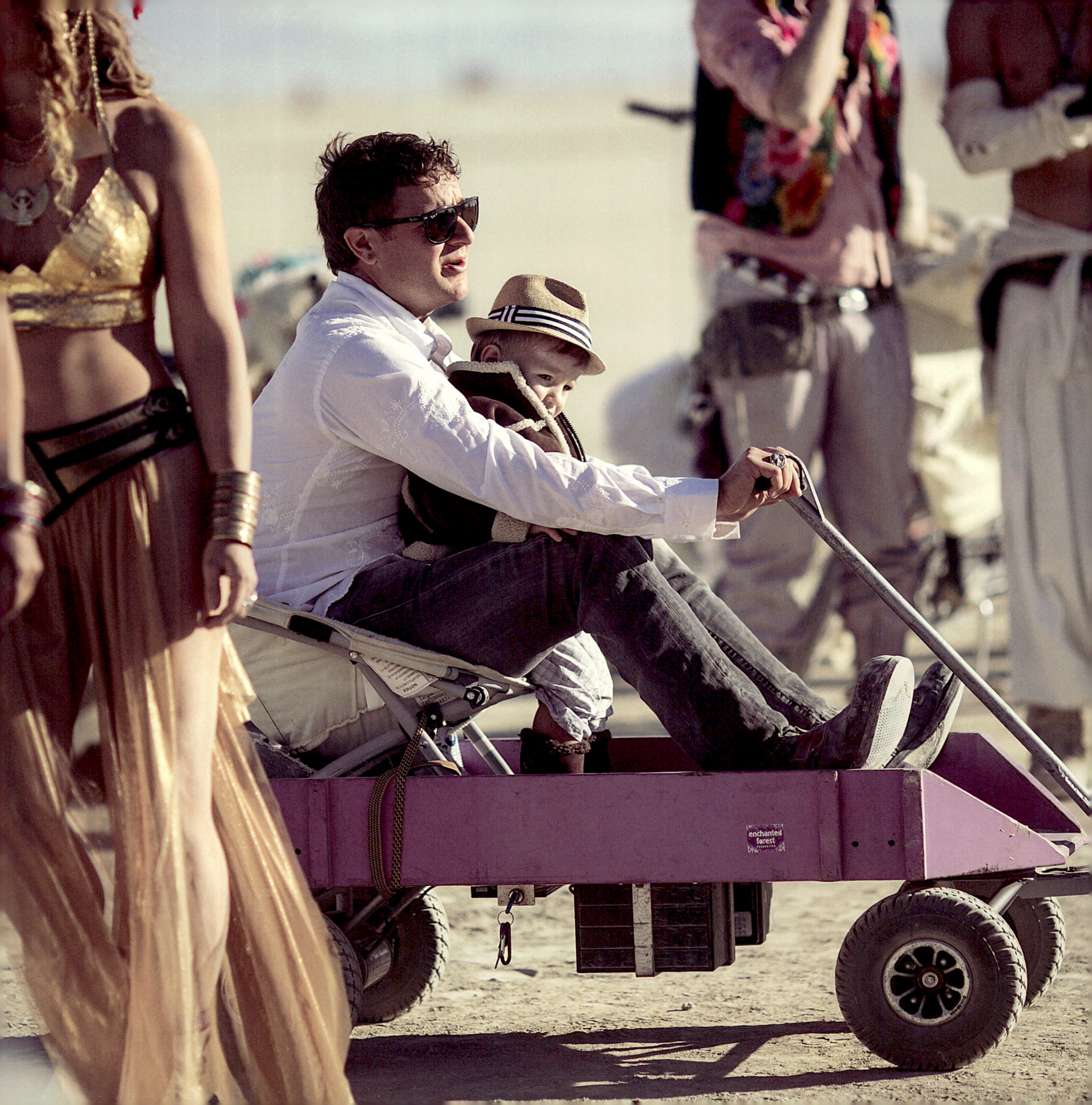
enchanted
forest

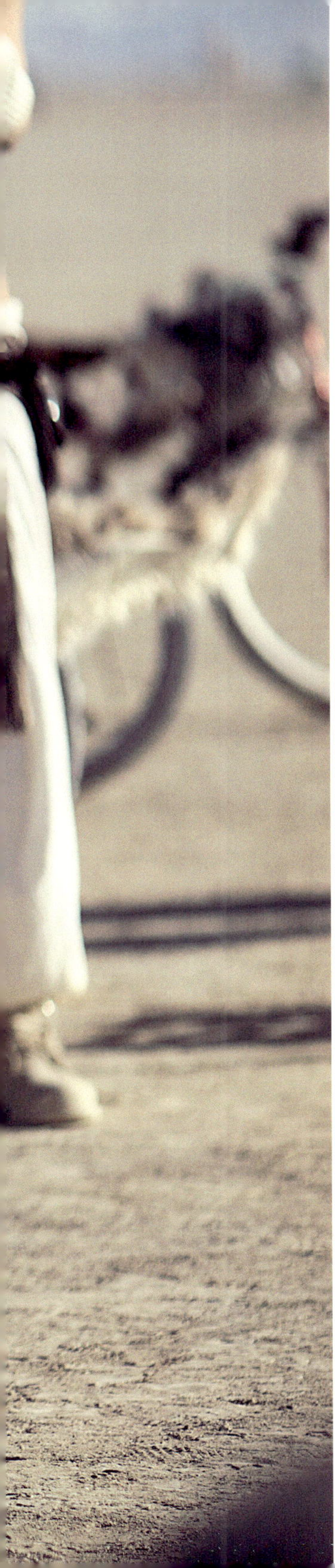

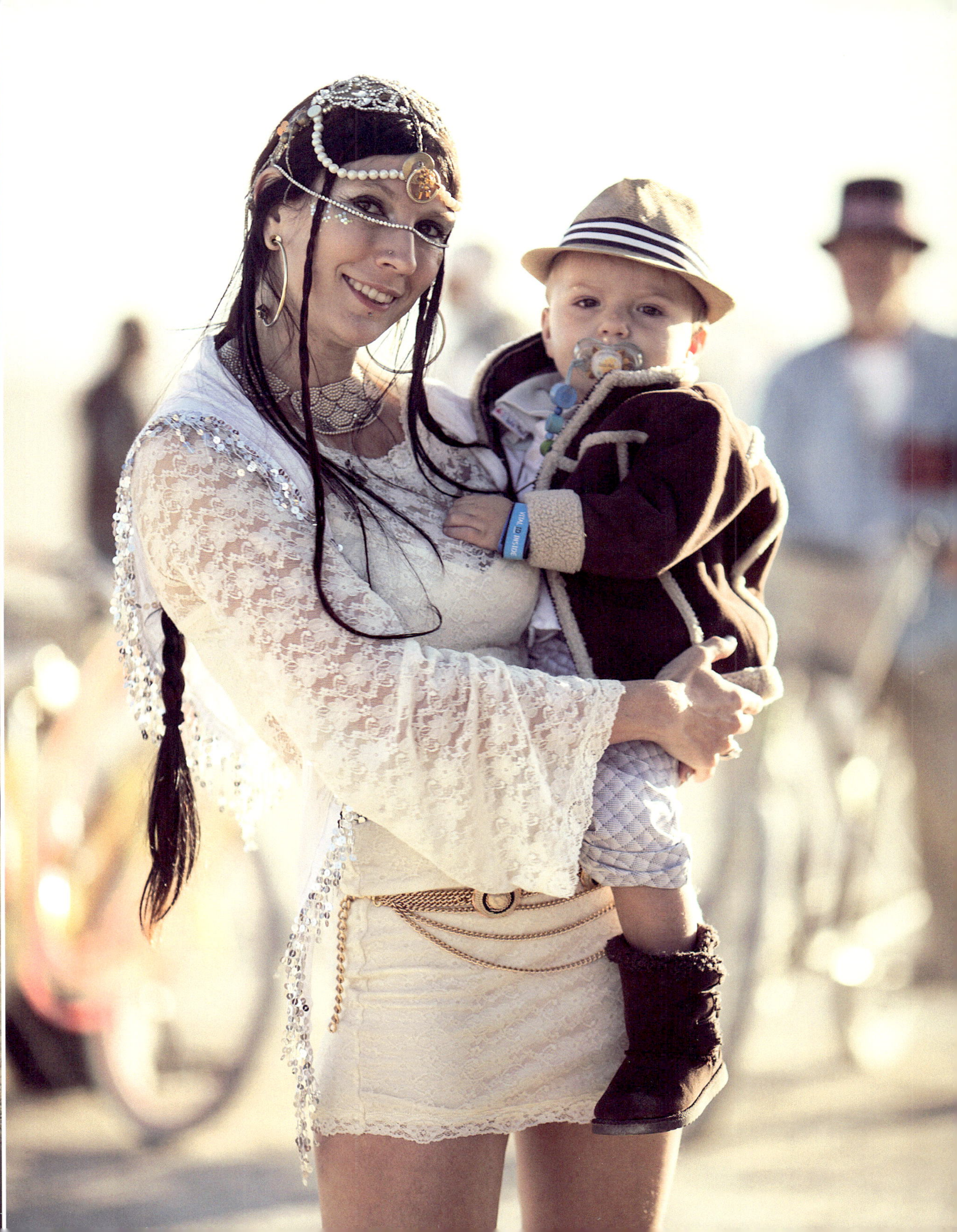

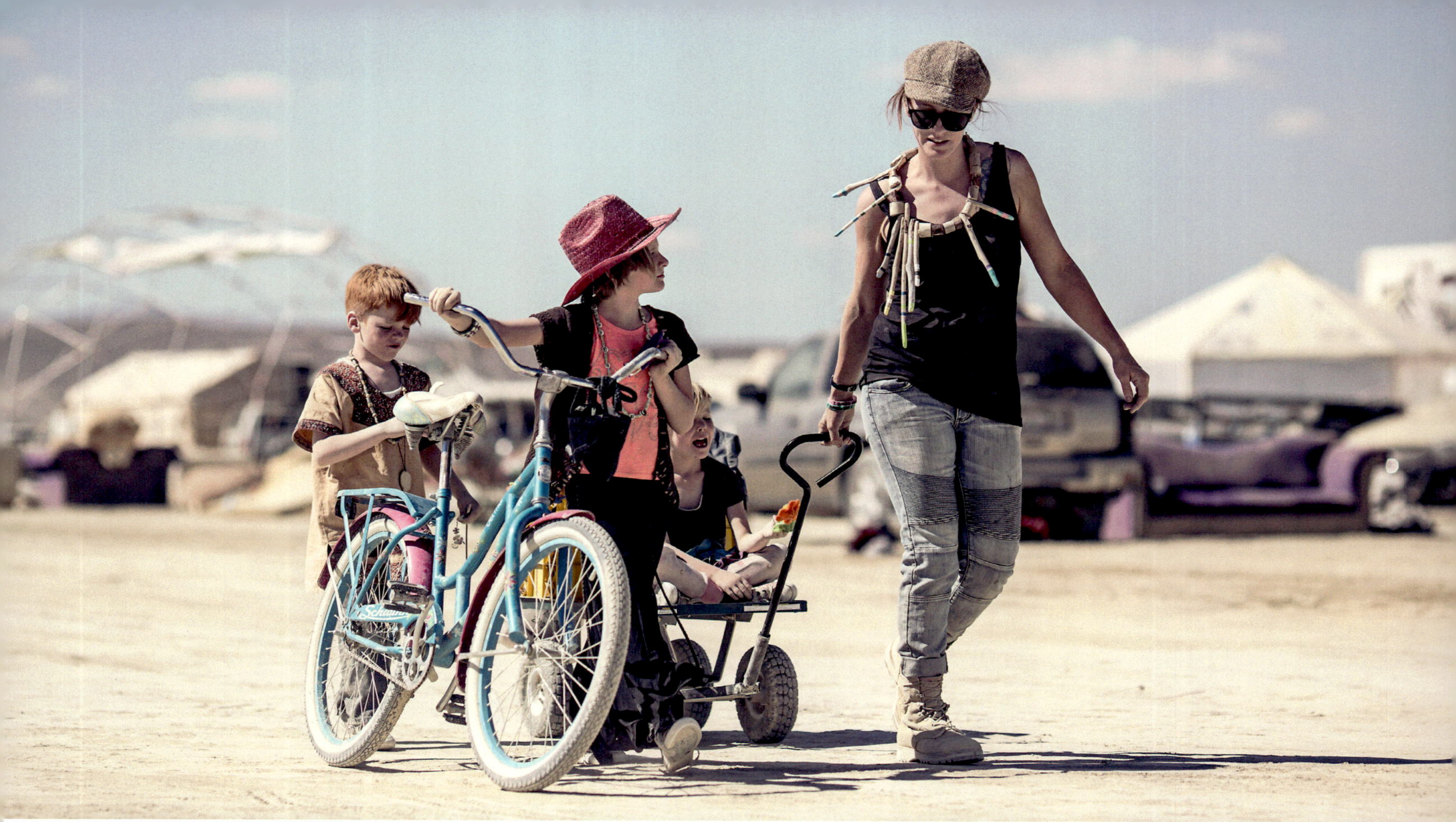

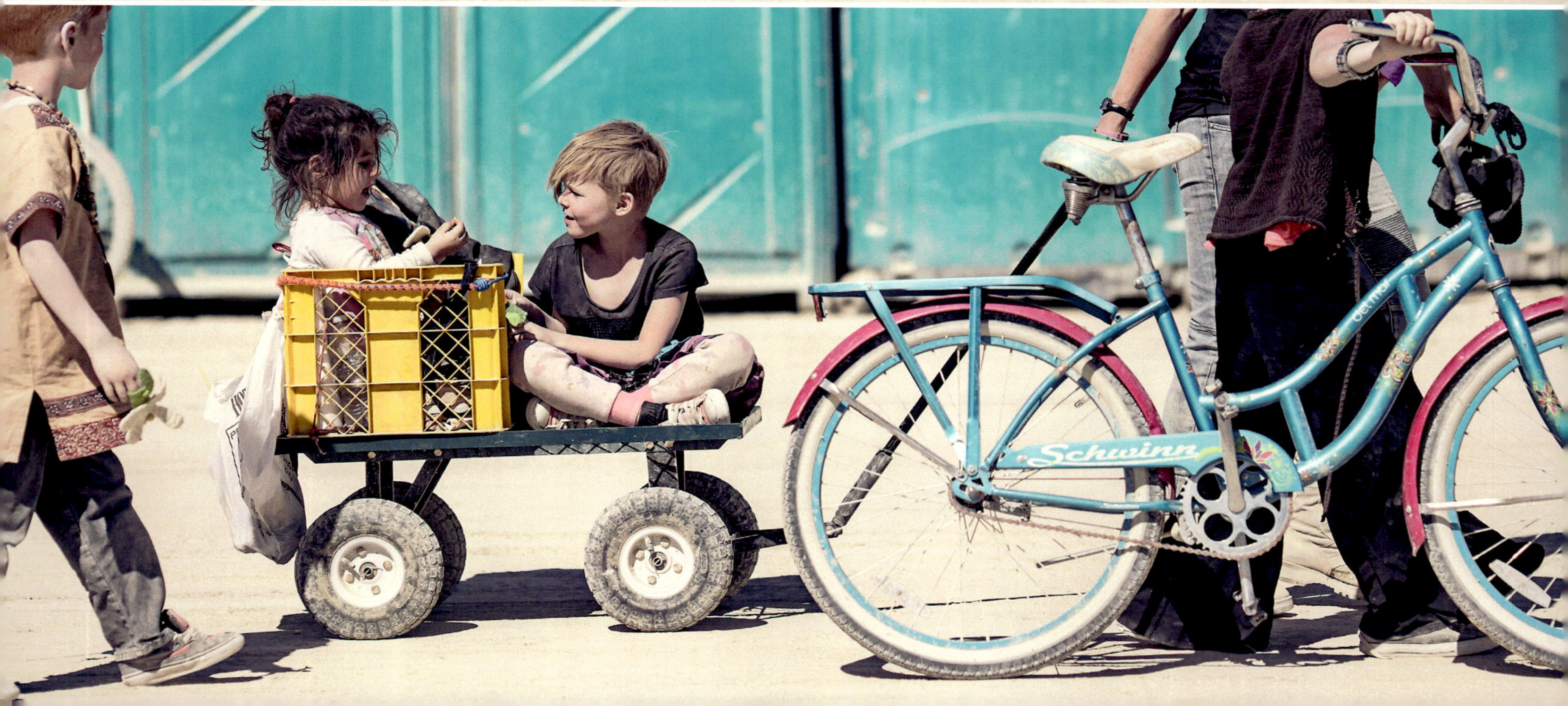
Schwinn

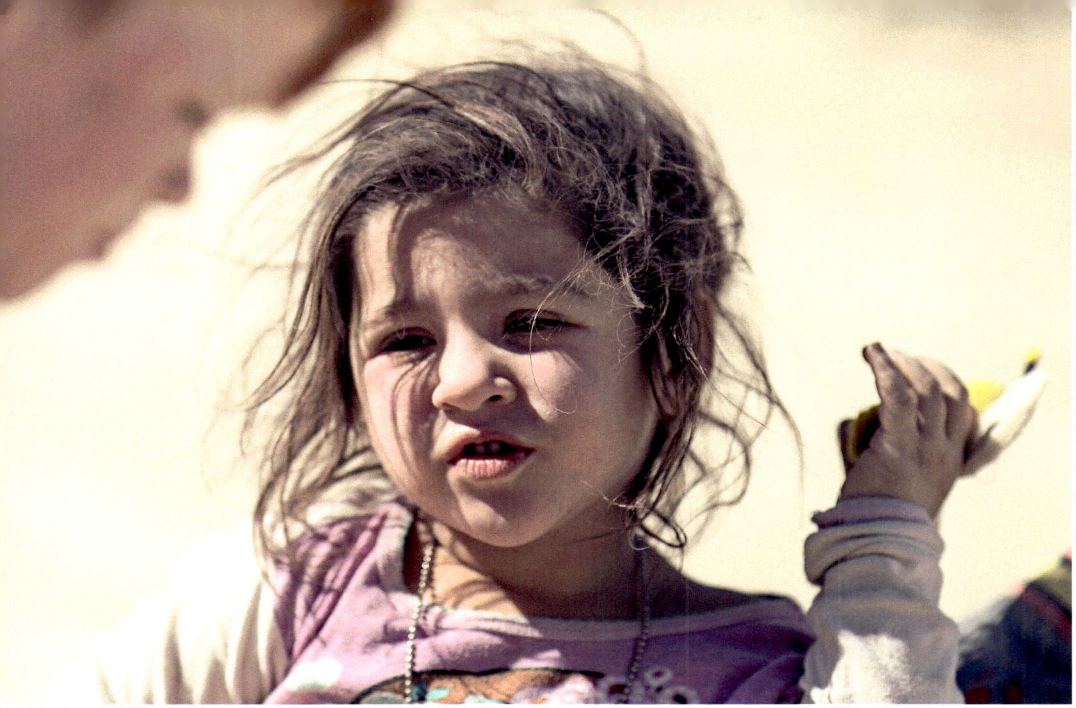

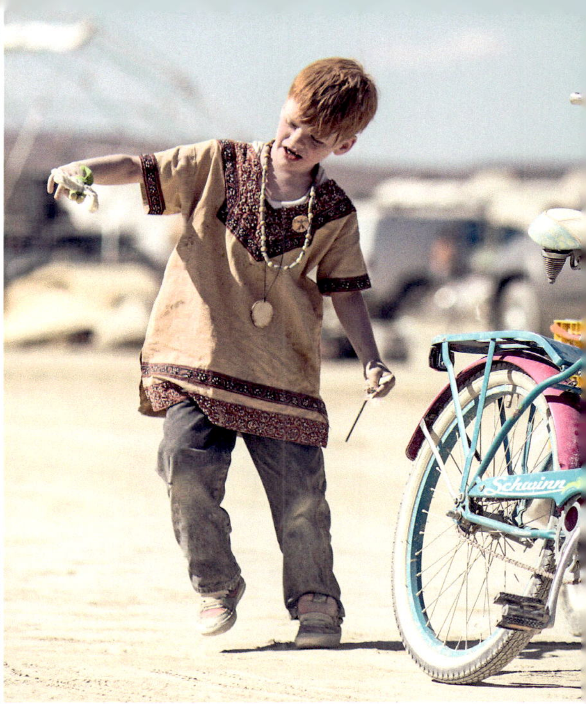

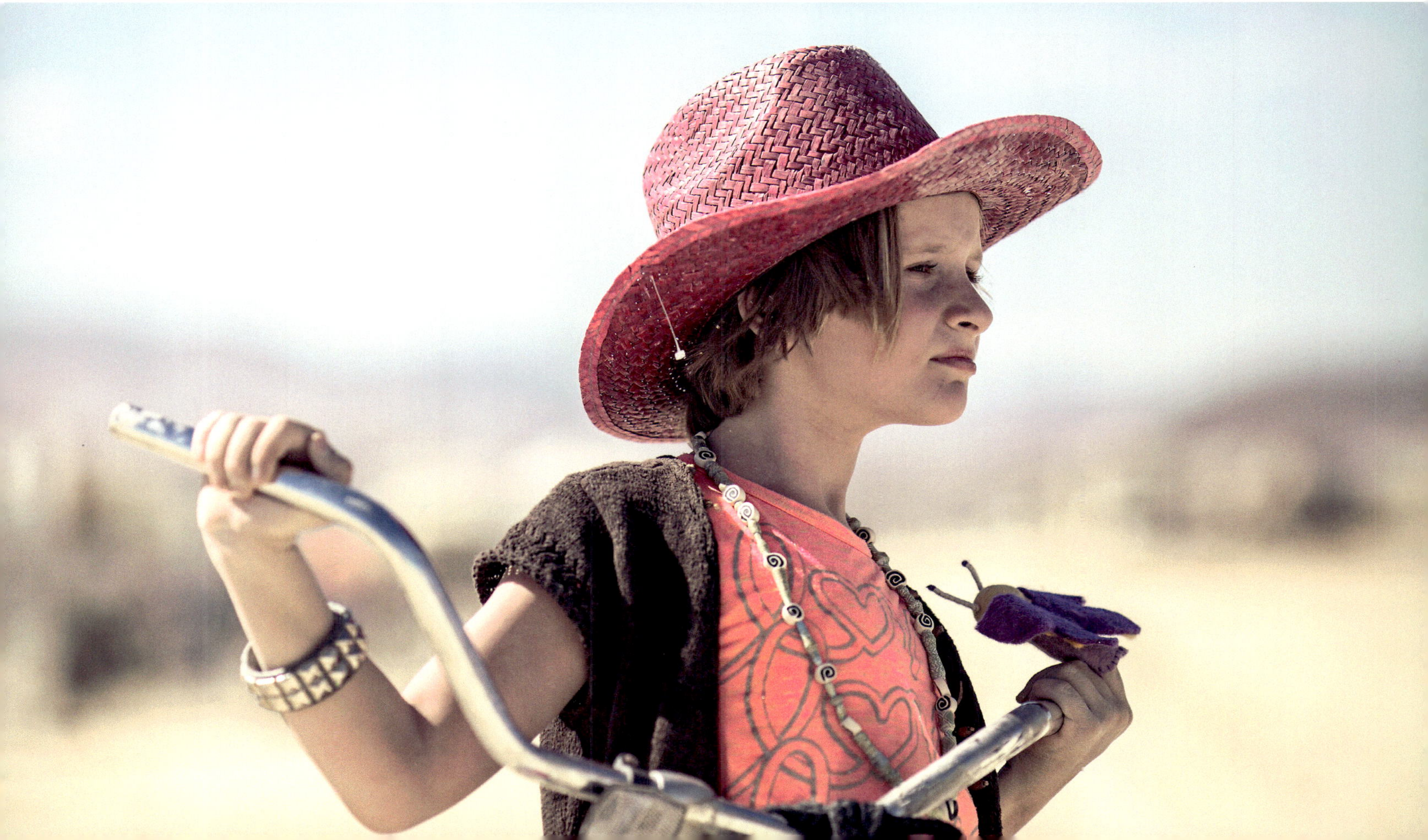

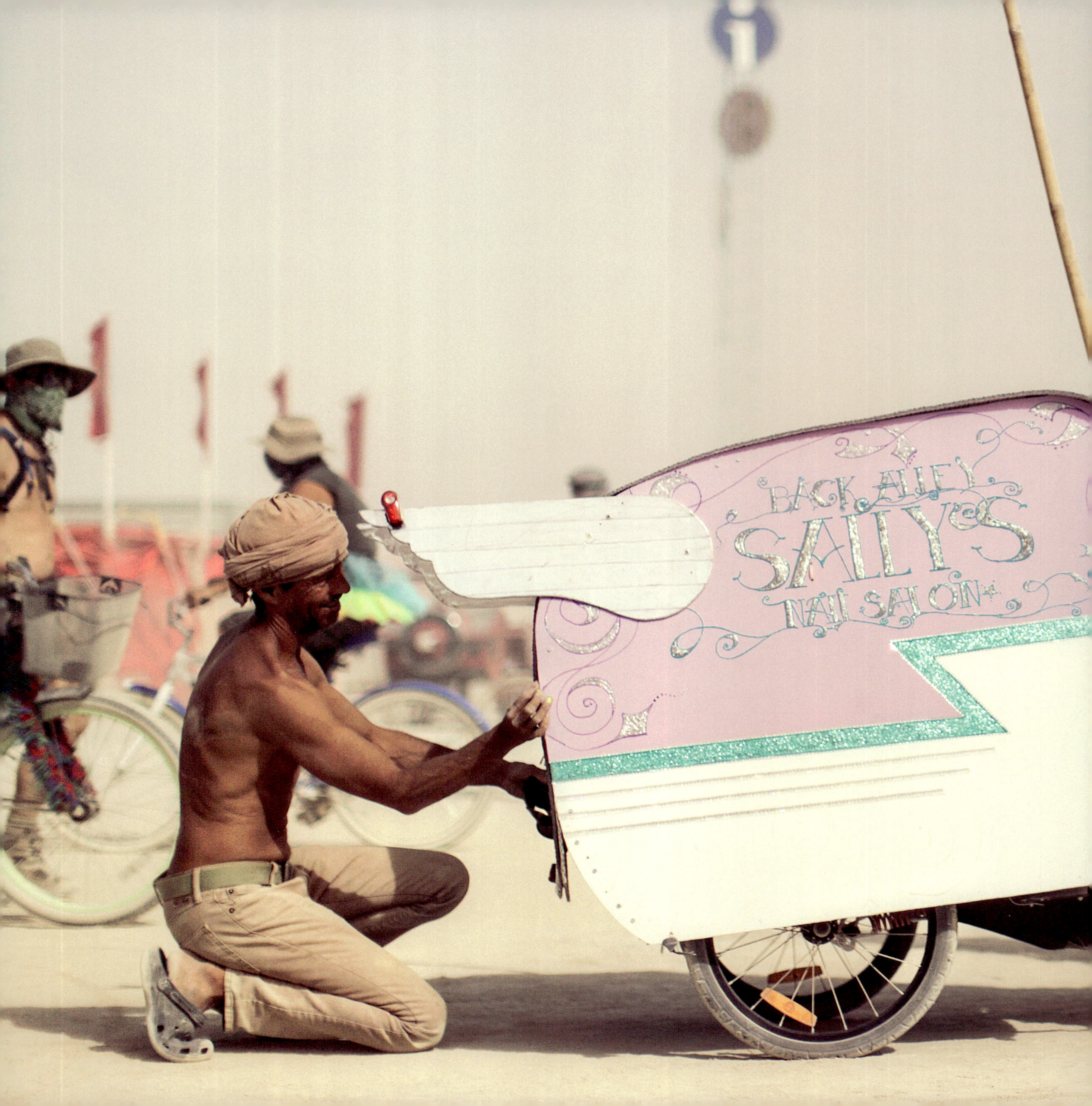
BACK ALLEY
SALLY'S
NAIL SALON

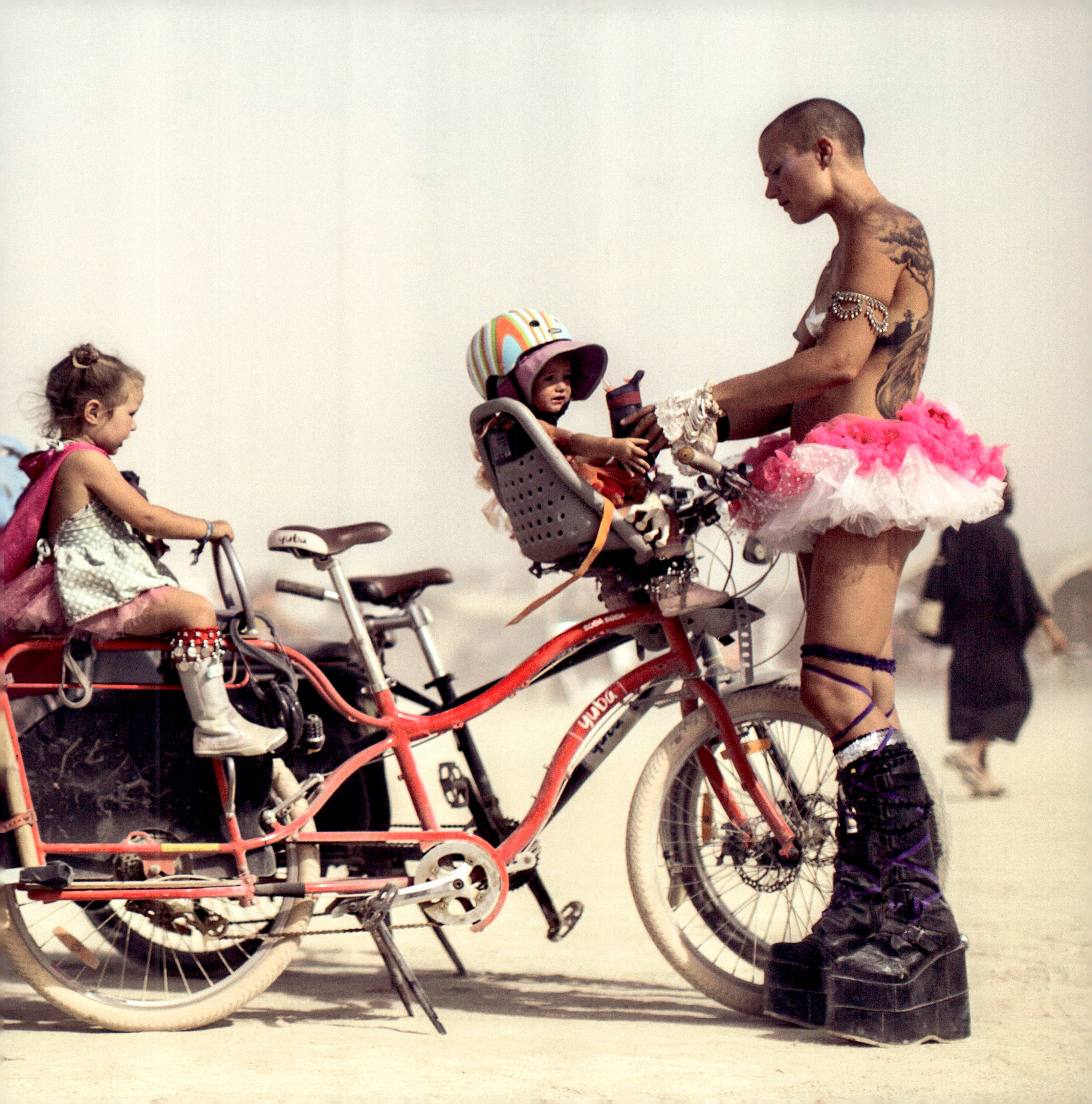
yuba

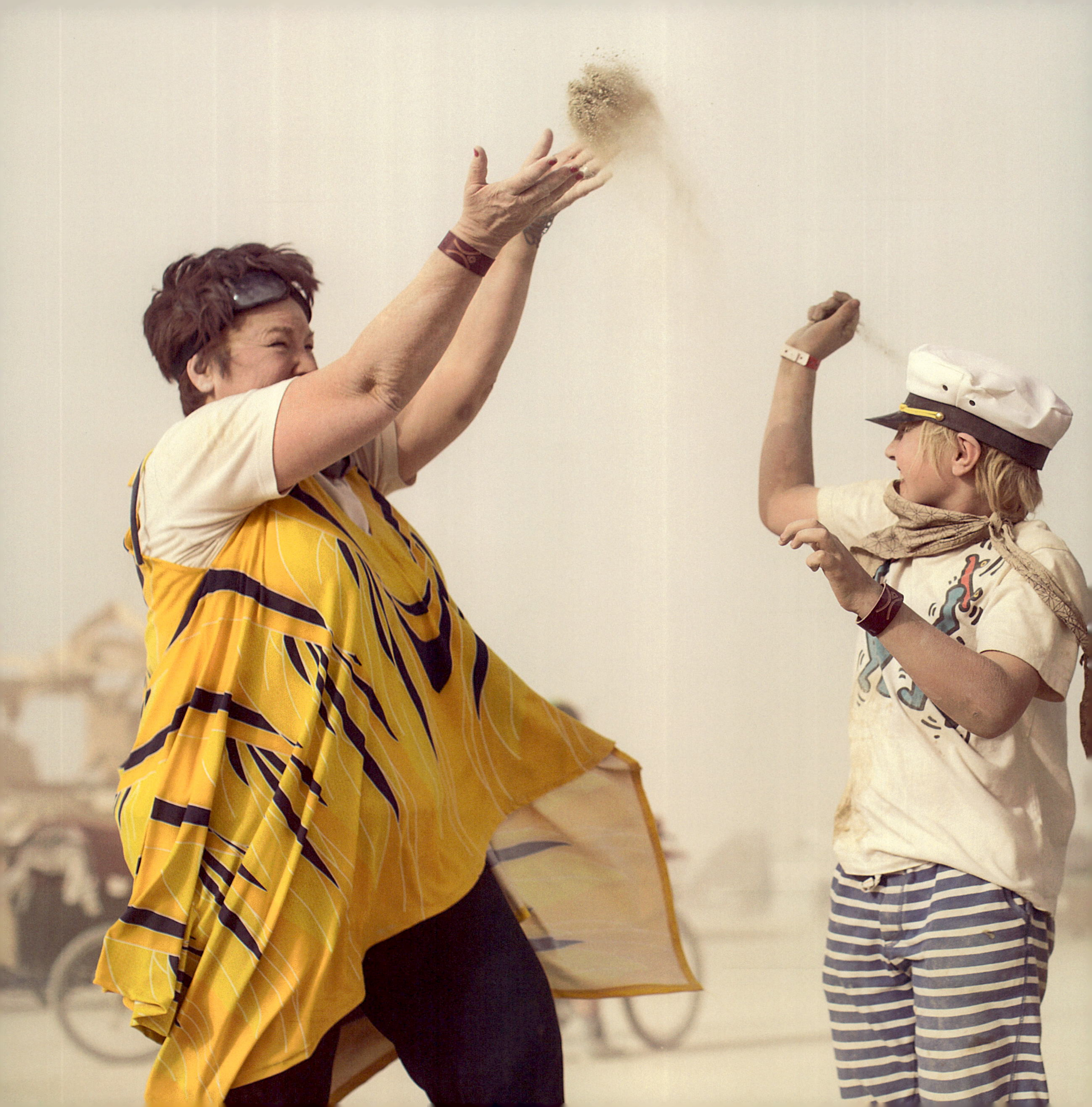

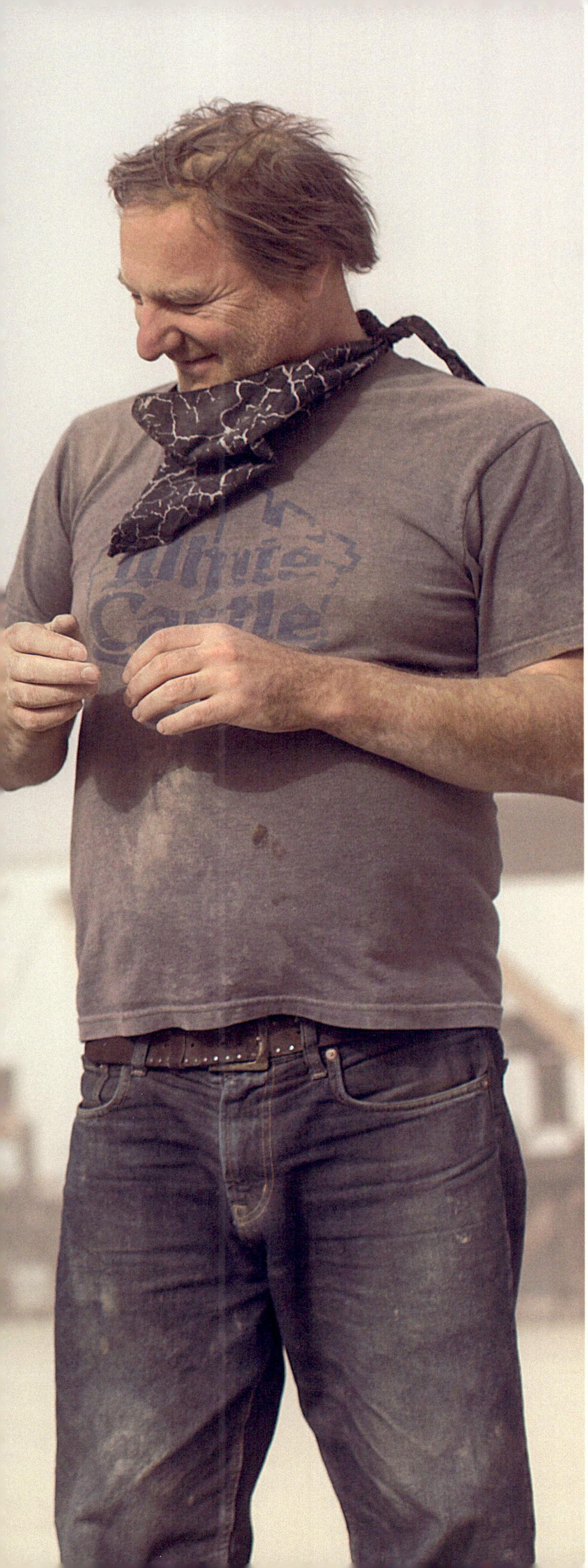
White Castle

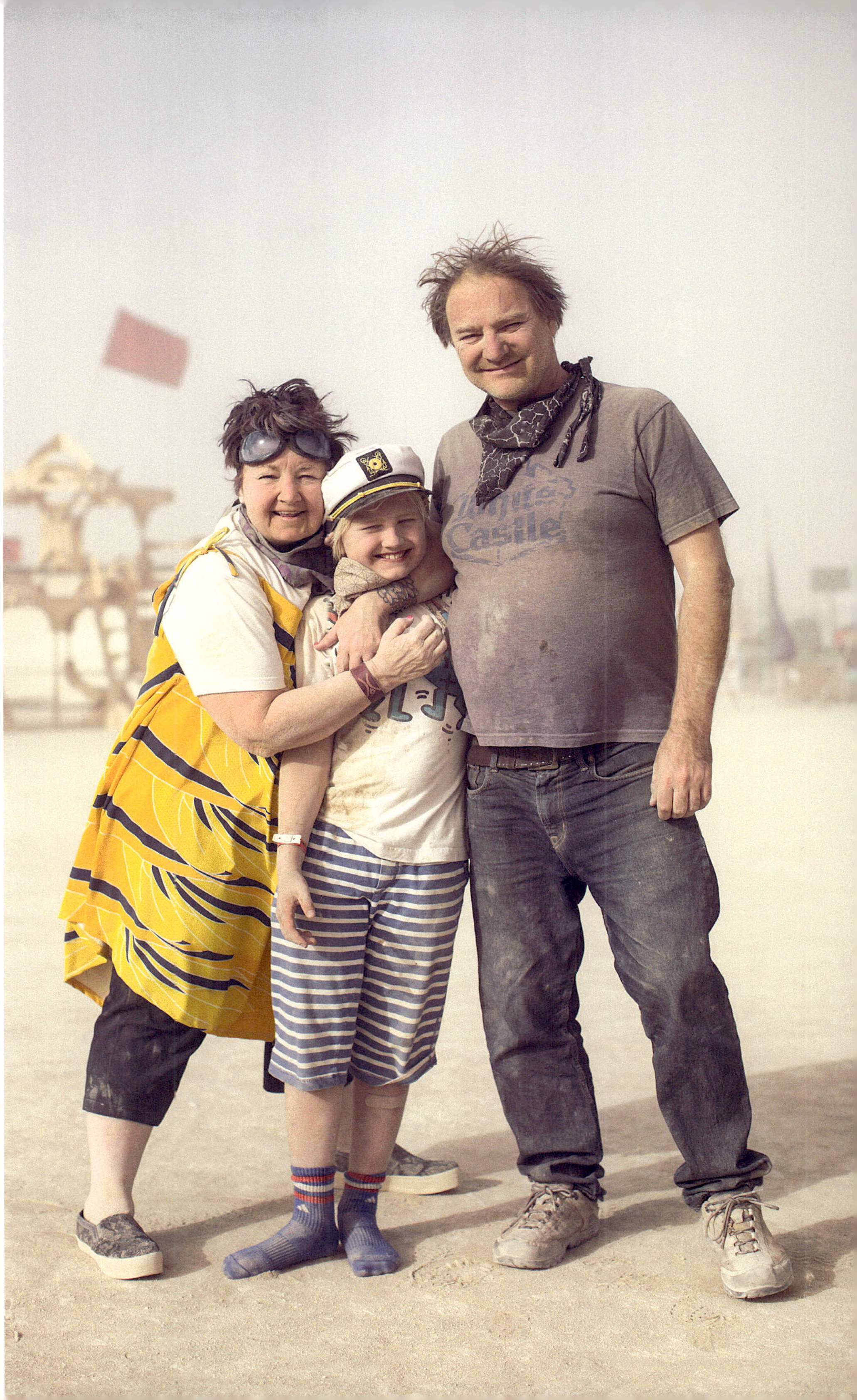
White Castle

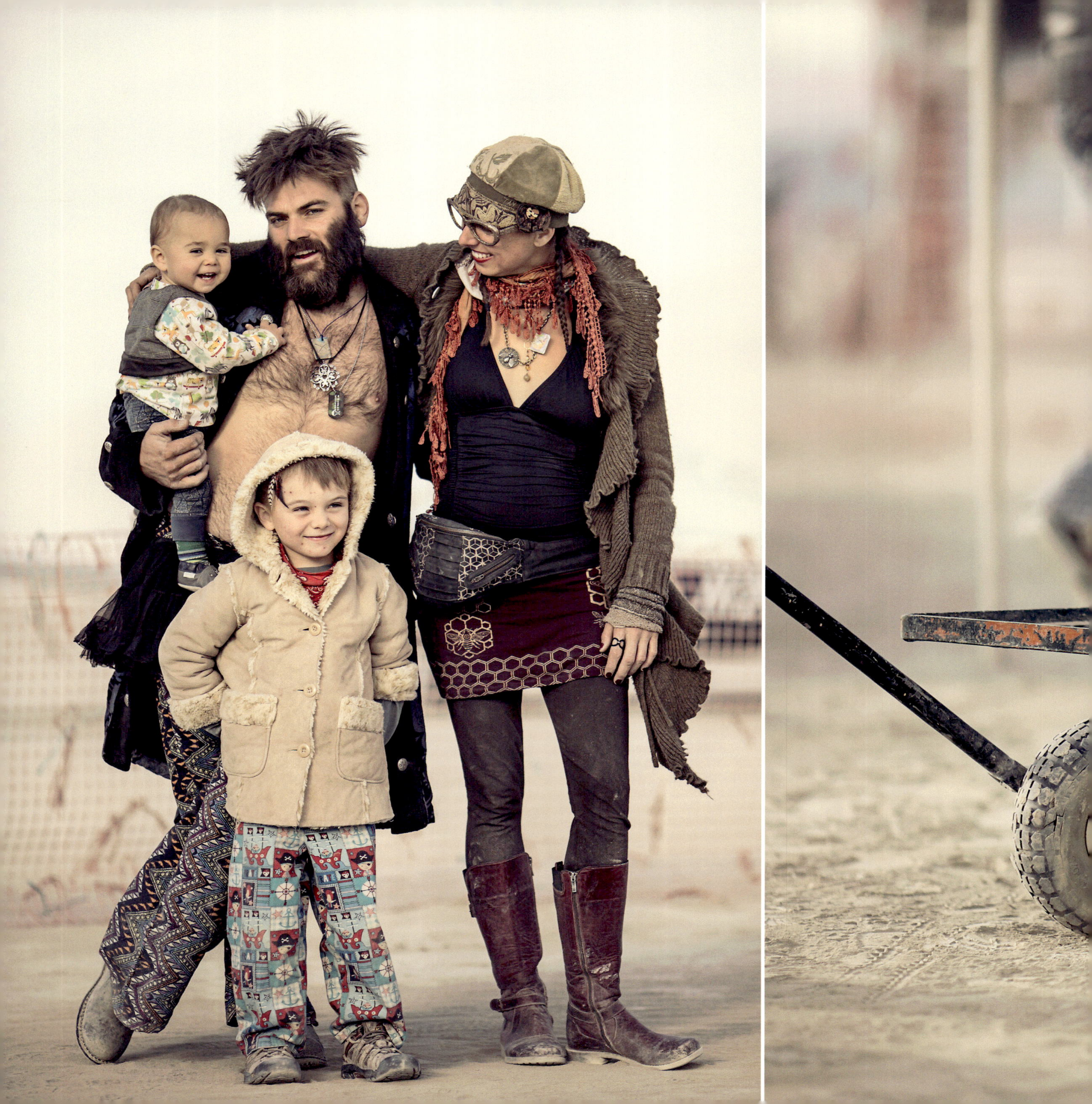

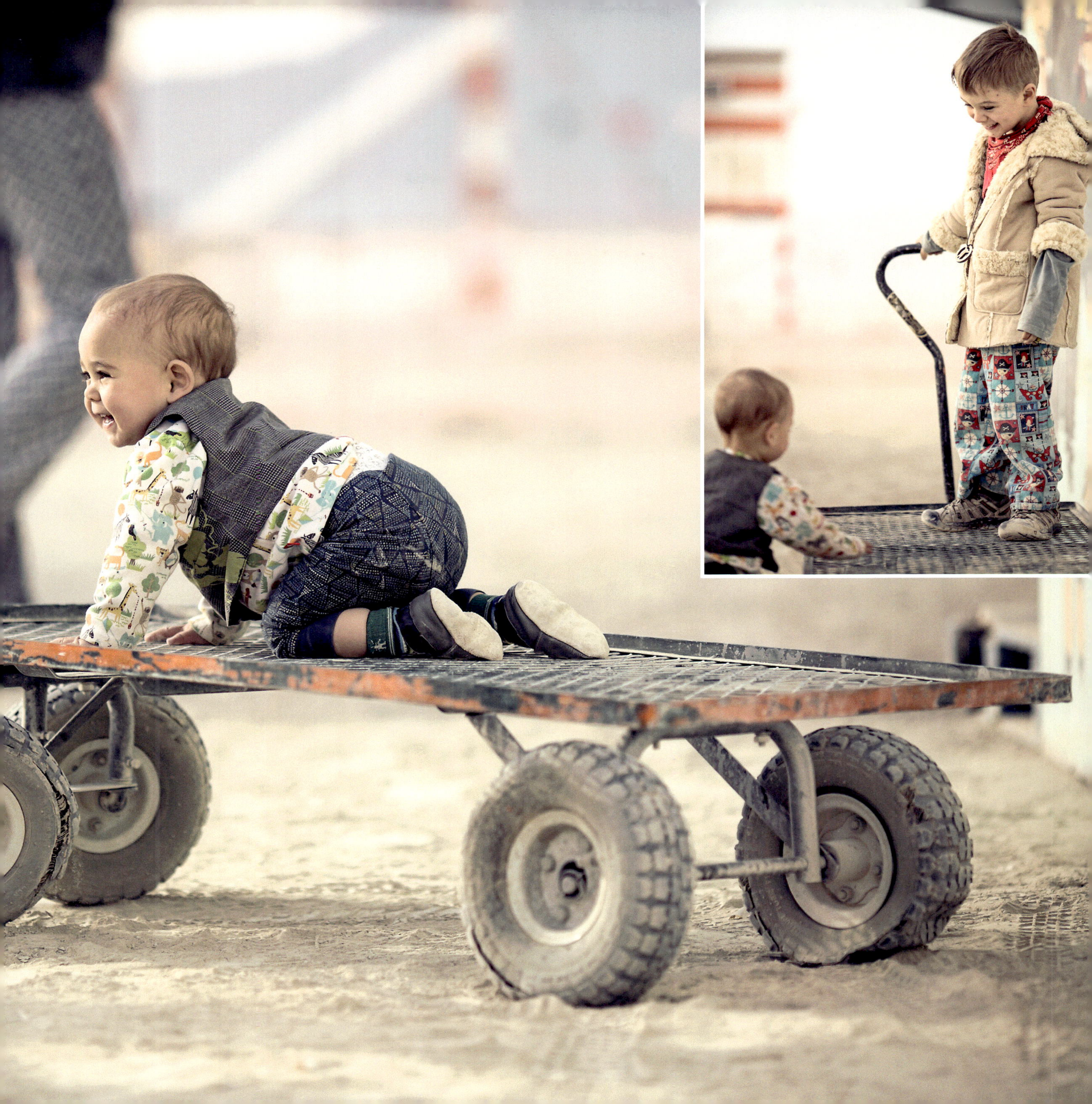

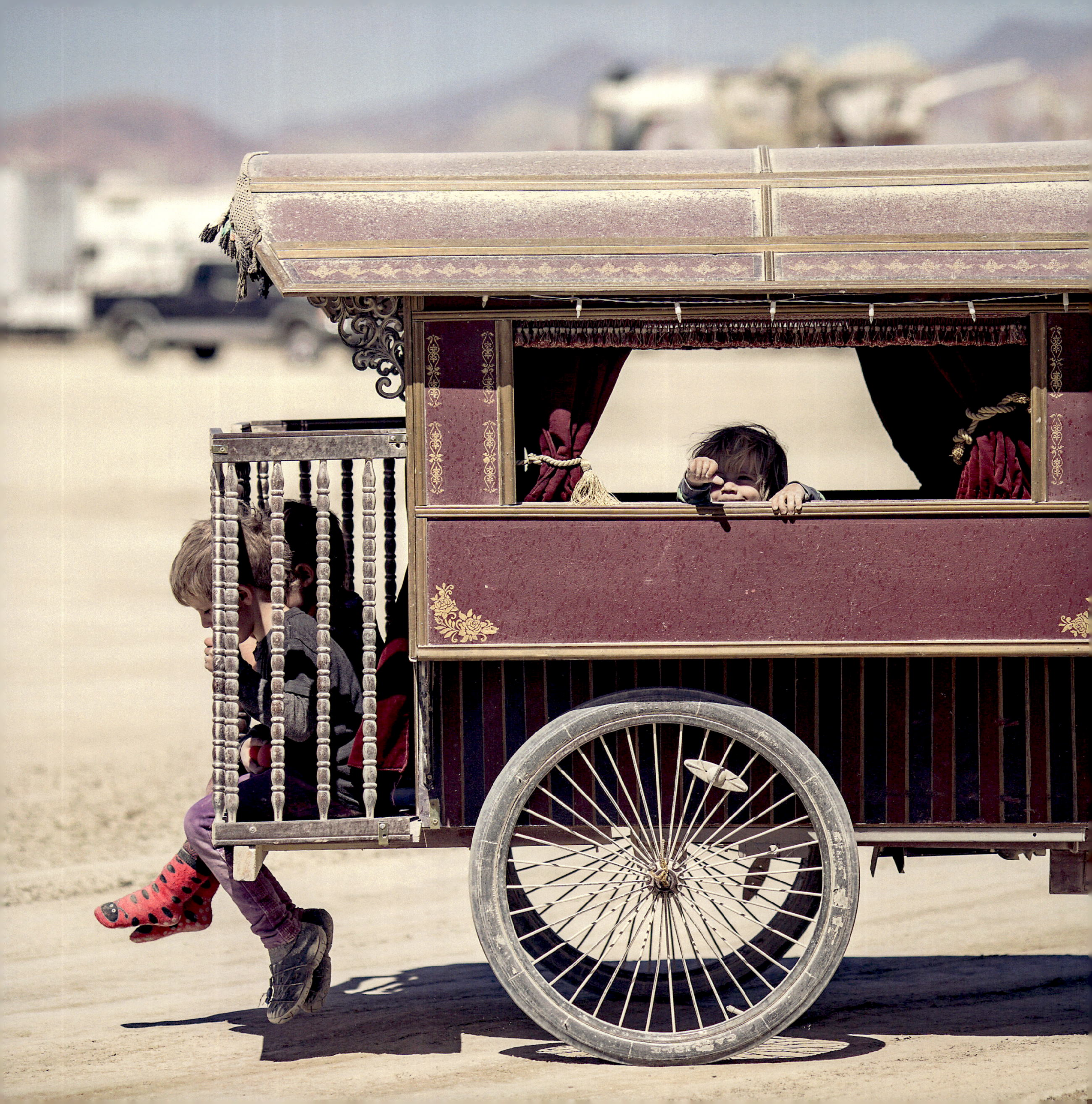

"We are are 21 year veterans of Black Rock City – a world of radical acceptance, free speech, self expression, and radical self reliance. It's been an honor to bring our sons and watch as the experience of life itself on the Playa has taught them more in those weeks than any books or classes could teach them in a lifetime. Bringing our sons has become our prayer for the future – we no longer see Burning Man as an isolated experience once a year, but rather, as an offering that will be carried on in the hearts of our children. For us, it's been a transformational experience every time; **for our children it is, in even greater magnitude, a formational experience, shaping the very people they are still becoming."**

ISAAC, JESSICA, JONAKAI & GAVILAN

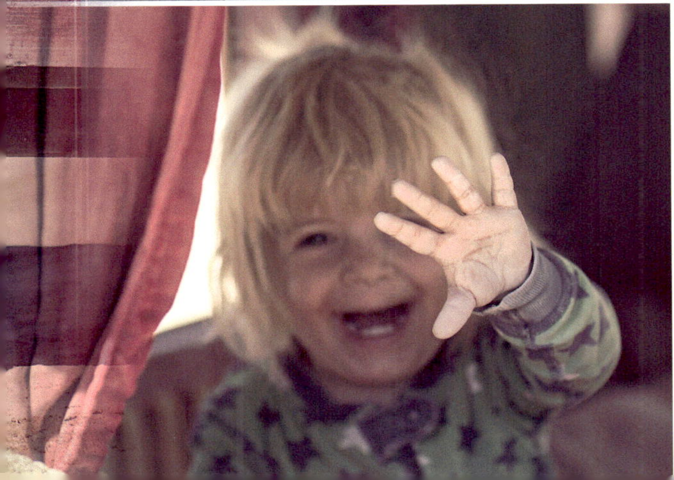

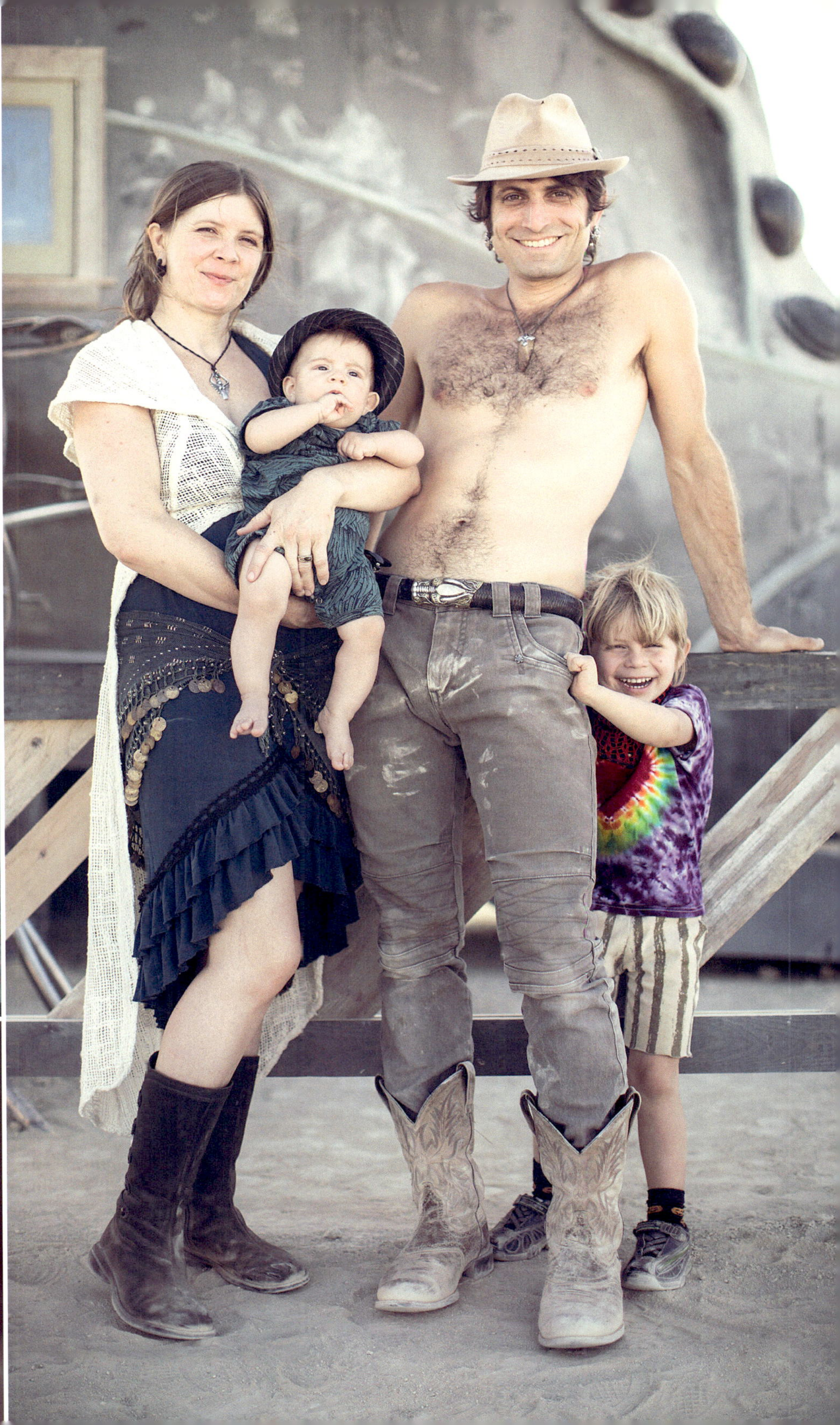

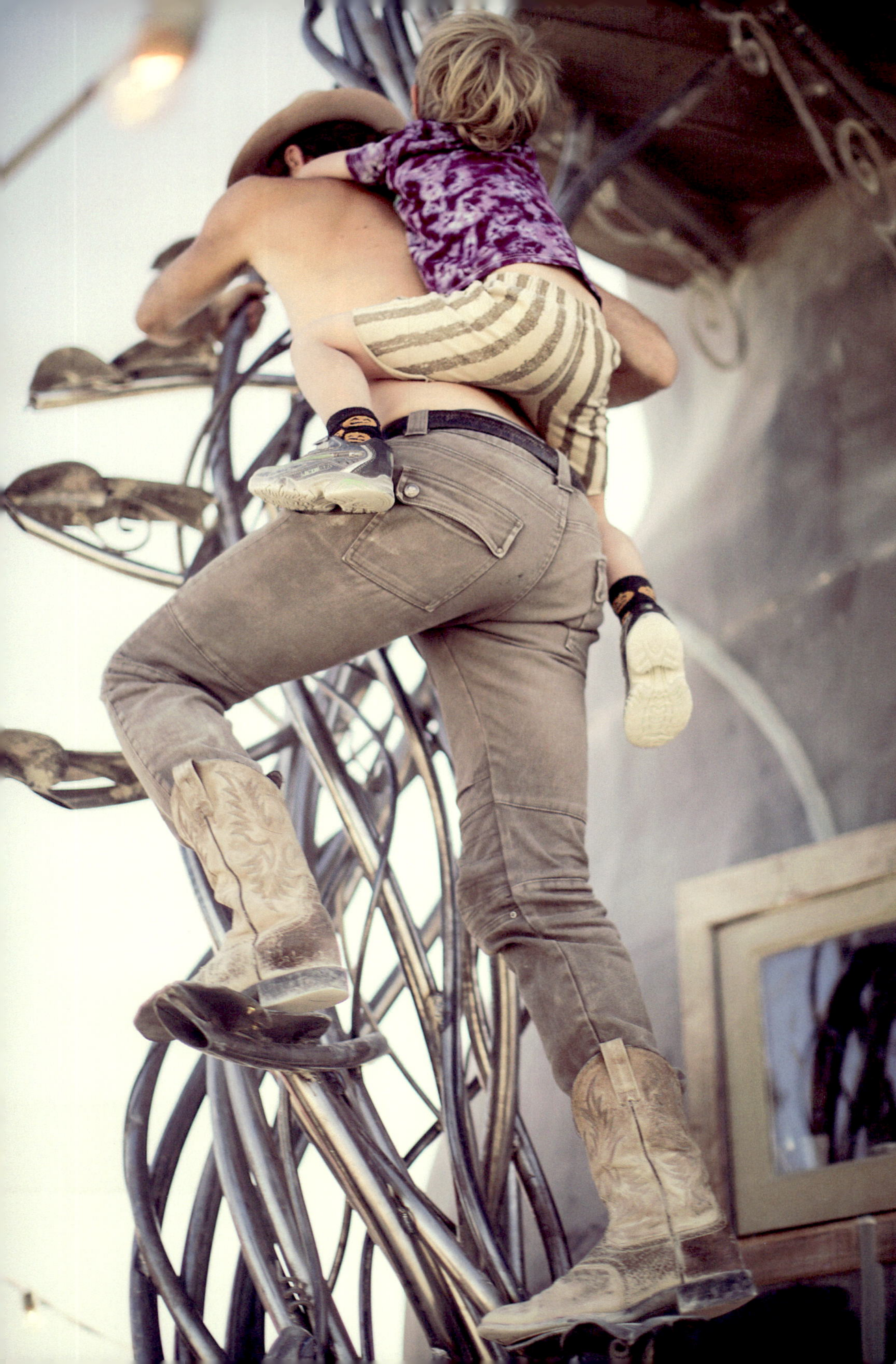
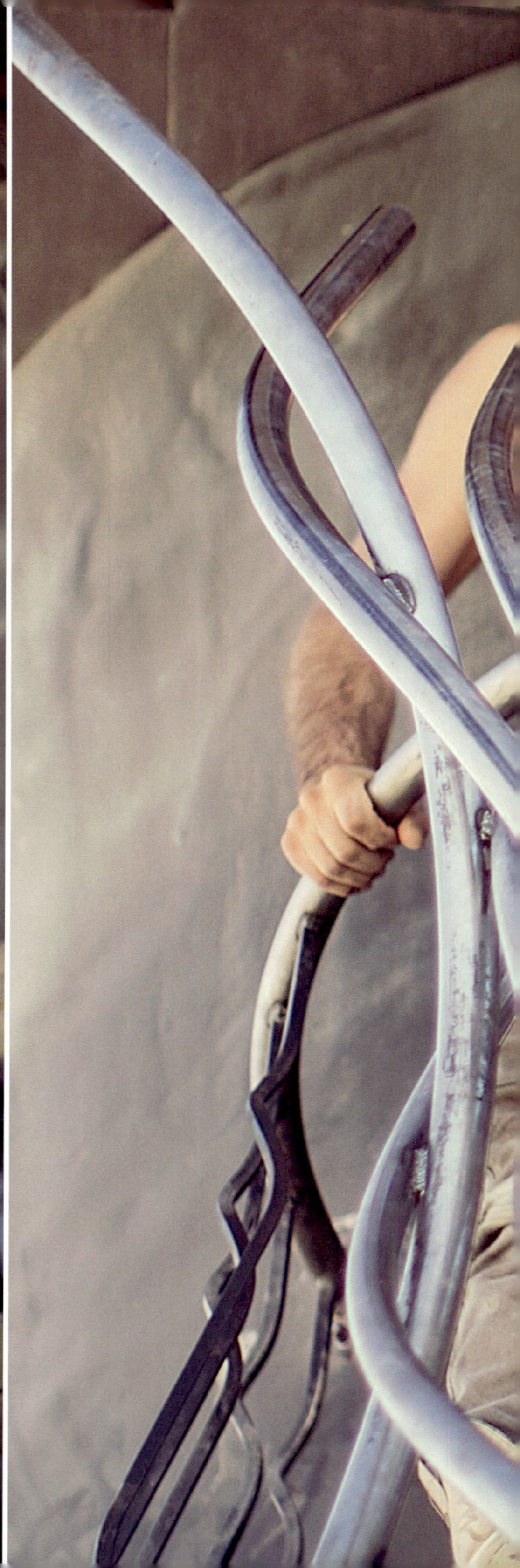

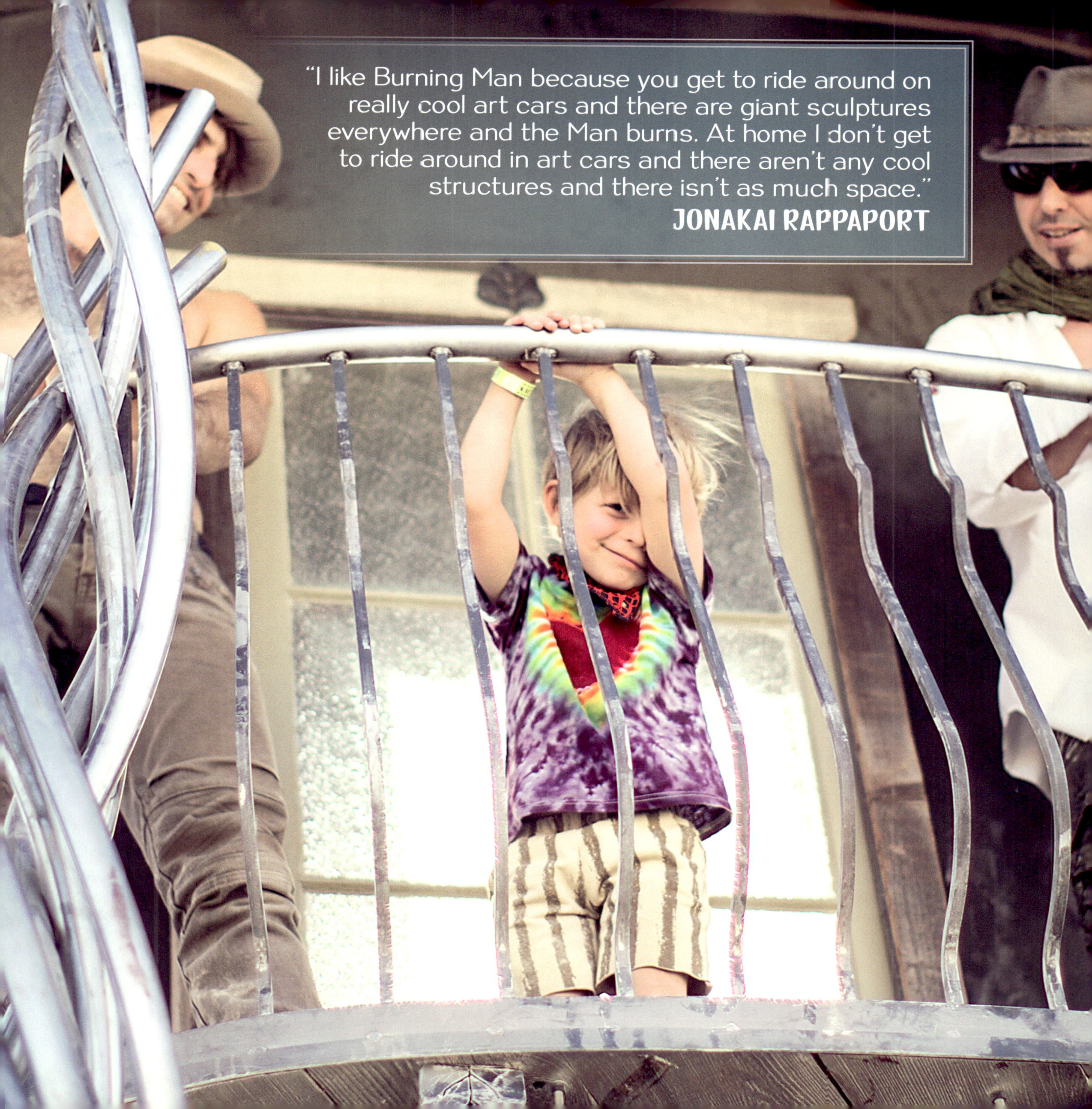

"I like Burning Man because you get to ride around on really cool art cars and there are giant sculptures everywhere and the Man burns. At home I don't get to ride around in art cars and there aren't any cool structures and there isn't as much space."

JONAKAI RAPPAPORT

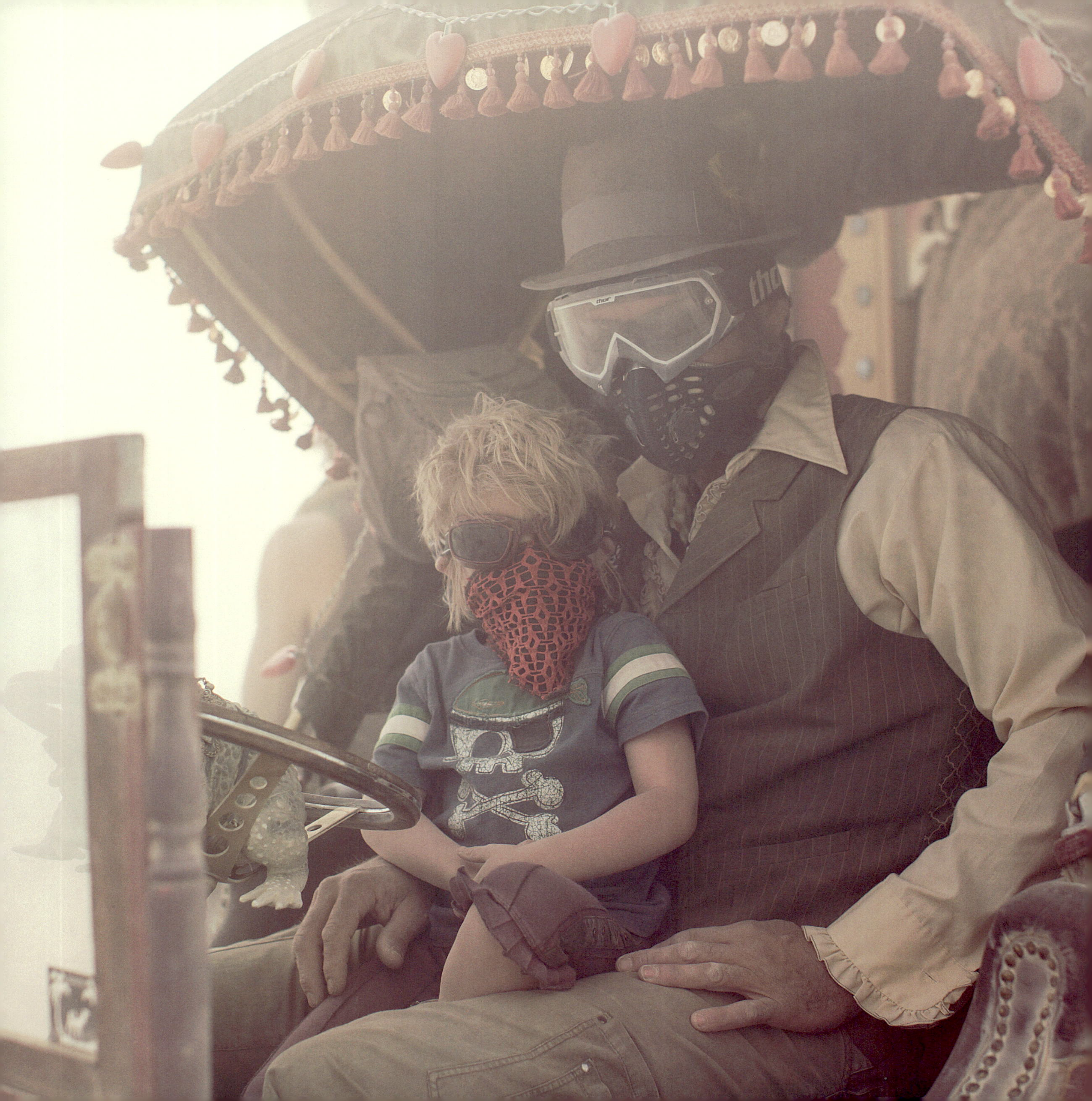
thor

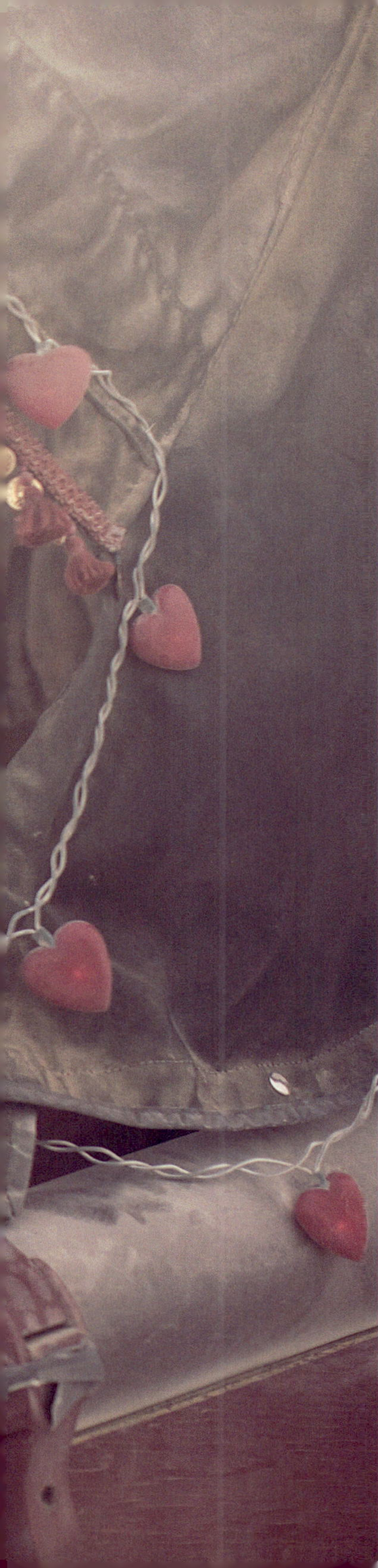

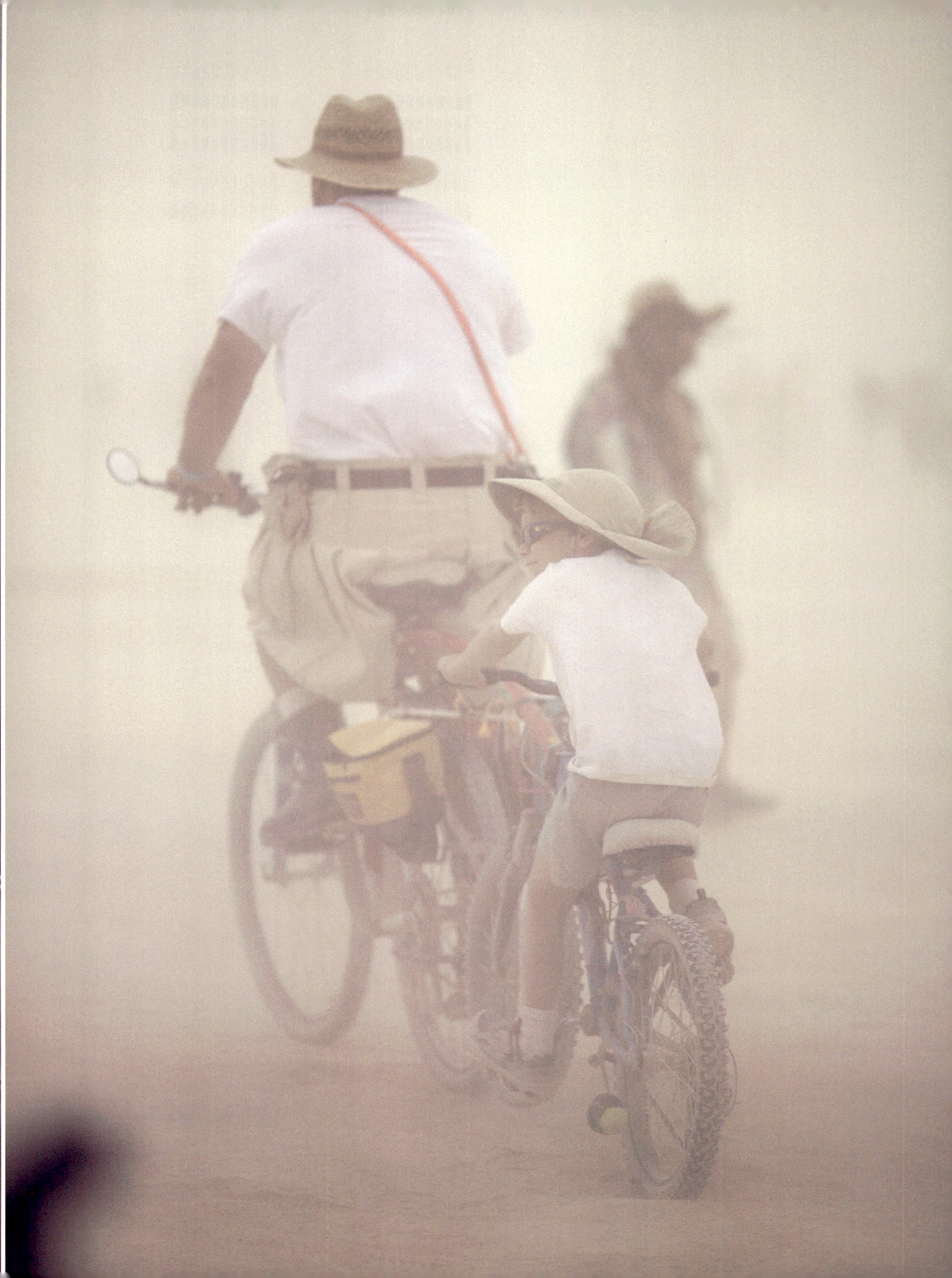

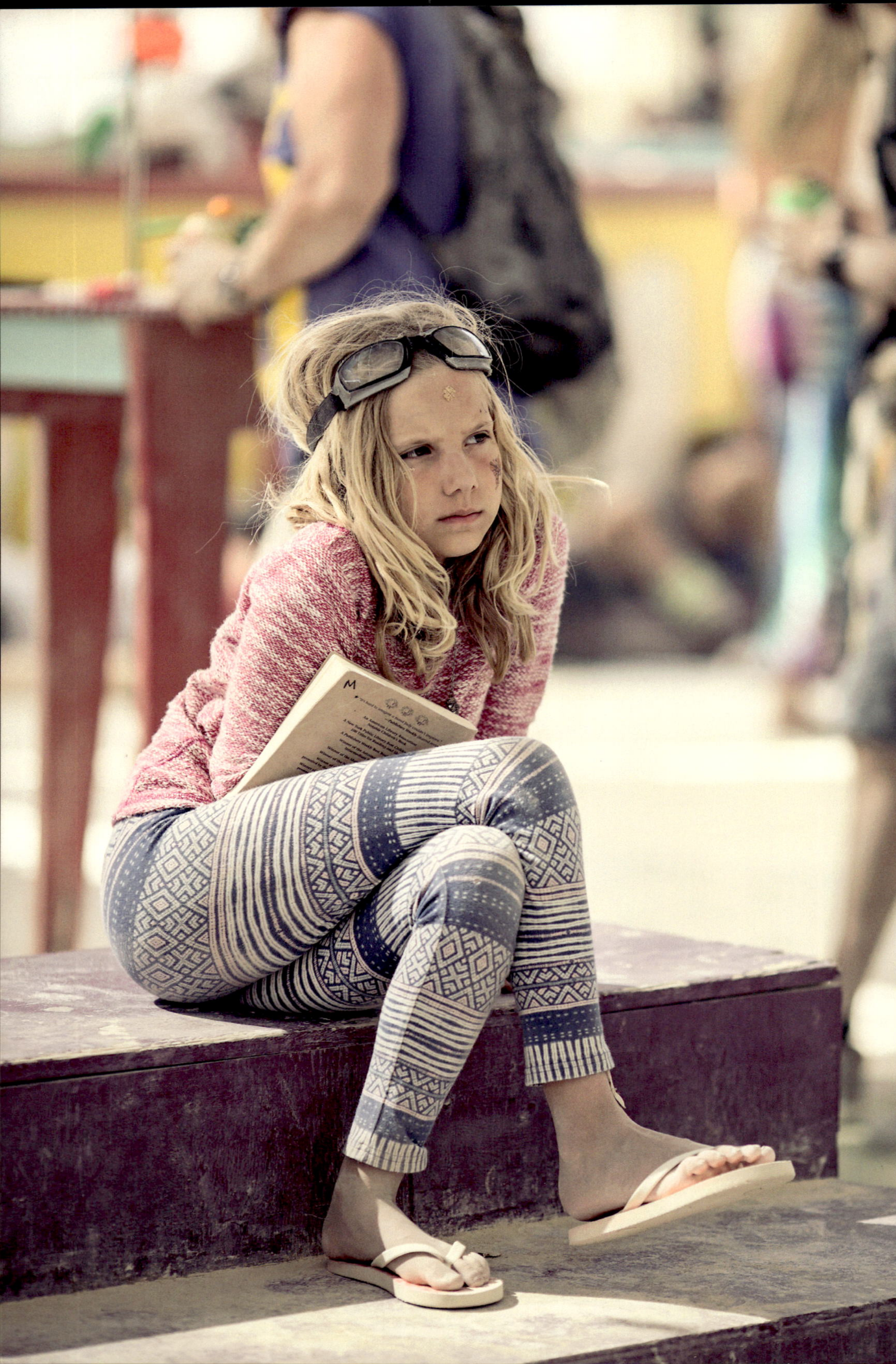

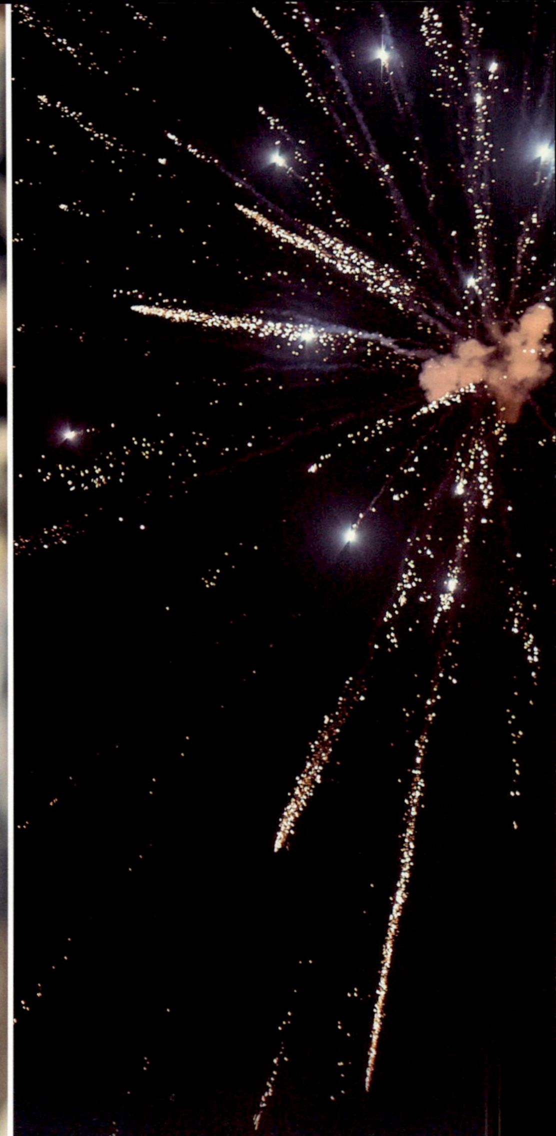

"The best part about Burning Man is that people are free to BE and express themselves, and I feel like the burning of the Man each year represents a fresh start."

ARTEMIS

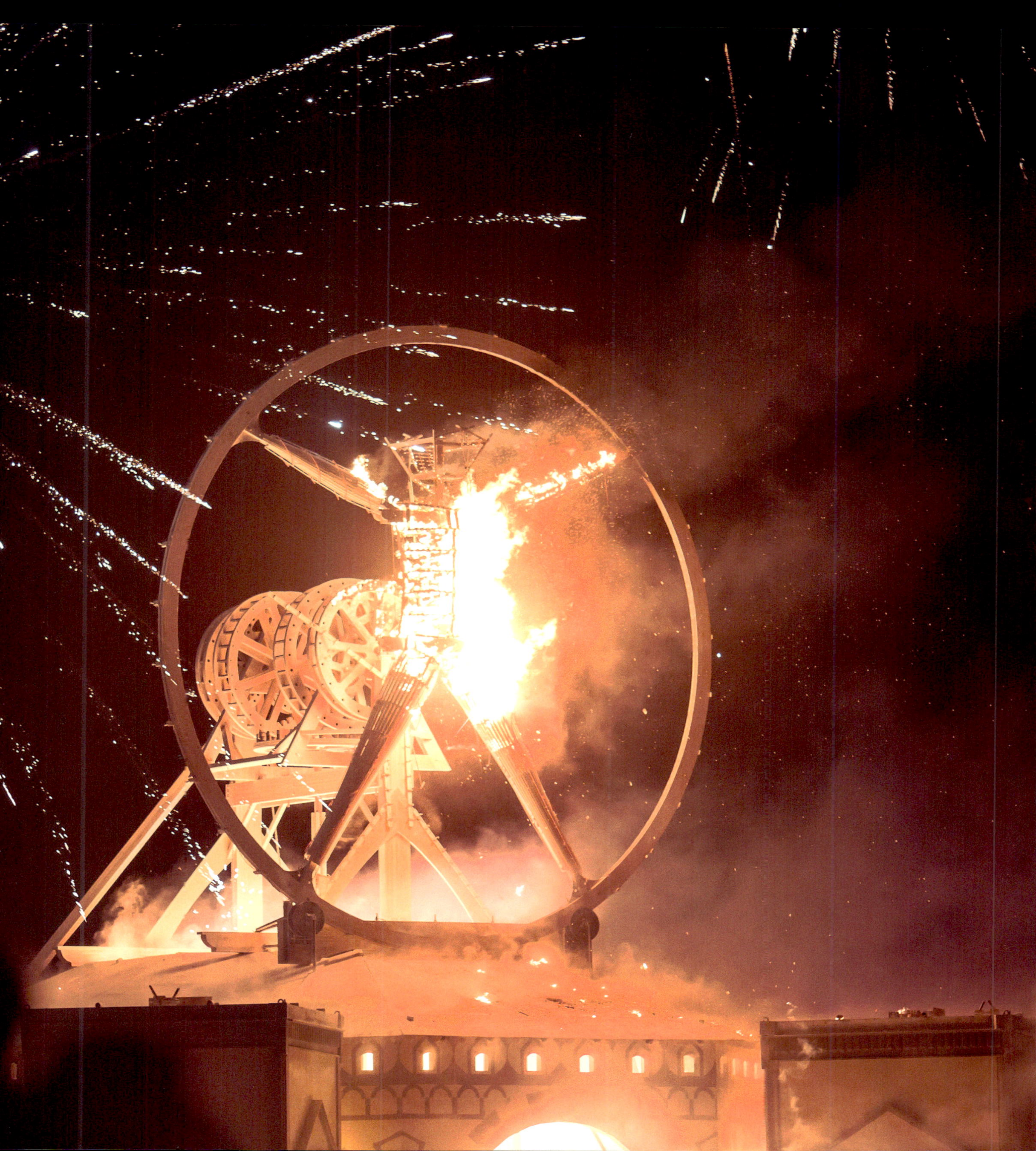

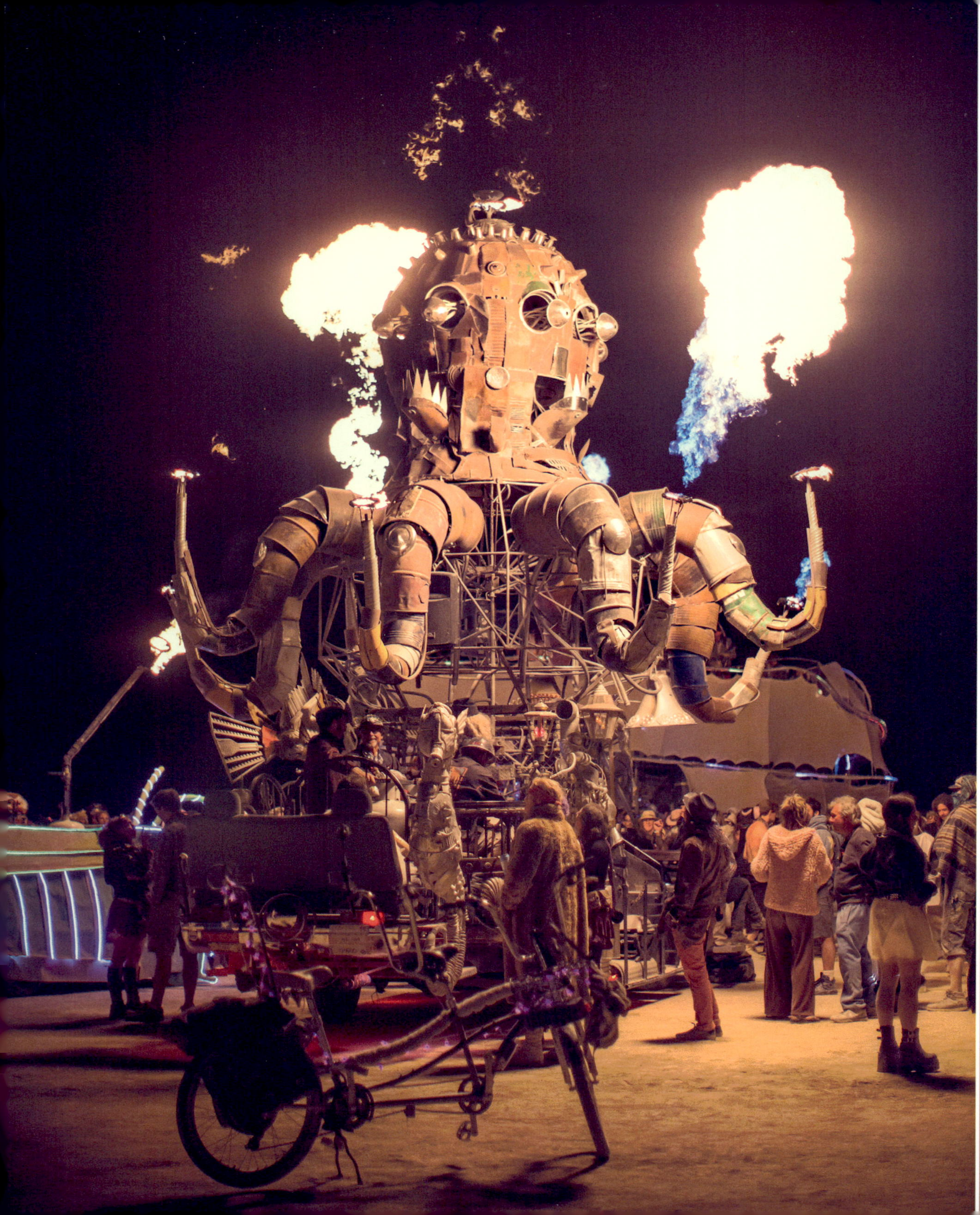

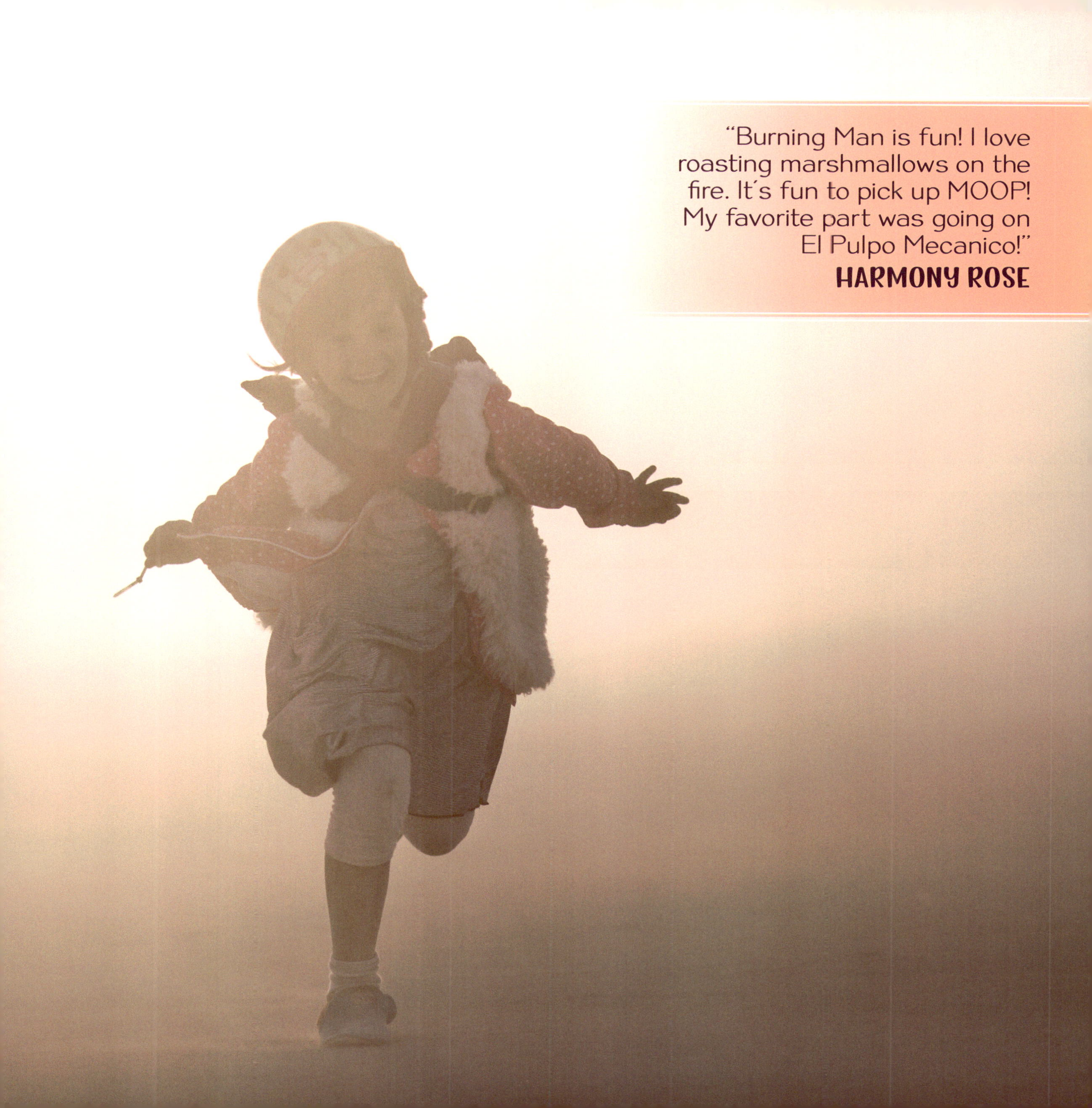

"Burning Man is fun! I love roasting marshmallows on the fire. It's fun to pick up MOOP! My favorite part was going on El Pulpo Mecanico!"

HARMONY ROSE

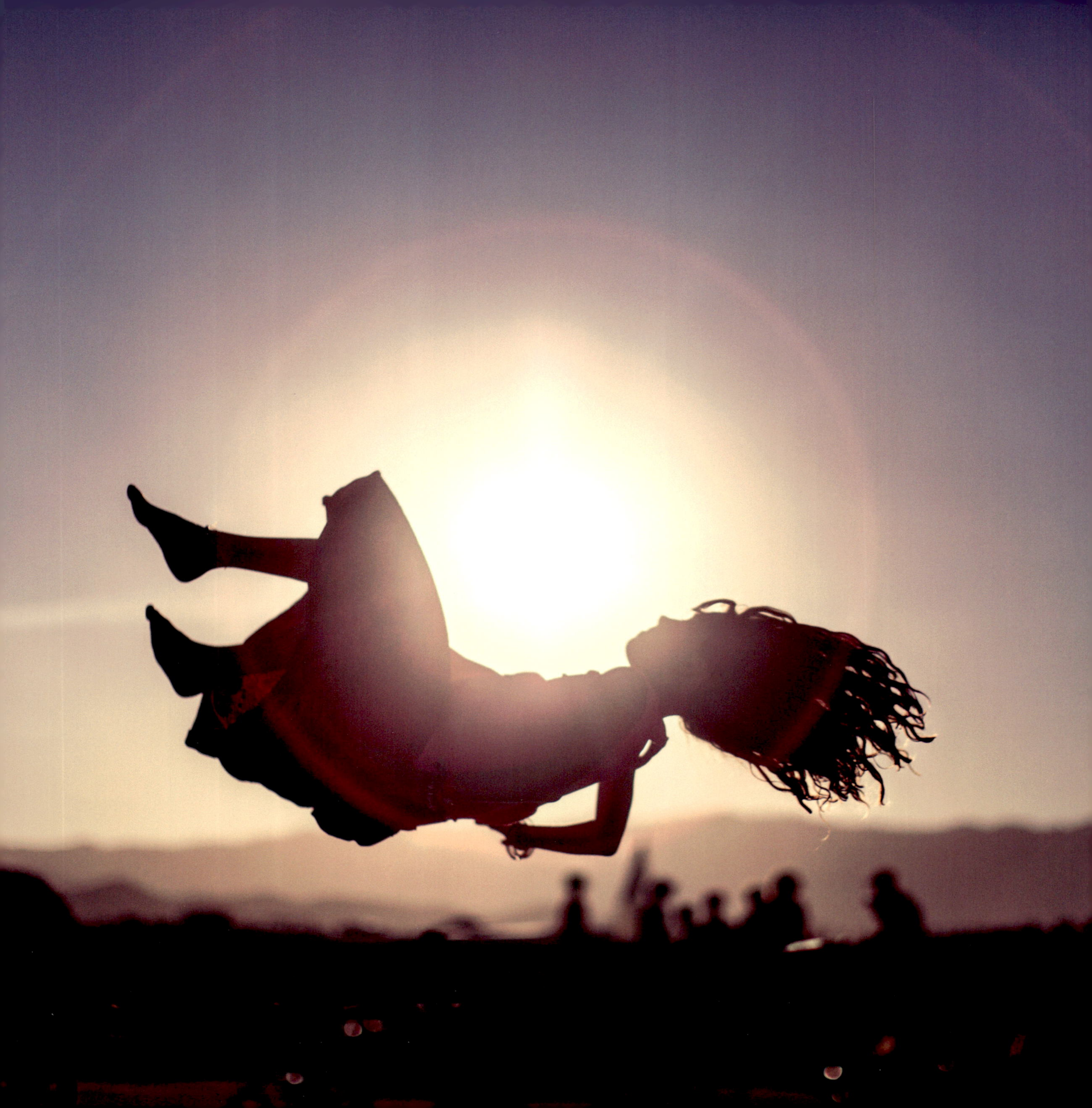

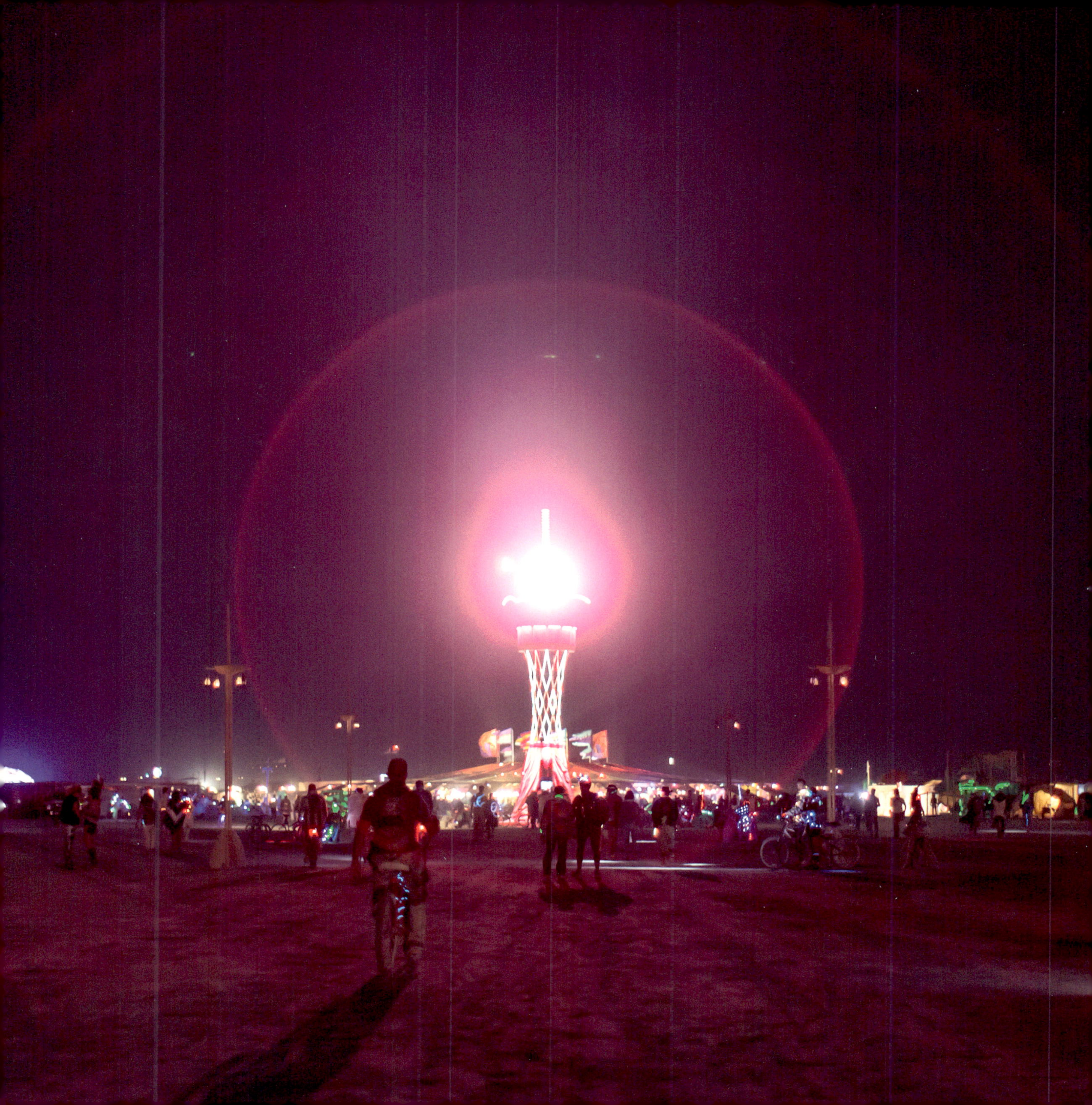

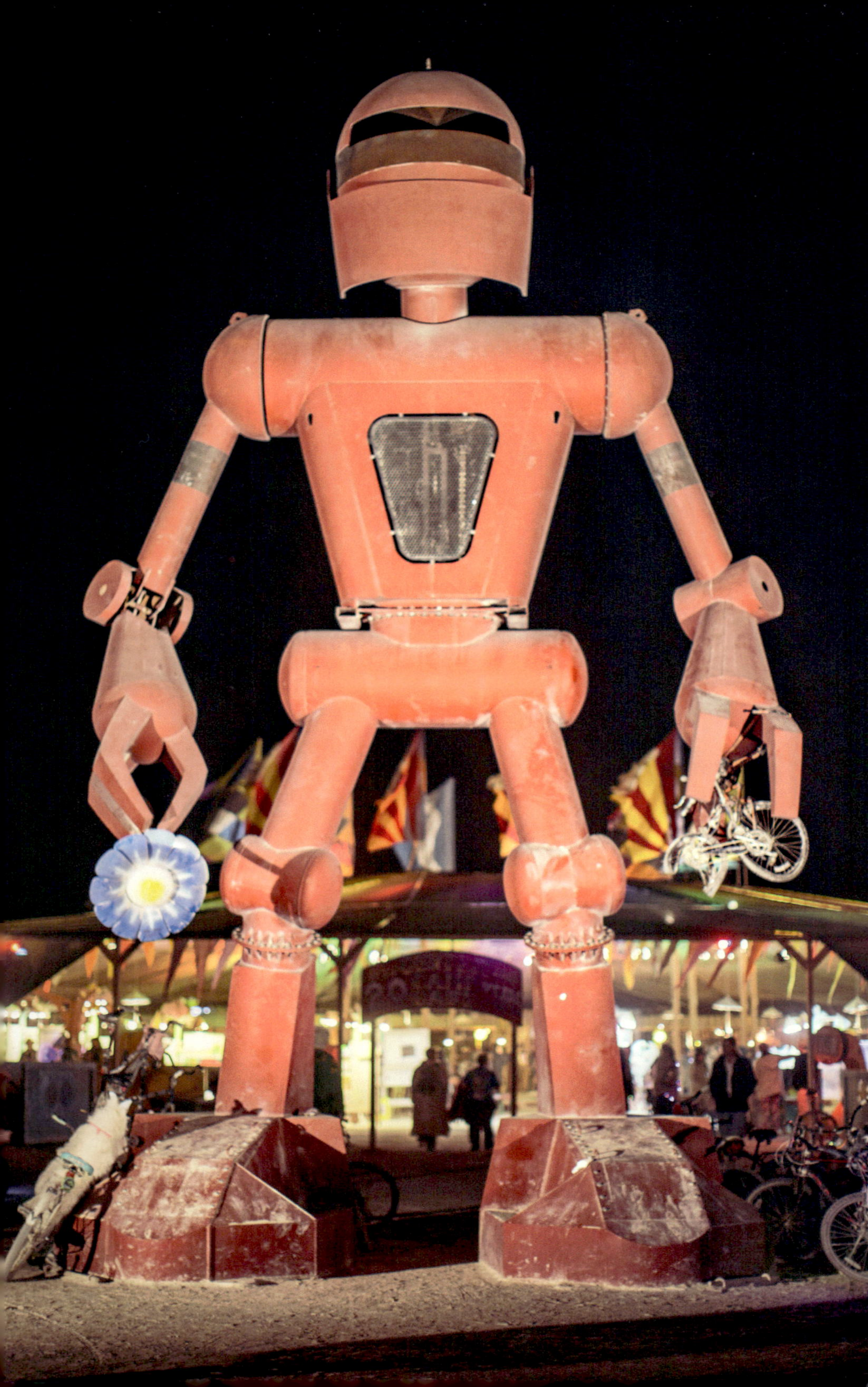

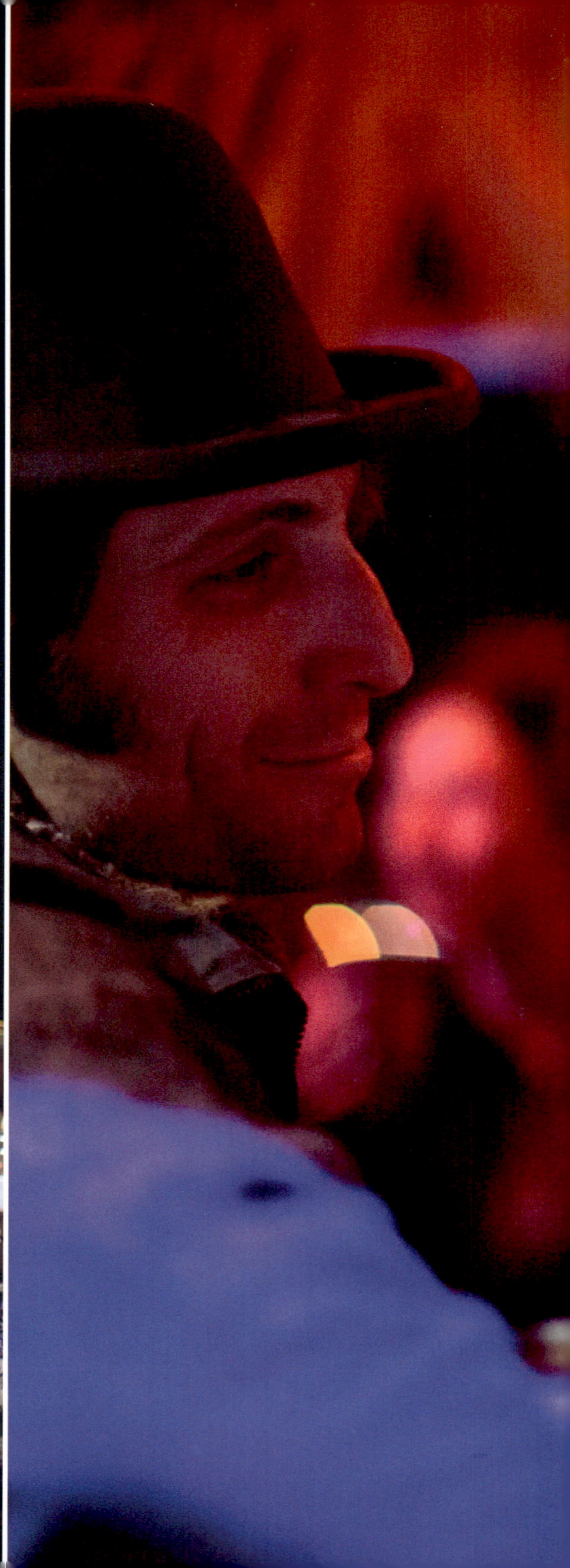

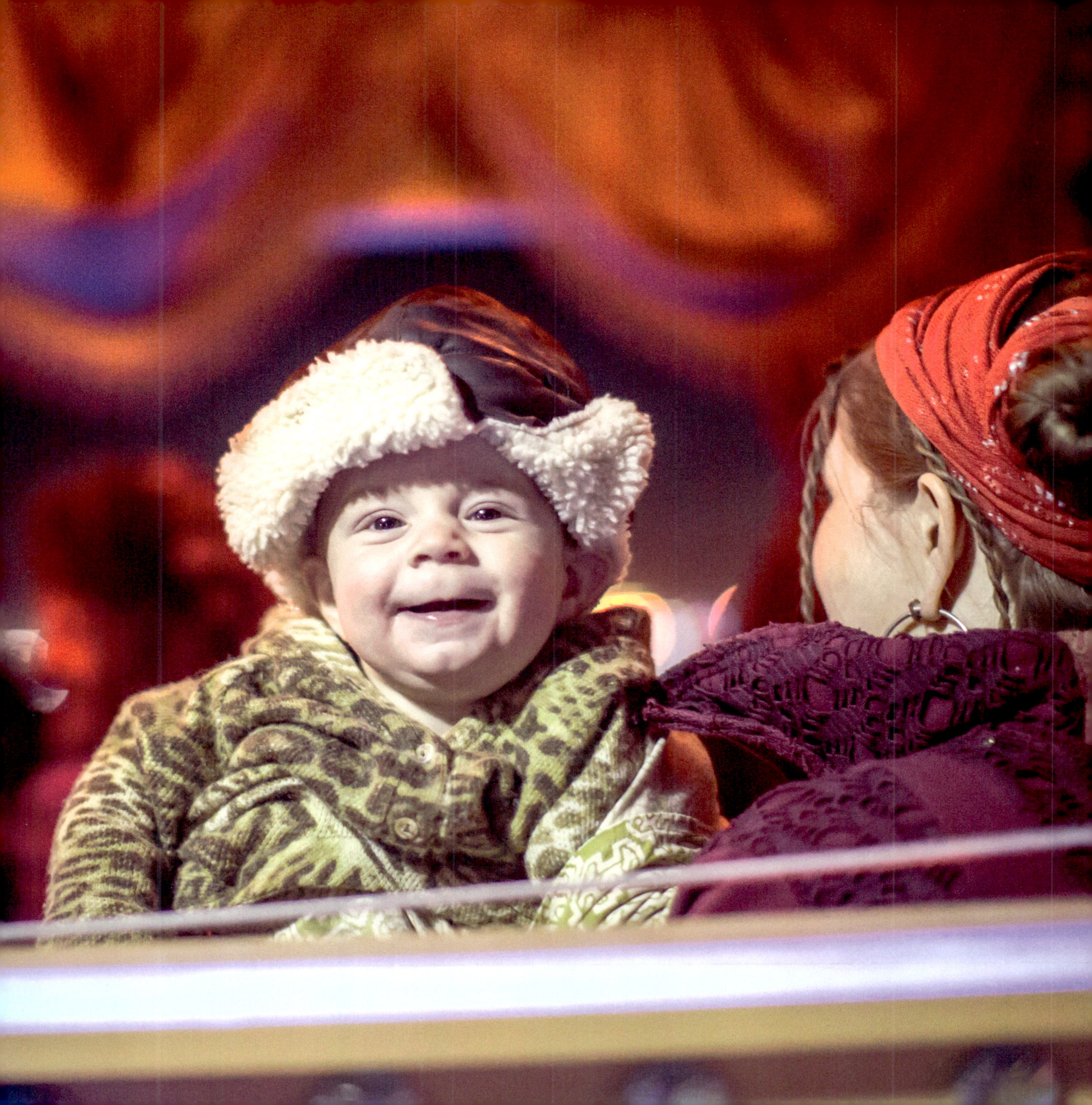

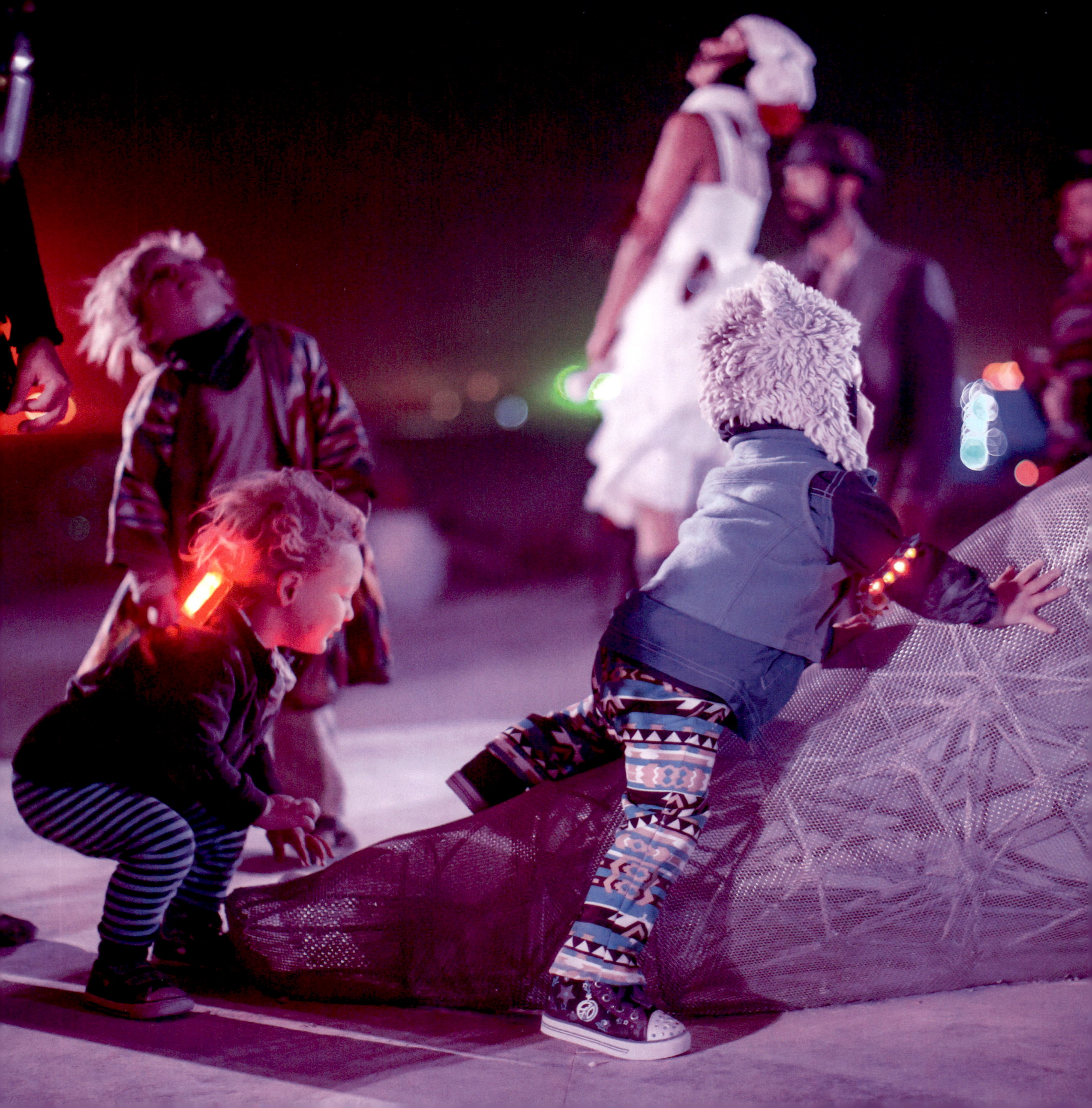

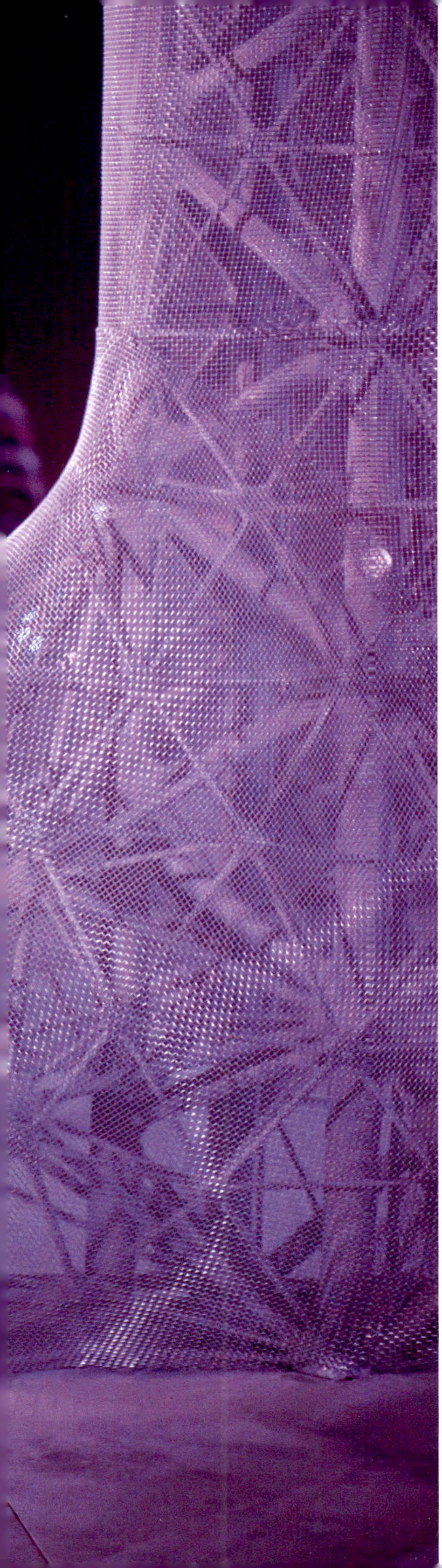

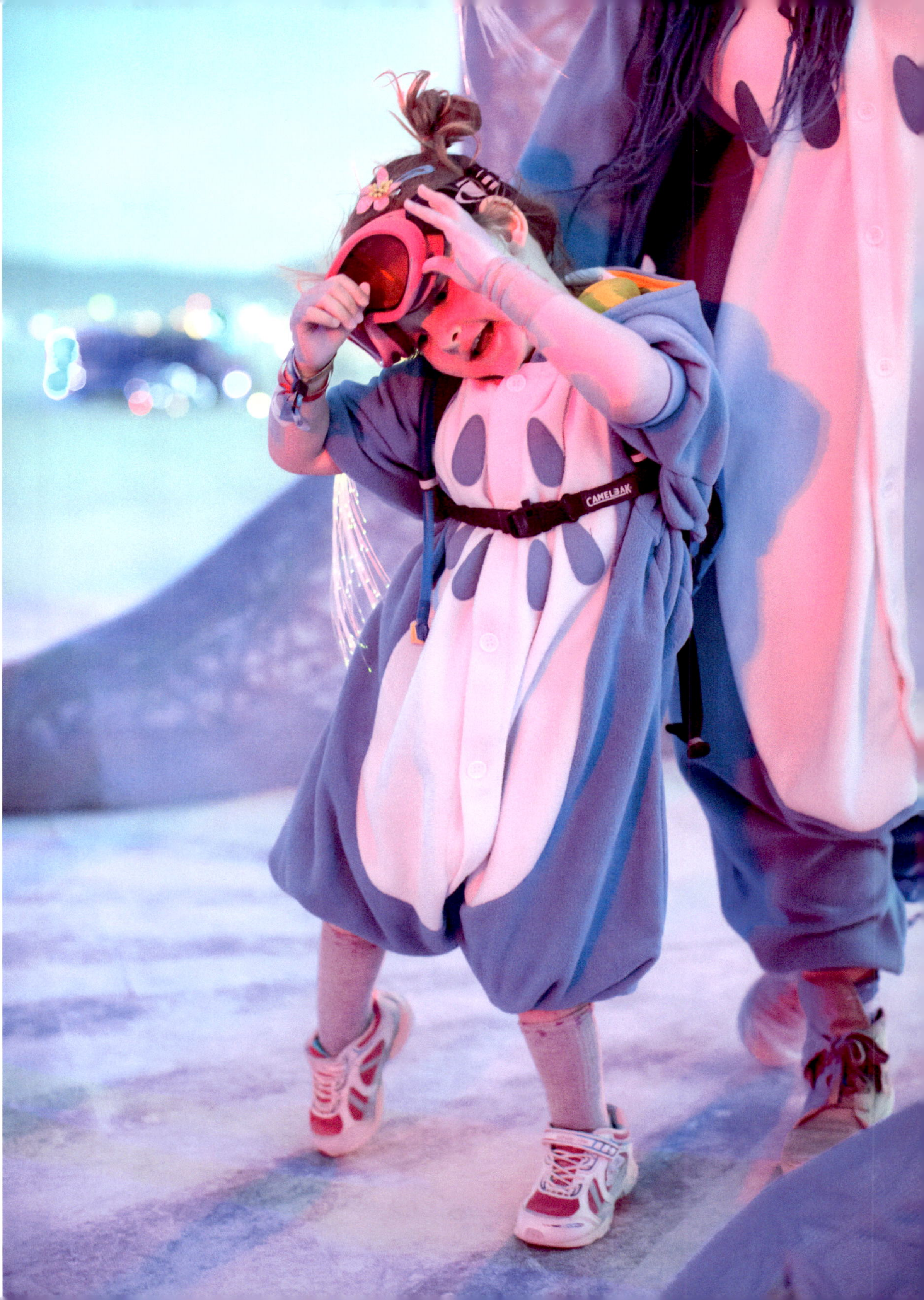
CAMELBAK

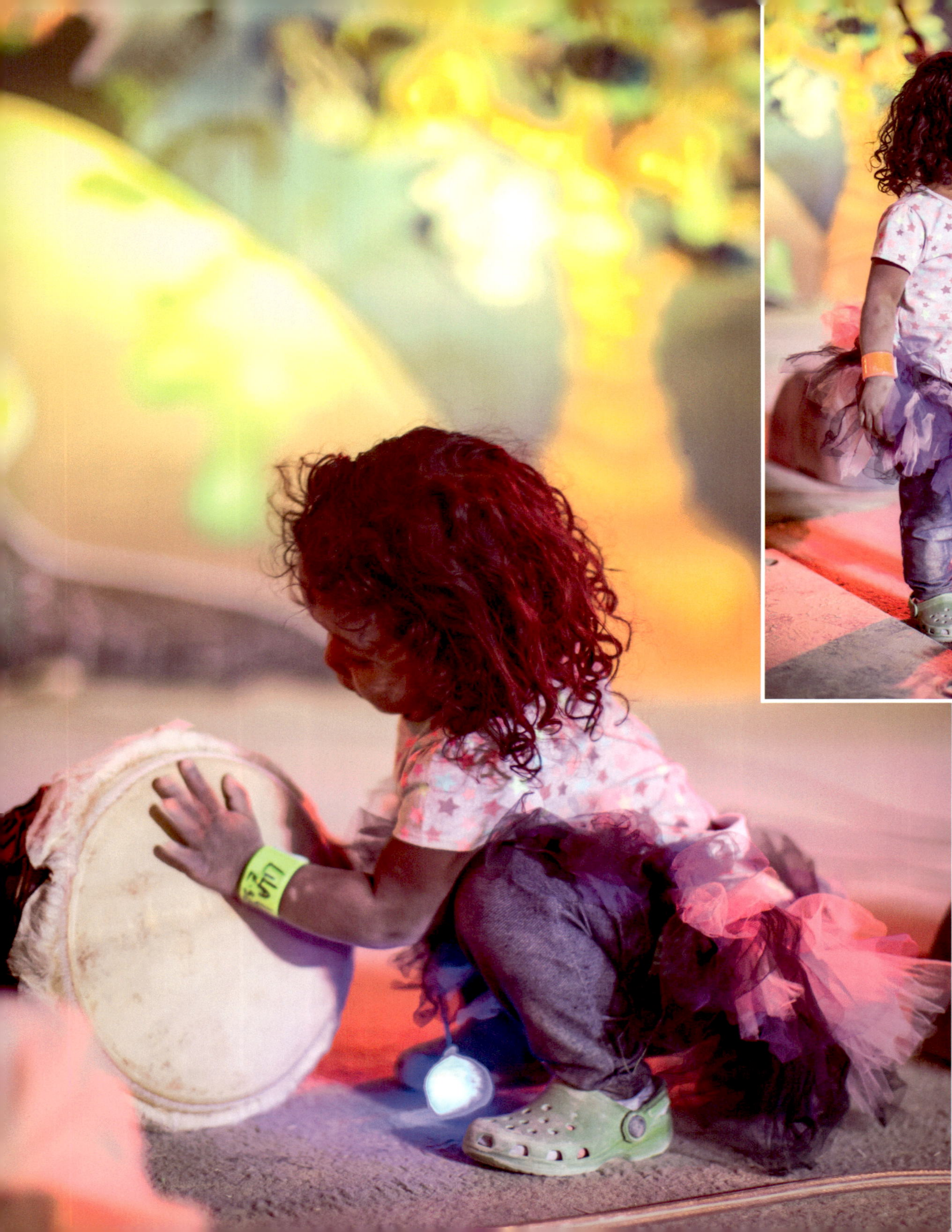

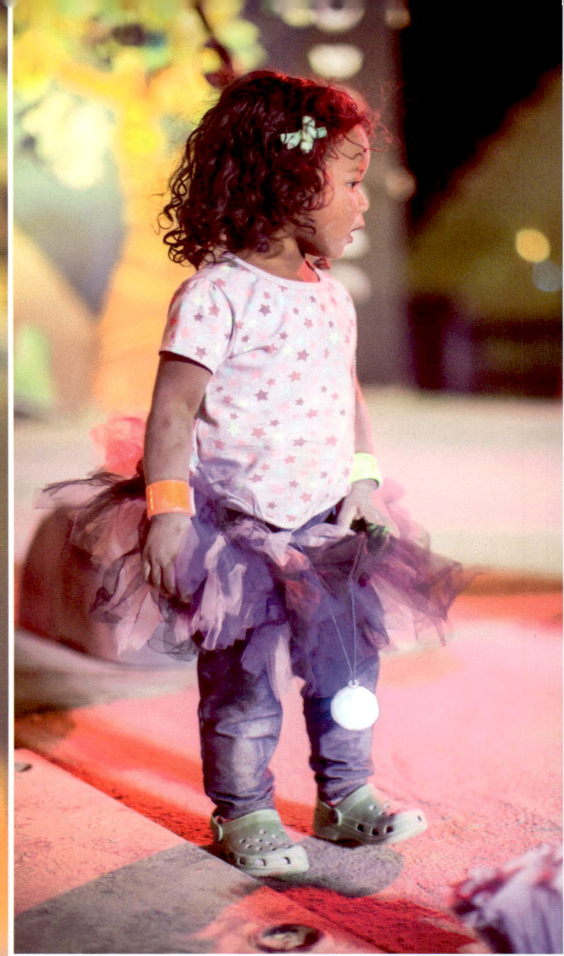

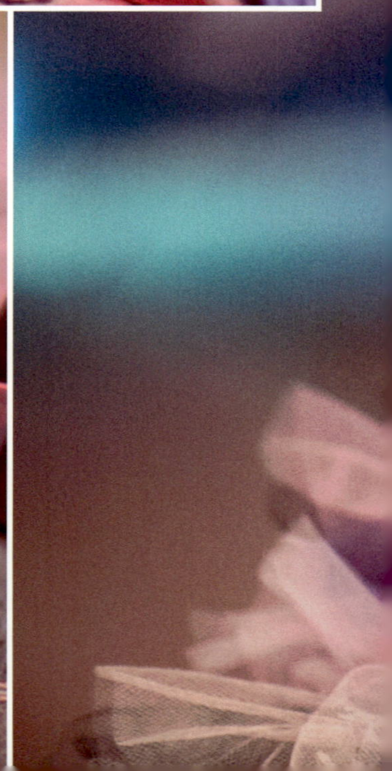

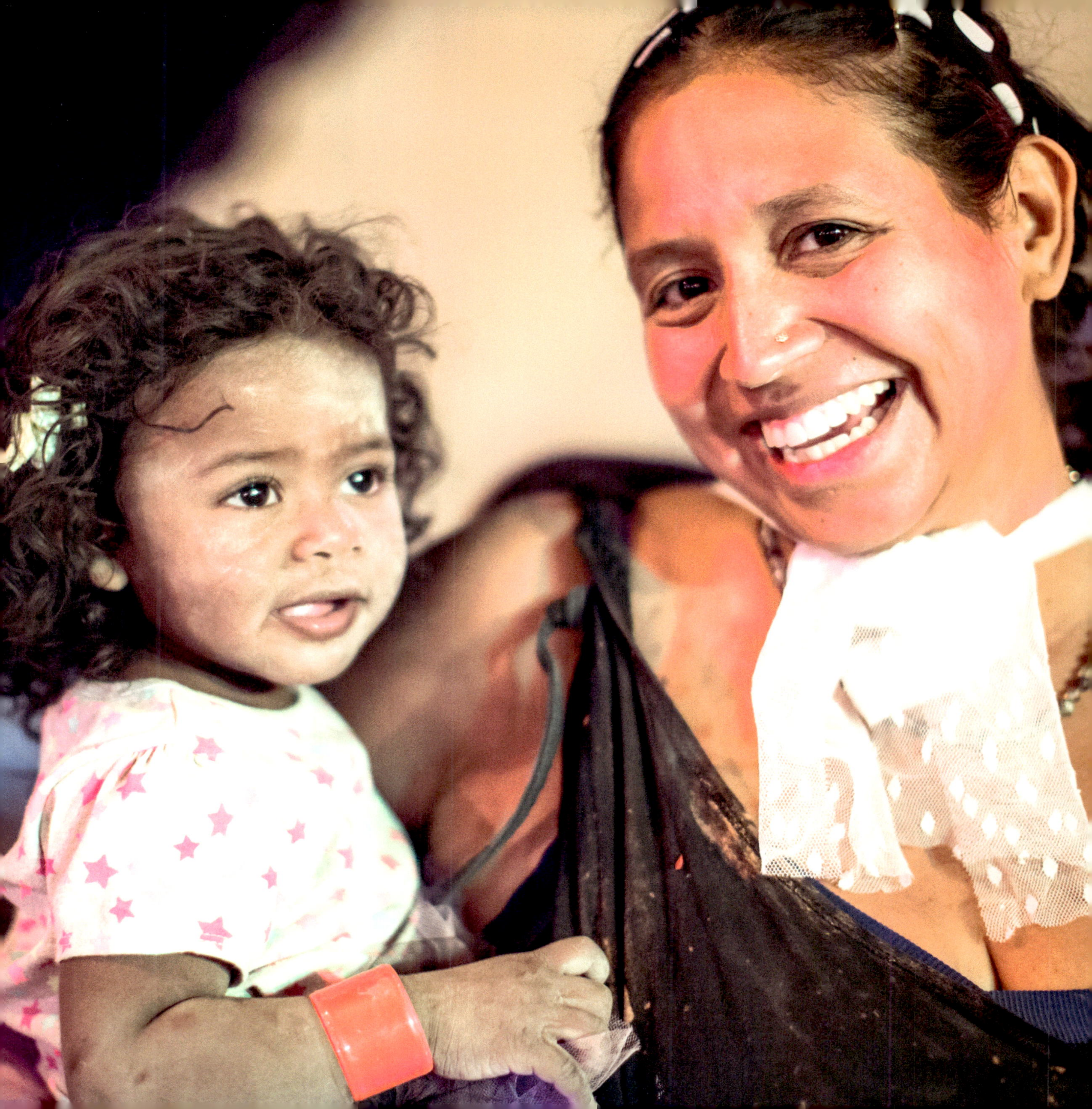

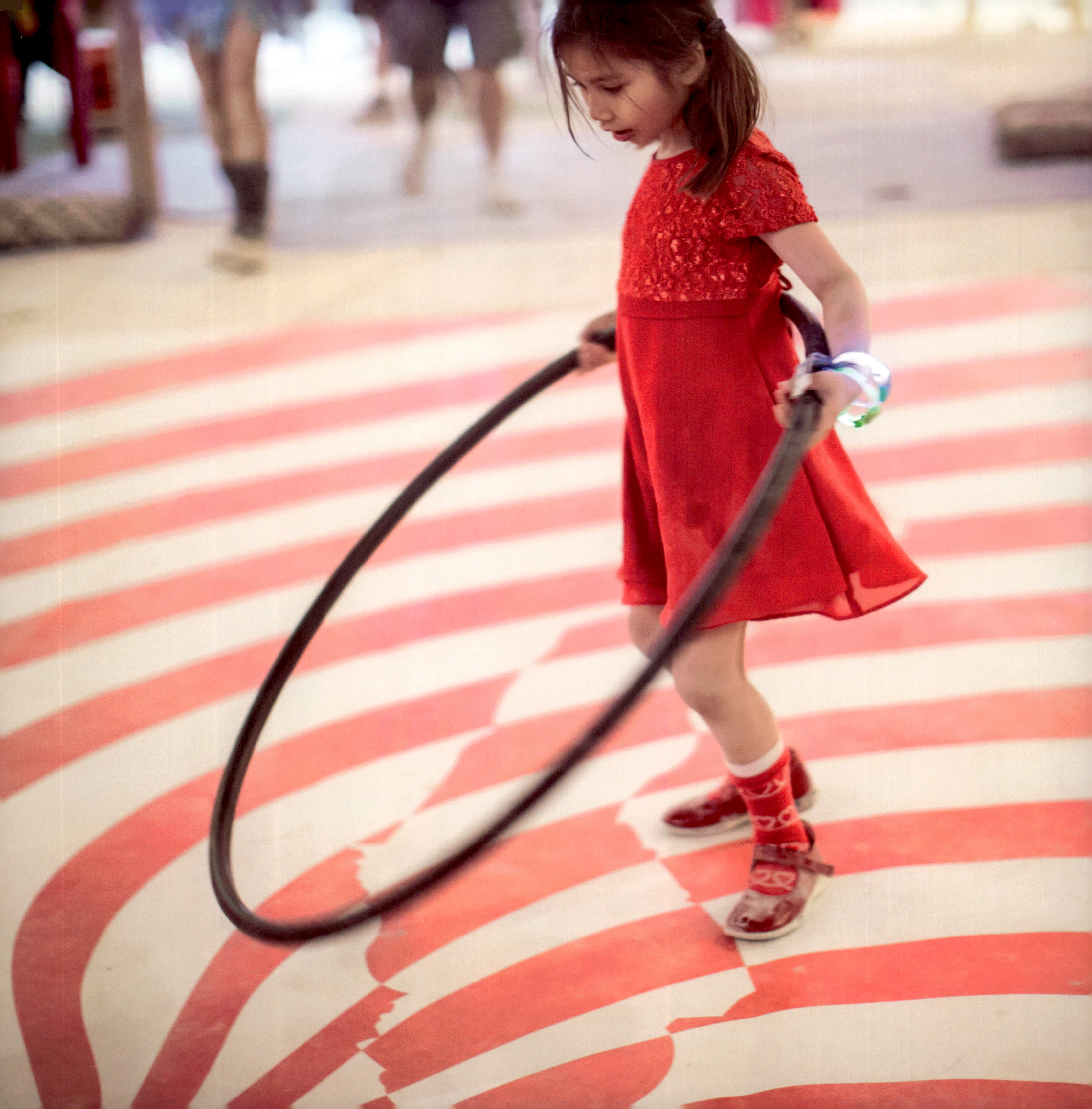

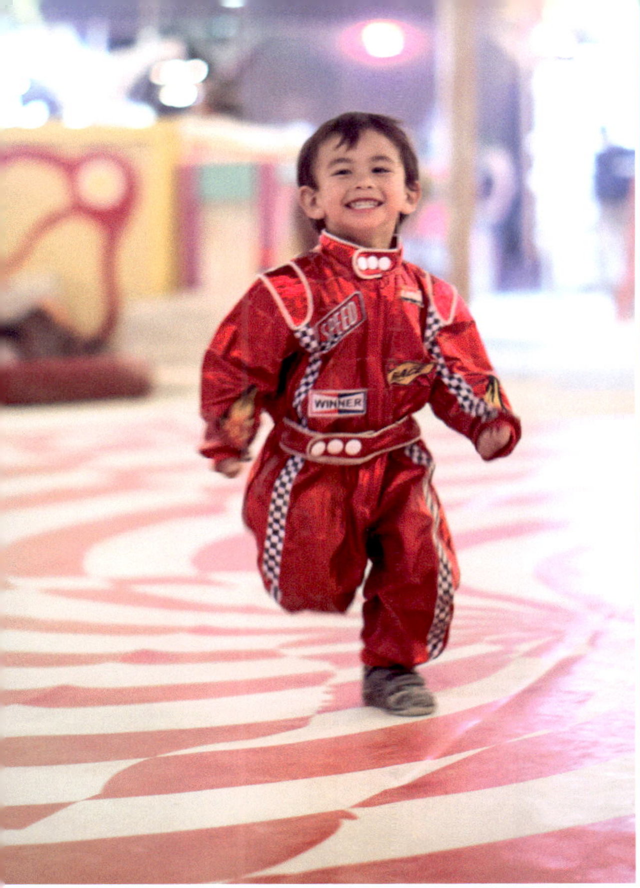
SPEED
WINNER

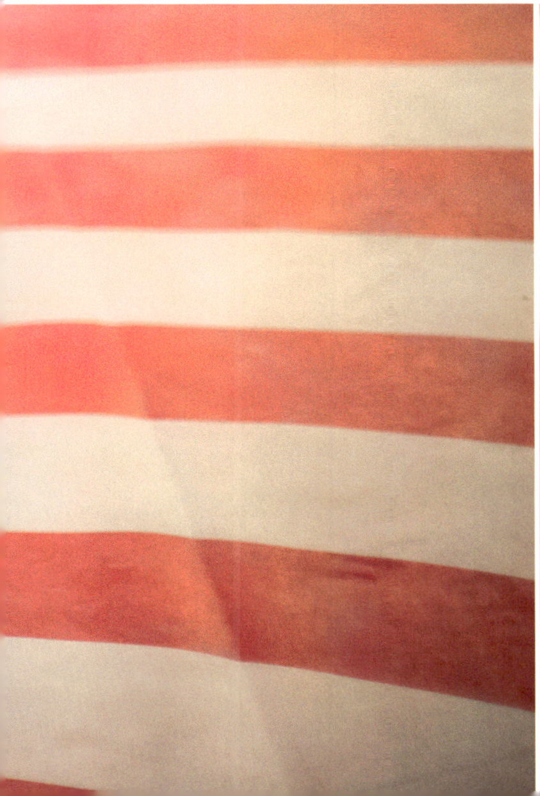

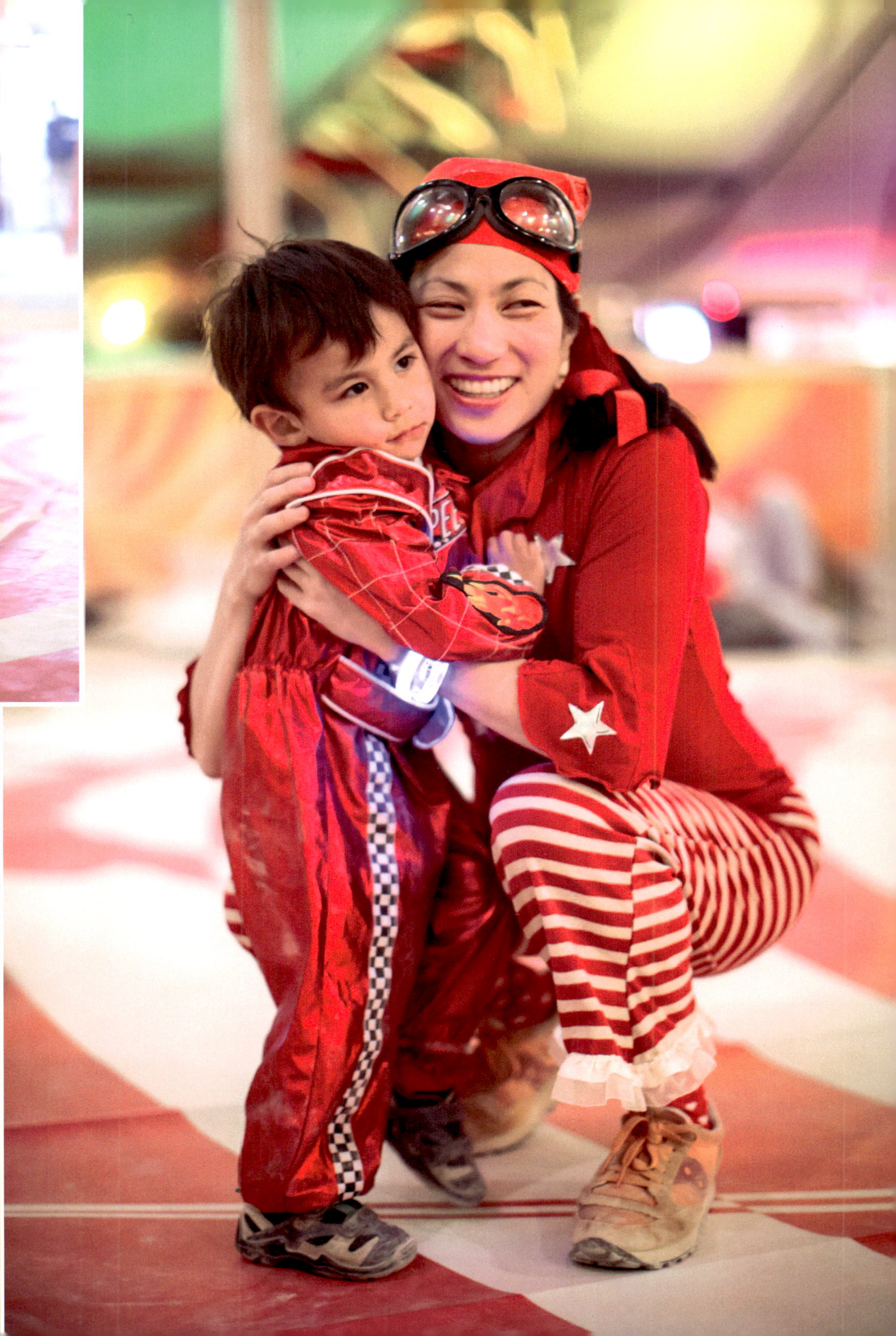

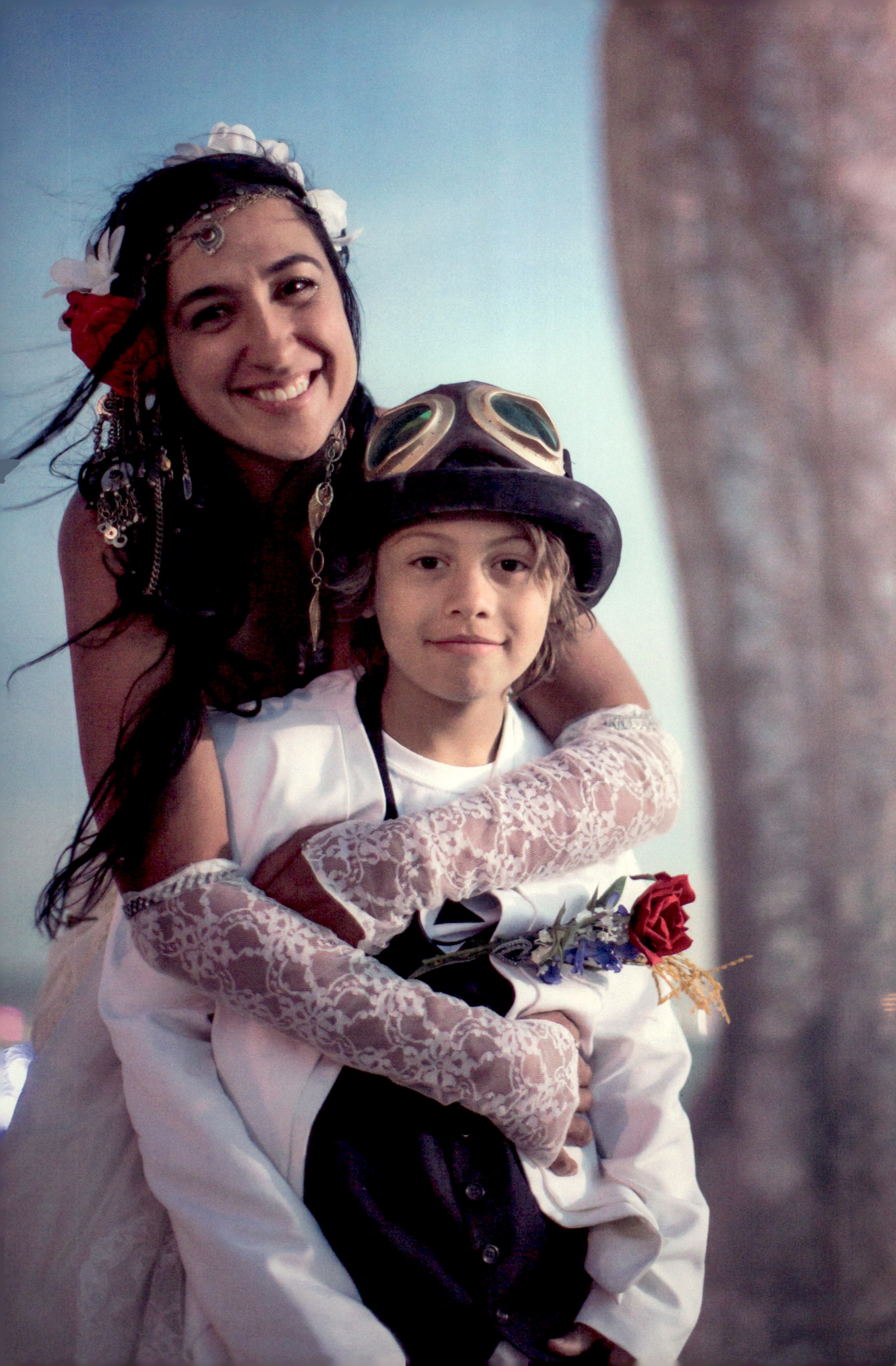

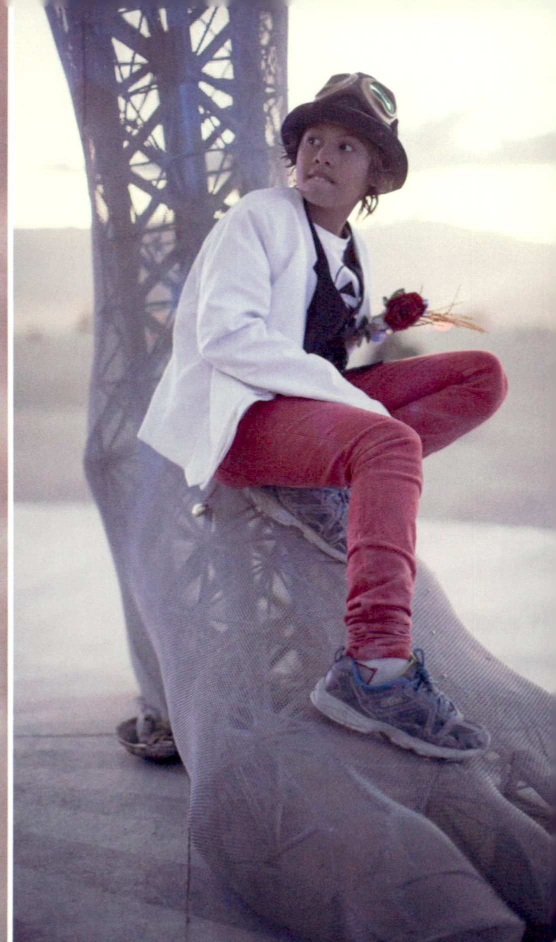

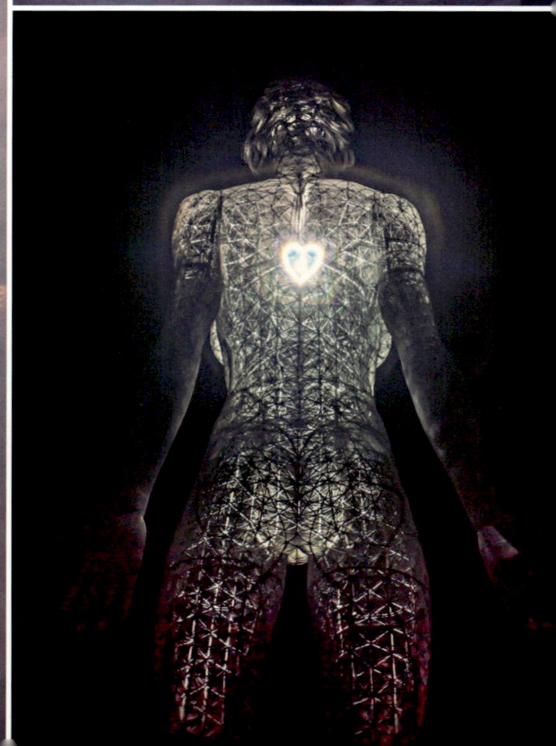

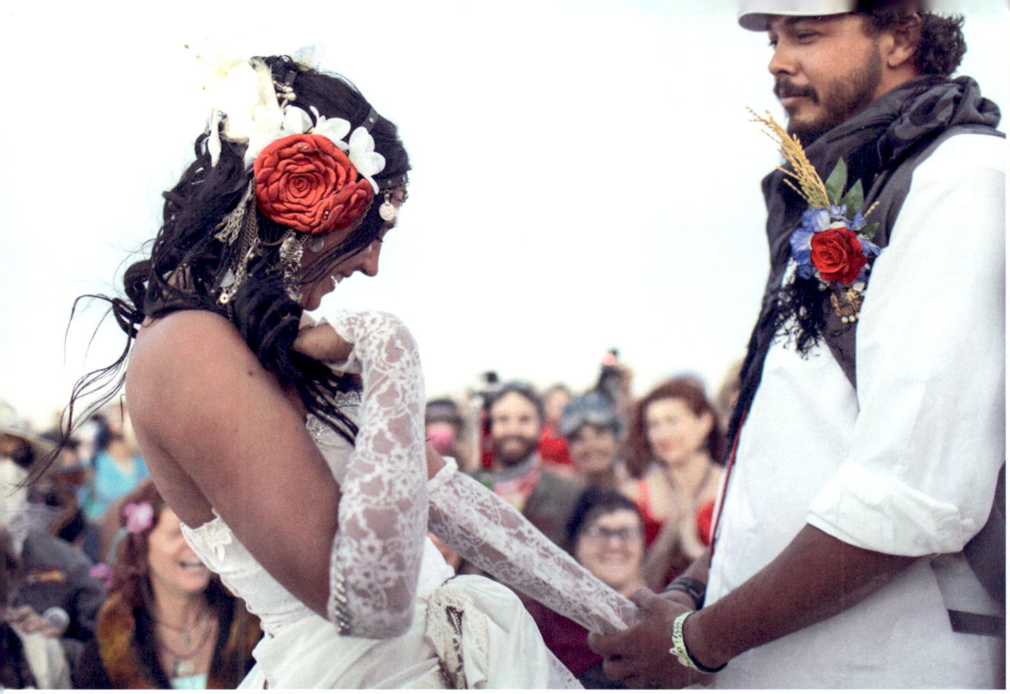

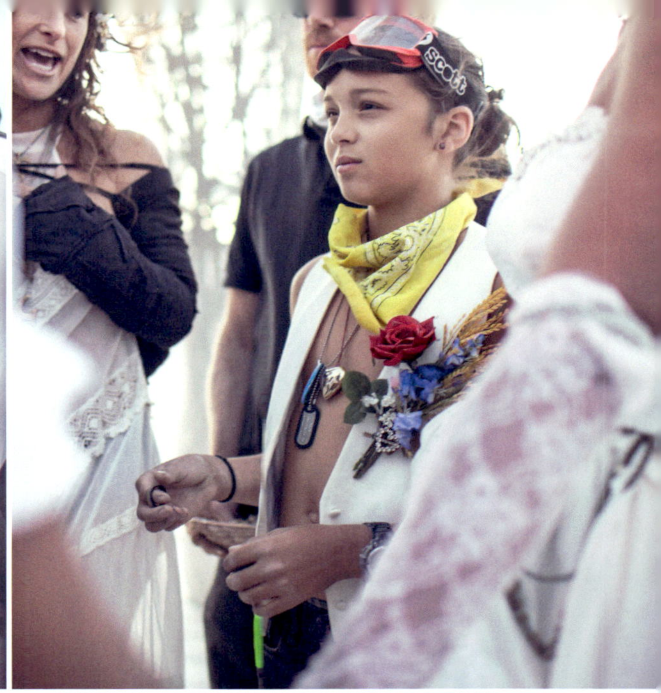

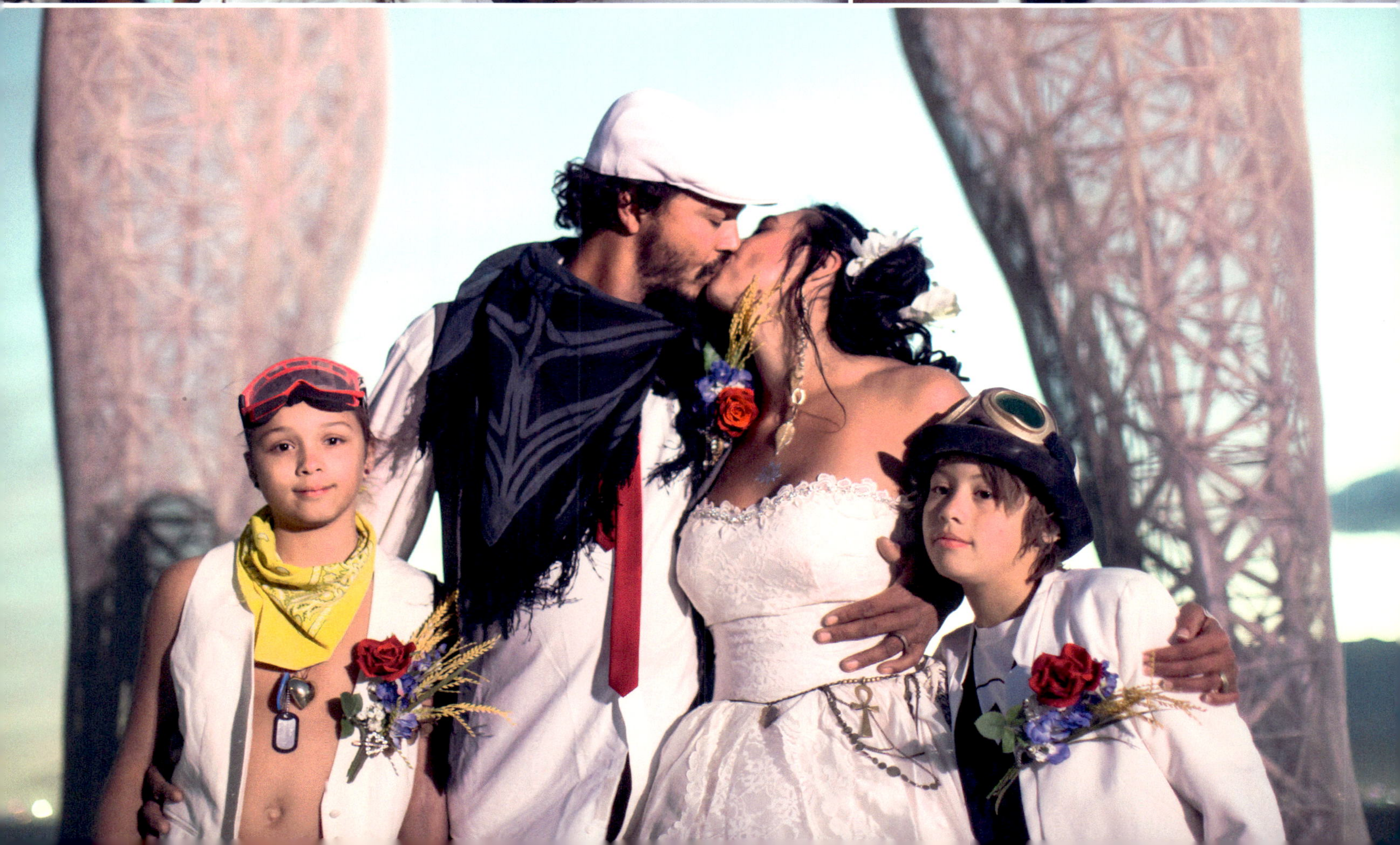

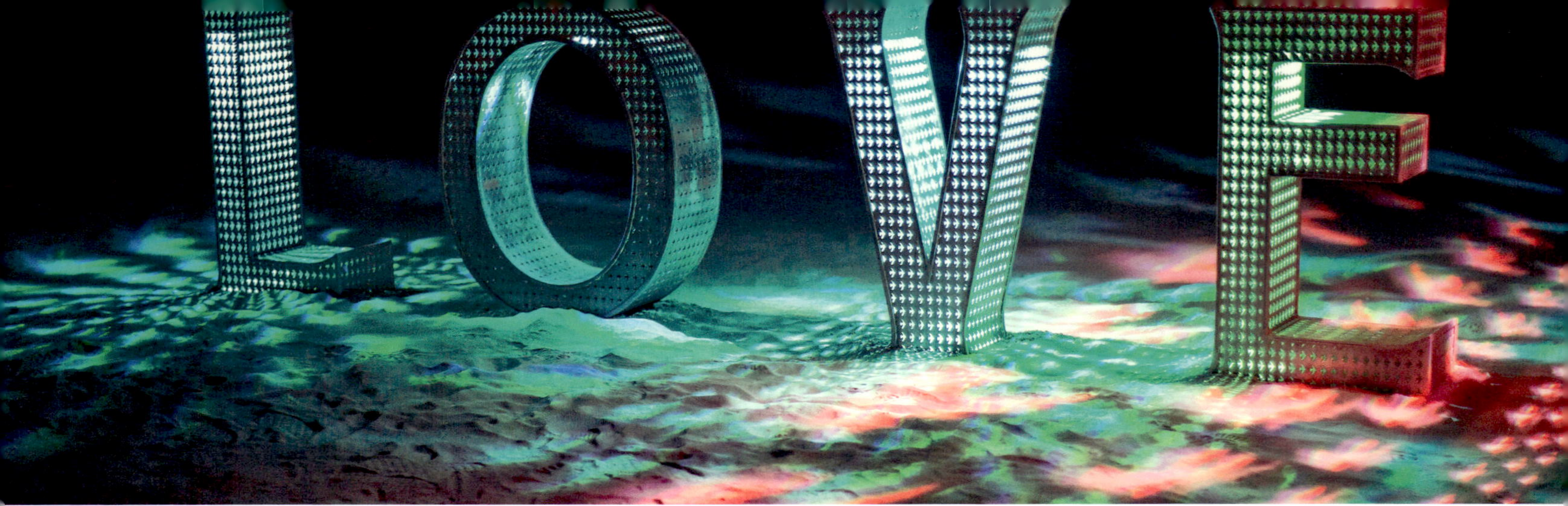
LOVE

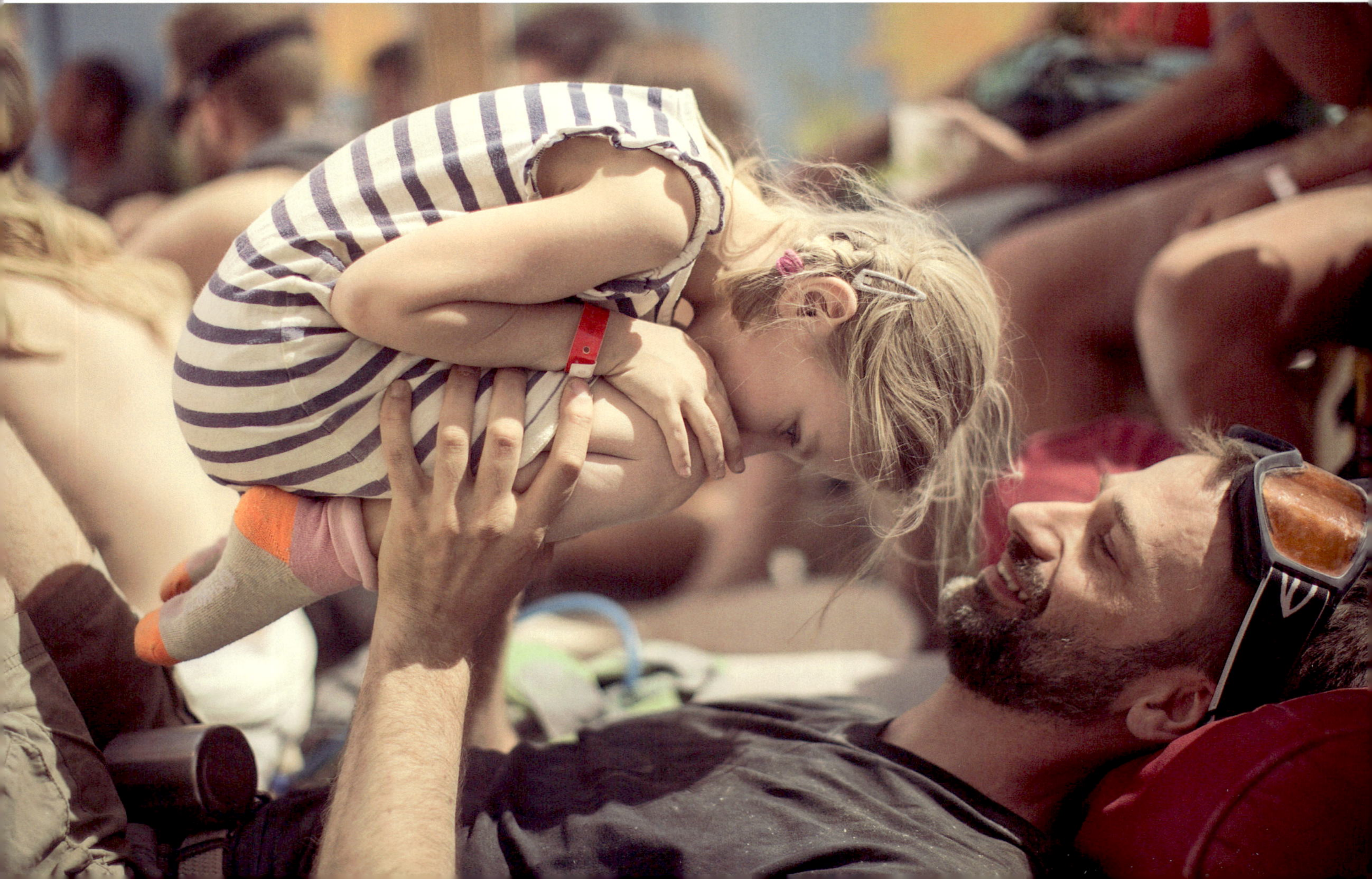

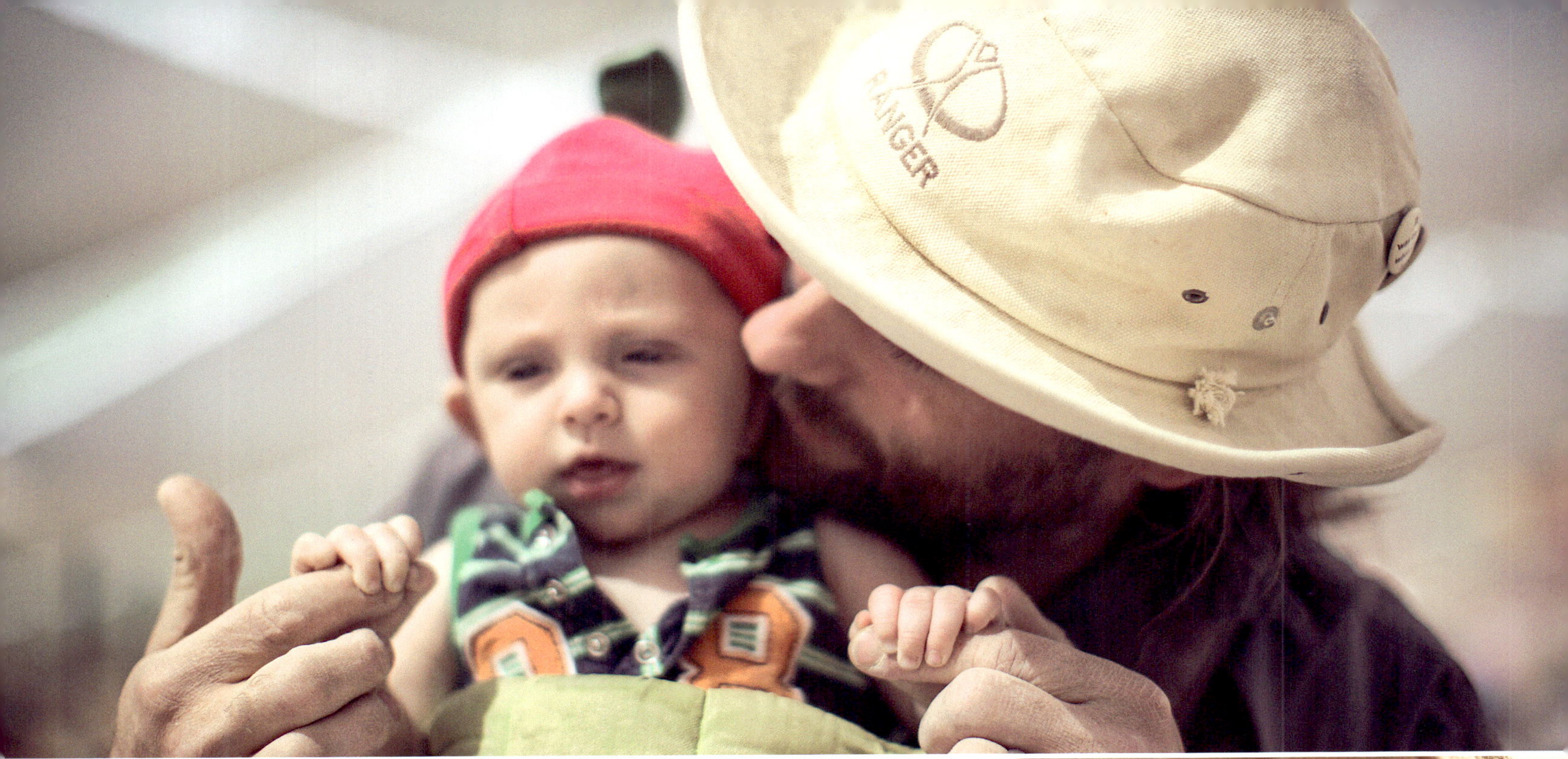
RANGER

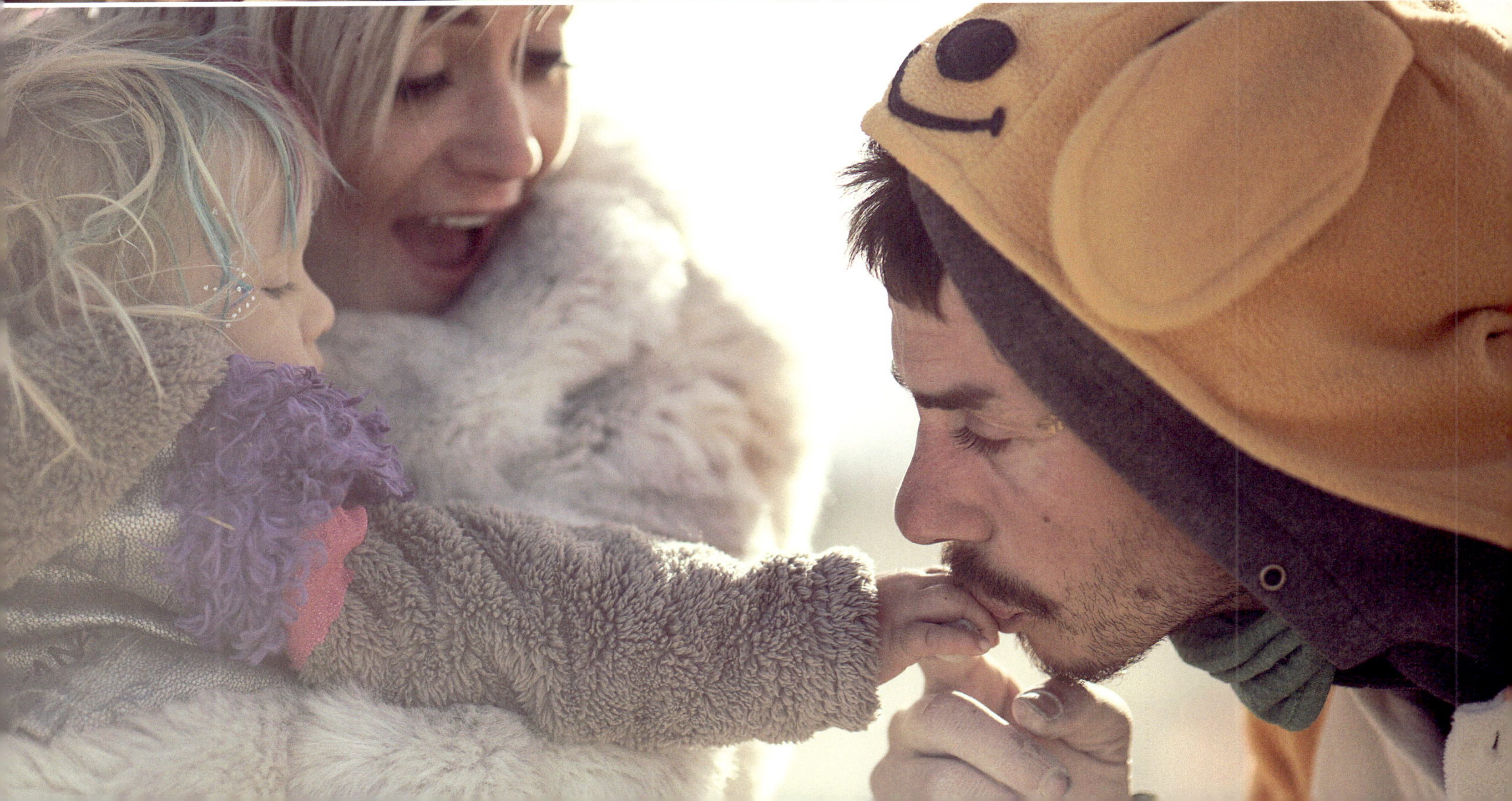

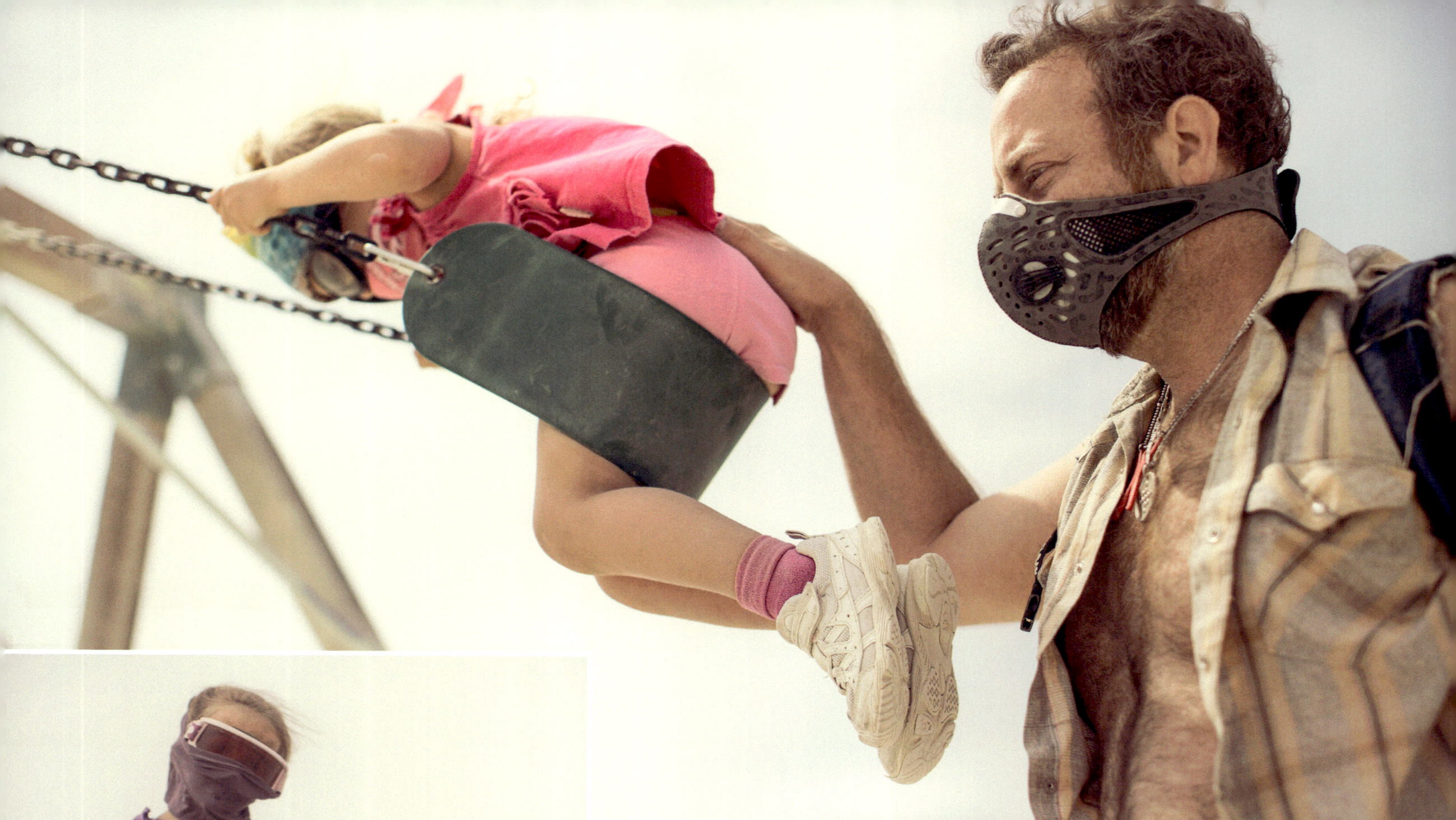

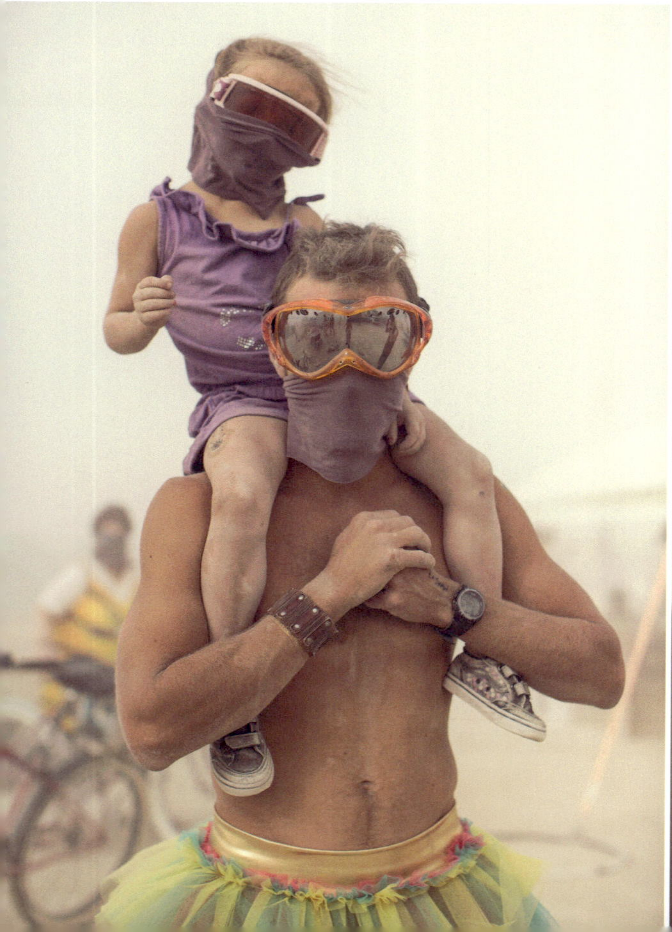

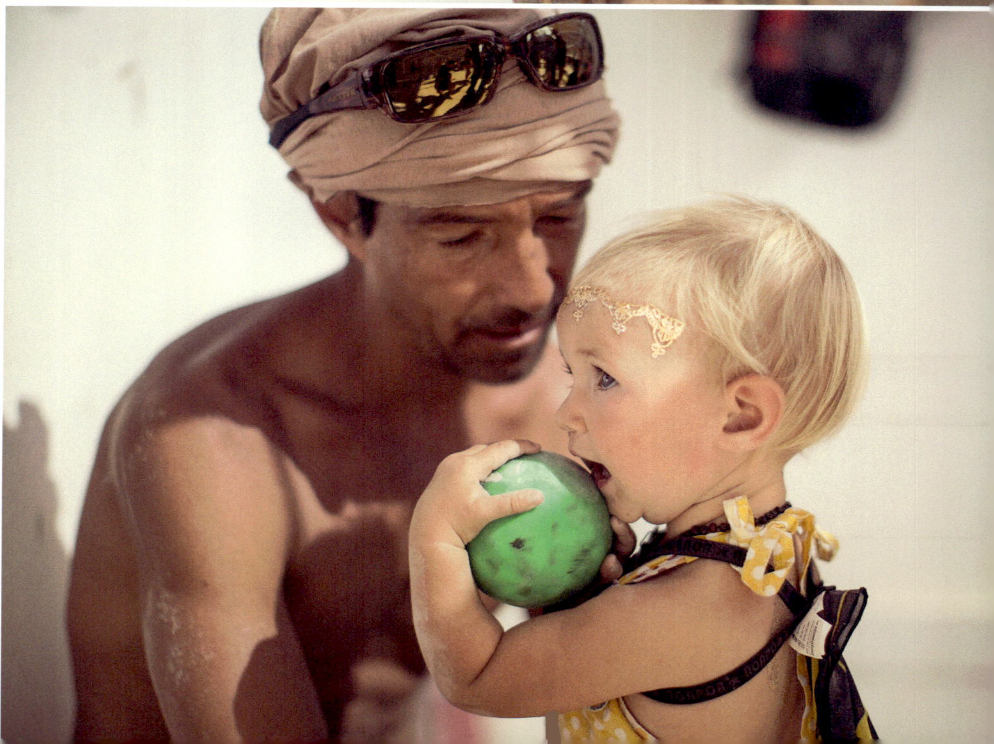

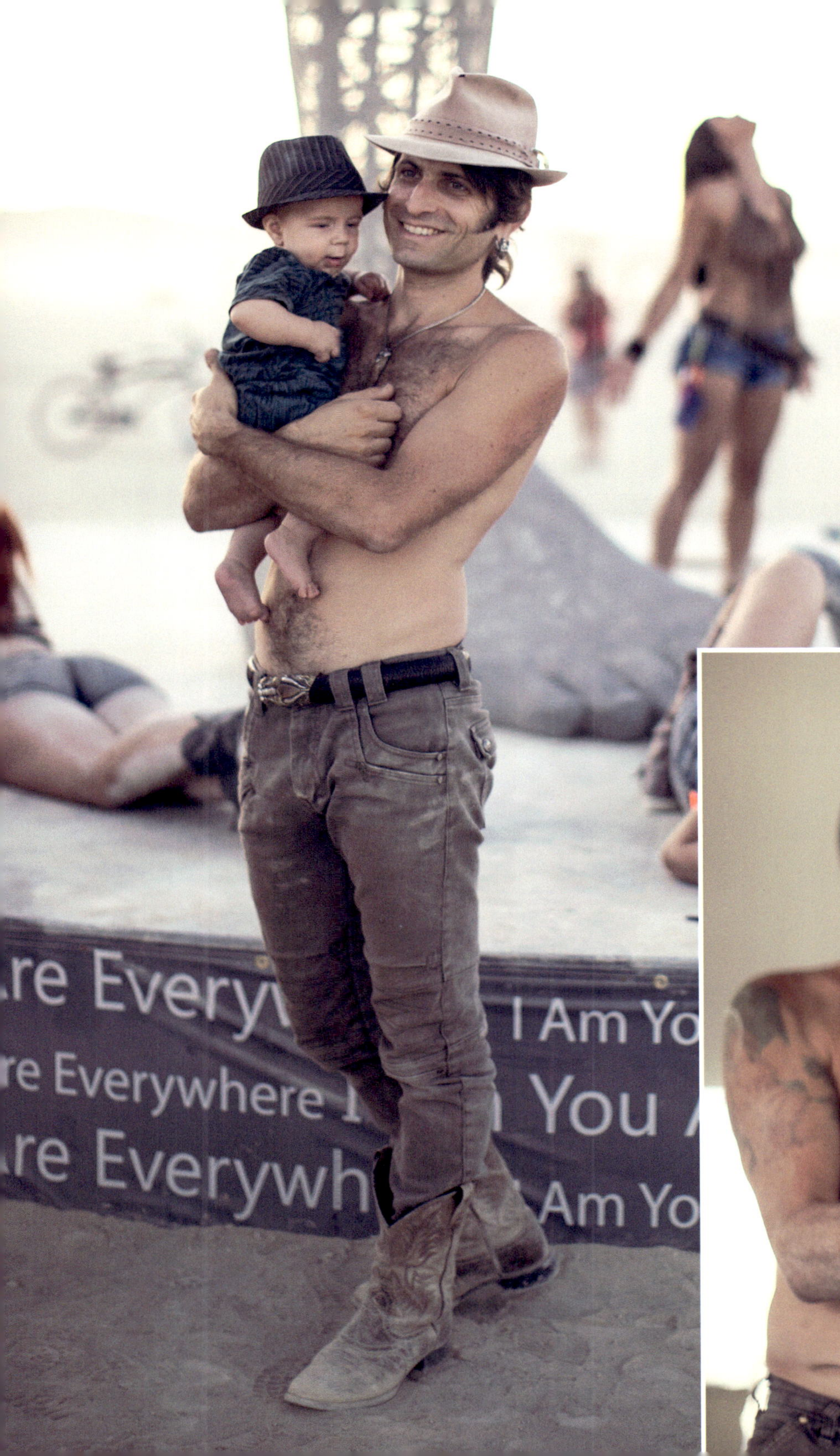
re Everyw
I Am Yo
re Everywhere I
n You
re Everywh
Am Yo

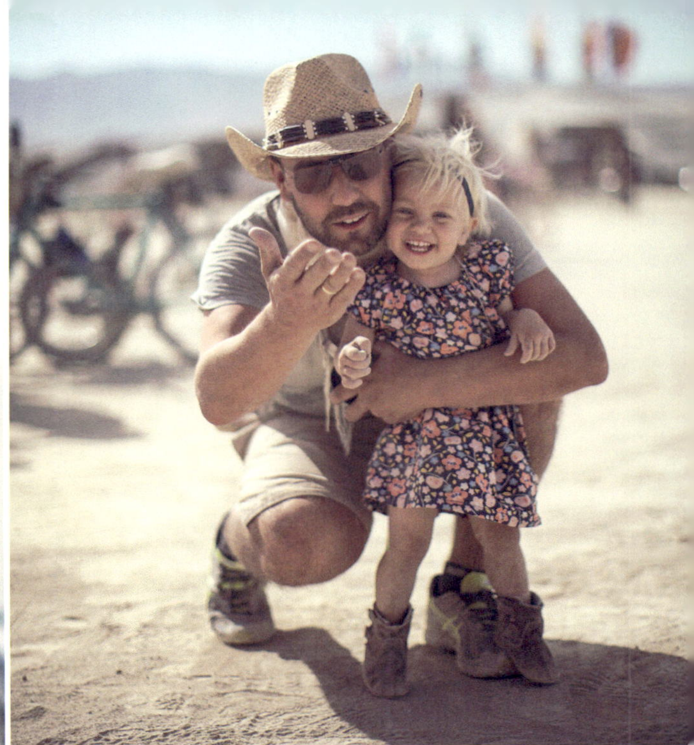

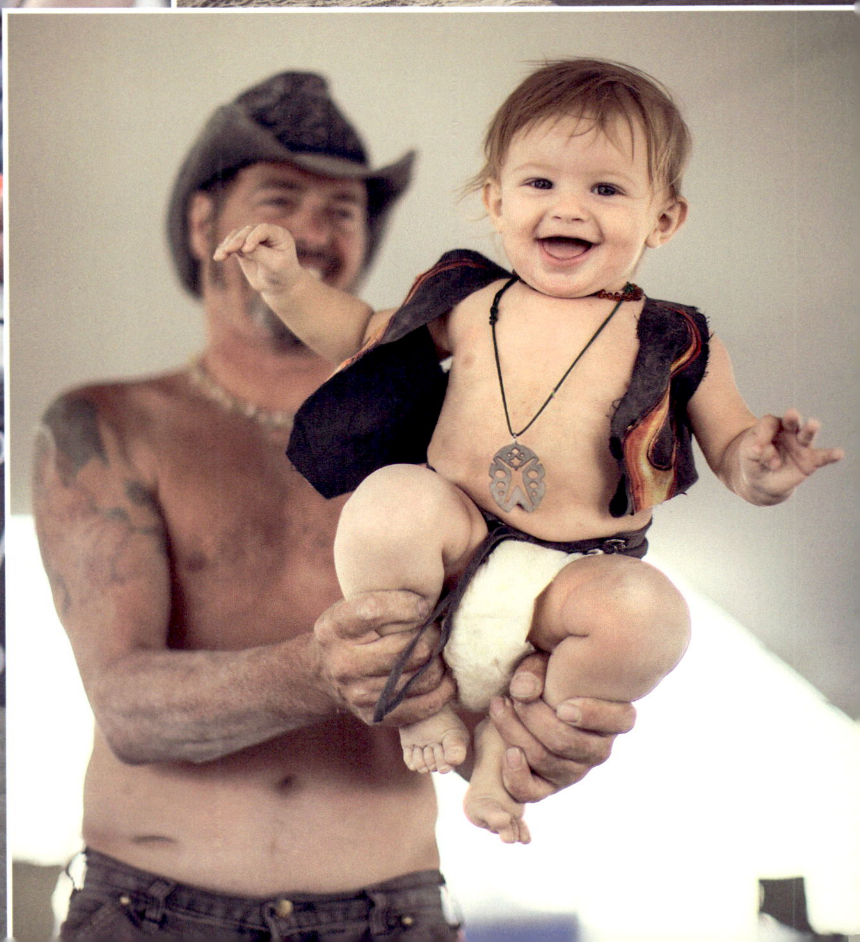

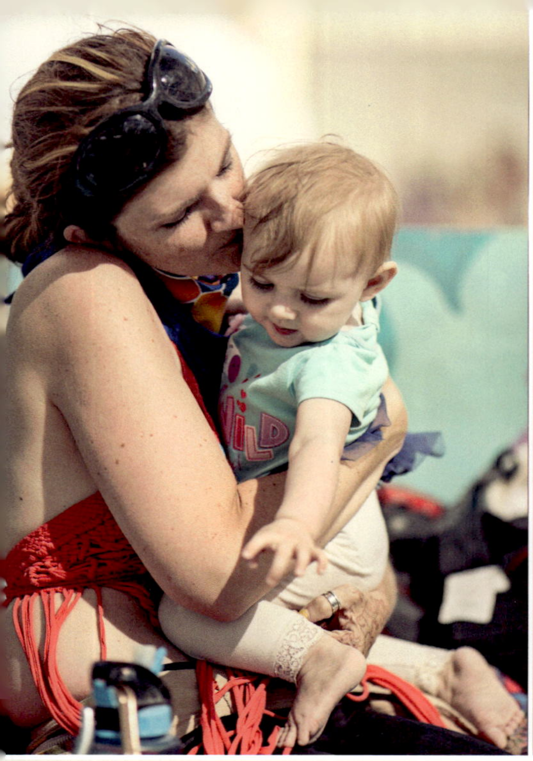
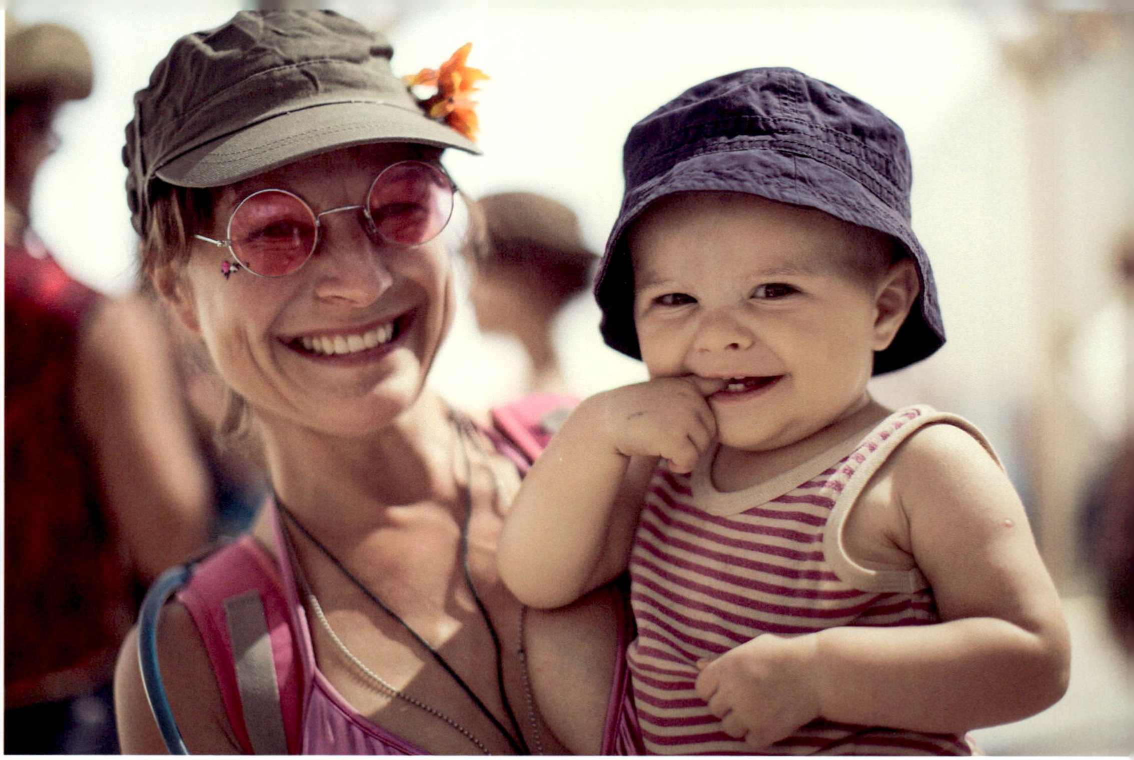
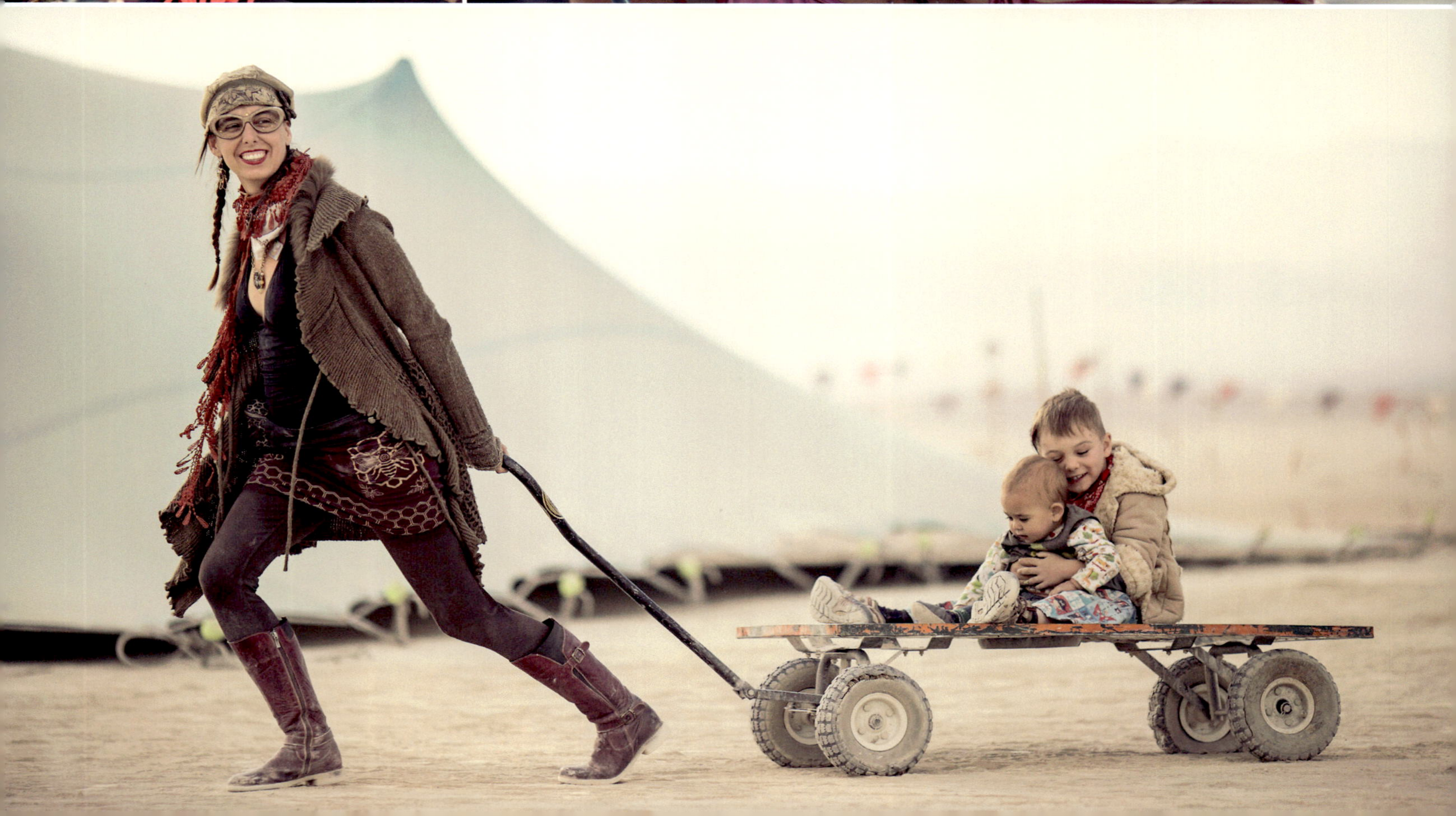

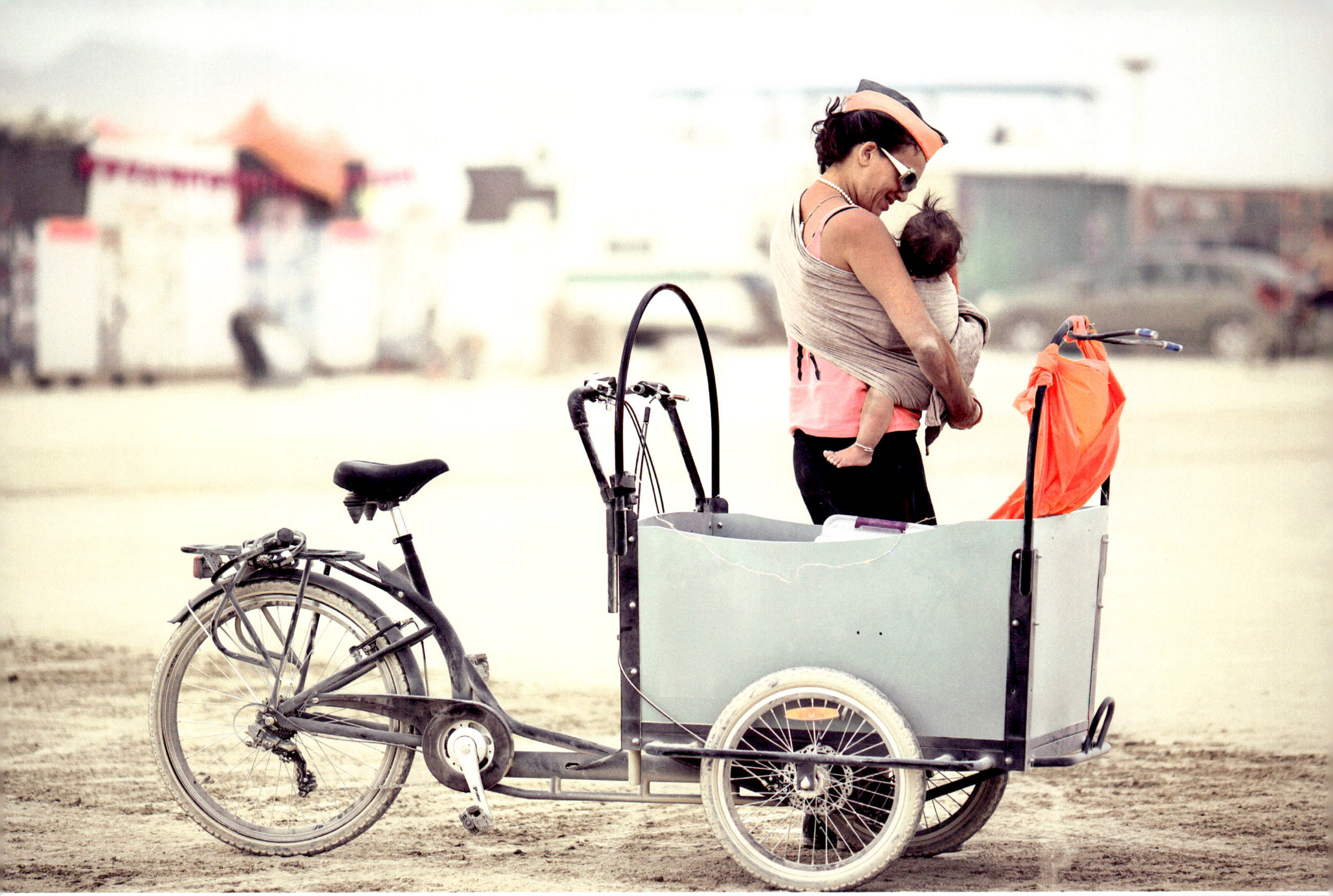

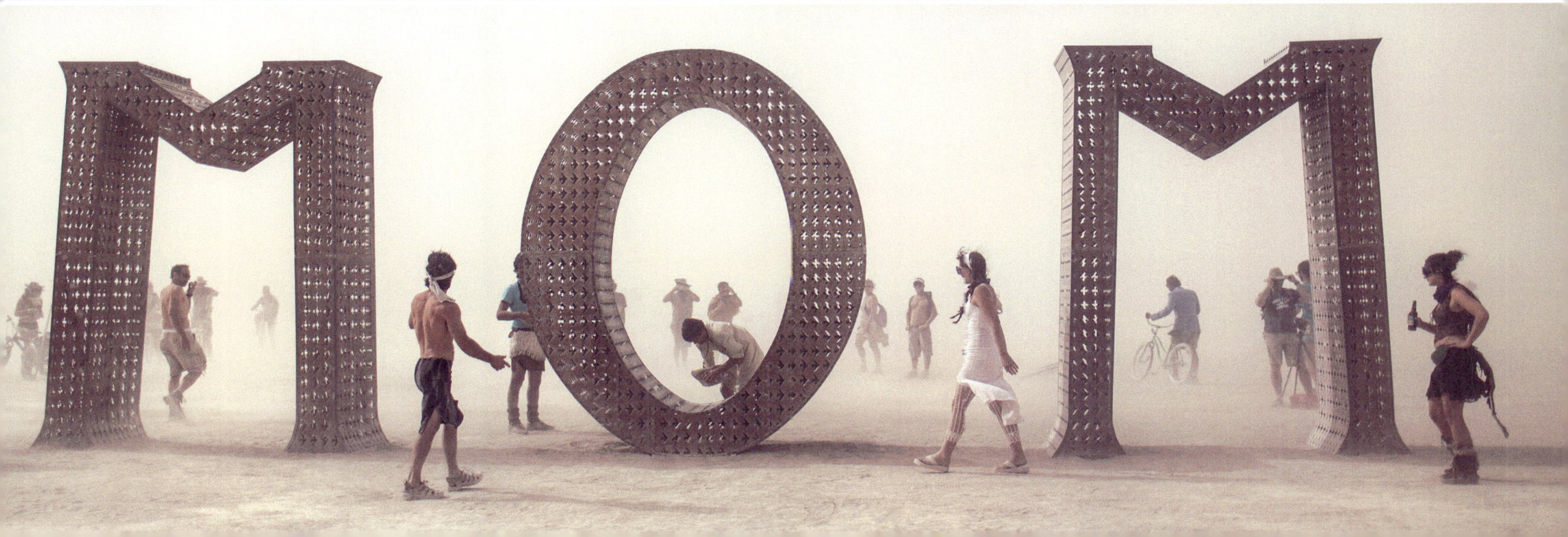
MOM

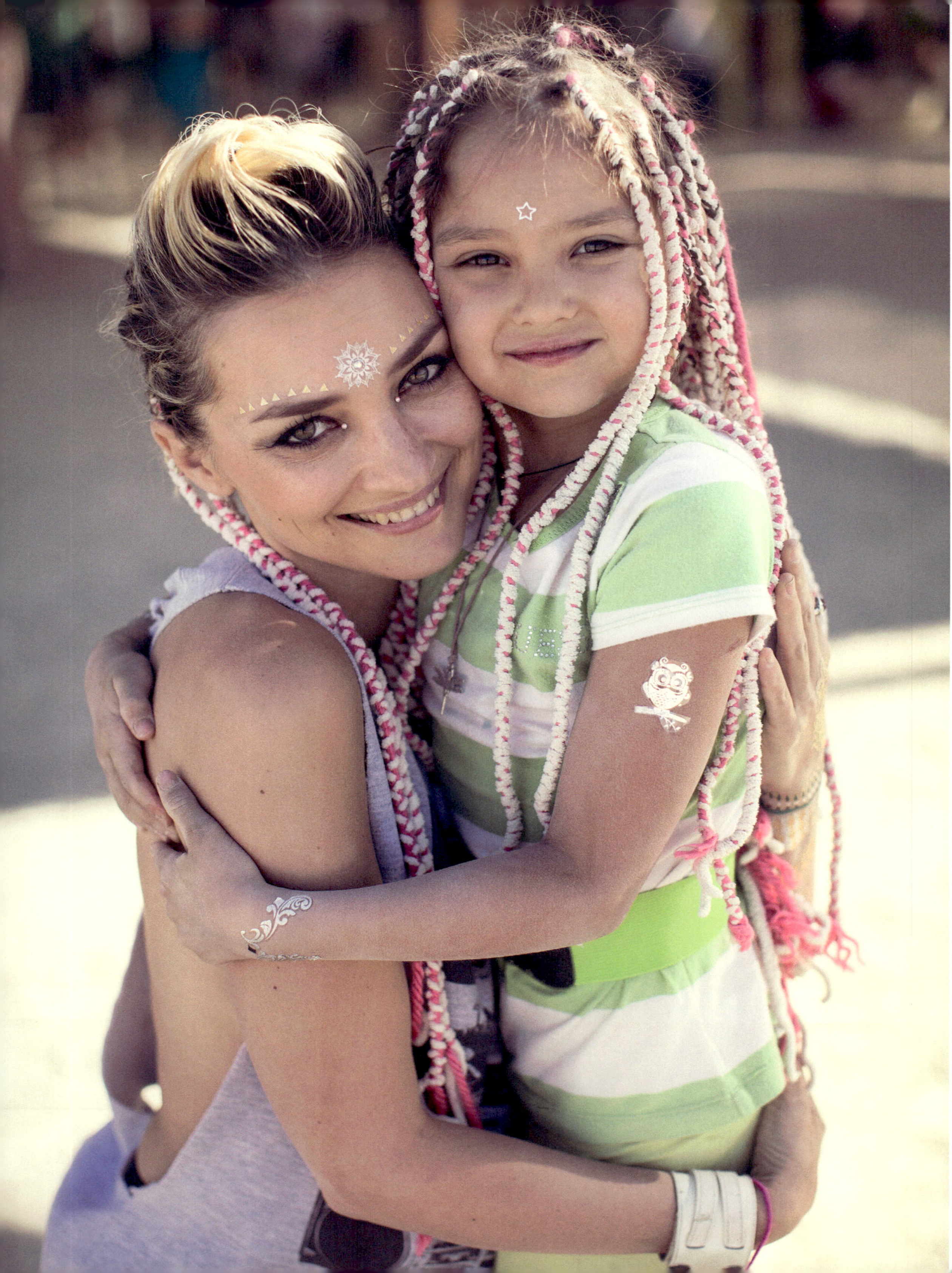

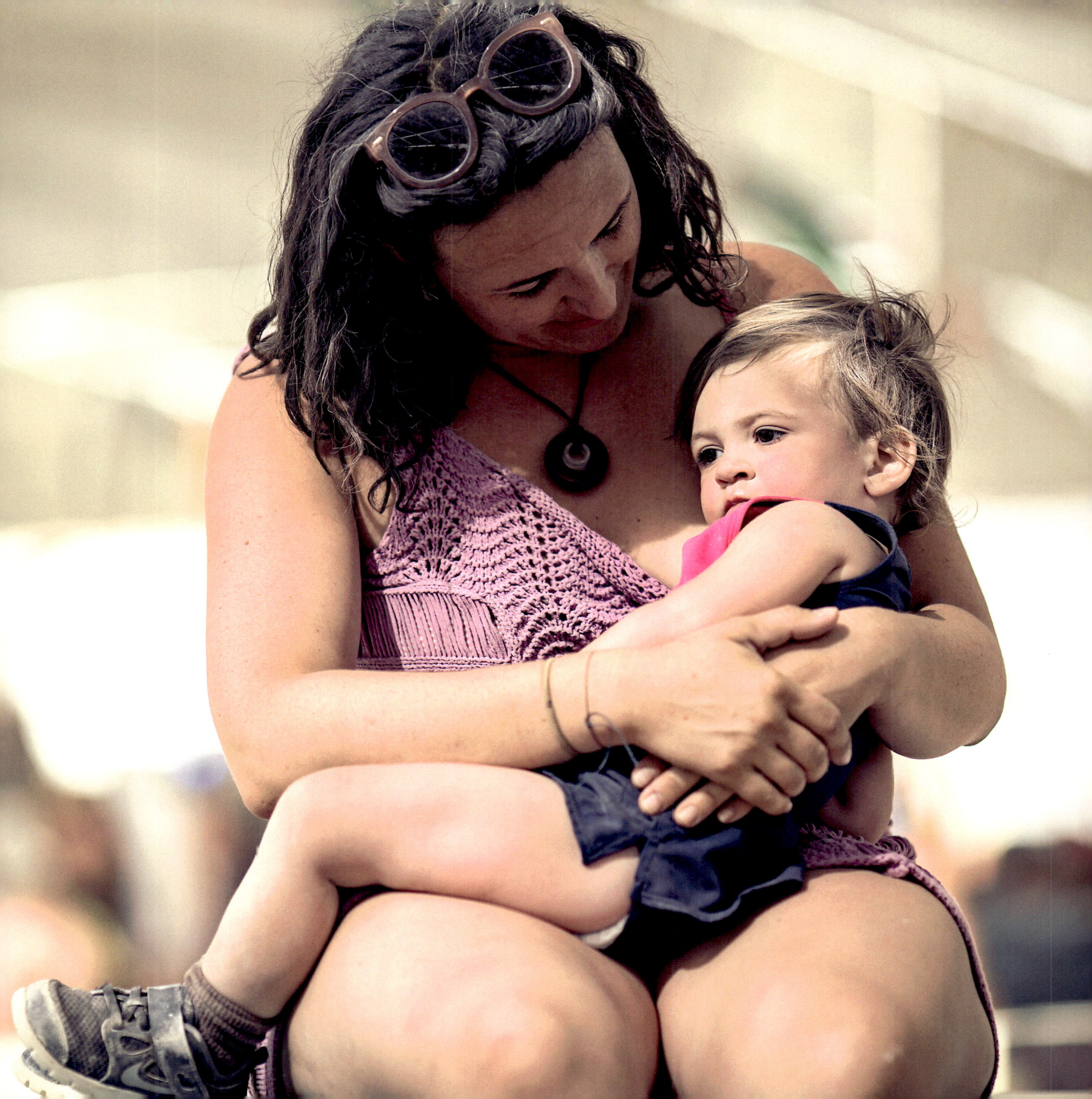

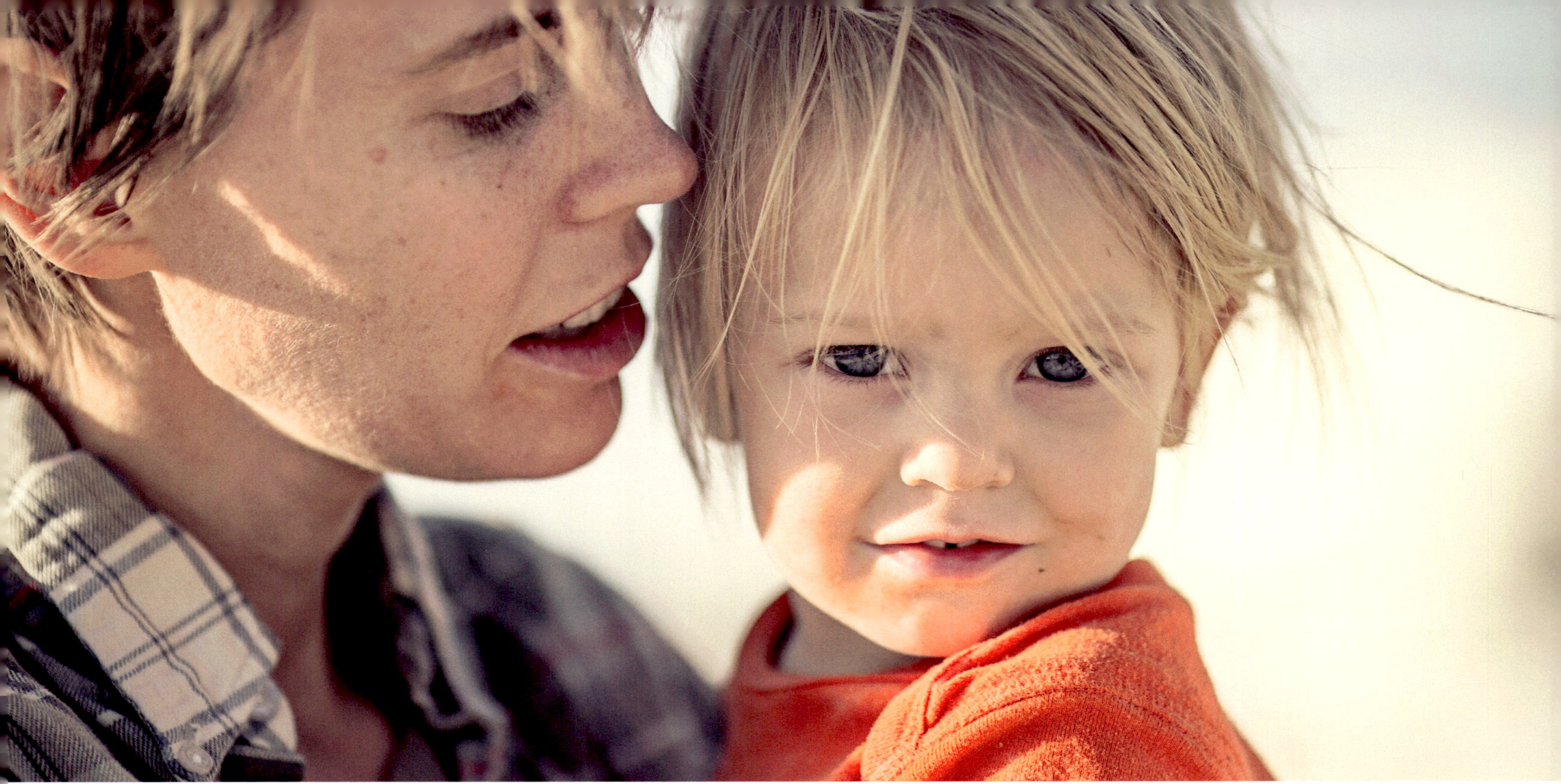

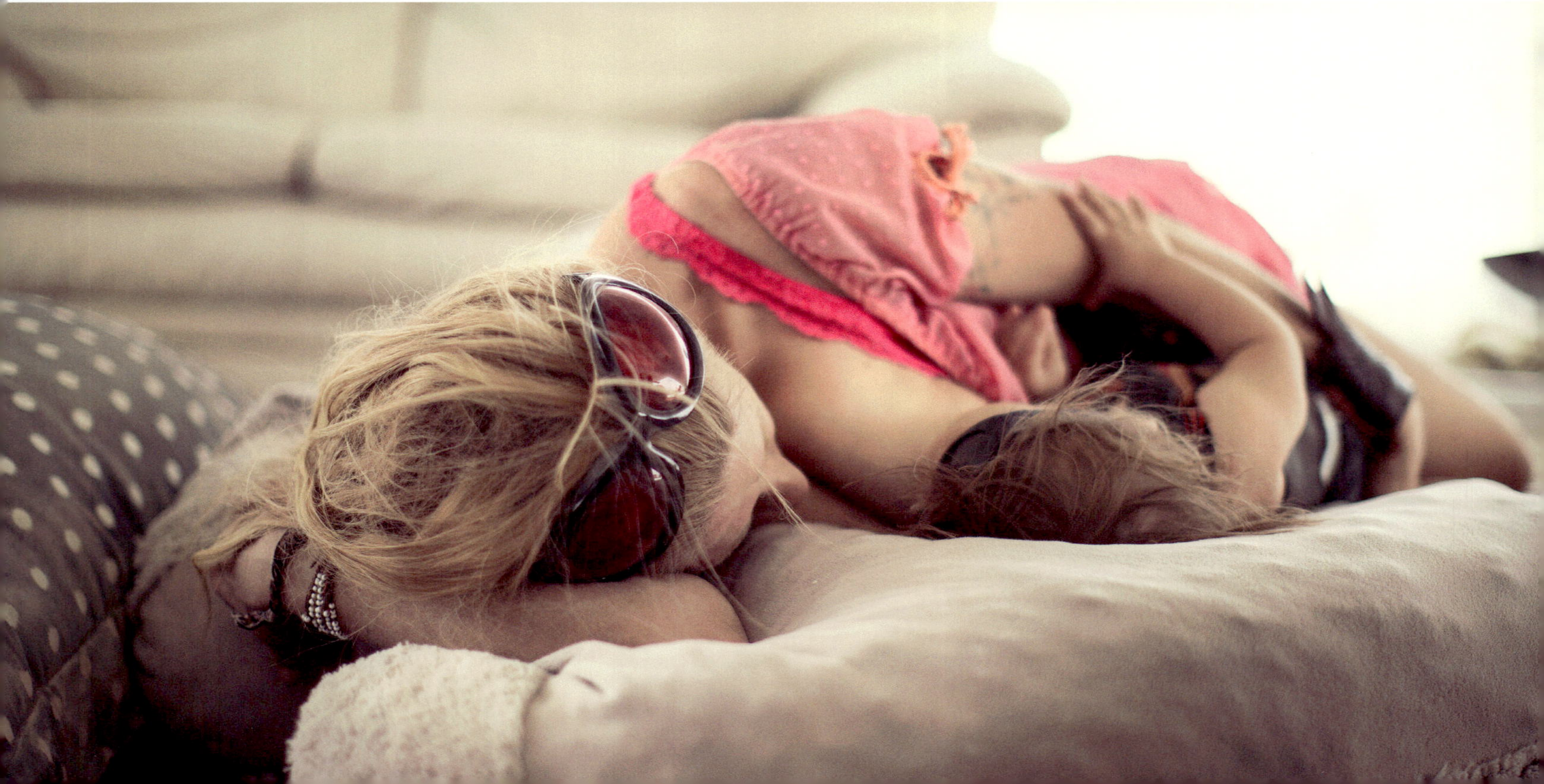

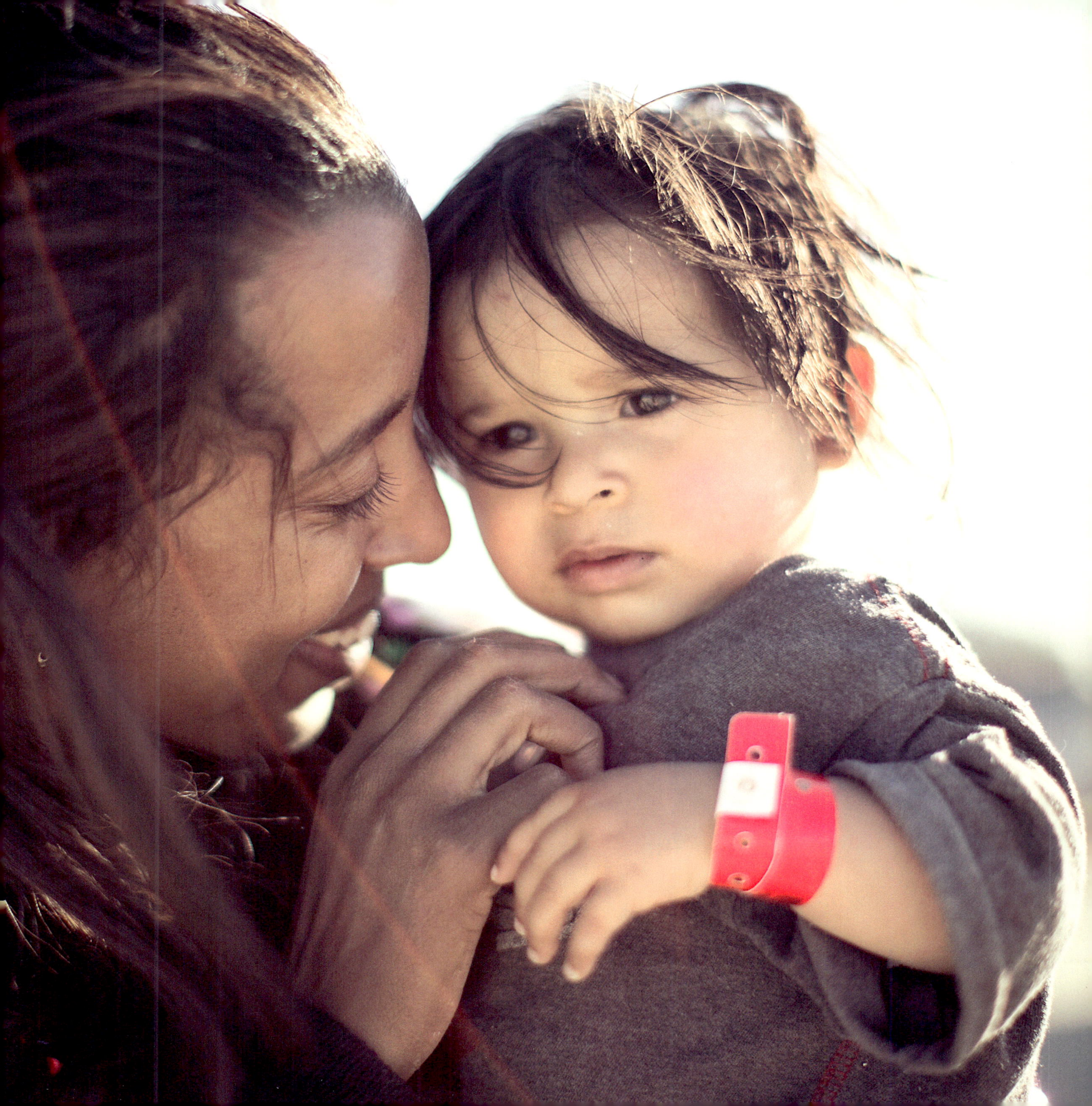

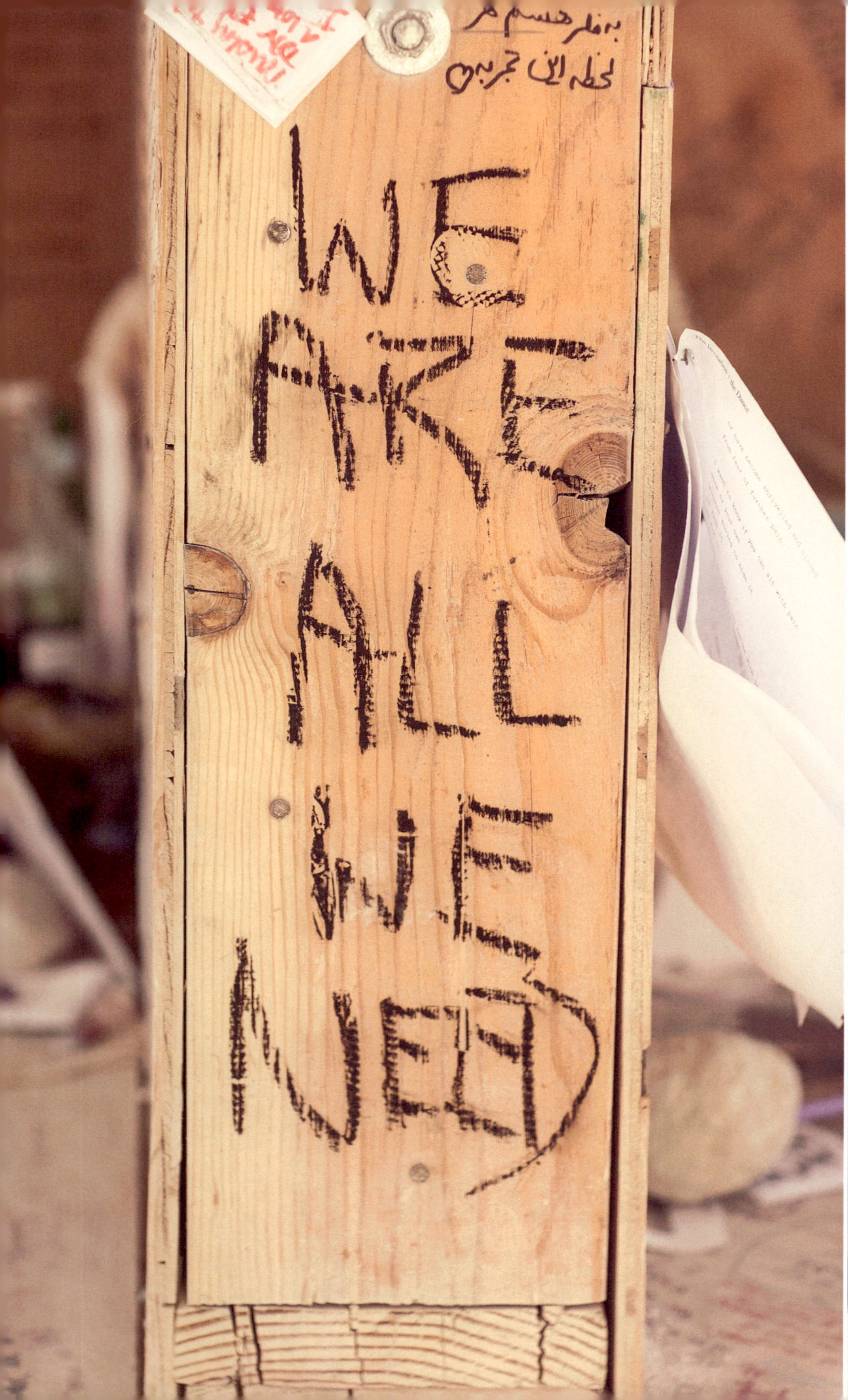
WE ARE ALL WE NEED

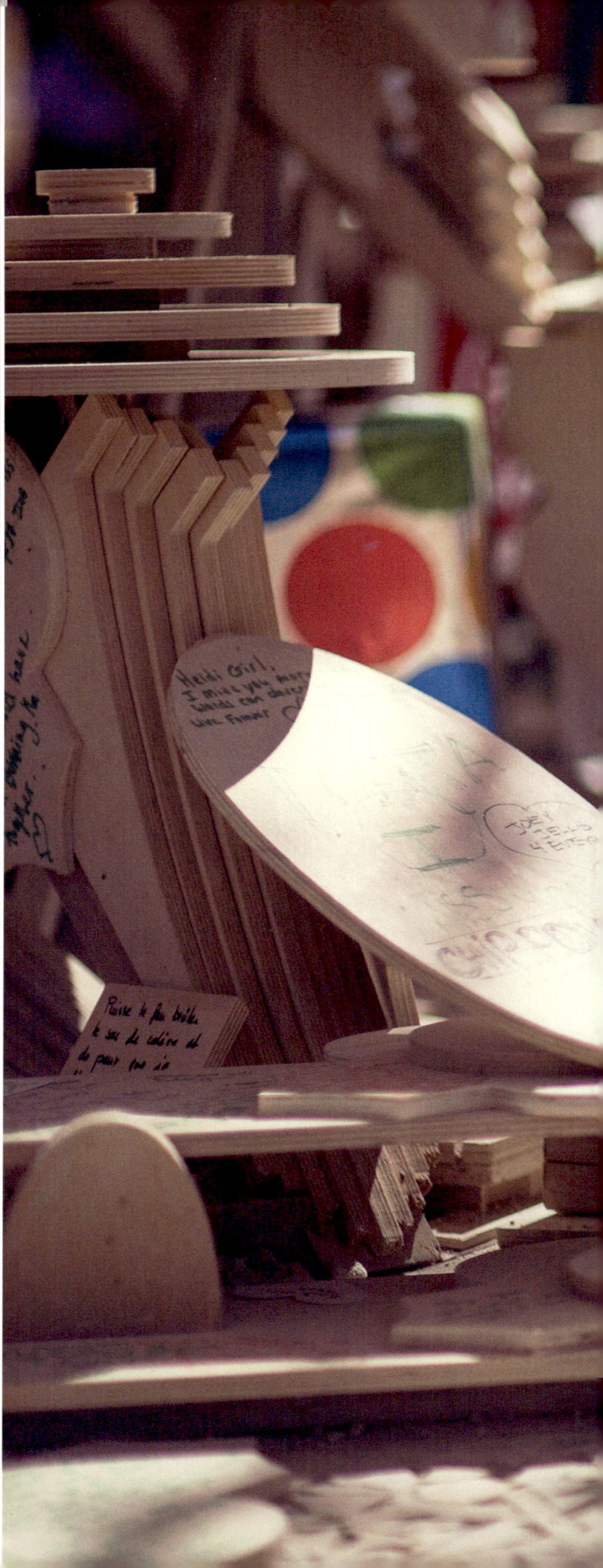

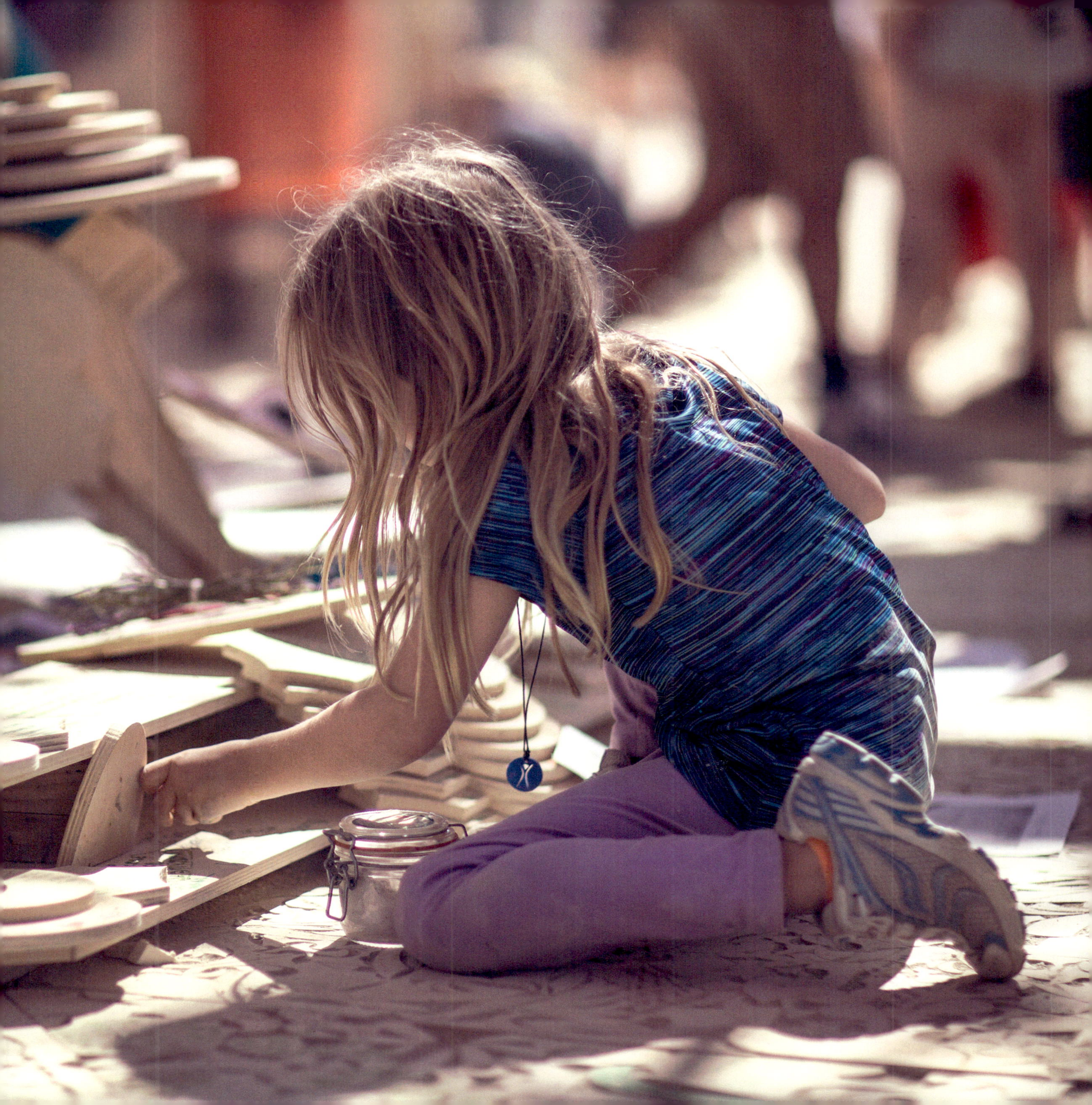

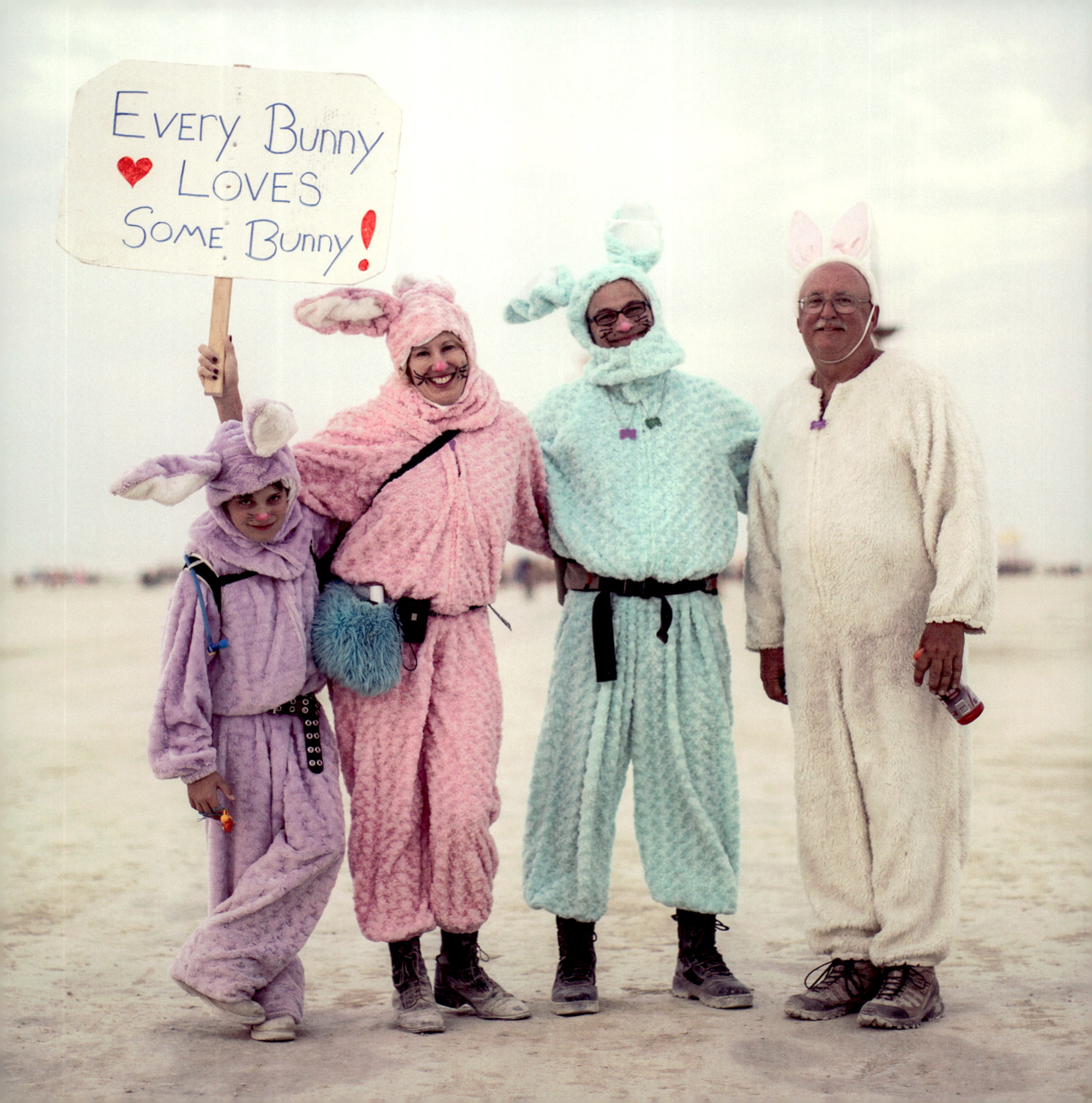
Every Bunny
LOVES
Some Bunny!

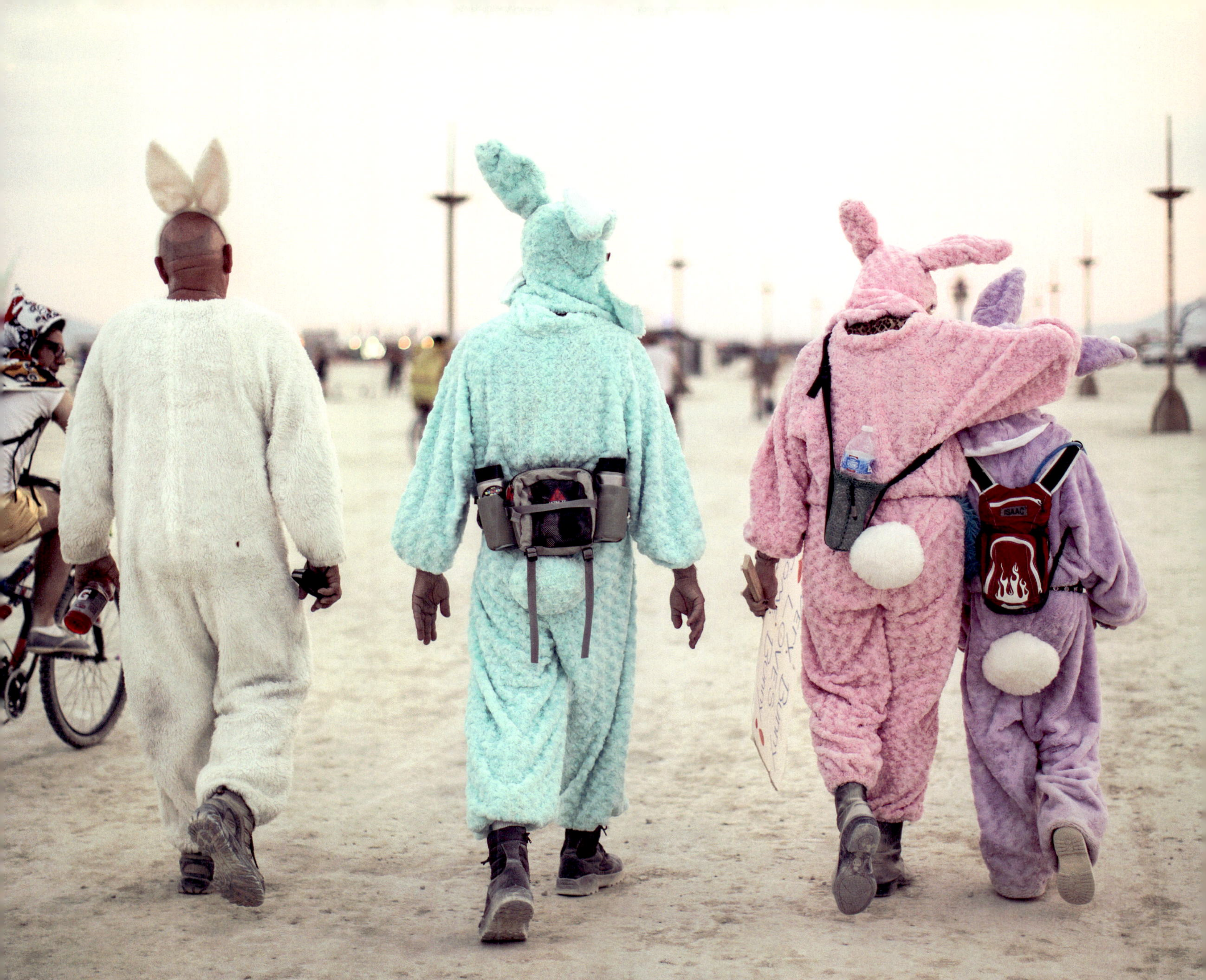

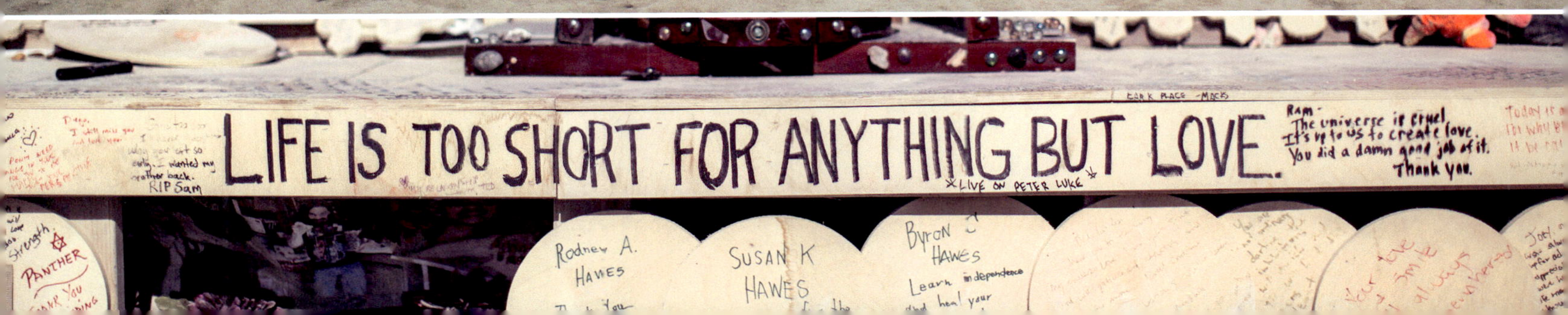

LIFE IS TOO SHORT FOR ANYTHING BUT LOVE.
Ram-
The universe is cruel.
It's up to us to create love.
You did a damn good job of it.
Thank you.
LIVE ON PETER LUKE
RIP Sam
Strength
PANTHER
Rodney A. Hawes
SUSAN K HAWES
Byron Hawes

• TO ALL THE BEAUTIFULLY DUSTY FAMILIES •

I adore you.

WITHOUT YOUR PARTICIPATION, THIS BOOK SIMPLY WOULDN'T EXIST.

Thank you for saying 'yes'.

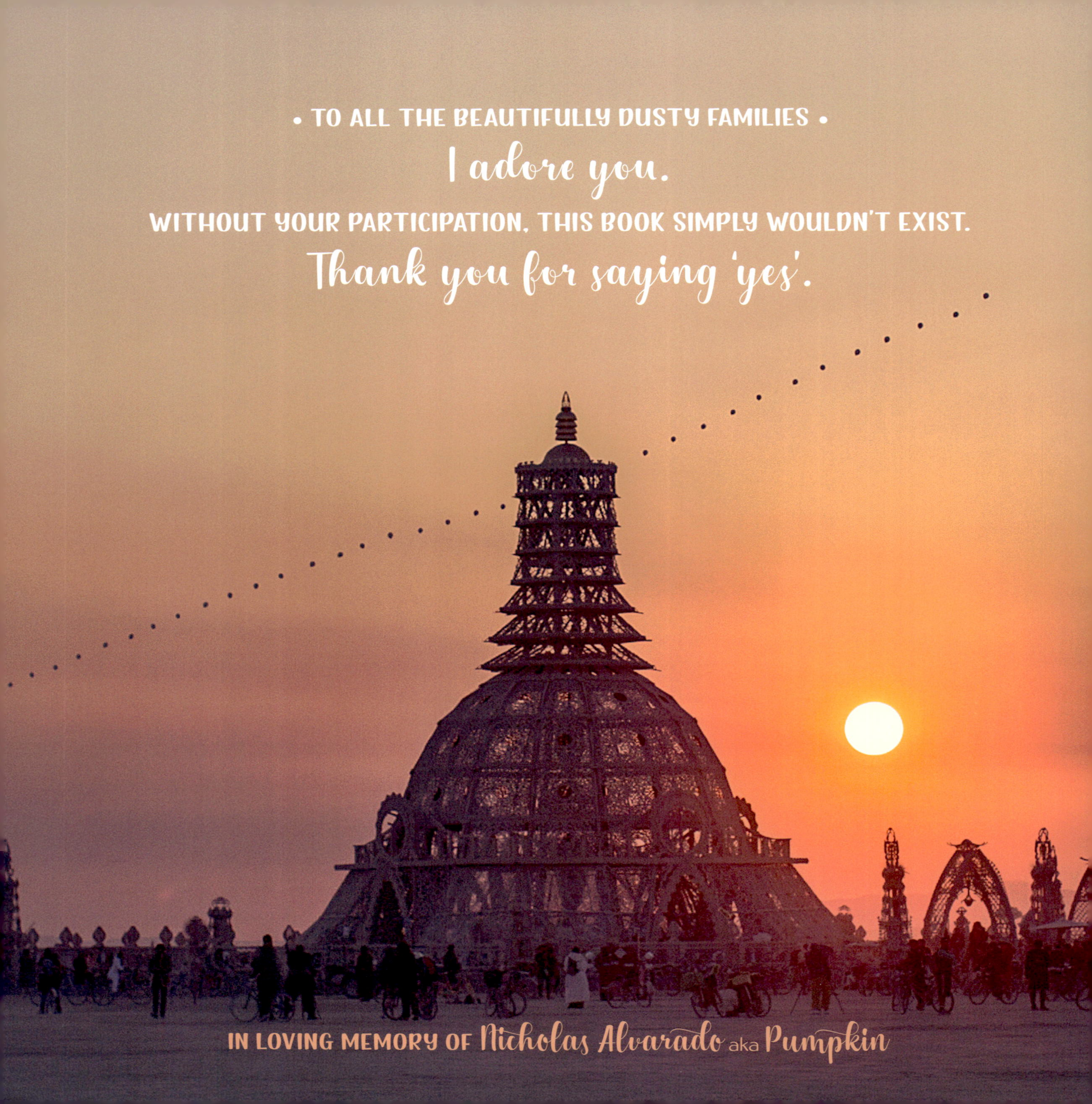

IN LOVING MEMORY OF *Nicholas Alvarado* aka *Pumpkin*

Heartfelt Gratitude

From concept to completion, I owe the strength of this project to the steadfast support of these exceptional humans...

• For building 'Hassy', keeping me well-nourished (in heart & body), being my trusted 2nd pair of eyes and reminding me, always, what matters most •

THADDEUS KOSTER

• For believing in me and silently moving mountains •

ZAC CIRIVELLO

• For trusting me with this delicate subject matter •

BURNING MAN COMMUNICATIONS TEAM (especially **MEGAN MILLER**)

• For your continued encouragement, expertise and reassurance •

MEGHAN LEGG, JP WITHAM & IVAN INNES of **HEMLOCK PRINTERS**

• For your endless patience, shared meals, pep talks and coffee breaks •

SHANNON SIMS • KAI DRUZDEL • MATTHEW BARRY • PATRICK GERAGHTY
LYNX DEMUTH & LUNA BRIE • FLORA BOWLEY & JONATHAN WOOD
JENNIFER LOVE, JONATHAN BRINKLEY & LITTLE LUCA

• For your invaluable crowd-funding guidance •

IAN MACKENZIE • KIANA PREMA

• For truly seeing me, long before I could see myself •

KAREN STEPP • LIZ CHINLUND • DAVID SIMON-BAKER • KRISTIN BORELLO
CHRISTY BOCSKAI • YOSHINORI TANAKA • MARGOT LEOM
RYAN MITCHELL • AKIRA CHAN

• For enduring and contributing to the evolution of ***me*** •

NASIMA & RAY BERNHARDT • ABDULRAHMAN LOMAX
ABE & PAIGE LOMAX • MIRM, STEPHEN, SKYLER & AIDEN STEELE
SAUL LOMAX & CORINNE FRANÇOISE A • ZED LOMAX, KELLY MCPEAK & JADE LOMAX
RACHEL, SAM & JOHNNY FIEDLER • LUCIA LOMAX • ASH LOMAX-GONZALES
JESSICA LOMAX • ARIANA LOMAX

• For helping me build the solid foundation of my photographic career •

PATRICK WILSON • GRAHAM & JOSEE WILSON

• TO MY AWESOME KICKSTARTER BACKERS NAMED ON THE FOLLOWING PAGES •

– your generosity brought this book to life...

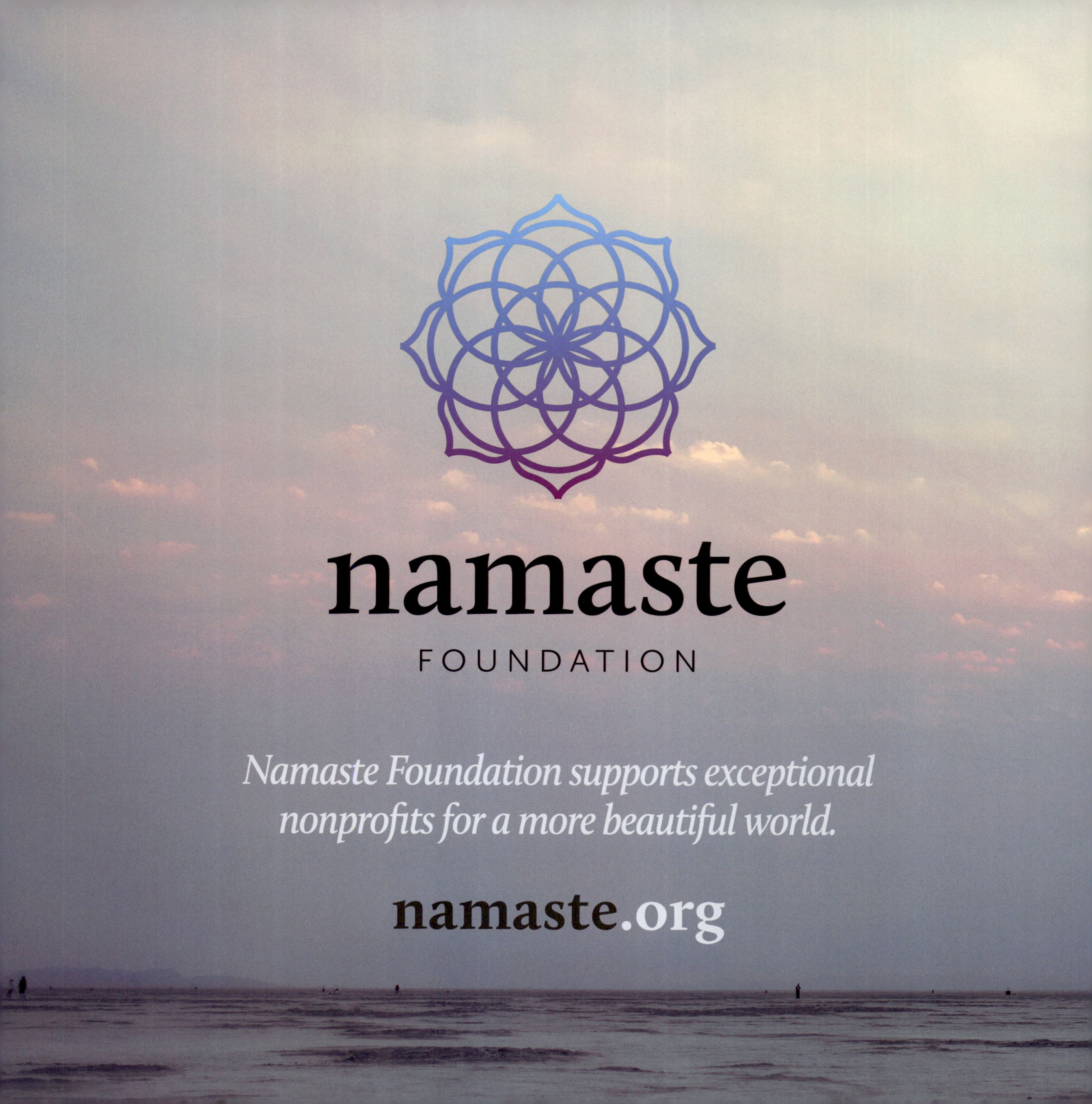
namaste
FOUNDATION
Namaste Foundation supports exceptional nonprofits for a more beautiful world.
namaste.org

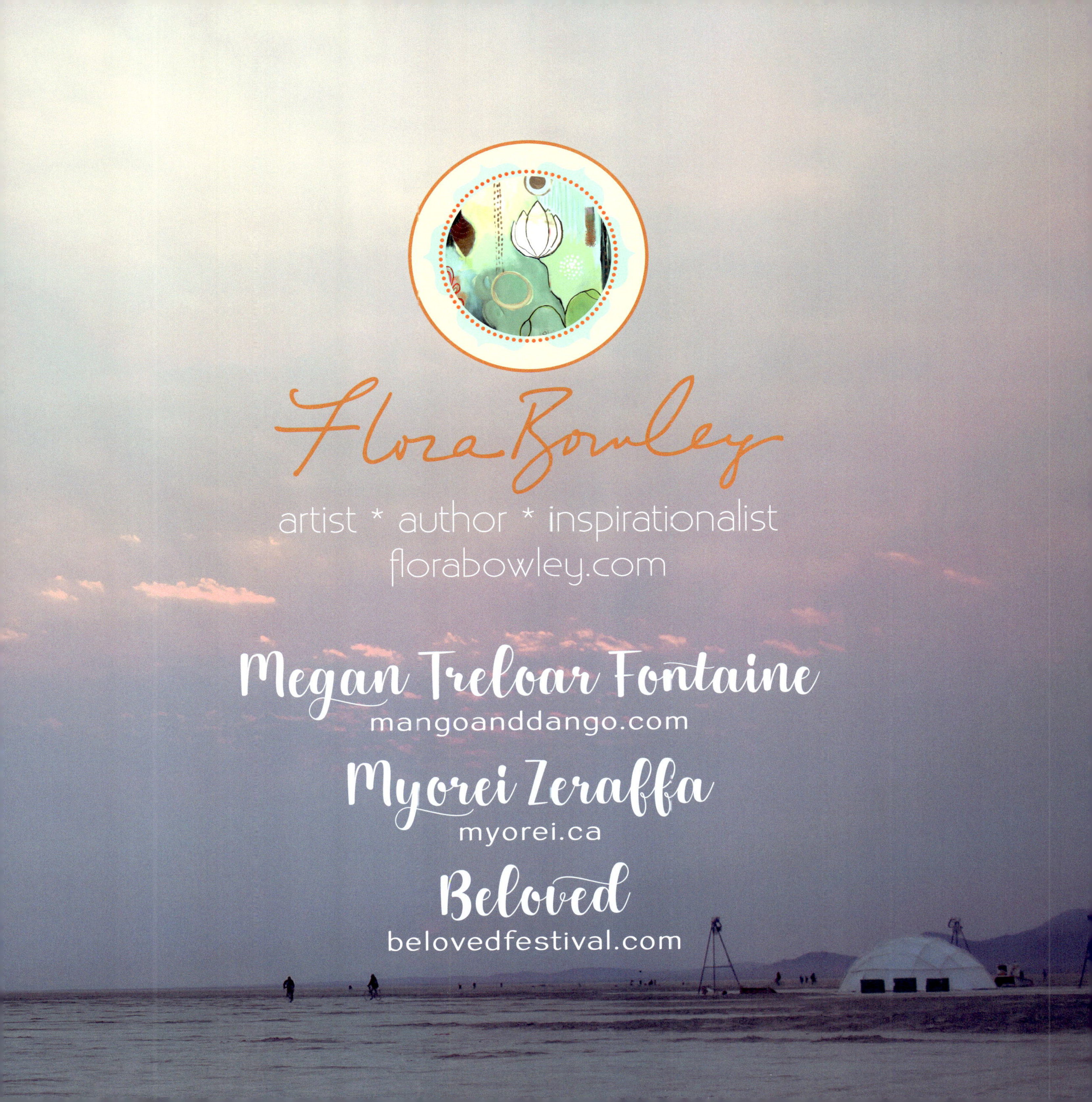
Flora Bowley
artist * author * inspirationalist
florabowley.com
Megan Treloar Fontaine
mangoanddango.com
Myorei Zeraffa
myorei.ca
Beloved
belovedfestival.com

CLAIRE COLAÇO • JOHN KHOURY • TONY.ANCIENT FRIEND
KELLI RUA KLEIN • DEVON AMELIA ~ WILD ABANDON JEWELRY ~´~

ABE & PAIGE LOMAX • CHARLES DIAMOND • GERASIMOS • HUMMERFLY/MARISA • MEGAN MILLER
JANE & JANE'S HUSBAND • JOSHUA LAWRENCE & ARIEL SUTRO • JOAN S. PERRY & CHRISTIAN MILLER

RISING APPALACHIA • LI BAI • KEVIN BATTEY • KRISTINE BATTEY • SEB BONFIRE & SUPAHEIST PETEY • JARED BRYANT • GAIA CONCEPTIONS • ALVIN, ANGIE & DEX • SHARON DIAMOND TAMER EL-SHAKHS • THE RAINBOW FACTORY • JEFF FALK • KAUTZ FAMILY • ROBIN DEL PINO FERRIES DAWN GOSLING • HOBO HAULIE • AMY HD • JENNIFER HOLM • DANIELLE HOOPER • DAVID & KAREN CHAD & KATIE JOINER • LAURENT LATHIEYRE & FAMILY • JEET-KE LEUNG • TARA MARSH HOLLY, BONES, KAI & MAX • MARY MCBRIDE • RYAN 'LITTLEKING' MITCHELL • AMAZING GAGE'S MOM AN INSPIRED MOM • DERRICK PAWLOWSKI • JANET E PLOSS • JENIFER REYNOLDS • BRAD RHADWOOD KELLY RAE ROBERTS • ROBINSUNNE • JEREMIE RODGER • BLAKELY STEIN • ADA SPENCER MICHAEL STEADMAN • MIRM, STEPHEN, SKYLER & AIDEN STEELE • TALLNEIL • CANDACE VERLEE

julietiare • Mark Achbar • William Ching • Buckman Coe • Jon Felix • Rosie Grey • Beth Haase • Jessica Haller • Sophie Cissa Fritzi Herting • Meta Method • Alec Vishal Rouben • Nomad Shev • Katrina Taylor & Christopher LaMarca

@amsterdamant • Alain • Craig Allen • Nicholas Alvarado aka Pumpkin • Rene Alvarez • Tracey Anderson Gail W Armand • Eamon Armstrong • Ali Avalon • Time & Indie Ballard & • Sarah Perry • Matthew Barry Robert Behounek • Juan Carlos Belair • Kristie & Jonathan Berger • David Block • S.G. Luperti Boehm & Family Boots • Chris Boraski • Stephan Bourke • Michelle Nayeli Bouvier • Brian Thomas Bradley • Pat Hansen Brooke Justin Brothers • Nicolai-Ajahni Brown • Darien Benjamin Kenobe Cross, Future Burner • Hilary Cantu Heather Cappelo~Cours • Kerissa Catania (Hemlock Printers) • Akira Chan • Cheeky • Liz Chinlund Jack Aroo Chriss-Donovan • Julie Clay • Edward Clynes • Melissa Iliana Cohen • Eunoia Confused Poppy CosmicLove • Cristina~Rivera • Ryan B Curtis • Randi Cuthbert • Cynthia • Rebecca Danielson Diamond Dave • Brian Davidson • Athena Demos • Will Dempster • McKenzie Dibble • Jean-Philippe Doucet Annie Kelly aka Dragonfly • Kai Druzdel • James Druzdzel • Jordan Easton • Gary Edmonstone • Om EduBen Fahad 'Eid' • Lela Pod Emad • EmSquared • Zac Fabian • Aden Jay Fardell • Sage Ferreira • Risa Fiorini Tammy FireFly • Michael & Elizabeth Flanagan • Gregg Fleishman • Luminous Flux! • Strawberri Fraiz Lovely Freaky • Buttercup, FarmerJohn, Aurora & Sawyer Frugoli • Warren Geisler • Kira & Geoff Patrick Geraghty • Anne Gerzin • Bribe, Lucy, Elo & Gigi • Gignilliat • White Feather & Mojave Glamour Teresa E Gonczy • Thomas D Gottwald, Sr • Jim Graham • David A Greene • Riley Bay Hamilton Greensberg Beth Grundvig • Anna-Lena 'Shama' Gustavsson • Jonah Haas • Halcyon • Adam Hammer George & Jacqueline Hampton • Jonathan Hanley • Jen Hart • Leigh-Anne Hazard • David A. Hedriana II Henk-Jan • HeyHey • Maggie Holley • Kate Hoyle • Holly F. Hudson • Manuel & Ildiko • Arielle & Jamil

Isaac & Jessica • Noëlle Hampton & André Moran • Jarin • Jessie • Camilla Johnson • Lynn Johnson Andrew Jones • Kirk Jorgensen • J9 • Matt Haze Kaftor • Jesse & Ryan Kaltio • Ali Kaukas • Kentucky Kimberlé • Lisa King • Sheree Knickel • Carrie Koester • Reni Kushim • Sharon LaMonica • Beth Laskin Peter Leal • Chelsey Lehl • Margot Leom • Lexicon Colin Liotta • Brian Lipps • Marçal llenas • LoveLee Philip Coldrey Lo • The Londons • Chris, Ariel & Mobius Loop • Victoria Grace Lopez • Alex LordThorsen Kelly Love • Sonia Lub • Brandon Luke • Scruffy, Lydia & Ruth • Celeste D. • Maisel • Goose Manriquez Sarah Marie • Mark Martinez • Mercedes Martinez • Elodie Massa • Massive • Michelle Matisse Riley McCormick • Festival Medical • Maia Mikulenka • Rob Mitchell • Diggable Monkey • Christina Montero Starfire & Moonbeam • Kristine Mooney • Tara Morris • Shannon Morse • Ryan Muckle • Russell T Murray Cameron Neilson • Ellia Nolan • Kristen Northrup • oRbiT • Owl • Lisa Parks • Audrey, Chris & Sidney Pratt of Kidsville! • Mike Pickett • Wesley Wolfbear Pinkham • Twisted • Pixie • Tobin Poppenberg Mia Quagliarello • Sarah Quirino • Sophie de Rakoff • Jahmez Reismiller • Stefanie Renee • Ally Roberton Ed Lizard Rosen • Megan Rubia • Ernest 'Hoodie' Salinas • Shimone Samuel • David Schnack • Chill Sea Ali Shanti • John Felix Shaw • Kyala Shea • Dan 'Corndog' Shick • Antonio Silva • Dave Slater • Ivy Smyth Marc Solondz • Stephanie Gehlen South • Aunty Steph • Robin Tala • Shambrai Todd • Mathew Troy • Annie Vail Marie Chantale & Hélia Vaillancourt • Jaclyn Varty • Jeffrey & Vicki • Giuseppe Vis • Holcombe Waller William Walsh • Josh Wendel • Pat Wheaton • Mark Wieder • Brittany, Worthy & Luna Williams • Jonathan Wood Keith Woodson • Mindful Mimi, Founder of createandconnect.org • Fatty Yuniverse • Daniel Zetterstrom

Susan Adams • Erin Alexandra • Amancala • Skyla & Travis Amazing • Karen Andersen • Tigre Bailando Tom Bassett • Kale Beaudry • Yelena Filipchuk & Serge Beaulieuw • Elynyd Benjamin • Jennifer Bobroff Papa J - Flattery Camp • Stephen Canino • Cristie Chamberland • Paul Chandler • Talya Christbason Gillian Cofsky • Shantala Davis • Lei Lei de Kirby • Pat Deegan • Jesselynn Desmond • John 'Instant Noodle' Early HÄANA • Harlin Emil • Gaby Esensten • Cadence Feeley • Andre Kitty Friemann • Celeste Galrao • Eric Giambrone Torin Gray Goodnight • Rosie Grey • Feather Groves • Harmony Haney • Richard Hartnell • Lydia Harutoonian Holly Hogan-Long • Anastasia Hope • Grace Kaplowitz • KarinAnn • Teresa Koberstein • Mandalyn Kruger Chandra Lebovitz • Zed Lomax • Anjali Magneron • Alexandra 'Ali Ma' Maida • Runa Wilhelmina Marrable Roger McShane • Christina Miglino • Mirra Misko • Bones & Holly Newstead • Cristina Orbe • Dani Palacio Ciel Patenaude • Persepsion • Yishai Potack • Idan Raz • Rachael Rice • Oliver Halsman Rosenberg • Betsy Sandlin Marta Sasinowska • Sean Micheal Eric Scarritt • Geneva Shanti • Tomer Shapira • Shauna • Silverback Brittni Smith • Jessica Smith • Daniel Tenenbaum • Katherine Tetz • Rachel Turiel • Rocco Tyndale • Cara Ucci Alexa <3 Webster • Carly Whitaker-Wilson • Nicholas Williams • Sandi Kovach-Long aka krzylade BRCMA WriteHand

Micheal Alahouzos • Agatha Bacelar • Katrina Bisonette • Cate • Ted Chu • Jess Coe • Sevonne Cohen Maurielle Daudalin • Heather Davies • Sugar Rebecca Day • Judy Delgado • Ari Fararooy • Aimee Flora-Mongroo Jasmine Fuego • Trammell Hudson • Rita Imecs • Todji Kurtzman • Bram Larrick • Scott Lewis • Niema Lightseed Lung Liu • Amy Secada Lopes • Woodburn PTY LTD • Jessica McStaverick • Danny Medoza • Eddy Moretti Tanya Norman • Adrianna Peters • Megan Powell • Amelia Rae • Djamilla Sad Ram • Alexa Rosenthal • Jean-Phillipe Roy Merdeka (Sandra) • Chris Schweizer • Jordan Tal • Vanessa • Tenaya Wieczorek • Jill Wone • Ron Worobec • Stav Zas

thank you!

Dusty Playground
For the Littlest Burners

*Image on page iii provided by Harley Dubois

Photographed, Designed and Published in the United States by Zippy Lomax

Zipporah LLC • PO Box 11175, Portland, OR 97211

zippy@dustyplayground.com

dustyplayground.com

zippylomax.com

First Edition, 2017

Library of Congress Control Number: 2017906475

ISBN: 0-9985794-0-8

The paper used in the production of this book was made from trees grown in independently inspected forests, and certified as meeting the highest standards for environmental, social and economic responsibility.

10 9 8 7 6 5 4 3 2 1

Printed and bound with care in Canada by

Hemlock

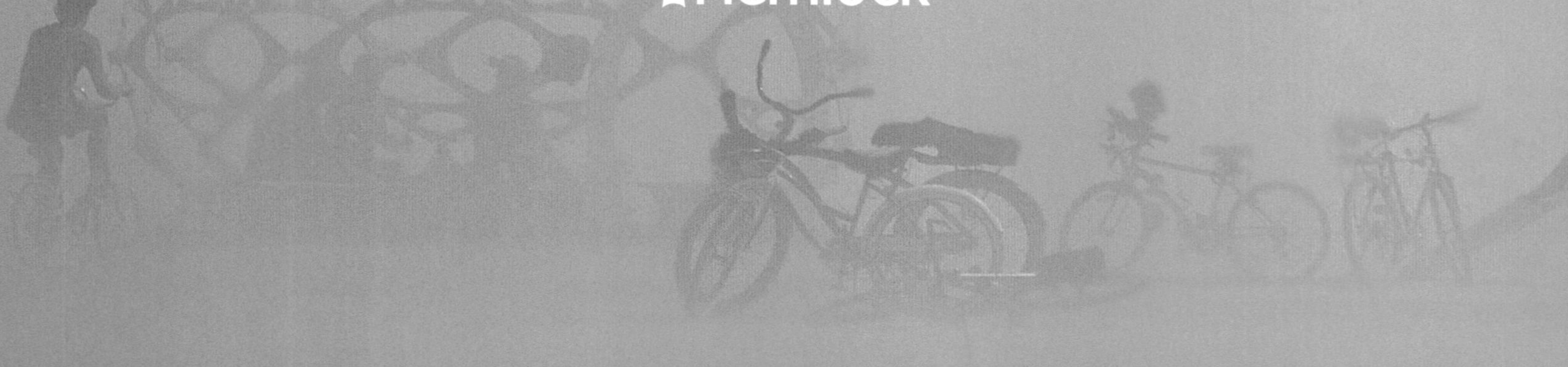

AdSense Unleashed

AdSense A-Z Plus 175 Killer Tips & Tricks

By

G. A. Barger

ADSENSE UNLEASHED
ADSENSE A-Z PLUS 175 KILLER TIPS & TRICKS

First Edition
Manufactured in the United States and/or the United Kingdom
10 9 8 7 6 5 4 3 2 1
ISBN: 978-1-933747-03-3

BottleTreeBooks.com

TABLE OF CONTENTS

I. Introduction

A. Huge Revenue Potential of AdSense

Google is one of the most widely used search engines. Neilsen/Net Ratings recently disclosed that Google accounts for over 45% of all US Internet searches. Google states that its network reaches 80% of all Internet users. It gains 60 million unique viewers per month with over 200 million searches conducted every day. This results in over 8 million searches per hour, 140 thousand searches each minute or over 2000 searches every *second*. In addition, Google has over 400,000 AdWords advertisers that pay Google anywhere from a few cents to fifty or more dollars when someone clicks on their ad. Almost solely from this advertising revenue Google has become one of the fast revenue growth companies. But Google does not keep all its advertising revenue to itself; it is willing to share it with some of the smallest Websites on the Internet. As you know, this program is called "AdSense" and with it AdWords text and Image Ads can be displayed on your own Web pages. The ads are linked to the content on your site. When a user clicks on an ad, Google shares a large percentage of the click revenue with *you*.

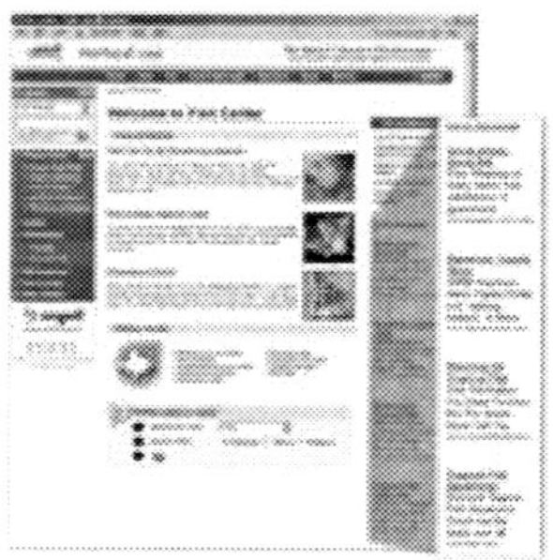

If you are not a Webmaster, you may be nervous about the technicalities of enabling ads on your site, but it is easy to get these ads up and running without a special technical background. Google has created HTML code that you copy and paste to enable AdSense ads on any Website page.

KEEP HTML CODE "AS IS"

Never modify the AdSense HTML code in any way, as this is a violation of the AdSense Terms & Conditions.

You do not even have to select ads. Google searches AdSense Websites and inserts AdWord ads that are tailored to the interests of visitors by the keywords displayed on your site. The potential to increase your Website revenues using Google AdSense is huge. Enabling AdSense will not, however, increase the ranking of your Website in Google search results.

In *AdSense Unleashed* you will learn how to mine the hidden revenue potential of your Website. We will show you what keywords are paying the most, what type of ads get the most clicks, what colors you should use for your ads, and where they should be placed on your Website.

INSERT CODE BETWEEN HTML BODYLINES

Copy and paste the AdSense HTML code between the <Body> tags of your Web page HTML code.

B. AdSense Sign-Up

Best of all, the AdSense sign-up process is easy. You simply input your account information to be an AdSense publisher, get approved by Google within a few working days, insert code on your enabled Web page, and Google will serve you ads that trigger off keywords on your site. You will begin sharing in click revenue immediately. Here is how you begin the sign-up process.

SIGN-UP FOR ADSENSE TODAY

Signing up at www.AdSense.Google.com is easy and it takes only a few minutes. This is done online with no sign-up fees.

How to Contact Google in General
Google Inc. 1600 Amphitheatre Parkway Mountain View, CA 94043 USA Tel: +1 (650) 253 0000 Fax: +1 (650) 618 1499

FREE ADSENSE SUPPORT

Google provides free AdSense support. If you have an issue, just send your question to adsense-support@google.com or adsense-tech@google.com. Google does not offer AdSense telephone support.

II. AdSense for Search

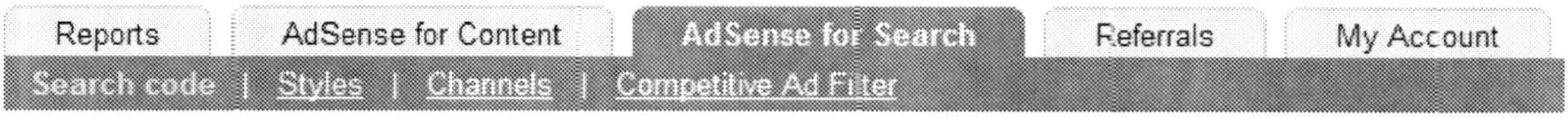

A. Search Box

The AdSense program has main two divisions: AdSense for Search and AdSense for Content. First, we will discuss AdSense for Search. Under AdSense for Search, Google allows you to install, for free, its search technology on your Website in the form of a Google search box. Users can then search the entire Web right from your site! AdWord Text Ads are displayed with the search results on your site. If the user clicks on one of those ads, you will share in the click revenue with Google. The chance of a user clicking on one of these ads is much higher than ads served down the traditional right-hand side of the page. All AdSense for Search ads are placed directly above the search results and because users scan the page from top to bottom, it means the ads receive more attention and more clicks.

NO PAYMENT FOR SEARCHES

> You do not receive AdSense revenue when users search on your site; only when they click on an ad generated from the search results.

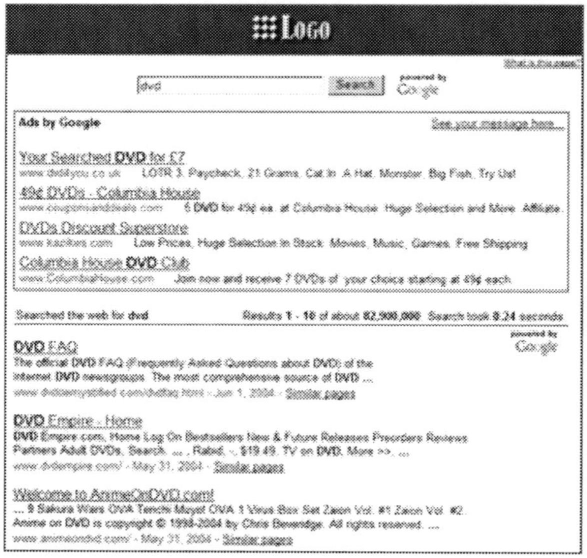

NO IMAGE AD RESULTS

> Google only serves Text Ads above the AdSense for Search results. It does not allow Image Ads to be shown.

With AdSense for search, Google lets you track all aspects of the search results as well as what terms your users are searching on. This occurs within the Reports tab. You can even display the top 25 search terms used on your site within a set time period. A search term must appear at least two times to show up on the list. When you first launch AdSense for search, there will be an initial period when few search terms show up as being popular. How is this beneficial to you? You may find that the content of your site is lacking information that your customers are looking for when visiting. We will discuss the various features and options of the Reports tab below.

BEST LOCATION FOR THE SEARCH BOX

> Most people look for a search box in either the upper right-hand corner or upper middle of the page, so these are the best locations.

Google states that AOL increased its search traffic by 33% using AdSense for search and increased customer satisfaction in the process. AdSense for search really is a win-win situation. Put the power of Google on your Website today and make money in the process!

ADS NOT TRIGGERED ON PAGE CONTENT

Unlike AdSense for Content, AdSense for Search ads are triggered from the particular search terms users input into the search box, not off keyword content on your Website page.

B. Search Languages

AdSense for Search ads can be displayed in twenty-two supported Google languages. Google continues to add new languages on a frequent basis.

Twenty-Two AdSense for Search Languages
Chinese (Simplified)
Chinese (Traditional)
Croatian
Czech
Danish
Dutch
English
Finnish
French
German
Hungarian
Italian
Japanese
Korean
Norwegian
Polish

Portuguese
Russian
Slovak
Spanish
Swedish
Turkish

C. Search Code

One does not have to be technically oriented to create the code needed for the AdSense for Search box. Google generates this HTML code for you and you merely copy and paste it into the HTML code on the Website page where you want your search box displayed.

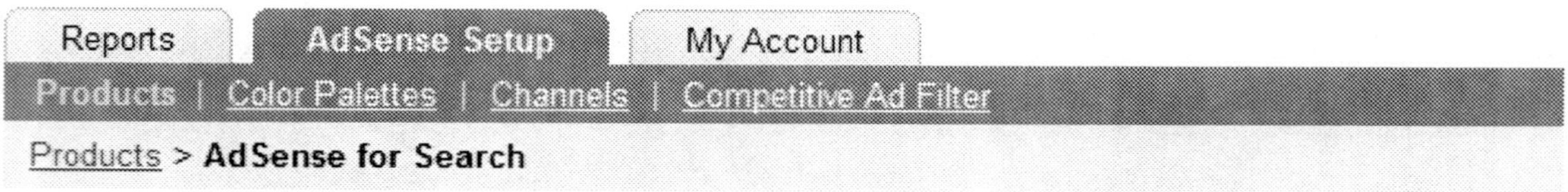

BEST PAGE FOR THE SEARCH BOX

On most Websites the homepage gets the highest traffic. By placing the AdSense search box on your homepage where you get the most traffic, you will not only get the most searches, but also greatly enhance the user experience. This will keep your users coming back for more.

If you do not open a new window when search results are served to your users, you stand the chance of losing a potential customer who may click on the search results and forget about your site. When developing your search code, check the open search results in a new browser box and Google will automatically add the HTML tag for you.

GOOGLE SEARCH CODE MARKINGS

So that you can easily where the Google for Search code begins and ends, Google will insert the following marker line: <!-- SiteSearch Google --> at the top and bottom of the HTML code. This makes it easy for you to find the Google on your HTML code page.

A good implementation practice to employ when placing the AdSense for Search box on your page, is to place the cursor at the spot where you want the box to appear. Many HTML editors such as FrontPage are "What You See is What You Get" (WYSWYG), which means the cursor location will be the insertion point of the search box when you flip to "Code View" and paste in the Java script.

TRICK TO CENTERING THE REFERRALS BUTTON

The AdSense for Search box will automatically be left justified when placed on your Web page even if that blank portion of the page is set to center justification. An easy trick to getting the button centered on the page is to type a few letters of centered text such as ZZZ, place your cursor to the right of the Zs, click over to the "Code" section of your page, and paste the button HTML code into your site. The box will be centered. Now just remove the three Zs from your page.

D. Search Styles

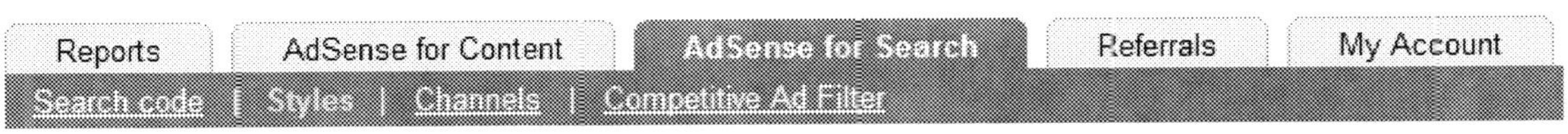

Google lets you customize almost every aspect of the AdSense search box. You can change the text size, font, text color, and background color (200 colors to choose). You can even include your company logo and customize the search button itself. By having the AdSense search box customizable, Google makes it easy for you to blend the search box into the look and feel of your Website. You can even allow users to conduct searches on your site. This will create great functionality to even the most static of Websites. The search box should compliment your site and thereby make searching on your site as seamless as possible. Increased searching means increased ads shown beneath the search results, more clicks on those ads, and more revenue for your site.

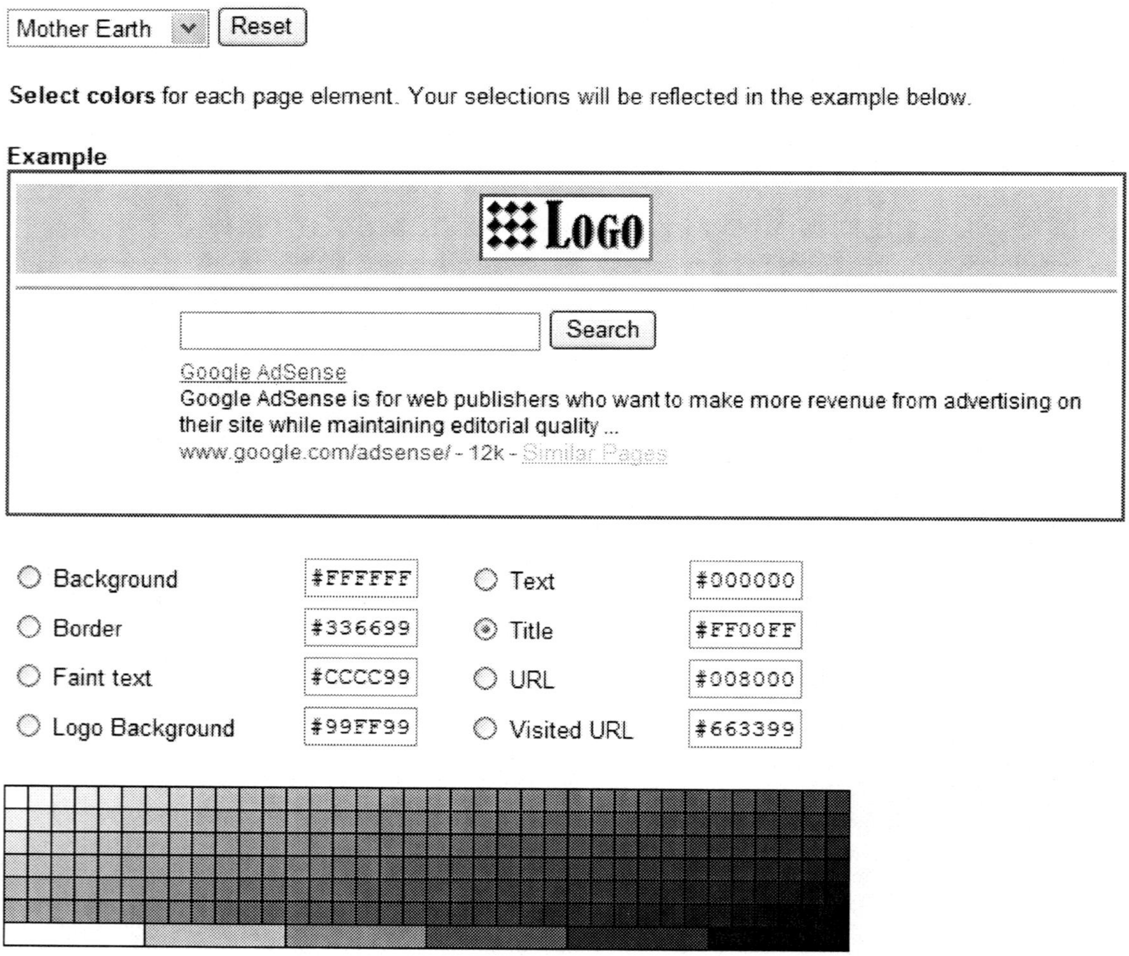

Google has developed a number of color schemes that you can start with when defining your AdSense for Search box colors.

Eleven Pre-designated AdSense for Search Color Schemes
Mother Earth
Blue Sky
Coffee Can
Contemporary
Marine
Mocha Fix
Seafoam
Seventies
Snowcone
Spearmint
Yellowjacket

LESS COLOR SCHEMES THAN ADSENSE FOR CONTENT

At present Google has less than half the number of color schemes within AdSense for Search than it does within AdSense for Content. Mother Earth is the only color scheme they have in common.

1. Search Results Background

Your search results background colors are virtually unlimited in AdSense as are the other various areas of the search box you have color control over. The goal with the background color is to blend it – or even match it – with your Web page background. This has the effect of stitching the search box onto your page and making it an integral part of your Website.

AVOID CLOSELY-RELATED COLORS

Tones that are closely related, for example: yellows-and-greens, reds-and-greens, etc., are "vibrating" colors. The human eye has difficulty distinguishing between the two. This is especially the case for "color blind" Internet users. Avoid use of these vibrating colors to ensure all parts of your ad can be seen clearly.

a. Apply the Four Color Rule

What is often mistakenly called the "Three Color Rule" is actually a guideline for applying background and foreground Web colors. Specifically, the rule states that one background color (preferably pale) should be used in conjunction with only three foreground colors, hence more aptly titled the "Four Color Rule." More than a subtle use of multiple background colors (this includes ad borders) will hamper reading of the foreground colors. The three-color foreground rule of thumb applies to any text within Text Ad Units shown on your site. Colored text, even if it is black or white, will use up one of your targeted three foreground colors.

REMEMBER LOGO COLORS

The color of your company logo will also use up one of your three foreground colors.

b. Universal Browser Color Palette

Various Web browsers may display some colors differently than intended. This can wreck havoc with ads on your site. To be safe, use one of the 216 browser-safe colors. They look the same on *every* browser for *every* color monitor. There is not enough space to display them here, but conduct an Internet search on the "216 browser-safe colors" to display them.

c. Match Background Colors - Microsoft FrontPage

Microsoft FrontPage is one of the most popular Web page design programs.

In *AdSense Unleashed* you will encounter a common theme regarding the blending of various AdSense background colors with background colors on your Website. It becomes difficult with all the color options Google provides to ensure you are matching the background colors exactly. Here is how to find out the precise background color being used on your Web page.

1. Right click on Website background

2. Select "Cell Properties"

3. Under "Background" click on "Color" down arrow

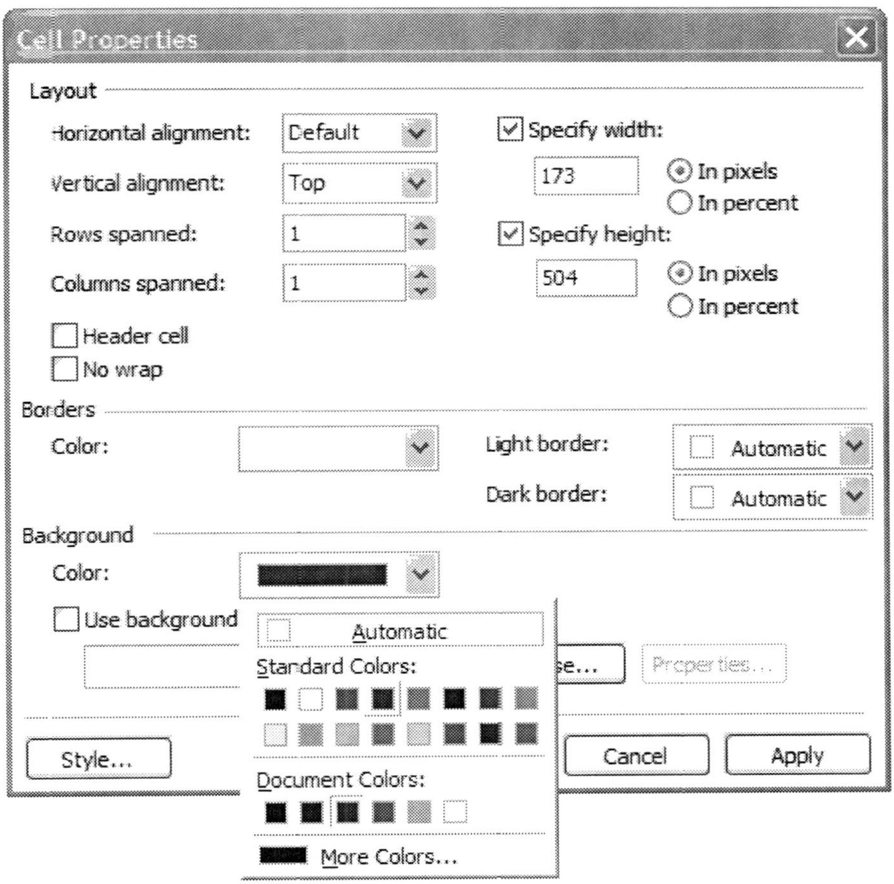

4. Select "More Colors" from drop down menu

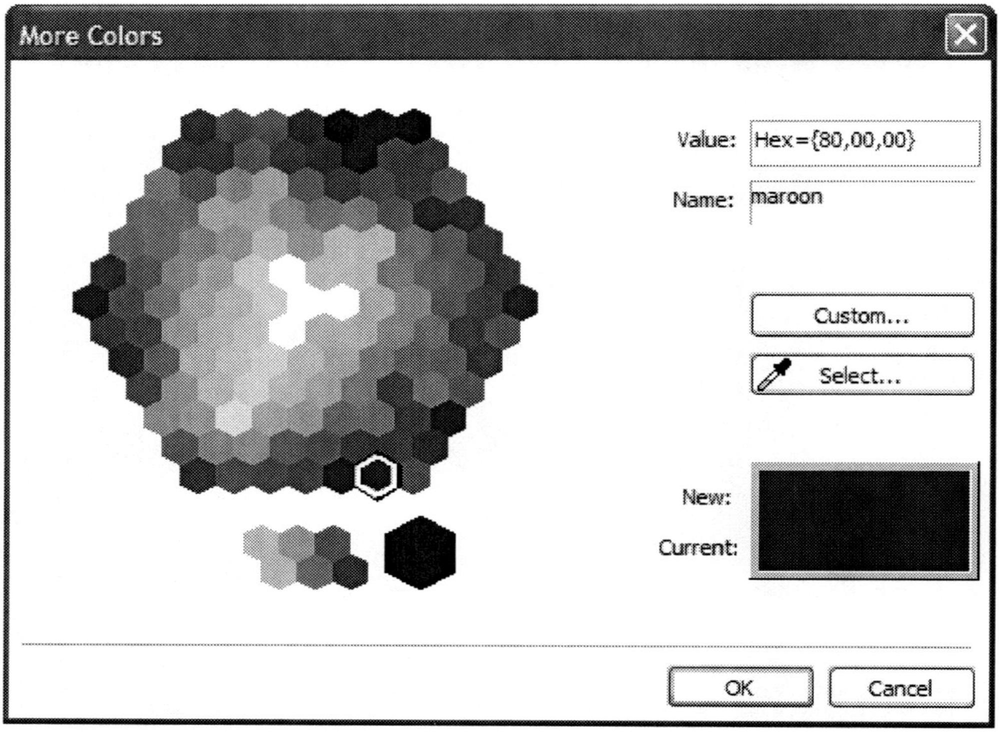

5. Write down hex number in "Value" box

6. Use hex number when setting AdSense background colors

2. Search Results Border

The strategy for the search results border is used in conjunction with the search results background. The quick solution is to make them identical so that the border of the search box window is not detectable by users.

3. Faint Text

Faint text is the text Google displays in the search results that is not as bright as the others such as the "Similar Pages" or "Cached" links. These are secondary information links. Keep this text unobtrusive by making it a lighter hue than the other text above and next to it: URL text color and bodyline text color.

4. Logo Background Color

The logo background color is a misnomer in that the color you pick will surround your logo, but not show *behind* your logo. For branding purposes alone, it is very important that you include your logo. It can be positioned either at the top of the search box or to the left of the search box. It is also a good idea to integrate your URL as part of the logo section. For many startup companies, the company name is the URL. Amazon.com, though not a startup anymore, is an example. The logo background color should blend with your logo colors (if any) and be uniform with any corporate color scheme you may have established. Remember, the logo and associated colors build brand identity, not Website identity. Sometimes, they will be one in the same.

MATCH LOGO BACKGROUND TO SURROUNDING BACKGROUND

> When creating the .jpg, .png or .gif logo for inclusion in AdSense for Search, match the background color to the color you are going to use to surround your logo. This is an impressive way to integrate your logo onto AdSense for Search box and give the logo an embossed look.

a. Logo Placement

Your logo can be positioned in two places relative to the Google search box. The first is above the search box and the second is to the left of the search box. If you have vertical space constraints or are trying to reduce the footprint of the search box on your site, put your logo off to the side. If you do not have space constraints, place your logo above the search box to increase brand recognition.

NO LOGO REQUIRED

Google does not require you to display a logo.

b. Logo Dimensions

The dimensions of your logo must be square and they are further limited by two sizes: 50 X 50 pixels (logos above the search box) or 100 X 100 pixels (logos next to the search box).

Three Logo File Types Accepted

1. .jpg
2. .gif
3. .png

GOOGLE MAY RESIZE YOUR LOGO

Adhere to Google's strict dimension guidelines or Google will resize your logo to make it fit the guidelines.

5. Search Button Background Color

Google gives you the option of including the Google logo, placing the words "Google Search" on the search button itself, and picking the background color for the search button. This is found under the AdSense Setup tab.

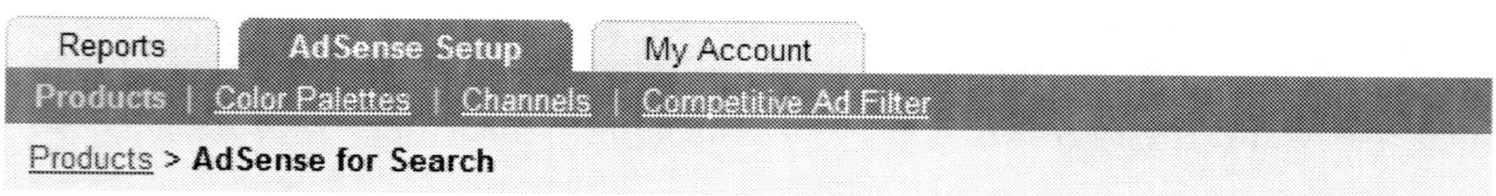

Three Search Button Background Colors

1. White
2. Black
3. Gray

Google also lets you adjust the width of the search box by specifying the number of characters allowed. You can also allow users to search the entire Web or your site within the AdSense for Search product beneath the AdSense setup tab.

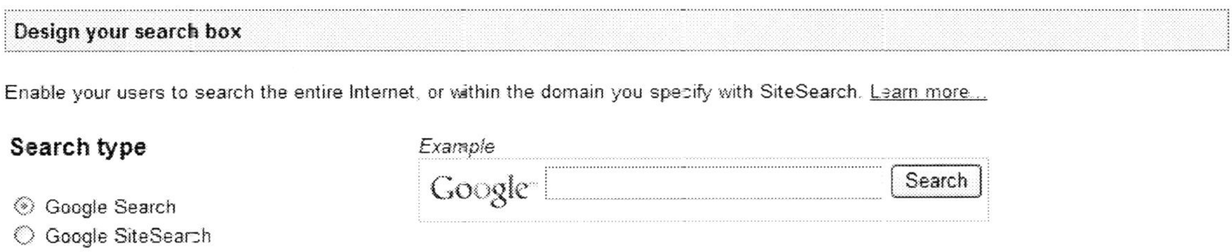

ENABLE SITESEARCH

It is a best practice to enable SiteSearch. Not only does it make your site more user friendly, but it also keeps your users right where you want them. Be mindful that AdSense ads for SiteSearch will be triggered off the search term instead of the content on your site.

6. Search Results Background Color

You typically want the search results background to blend or match with your Website background color. Whatever color you pick, ensure that the search results text is easily readable against the background. As a general rule of thumb, try not to get too flamboyant with the search results background color. Remember the "Four-Color" rule.

SELECT THE SAFESEARCH BUTTON

The majority of AdSense publishers will want to click the SafeSearch button so that adult ads are not shown in the search results on their site.

7. Search Results Text Color

Picking colors for your search results is a contrast in background and foreground hues. Try to match your search results text color to other text on your page. This will give your search results an integrated feel.

TEST DIFFERENT FONT COLORS

Even a small adjustment in font color can have a dramatic effect on your CTR. Channels let you test this. We will discuss channels in great detail below.

8. Search Results Border Color

You typically want the search results border eliminated. To do this, either make it the identical color to your page background or your search results background color. If, however, you have a site that is segmented with multiple content boxes each having borders, match your search results border to the other borders.

AD AND SEARCH RESULT COLORS IDENTICAL

You cannot make the search results and ad text different. They will always be the same. In addition, the search term(s) used will be bolded within both the ads and search results.

9. Visited URL Color

The visited URL color is the color the text will change after your users have clicked on link. It lets them know they have been there and done that. Err on the subtle side. The visited URL color should be of a softer hue than the non-visited URL colors.

MATCH TO FAINT TEXT COLOR

One good option is to make the visited URL color the same as the faint text color.

E. Site-Flavored Search

We have learned that Google lets you tailor the search box and the search results pretty much anyway you please. You can even include your own logo. Now, with Site-Flavored Search, you can incorporate Google's artificial intelligence to learn the underlying theme of your Website. To get started, simply click on the Site-Flavored Search box under the AdSense Setup tab. Once you have customized the other areas of the search and results box, Google then generates the HTML code and you paste it into your HTML Website code. Easy enough.

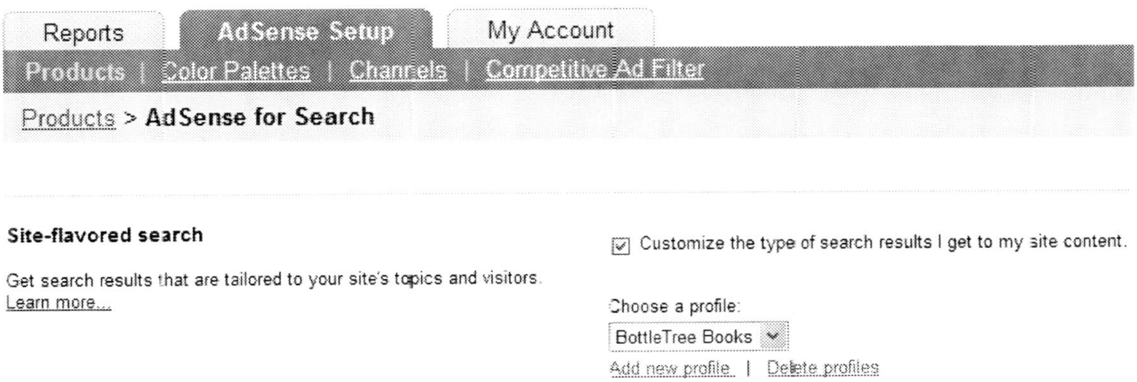

SEARCH RESULTS WILL NOT CHANGE AT FIRST

The Google AI takes time to learn your site. In the beginning you may not see your search results change very much.

Here's how Site-Flavored Search works. Let's say you have a Website that sells digital music. Over time Google's algorithm will learn that when users search for "Fish" on your site they are looking for information about the band Fish instead of what they want for dinner.

F. Search Channels

What are AdSense for Search Channels? They are free ad evaluator tools that tell you full details regarding which size, position, and type of ads are getting you the most AdSense revenue. They also provide invaluable data regarding what terms users are searching on at your Website. Configuration for search Channels is found beneath the AdSense for Search tab.

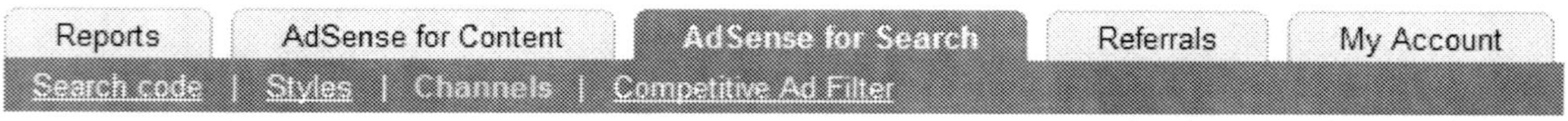

Channels are actually dedicated Google computer algorithms that monitor the AdSense for Search box on your site and give detailed reports. Since location is the name of the game on AdSense, you must find which search box location, background color, text color, etc. will produce the best results.

Four Steps to Channel Tracking Success

1. Create a Channel for *each* search box on your page (you are allowed 2 per page)
2. Include the following in each Channel name:
   - Search results color scheme
   - Search box position
   - Page name (ex, "HomeTopRightMotherEarth")
3. Test the Channels for 2 weeks (for each position and color scheme) and see which has the greatest CTR
4. Use the search box position and color scheme with the highest CTR.

TINY CHANGES, BIG SUCCESS

Even changing something as minor as the search results Title color can have a dramatic effect on your CTR.

G. Search Filters

Google lets you filter ads that you may not want displayed when a search is conducted, such as ads from competitors. Filters are important for a successful AdSense for Search campaign, and they are under used. Just as negative keywords are vital to a successful AdWord campaigns, filters are just as important for AdSense.

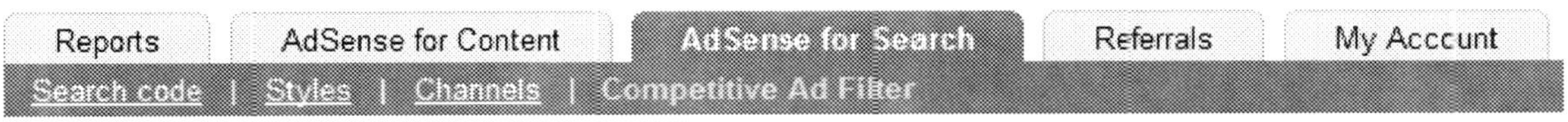

It is problematic that if you are going to participate in the AdSense program, you may receive competitor ads on *your* Website. You run the risk that a competitor's ad may be more compelling than even your content and you may not only lose a sale, but also gain one for your competition while merely sharing in a percentage of the click revenues. Sometimes, you may even filter your competitor's URL and its ads will keep showing. Here are four tips to zap the competition through AdSense filters.

Four Tips to AdSense Filter Success

1. Place competitor URLs in both AdSense Content and Search filters
2. Filter both the destination URL and the URL shown in the ad text
3. When entering the destination URL, drop the "www" and any other data before the name (i.e., just enter Website.com)
4. Your competitor may have multiple URLs so ensure that all

	are filtered out

FILTERING IS NOT INSTANTANEOUS

When setting up a filter so that a competitor cannot advertise on your AdSense-enabled site, it takes about three hours for the filter to begin working.

III. AdSense for Content

AdSense for Content is the most commonly used part of the AdSense program. It is the traditional model where Ad Units are placed at various spots within your Web page so that Google can serve tailored ads in these locations. Your users benefit since they may be alerted to discounts or programs in their areas of interest (i.e., the areas that attracted them to your site in the first place). Google provides the ad layout code that you cut and paste into the HTML code of your Website. This code is found under the AdSense for Content tab.

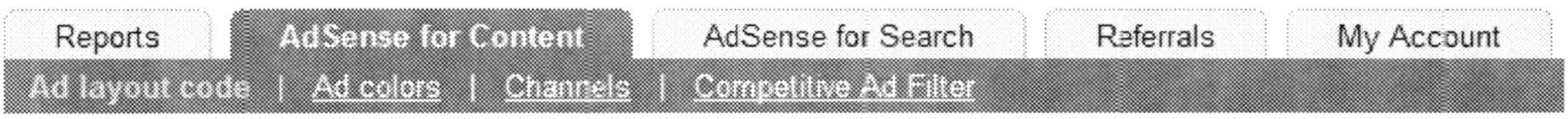

PAGE TITLE AND FIRST SENTENCES IMPORTANT

In determining Website content, Google places high importance on the Title of your page and the first few sentences. Put keywords in bold (<b> HTML tags) and/or in the header HTML tags: h1, h2, . . .). If a certain page is getting low Click-Through-Rates, change the Title to reflect the most important keyword on the page.

A. Cost-Per-Click Model

Okay, how to AdWords bid to serve ads to the Google Content Network? AdWords advertisers bid on certain keywords, which trigger impressions of their ads. When a visitor clicks on one of the AdSense ads, Google shares the revenue with the Website owner; i.e., the CPC, just as it does for book publishers with Google Books. We will explore the percentage Google shares with you below. Amazon.com is a great example of a large Website putting AdSense to work for it.

amazon.com

It commonly displays three advertisements when users search for books and other products. They are listed under the "Customers who are interested in this title may also be interested in:" portion of the results page. Although not an official Google partner (Amazon has it own search engine called A9), Amazon uses Google's AdSense program to increase its revenues. When someone clicks on an ad, Amazon gets additional revenue from Google. What this means for AdWords advertisers is that in addition to having their ads displayed during the 200 million searches conducted on Google each day, their ads can further be displayed on millions of other Websites and AdSense sites, including massive retail Websites such as Amazon.com.

DO NOT CLICK ON YOUR OWN ADSENSE ADS

Clicking on AdSense ads shown on your Website will not generate you revenue since Google tracks IP addresses from where clicks emanate. In fact, this is a violation of Google's AdSense Terms & Conditions and you risk being barred from the program.

B. How CPC Ads Are Ranked on Your Site

The traditional AdWords model of bidding for ad placement was based on the Cost-Per-Click (CPC) model. At first glance it appeared that Google's pay-for-performance system appears to reward those bidding the highest amount with top placement in AdWords. The logic follows that if one advertiser is paying $10 each time a customer searches on "cars" and clicks on its ad, while the next bidder is paying $2.50, the higher bidder should receive top placement. Surprisingly, this is not the case. The number of *clicks* an ad receives on Google is the most important factor to gaining top placement! These are the ads that will bring you the most revenue as an AdSense publisher; not because they pay the most per click, but as result of them getting clicked on the most. In other words, the most popular ads bring you the most revenue.

Ad Rank is the term used to describe ad placement within Ad Units shown on your Website. Google determines this ranking for Cost-Per-Click ads by multiplying the Quality Score by the maximum CPC. This simple mathematical formula is how placement is calculated:

Ad Rank = (QS)(Max. CPC)

What does this mean for you? It means more revenues since only the highest quality, highest paying ads will be served against your content.

1. CPC Optimization Method

The higher an advertiser's Quality Score, the lower they will pay per click no matter how much their maximum CPC. This is the smart advertiser's formula to driving more clicks at less CPC. For the smart advertiser, quality remains the best tool to a lower CPC and higher Ad Ranking on AdWords. Click-Through-Rate (CTR) is the key component of the Quality Score. It therefore follows that when the number of clicks increase, so will the Ad Rank of a particular ad in the Ad Unit on your Website. Ads with a high CTR are the ads making Google the most money and therefore they will also make *you* the most money as an AdSense publisher. The amount of users clicking on an ad is more vital to Ad Unit placement or rank than the maximum amount an advertiser pays Google per click.

In limited circumstances you may have ads placed by Google for its *own* products showing up on your site. Does Google always reserve for itself the top spot? In the test we conducted the answer is NO. A Google advertisement for AdWords was ranked second. Google's ads appear to be under the same rules as all other ads. They must have high Quality Scores to rank first.

For instance, if an ad shows on your site with a maximum CPC of $50 but it only gets one click-through per week, an ad with a CPC of $1 getting 51 click-throughs will rank above the $50 CPC ad. A competitor that is only paying $1 each time a user visits its Website will be placed higher in the

Google ranking system than a company paying $50 for each click! Regardless, you will be the one getting the most revenues by having the most popular ad ranked first.

2. CPC Brute Strength Method

The alternate way of looking at the AdRank formula is the brute strength method. If an AdWords advertiser has a lot of cash to spend on each click, their Quality Score can be lower and they will still rank first since they are making Google the most money with less clicks. Regardless, the top ad being displayed in your Ad Unit will be getting you the most revenue. Period.

C. Cost-Per-Impression Model

Did you know that you can receive money from Google even if no one clicks on the ads shown on your AdSense site? It is called the Cost-Per-Impression model (CPM) and with it AdWord advertisers pay Google to show their ads 1000 times on a Website they designate through Site Targeting. These advertisers pay the same amount no matter how many clicks are received. This works the same way for you as an AdSense publisher. Google will pay you a percentage of the CPM the AdWords advertiser is paying to show ads on your site.

TEXT AND IMAGE CPM ADS

Both Image Ads and Text Ads can be displayed on a CPM basis by AdWords advertisers.

If you have tried the Cost-Per-Click model and are not getting many clicks but lots of traffic, one way to increase revenues is switching to the CPM Model. Better yet, employ both models.

CPC & CPM INCREASE REVENUES

By showing both CPC and CPM ads on your site, you will greatly increase the chances Google has ads in its inventory that will be a fit for content on your site.

1. Site Targeting

a. Introduction

Google's Content Network reaches some of the most visited sites on the Internet—including AdSense sites. Some of your content will attract the very kind of high paying ads you desire for maximum revenue. Other content may attract low-paying ads. Now you no longer have to guess which AdWord ads will show up on your site and advertisers no longer have to hope their ads are shown on sites that will get them the most clicks and ultimate product sales. Enter the powerful tool called "Site Targeting."

ALL CPM ADS ARE SITE TARGETED

CPM ads are Site Targeted only. This means your site will only show these ads if an AdWords advertiser has *selected* your site to show CPM ads. Otherwise, you will be showing all CPC ads on your site.

Site Targeting changes the rules for traditional Google advertising. With Site Targeting, AdWords advertisers can pick the particular AdSense sites on the Content Network where they want their ads to run. *And*, AdSense publishers can now extend an open invitation for advertisers to display impressions of their ads on their site. This is called "Onsite Advertiser Sign-Up" and we discuss it in detail below. The coupling of AdWords advertisers and AdSense publishers is a marriage made in revenue heaven.

WATCH YOUR CLICK REVENUE INCREASE

> The more advertisers jockeying to display ads on your site, the more your click revenues will increase by higher average CPCs.

Here is a chart that will eliminate some of the confusion among Image and Text Ads, CPC ads and CPM ads. Once again, note that CPM are only Site Targeted.

	Image Ads	**Text Ads**	**Expanded Text Ads**
CPC (Content Network)	Yes	Yes	Yes
CPM (Site Targeted)	Yes	Yes	Yes

b. CPM Model of Pricing

To fully understand how Site Targeting can benefit your AdSense site, let's first take a look at this model from the advertiser's perspective. By knowing what tools are available to those advertising on your site and their mindset for getting traffic, you can greatly increase the effectiveness of your AdSense campaign. Fundamental to this review is a unique way that ads are priced using Site Targeting. Under the traditional model, AdWord advertisers pick the *keywords* that will run across the entire Content Network and the associated maximum CPC. Advertisers then only pay when their ad is clicked on and likewise you, the AdSense publisher, only get revenues when an ad is clicked on.

Site Targeting, however, is a Cost-Per-Impression ("CPM") model that is based on 1000 impressions of an AdWords ad. As discussed above, you make money even when ads are not getting clicked on. Each *impression* of an ad now brings in revenue for your Website. If a Site Targeted ad appears on your Website, it means that the advertiser is paying more on a CPM basis than any regular CPC ad with an established Click-Through-Rate. Period. This is great news, but there is a perceived downside in the pricing model Google has established.

PAID FOR ANY CPM IMPRESSION

You do not have to wait until 1000 impressions are shown of an ad on your site to get CPM revenue. If, for example, you only have 10 impressions of a CPM ad, Google will pay you 10/1000 of the ad revenue.

Google has set the minimum CPM to only $0.25 USD. AdWords advertisers on the Content Network can now get 1000 impressions of their ads shown for only $0.25. If an advertiser's CTR is around the normal 1.0% level, this means they will be getting 10 clicks for $.25, which equals $0.025 per click! If the advertiser's CTR is around 5%, they will get 50 clicks per 1000 and have the potential of paying only $0.005 per click (i.e., less than a penny per click).

Minimum CPM	Maximum CPM
$0.25 USD	Unlimited

ADVERTISERS NOT LOCKED INTO 1000 IMPRESSIONS

At any time an AdWords advertiser can stop impressions of its ads on your site before reaching the 1000 impression stage. If this occurs, Google will charge the advertiser on a pro rata basis for the impression that did occur.

A slight downside to Site Targeting is that advertisers dictate which ads will appear on your site, not Google's computer search algorithms. For instance, your site may feature content about mortgages, but you might find ads showing on your site about "Secured Loans." This variation of ads to content may at first appear to result in lower revenue. But remember that Site Targeted ads must outperform CPC ads to replace. The AdWord advertisers targeting your site believe that your Website audience will be interested in their ads. With Site Targeting you are assured to get the highest paying ads and fresh ad content transitioning in and out of your site.

HOW TO BLOCK CPM ADS

If for some reason you do not want certain CPM ads showing on your site, you can block them by adding the ad URL to your AdSense filter. Be aware that the more CPM ads you block, the fewer ads served to your site. This will drop the CPC bids. Less advertisers=Less revenue.

2. All About eCPM

There is an acronym Google likes to use that is closely related to the Cost-Per-Impression model. It has caused some confusion among AdSense publishers and is called "eCPM." This term stands for the "effective Cost-Per-Impressions" of an AdWords ad. It applies to both CPC and CPM ads.

$$eCPM = 1000 \times \frac{Earnings}{Impressions}$$

What this means for you is an easy way to calculate your earnings based upon the number of impressions your ads are receiving and is a way to compare performance of both CPC and CPM ads. For instance, if your CPM ad make $1 per 100 impressions, your eCPM would equal 1000x$0.1 or $100. This means that for every 1000 impressions you receive, you can estimate earnings of $100. Similarly, if a CPC ad pays $1 for each click and the ad receives $15 clicks per 1000 impressions, its eCPM would be $15.

SITE TARGETED ADS CAN ONLY MEAN GREATER REVENUES

It is important to realize that Site Targeted ads compete for placement with normal CPC ads. This means that no matter how low an advertiser's CPM is, it still must have an eCPM greater than the CPC eCPM ad it is replacing on your site. In other words, CPM advertisers must still bid competitively on your site to get top placement.

Below we discuss the often-confusing world of how ad impressions are calculated. For now, know that you can track eCPM in your AdSense reports, which are updated every few minutes, and that eCPM is a great way to determine a run rate for your click revenue. In other words, your eCPM report gives you a snapshot not only of what you are earning on a Cost-Per-Impression basis, but also what you *could* be earning if you were to increase traffic to your site. Think of eCPM as your crystal ball for future click revenues.

Google ensures that ads served to Ad Units on Content Network sites will yield the highest eCMP, regardless of whether they are Image Ads or Text Ads; CPC or CPM ads. If an AdWords advertiser is bidding under the Site Targeted CPM model and this ad is showing on your site, its ad must be earning you more money than the normal CPC ad(s) that it is displacing, which means it will earn you more revenue as an AdSense publisher. You can rest assured that this is always the case with Google's AdSense program.

eCPM ADVANCED REPORTS

Both Content Network and Site Targeted ad revenue can be displayed separately in the AdSense Advanced Reports section.

3. How Google Calculates Ad Impressions

How does Google calculate an impression? Every time a user enters your Website and a particular ad is shown, that is an ad impression. You can have multiple ad impressions per page. An Ad Unit can have up to five Text Ads shown at any time within it, thus resulting in five ad impressions at a time.

Google allows you to display two search boxes, one Link Unit, five Referral Buttons, and up to three Ad Units on any page of your site. If a user views a page with two Ad Units and one Link Unit, Google will record three Ad Unit impressions but only one page impression.

RUN BOTH ADSENSE PROGRAMS

Run both AdSense for search and content on your Website to maximize clicks and AdSense revenue.

D. How CPM Ads Are Ranked on Your Site

The other types of ads that can be shown on your site are based on a Cost-Per-Thousand-Impressions (CPM) model. Here AdWord advertisers pay to have their ads shown 1000 times regardless of the number of times the ad is clicked on. Here, the CPM is the most important factor to gaining top placement! These are the ads that will bring you the most revenue as an AdSense publisher and you get paid regardless of whether the ad is clicked on. What's more, CPM ads can displace CPC ads is they will make you (and hence Google) more money. Regardless, you can always rest assured that the ads Google serves to your AdSense Ad Unit will get you the most revenue.

Google determines the Ad Rank for CPM ads by multiplying the Quality Score by the CPM. This simple mathematical formula is how placement is calculated:

Ad Rank = (QS)(CPM)

What does this mean for you? It means more revenues since only the highest quality, highest paying ads will be served against your content.

1. CPM Optimization Method

The higher an advertiser's Quality Score, the lower they will pay per thousand impressions and still get top ranking. For the smart advertiser, quality remains the best tool to a lower CPM and higher Ad Ranking on AdWords. Unlike CPC ads, Click-Through-Rate (CTR) is not a component of the Quality Score for CPM ads. Ads with a high CPM are the ads making Google the most money and therefore they will also make *you* the most money as an AdSense publisher. They will even displace CPC ads.

For instance, if an ad shows on your site with a maximum CPC of $50 but it only gets one click-through per week, the AdWords advertiser is paying Google $200 a month in advertising fees. If a CPM ad is paying $25 per 1000 impressions on your site and you site serves up 10,000 impressions of the ad, the AdWords advertiser is paying Google $250 a month in advertising fees. This means Google will replace the CPC ad with the CPM ad (assuming the Quality Scores are equal)! Regardless, you will be the one getting the most revenues by having the most popular ad ranked first.

2. CPM Brute Strength Method

The alternate way of looking at the AdRank formula is the brute strength method. If an AdWords advertiser has a lot of cash to spend per 1000 impressions, their Quality Score can be lower and they will still rank first since they are making Google the most money. Regardless, the top ad being displayed in your Ad Unit will be getting you the most revenue.

E. AdSense for Content Languages

You may wonder if AdSense ad languages are limited to English or to the language on your Website. The answer is NO on both accounts. AdSense for Content ads can be displayed in eighteen supported Google languages. AdSense for Content has four less languages than AdSense for search.

These are Croatian, Czech, Slovak, and Traditional Chinese.

Eighteen AdSense Content Languages
Chinese (Simplified)
Danish
Dutch
English
Finnish
French
German
Hungarian
Italian
Japanese
Korean
Norwegian
Polish
Portuguese
Russian
Spanish
Swedish
Turkish

When you establish your AdSense publisher account, you will be asked what is the primary language on your site. Ads will be served in this language regardless of whether you also have content in other languages.

GEOTARGETED LANGUAGES

If you do not select a primary language when creating your account, Google will use geotargeting to serve AdSense ads such that ads are relevant to a particular user's language and local based on the relevant IP address.

Last, you may not show AdSense ads on pages written in languages unsupported by Google. For instance, if your page is written in an unsupported language such as Latin, you may not show AdSense ads since they can only be served in the eighteen languages listed above for the Content Network. Below are all languages supported by Google along with the associated Websites for the various countries. Languages that are supported by either AdSense for Content and AdSense for Search are in bold. The letters [AS] denote the four added languages supported in AdSense for Search. The type of language you pick as your primary will determine the ads that get served on your site by businesses from countries that speak the language.

Countries	Languages	Google Website
Andorra	Catalan	www.google.com/intl/ca/
Anguilla	**English**	www.google.off.ai/
Antigua and Barbuda	**English**	www.google.com.ag/
Argentina	**Spanish** Guarani	www.google.com.ar/ www.google.com/intl/gn/
Armenia	Armenian Kurdish	www.google.com/intl/hy/ www.google.com/intl/ku/
Austria	**German**	www.google.at
Albania & Kosovo	Albanian/Tosk	www.google.com/intl/sq/
Australia	**English**	www.google.com.au/
Azerbaijan & Georgia & Iran & Turkey	Azeri, **Russian** Azerbaijani	www.google.az/ www.google.com/intl/az/
Belgium	**French, Dutch, German, English**	www.google.be/
Belize	**English, Spanish**	www.google.com.bz/
Bangladesh	Bengali	www.google.com/intl/bn/
Belarus	Byelorussian	www.google.com/intl/be/
Bolivia	Spanish	www.google.com.bo/
Bosnia & Herzegovina	Bosnian, Serbian, **Croatian**[AS]	www.google.com/intl/bs/ www.google.com/intl/sr/

		www.google.com/intl/hr/
Brazil	**Portuguese** Guarani	www.google.com.br/ www.google.com/intl/gn/
Burundi	**French**	www.google.bi/
Bulgaria	Bulgarian	www.google.com/intl/bg/
Canada	**French**, **English**	www.google.ca/
Chad	**French**	www.google.td/
Chile	**Spanish**	www.google.cl/
China	**Chinese (Simplified)** **Chinese (Traditional)**[AS] Mongolian Uighur	www.google.com/intl/zh-CN/ www.google.com/intl/zh-TW/ www.google.com/intl/mn/ www.google.com/intl/ug/
Colombia	**Spanish**	www.google.com.co/
Congo (Republic of)	**French**	www.google.cg/
Congo (Democratic Republic of)	**French**	www.google.cd/
Cook Islands	**English**	www.google.co.ck/
Czech Republic	**Czech**[AS]	www.google.com/intl/cs/
Cocos Islands	**English**	www.google.cc/
Costa Rica	**Spanish** **English**	www.google.co.cr/
Cote D'Ivoire	**French**	www.google.ci/
Croatia	**Croatian**[AS] Serbo-Croatian	www.google.com/intl/hr/ www.google.com/intl/sh/
Cuba	**Spanish**	www.google.com.cu/
Denmark	**Danish**, Faroese	www.google.dk/ www.google.com/intl/da/
Djibouti	**French**, Arabic	www.google.dj/
Dominican Republic	**Spanish**	www.google.com.do/
Dubai, Egypt, Iraq, Jordan, Kuwait, Lebanon, Oman, Sudan, Saudi Arabia, Syria, UAE	Arabic	www.google.com/intl/ar/ www.google.com.sa/
Ecuador	**Spanish**	www.google.com.ec/
El Salvador	**Spanish**	www.google.com.sv/
English-Speaking Countries	Pig Latin	www.google.com/intl/xx-piglatin/

Eritrea & Ethiopia (North)	Tigrinya	www.google.com/intl/ti/
Estonia	Estonian	www.google.com/intl/et/
Ethiopia (south)	Amharic	www.google.com/intl/am/
Faeroe Islands	Faroese, **Danish**	www.google.com/intl/fo/ www.google.com/intl/da/
Fiji Islands	**English**	www.google.com.fj/
France -Bretagne -Languedoc Roussillon, Midi-Pyrénées -Basque	**French**, Berrichon -Breton -Occitan -Catalan -Basque	www.google.fr/ www.google.com/intl/br/ www.google.com/intl/oc/ www.google.com/intl/ca/ www.google.com/intl/eu/
Finland	**Finnish** **Swedish**	www.google.fi/ www.google.com/intl/sv/
Gambia	**English**	www.google.gm/
Georgia & Azerbaijan & Iran & Turkey	Georgian	www.google.com/intl/ka/
Germany -Schleswig-Holstein	**German** -Frisian	www.google.de/ www.google.com/intl/fy/
Ghana	Twi	www.google.com/intl/tw/
Gibraltar	**English, Spanish, Italian, Portuguese**	www.google.com.gi/
Greece	Greek	www.google.com/intl/el/ www.google.com.gr/
Greenland	**English, Danish**	www.google.gl/
Guatemala	**Spanish**	www.google.com.gt/
Guam, Saïpan, Oceania	Chamorro	www.google.com/intl/gu/
Guernsey	**French, English**	www.google.co.gg/
Honduras	**Spanish**	www.google.hn/
Hong Kong	**Chinese (Traditional)**[AS]	www.google.com.hk/
Hungary	**Hungarian**	www.google.co.hu/ www.google.com/intl/hu/
Korea	**Korean**	www.google.co.kr/
India	**English** Hindi Kannada Marathi Oriya Punjabi Tamil	www.google.co.in/ www.google.com/intl/hi/ www.google.com/intl/kn/ www.google.com/intl/mr/ www.google.com/intl/or/ www.google.com/intl/pa/ www.google.com/intl/ta/

	Telegu Urdu Bengali (Bengla) Bihari Malayalam Uighur Sindhi	www.google.com/intl/te/ www.google.com/intl/ur/ www.google.com/intl/bn/ www.google.com/intl/ml/ www.google.com/intl/ug/ www.google.com/intl/sd/
Indonesia	Indonesian Bahasa, Indonesian Sudanese	www.google.co.id/ www.google.com/intl/id/ www.google.com/intl/su/
Indonesia-Jawi Island	Javanese	www.google.com/intl/jw/
Iran & Iraq & UAE	Perse (Farsi) Kurdish	www.google.com/intl/fa/ www.google.com/intl/ku/
Ireland	**English** Gaelic Irish	www.google.ie www.google.com/intl/ga/
Iceland	Icelandic	www.google.com/intl/is/
Israel	Hebrew Arabic Yiddish	www.google.co.il/ www.google.com/intl/ar/ www.google.com/intl/yi/
Italy -Piemonte, Liguria, Calabria -Sardinia	**Italian** • Occitan • Catalan	www.google.it/ www.google.com/intl/oc/ www.google.com/intl/ca/
Jamaica	**English**	www.google.com.jm/
Japan	**Japanese**	www.google.co.jp/
Jersey Island	**French**, **English**	www.google.co.je/
Kazakhstan	Kazakh Uighur	www.google.kz/ www.google.com/intl/ug/
Kenya	**English** Kiswahili	www.google.co.ke/ www.google.com/intl/sw/
Kyrgyzstan	Kyrgyz Uighur	www.google.kg/ www.google.com/intl/ky/ www.google.com/intl/ug/
Laos	Laotian	www.google.com/intl/lo/
Latvia	Latvian	www.google.lv/
Lesotho	**English**, Zulu Sesotho	www.google.co.ls/ www.google.com/intl/st/
Libya	Arabic, **Italian**, **English**	www.google.com.ly/
Liechtenstein	**German**	www.google.li/

Lithuania	Lithuanian	www.google.lt/
Luxembourg	**German**	www.google.lu/
Macedonia	Macedonian, Serbian, **Croatian**[AS]	www.google.com/intl/mk/ www.google.com/intl/sr/ www.google.com/intl/hr/
Malaysia	Bahasa Melayu, **English** Bahasa Melayu Tamil Malayalam	www.google.com.my/ www.google.com/intl/ms/ www.google.com/intl/ta/ www.google.com/intl/ml/
Malawi	**English**	www.google.mw/
Malta	Maltese	www.google.com/intl/mt/ www.google.com.mt/
Mauritius	**French, English**	www.google.mu/
Mexico	**Spanish**	www.google.com.mx/
Micronesia	**English**	www.google.fm/
Mongolia	Mongolian	www.google.com/intl/mn/ www.google.mn/
Montserrat	**English**	www.google.ms/
Mozambique	Zulu, **Portuguese**	www.google.com/intl/pt/ www.google.com/intl/zu/
Namibia	**English**, Afrikaans	www.google.com.na/
Nepal	Nepali	www.google.com/intl/ne/ www.google.com.np/
Netherlands -Friesland	**Dutch** -Frisian	www.google.nl/ www.google.com/intl/fy/
New Zealand	**English**	www.google.co.nz/
Nicaragua	**Spanish**	www.google.com.ni/
Norfolk	**English**	www.google.com.nf/
Norway	**Norwegian** Norwegian (Bokmål) Norwegian (Nynorsk)	www.google.no/ www.google.com/intl/no/ www.google.com/intl/nn/
Pakistan	Punjabi Sindhi Uighur	www.google.com.pk/ www.google.com/intl/sd/ www.google.com/intl/ug/
Panama	**Spanish, English**	www.google.com.pa/
Paraguay	**Spanish** Guarani	www.google.com.py/ www.google.com/intl/gn/
Peru	**Spanish**	www.google.com.pe/

Philippines	Filipino Tagalog	www.google.com.ph/ www.google.com/intl/tl/
Pitcairn (Islands)	**English**	www.google.pn/
Poland & Lithuania	**Polish**	www.google.pl/
Portugal & Angola & Brazil & Mozambique	**Portuguese**	www.google.com/intl/pt/
Puerto Rico	**Spanish**	www.google.com.pr/
Roman Empire	Latina	www.google.com/intl/la/
Romania & Moldova	Romanian, **German**, **Hungarian**	www.google.ro/ www.google.com/intl/ro/
Russia	**Russian**	www.google.com.ru/ www.google.com/intl/ru/
Rwanda	**French**, Swahili, **English**	www.google.rw/
Saint Helena	**English**	www.google.sh/
Saint Vincent and the Grenadines	**English**	www.google.com.vc/
Samoa	**English**	www.google.as/
San-Marino	**Italian**	www.google.sm/
Scotland	**English**, Scots Gaelic	www.google.com/intl/gd/
Seychelles	**French**, **English**	www.google.sc/
Serbia	Serbian Serbo-Croatian	www.google.com/intl/sr/ www.google.com/intl/sh/
Singapore	Tamoul Malay Bahasa	www.google.com.sg/ www.google.com/intl/ta/ www.google.com/intl/ms/
Slovakia	**Slovak**[AS], **Hungarian**	www.google.sk/ www.google.com/intl/sk/
Slovenia	Slovenian	www.google.com/intl/sl/
Somalia	Somalia	www.google.com/intl/so/
South Africa	**English** Afrikaans Xhosa Zulu Sesotho	www.google.co.za/ www.google.com/intl/af/ www.google.com/intl/xh/ www.google.com/intl/zu/ www.google.com/intl/st/

Spain -Basque Country -Cataluna -Galicia -Val D'Aran	**Spanish**, Basque, Catalan, Galician, • Basque • Catalan • Galician • Occitan	www.google.es/ www.google.com/intl/es/ www.google.com/intl/eu/ www.google.com/intl/ca/ www.google.com/intl/gl/ www.google.com/intl/oc/
Sweden	**Swedish**	www.google.se/ www.google.com/intl/sv/
Sri Lanka	Tamil Sinhalese	www.google.com/intl/ta/ www.google.com/intl/si/
Switzerland	**German, Italian,** Romanche	www.google.ch/ www.google.com/intl/rm/
Taiwan	**Chinese (Traditional)**[AS]	www.google.com.tw/
Tajikistan	**English**, Tajik	www.google.com.tj/
Tanzania	Kiswahili	www.google.com/intl/sw/
Thailand, Vietnam	Thai	www.google.com/intl/th/ www.google.co.th/
Tonga	**English**	www.google.to/
Trinidad and Tobago	**English, French, Spanish, Chinese (Traditional)**[AS]**, Chinese (Simplified)**	www.google.tt/
Turkey	**Turkish** Kurdish Uighur	www.google.com/intl/tr/ www.google.com.tr/ www.google.com/intl/ku/ www.google.com/intl/ug/
Turkmenistan	Turkmen	www.google.com/intl/tk/ www.google.tm/
Uganda	**English**	www.google.co.ug/
Ukraine	Ukrainian	www.google.com/intl/uk/ www.google.com.ua/
United Arab Emirates	Arabic	www.google.ae/
United States of America	**English** **Spanish**	www.google.com/ www.google.com/intl/es/
Uruguay	**Spanish**	www.google.com.uy/
Uzbekistan & Afghanistan & Kazakhstan & Tajikistan & Turkmenistan	Uzbek Uighur	www.google.com/intl/uz/ www.google.uz/ www.google.com/intl/ug/
United Kingdom	**English**	www.google.co.uk/

	Scots Gaelic Gaelic Irish Welsh	www.google.com/intl/gd/ www.google.com/intl/ga/ www.google.com/intl/cy/
Ukraine	Ukrainian	www.google.com/intl/uk/ www.google.com.ua/
Vietnam & Cambodia & Laos	Vietnamese, **French, Chinese (Traditional)**[AS]	www.google.com.vn/ www.google.com/intl/vi/
Virgin Islands	**English**	www.google.vg/ www.google.co.vi/
Wales	Welsh	www.google.com/intl/cy/
World	Interlingua Esperanto	www.google.com/intl/ia/ www.google.com/intl/eo/
Yugoslavia	Serbian, Montenegrin, Albanian, **Hungarian, Slovak**[AS], Romanian, Serbo-Croatian	www.google.com/intl/sr/ www.google.com/intl/sq/ www.google.com/intl/hu/ www.google.com/intl/sk/ www.google.com/intl/ro/ www.google.com/intl/sh/

F. AdSense for Content Code

One does not have to be technically oriented to create the code needed to display AdSense for Content ads on your site. Google generates this HTML code for you and you merely copy and paste it into the HTML code on the Website page where you want your ads to appear.

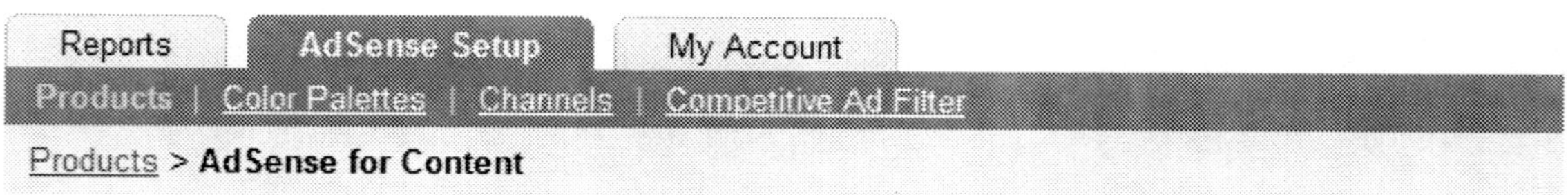

BEST PAGE FOR AD UNITS

On most Websites the homepage gets the highest traffic. By placing the AdSense Ad Units on your homepage (assuming it gets the most traffic), you will not only get the most clicks, but also enhance the user experience. This will keep your users coming back for more.

The AdSense for Content code is actually Java script that you paste into the HTML code of your particular Website page. It must be inserted between the <Body> tags of the HTML code to be operational. A good implementation practice for you to employ when placing Ad Units on your page is to place the cursor at the spot where you want your first Ad Unit to appear. Many HTML editors such as FrontPage are "What You See is What You Get" (WYSWYG), which means the cursor point will be the insertion point of the Ad Unit when you flip to "Code View" and paste in the Java script.

SECTION OFF YOUR ADSENSE FOR CONTENT CODE

Unlike the AdSense for Search code, Google does not section off the AdSense for Content code by a marker, which makes the code difficult to find if you want to move the Java script when you are moving Ad Units around on the page. Use the following marker line: <!-- Google Content Ad Unit# --> at the top and bottom of the HTML code. Where the # will be the actual number of the Ad Unit on the page. For example: <!-- Google Content Ad Unit2 -->.

A good implementation practice to employ when placing the AdSense for Content Ad Units on your page, is to place the cursor at the spot where you want the first Ad Unit to appear. Many HTML editors such as FrontPage are "What You See is What You Get" (WYSWYG), which means the cursor location will be the insertion point of the Ad Unit when you flip to "Code View" and paste in the Java script.

TRICK TO CENTERING YOUR AD UNITS

The Ad Unit will automatically be left justified when placed on your Web page even if that blank portion of the page is set to center justification. An easy trick to getting the Ad Unit centered on the page is to type a few letters of centered text such as ZZZ, place your cursor to the right of the Zs, click over to the "Code" section of your page, and paste the HTML code into your site. The Ad Unit will be centered. Now just remove the three Zs from your page.

G. Ad Format Colors and Text

Google offers many different shapes and sizes of ads that can be displayed on your AdSense site. Add to the mix that they can be text or Image Ads, CPC or CPM, and you have a lot of variety.

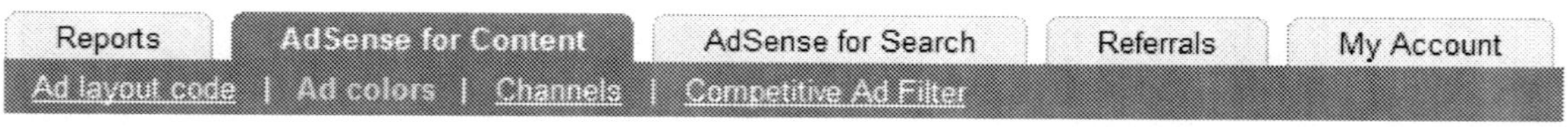

1. AdSense for Content Ad Color Schemes

The colors you pick for your AdSense ads are vitally important to the number of clicks you will receive on those ads. The color options are found under the AdSense for Content tab. Ad Units should enhance your site instead of detract from it. This is accomplished by blending ad font and background colors with the look-and-feel of your site. Google provides a huge number of options for your Ad Unit color choices.

Twenty-Six Pre-designated AdSense for Content Color Schemes
Mother Earth
Black & Blue
Fresh Mint
Cut Grass
Raspberry Smoothie
Vanilla Cream
Green Taffy
It's a Girl!
Aquadoodle
Popcorn
Blue Whale
Cumulous Cloud
Blue Bird
Peach Melba
Wicked Witch
Swamp Green
Grape Skin
Melancholy Blue
Steely Gaze
Black Knight
Robin's Egg
Green Tea
Blue Suey
Pot Roast

Google allows you to create up to 100 custom colors for the ads displayed on your site apart from the 26 listed above. You can go with one of the twenty-six pre-designated color schemes or use one as your base to create a launching pad for a custom color scheme. Within the "AdSense for Content" tab, if you click on "manage colors" under "Ad Layout Code" selection, or select "Ad Colors" you can pick from the following color palette. First, however, you must select a base color scheme as your starting point.

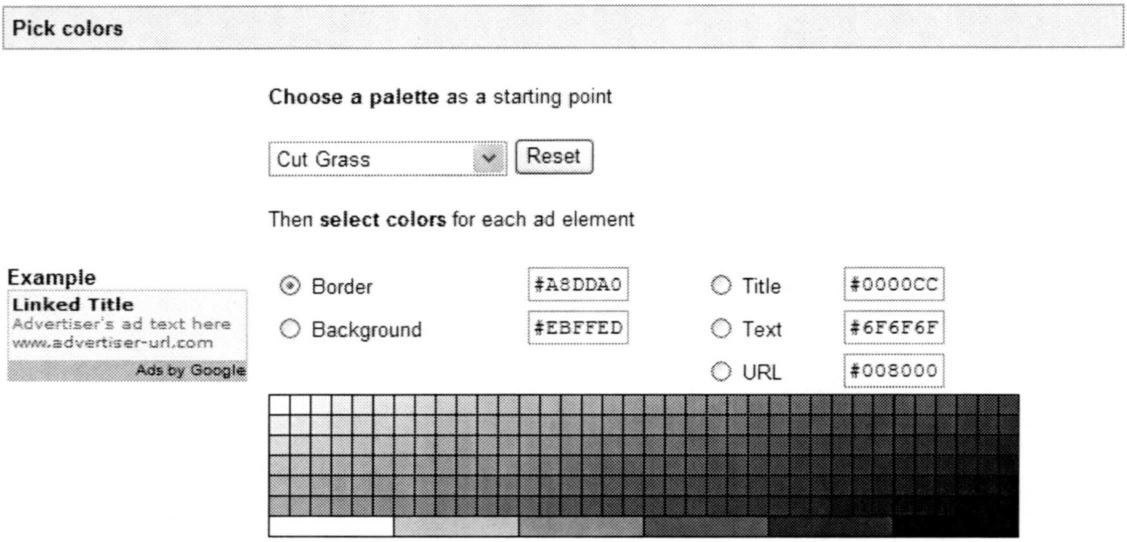

CREATE CUSTOM AD COLORS

> The majority of times your Website colors will not exactly match Google's pre-set colors listed above. To ensure proper blending, use custom colors so that your ad colors match your site colors. As a helpful shortcut trick, hold down the Ctrl key when choosing to select up to four color palettes.

Be sure to set your browser to allow both cookies and JavaScript or you may be unable to save your custom color palettes. If you have both enabled and are still unable to save your custom color palettes, your browser's cache may be full. Clear your browser cache and delete all cookies before trying to save your color palettes again. Under the "Tools" tab in Internet Explorer select "Internet Options" and click on the "Delete Cookies" button.

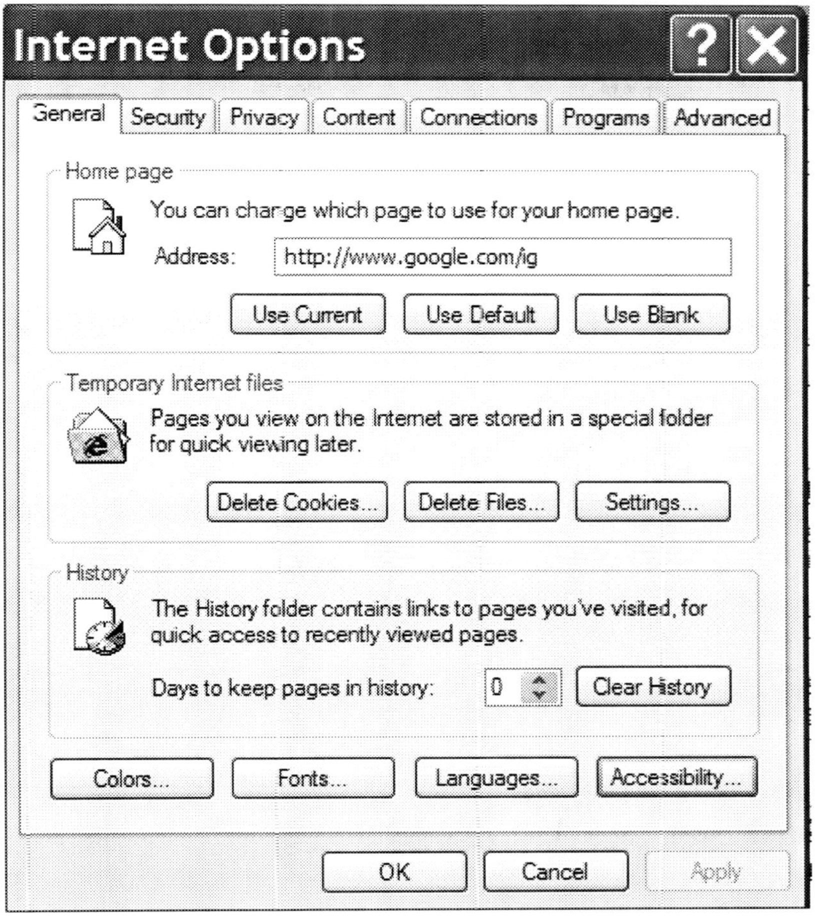

MORE COLOR SCHEMES THAN ADSENSE FOR SEARCH

At present Google has more than double the number of color schemes within AdSense for Content than it does within AdSense for Search. Mother Earth is the only color scheme they have in common.

2. Ad Background

Your Ad Unit background colors are virtually unlimited in AdSense as are the other various areas of the Ad Unit you have color control over. At first it would appear that you should make the AdSense for Content background colors flamboyant so they standout on the page and draw attention to the ads. This has been shown time and time again to be the wrong approach with clicks dropping by up to 65%. Ads where the background color matches the Website page color get more clicks. Period.

> AdWords A-Z Book
> + 150 Guerrilla Tactics Only $14.98.
> www.bottletreebooks.com/GuerrillaTactics.htm

Background

The goal with the background color is to blend it – or even match it – with your Web page background. This has the effect of stitching the Ad Unit onto your page and making it an integral part of your Website.

AVOID CLOSELY-RELATED COLORS

> Tones that are closely related, for example: yellows-and-greens, reds-and-greens, etc., are "vibrating" colors. The human eye has difficulty distinguishing between the two. This is especially the case for "color blind" Internet users. Avoid use of these vibrating colors to ensure all parts of your ad can be seen clearly.

AdSense ad colors should blend with the site, which means the background color for each ad should generally be a similar color hue (avoiding vibrating colors). This also includes any Link Units you might employ. Using a light background color with dark text is preferred. This way the text jumps off the page at searchers. This is the same technique Web designers use. The title of your ads should jump out at users to draw attention to the ads and provide further clarification to users that it is an ad they are viewing instead of content.

a. Apply the Four Color Rule

What is often mistakenly called the "Three Color Rule" is actually a guideline for applying background and foreground Web colors. Specifically, the rule states that one background color (preferably pale) should be used in conjunction with only three foreground colors, hence more aptly titled the "Four Color Rule."

AVOID AD BLINDNESS

> So called "ad blindness" occurs when ads stand out so much that users of your site identify them as such and do not pay attention to them.

We are all familiar with those flashing banner ads that do everything but leap off the computer screen and bite you in the nose to get your attention. And we are equally aware at what a turn off those ads are. Not only do they drive users away from clicking on them, they actually compel you to jump pages so that they no longer flash in your eyes. Google does not allow these types of Image Ads, by the way. Your AdSense background colors should be an extension of your site and the ads should stand out slightly while still complementing your site colors such as beige/tan.

CHANGE IMAGE AD BORDER COLORS IF NEEDED

> As an AdSense participant you can change the border colors of Image Ads shown on your site. Change them to blend in with your site.

More than a subtle use of multiple background colors (this includes ad borders) will hamper reading of the foreground colors. The three-color foreground rule of thumb applies to any text within Text Ad Units shown on your site. Colored text, even if it is black or white, will use up one of your targeted three foreground colors.

b. Universal Browser Color Palette

Various Web browsers may display some colors differently than intended. This can wreck havoc with ads on your site. To be safe, use one of the 216 browser-safe colors. They look the same on *every* browser for *every* color monitor. There is not enough space to display them here, but conduct an Internet search on the "216 browser-safe colors" to display them.

ROTATE AD COLORS

Always eating the same leftovers gets old and so does viewing the same ad colors on a page. Once in a while you should rotate ad colors on your site to keep ads looking fresh, new and exciting. Simply depress the Control key (Ctrl) when generating HTML ad code and select up to four color palettes in the ad layout code of your AdSense account. Another great way to keep your ads fresh is to alternate between text and Image Ads. This will help lessen "ad block" on your page.

c. Match Background Colors - Microsoft FrontPage

Microsoft FrontPage is one of the most popular Web page design programs. In *AdSense Unleashed* you will encounter a common theme regarding the blending of various AdSense background colors with background colors on your Website. It becomes difficult with all the color options Google provides to ensure you are matching the background colors exactly. Here is how to find out the precise background color being used on your Web page.

1. Right click on Website background

2. Select "Cell Properties"

3. Under "Background" click on "Color" down arrow

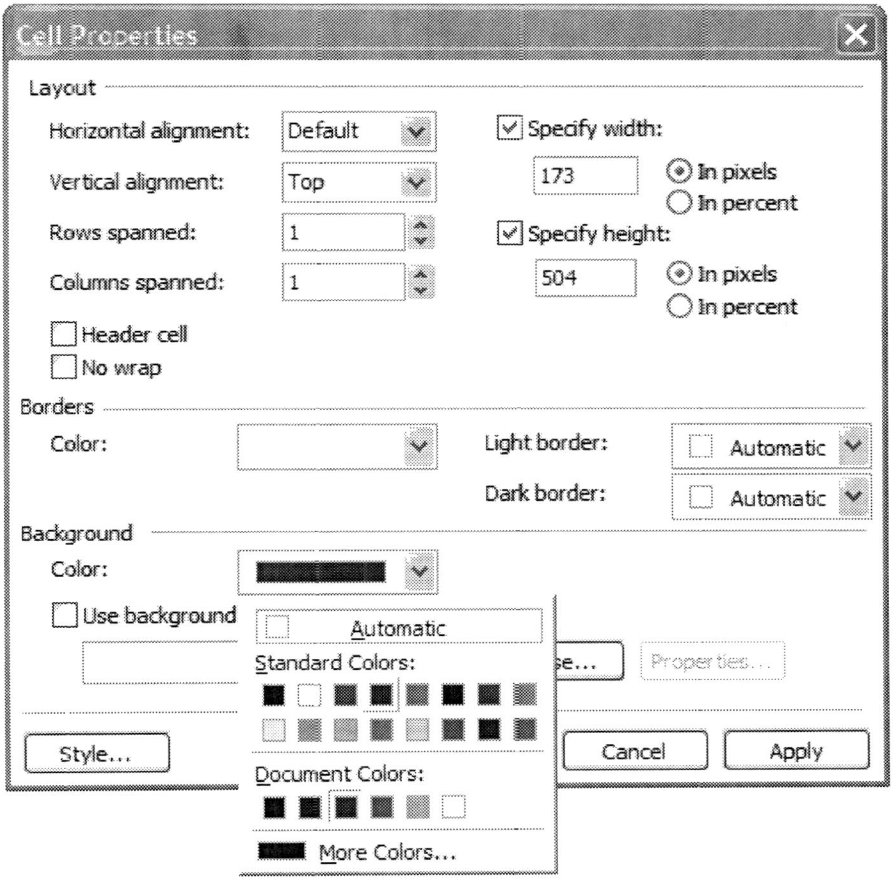

4. Select "More Colors" from drop down menu

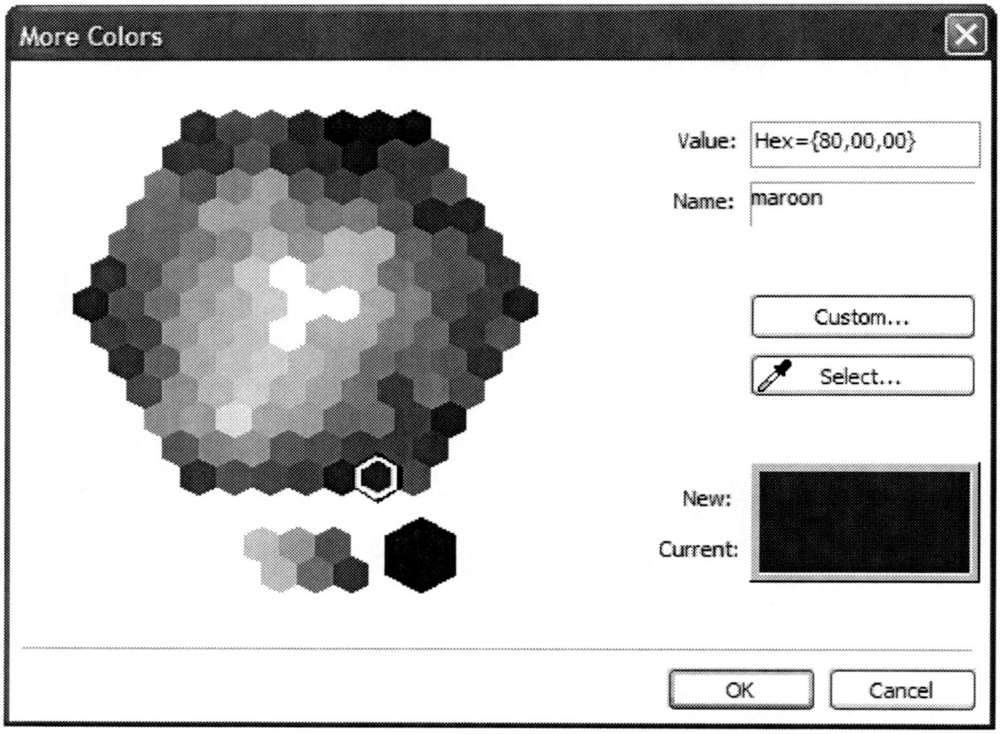

5. Write down hex number in "Value" box

6. Use hex number when setting AdSense background colors

3. Ad Border

Google even lets you decide if you want a border to surround your AdSense ads. On "busy" content sites, borders are recommended to block off ads, but in most cases borders do little to help with clicks. You cannot remove borders for Image Ads. Text Ads are the most popular ones that are used with surrounding borders.

The strategy for the Ad Unit border color is to match it or blend it with the background. The quick solution is to make them identical so that the border of the Ad Unit is not detectable by users. Blondes have more fun and Ad Units without borders gets more clicks!

Border

AdWords A-Z Book
+ 150 Guerrilla Tactics Only $14.98.
www.bottletreebooks.com/GuerrillaTactics.htm

Alternatively, if you have a Website with segmented boxes and rectangles that define certain areas such as articles, navigation, affiliations, and industry links, create an ad border that matches the other page borders.

BORDERLESS ADS GET MORE CLICKS

It has been shown that ads without borders get more clicks on the AdSense Content Network than those with borders.

4. Ad Titles

The color of the AdWord ad Titles shown in your Ad Units is very important. These are the first part of the ad users see and read. If it stands out, you are likely to get more clicks. You can also match it to other Title text on your page to give the ads an integrated feel.

Title

AdWords A-Z Book
+ 150 Guerrilla Tactics Only $14.98.
www.bottletreebooks.com/GuerrillaTactics.htm

5. Ad Text

Ad text (font and size) can both be adjusted by you, the AdSense publisher. Just as with ad colors, you should match the font and size to that of your Website to blend the ads even more.

YOU CANNOT ADJUST IMAGE AD TEXT

Remember that you can only adjust the text font and size for text and Link Units. This does not apply to Image Ads, which makes them difficult to blend into your site.

Also be sure to make the URL text color of the ad the same color as the other text of the ad to make it appear obvious.
Picking colors for the ad text is a contrast in background and foreground hues. Do not get too fancy here. You want users to easily read the Bodylines of the ads. Try to match your ad text color to other text on your page. This will give your search results an integrated feel. Remember, Titles draw users' attention to the ads and the Bodylines deliver the heart of the advertising message.

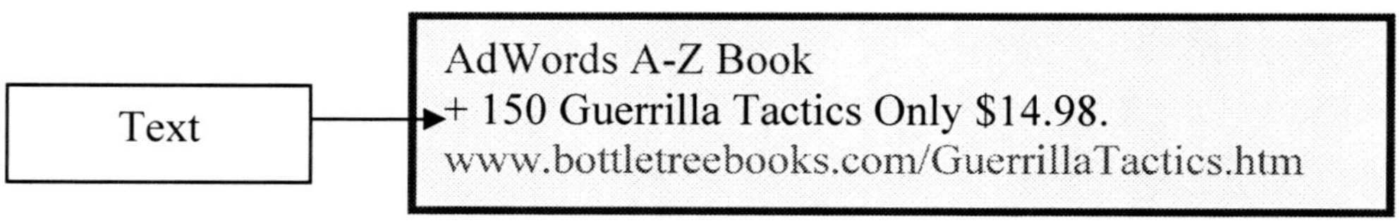

TEST DIFFERENT FONT COLORS

Even a small adjustment in font color can have a dramatic effect on your CTR. Channels let you test this. We will discuss AdSense for Content channels in great detail below.

6. Ad URL

The URL color is of least importance in the ad. Err on the subtle side. The URL color should be of a softer hue than the other ad colors. This also makes the ad seem less like an advertisement.

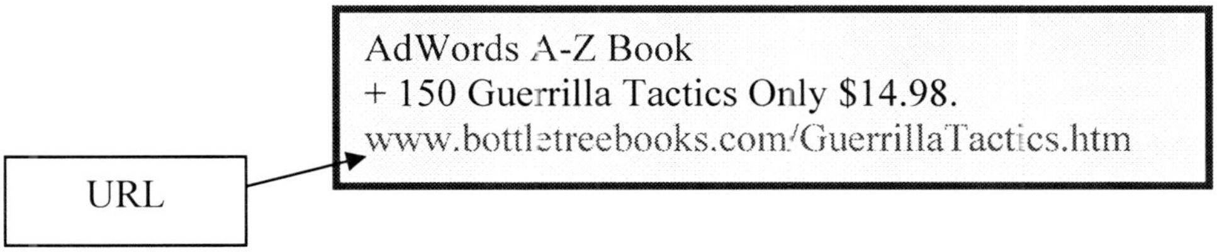

It may seem that to reach the goal of making ads blend in with your Website that you should make the URL color in the Ad Unit the same as the background color of your site. Google will not let this happen. Within your AdSense account you will see the URL colors change to your background color, but Google will switch them to black for display on your site. Now, the question remains as to what Google will do (if anything) if your background color is black and you change your URL color to black? We know that Google's default URL color is also black.

DO YOU WANT LINKING URLS DISPLAYED?

Link Units and the Leaderboard, Banner, and Half Banner Text Ads are the *only* AdSense ads where an ad URL is not displayed on your site.

Here is a comparison chart that will help you match various colors on a typical Website to their corresponding ad colors.

Website Colors	**Ad Match Colors**
Background	Ad Background
Border	Ad Border or Ad Titles
Text	Ad Titles and/or Ad Text
Underlines	Ad Title

7. "Ads by Google"

Below you will see that an "Ads by Google" stamp is placed on *all* Ad

Units. Its placement within the ad in relation to the location of the ad on your Web page can increase or decrease users' notice of the marking. If they are less likely to notice, you may get more clicks. We suggest picking Ad Units with ads at opposite locations of the "Ads by Google" text.

"Ads by Google"	Text Ads	Image Ads	Link Units
Lower Right	Leaderboard, Banner, Half Banner	Leaderboard, Banner, Medium Rectangle	None
Upper Left	Button, Small Rectangle, Vertical Banner, Medium Rectangle, Square, Large Rectangle, Skyscraper, Wide Skyscraper	None	All Vertical
Bottom Center	None	Skyscraper, Wide Skyscraper	None
Left	None	None	All Horizontal

ONLY CERTAIN AD UNITS HAVE "ADS BY GOOOOOOGLE"

Link Units and AdSense for Search results are the only Ad Units that use the term "Ads by Goooooogle" instead of the normal "Ads by Google."

By clicking on the "Ads by Google" or "Ads by Goooooogle" links, Internet users can give Google feedback on what they like and dislike about Ad Units. In addition, if you notice an ad on your site that is unwanted, you can simply click on the "Ads by Google" link and tell Google about it.

Alternatively, you can use filters to keep the ad from showing in the future. We will discuss filters later on.

H. AdSense Text Box Shapes and Sizes

Google is one short of a dozen text boxes. Below are the eleven text box shapes and sizes. Notice the "Ads by Google" link in all of them.

Leaderboard (728 x 90)

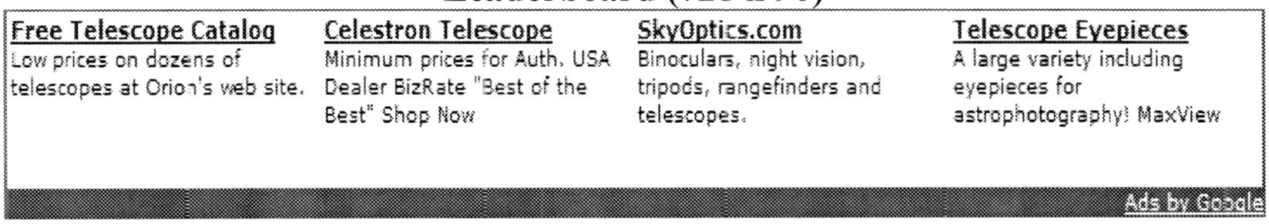

Banner (468 x 60)

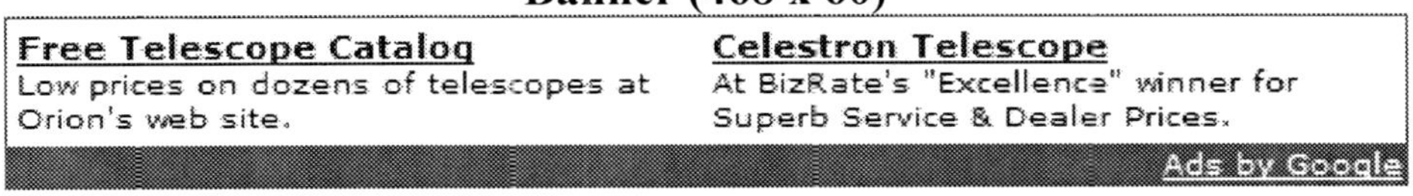

Half Banner (234 x 60)

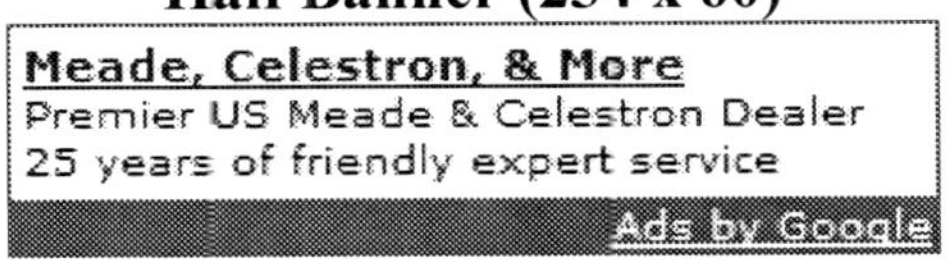

Button (125 x 125)

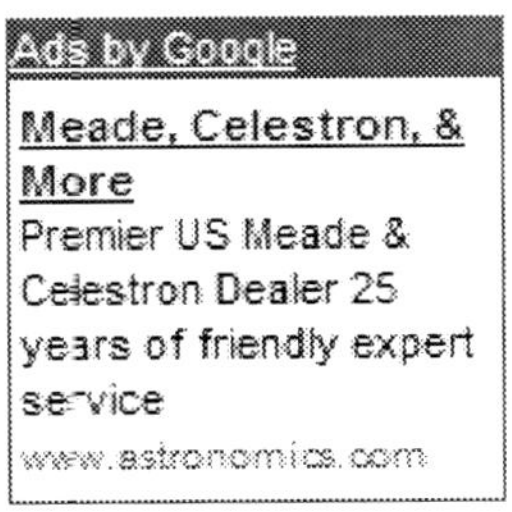

Small Rectangle (180 x 150)

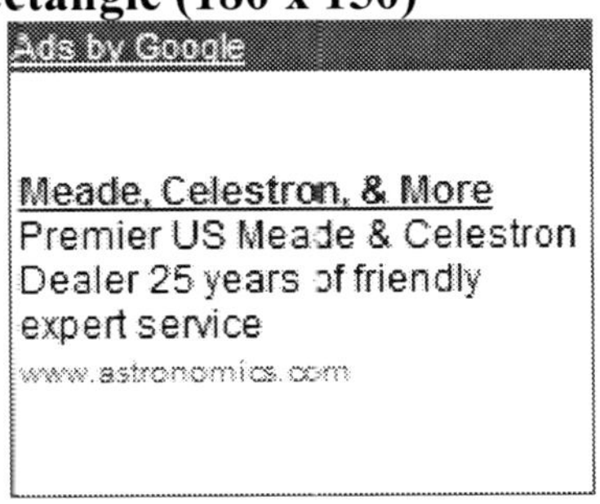

ADSENSE TEXT AD CLICK ADVANTAGE

For a Text Ad only the Title can be clicked if shown in the normal Google Search Network. For ads on the Content Network, which includes AdSense, *any* part of the ad can be clicked. This is another way Google helps you get click revenue. A user can also click to the right of the text in the empty space between the text and border, but cannot click in the empty space between the left of the ad text and border. Note the Small Rectangle has the deadest space.

Vertical Banner (120 x 240)

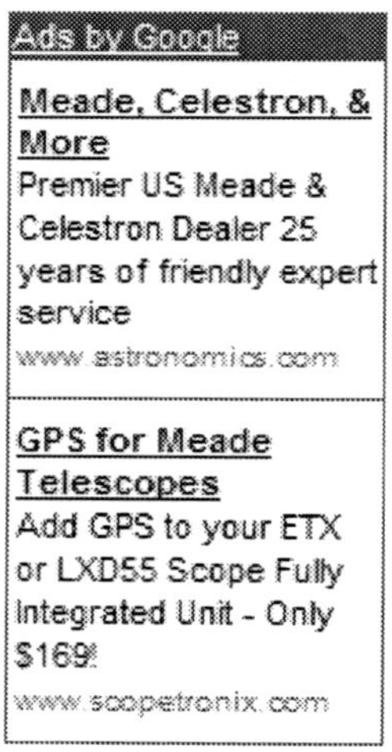

Medium Rectangle (300 x 250)

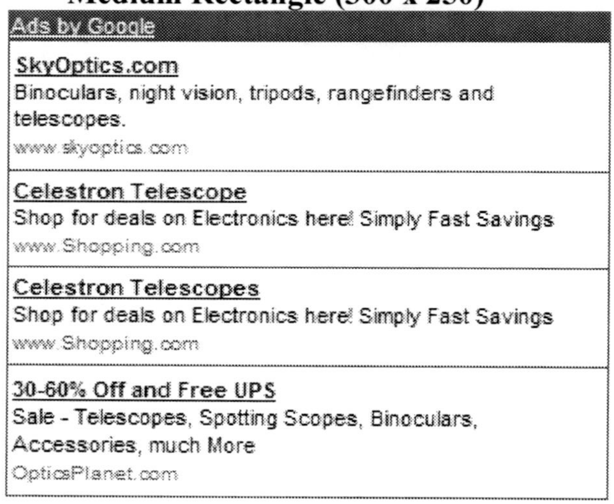

Square (250 x 250)

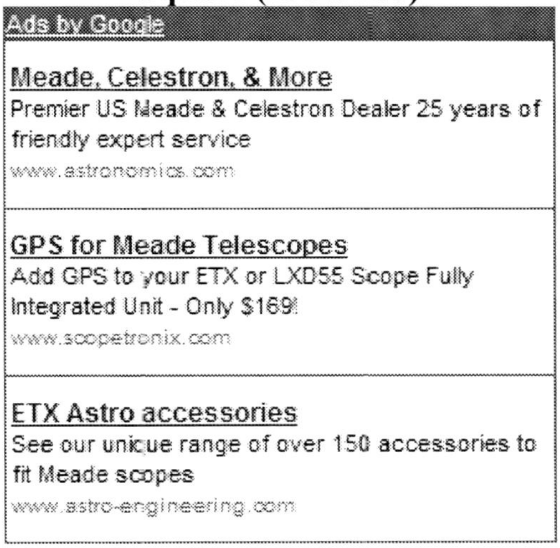

PLACE ADS NEAR IMAGES

If you have images on your site users will be drawn to those images. If you place an ad near an image that gets a lot of attention, the ad itself will get more clicks.

Large Rectangle (336 x 280)

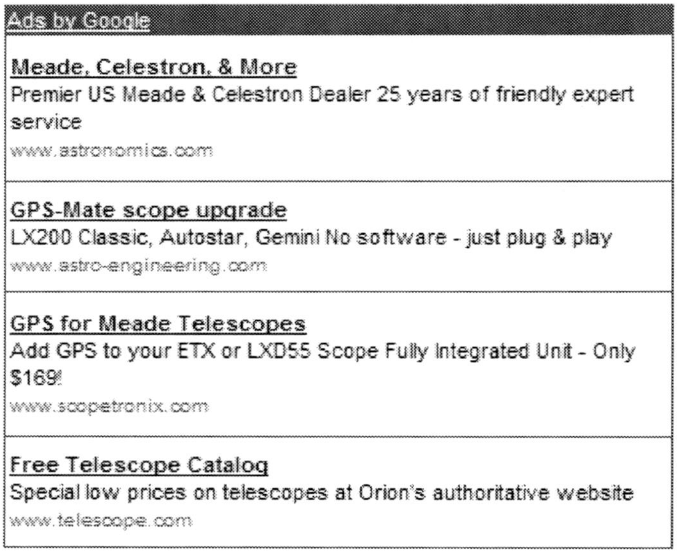

THE BEST AD UNIT FORMAT

One text format outshines them all! It is the Large Rectangle and if there is no other place to squeeze in ads on your AdSense page, use this format.

Skyscraper (120 x 600)

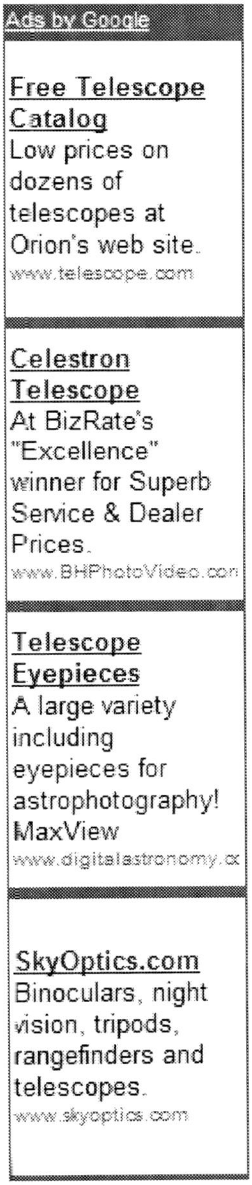

Wide Skyscraper (160 x 600)

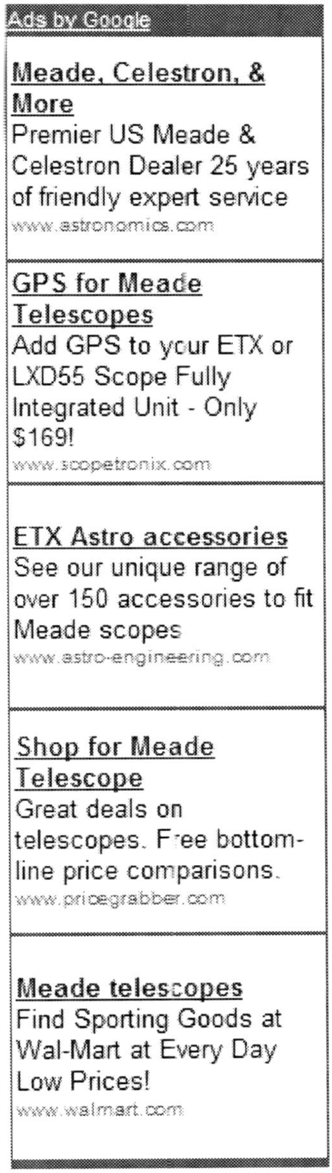

1. Best Performing Text Ad Sizes

The wide ad formats get more clicks than normal size Text Ad Units since they take up fewer horizontal lines on the page and allow users to read several words before having to scan back to the left of the next line. Hence, users stay focused on the Ad Unit. This is very important to your AdSense success. For instance, the Large Rectangle gets more clicks than the Medium Rectangle and the Wide Skyscraper receives more traffic than the normal Skyscraper. Place the Ad Unit with the best performance potential *first* in your HTML code (i.e., above the other AdSense HTML scripts and always between the <Body> tags). This will ensure ads are served into this Ad Unit on a first-come, first-served basis. If Google runs out of ads to serve to your other Ad Units, at least the one with best placement and size will get available ads first on your site.

PAGE LOAD TIME HARDLY SLOWS

Enabling AdSense on your site - even though Java script is added to your page - will do little to slow the loading of your page into a Web browser. In our tests the change was not noticeable.

2. Expanded Text Ads

Sometimes Google may not display all of the ads in the Ad Unit space. This occurs for both Site Targeted CPM ads and keyword targeted CPC ads.

First, let's consider CPC Expanded Text Ads. In this instance Google's algorithms may determine that expanding one or two ads to fill up and entire Ad Unit will result in greater revenues. In this case text size will be increased to expand the ad into the void left when the other ads are eliminated. Think of these as the "elephant in the room" ads. They cannot be ignored.

Second, we've learned that Site Targeted ads are bid on a Cost-Per-Thousand-Impressions (CPM) basis. If you will make more money off a

CPM ad than the multiple CPC ads it replaces, the CPM ad will be expanded to take up the entire Ad Unit. For example, only one ad may be shown in the Square Ad Unit instead of the normal three ads. Do not panic. This usually will not mean that Google has a shortage of ad inventory. When Google does this less ads are displayed, but the increased font size of the ad(s) shown – and high Quality Score – will result in more clicks even with less ads.

WHEN EXPANDED ADS DO NOT APPLY

The Half Banner, Button, and Small Rectangle Text Ad Units only have one ad to begin with, so Expanded Ads will not apply.

Expanded Text Ads are a great way to get more clicks/revenue. Google provides this service automatically and since Expanded Text Ads stand out more and are easier for your users to read, their experience will be enhanced on your Website.

LINK UNITS DO NOT APPLY

Expanded Ads do not apply to Link Units, which we will discuss in greater detail below.

Let's compare the number of normal Text Ads that an Expanded Text Ad displaces. We will assume one Expanded Text Ad will replace all ads within the Ad Unit. We will also chart the resulting eCPM needed for an Expanded Text Ad to displace normal CPC contextual ads and begin showing on your site.

Text Ad Formats	Number of Text Ads Displaced	eCPM for Expanded Text Ads
Banner 468X60 pixels (28,080 Total Area)	Two	$ECPM_{et} > eCPM_{CT1} + eCPM_{CT2}$
Vertical Banner 120X240 pixels (28,800 Total Area)	Two	$ECPM_{et} > eCPM_{CT1} + eCPM_{CT2}$
Square 250X250 (62,500 Total Area)	Three	$ECPM_{et} > eCPM_{CT1} + eCPM_{CT2} + eCPM_{CT3}$
Leaderboard 728X90 pixels (65,520 Total Area)	Four	$ECPM_{et} > eCPM_{CT1} + eCPM_{CT2} + eCPM_{CT3} + eCPM_{CT4}$
Medium Rectangle 300x250 pixels (75,000 Total Area)	Four	$ECPM_{et} > eCPM_{CT1} + eCPM_{CT2} + eCPM_{CT3} + eCPM_{CT4}$
Large Rectangle 336X280 pixels (94,080 Total Area)	Four	$ECPM_{et} > eCPM_{CT1} + eCPM_{CT2} + eCPM_{CT3} + eCPM_{CT4}$
Skyscraper 120x600 pixels (72,000 Total Area)	Four	$ECPM_{et} > eCPM_{CT1} + eCPM_{CT2} + eCPM_{CT3} + eCPM_{CT4}$
Wide Skyscraper 160 X 600 pixels (96,000 Total Area)	Five	$ECPM_{et} > eCPM_{CT1} + eCPM_{CT2} + eCPM_{CT3} + eCPM_{CT4} + eCPM_{CT5}$

The Expanded Text Ad must have an eCPM greater than the sum of the eCPM ads that it displaces within the Ad Unit. What this tells us is that Banner Expanded Text Ads must have an eCPM greater than the combination of the two Text Ads they replace. The Leaderboard, Medium Rectangle, and Skyscraper Expanded Text Ads must have an eCPM greater than the summation of the four Text Ads they replace and the Wide Skyscraper Expanded Text Ad must have an eCPM greater than the sum of the five Text Ad eCPMs it displaces. From a pure analysis of Text Ad pixel area versus the number of Text Ads displaced, the Medium Rectangle and Wide Skyscraper are the best footprint value. This is no coincidence. Per

Google, the Medium Rectangle and Wide Skyscraper are the *two best* performing Image Ads and Text Ads. We will discuss Image Ads in great detail below.

3. AdSense for Content and Frames

You can employ AdSense ads on a frames-based Website, but it requires a few extra steps. Understanding this also gives insight into how Google crawls frames-based sites. It is the primary content frame that Google crawls to categorize frames-based sites. The vast majority of times this is content laid out right down the middle of the page.

Two Steps to Enabling AdSense Ads on Frames-Based Sites

1. Check the "Framed Page" box when generating AdSense for Content code
2. Copy and paste AdSense code into the *primary* content frame (usually the middle of the page) of your Website

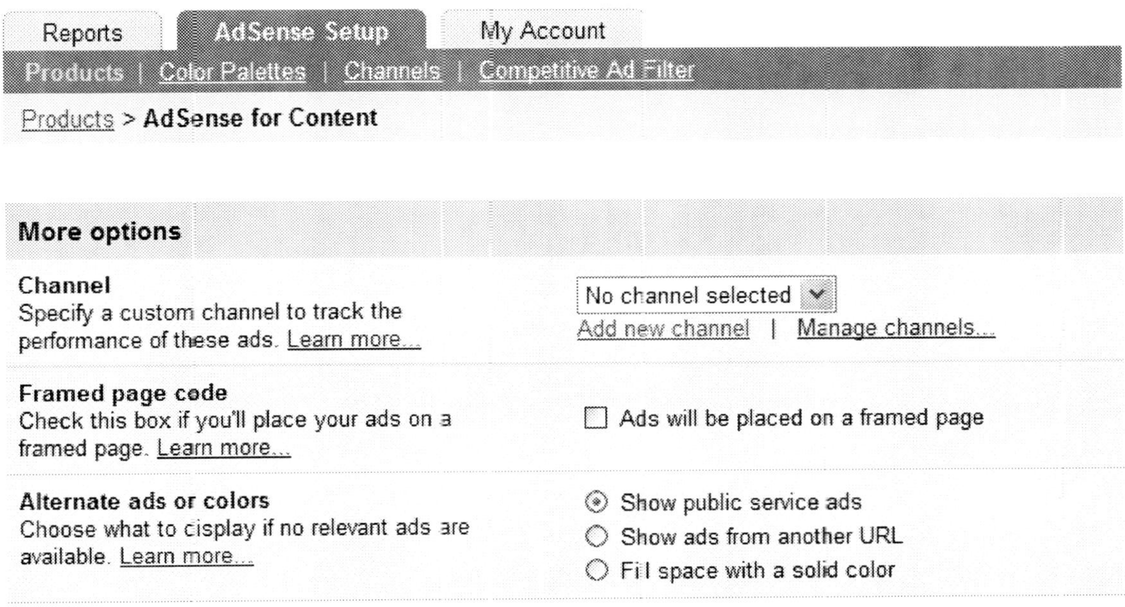

I. Image Ads

You have the option of requesting that Google show either Text Ads on your AdSense site or Image Ads or *both*. Google states that to maximize AdSense click revenue you should enable both Image Ads and Text Ads on your site. Since Image Ads replace four AdWord Text Ads, their eCPM must be high if they appear on your site when you have both Text and Image Ads enabled. This strategy, like any, can backfire if you have the type of Website that may cause users to be turned off by Image Ads. Here is how you enable Image Ads. Under the "My Account" tab select "Ad Type Preferences."

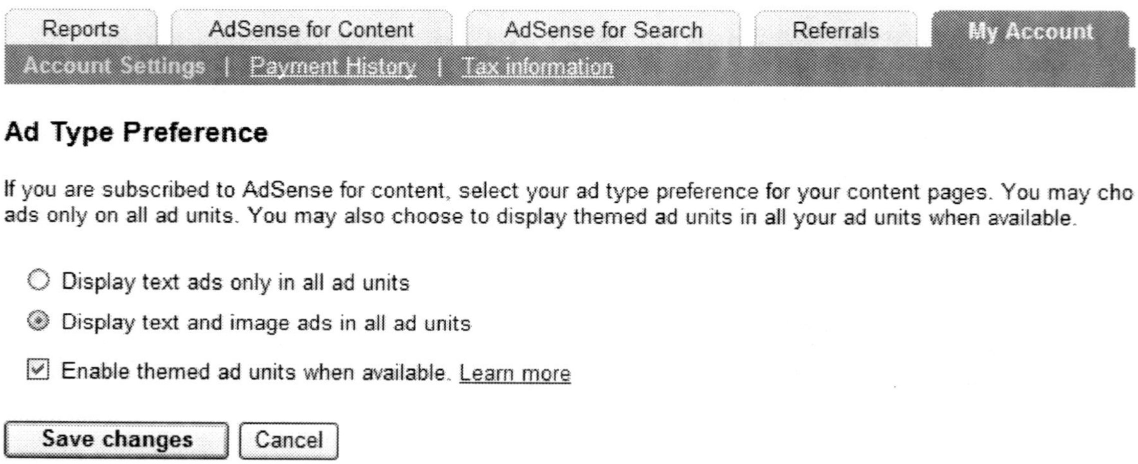

Colors are vital to any AdSense site, especially those running Image Ads. We will discuss color integration in detail below. It is often unclear what is meant by enabling Image Ads to run on the AdSense designated areas on your Website. This does not mean that Google will exclusively show Image Ads (unless you have instructed Google to do so). Just like on the rest of the Content Network, Image Ads vie for ad space with AdWords Text Ads. If one Image Ad is resulting in more clicks and higher revenue for Google, then it will be displayed in place of four Text Ads. Usually, this is not the case, however, and regular Text Ads are shown.

1. Static Image Ad Shapes and Sizes

Static ads are the traditional Google Image Ads. The ads can be uploaded to Google in the following formats:

- .JPG (Static Graphic)
- .GIF (Static Graphic)
- .PNG (Static Graphic)

Google does not show Image Ads on its Website or within the AdSense for Search Network.

a. Static Ad Sizes

Of the eleven square and rectangle sizes in which AdSense ads are displayed, Image Ads may only be served into seven sizes. If you are not using one of these size Ad Units, you are potentially limiting the best ads (if they are Image Ads) from being served to your pages.

Image Ad Formats
• Medium Rectangle [Vertical Rectangle] (300x250) • Banner [Horizontal Rectangle] (468x60) • Skyscraper [Vertical Rectangle] (120x600) • Wide Skyscraper [Vertical Rectangle] (160 X 600) • Leaderboard [Horizontal Rectangle] (728x90) • Square [Square] (250 X 250) • Large Rectangle [Vertical Rectangle] (336 X 280)

In the Text Ad section above we learned that wider sizes get more clicks than regular sizes. Is this the same for Image Ads? Yes!

RUN AD UNITS WITH THE MOST ADVERTISING OPTIONS

Your initial goal is to pick Ad Units that can run both Text and Image Ads to increase the scope of ads that can be served on your site, and at the same time pick Ad Units that have the highest CTRs. There are two "wide format" Ad Units that fit this model. Use the 300 x 250 medium rectangle and 160 x 600 wide skyscraper. The best placement is to put the wide skyscraper down one side of the page and the medium rectangle near the top middle.

The various Image Ad shapes and sizes are shown below, but not necessarily to actual size given margin size constraints.

Medium Rectangle (300 x 250)

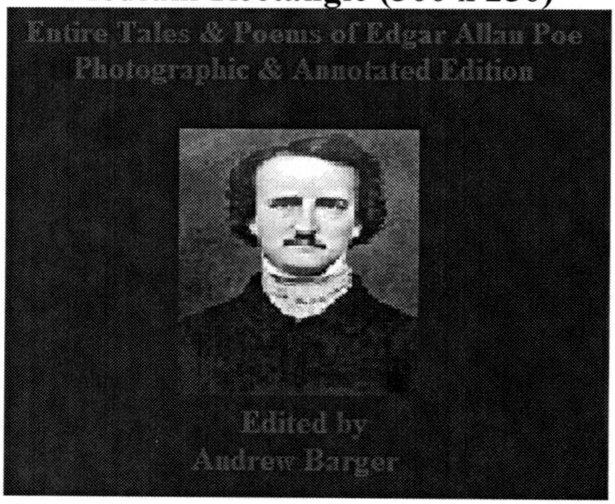

Large Rectangle (336x280)

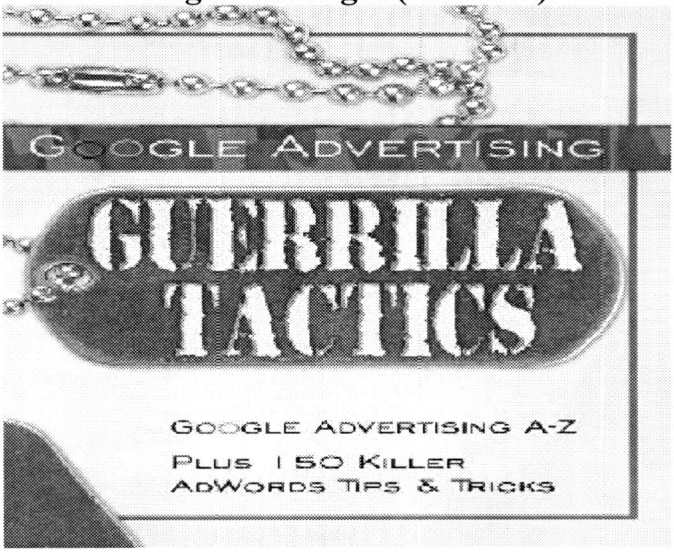

Leaderboard (728 x 90)

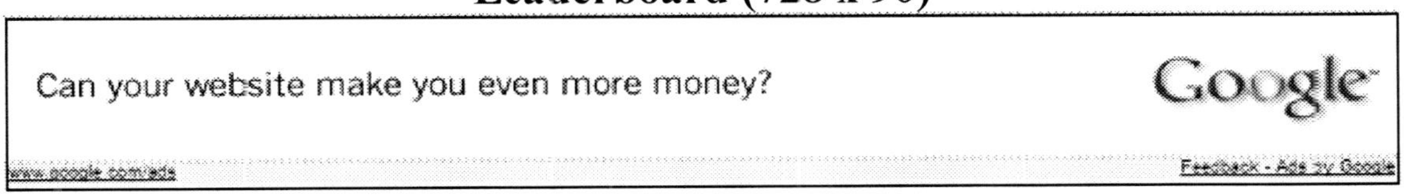

Banner (468 x 60)

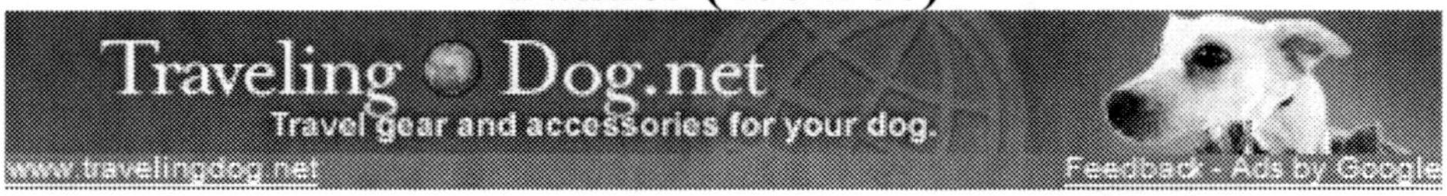

Square (250x250)

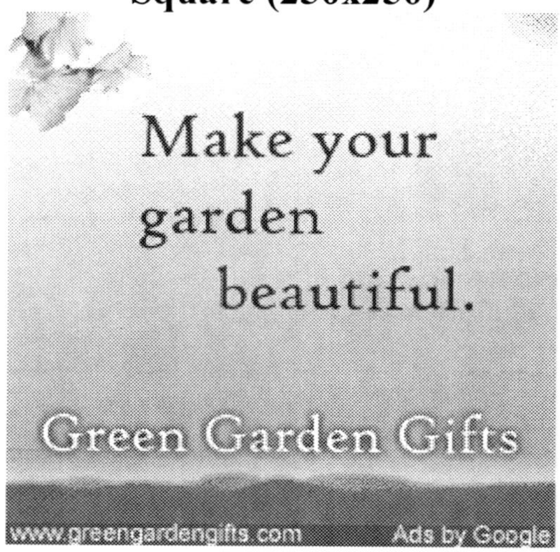

Skyscraper (120 x 600)

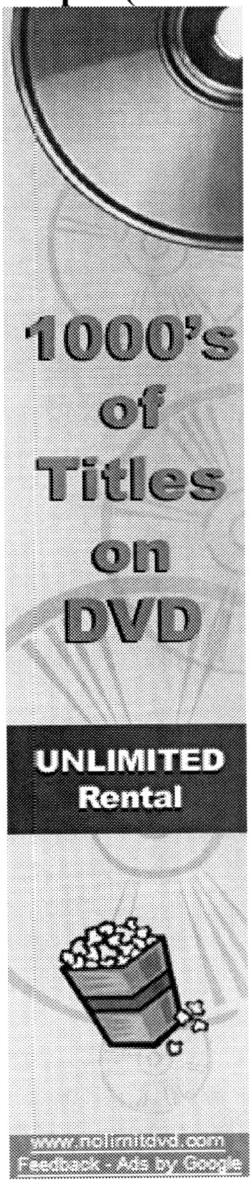

Wide Skyscraper (160 x 600)

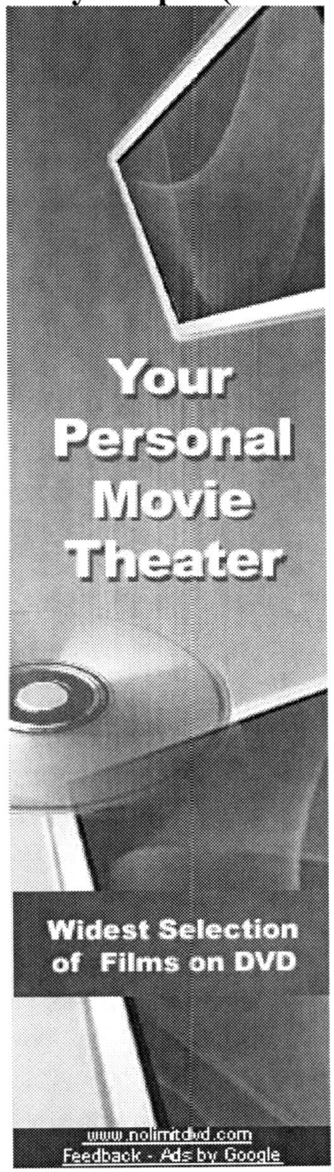

EDITORIAL GUIDELINES SIMILAR TO TEXT ADS

Only "family safe" graphics are allowed on Image Ads and the images must not be misleading as to the product/service being sold or act like Windows/Mac error boxes. Competitive claims and product discounts or "free" ads must be supported on the Website landing page. Here are Google's trademark usage guidelines:
http://www.google.com/permissions/trademarks.html

b. Static Ad Style Guidelines

Static ads have the ability to draw even more user attention, and therefore more clicks, than text ads. If they are not done correctly, however, they have the potential of ruining your AdSense campaign. Acutely aware of this, Google has set forth a number of static ad style guidelines.

Static Ad Style Guidelines
➢ Text ads may not be mimicked (i.e., AdWords advertisers may not make their Image Ad look like it is a block of text ads). ➢ Ad must occupy entire space of ad block. ➢ Prizes may not be offered for clicking on the ad. ➢ Ads cannot be sideways in the ad space or upside down. ➢ Ads must not extend out of the ad space allotted. ➢ Ads may not be divided to appear like two or more ads.

2. Animated Ads

At first Google did not allow Image Ads to move, but that has all changed. Image ads can move if desired. Google calls these animated ads. Contrary to popular belief, Google allows flash ads to be included as Image Ads on your AdSense page. Animated file sizes are limited to 50 Kilobytes so they cannot be too complex. The ads can be uploaded to Google in the following formats:

- .GIF (Animated Graphic)
- .SWF (Animated Graphic)

CANNOT DISABLE ANIMATED ADS

If you select to show Image Ads, Google does not allow you to pick between static and animated ads. Both will show on your site.

a. Flash Ads

Flash ads are unique types of animated ads that are uploaded in the same manner as other graphic files, but must be formatted in flash versions 4-6. Flash ads must also support clickTAG. This is the tracking code Google assigns to flash ads to track where it is advertised and the number of clicks. Redirection in the ad when clicked upon must be sent to the URL listed in the clickTAG only.

FLASH AD EDITORIAL GUIDELINES

The same editorial guidelines that apply to other Image Ads also apply to flash ads. Please visit https://adwords.google.com/select/imageguidelines.html for Google's latest guidelines.

b. Animated Ad Style Guidelines

Animated ads have the ability to draw even more user attention, and therefore more clicks, than static ads. If they are not done correctly, however, they have the potential of ruining your AdSense campaign. Acutely aware of this, Google has set forth a number of strict animated ad style guidelines.

Animated Ad Style Guidelines
➢ Animated ads cannot flash or strobe. *Thanks Google!* ➢ Ads that simulate computer functions ("Trick-to-Click") are not allowed. ➢ Prizes may not be offered for clicking on the ad. ➢ No looping animation is allowed. All animation must be finished within 30 seconds of the ad being displayed. ➢ Ads must not extend out of the ad space allotted.

3. Image Ad Text Displacement

Image Ads displace a number of Text Ads if both are enabled on your site. Let's compare the number of Text Ads the five Image Ad sizes displace and the resulting eCPM needed to begin showing on your site.

Image Ad Formats	Number of Text Ads Displaced	eCPM for Image Ads
Banner 468X60 pixels (28,080 Total Area)	Two	$ECPM_{IA}>eCPM_{CT1}+eCPM_{CT2}$
Leaderboard 728X90 pixels (65,520 Total Area)	Four	$ECPM_{IA}>eCPM_{CT1}+eCPM_{CT2}+eCPM_{CT3}+eCPM_{CT4}$
Medium Rectangle 300x250 pixels (75,000 Total Area)	Four	$ECPM_{IA}>eCPM_{CT1}+eCPM_{CT2}+eCPM_{CT3}+eCPM_{CT4}$
Skyscraper 120x600 pixels (72,000 Total Area)	Four	$ECPM_{IA}>eCPM_{CT1}+eCPM_{CT2}+eCPM_{CT3}+eCPM_{CT4}$
Wide Skyscraper 160 X 600 pixels (96,000 Total Area)	Five	$ECPM_{IA}>eCPM_{CT1}+eCPM_{CT2}+eCPM_{CT3}+eCPM_{CT4}+eCPM_{CT5}$
Square 250x250 pixels (62,500 Total Area)	Three	$ECPM_{IA}>eCPM_{CT1}+eCPM_{CT2}+eCPM_{CT3}$
Large Rectangle 336x280 (94,080)	Four	$ECPM_{IA}>eCPM_{CT1}+eCPM_{CT2}+eCPM_{CT3}+eCPM_{CT4}$

The Image Ad must have an eCPM greater than the sum of the eCPM contextual click ads that it displaces within the Ad Unit. What this tells us is that Banner Image Ads must have an eCPM greater than the combination of the two Text Ads they replace. The Leaderboard, Large Rectangle, Medium Rectangle, and Skyscraper must have an eCPM greater than the summation of the four Text Ads they replace and the Wide Skyscraper must have an eCPM greater than the sum of the five Text Ad eCPMs it displaces. From a pure analysis of Image Ad area versus the number of Text Ads displaced, the Medium Rectangle and Wide Skyscraper are the best footprint value. This is no coincidence as we have learned. Per Google, the Medium Rectangle and Wide Skyscraper are the *two best* performing Image Ads and Text Ads.

J. Link Units

What is a Link Unit? Well the answer is simple and there are many reasons why you should be using them in your AdSense campaign. You can think of Link Units as title/keyword only AdWord ads. Link Units are triggered off the content of your Website and automatically served by Google just like AdWords or Image Ads. Once a user clicks on one of the Link Unit topics, they are taken to a page that displays a group of normal AdWord ads.

LINK UNIT EARNINGS

Realize that initial clicks on Link Units do not earn you click revenue. Only when the user clicks on the *underlying* ad on an AdWords page do you earn a percentage of the CPC.

1. Link Unit Sizes and Shapes

As you will see below, Link Units come in various sizes. The first 8 typically work best on a vertical navigation bar of a Website, while the "horizontal" Link Units work best across the top or middle of the screen. Link Units also take up less space than a block of AdWords text or Image

Ads. Therefore, they appear more inconspicuous on your Website and less likely to turn off users. Their small footprint also gives you the flexibility to add more content, which will only attract more users.

INTEGRATE LINK UNITS INTO TEXT

> The small footprint of Link Units allows you to place them just outside or inside the text of your Website so that the text wraps around the Link Units. In a Blog that is essentially a vertical column of text and photos, you can place horizontal Link Units as dividers to maximize their usage. For example, a horizontal Link Unit could be placed at the end of each day of updates.

Link Units are a way to add clickable content to your Website, which allows users to drill down for more information that may not be found within your Website text. Here are the various Link Unit sizes.

5 Links or Less
(120 x 90)

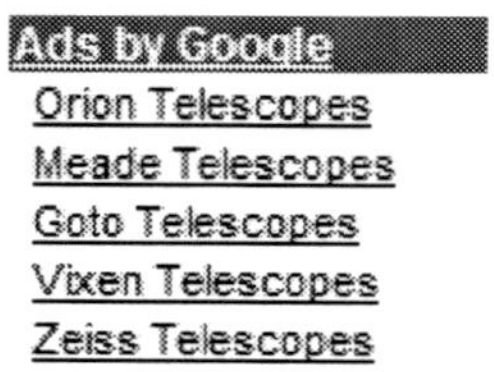

4 Links or Less
(120 x 90_4)

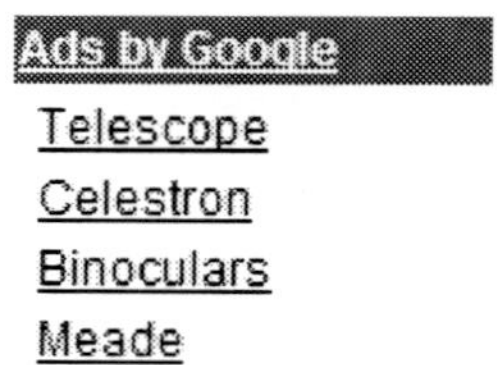

5 Links or Less
(160 x 90)

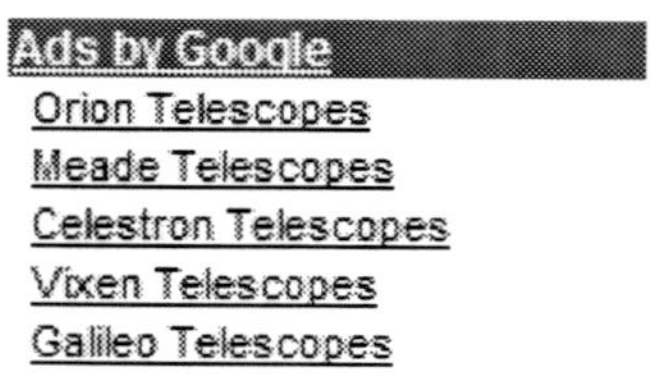

4 Links or Less
(160 x 90_4)

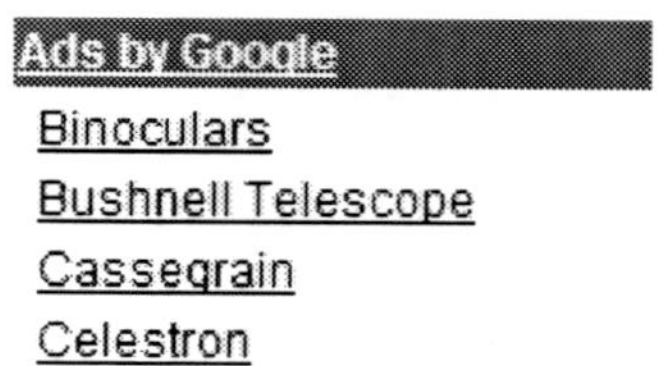

5 Links or Less (180 x 90)

Ads by Google
- Binoculars
- Bushnell Refractor Telescope
- Canon Telescope
- Cassegrain
- Celestron

4 Links or Less (180 x 90_4)

Ads by Google
- Binoculars
- Bushnell Telescope
- Cassegrain
- Celestron

5 Links or Less (200 x 90)

Ads by Google
- Binoculars
- Bushnell Refractor Telescope
- Canon Telescope
- Cassegrain
- Celestron

4 Links or Less (200 x 90_4)

Ads by Google
- Orion Telescopes
- Celestron Telescopes
- Meade Telescopes UK
- Refractor Telescopes

PLACE ADS ABOVE ARTICLE/REFERENCE LINKS

> If your Website links to important articles, Websites, or references relating to your content, try placing Ad Units above these links to get more clicks. Link Units are especially valuable in this case.

(458 x 15) – 5 Links or Less

Ads by Google Telescopes Meade ETX Celestron Meade LXD75 Meade

(458 x 15_4) – 4 Links or Less

Ads by Google Telescopes Meade ETX Celestron Meade ETX-70AT

(728 x 15) – 5 Links or Less

Ads by Google Meade Telescopes Refractor Telescopes Meade ETX Celestron Telescope Reflector Telescope

(728 x 15_4) – 4 Links or Less

Ads by Google Meade Telescopes Celestron Telescopes Refractor Telescopes Cassegrain Telescopes

TRACK LINK UNIT CLICKS SEPARATELY

Link Units can be included on a page with regular Ad Units and Image Ads. Use custom Channels, which will be discussed in detail below, to track Link Unit earnings. They will also give you visibility into how your Link Units are performing in relation to the other Ad Units.

2. Link Unit Strategies

Here is the skinny on Google's thinnest ads. Think of the three types of AdSense ads like this: Image Ads shout, Text Ads talk, and Link Units whisper to your users. The Link Units above may look familiar to you even if you have never seen one in the formal sense. The reason why is because Link Units resemble a typical Website navigation system. Menu or navigation links on a Website are commonly configured down the right- or left-hand sides of the page, across the top, or across the bottom.

ONLY ONE LINK UNIT ALLOWED PER PAGE

Google limits the number of Link Units on a page to only one.

Many times Web surfers will click through Website navigation menus trying to find the content that they are looking for on a site. With Link Units, this rapid click behavior works to your advantage. Configure your Link Unit to be within the menu navigation system of your page. Since we've learned that ads above the fold, near the top left of the page get more clicks, place your vertical Link Unit on the top of your left-hand column navigation system or a horizontal Link Unit across the top of your page to get the most clicks. These are the two places the vast majority of Websites place their navigational structure.

MATCH LINK UNIT COLOR TO NAVIGATION SYSTEM

It is an easy mistake to pick the colors of your Link Units to match your Website when your navigation menu may have an entirely different color scheme, or at least a different font color.

Be careful not to use Link Units in a way that can be misleading. For example, placing small images above each Title in a horizontal Link Unit will make them appear as image captions instead of ads. This may violate Google's AdSense policy.

If your Web page seems bare down the left-hand column, Link Units are a great way to add secondary content to your site. By secondary content, we mean that users must click on the Title to be directed to the page where the AdWord ads are listed in full. To implement this strategy, place a 120 X 90 or 160 X 90 Link Unit in vertical fashion down the left-hand side of the page. Both of these sizes provide the maximum five Title lines for Link Units. Remember that you cannot stack Link Units since Google allows only one per page. Also, ads to the left and above the fold get the most clicks.

PLACE VERTICAL LINK UNITS IN LEFT-HAND COLUMN

If lacking left-hand content, place a 120 X 90 or 160 X 90 Link Unit in vertical fashion down the left-hand side of the page.

3. Maximum Ad Units Supported on a Page

In the past Google only allowed one Ad Unit to be displayed per page, but now you can run multiple Ad Units on each page. In your search for higher click revenues, be careful of ad overkill. Below is the maximum number of Ad Units Google is currently able to support.

Maximum Ad Units Supported on a Page

- 2 AdSense Search Boxes
- 1 Link Unit
- 5 Referral Buttons (One for Each Referral Product)
- 3 Ad Units (Combination of Text or Image Ads)

This begs the question whether you should have AdSense ads displayed on *every* page of your Website. The answer is generally NO, but you should have ads on a large majority of pages. If you are trying to give the initial appearance that your site is not overly populated with ads, keep them off your homepage. This strategy may hurt your revenues if your homepage is the most highly trafficked on your site.

THE "VIEW ADS ABOUT" DARK CLOUD

If you have insufficient content on your site for Google to serve Link Units, its default is to place a search box with the term "View ads about" next to it. If users search and then click on an ad after the results are received, you will share in this revenue in similar fashion to AdSense for Search.

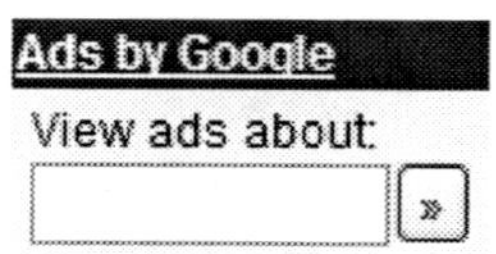

4. Ad Location

A successful AdSense site is no different than the real estate market. It's all about location, location, location. Here we are talking about the location of the ads on your Website. Are there some locations that result in more clicks than others? You bet.

CENTERED ADS ABOVE THE "FOLD" PERFORM BEST

Centered ads displayed above the "fold" (i.e., the middle of the screen) get more clicks than those below the fold. The second best location is the top left of the screen.

Ads placed adjacent to rich content on your site perform well. The same results go for Link Units placed near the navigational structure on your Website.

ATTRACT CONTENT EYES, ATTRACT AD CLICKS

A great rule of thumb is that if users' eyes are attracted to a particular content/navigational area of your screen, ads in this area will get the most clicks. See the heat map section below for more info. Note that this does not work in reverse. Trying to attract attention to ads (instead of content/navigation) by using wild colors or large text will result in less clicks.

The *worst* place to put an ad is on the sides, at the bottom of your Website such that a user has to scroll to view it. If you have a long article, an ad at the bottom of the article gets decent results, although an ad in the *middle* of the text will get a fair number of clicks. Flow content text around ads in the middle of the page.

MOVE ADS AROUND

Frequent visitors may come to identify certain areas of your Website as the "ad area" and therefore avoid it. This is a common occurrence with Blogs that may have daily readers. To remedy this, move the location of your ads around every so often.

K. AdSense Heat Maps

Google has provided Heat Maps that display "hot" click areas on sample Websites for AdSense publishers. Dark colors are the best areas with light colors being less click-active. Below we will investigate Google's heat maps for a traditional content site and a forum/Blog site. Along the way we'll point out which ad types and sizes will work best in the hottest click areas.

a. Traditional Website Layout

In a traditional Web page layout content is centered on the page, usually around the fold line. From the heat map below you will see what spots surrounding the center content get the most clicks. The lighter-colored areas do not work well and so we have flagged them of "Little Value." Let's make clear that we are not advocating the use of ads in all the hot areas. This would be ad overkill and drive users away from your site. Instead, test the hot spots, see what works best for you and use a *few* ads in key places.

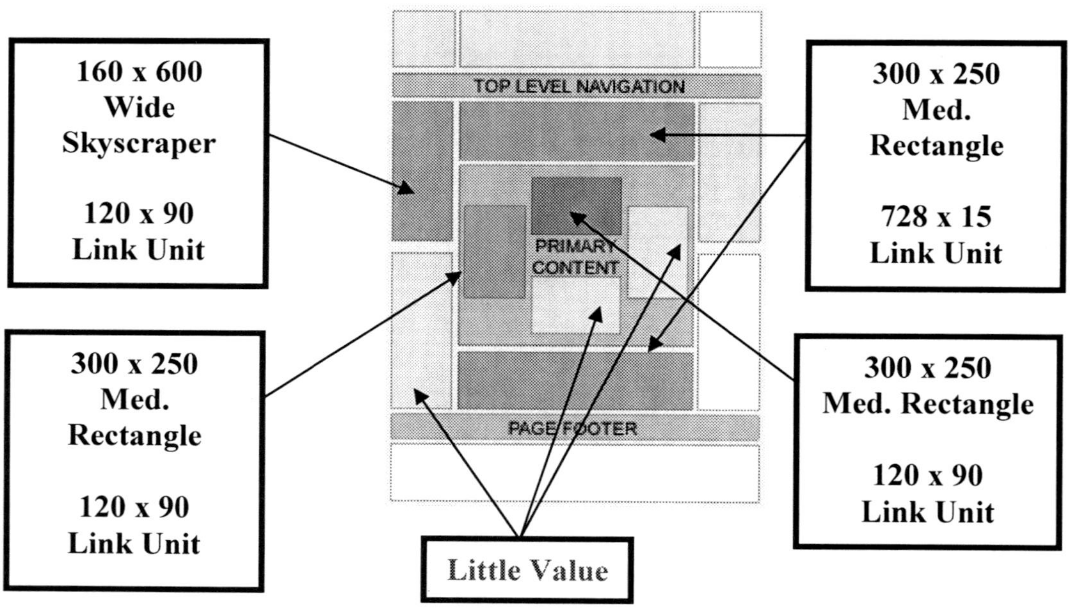

WIDE FORMATS MAXIMIZED

Note that both the 300 x 250 Medium Rectangle and 160 x 600 Wide Skyscraper are not only the best performing ads sizes, but also each supports Text Ads *and* Image Ads.

Ad Units placed directly below an article on a page are an exception to the general rule that ads above the fold get more clicks.

2. Blog Ad Optimization

The traditional Blog layout is vertical in nature and content is usually centered down the page. Again, the upper left, above the fold positions get the most clicks as demonstrated.

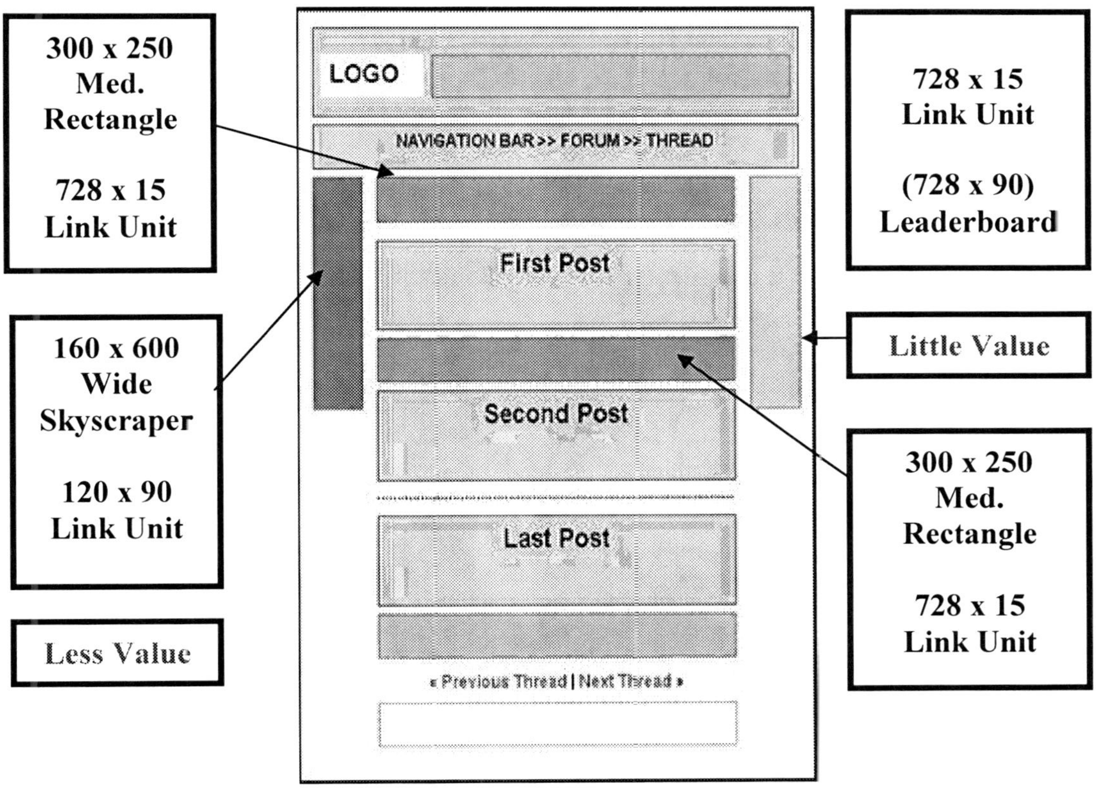

Layer ads and posts within your forum. The Ad Units can serve as commercial breaks for your readers. For individual post sections, adding a horizontal banner at the end will help, but it will not get more clicks than a medium rectangle blended into the post content. Last, Link Units are suggested in multiple places, but currently only one Link Unit is allowed by Google per page. Experiment and see which one performs the best in a certain location.

PLACE BANNER ADS OR LINK UNITS ABOVE COMMENT BOX

Many times Blogs have a comment section for users to post. Comment sections are usually at the bottom of the page. Use a horizontal Link Unit to provide a break and to offer additional topics for your users.

Section Targeting, which will be discussed in detail below, is a great way to hone in on your most recent posts so that relevant content ads are served in this physical location on the screen.

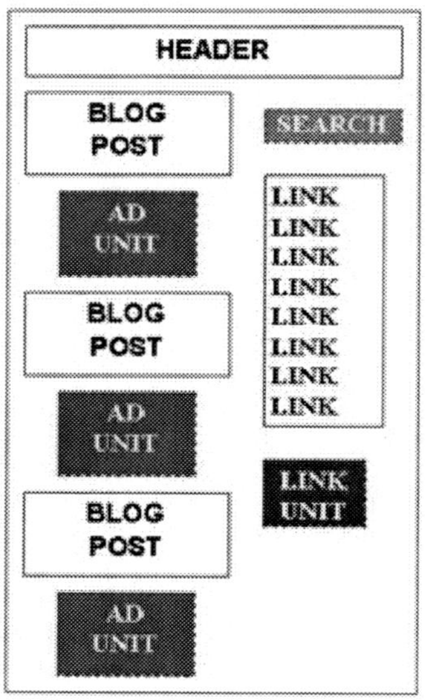

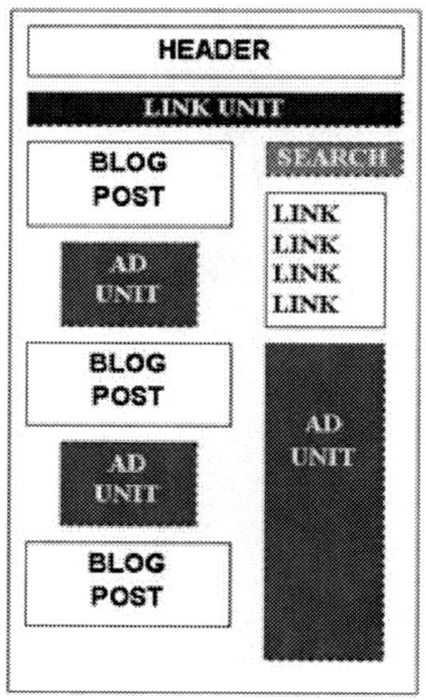

3. Page with List Layout

It is becoming popular to have a Website page with a list of words or terms that are relevant in a particular industry. For example, pages have been created that list, in long column form, top industry distributors or manufacturers of a particular product. Technology sites might want to list the top patents of the year. These lists are also coming into fashion on entertainment Websites that list "buzz" in certain categories.

Extensive lists may go on for pages, which requires users to scroll down to view it in the entirety. They may easily miss any AdSense ads at the top or even along the sides. Link Units can be used for great effect in list pages. That being said, below is a heat map for a list Web page that is similar to one used for Blogs.

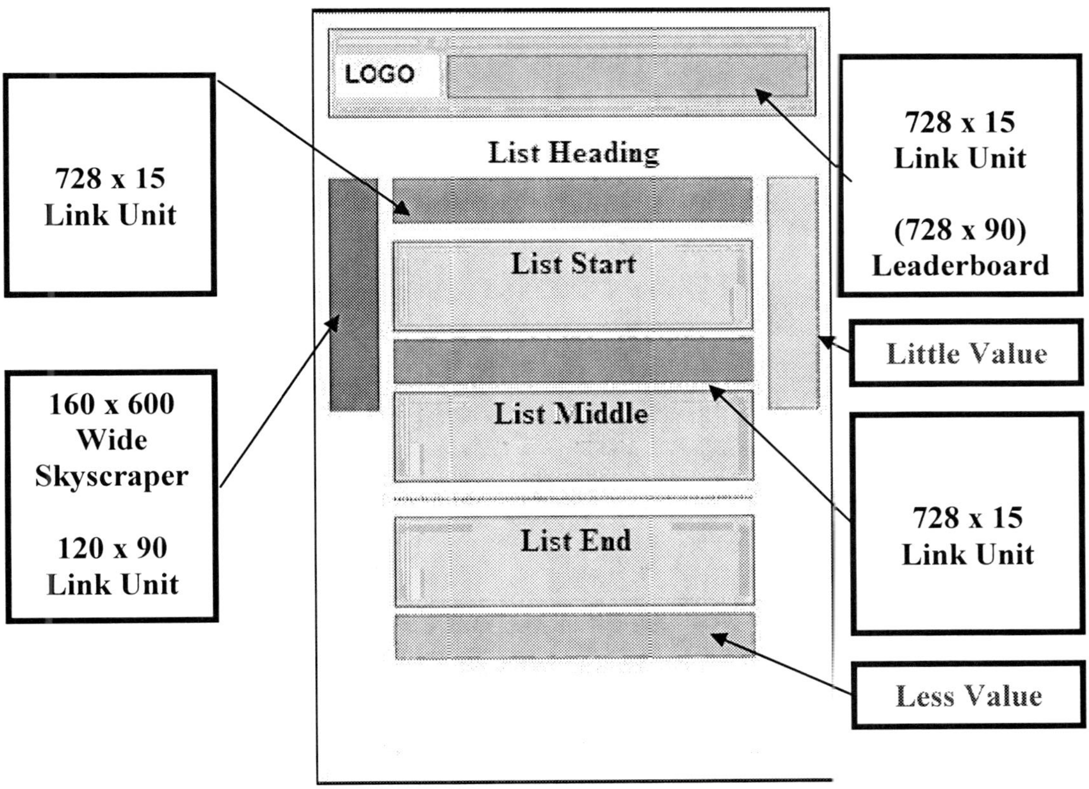

USE AD UNITS HORIZONTAL LINES ON LIST PAGES

Horizontal Ad Units are a great way to bust up an extensive list so you have multiple chances for users to click on ads as they scroll down the page.

5. Really Simple Syndication (RSS) Feeds

RSS feeds are the latest Wed advertising tool. They allow publishers to compile information from related news sites, Blogs and informational Websites and send these out in an abbreviated form. Think of them like the news briefings that are compiled in large companies and sent out periodically to top management. With RSS feeds, publishers send out content data such as news articles to subscribers. This used to be called "push" content on the Web. Regardless, Google places targeted ads within these feeds, which are typically only a few lines of text contained in a border. AdSense publishers are paid by Google for including the ads in the RSS feeds shown on their sites. Google then shares click revenues with the AdSense publisher just like under the traditional model.

ONE AD PER ARTICLE

Google cites best practices for RSS publishers as being one ad per article. Google does not want ad overload being sent to RSS subscribers.

L. Themed Ad Units

In late 2005 Google introduced Themed Ad Units, which allow AdWords advertisers to display ads that have a background watermark drawing. The watermark appears behind the words of Text Ads shown on your site. Here is an example.

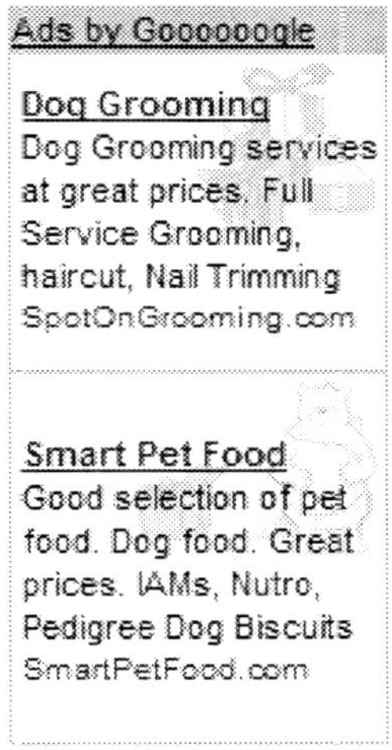

NO CONTROL OVER THE GRAPHICS

> At present, Google does not let AdWords advertisers select the graphic that will appear behind the text of ads shown on your site.

Themed ads units stand out on your site. They are the spice to your content soup. Google has total control over the watermark displayed on Themed Ad Units and the duration they will show. For example, AdWord advertisers who have this feature enabled will have holiday-themed graphics shown behind the text of their ads from the day after Thanksgiving in the United States until December 26th, the day after Christmas. Google will introduce other graphics for other holidays and special events through out the year, such as the Superbowl. Think of Google as having a giant themed ads switch.

ADWORDS ADVERTISERS CAN DISABLE THEMED ADS

> Be mindful that some ads may show the watermark and some will not due to whether a particular AdWords advertiser has them enabled.

The graphics are shown in the upper right-hand corner of the ad and may slightly affect the readability of text that is laid over the graphics. You are always under control with the AdSense program and can disable the showing of themed ads at any time. This is accomplished under the "Ad Type Preference" section beneath the My Account tab.

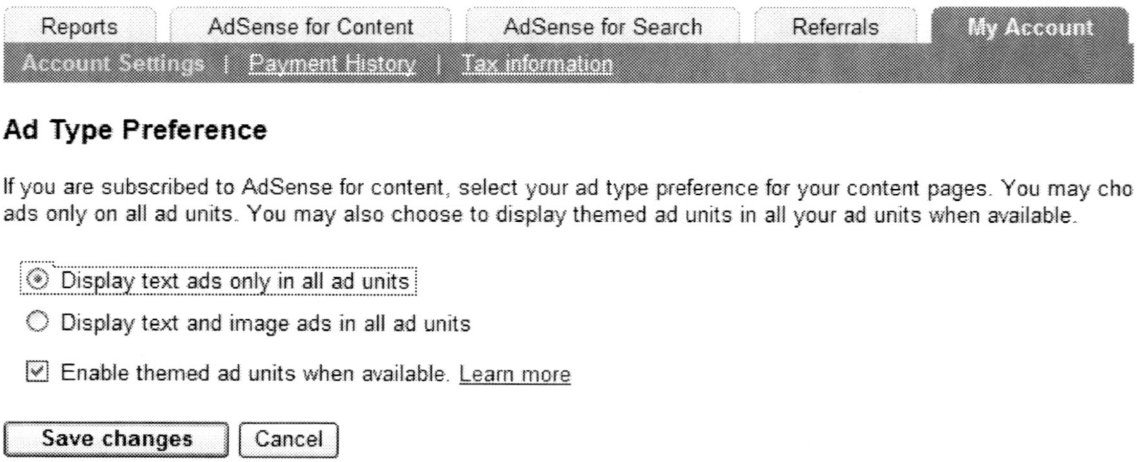

DISABLE THEMED AD UNITS FOR GRAPHIC SITES

If you have a graphics intensive site, make sure you turn off themed Ad Units as they create confusion for users.

M. Alternate Ads

Alternate ads prevent the showing of public service announcement ads on your site. Since Google serves ads to the first Ad Unit in your HTML code, a shortage of ads means public service announcements will be shown in the first Ad Unit if there is a shortage of ads. The other Ad Units on the page will be displayed as clear rectangles by default. We have learned that you should put your most prominent Ad Unit first in your HTML code to increase the likelihood of getting ads served to the Ad Unit that will get you the most clicks. If Google, however, does not have ads with keywords linked to your content, this strategy can backfire. Public service ads will be displayed in your most prominent Ad Unit.

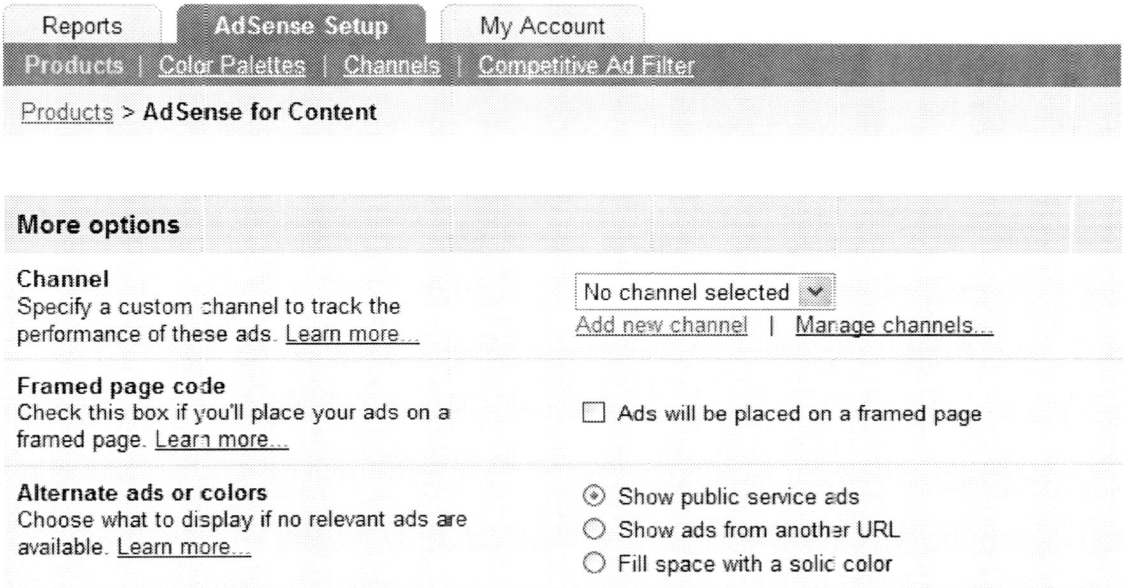

Alternate ads serve as a stopgap measure against public service ads on your site. Think of alternate ads as your defensive public service ad shield. Below are the four primary ways to prevent public service ads from showing in your Ad Units.

1. Ad Unit Color Blending or Alternate URL

Google lets you designate any of its custom or standard colors that will be used to fill in any Ad Unit for which there is a shortage of AdWord ads. Alternatively, you can input a URL address for an alternate ad server from which Google will display ads on your site if there is a shortage of AdWord ads. Here is how you can pick alternate ad colors or input an ad server URL. First, select the “AdSense for content” tab within your account. The following “Alternate ad URL or color” box will be displayed. You can simply input your URL into this box and click the “Update code” button or select “Choose a color. . .” to pick from Google’s list.

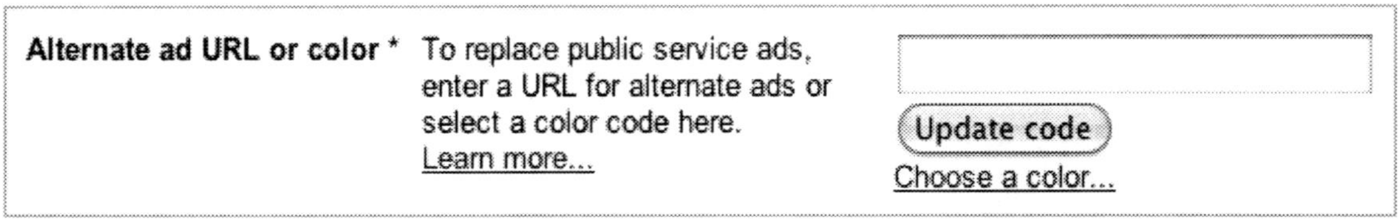

Once you pick your palette color, select "Save and get code." This will have the effect of updating your Ad Units with the alternate ad colors. Be sure to also click the "Update code" button upon return from the color palette to update the layout code.

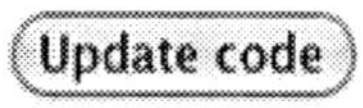

ALTERNATE AD CLICKS NOT COUNTED

Google neither pays revenue for clicks on alternate ads nor tracks these clicks within your AdSense account. They do, however, count as normal ad page impressions.

2. HTML Page Fillers

HTML page fillers are often mislabeled as clickable images. They are to a certain extent, but actually much more. Think of them as clickable Web pages with images. When you enable HTML page fillers, you are allowing Google to display an image as your alternate ad that when clicked on will take your users to another page via your designated link. The image that will be loaded must be in HTML format. A standard image format such as .jpg or .tif will not work in this instance. Instead, you will have to create a page that points a browser to this image. HTML page fillers are also the most complicated to implement. There are three steps to enabling HTML pages on your site.

a. HTML Page Creation

First, use your HTML code generation software to create a new Web page that contains the *full* hyperlink to your image. Google also recommends using an HTML code in your new page called TARGET="_TOP": that instructs your browser to load the clickable image only into the Ad Unit instead of the entire HTML page. Here is an example:

Sample HTML Page Creation Code

```
</head>
<body>
<a href="www.google.com" target="_top":> img src= "http://www.yourwebsite.com/images/alt_ad_skyscraper.jpg"></a>
</body>
</html>
```

Let's break down the key line of code with the TARGET="_TOP": reference.

www.google.com ← Destination URL

target="_top": ← Instructs browser to load the destination in a full window instead of the designated Ad Unit

http://www.yourwebsite.com/images/alt_ad_skyscraper.jpg ← Full URL path to your image

FILLING OF ALL AD UNITS

Be sure not to fill all Ad Units on your page with the same image as this will make your page look unprofessional.

b. Uploading HTML Page

Now that you have created your HTML page and image to be displayed in your Ad Unit when Google has a shortage of AdWord ads, you must upload it to the server that hosts your Website. To tell Google where the image is located, simply input the full URL into the "Alternate ad URL" box.

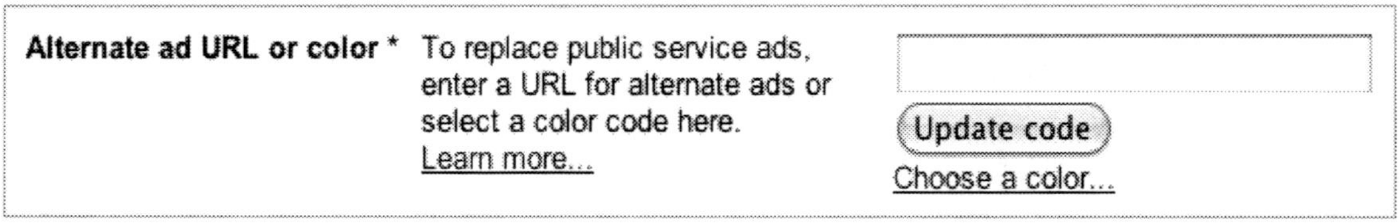

http://www.yourwebsite.com/page1/alternatehtmlpage.html ← Full URL path to your HTML page

UPLOAD TO ANY WEB SERVER

You are not limited to your host sever. You may upload your HTML page to any server on the Web.

If you are running AdSense ads on a number of different Websites, ensure that this code is uploaded to each of them so that HTML page filler Ad Units are enabled.

c. Update Code

Remember that once you type in the full HTML page URL, you are not finished until you click on the Update Code button.

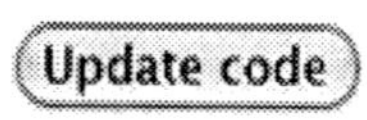

3. Image Fillers

If you would like to display your own non-clickable image as an alternate ad, Google lets you do this, too. Think of image fillers as a cousin to Themed Ad Units. Here, the size of the image is only limited by the size of the Ad Unit. To add your image to an Ad Unit you need only type the full URL of the image's location into the "Alternate ad" box and click Update Code when finished.

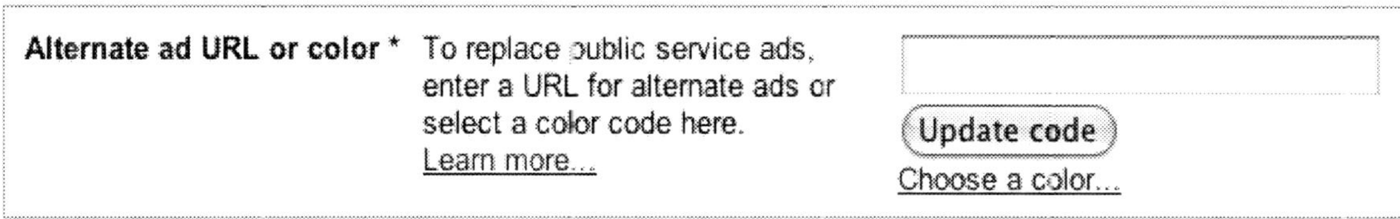

http://www.yourwebsite.com/images/alt_ad_skyscraper.jpg ← Full URL path to your image

IMAGE SIZE DOES MATTER

Ensure that your image will fit within the designated Ad Unit. If your image is too small to fit the entire Ad Unit, either increase its size or ensure that the background color of your Ad Units match the background color of your site. If your image is too big, it will be cropped at the right and bottom edges.

4. Disappearing Ad Units

While Google commonly refers to these as "collapsing Ad Units," it is more appropriate to title them "disappearing Ad Units" since they are no longer visible on your Website if Google has a shortage of ads. Disappearing Ad Units are a great advantage in that they save you space on your Website. Be mindful that, depending upon how your page is structured, their disappearance may leave blank spaces on your page.

BEST PAGE CONFIGURATION FOR DISAPPEARING AD UNITS

If you are going to have an Ad Unit disappear on your page, the best layout is when you have text wrapping around the Ad Unit. Its disappearance will then make the text flow as one cohesive unit. Other configurations that work well with disappearing Ad Units are the use of horizontal banners above or below text.

Watch out for disappearing Leaderboard Ad Units at the top of a Webpage and skyscrapers down the sides of a page. These sections may be left blank at the disappearance of the Ad Unit or content may get slid together that you do not wish to be adjacent.

NO NEED TO BLEND COLORS

> Unlike color alternate ads, with disappearing Ad Units there is no need to blend the background color of the ads if you do not wish. They will entirely disappear.

Below we will show you the five-step process to enabling disappearing Ad Units on your site.

Step 1 – Download Disappearing Ad Unit File
To download the disappearing Ad Unit file to your computer, simply visit: http://pagead2.googlesyndication.com/pagead/google_adsense_script.html. If you receive a blank page when visiting the link, just right click on the page and select “View source” from the dropdown menu. You can then manually copy and paste the HTML code or you can copy it below.

Disappearing Ad Unit Code

```
<!DOCTYPE html PUBLIC “-//W3C//DTD XHTML 1.0 Transitional//EN”
“http://www.w3.org/TR/xhtml1/DTD/xhtml1-transitional.dtd “>
<html xmlns=“http://www.w3.org/1999/xhtml” xml:lang=“en” lang=“en”>
<head>
<meta http-equiv=“Content-Type” content=“text/html; charset=iso-8859-1” />
<title></title>
<script src=“http://pagead2.googlesyndication.com/pagead/google_adsense_script.js”
type=“text/javascript”></script>
</head>
<body style=“background-color: transparent;”>
</body>
</html>
```

Step 2 – Upload File to Web Host Domain
Under the next step you need to copy this HTML code to a file and upload it to your host Web server.

PLACE CODE ON ALL DOMAINS

> If you are running AdSense ads on a number of different Websites, ensure that this code is uploaded to each of them so that disappearing Ad Units are enabled.

Step 3 – Input Entire URL Path to File in "Alternate Ads URL" Box
Once again, you must now tell Google where the disappearing Ad Unit HTML file is located on your Web server by typing the full URL into the "Alternate ad URL."

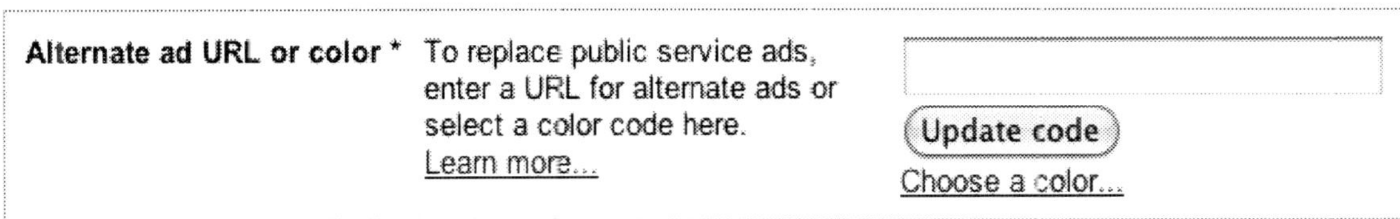

http://www.yourwebsite.com/page1/disappearinghtmlpage.html ← Full URL path to your HTML code

Step 4 – Click Update Code Button
Always remember to click on the Update Code button.

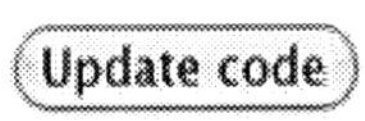

Step 5 – Place Generated Ad Code Into Web HTML of Website
The last step is to insert the generated code into all Web pages where you are running AdSense ads and you want to enable disappearing Ad Units. Be certain that your code points to the right domain. If you own Website1.com, Website2.com and Website3.com, use the right URL for where you have placed your code.

N. Filters

Filters are important for a successful AdSense for Content campaign, and they are underutilized. Just as negative keywords are vital to successful AdWords campaigns, filters are just as important for AdSense.

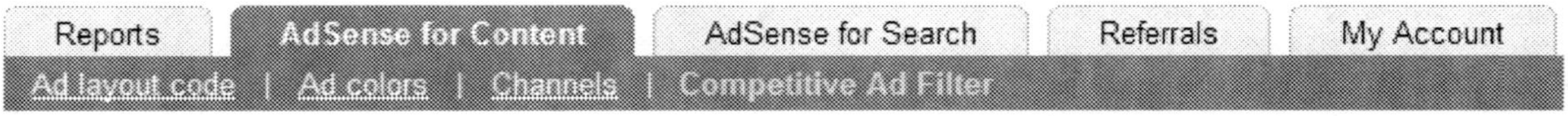

It is problematic that if you are going to participate in the AdSense program, you may receive competitor ads on *your* Website. You run the risk that a competitor's ad may be more compelling than even your content and you may not only lose a sale, but also gain one for your competition. Sometimes, you may even filter your competitor's URL and its ads will keep showing. Here are four tips to zap the competition through filters on AdSense.

Four Tips to AdSense Filter Success
➢ Place competitor URLs in both AdSense Content and Search filters; ➢ Filter both the destination URL and the URL shown in the ad text; ➢ When entering the destination URL, drop the "www" and any other data before the name (i.e., just enter Website.com); ➢ Your competitor may have multiple URLs so ensure that all are filtered;

FILTERING IS NOT INSTANTANEOUS

Be mindful that you when set up a filter so that a competitor cannot advertise on your AdSense-enabled site, it takes about three hours for the filter to begin working.

Remember that filtering will reduce the number of ads in the AdWords pool that will match with content on your site. As an alternative to filtering out ads served from an entire URL, you may only want to limit your filtering to a specific URL page within an overall site.

O. AdSense for Content Channels

What are AdSense for Content Channels? They are free ad evaluator tools that will tell you full details regarding which size, position and type of ads are getting you the most AdSense revenue. Configuration for Channels is also found beneath the AdSense for Content tab.

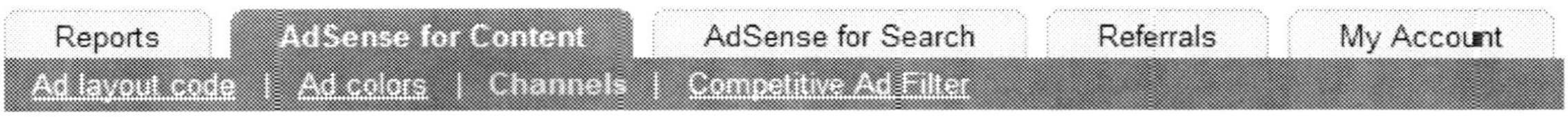

Channels are actually dedicated Google computer algorithms that monitor ads on your site and give detailed reports. Since location is the name of the game on AdSense, you must find which Ad Unit location is producing the best results. Here is how.

Four Steps to Channel Tracking Success

1. Create a Channel for *each* Ad Unit on your site
2. Include the following in each Channel name:
   - Ad color
   - Ad format
   - Ad position
   - Page name (ex, "HomeLeftSkyscraperMagenta")
3. Test the Channels for 2 weeks and see which Ad Unit position has the greatest CTR
4. Ensure Ad Unit with highest CTR is the first instance of ad code that appears in HTML for that page. Google fills the first Ad Unit with ads before the rest.

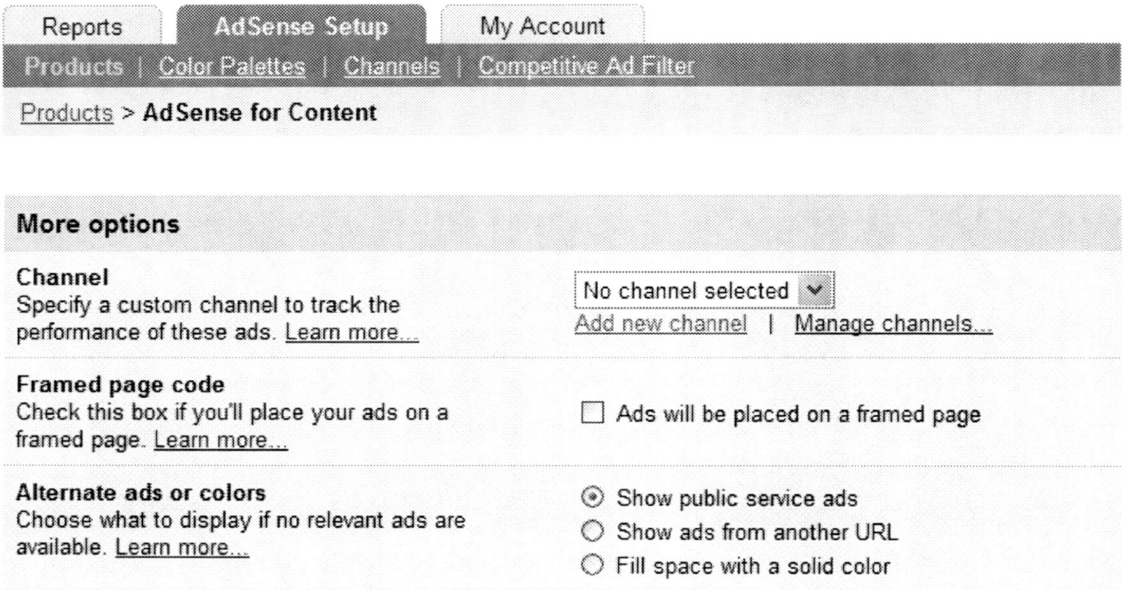

TINY CHANGES, BIG SUCCESS

Channels allow you to test different positioning and formats. Even something as minor as changing Ad Unit colors can have a dramatic effect on your CTR.

IV. AdSense Revenue

Okay, so Google shares click revenues with you as an AdSense publisher. This begs the question: "What *percentage* of click revenues does Google give me?" Which leads into the next burning question: "How can I learn what advertisers are bidding per click on my site?" You may find it surprising that you can know, with relative certainty, the answers to both these questions.

A. Sharing of Click Revenues

The percentage of click revenues Google pays its AdSense publishers was recently a closely guarded secret. The common consensus in the Internet community was 50%. A New York Times article changed this perception in 2006, which stated that Google pays about 78.5% to AdSense publishers and keeps only 21.5% for itself. It is believed this amount varies slightly due to various factors just as the amount AdWords advertisers pay per click changes based upon relevance, quality, popularity, maximum CPC, etc. It is also speculated that Google may have struck separate deals with large AdSense users such as Amazon.com to share a larger percentage of revenues for high traffic customers.

1. Ascertaining Click Revenue Sharing

There *is* one method that will give you a peek at the wizard behind Google's click sharing curtain. It is Google's Bid Tool, which shows you how much AdWords advertisers are bidding on various keywords. If you have a handful of keywords that are prominent on your site, see what people are bidding, track the top bids to particular advertisers, watch for these bids on your AdSense site, and monitor how much Google is paying you per click. You will then be able to estimate the click revenue sharing amount to a large extent.

Four Steps to Ascertaining Click Revenue Sharing
➢ Use Bid Tool for Top Site Keywords ➢ Track Bids to Particular Advertisers

- Watch for Advertiser Ads on Your Site
- Compare to How Much Google Pays Per Click, Realizing that the Top Ads are Likely Getting the Most Clicks

USE BID TOOL DATA TO EXCLUDE LOW BIDDERS

You only want advertisers with the highest combination of CPC and CTR showing ads on your site. If you have advertising "dogs" repeatedly displaying impressions of their ads on your site, not only do your revenues drop, but also you are providing less and less content value for your users. This obviously means they will not visit as often. To stop this vicious cycle, use Bid Tool data to see who is bidding the most for keywords highly relevant to your site, then use filters to exclude certain "dog" advertisers from your site.

Did you know there is actually an AdSense industry-wide average of 1% Click-Through-Rate? If you are scoring above this average, your AdSense program is optimized and if you are consistently below this average, use the tips and tricks in *AdSense Unleashed* to get your clicks humming. Another good rule of thumb is that per 1000 impressions you should receive about $1 in click revenue. Again, if you are over this amount, your AdSense program is doing well.

2. Remember the $0.01 Minimum Bid

Google has lowered the minimum bid on the Content Network to only $0.01 USD. Google also lets AdWords advertisers bid a separate (and usually lesser) amount for clicks on the Content Network, which also hurts your revenues. Since the AdSense Network is part of the Content Network, you may have a group of $0.01 bidders advertising on your site. Sharing click revenues with these bidders is, well, no fast way to riches. Smart Pricing on the Content Network, where Google automatically lowers bids for low Click-Through-Rates, may also work against your revenue sharing endeavors. Since $0.01 is the lowest amount of revenue Google displays in AdSense, we surmise that Google will share 100% of the click revenue with you if the minimum bid is $0.01. Regardless, if you continually see $0.01 showing up as your part of the click revenue, filter out these low-bidding ads in the hopes of getting those with higher CTRs and minimum CPCs served on your Website. Filtering will be discussed in detail below. Of course Google wants the highest paying ads shown on your site because they result in the most revenue for both you (Google's customer) and Google. You both have a common goal in this regard.

SMART PRICING APPLIES TO IMAGE ADS

> Google's Smart Pricing feature applies to Image Ads so if Google determines that clicks are less likely to convert on a Content Network site, the CPC will automatically be reduced.

3. When Google Will Not Share Revenue

As mentioned, Google splits the click or impression revenue with you as an AdSense publisher. We've learned that it's a no-no to click on AdSense ads on your own Website. The only exception is under Link Units. AdSense publishers can click on the initial topic link, but cannot click on the underlying ads displayed. Here are all the instances where Google will not share revenue with you for clicks on AdSense ads as stated by Google.

Five Instances of No AdSense Revenue Sharing
"Google shall not be liable for any payment based on (a) any amounts which result from invalid queries, or invalid clicks on Ads generated by any person, bot, automated program or similar device, including, without limitation, through any clicks or impressions (i) originating from Your IP addresses or computers under Your control, or (ii) solicited by payment of money, false representation or request for users to click on Ads; (b) Ads delivered to end users whose browsers have JavaScript disabled; (c) Ads benefiting charitable organizations and other placeholder or transparent Ads

that Google may deliver; (d) Google advertisements for its own products and/or services; or (e) clicks co-mingled with a significant number of invalid clicks described in (a) above, or as a result of any breach of this Agreement by You for any applicable pay period."

INVALID CLICKS APPEAR IN REPORTS

Even though you will receive no revenue recognition, Google reports to you clicks deemed invalid in your AdSense reports.

B. Learning Competitor Gross Payments

As part of Google's AdSense terms and conditions, you can disclose to the world your gross payments. Successful AdSense publishers love to show off their earnings and you can view them at www.AdMoolah.com to see how the competition is doing. If you notice a competitor site that is outperforming you, take a look at its advertising/page layout and see if you can improve your site accordingly. Also, see which content sites are getting the most revenue in general and point your content in that direction.

C. AdWords-AdSense Loop Revenue Strategies

Let's discuss a little known AdWords-AdSense revenue tactic. This is a great revenue strategy if you can get it to work properly, but you must be both an AdWords advertiser and AdSense publisher.

1. Direct Advertising

In essence, you develop an AdWords ad that drives traffic to your site based upon a few keywords. Ideally this will be a high performing ad that gets a lot of clicks at a low CPC. Once at your site, users can view *multiple* AdSense ads. We have learned that each Web page can have a maximum of two search boxes, one Link Unit, five referral buttons and three Ad Units. A maximum of five link titles can be shown per Link Unit and five Text Ads for each Ad Unit for a total of fifteen Text Ads on a page. What this means is that one AdWords ad can direct traffic to a page with fifteen Text Ads and five link titles. This does not include potential clicks off search box ads or the referral button.

DO NOT ADBOMB

Having more ads than content will give your page a cheap feel and result in less clicks. The more ads, the more content needed. Avoid adbombing.

You will know when your AdWords and AdSense programs are working in synch when clicks on your AdSense ads generate more revenue than what you are paying for AdWords clicks. This is what we call the AdSense-AdWords loop and it is a good measure of your advertising success. A downside to the AdSense-AdWords loop is that once users click on your AdWords ad, they are less likely to click on yet another ad on your Website.

2. Link Advertising

After reading *AdSense Unleashed* you have learned a number of ways to add new content that will bring in higher click revenue, especially after reviewing the top paying keywords section. When you create the new pages, be sure to include links to those pages from lower paying content pages. This is a "link advertising" strategy under the AdWords-AdSense loop and here is how it works. Let's say you have a content page that focuses on a low cost keyword such as "roof shingles," which is a $0.10-$0.15 per click keyword. You run AdWord ads that direct traffic to this Web page within your site. Next you create hyperlinks to your new content page where you offer ten affiliated roof repair services since the keywords "roof shingles" are closely related to roof repairs. The AdSense ads on the new roof repair pages will serve keywords that pay between $3.00 and $5.00 per click! Therefore hyperlinks to these newly created content pages allow users interested in roofing shingles to easily click over to your page with much higher paying keywords.

V. AdSense Referrals

There are other ways to get additional AdSense revenue apart from traditional ad clicks. To maximize your revenues with the AdSense program, consider AdSense referrals.

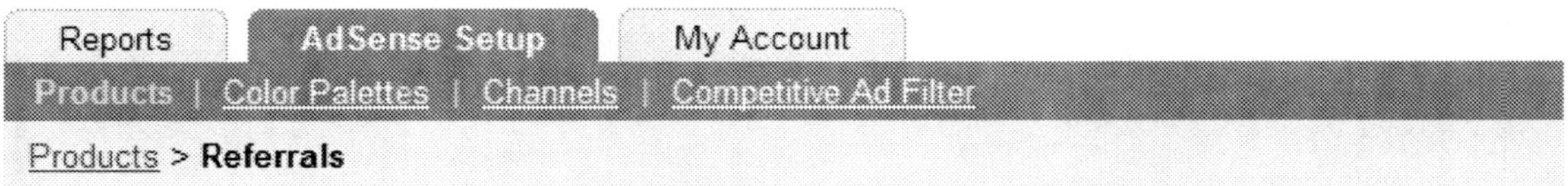

This is the third main area of the Google AdSense program. While at first it was the least used, Google continues to make AdSense referrals more user friendly and the revenue potential greater. There are five referral options: AdSense, AdWords, Google Toolbar with Firefox, Google Pack and Picasa.

A. Referrals Buttons and Text Link Codes

Like all other AdSense code, Google generates this for you automatically. You only need to paste the Java script into the code of your HTML page. Remember that the code must be inserted somewhere between the top and bottom <Body> tags of your site.

SECTION OFF YOUR REFERRALS CODE

Unlike the AdSense for Search code, Google does not section off the referral code by an HTML marker, which makes the code difficult to find within your HTML code if you want to move the Java script around such as when you are moving the button or text link around on the page. Use the following marker line: <!-- Google *type* Referral Button --> at the top and bottom of the HTML code; where the *type* will be either "AdSense" "Firefox" or "AdWords". For example: <!-- Google Firefox Referral Button -->

A good implementation practice to employ when placing a referral button or text link on your page, is to place the cursor at the spot where you want your first Ad Unit to appear. Many HTML editors such as FrontPage are "What You See is What You Get" (WYSWYG), which means the cursor location will be the insertion point of the referral button when you flip to "Code View" and paste in the Java script.

TRICK TO CENTERING THE REFERRALS BUTTON AND TEXT LINK

The AdSense referral button and text links will automatically be left justified when placed on your Web page even if that blank portion of the page is set to center justification. An easy trick to getting them centered on the page is to type a few letters of centered text such as ZZZ, place your cursor to the right of the Zs, click over to the "Code" section of your page, and paste the HTML code into your site. The button or text link will be centered. Now just remove the three Zs from your page.

B. AdSense Referrals Program

Beneath the "Referrals" tab you select the type of button or text link for your page and Google will generate the HTML code that can be easily inserted into your Website. This will display an AdSense referral button or text link that users can click on to sign up for AdSense. What is the upside for you? You will receive $100 USD when each user you refer incurs $100 in click revenues on their site. For many AdSense publishers this is the quickest way to start receiving AdSense money since it will not make any payments to you until you have reached at least $100 in your account.

REFERRAL BUTTON REDUCES AD & CONTENT SPACE

Using the AdSense referral button on your site will reduce ad and content space. We recommend trying the referral button for a period to see if it is working for your site, and if not, replace this space with regular AdSense ads or content.

Smart Pricing automatically adjusts AdWord ads CPC lower on the Content Network if an ad is not performing as well there as on Google's Search Network. Referral clicks on your site have only a minuscule effect on Smart Pricing. While clicks on the referral button will not directly affect Smart Pricing, they do (potentially) reduce the number of ad clicks on your site and therefore lower the CTR for ads on the Content Network.

TIME LIMIT FOR ADSENSE REFERRAL SIGNUP

It used to be that Google required referrals to signup within 90 days for you to get credit, but now referrals have 180 days in which to signup. You have double the time to receive your $100!

AdSense referral clicks and ad clicks on your site are tracked separately.

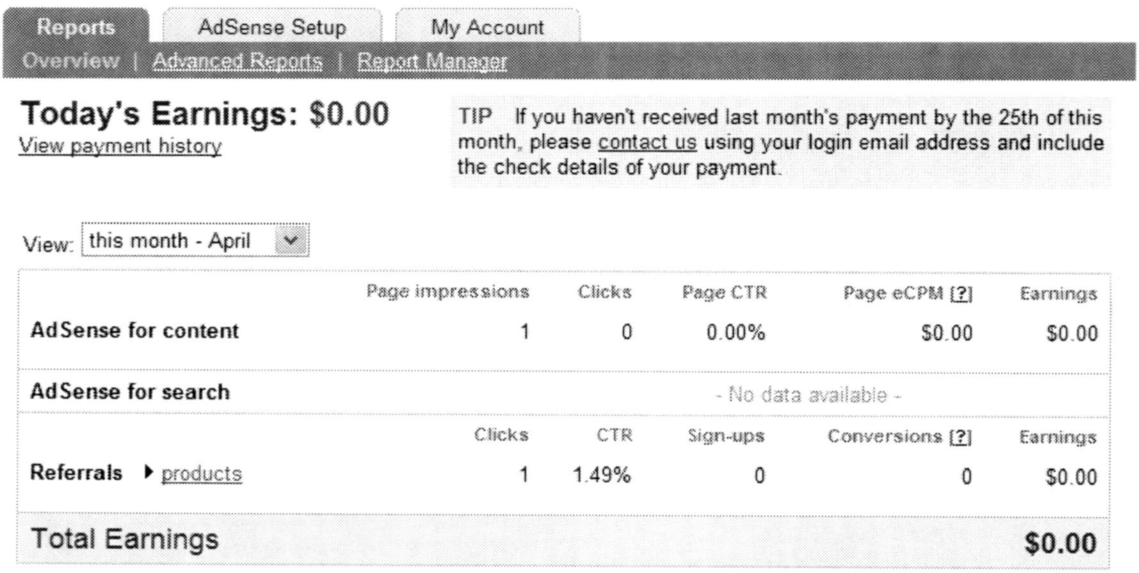

1. AdSense Referral Buttons

Google provides a wide range of referral buttons you can insert on your site. They range from square, horizontal and vertical ads. Below are the six categories.

a. Large Vertical Rectangle

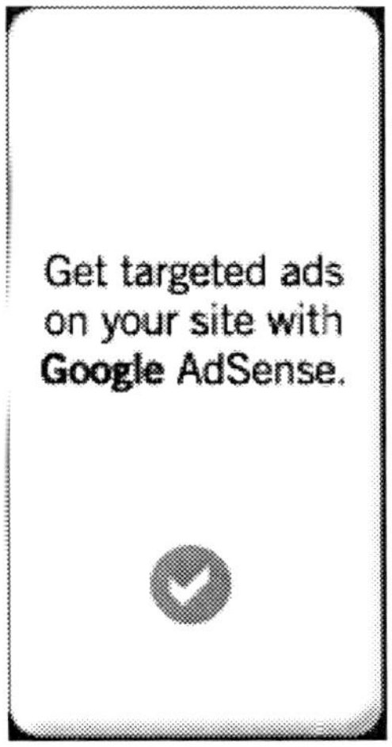

b. Medium Rectangle

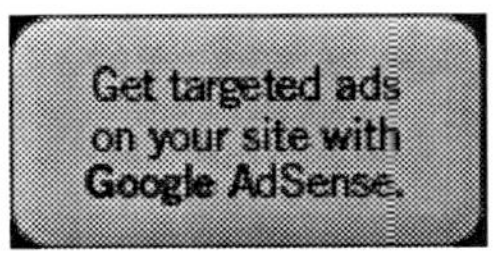

c. Medium Square

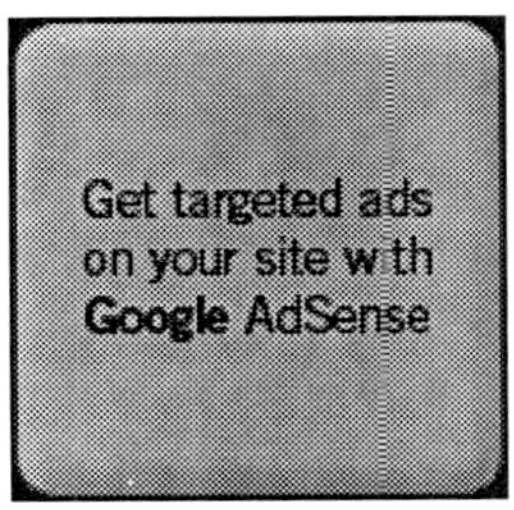

d. Large Rectangle

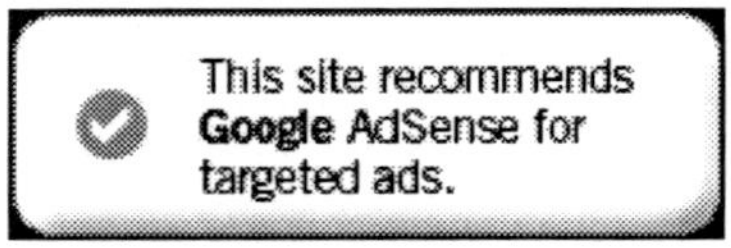

e. Extra Large Rectangle

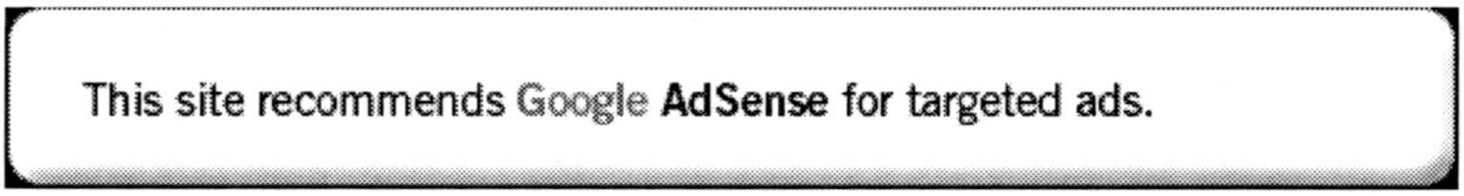

f. Small Rectangle

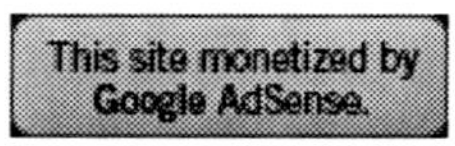

2. AdSense Referral Text Links

In 2006 Google added AdSense referral text links to your referral arsenal. Now you can use text links instead of bulky graphics. You cannot change the font size or color of the text links or the text itself. The four options are listed below.

- (•) This site monetized by Google AdSense
- ( ) Generate revenue from your website. Google AdSense.
- ( ) This site recommends Google AdSense for targeted ads
- ( ) Get targeted ads on your site with Google AdSense

TEXT LINKS LESS INVASIVE

One overarching them in *AdSense Unleashed* is the integration of AdSense components into your Website. Text links are a great way to save content space and include referral links without intruding too much on you Website design.

C. Firefox with Google Toolbar Referral Program

You may also add a Firefox (Web Browser) with Google Toolbar referral button to your site. Here you will receive $1 USD for each user that downloads and installs Firefox. If a user clicks on the referral button and already has Firefox installed on their computer, they will be redirected to the Google Toolbar with Firefox page. You will not, however, receive referral money in this case. Firefox with Google Toolbar referrals is available to *both* U.S. and international AdSense publishers.

REFERRAL ENDORSEMENT LANGUAGE

> Google allows you to use referral endorsement language on your Website such as "AdSense works for me and it can work for you too," or "Use Firefox with Google Toolbar for great integration." You cannot, though, use endorsement language adjacent the referral button itself like "Click on me," or "Press my button!"

1. Firefox with Google Toolbar Referral Buttons

Below are the six categories of Firefox with Google toolbar buttons

a. Medium Rectangle

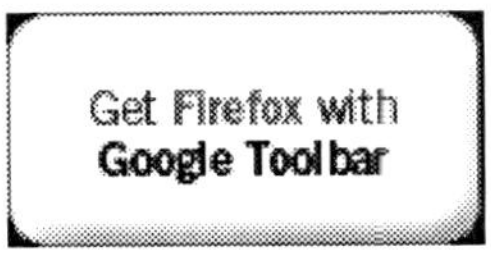

b. Vertical Rectangle

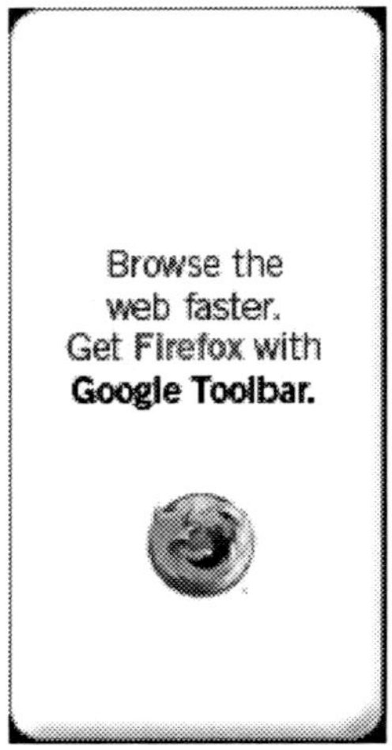

c. Square

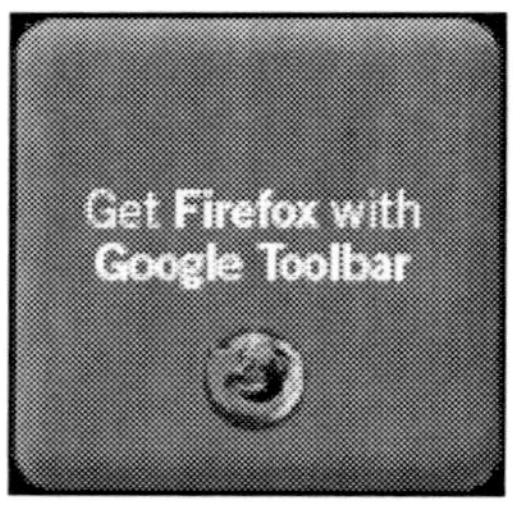

d. Large Rectangle

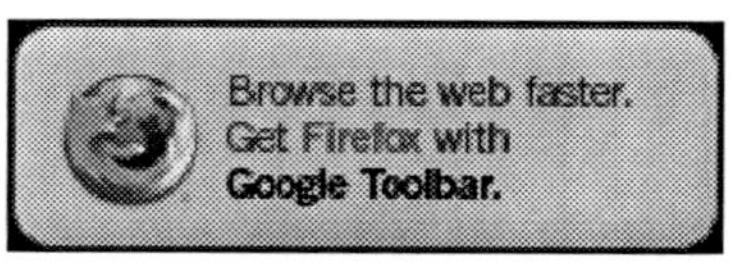

e. Extra Large Rectangle

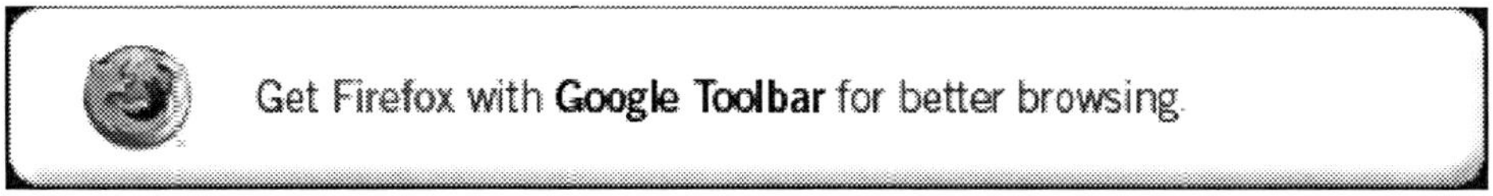

f. Small Rectangle

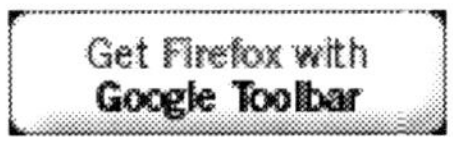

BUTTON CREATIVITY LIMITED

At present Google does not allow you to get creative with the referral buttons such as turning the buttons into different shapes, using splashy colors, or text links instead of the buttons. Google is seeking uniformity of design and in its corporate logo on the Web.

2. Firefox with Google Toolbar Referral Links

In 2006 Google added Firefox with Google Toolbar referral text links to your referral arsenal. Now you can use text links instead of bulky graphics. You cannot change the font size or color of the text links or the text itself. The four options are listed below.

- Get Firefox with Google Toolbar
- Get Firefox with Google Toolbar for better browsing
- Browse the web faster. Get Firefox with Google Toolbar
- Firefox with Google Toolbar

D. AdWords Referral Program

Google also lets you place an AdWords referral button on your site. When users of your site click on the button or text link, sign up for an AdWords account, *and* spend their first $100 with AdWords, you receive $20.

NINETY DAY TIME LIMITATION

In order for you to receive your $20, the new AdWords advertiser must spend its first $100 within the first 90 days after opening the account. You may be signing up many new advertisers, but if they are not spending $100 in advertising money in the first 90 days you will not be receiving your referral money.

1. AdWords Referral Buttons

Most of the AdWords referral buttons come in sets or groups of three. Each is shown below.

a. Large Horizontal Rectangle Group

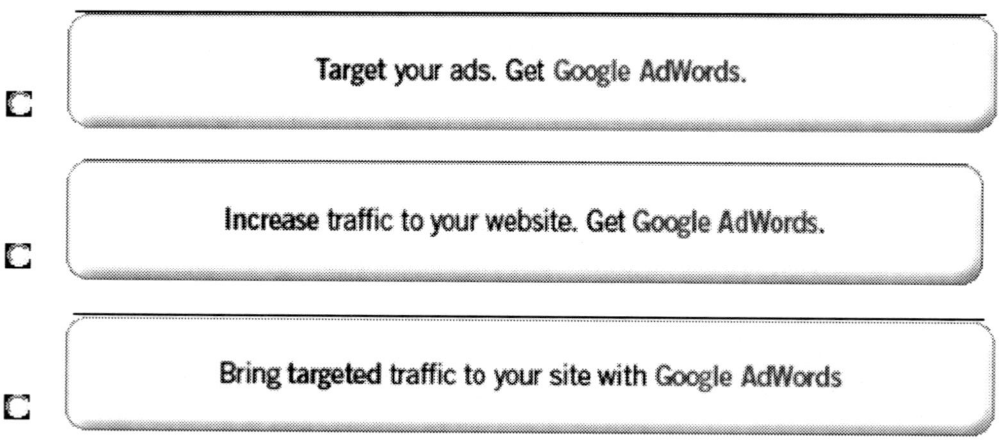

b. Small Rectangle

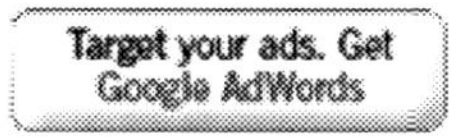

c. Vertical Rectangle Group

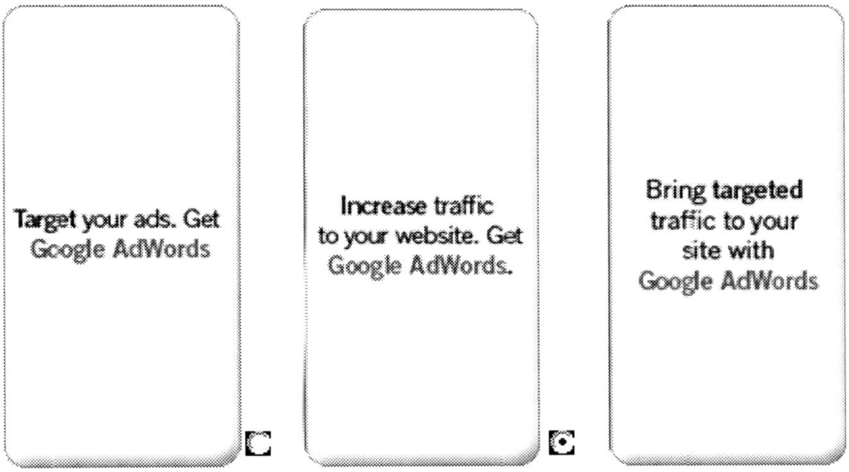

d. Large Rectangle

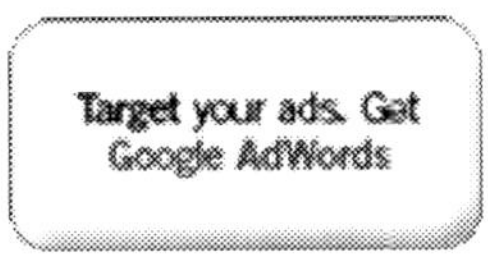

e. Square Group

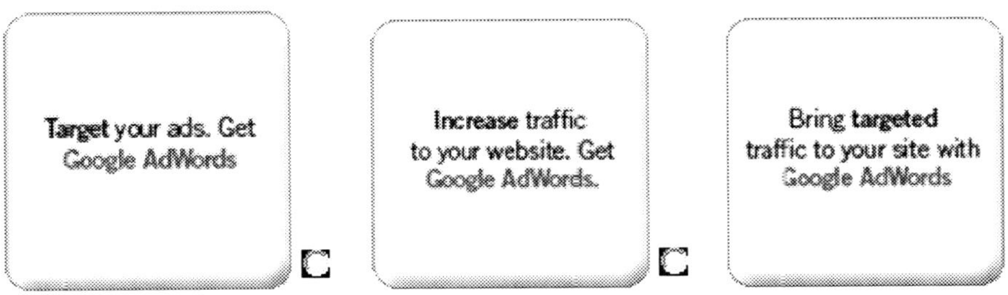

f. Small Horizontal Rectangle Group

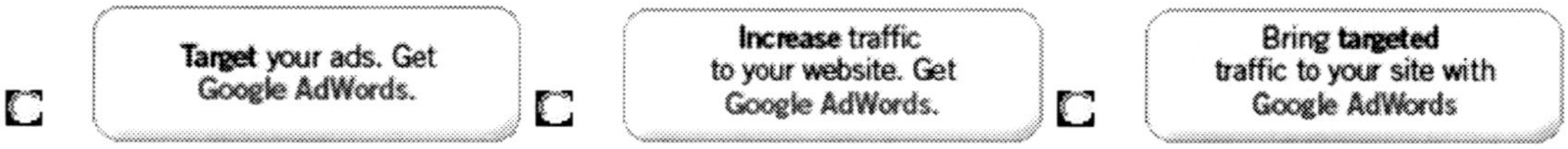

ADWORDS REFERRALS LIMITED

> You can only refer new AdWord advertisers in countries and for languages where AdSense for Content is available. Please see the AdSense for Content section of *AdSense Unleashed* for a complete list of those countries and languages.

2. AdWords Referral Text Links

In 2006 Google added AdWords referral text links to your referral arsenal. Now you can use text links instead of bulky graphics. The text links are set off by radio buttons. You cannot change the font size or color of the text links or the text itself. The four options are listed below.

- Bring targeted traffic to your site with Google AdWords
- Target your ads. Get Google AdWords.
- Increase traffic to your website. Get Google AdWords.
- Target a specific audience. Get Google AdWords.

E. Google Pack Referral Program

Google Pack is a suite of free software that Google provides for download. The software includes everything from virus protection to Google Desktop Search to the Google Toolbar. When users of your site click on the button or text link and download the Google Pack for the first time, you receive up to $2. If they download the full Google Pack you receive the full $2.

U.S. ONLY

Only users from the United States will be shown the Google Pack download buttons or text. If they are from another country, Google will automatically display the Firefox referral button or text link.

1. Google Pack Referral Buttons

Most of the Google Pack referral buttons come in sets or groups of three. Each is shown below.

a. Large Horizontal Rectangle Group

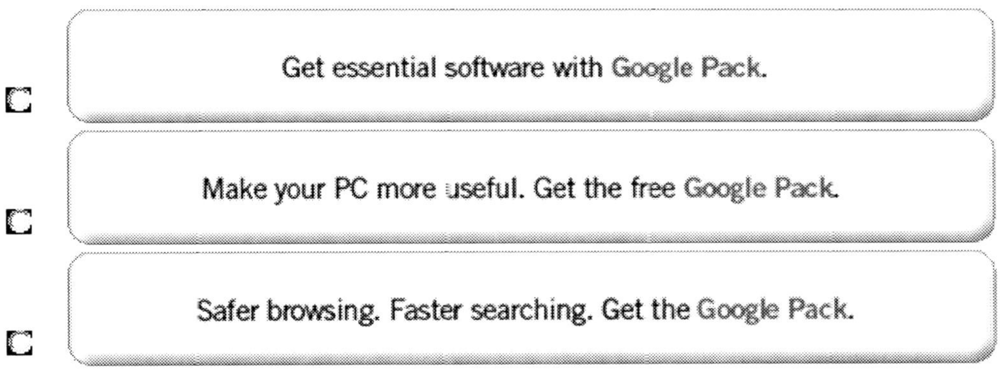

b. Small Rectangle

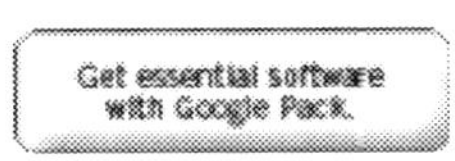

c. Large Rectangle

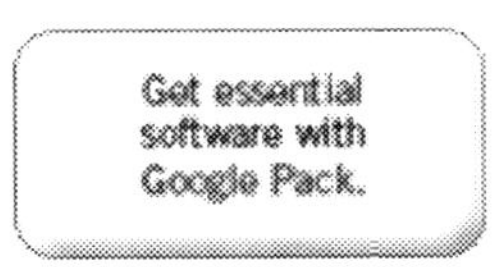

d. Vertical Rectangle Group

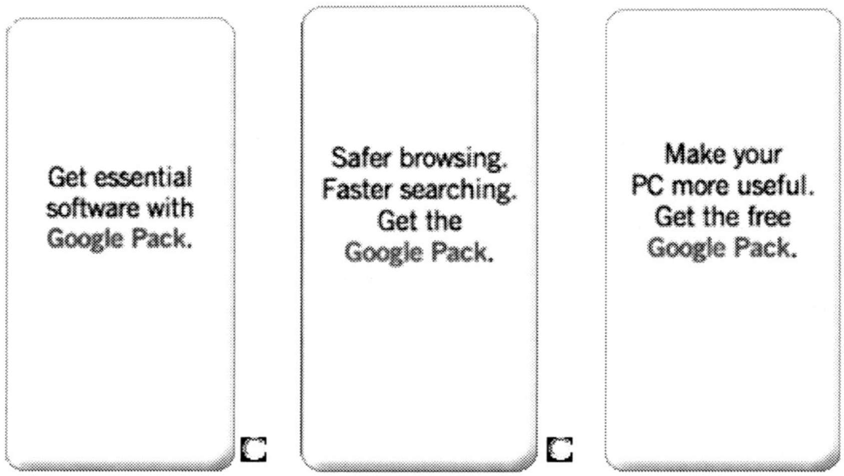

e. Square Group

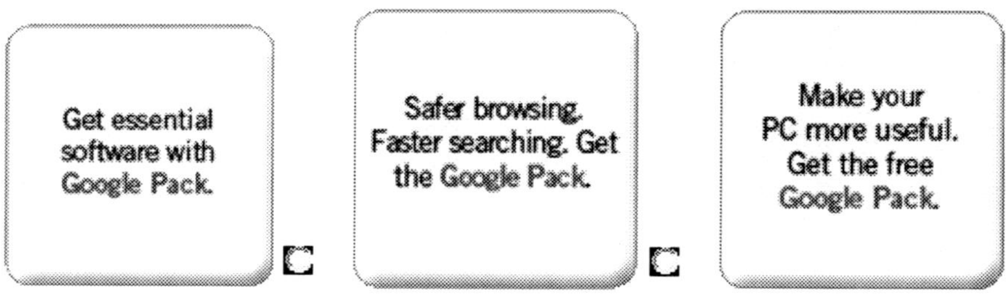

f. Small Horizontal Rectangle Group

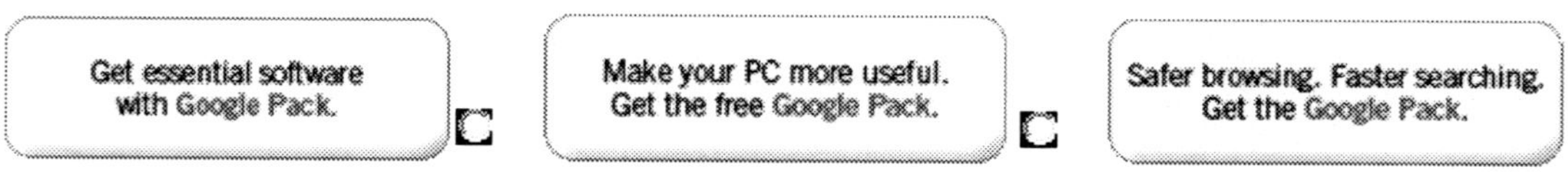

GOOGLE PACK REFERRALS LIMITED

Only Windows's users can download the Google Pack for you to get credit and it must be a first time installation.

2. Google Pack Referral Text Links

Google Pack text links can be employed instead of bulky graphics. The text links are set off by radio buttons. You cannot change the font size or color of the text links or the text itself. The three options are listed below.

- (•) Get essential software with Google Pack.
- ( ) Safer browsing. Faster searching. Get the Google Pack.
- ( ) Make your PC more useful. Get the free Google Pack.

GOOGLE PACK TEXT LINKS LIMITED

Note that you only have three text link options with Google Pack and Picasa referrals, but four for the other referral programs.

F. Picasa Referral Program

Picasa is Google fabulous digital photo software that Google provides for free download. With it you can automatically search your computer for photos, label them, email them and order prints. When users of your site click on the button or text link and download Picasa for the first time, you receive $1 USD.

NOT LIMITED TO U.S. USERS

Unlike Google Pack Referrals, Picasa Referrals are not limited to users from the United States.

1. Picasa Referral Buttons

Most of the Picasa referral buttons come in sets or groups of three. Each is shown below.

a. Large Horizontal Rectangle Group

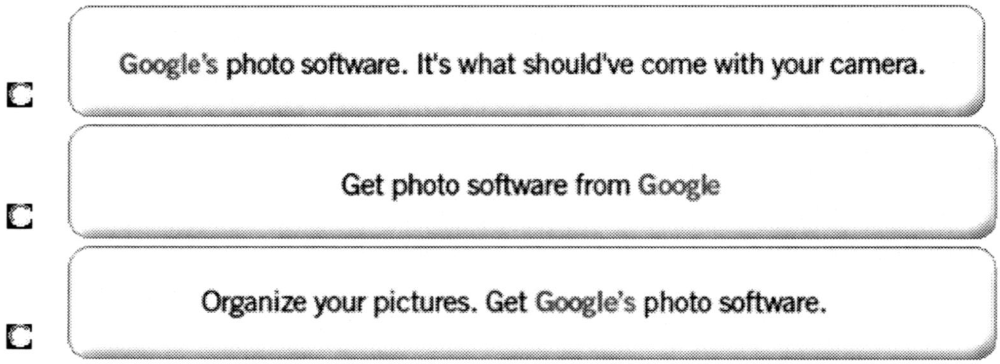

b. Small Rectangle

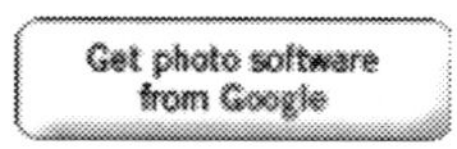

c. Large Rectangle

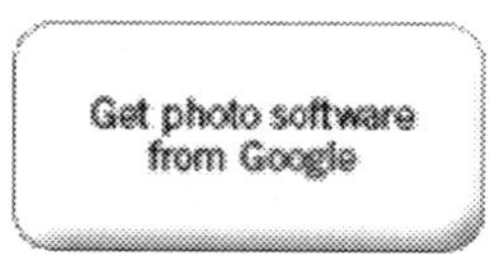

d. Vertical Rectangle Group

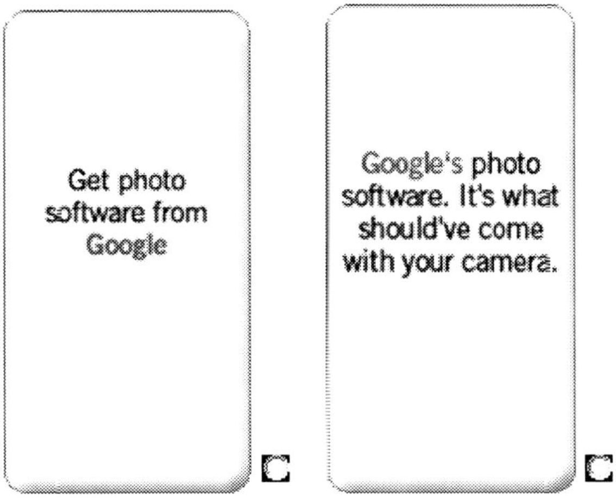

e. Square Group

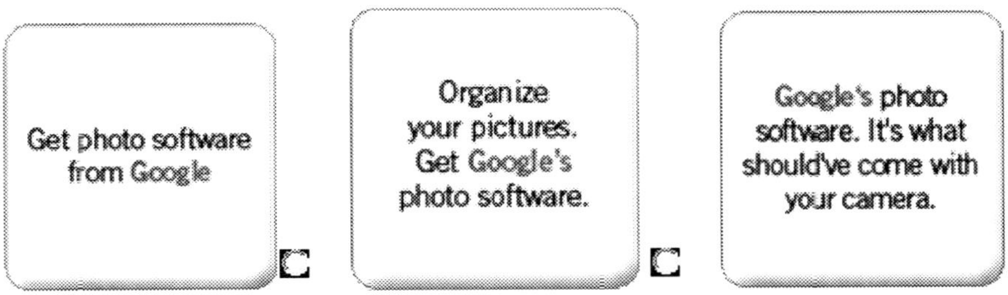

f. Small Horizontal Rectangle Group

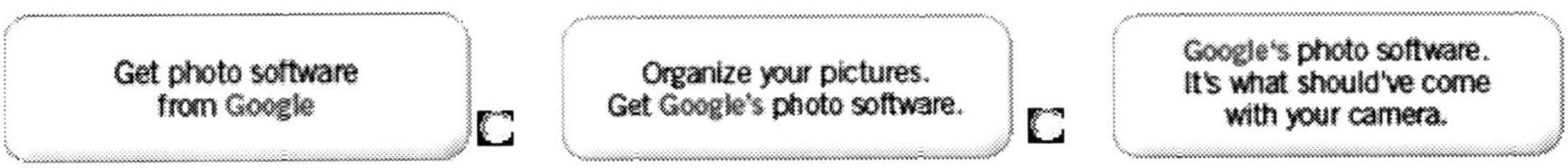

PICASA REFERRALS LIMITED

Only Windows's users can download Picasa for you to get credit and it must be a first time installation.

2. Picasa Referral Text Links

Picasa text links can be employed instead of bulky graphics. The text links are set off by radio buttons. You cannot change the font size or color of the text links or the text itself. The three options are listed below.

- Google's photo software. It's what should've come with your camera.
- Organize your pictures. Get Google's photo software.
- Get photo software from Google

ONE REFERRAL BUTTON PER PRODUCT PER PAGE

Keep in mind that you can have five Referral Buttons/text links on a page, but they are limited to one per referral product for a total of five.

VI. AdSense Payments and Accounting

A. Monthly Payments

Under the AdSense payment system Google sends you a fat monthly check every time you are due $100 or more. If you are signed up for electronic funds transfer, you will get money wired to your designated bank account once you reach the $100 threshold.

WHEN PAYMENT IS SENT

Payment is sent within 30 days after the end of the month when you reach $100 USD or more of click revenue in your account.

Ensure You Have the Correct Address

It sounds rudimentary, but little typos in your address can delay payment or even cause your AdSense payments to be sent to the wrong address. If you want Google to mail a check to your business or residence when you have reached $100 in click revenue, then verify your correct address.

- Account tab;
- Select "edit" next to the "Payee Information" link;
- Input correct address; and
- Save changes and exit.

COUNTRY FIELDS & PAYEE NAME DIFFICULT TO CHANGE

At present Google does not allow you to modify the "Country" or "Payee Name" fields once the initial application has been approved. This is apparently to prevent fraud.

Let's say you are simply not getting enough AdSense clicks to reach the $100 threshold required for Google to pay you. When you have only $65 in your AdSense account you decide you would rather devote the space on your Website to content or another click revenue venture such as Amazon.com's Affiliates program. Will Google ever pay you the $65? The answer is yes, but you will have to wait until the end of its fiscal year when it cleans up its books. February is usually when Google sends out checks to those who have stopped publishing under the AdSense program and have click revenues left in their accounts.

UNDER 18?

Signing up for AdSense can be accomplished if you are under 18 years old by submitting a parent or guardian as the payee for AdSense revenue.

At present Google does not issue a yearend statement of earnings that you can use for tax purposes. Google suggests printing bank account statements or copying AdSense checks. Let's hope Google fixes this in the near future.

CONTACT GOOGLE IF NO PAYMENT BY 25TH

If you have not been paid by the 25th of any month in which you are due payment, contact Google at adsense-support@google.com and be sure to include your login email address along with details of the payment you were to receive.

B. What to Do If You Move

Google sends your AdSense checks to the address you specified in your account application. Fair enough. What do you do if you move? If it is within the same country, log into your AdSense account, visit the "Payee Information" section under the "My Account" tab, and enter your new address. If, however, you are moving to a different country, Google prevents the country field from being changed for various legal, identity verification, and tax purposes. Here are the four steps you must take to transition your address to the new country:

Four Country Change of Address Steps in AdSense
1. Place AdSense Account on Payment Hold Status 2. Email Google with Answers to the Following 3 Questions: ➢ Amount of Last AdSense Payment ➢ First Day You Received a Page Impression ➢ Page Impressions Received on First Day 3. Close Existing Account 4. Submit New Application with New Address in Foreign Country

C. What to Do If You Change Names

Since Google will not let you change the payee name yourself, what should you do if you get married and adopt the surname of your spouse? Unfortunately, there are no quick solutions. Google prevents the payee field from being changed for various legal, identity verification, and tax purposes. Here are the steps you must take to transition to a new surname:

Five Change of Name Steps in AdSense
1. Place AdSense Account on Payment Hold Status 2. Email Google with Answers to the Following 3 Questions: ➢ Amount of Last AdSense Payment ➢ First Day You Received a Page Impression ➢ Page Impressions Received on First Day 3. Inform Google About Your Name Change 4. Close Existing Account 5. Submit New Application with New Name

Google is an American-based company. If you have foreign characters in your name or address that are nonstandard English characters, this may create a problem when Google prints your check. Fortunately, when you signup for AdSense you can add special characters in your name or address such as the Greek characters: ∀, **0**, **H**, and **P**.

FOREIGN CHARACTERS PRINTED A BIT DIFFERENTLY ON CHECKS

Because of printing limitations, Google may print foreign characters in your name or address differently on your checks. For instance, **ö** will be printed as **oe**. Google asserts that this *usually* does not cause problems with cashing checks.

You can email Google to change characters in your payee name if needed. Simply send your request to adsense-support@google.com. Be sure to include your AdSense account number in the email.

D. How to Add Another Site to Your Account

If you want to add another Website to your AdSense account, you do not have to fill out a new application for that site. As long you meet the AdSense criteria for content and other policies on the new site.

Five Steps to Setting Up a New Website in Your Account

1. Select Either AdSense for Search or Content Under the AdSense Setup tab
2. Follow the Normal Ad Setup Guidelines
3. Generate the AdSense Code
4. Copy the AdSense HTML Code
5. Paste the HTML Code Into the HTML Code on the Appropriate Page within Your New Site

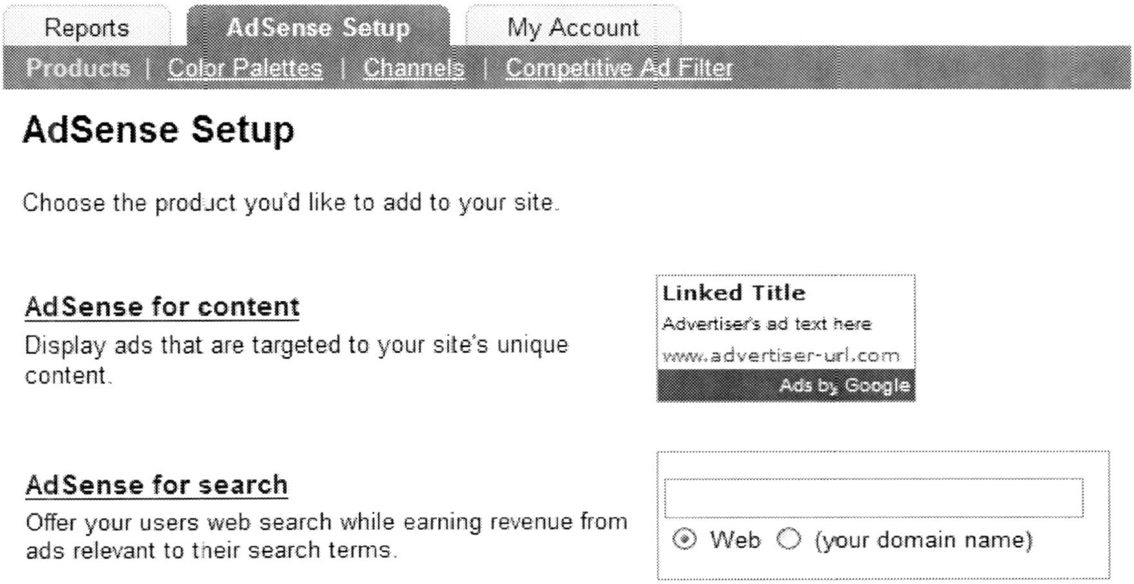

E. How to Select Your Form of Payment

Google provides two main forms of payment that you can receive. We will discuss both below.

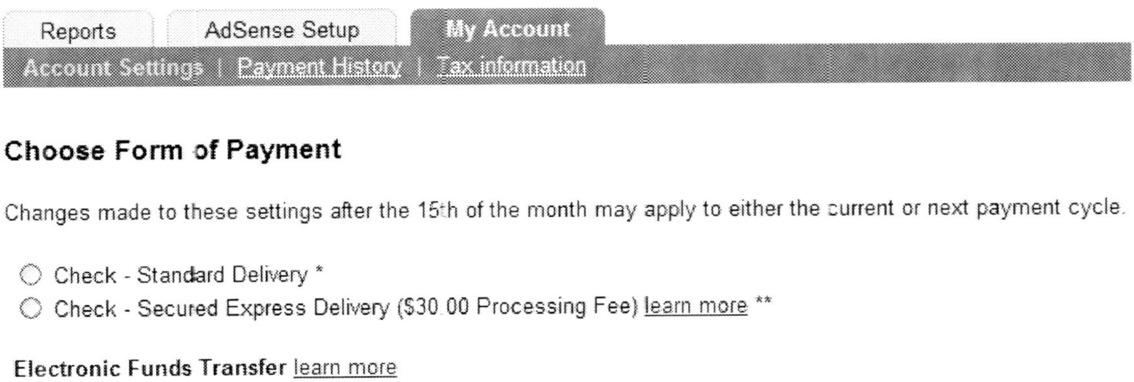

1. Payment by Check

Payment by check is the first option. There are few advantages to payment by check. The checks take longer to reach you, they may get lost in the mail, you must deposit the checks yourself in the bank, and if you have foreign characters in your name a slightly changed printing of your name may cause issues in getting the check cashed.

If you live a country other than the United States, you will get paid in your local currency. The conversion from U.S. dollars to the local currency takes place on the day the check is cut from Google's account. The exchange rate is calculated using standard conversion data on the day of transfer. Google lets you view the exchange rate it used for your conversion within your account. Simply click on the earning's line for the month in question on the Payment History page beneath the My Account tab.

EXTRA FEE FOR SECURED EXPRESS DELIVERY

Be aware, Google charges a $30 USD fee for secured express delivery of checks.

2. Payment by Electronic Funds Transfer

The second payment option is by electronic funds transfer directly to your bank account. This is the preferred method of payment as it gets your money to you safely and quickly. The money is typically deposited by the 5th day of the month. As the accountants say, this is a great way to manage your working capital. The quicker your payments are in your bank account, the more you can leverage this money for your business.

SIGN UP FOR EFT ADSENSE PAYMENTS

Signing up for EFT payments is easy. Click on the "My Accounts" tab and then the "Payment Details" section. Select "Edit" and input your bank account and routing numbers. Google will send a small amount to your account. Once your verify this exact amount, you will be signed up for EFT payments.

Countries Where EFT AdSense Payments are Enabled
Austria Belgium Canada Denmark France Germany Great Britain Ireland Italy Japan Netherlands Portugal Spain Sweden Switzerland United States

Google allows you to name your various EFT accounts. Apply easy to remember monikers such as ones named after different Websites, businesses or even bank accounts. To rename your accounts, select "Edit" under your Accounts Settings page. When selecting EFT payments, you will be asked for a nickname along with your bank routing information for the EFT.

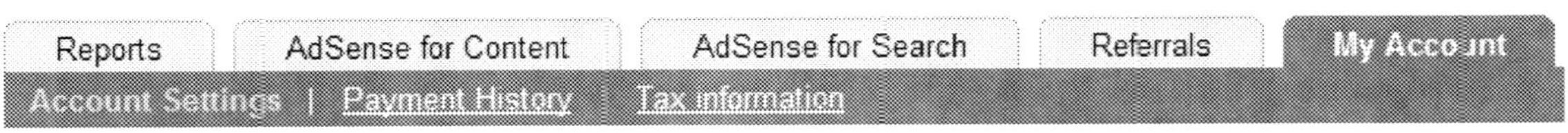

Account Holder Name: BottleTree Books LLC

Account Nickname:

Routing Number:

Account Number:

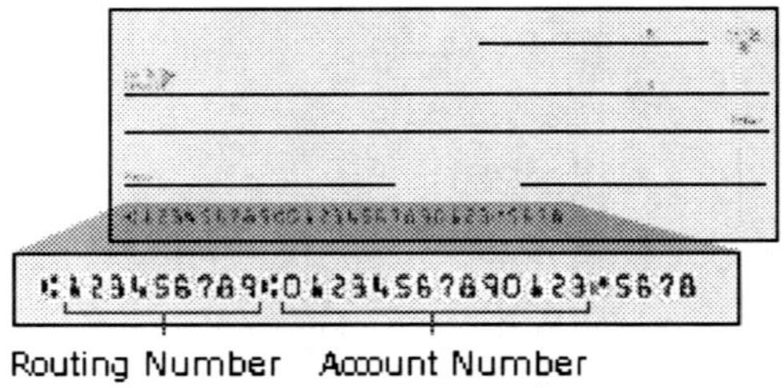

MULTIPLE BANK ACCOUNTS ALLOWED

It is little known that you can have *multiple* EFT bank accounts within your AdSense account. This is advantageous if you have multiple Websites and/or businesses running AdSense ads.

If you receive EFT payments in a bank located outside of the United States, the conversion from U.S. dollars to the local currency takes place on the day the money is wired from Google's account. The exchange rate is calculated using standard conversion data on the day of transfer.

VIEW THE EXCHANGE RATE

Google lets you view the exchange rate it used for your conversion within your account. Simply click on the earning's line for the month in question on the Payment History page beneath the My Account tab.

3. Ensure You Have the Correct Tax Information

As a payment service provider, Google must collect tax information from all AdSense publishers prior to enabling payments. This applies both to U.S. and foreign countries. Google's tax information wizard will guide you through this process. Follow the link below.

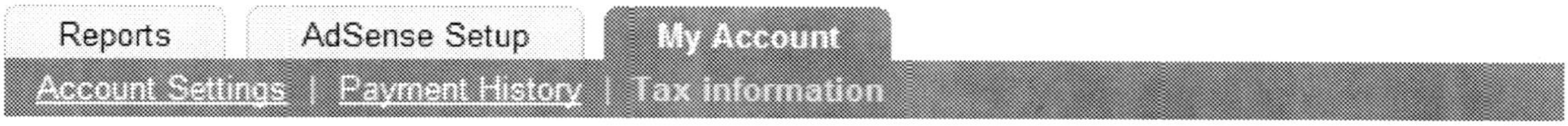

4. How to Get Your PIN

Like most online companies, Google uses Personal Identification Numbers (PINs) as a type of password into your AdSense account. When you reach the $50 threshold of click revenues, Google will establish a unique PIN and mail it to you. This is yet another reason to ensure your mailing information is accurate.

PINs by Snail-Mail

> On average PINs take 2-3 weeks to reach you after cresting the $50 PIN initiation level. Currently, Google will not email PINs to you.

Before you can receive payments from Google (after reaching the $100 in click revenues required for payment), you must input this unique PIN for verification. Be sure to keep your PIN in a place where you can easily locate it. For smaller Websites, it can take months to reach $100 in clicks after passing the $50 PIN initiation level. Remember, if you lose your PIN you can always request another from Google within your AdSense account.

Replacement PINs Never Change

> Any replacement PINs you request from Google will be the same as the original. They do not change.

F. How to Put Payments on Hold

There may be times when you need to place your AdSense payments on hold if you are traveling or moving. Google lets you easily place a "self-hold" on your account. Under the My Account tab select "account settings" and then "Hold Payment." By selecting this option, Google will hold your AdSense revenue payments.

PAYMENTS HELD INDEFINITELY

Once the "Hold Payment" option is selected, Google will hold all payments until you unselect the "Hold Payment" box. Right now you cannot specify the duration for the hold payment to last. It is indefinite.

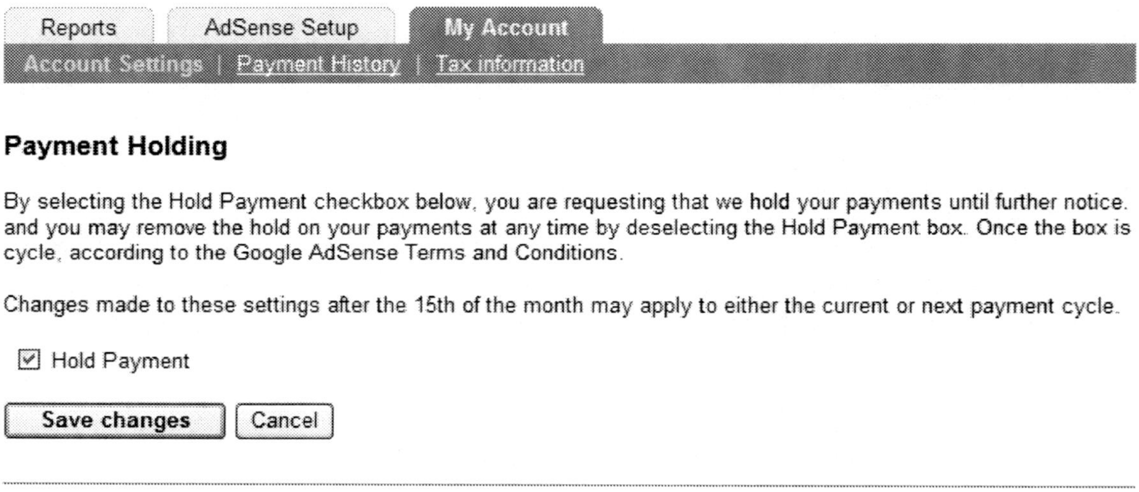

HOLD PAYMENT BEFORE 15TH OF THE MONTH

Ensure that you hold AdSense revenue payments before the 15th of the month or Google cannot guarantee that the next month's payment will be held.

VII. How AdWords Advertisers Find Your Website

If advertisers do not have a particular site in mind, but would like to find out which sites relating to their keywords are showing Google ads, they can search for AdSense sites in two main ways. These are the Site Tool and the "Advertise on This Site" link.

A. Site Tool

The Site Tool is an AdWords tool. It is *not* found under the "Tools" tab within AdWords. It is actually built within the "Site Targeted Campaign Setup" link on the Campaign Summary page. There are three components to the tool that can be employed by AdWords advertisers to find your direct URL, Website topics, or to target demographics of your users.

1. List URLs

If an AdWords advertiser would like to learn if a group of Websites are part of the Google AdSense network or whether sites with similar content are available, they can manually list the URLs. This is the primary way that AdWord advertisers find your Website. They can then submit a bid, on a Cost-Per-Thousand-Impressions model, to serve ads on your site. Google also returns a list of similar sites on the AdSense network.

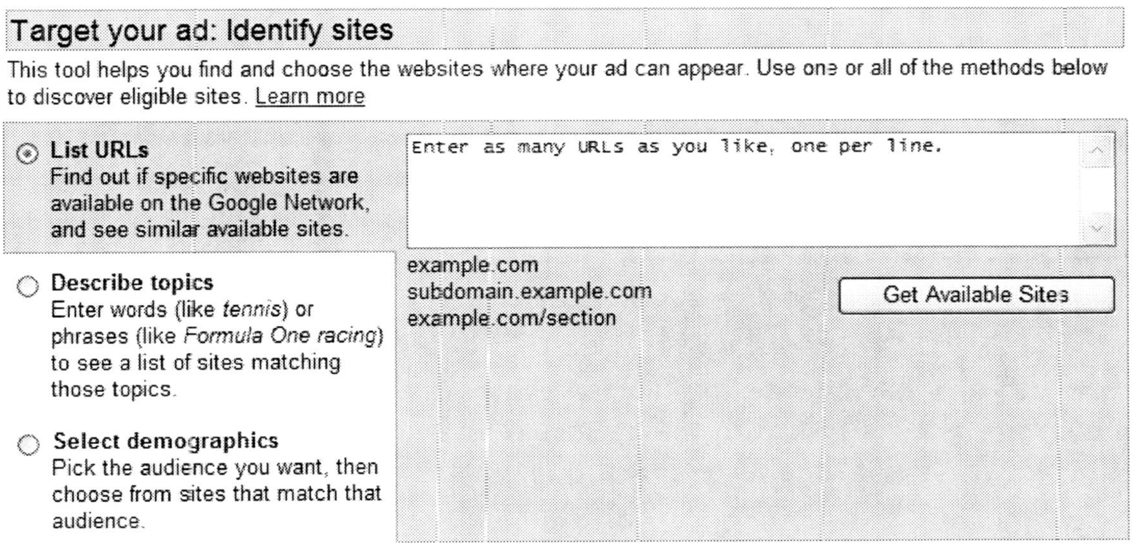

ADVERTISERS CAN ENTER SPECIFIC WEB PAGES

Google lets advertisers target specific *pages* of your Website also. All they need to do is type it in such as www.bottletreebooks.com/GuerrillaTactics

Google will list the available sites and then AdWord advertisers can simply click on the link to view the sites. If they like the content, they can check the box next to the site and then add it to the list of sites on which they are willing to advertise.

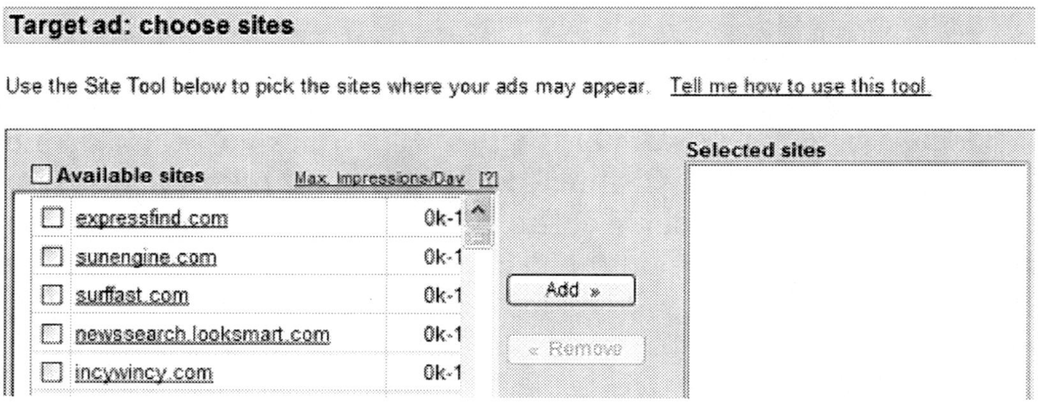

WEBSITES NOT IN THE CONTENT NETWORK

If AdWords advertisers search on a site that is not in Google's Content Network, it will list them as not available.

2. Describe Topics

Here AdWord advertisers simply enter keywords into Google's Site Tool and it returns a list of AdSense Websites relevant to those keywords. Not only will the list of sites be returned, it estimates the number of impressions that will be shown of the ad. Advertisers can also type in key phrases to narrow the focus of their search.

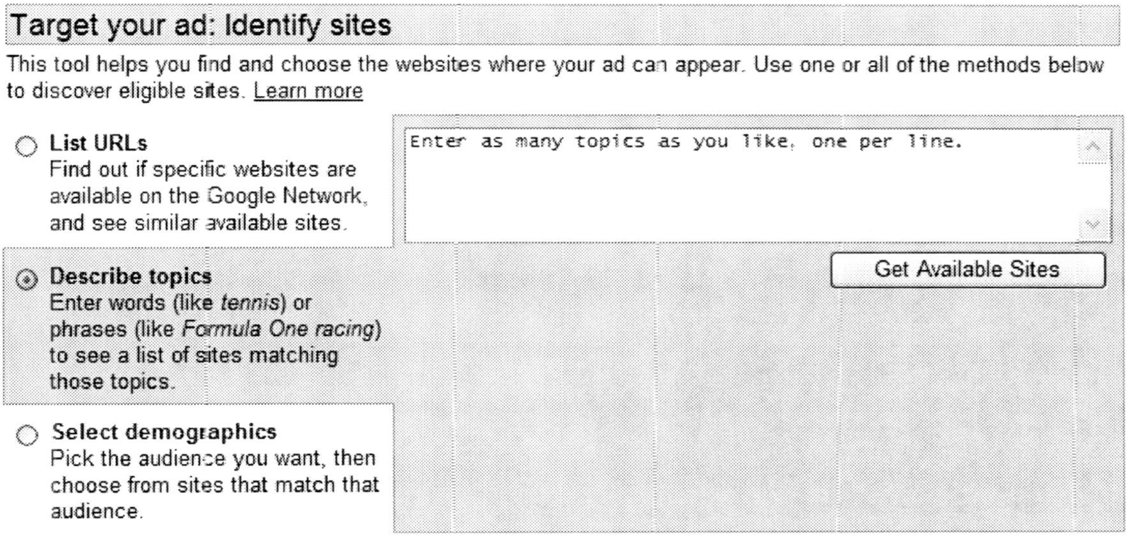

Google will then list the available sites and then AdWords advertisers can simply click on the link to view the sites. If they like the content, they can check the box next to the site and then add it to the list of sites on which they are willing to advertise.

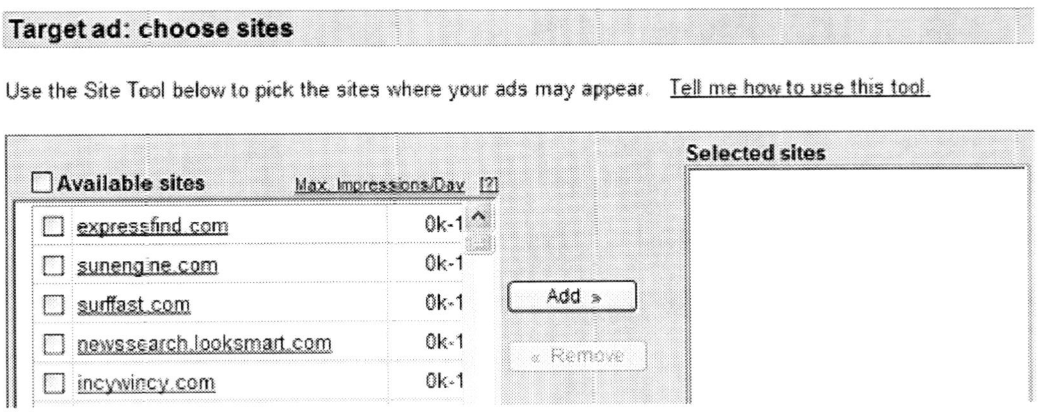

3. Select Demographics

Demographic selection is audience targeting to the max. With this powerful sub-tool of Site Targeting, AdWord advertisers can seek out and focus in on the exact demographic that buys their products or services. No longer do advertisers have to guess at what type of people are visiting sites they want to target. Google now provides twenty-two demographics from which your CPM advertisers can pick. Obviously, the less demographic selection, the fewer sites that will be returned in the results. Where does Google get this data? It uses data from comScore Media Metrix, which has compiled some of the most extensive user data on the Internet.

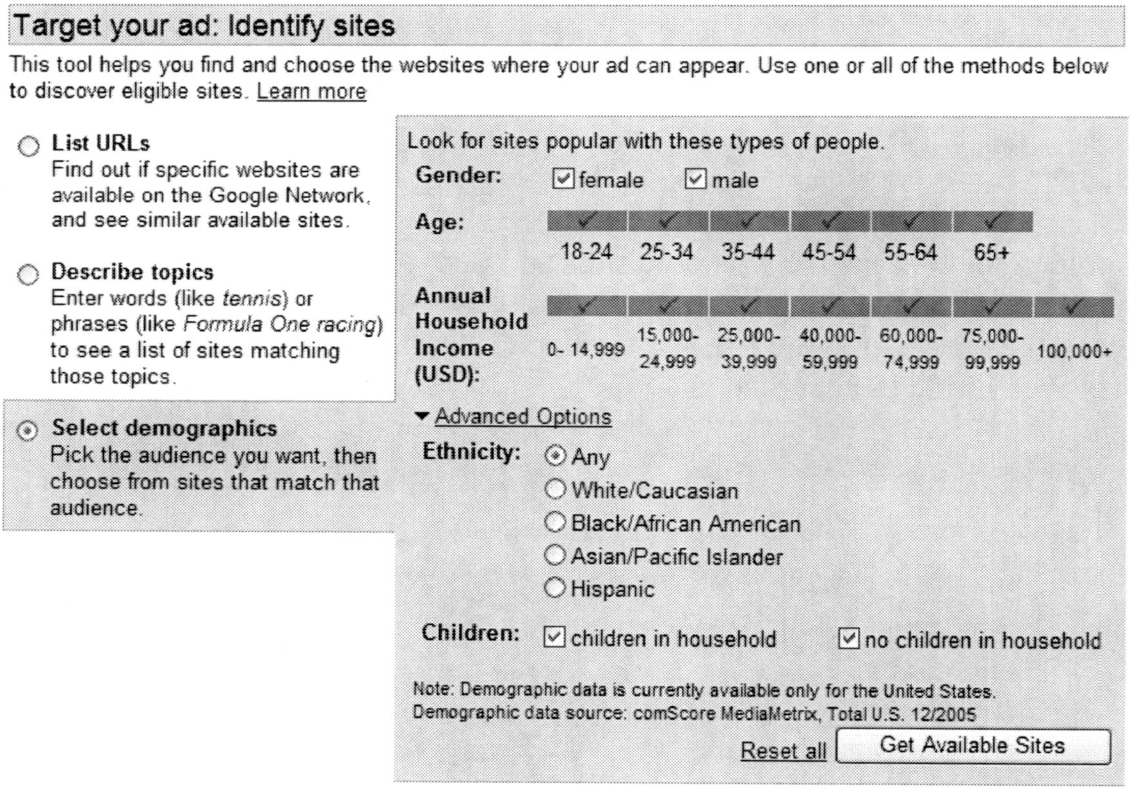

DATA LIMITED TO UNITED STATES USERS ONLY

At this time Google data via comScore is limited to U.S. users only. If you do not target the United States, you will not be presented with demographic site selection in the Site Targeting tool.

Google will list the available sites and then AdWord advertisers can simply click on the link to view the sites. If they like the content, they can check the box next to the site and then add it to the list of sites on which they are willing to advertise.

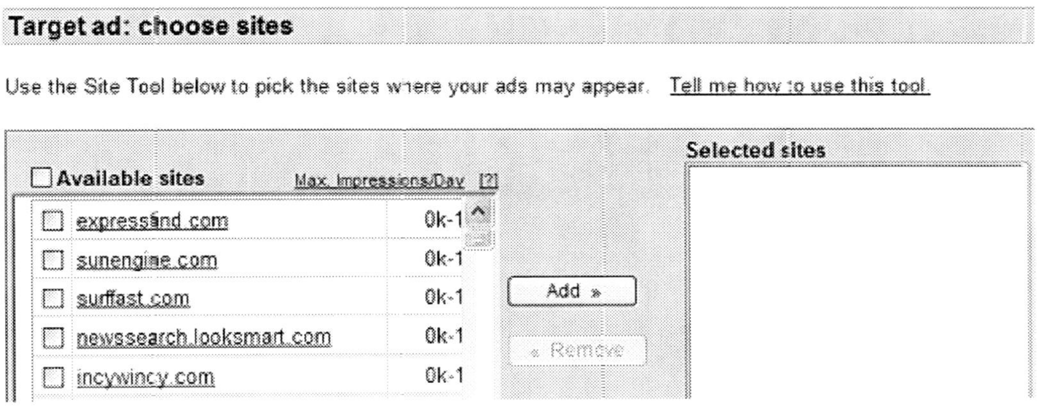

MAXIMUM 100 AVAILABLE SITES LISTED

Google will return up to one hundred sites based upon demographic data.

After the list is returned, advertisers can click on the URL links to visit the sites or select the “Find more sites like these” link to generate a new batch of demographic focused sites with similar content. Next Google asks for the amount advertisers are willing to pay per 1000 impressions of an ad on these sites.

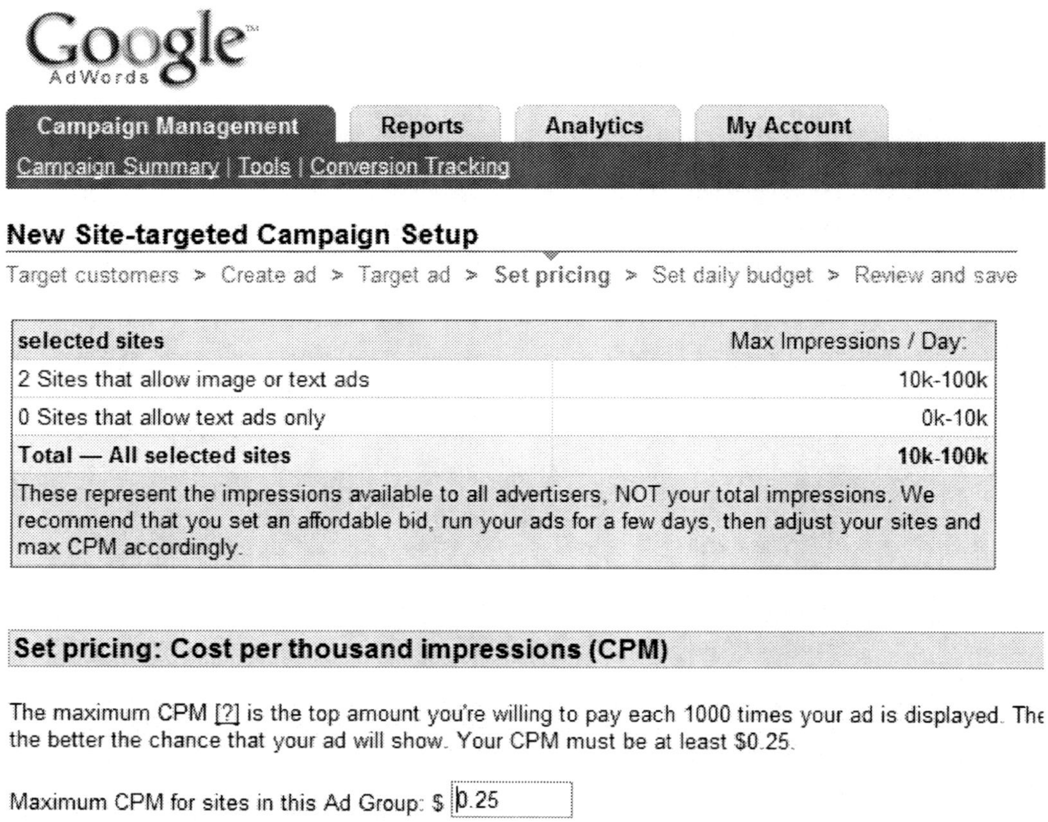

Finally, advertisers set their daily budget, review their selections, and their CPM ads begin showing. Google also allows them to *exclude* sites where they do not want impressions of ads being shown.

EXCLUDE UP TO 500 SITES

Google's powerful Site Exclusion Tool allows advertisers to block ads from showing on up to 500 Websites. This is like the Filtering Tool on steroids. Excluding a site keeps ads from showing on *all* pages of that Website.

B. "Advertise on This Site" Link

The second main way that advertisers learn how to advertise on your site is the "Advertise on This Site" link where advertisers signup right on your Website. That way advertisers targeting your site are ensured of ad inclusion. The process is simple. You display an "Advertise on this site" link on your Ad Units. When it is clicked on, users are taken to a unique landing page that contains your logo (generally you want to make this the same as the logo for your AdSense for Search box). Then users can create a new AdWords account (if they do not have one already) and make unique ads that will only show on your Website. With direct advertiser signup it is now much easier for advertisers to start targeting your site for their ads, which can only mean increased revenue for you, the AdSense publisher. Enter "Advertise on this site" links.

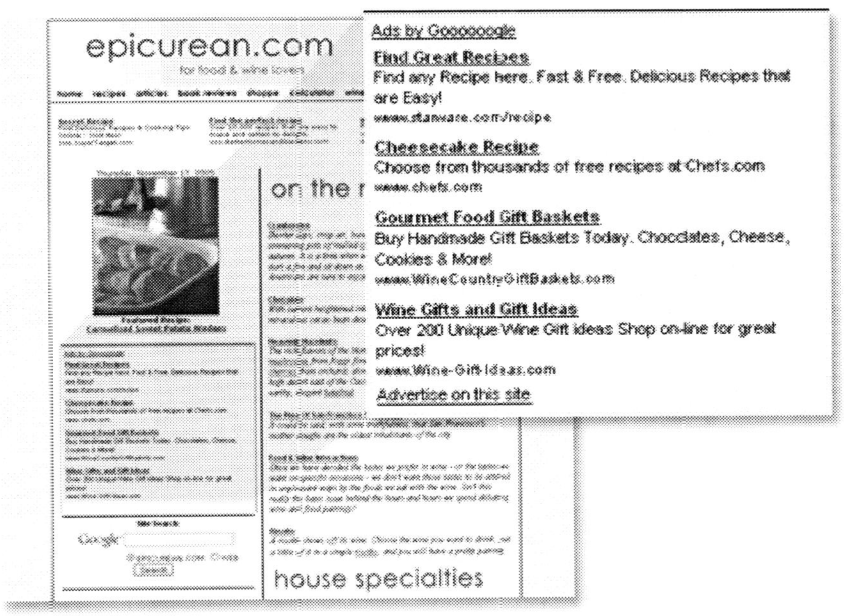

If you are an AdSense publisher, this link is a powerful tool to enable impressions of high paying ads on your site. For instance, let's say you offer counseling help for those convicted of DUI (driving while under the influence). The content you have posted on your site is about your services, the dangers of DUI, and various DUI statistics in all 50 of the United States is driving traffic. Your AdSense ads are getting clicks and you have seen an increase in revenue. By adding the "Advertise on this site" link to your Ad Units, you subsequently notice that a prominent law firm in New York, representing clients in various DUI charges, has begun showing ads simply by clicking on the "Advertise on this site" link on the Ad Unit and completing the easy sign-up process.

Three-Step "Advertise on This Site" Sign-Up
➢ Advertisers Click on the "Advertise on this site" Link; ➢ Advertisers Log Into Their AdWords Account or Create a New One; ➢ They Complete Three Step Site Targeted Campaign Wizard;

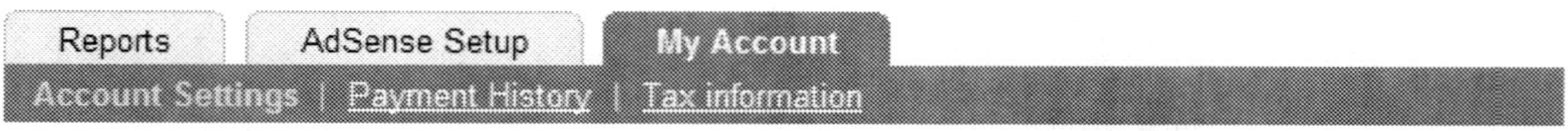

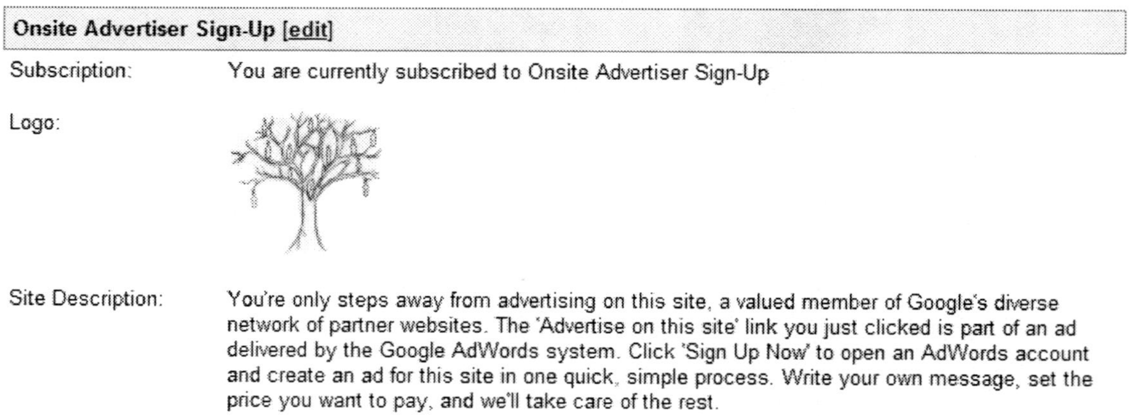

Direct signup is a huge advantage for AdSense publishers. You now receive highly tailored ads for your site that are likely to result in higher Click-Through-Rates and hence more money for you. Plus, these tailor ads must make you more money than ads generally served to your site or they will not show. This is actually Site/Segment Targeting on the Content Network where advertisers can hone ads for particular sites or pages within a site. In addition, the more advertisers you have vying for ads on your site, the higher the amount they will pay per click, which means you will make even more money for each click.

CUSTOMIZE THE LANDING PAGE

> Google lets you customize almost every aspect of the Onsite Advertiser Signup landing page. You can change the text size, font, color, and background color (200 colors to choose). You can even insert your company logo. Take every opportunity to build brand/site awareness. Also, your landing page should have the look and feel of your Website.

Here is the standard language Google displays when a potential advertiser clicks on this link:

> **You're only steps away from advertising on this site, a valued member of Google's diverse network of partner websites. The 'Advertise on this site' link you just clicked is part of an ad delivered by the Google AdWords system. Click 'Sign Up Now' to open an AdWords account and create an ad for this site in one quick, simple process. Write your own message, set the price you want to pay, and we'll take care of the rest.**

While Google's general language generally works, here are our suggested changes:

> **You're only steps away from advertising on ~~this site~~ Name of Website *or* Language Such as "The Internet's Best Sporting Goods Site", a valued member of Google's diverse**

network of partner websites. The 'Advertise on this site' link you just clicked is part of an ad delivered by the Google AdWords system. Click 'Sign Up Now' to open an AdWords account and create an ad for ~~this site~~ Name of Website *or* Language Such as "The Internet's Best Sporting Goods Site", in one quick, simple process. Write your own message, set the price you want to pay, and ~~we'll~~ Google will take care of the rest. Follow this link www.[URL].com to visit our homepage.

You can change this language at any time. Do not use all capital letters for the welcome language. Not only is all caps harder to read for the human eye, but also it is considered shouting on the Internet.

LANDING PAGE ADWORDS REFERRAL BUTTON?

Now that Google offers AdWords referrals revenue, you may wish to add an AdWords referral button on your landing page. Since the landing page does not have editable HTML, you are unable to add this button. Hopefully Google will change this in the future.

VIII. Section Targeting

A. Introduction

Section Targeting is a more highly focused version of Site Targeting. With Section Targeting you can specify the area on your Website from where Google will draw keywords to be used in serving ads. This prevents unwanted keywords from being taken into consideration by Google such as those used in your site navigation structure.

For example, consider a laser hair removal (and very popular) Blog that shows AdSense ads in Wide Skyscraper format down one side and a Wide Rectangle format near the top of the Blog. Knowing that regular readers of this Blog (those contemplating laser hair removal procedures) typically read only the most recent posting, which is at the top of the screen next to the Wide Rectangle unit of AdSense ads focused on laser hair removal. Since you want ads relevant to your latest posting, you can Section Target this area. You can also instruct Google to downplay older posts sitting below that text. This will prevent ads being served with information about old posts that users of your site may not be interested in at the moment.

SECTION TARGETING NOT LIMITED

> You can have unlimited Section Targeting within your Website.

Likewise, AdWord advertisers can target this section of the page to show ads on a CPM basis. Here AdWord advertisers can outsmart their keyword targeting competition that is using a scattershot approach to hopefully get their ads running on the most popular Blog in the laser hair removal industry. Once again, Google provides the tools for smart advertisers to flourish. With Section Targeting, you specify to Google which areas of text/HTML code on your Website it should key upon when serving AdSense ads. This option could easily be called "Content Section Targeting" because it lets you focus on page content to determine the keywords that will be derived for serving ads on a section of your Web page.

B. How to Add Section Targeting to Page Content

Okay, here is more HTML code that you must insert into the HTML code of your Website. Google simply needs you to define the area of content on your page that it should serve ads to. This definition is accomplished by two lines of HTML tags:

```
<!-- google_ad_section_start -->
```

Section Targeted Content

```
<!-- google_ad_section_end -->
```

SECTION TARGETING AND AD UNIT LOCATIONS

> Remember that Google will serve ads into the first Ad Unit laid out in your HTML code. If you Site Target content at the bottom of the page and your first Ad Unit is at the top of the page, you will get ads served into that Ad Unit that are unrelated to the content near the Ad Unit.

Ensure you only use Section Targeting on large portions of Website content. It is against Google's AdSense policy to focus on small portions of your content in an effort to change the appearance of your content in the eyes of Google's crawlers. Insufficient content being targeted may also result in a drop of AdSense ads that will be served to your page and/or Public Service Ads being shown.

C. How to Quarantine Content Sections

Likewise you can quarantine sections of your page that you do not want Google's crawlers to see. Let's say you have a site that focuses on camping gear, but you have a small section devoted to your favorite snack food: Pink Sno-Balls. If Google crawls this content area you may get Pink Sno-Ball ads. To block off sections of your page add the following tag line before the content in question:

```
<!-- google_ad_section_start(weight=ignore) -->
```

Content to be Blocked from Google Crawlers

```
<!-- google_ad_section_end -->
```

UP TO TWO WEEK DELAY

> It may take up to two weeks for Google's crawlers to visit and record the Section Targeting on your Website.

D. Example of HTML Section Targeting

Below is an example of how sample Section Targeting tags may look in your HTML. Note that we have blocked a section of content from being crawled.

```
<html><head><title>Section targeting</title></head>
<body>
<!-- google_ad_section_start -->
```

Text of Your Page Where Most of Your Content Resides

```
<!-- google_ad_section_start(weight=ignore) -->
```

Content to be Blocked from Google Crawlers

```
<!-- google_ad_section_end -->
```

```
<!-- google_ad_section_end -->
</body>
</html>
```

TARGET WEBSITE HOMEPAGES IF RELEVANT

> For the vast majority of Websites, the homepage gets the most traffic. Whether through direct traffic or internal clicks once users deep link into a site. Keep this in mind when setting up your Section Targeting campaign.

IX. Little Used AdSense Tools

A. AdSense Preview Tool

The AdSense Preview Tool is a downloadable application that allows you to learn what ads from what countries will be delivered to a particular page of your Website. Its operation is simple; you merely right-click on a particular page of your Website and the results will be displayed. Note that this application currently only works for Internet Explorer 6.x browsers.

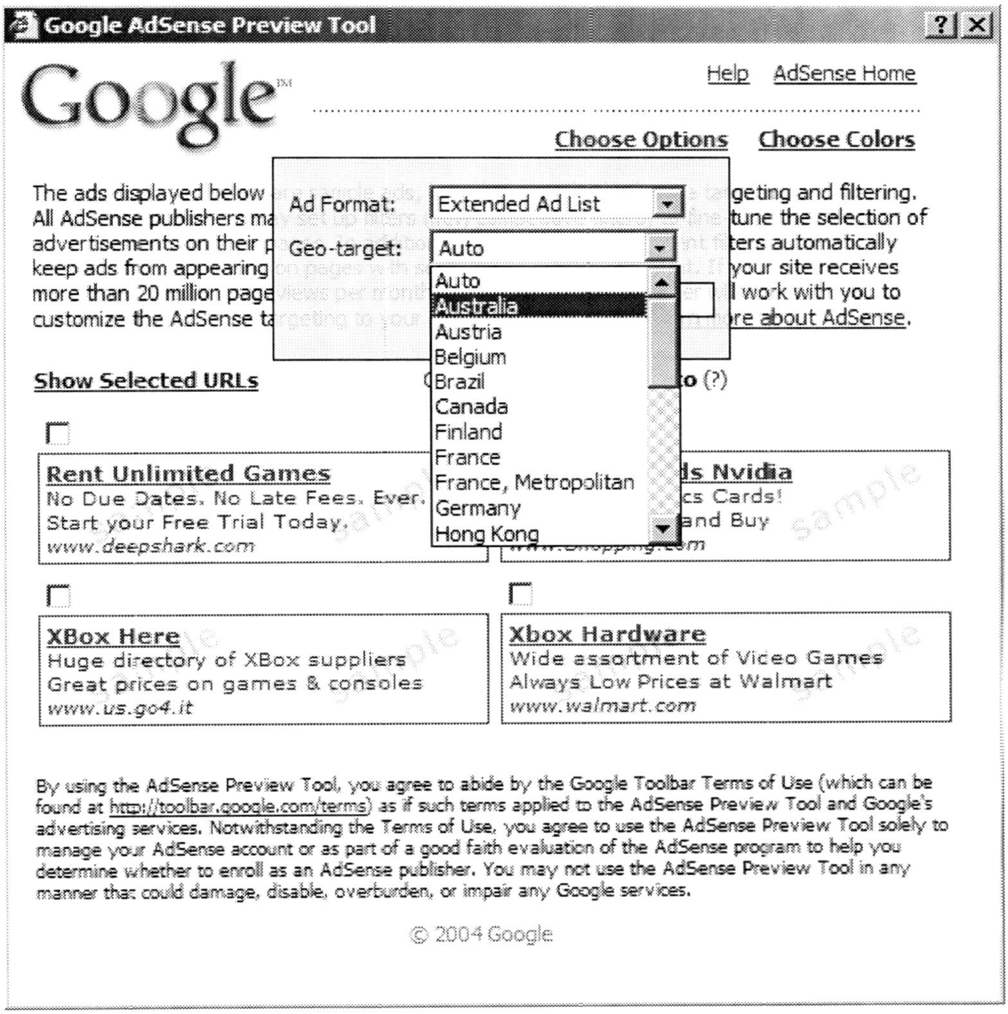

DOWNLOAD THE ADSENSE PREVIEW TOOL TODAY

To download this free and powerful tool, simply point your browser to: https://www.google.com/adsense/previewtool.

B. Sitemap Your Way to Success

With Sitemaps you can easily keep Google updated with any changes made on your site. What this means for you as an AdSense publisher is that you will be served the most relevant, content matching ads on a timely basis. Which, in turn, means more ad clicks and revenues. With Sitemaps you no longer have to wait for the Googlebots to crawl your Web pages – which can take two weeks – for changes to be logged into its site index. Now the Googlebots will be notified when changes occur. They will crawl the exact pages where changes have been made and update it.

SIGN UP FOR SITEMAPS TODAY

To get your Website registered with Sitemaps for free, visit http://www.google.com/webmasters/sitemaps/login and open your account today.

1. How to Submit Sitemaps to Google

In fact, you do not need a sitemap at your Web domain to get Google's detailed tracking. When signing up for Sitemaps, Google will ask you if you have a sitemap. If the answer is no, simply input your tracking URL. Google will then generate a unique code that will look something like this: Goog2389djiej38d. To verify you are the owner of the URL so that detailed tracking can begin, Google next requires you to create an HTML file with the code as the title (ex., Goog2389djiej38d.html). When you click the "Verify" button, the Googlebots will search the files on your domain server. If the file is there, you will begin receiving detailed stats.

Three Ways to Submit Sitemaps to Google

- Sitemap Generator http://www.google.com/webmasters/sitemaps/docs/en/sitemap-generator.html
- XML Sitemap http://www.google.com/webmasters/sitemaps/docs/en/protocol.html
- Submit a Text File with URLs

2. Sitemap Statistics

Another great feature of Google Sitemaps is the built-in statistics tools. Using Sitemaps you can easily learn which search terms users are employing to find content on your site. You can find this information under the Stats tab within the Query Stats subsection.

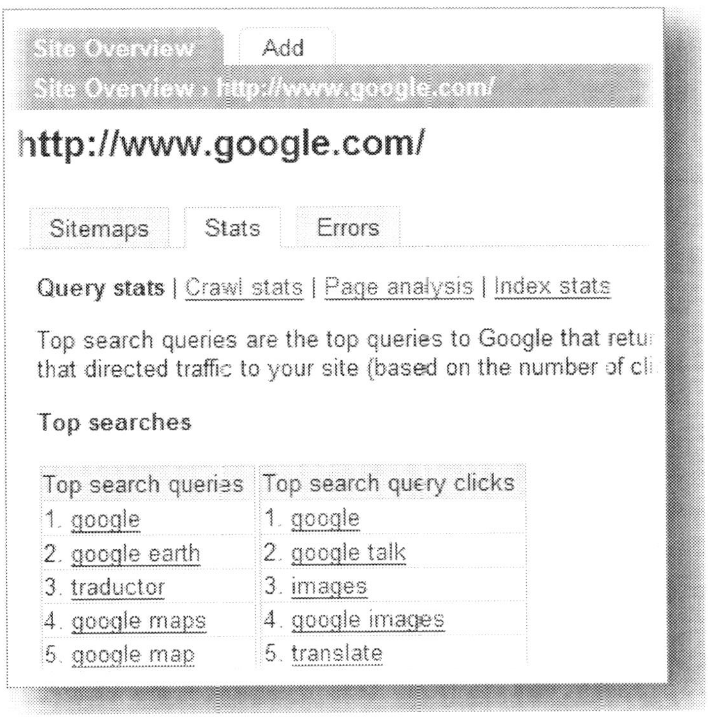

It tells you PageRank for all your pages, which search queries are driving traffic to your site, and which pages returned errors such as the dreaded 404 error. Sitemaps also give detailed stats on searches conducted within Google search and how free traffic based off these searches are finding your site (i.e., what search terms they are using and where your site is ranking for those search results). Beneath the Stats tab you will also find such valuable information as Crawl Stats, Page Analysis, and Index Stats. The later provides a tally of keywords that link to your site and common keywords found on sites that link to your site.

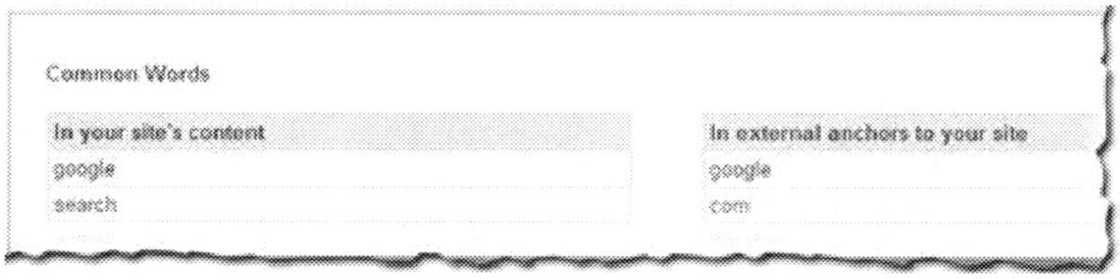

USE SITEMAP DATA FOR SECTION TARGETING

If you learn from Sitemap data that certain search terms are being used to find your site, focus your Section Targeting on that area of content to ensure the right AdSense ads are getting served.

3. How to Ensure Googlebots are Not Blocked

To review the content on your site, Google launches an army of Googlebot scouts across the Web that return with information. You can inadvertently block Googlebots from searching all or portions of your site. This could tank the number of clicks you receive since Google may start serving public service announcements or misdirected ads on your site. How this works is that the Googlebots first review a robots.txt file located on your domain server. You may not even know you have one, but if it is set to refuse entrance by the Googlebots, they will be turned away and return to Google empty handed.

Luckily, Google lets you generate a report within Sitemaps that tells you key information about your robots.txt file such as: (1) the last time the Googlebots crawled your site; (2) whether specific URLs within your site are blocking the Googlebot and Google content, image and search crawlers; and (3) test changes. This report is found under the Robots.txt tab within Sitemaps.

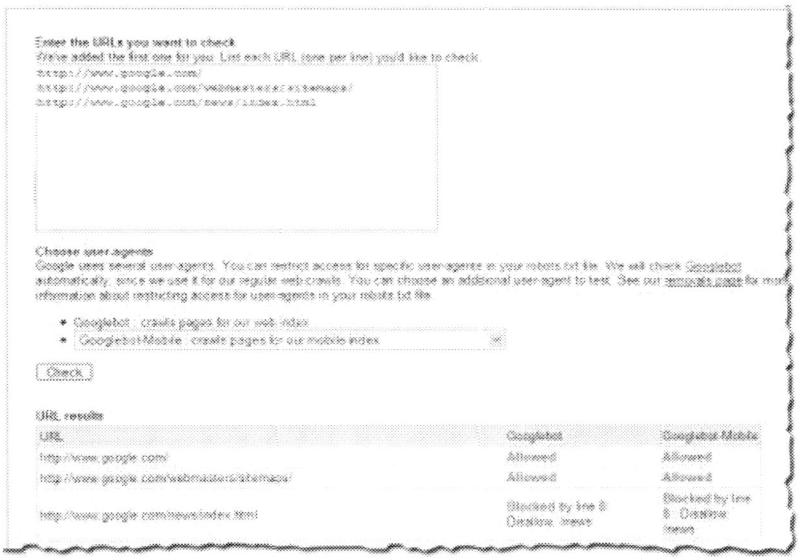

TEST ROBOT.TXT CHANGES FIRST

A powerful feature of Sitemaps is the ability to test changes to your robot.txt file *without* modifying it at your Website. See how the various Googlebots and crawlers will react first.

4. Mobile Sitemaps

Google Mobile Sitemaps allow you to submit URLs to the Google index that have been specifically set up for mobile device use such as cellphones and Palm devices.

MOBILE SITEMAPS FOR WEBMASTERS

Google has very specific rules for mobile Sitemaps. It is highly recommended that you visit http://www.google.com/webmasters/sitemaps/docs/en/mobile.html for the latest information.

C. Test Keyword Density

It is important to ascertain the keyword density on your page before it is crawled by GoogleBots. If you have the wrong keyword density, you will get AdSense ads served that will result in less clicks and less money. Here is a great Website that will let you calculate your keyword density for free: www.ranks.nl/tools/spider.html

D. View Ads Based on Content

You now know how to test the keyword density of your site. It is little known that you can actually view sample ads that will be served to your Website *before* enabling AdSense. These are typically sandbox tools since they let you play in the AdSense sandbox before committing. A great sandbox tool can be found at: http://www.digitalpoint.com/tools/adsense-sandbox/ The content this tool considers is both word content and Website URL name. The later should not be overlooked when setting up your Website. Subdomain extensions should also be picked carefully based upon the content of your particular page.

E. Add Google Maps API

With the Google Maps API you can now include a tailored map on your Website to your place of business, where your products are made, or any pretty much any location that you want to show on a map. Google now allows you to incorporate its leading Internet mapping technology you're your Website. You can add markers to the map, graphics, and information balloons. Best of all – it's free!

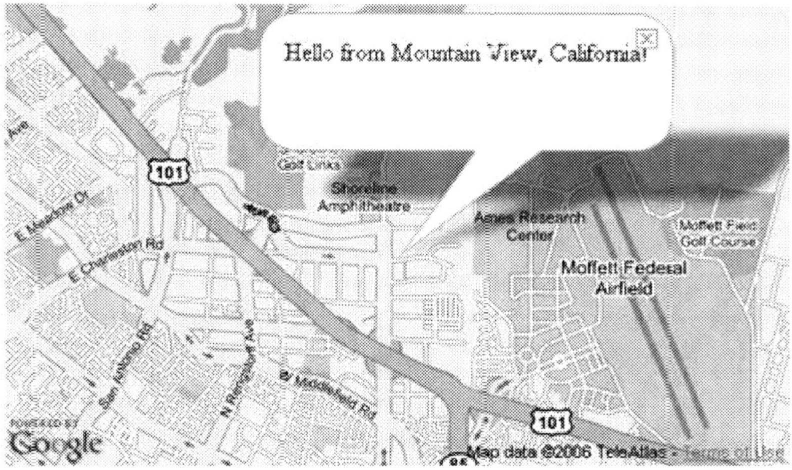

SIGNUP FOR THE MAPS API TODAY

To get the free Google Maps API for your Website, please visit: http://www.google.com/apis/maps/.

The Google Maps API is free for any Website that does not charge a fee to use the Website. In other words, it must be free to consumers to use. Certain pay per usage or monthly fee sites are there excluded from using the Google Maps API. Incorporating the Google Maps API for your Website is a great way to add content that will get you more clicks on relevant Ad Units placed near the map itself. Place your Ad Units near any information balloon you may have on your map as this will attract eyeballs.

MAPS WILL NOT IMPROVE SITE RANKING

Adding Google Maps API to your Website will not improve your site ranking within Google's ranking system.

X. Top Paying AdSense Keywords

A. Introduction

Okay. We've learned that Google pays you a percentage of the CPC for ads served on your site and we've also learned that by doing a little homework you can reach a good estimate as to what that percentage is. In light of this, serving content on your site, focused on some of the top paying keywords, can result in huge revenue increases. Before we begin showing how to find these words, let's make clear that we are not advocating so called "keyword farm" sites that merely list top paying keywords with no content behind them. Instead, we'll show you how to spot the top paying keywords in *your* market. Once you know these words, include a section of content, perhaps a series of articles, directed toward them to increase revenue. You may also want to update the content in your existing articles.

Here's an example. Let's say you are the world's foremost expert on tort reform law. You have been following this convoluted area for years and recently have started your own Blog that is fast becoming the hot place to get the latest information on which states are passing legislation. You are so involved with this subject that you frequently Blog about various state senators who vote for or against portions of the tort reform bills. Your users are eating it up, but you notice that few ads are being served deal with senator ad campaigns for or against reelection. Suddenly you see your revenue drop because 95% of your readers do not live in the particular state of that senator. What has happened? Your Blog has gone down the wrong path, but all is not lost. Tort lawyers pay some of the highest amounts for keywords (upwards of $50 a click) such as "Mesothelioma," "Birth Defects," "Doctor Malpractice," "Asbestos," and "Vioxx." You get the picture. Realizing this you begin writing content that goes deeper into the different types of tort reform that uses many of these keywords, which in turn results in high paying ads being served and revenues skyrocketing for your Website.

B. Top Keyword Groups in Major English Speaking Countries

Below is a selection of top paying keywords in five major English speaking countries: Australia, Canada, Ireland, United Kingdom, and United States. The maximum CPC amounts change often, but the pattern of keywords do not. Like you may expect, some of the keywords with the highest average CPC are found with words relating to the three lucrative professions of finance, law and the medical industry. All of the terms shown below have *average* CPCs above $15 USD per click.

1. Australia

a. Australian Domain Name Terms

We are all familiar with Internet domain names. They are the unique URL names you register with a Top Level Domain ("TLD") extension such as www.BottleTreeBooks.com or a country level domain such as BottleTreeBooks.com.au. There are also regional domain extensions such as the relatively new .eu extension. Australian domain names, and many functions associated with Australian domain names, continue to be highly sought after by advertisers. What advertisers are seeking in this instance is a yearly or monthly flow of income from domain registration or hosting. Some of the most lucrative businesses regarding Australian domain names relate to domain search, how to register a domain name, and domain hosting. The clusters of terms below are very telling in this regard. All are important if you have content that will attract Australian domain name searchers. The *average* CPC for the following terms range from $15 to $29 USD.

Australia Domain Names
Australian Domain
Available Domain
Available Domain Name
Buy a Domain Name
Cheap Domain
Cheap Domain Hosting

Cheap Domain Names
Cheap Web Hosting
Domain Australia
Domain Check
Domain Name Availability
Domain Names
Domain Names Search
Domain Register
Domain Registering
Domain Registers
Domain Registration
Domain Search
Domain Searches
How to Register a Domain Name
Low Cost Domain
Low Cost Domain Registration
Register a Domain Name
Register a Website
Register Domain Names
Registering Domain Names
Search Domain Name
Website Monitoring
Website Registration
Web Host

b. Australian Mortgage Terms

Mortgage related terms are very popular in Australia. We are all familiar with most of them. Both commercial and residential mortgages offer an ongoing revenue stream to the mortgagor. You will see below all the terms you would expect to see such as "Mortgage Application," "Mortgage Lenders," and "Refinancing a Mortgage." Australian mortgage and lending terms, and many functions associated with these Australian financing terms, continue to be highly sought after by advertisers. Again, what they are seeking in this instance is a yearly or monthly flow of income from a mortgage loan. The clusters of terms below are very telling in this regard. All are important if you have content that will attract Australian mortgage and lending searchers. The *average* CPC for the following terms range from $15 to $36 USD.

Champion Mortgage
Countrywide
Debt Consolidation
Debt Consolidation Mortgage
Equity Mortgage
Lender
Mortgage Application
Mortgage Applications
Mortgage Companies
Mortgage Leads
Mortgage Lenders
Mortgage Loans
Mortgage Loans
Mortgage Payment Protection
Mortgage Protection
Mortgage Rates
Mortgage Refinance
Pre Approval
RE Mortgage
Refinancing
Refinancing a Mortgage
Refinancing Mortgage
Second Mortgages

c. Australian Online Degree Terms

Online degrees where a student can learn over the Internet are popular in Australia as in most countries. With online education, students benefit from learning in the comforts of their own home. They no longer have to commute or live on campus, which can substantially add to the cost of education. One of the best advantages to getting a degree over the Internet, such as a psychology degree online, is that students can attend online classes at some of the best universities in the country of Australia without leaving their own home. Below is a list of the terms you would expect to see such as the general "Online Colleges" to more specific areas of online education such as "Criminal Justice Degree Online" and "Psychology Degree Online." Australian online degree terms, and specific degrees associated with these Australian online degree terms, continue to be highly sought after by advertisers. New students provide a yearly or monthly flow of income. Classes can be much larger than traditional "presence" education where there are no building constraints. The clusters of terms below are telling in this regard. All are important if you have content that will attract Australian online college searchers. The *average* CPC for the following terms range from $15 to $32 USD.

Accounting Degree Online
Criminal Justice Degree Online
Marketing Degree Online
Online Colleges
Paralegal Degree Online
Psychology Degree Online

d. Australian Insurance Terms

The popularity of insurance products is no different in Australia than in other countries. The four main insurance categories continue to be the best sellers: Auto Insurance, Health Insurance, Home Insurance, and Life Insurance. Comparative rates can be gathered quickly and easily on the Internet. Purchasers are no longer limited to their local insurance agent. Quotes can be gotten from all over Australia using the Internet. While insurance products themselves are obviously popular, quotes on various insurance products are also used often. Below is a list of popular terms in this content area such as the general "Auto Insurance Quote" to more price specific insurance terms such as "Cheap House Insurance," "Content Insurance," and the life insurance product "Term Insurance." Australian insurance terms continue to be highly sought after by advertisers and the trend shows no signs of abating. Again, what advertisers are seeking in this instance is a yearly or monthly flow of income from insurance policies in the four main categories listed above. All are important if you have content that will attract Australian online insurance searchers. The *average* CPC for the following terms range from $15 to $46 USD.

Auto Insurance Quote
Car Insurance Quote
Cheap Car Insurance
Cheap House Insurance
Commercial Vehicle Insurance
Content Insurance
Discount Car Insurance
Discount Life Insurance
Dog Insurance
Health Insurance Quote
Health Insurance
Income Protection
Insurance Cover
Insurance Wedding
International Health Insurance
Landlords Insurance
Life Assurance
Life Insurance
Life Insurance Quote Online
Medical Insurance
Online Car Insurance
Online Insurance Quotes
Short Term Insurance
Temporary Insurance
Term Insurance

e. Australian Legal Terms

Attorneys. As you may have guessed, the legal profession continues to offer some of the most lucrative content in Australia. We can bunch these into three main categories. The first is criminal defense and those terms associated with a defense attorney or criminal attorney. The second type of classification can be noticed by so called "no win no fee" attorneys. These attorneys, or solicitors under the British common law system, typically do not charge a fee for their services but rather take a percentage of any settlement or court win. This percentage is usually in the range of twenty-five to fifty percent. While no win no fee attorneys in Australia are sometimes looked down upon as being litigious or "ambulance chasers," they give a voice to some injured people who could not otherwise afford the billing rates of most attorneys. Australian personal injury lawyer terms continue to be highly sought after, too. Personal injury attorneys can get big fees or a share of large verdicts and they use advertising money to reflect the potential of getting new clients. The last category is related to taxes. Tax attorneys continue to be popular in Australia as in most countries. All the terms below are important if you have content that will attract Australian online searchers in need of an attorney. The *average* CPC for the following terms ranges from $15 to $37 USD.

Attorneys
Criminal Attorney
Criminal Defense
Defense Attorney
DUI
Drug Lawyer
Injury Lawyer
Medical Malpractice Lawyer
Mesothelioma Attorney
No Win No Fee
No Win No Fee Solicitor
Personal Injury
Personal Injury Lawyer

Personal Injury Solicitor
Slip and Fall
Solicitor Fee
Tax Attorney

f. Australian Mesothelioma Terms

Mesothelioma is a big word for a big disease, a rare form of lung cancer, caused by asbestos exposure. The evidence of mesothelioma cancer does not appear for up to thirty years after the asbestos exposure. Pleural mesothelioma cancer is a type of malignant mesothelioma that affects the outer lining of the lungs. It is rare but deadly. There apparently is no universal screening method for mesothelioma cancer. Driven by mesothelioma attorneys, mesothelioma terminology has become highly valued in Australia. Misspellings of the lengthy word are also popular. These include words such as "Mesotelioma," "Mesotheloma," and "Mesothilioma." Mesothelioma attorneys can get big fees or a share of large verdicts from these types of suits, and they use advertising money to reflect the potential of getting new mesothelioma cancer clients. All the terms below are important if you have content that will attract Australian online users in search of mesothelioma research or a mesothelioma attorney. The *average* CPC for the following terms range from $15 to $45 USD.

Asbestosis Mesothelioma
For Mesothelioma
IS Mesothelioma
Malignant Mesothelioma
Malignant Pleural Mesothelioma
Mesotelioma
Mesotheloma
Mesothilioma
Mesothelioma Attorney
Mesothelioma Cancer
Mesothelioma Legal
Mesothelioma Lung

Mesothelioma Prognosis
Mesothelioma Research
Mesothelioma Symptoms
Peritoneal Mesothelioma
Pleural
Pleural Mesothelioma
What is Mesothelioma

g. Australian Cord Blood Terms

A decade ago the term cord blood, which is blood from a baby's umbilical cord or mother's placenta, was little used. Great strides in the medical profession have uncovered the value of stem cells taken from a baby's umbilical cord or mother's placenta. Cord blood is delivered from the hospital to a cord blood center that tests the blood and stores it. Private cord blood banks charge a few thousand dollars for collection and then ongoing storage fees. The number of highly valued cord blood terms are somewhat limited, but the terms below are important if you have content that will attract Australian online users in search of cord blood research or a cord blood bank. One of the most lucrative areas for blood banks is the ongoing storage fees for cord blood that can last decades. The *average* CPC for the following terms range from $15 to $36 USD.

Cord Blood
Cord Blood Bank
Cord Blood Cells
Cord Blood Collection
Cord Blood Donation
Cord Blood Stem Cells
Cord Blood Storage
Cord Blood Transplant
Umbilical Cord Blood
Umbilical Cord Blood Bank

h. Australian Laser Hair Removal Terms

Permanent hair removal has become an obsession in many parts of the world. This is especially true in areas near the ocean. The prime season for hair removal procedures is early spring. In Australia, laser hair removal is both popular and expensive. Patients are typically charged for each session of permanent hair removal, which can take numerous visits for just a small area. These ongoing hair removal treatments, which may address only a patch of skin at a time, are costly and typically not covered by medical insurance. Since permanent laser hair removal is expensive in Australia, doctors are willing to pay larger advertising sums to attract new clients and this is where you benefit. The terms below are important if you have content that will attract Australian online users in search of laser hair removal procedures. Also keep in mind that hair removal equipment itself costs a lot of money and therefore attracting doctors and medical professionals who may purchase this equipment is desirable. The *average* CPC for the following terms range from $15 to $23 USD.

Back Hair Removal
Facial Hair Removal
Hair Removal
Hair Removal Clinic
Hair Removal Equipment
Hair Removal Machine
Hair Removal Treatment
Laser Hair Removal
Laser Hair Removal Clinic
Laser Hair Removal Clinics
Laser Hair Removal Costs
Laser Hair Removal Equipment
Laser Hair Removal for Men
Laser Hair Removal Machine
Laser Hair Removal Treatment
Lazer Hair Removal
Lasor Hair Removal

Permanent Hair Removal
Permanent Laser Hair Removal
Permanent Hair Removal
YAG Laser Hair Removal

i. Australian Nursing Terms

Nursing continues to be one of the most in demand professions not just in Australia, but also across the world. As health problems continue to increase and hospitals continue to expand, proper nurse staffing is of utmost importance in the medical community. Registered nurse jobs are the hottest of this group. Any search of help wanted ads in a newspaper or online will most likely uncover nurse staffing ads. "Nurse recruiting" is also a popular term. Another stems from universities offering "nurse scholarships." The terms below, though limited compared to some other categories in Australia, are important if you have content that will attract Australian doctors and hospitals in search of nurse staffing. The *average* CPC for the following terms range from $18 to $24.

Nurse Recruiting
Nurse Scholarship
Nurse Staffing
Registered Nurse Jobs

j. Australian Secured Loan Terms

Secured loans are loans guaranteed by property that is used as collateral for the loan. If the purchaser should default on the loan, the lender for the property will receive the collateral, which is forfeited by the purchaser. There are many types of secured loans in Australia with personal debit consolidation loans—typically to pay off higher interest rate loans such as credit card and student debt—and mortgage loans being the most popular. Please see the mortgage terms section for the best uses of terminology in this area. Use the secured loan terms below in your content to attract online Australian Internet users in search of various types of secured loans. The *average* CPC for the following terms range from $15 to $34 USD.

Bridging Loans
Consolidate
Consolidate Debt
Consolidating
Consolidation
Debit Consolidation
Debit Buster
Debit Consolidation
Debit Consolidation Secured Loan
Loans4u
Lombard Direct
Low Interest Rate
Non Secured Loans
Secure Loans
Secured
Secured Finance
Secured Loans
Secured Personal Loan
Unsecured Debt Consolidation Loan
Unsecured Debt Consolidation Loans
Secured

2. Canada

a. Canadian Domain Name Terms

We are all familiar with Internet domain names. They are the unique URL names you register with a Top Level Domain ("TLD") extension such as www.BottleTreeBooks.com or a country level domain such as BottleTreeBooks.ca. There are also regional domain extensions such as the relatively new .eu extension. Canadian domain names, and many functions associated with Canadian domain names, continue to be highly sought after by advertisers. What they are seeking in this instance is a yearly or monthly flow of income from domain registration or hosting. Some of the most lucrative businesses regarding Canadian domain names relate to domain search, how to register a domain name, and domain hosting. Since the dot com bubble burst in 2001, the same of domain names on the open market has been heating up. The clusters of terms below are very telling in this regard. All are important if you have content that will attract Canadian domain name searchers. The *average* CPC for following terms range from $15 to $25 USD.

Available Domain
Available Domain Name
Buy a Domain Name
Cheap Domain
Cheap Domain Names
Cheap Web Hosting
Dedicated Hosting
Domain Check
Domain Name Availability
Domain Names
Domain Names Canada
Domain Names Search
Domain Register
Domain Registering
Domain Registration
Domain Searches
Domainnames
How to Register a Domain Name
Inexpensive Domain
Low Cost Domain
Low Cost Domain Registration
Register a Domain Name
Register a Website
Register Domain Names
Registering Domain Names
Web Address

Web Host
Website Monitoring
Website Registration

b. Canadian Mortgage Terms

Mortgage related terms are very popular in Canada. We are all familiar with most of them. If interest rates are high, mortgage seek to lock in adjustable rate mortgages. If interest rates are low, homeowners seek to lock in fixed rate mortgages. Both commercial and residential mortgages offer an ongoing revenue stream to the mortgagor. You will see below all the terms you would expect to see such as "Mortgage Application," "Mortgage Lenders," and "Refinancing a Mortgage." Canadian mortgage and lending terms, and many functions associated with these Canadian financing terms, continue to be highly sought after by advertisers. Again, what they are seeking in this instance is a yearly or monthly flow of income from a mortgage loan. The clusters of terms below are very telling in this regard. All are important if you have content that will attract Canadian mortgage and lending searchers. The *average* CPC for the following terms range from $15 to $36 USD.

Apply for Mortgage
Canadian Mortgage Rates
Lender
Low Mortgage Rate
Mortgage Application
Mortgage Applications
Mortgage Insurance
Mortgage Leads
Mortgage Notes
Mortgage Protection
No Down Payment
Pre Approval
Preapproval
Refinancing a Mortgage

Second Mortgages
Sell Mortgage
Wells Fargo Mortgage
Zero Down Mortgage

c. Canadian Online Degree Terms

Online degrees, where a student can learn over the Internet, are popular in Canada as in most countries. With online education, students benefit from learning in the comforts of their own home. They no longer have to commute in the cold Canadian winter or live on campus, which can substantially add to the cost of education. One of the best advantages to getting a degree over the Internet, such as a psychology degree online, is that students can attend online classes at some of the best universities in the country without leaving their own home. Below is a list of the terms you would expect to see such as the general "Online Colleges" to more specific areas of online education such as "Criminal Justice Degree Online" and "Psychology Degree Online." Canadian online degree terms, and specific degrees associated with these Canadian online degree terms, continue to be highly sought after by advertisers. New students provide a yearly or monthly flow of income. Classes can be much larger than traditional "presence" education where there are no building constraints. The clusters of terms below are telling in this regard. All are important if you have content that will attract Canadian online college searchers. The *average* CPC for the following terms range from $15 to $24 USD.

Accounting Degree Online
Colleges Online
Criminal Justice Degree Online
IT Degree Online
Marketing Degree Online
Network Security Degree
Online College Degree
Online Criminal Justice Degrees
Online Marketing Degree

Online MBA Degrees
Online Psychology Degree
Online Teaching Degree
Paralegal Degree Online
Psychology Degree
University of Phoenix Online Degree

d. Canadian Insurance Terms

The popularity of insurance products is no different in Canada than in other countries. The four main insurance categories continue to be the best sellers: Auto Insurance, Health Insurance, Home Insurance, and Life Insurance. Comparative rates can be gathered quickly and easily on the Internet. Purchasers are no longer limited to their local insurance agent. Quotes can be gotten from all over Canada using the Internet. While insurance products themselves are obviously popular, quotes on various insurance products are also used often. Below is a list of popular terms in this content area such as the general "Auto Insurance CA" to more price specific insurance terms such as "Cheap Car Insurance," "Commercial Vehicle Insurance," and the life insurance product "Term Insurance." Canadian insurance terms continue to be highly sought after by advertisers. Again, what advertisers are seeking in this instance is a yearly or monthly flow of income from insurance policies in the four main categories listed above. All are important if you have content that will attract Canadian online insurance searchers. The *average* CPC for the following terms range from \$15 to \$49 USD.

Auto Insurance CA
Cheap Car Insurance
Commercial Vehicle Insurance
Dog Insurance
House Insurance
International Health Insurance
Safe Auto Insurance
Temporary Health Insurance

Temporary Insurance
Term Insurance
Term Life Insurance Quotes

e. Canadian Legal Terms

Attorneys. As you may have guessed, the legal profession continues to offer some of the most lucrative content in Canada. Bidding is intense for popular terms. We can bunch these into three main categories. The first is criminal defense and those terms associated with a defense attorney or criminal attorney. People want to stay out of jail and they will pay a lot of money to keep it that way. The second type of classification rests with so called personal injury lawyers. These attorneys typically do not charge a fee for their services but rather take a percentage of any settlement or court win. "No win, no fee" is a common phrase in their part of the world. The percentage is usually in the range of twenty-five to fifty percent. While personal injury attorneys in Canada are sometimes looked down upon as being litigious, they give a voice to some injured people who could not otherwise afford the billing rates of most attorneys. The third category of legal terms is related to auto accident attorneys, especially given the winter road conditions in Canada. Tax attorneys also continue to be popular in Canada as in most countries. All the terms below are important if you have content that will attract Canadian online searchers in need of an attorney. The *average* CPC for the following terms ranges from $15 to $37 USD.

Attorneys
Auto Accident Attorney
Auto Accident Lawyer
Car Accident Lawyer
Criminal Attorney
Criminal Defense
Criminal Defense Law
Criminal Defense Lawyer
Criminal Defense Lawyers
Defense Attorney

Drug Lawyer
Federal Lawyer
Injury Lawyer
Malpractice Lawyers
Medical Malpractice Lawyer
Mesothelioma Attorney
Mesothelioma Lawyer
Personal Injury
Securities Lawyer
Slip and Fall
Tax Attorney

f. Canadian Mesothelioma Terms

Mesothelioma is a big word for a big disease (lung cancer) caused by asbestos exposure. The evidence of mesothelioma cancer does not appear for up to thirty years after the asbestos exposure. Pleural mesothelioma cancer is a type of malignant mesothelioma that affects the outer lining of the lungs. Attorneys focus in on these very specific search terms. There apparently is no universal screening method for mesothelioma cancer. Driven by mesothelioma attorneys, mesothelioma terminology has become highly valued in Canada. Misspellings of the lengthy word are also popular. These include words such as "Mesotelioma," "Mesotheloma," and "Mesothilioma." Mesothelioma attorneys can get big fees or a share of large verdicts from these types of suits, and they use advertising money to reflect the potential of getting new mesothelioma cancer clients. All the terms below are important if you have content that will attract Canadian online users in search of mesothelioma research or a mesothelioma attorney. The *average* CPC for the following terms range from $19 to $42 USD.

Asbestosis Mesothelioma
Malignant Pleural Mesothelioma
Mesotelioma
Mesotheloma
Mesothilioma

Mesothelioma Attorney
Mesothelioma Cancer
Mesothelioma Lawsuit
Mesothelioma Lawyer
Mesothelioma Lawyers
Mesothelioma Legal
Mesothelioma Lung
Mesothelioma Prognosis
Mesothelioma Research
Mesothelioma Symptoms
Pericardial Mesothelioma
Peritoneal Mesothelioma
Pleural Mesothelioma

g. Canadian Cord Blood Terms

A decade ago the term cord blood, which is blood from a baby's umbilical cord or mother's placenta, was little used. Great strides in the medical profession have uncovered the value of stem cells taken from a baby's umbilical cord or mother's placenta. Cord blood is collected at the hospital and delivered from the hospital to a cord blood center that tests the blood for various diseases. Finally the cord blood is stored by the center. Private cord blood banks charge a few thousand dollars for collection and then ongoing storage fees, which can generate revenues for decades. The number of highly valued cord blood terms is not limited in Canada. The terms below are important if you have content that will attract Canadian online users in search of cord blood research or a cord blood bank. The *average* CPC for the following terms range from $15 to $33 USD.

Baby Cord Blood
CBR Cord Blood
Cord Blood
Cord Blood Bank
Cord Blood Banking
Cord Blood Banks

Cord Blood Cell
Cord Blood Cells
Cord Blood Collection
Cord Blood Donation
Cord Blood Donations
Cord Blood Preservation
Cord Blood Program
Cord Blood Registry
Cord Blood Research
Cord Blood Services
Cord Blood Stem Cells
Cord Blood Stem Cells
Cord Blood Storage
Cord Blood Transplant
Cord Blood Transplants
Donating Cord Blood
Public Cord Blood Bank
Saving Cord Blood
Stem Cell Cord Blood
Umbilical Cord Blood
Umbilical Cord Blood Bank
Umbilical Cord Blood Banking
Viacord

h. Canadian Laser Hair Removal Terms

Permanent hair removal has become an obsession in many parts of the world. This is especially true in areas near the ocean. The prime season for hair removal procedures is early spring. In Canada, laser hair removal is both popular and expensive. Men and women seek the treatments in almost equal percentages. Patients are typically charged for each session of permanent hair removal, which can take numerous visits for just a small area. These ongoing hair removal treatments, which may address only a patch of skin at a time, are costly and typically not covered by medical insurance. Since permanent laser hair removal is expensive in Canada, doctors are willing to pay larger advertising sums to attract new clients and this is where you benefit as a content provider in this area. The terms below are important if you have content that will attract Canadian online users in search of laser hair removal procedures. Also keep in mind that hair removal equipment itself costs a lot of money and therefore attracting doctors and medical professionals who may purchase this equipment is desirable online. The *average* CPC for the following terms range from $15 to $23 USD.

Facial Hair Removal
Facial Laser Hair Removal
Hair Removal Treatment
Laser Hair Removal Clinic
Laser Hair Removal Cost
Laser Hair Removal Costs
Laser Hair Removal Edmonton
Laser Hair Removal Equipment
Laser Hair Removal Machine
Lazer Hair Removal
Lazor Hair Removal

i. Canadian Secured Loan Terms

Secured loans are loans guaranteed by property used as collateral for the loan. If the purchaser should default on the loan, the lender for the property will receive the collateral, which is forfeited by the purchaser. Much forfeiture involves court proceedings so these terms are sought after by those in the legal field and finance industry alike. There are many types of secured loans in Canada with personal debit consolidation loans—typically to pay off higher interest rate loans such as credit card and student debt—and mortgage loans being the most popular. Please see the mortgage term section for the best uses in this area. Use the secured loan terms below in your content to attract online Internet users in search of various types of secured loans in Canada. The *average* CPC for the following terms range from $16 to $34 USD.

Bridging Loans
Cheap Secured loan
Consolidate
Consolidate Debt
Consolidating
Consolidation
Debit Buster
Debit Consolidation
Debt Consolidation Secured Loan
Debitbuster
Fast Secured Loan
Loans Secured
Loans4u
Low Interest Rate
Remortgages
Secured
Secured Finance
Secure Loans
Secured Loans
Secured Personal Loan
Unsecured Debt Consolidation Loan

3. Ireland

a. Irish Domain Name Terms

Internet domain names are the unique URL names you register with a Top Level Domain ("TLD") extension such as www.BottleTreeBooks.com or a country level domain such as BottleTreeBooks.us. There are also regional domain extensions such as the .eu extension. Irish domain names, and many functions associated with Irish domain names, continue to be highly sought after by advertisers in Ireland and worldwide. What domain name registration and hosting companies are seeking in this instance is a yearly or monthly flow of income from such domain registration or hosting. Some of the most lucrative businesses regarding Irish domain names relate to domain search, how to register a domain name, and domain hosting. The clusters of terms below are very telling in this regard. All are important if you have content that will attract domain name searchers in Ireland. The *average* CPC for following terms range from $15 to $29 USD.

Available Domain
Available Domain Name
Buy a Domain Name
Cheap Domain
Cheap Domain Names
Domain Check
Domain Name Availability
Domain Names
Domainnames
Domain Register
Domain Registers
Domain Registering
Domain Registration
Domain Search
Domain Searches
How to Register a Domain Name
Register a Website
Register a Domain Name
Register Domain Names
Registering Domain Names
Website Monitoring
Website Registration

b. Irish Mortgage Terms

Mortgage related terms are very popular in Ireland as property values continues to escalate. They consist of the familiar terms. Both commercial and residential mortgages offer an ongoing revenue stream to the mortgagor. You will see below all the terms you would expect to see such as "Mortgage Application," "Mortgage Lender," and "Refinancing." Irish mortgage and lending terms, and many functions associated with these financing terms in Ireland, continue to be highly sought after by advertisers. Again, what financial companies are seeking in this instance is a yearly or monthly flow of income from mortgage loans. The clusters of terms below are very telling in this regard. All are important if you have content that will attract mortgage and lending searchers in Ireland. The *average* CPC for the following terms range from $15 to $32 USD.

Apply for Mortgage
Buy to Let Mortgages
Cheap Loans
Equity Mortgage
Loan Rates
Mortgage Application
Mortgage Applications
Mortgage Leads
Mortgage Lender
Mortgage Loan
Mortgage Loans
Mortgage Payment Protection
Mortgage Rates
Mortgage Refinance
Mortgage Protection
RE Mortgage
Refinance
Refinancing
Remortgage

c. Irish Insurance Terms

The popularity of insurance products is no different in Ireland than in other countries. The four main insurance categories continue to be the best sellers: Auto Insurance, Health Insurance, Home Insurance, and Life Insurance. Comparative rates can be gathered quickly and easily on the

Internet. Purchasers are no longer limited to their local insurance agent. Quotes can be gotten from all over Ireland using various online quote sites. While insurance products themselves are obviously popular, quotes on various insurance products are also used often. Below is a list of popular terms in this content area such as the general "Auto Insurance Quotes" to more price specific insurance terms such as "Cheap House Insurance," "Content Insurance," and the life insurance product "Term Insurance." Irish insurance terms continue to be highly sought after by advertisers and there is no sign of this abating. Again, what insurance companies are seeking in this instance is a yearly or monthly flow of income from insurance policies in the four main categories listed above. This ongoing income stream can, and typically does, last decades. All terms below are important if you have content that will attract online insurance searchers in Ireland. Note the misspelling of "Ensurance." The *average* CPC for the following terms range from $15 to $48 USD.

Auto Insurance
Auto Insurance Quote
Auto Insurance Quotes
Best Insurance
Boat Insurance
Car Insurance
Car Insurance Companies
Car Insurance Quote
Car Insurance Quote
Cheap Car Insurance
Cheap House Insurance
Commercial Vehicle Insurance
Content Insurance
Contents Insurance
Dog Insurance
Ensurance
Health Insurance
Health Insurance Quote

Heath Insurance
House Insurance
Insurances
Insurance Cover
Insurance Online
Insurance Quote
Insurance Quote
Insurance Young
International Health Insurance
Landlords Insurance
Life Assurance
Life Insurance
Life Insurance Quote
Life Insurance Quote Online
Motorcycle Insurance
Online Car Insurance
Online Insurance Quotes
Short Term Insurance
Temporary Insurance
Term Insurance
Term Life Insurance Quote

d. Irish Legal Terms

Attorneys. As you may have guessed, the legal profession continues to offer some of the most lucrative content in Ireland. We bunch these into three main categories. The first is criminal defense and those terms associated with a defense attorney or criminal attorney. The second type of classification can be noticed by so called "no win no fee" attorneys. These attorneys typically do not charge a fee for their services but rather take a percentage of any settlement or court win. This percentage is usually in the range of twenty-five to fifty percent. While no win no fee attorneys in Ireland are sometimes looked down upon as being litigious, they give a voice to some injured people who could not otherwise afford the billing rates of most attorneys. The third category is related to aviation. Aviation attorneys are popular in Ireland. Aviation lawyers handle complex aviation buying and selling contracts as well as injuries caused during aviation accidents. Irish personal injury lawyer terms continue to be highly sought after, too. Personal injury attorneys can get big fees or a share of large verdicts and they use advertising money to reflect the potential of getting new clients. All the terms below are important if you have content that will attract online searchers in need of an attorney in Ireland. The *average* CPC for the following terms ranges from $15 to $40 USD.

Aviation Lawyers
Criminal Defense
Criminal Lawyers
Defense Attorney
DUI
No Win No Fee
No Win No Fee Solicitor
Personal Injury
Personal Injury Lawyer
Solicitor Fee
Vioxx Lawyer

e. Irish Mesothelioma Terms

Mesothelioma is a big word for lung cancer caused by asbestos exposure. The evidence of mesothelioma cancer does not appear for up to thirty years after the asbestos exposure. Pleural mesothelioma cancer is a type of malignant mesothelioma that affects the outer lining of the lungs. There apparently is no universal screening method for mesothelioma cancer. Driven by mesothelioma attorneys, mesothelioma terminology has become highly valued in Ireland, although the amount of terms is more limited than in other industrialized nations, they are valuable nonetheless. Misspellings of the lengthy word are also popular. These include words such as “Mesotelioma,” “Mesotheloma,” and “Mesothilioma.” Mesothelioma attorneys can get big fees or a share of large verdicts from these types of suits, and they use advertising money to reflect the potential of getting new mesothelioma cancer clients. All the terms below are important if you have content that will attract Irish online users in search of mesothelioma symptoms or mesothelioma in general. The *average* CPC for the following terms range from $17 to $33 USD.

Mesothelioma
Mesothelioma Symptoms
Pleural

f. Irish Cord Blood Terms

A decade ago the term cord blood, which is blood from a baby's umbilical cord or mother's placenta, was little used. Great strides in the medical profession have uncovered the value of stem cells taken from a baby's umbilical cord or mother's placenta. Cord blood is delivered from the hospital to a cord blood center that tests the blood and stores it. Private cord blood banks charge a few thousand dollars for collection and then ongoing storage fees that can last decades. The number of highly valued cord blood terms is limited in Ireland just as it is in Australia. The terms below are important, however, if you have content that will attract online users in search of cord blood research or a cord blood bank in Ireland. The *average* CPC for the following terms range from $16 to $29 USD.

Cord Blood
Cord Blood America
Cord Blood Bank
Cord Blood Storage

g. Irish Laser Hair Removal Terms

Permanent hair removal has become an obsession in many parts of the world. This is especially true in areas near the ocean. The prime season for hair removal procedures is early spring. In Ireland, laser hair removal is popular and expensive, as in most countries. Patients, both men and women alike, are typically charged for each session of permanent hair removal, which can take numerous visits for just a small area. These ongoing hair removal treatments, which may address only a patch of skin at a time, are costly and typically not covered by medical insurance. Since permanent laser hair removal is expensive in Ireland, doctors are willing to pay larger advertising sums to attract new clients and this is where you benefit. The terms below are important if you have content that will attract online users in search of laser hair removal procedures in Ireland. Also keep in mind that hair removal equipment itself costs a lot of money and therefore attracting doctors and medical professionals who may purchase this equipment is desirable online. Note the different spellings for the word Laser. The *average* CPC for the following terms range from $15 to $21 USD.

Back Hair Removal
Facial Hair Removal
Hair Removal
Hair Removal Laser Treatment
Hair Removal Treatment
Laser Hair Removal
Laser Hair Removal Clinic
Laser Hair Removal Clinics
Laser Hair Removal Equipment
Laser Hair Removal Machine
Lazer Hair Removal
Lazor Hair Removal
Permanent Facial Hair Removal
Permanent Hair Removal

h. Irish Secured Loan Terms

Secured loans are loans guaranteed by property that is used as collateral for the loan. If the purchaser should default on the loan, the lender for the property will receive the collateral, which is forfeited by the purchaser. There are many types of secured loans in Ireland with personal debit consolidation loans—typically to pay off higher interest rate loans such as credit card and student debt—and mortgage loans being the most popular. The loan amounts can be large or small, but most are related to consumer related debt. Please see the mortgage term section above for the best uses in this area. Use the secured loan terms below, however, in your content to attract online Internet users in search of various types of secured loans in Ireland. The *average* CPC for the following terms range from $16 to $34 USD.

Bridging Loans
Consolidate
Consolidate Debt
Consolidating
Consolidation
Debit Buster
Debit Consolidation
Debitbuster
Loans4u
Low Interest Rate
Remortgages
Secured
Secured Finance
Secure Loan
Secured Loans
Secured Personal Loan
Unsecured Debt Consolidation Loan
Unsecured Debt Consolidation Loans
Secured

4. United Kingdom

a. UK Domain Name Terms

Internet domain names are the unique URL names you register with a Top Level Domain ("TLD") extension such as www.BottleTreeBooks.com or a country level domain such as BottleTreeBooks.co.uk. There are also regional domain extensions such as the relatively new .eu extension. United Kingdom domain names, and many functions associated with United

Kingdom domain names, continue to be highly sought after by advertisers. What they are seeking in this instance is a yearly or monthly flow of income from domain registration or hosting on the Web. Some of the most lucrative businesses regarding UK domain names relate to domain search, how to register a domain name, and domain hosting. Domain name selling is also hot again just as it was before the dot com bubble burst. The clusters of terms below are very telling in this regard. All are important if you have content that will attract UK domain name searchers. The *average* CPC for following terms range from $15 to $26 USD.

Available Domain
Available Domain Name
Buy a Domain Name
Cheap Domain Hosting
Domainnames
Domain Name Availability
Domain Name Registrations
Domain Names Search
Domain Registers
Domain Searches
How to Register a Domain Name
Low Cost Domain
Low Cost Domain Registration
Register a Domain Name
Register Domain Names
Registering Domain Names
Web Address

b. UK Mortgage Terms

Secured loans in the form of mortgage related terms are very popular in the United Kingdom. We are all familiar with most of them. Both commercial and residential mortgages offer an ongoing revenue stream to the mortgagor. You will see below all the terms you would expect to see such as “Mortgage Applications,” “Mortgage Lenders,” and “Refinancing a

Mortgage." UK mortgage and lending terms, and many functions associated with these UK financing terms, continue to be highly sought after by advertisers. Again, what they are seeking in this instance is a yearly or monthly flow of income from a mortgage loan. The clusters of terms below are very telling in this regard. All are important if you have content that will attract mortgage and lending searchers in the United Kingdom for these types of secured loans. There are a healthy number of terms in this space. The *average* CPC for the following terms range from $15 to $64 USD.

2nd Mortgage Loans
Apply for Mortgage
Bank Loans
Buy to Let Mortgages
Car Loans
Cheap Loans
Debt Consolidation Mortgage
Equity Mortgage
Financing
Lender
Lenders
Loan
Loans
Loans UK
Mortgage Applications
Mortgage Broker
Mortgage Broker Leads
Mortgage Companies
Mortgage Company
Mortgage Insurance
Mortgage Lenders
Mortgage Loan
Mortgage Loans
Mortgage Payment protection
Mortgage Protection

Mortgage Protection UK
Mortgage Refinance
Mortgage to Let
National Mortgage
Personal Loan
Personal Loans
RE Mortgage
Refinance
Refinancing
Refinancing a Mortgage
Refinancing Mortgage
Remortgage
Second Mortgage Rate
Second Mortgages
Secured Loans
Sell Mortgage
Unsecured Mortgage
Zero Down Mortgage

c. UK Online Degree Terms

Online degrees, where a student can learn over the Internet, are popular in the United Kingdom as in most countries. With online education, students benefit from learning in the comforts of their own home. They no longer have to commute or live on campus, which can substantially add to the cost of education. Rising fuel costs also are make commuting to school more cost prohibitive. One of the best advantages to getting a degree over the Internet, such as a psychology degree online, is that students can attend online classes at some of the best universities in the country without leaving their own home. Below is a list of the terms you would expect to see such as the general "Colleges Online" to more specific areas of online education such as "Online Teaching Degree" and "Online Psychology Degree." UK online degree terms, and specific degrees associated with these UK online degree terms, continue to be highly sought after by advertisers. New online students provide a yearly or monthly flow of income. Classes can be much larger than traditional "presence" education where there are no building constraints. The clusters of terms below are telling in this regard. All are important if you have content that will attract online college searchers in the United Kingdom. The *average* CPC for the following terms range from S15 to $32 USD.

Accounting Degree Online
Colleges Online
Network Security Degree
Online College Degree
Online IT Degree
Online Marketing Degree
Online Psychology Degree
Online Teaching Degree

d. UK Insurance Terms

Buyers are in control for insurance related products on the Internet. The popularity of insurance products is no different in the United Kingdom than in other countries. Those in need of insurance products can easily compare multiple options online with pricing given immediately. The four main insurance categories continue to be the best sellers: Auto Insurance, Health Insurance, Home Insurance, and Life Insurance. Comparative rates can be gathered quickly and easily on the Internet. Purchasers are no longer limited to their local insurance agent. Quotes can be gotten from companies across the United Kingdom and worldwide using the Internet. While insurance products themselves are obviously popular, quotes on various insurance products are also used often. Below is a list of popular terms in this content area such as the general "Auto Insurance Quote" to more price specific insurance terms such as "Cheap House Insurance," "Content Insurance," and the life insurance product "Term Insurance." "Building Insurance UK" is one of the most valued terms. UK insurance terms continue to be highly sought after by advertisers. Again, what they are seeking in this instance is a yearly or monthly flow of income from insurance policies in the four main categories listed above. All are important if you have content that will attract online insurance searchers in the United Kingdom. The *average* CPC for the following terms range from $15 to $54 USD.

Auto Insurance
Auto Insurance Quote
Building Insurance UK
Car Insurance
Car Insurance in the UK
Car Insurance in UK
Car Insurance Quote
Cheap Car Insurance
Cheap House Insurance
Cheap Insurance UK
Commercial Vehicle Insurance
Content Insurance
Contents
Discount Car Insurance
Dog Insurance
Health Insurance
Homeowners
House Insurance
Insurance
Insurance Wedding
Insurance Young
Insurances
Insure
International Health Insurance
Landlords Insurance
Life Insurance
Life Insurance Quote Online
Low Cost Life Insurance
Medical Insurance
Online Car Insurance
Online Insurance Quotes

Short Term Insurance
Term Insurance
Term Life Insurance Quotes
Whole Life Insurance

e. UK Legal Terms

Attorney related terms are hot in the UK. As you may have guessed, the legal profession continues to offer some of the most lucrative content in the United Kingdom. We can bunch these into three main categories. The first is criminal defense and those terms associated with a defense attorney or criminal attorney. These attorneys try to keep clients out of jail and the clients usually pay a healthy fee to keep out of jail. The second type of classification can be noticed by so called "no win no fee" attorneys. These attorneys, or solicitors under the British common law system, typically do not charge a fee for their services but rather take a percentage of any settlement or court win. This percentage is usually in the range of twenty-five to fifty percent. While no win no fee attorneys in the United Kingdom are sometimes looked down upon as being litigious, they give a voice to some injured people who could not otherwise afford the billing rates of most attorneys. The third category is related to taxes. Tax attorneys are popular in the United Kingdom as in most countries. UK personal injury lawyer terms continue to be highly sought after, too. Personal injury attorneys can get big fees or a share of large verdicts and they use advertising money to reflect the potential of getting new clients. All the terms below are important if you have content that will attract UK online searchers in need of an attorney. The *average* CPC for the following terms ranges from $15 to $47 USD.

Attorneys
Attorney Malpractice
Car Accident Lawyer
Criminal Attorney
Criminal Defense
Criminal Defense Attorney

Defense Attorney
Drug Lawyer
DUI
Federal Lawyer
Injury Lawyer
Lemon Law Attorney
Medical Malpractice Lawyer
Mesothelioma Attorney
Mesothelioma Lawyer
No Win No Fee
No Win No Fee Solicitor
Personal Injury
Personal Injury Attorneys
Personal Injury Lawyer
Personal Injury Solicitor
Securities Lawyer
Solicitor Fee
Tax Attorney

f. UK Mesothelioma Terms

Mesothelioma is a shortened term for mesothelioma cancer that is caused by asbestos exposure. It is a rare disease, but obviously deadly. The evidence of mesothelioma cancer does not appear for up to thirty years after the asbestos exposure. Pleural mesothelioma cancer is a type of malignant mesothelioma that affects the outer lining of the lungs. There apparently is no universal screening method for mesothelioma cancer. Driven by mesothelioma attorneys, mesothelioma terminology has become highly valued in the United Kingdom. Misspellings of the lengthy word are also popular. These include words such as "Mesotelioma," "Mesotheloma," and "Mesothilioma." Mesothelioma attorneys can get big fees or a share of large verdicts from these types of suits, and they use advertising money to reflect the potential of getting new mesothelioma cancer clients. All the terms below are important if you have content that will attract online users in search of mesothelioma research or a mesothelioma attorney in the United

Kingdom. The *average* CPC for the following terms range from $15 to $49 USD.

Asbestosis
Asbestosis Mesothelioma
Malignant Mesothelioma
Malignant Pleural Mesothelioma
Mesotheloma
Mesothilioma
Mesothelioma Attorney
Mesothelioma Attorneys
Mesothelioma Cancer
Mesothelioma Information
Mesothelioma Lawyer
Mesothelioma Lawyers
Mesothelioma Prognosis
Mesothelioma Research
Mesothelioma Symptoms
Peritoneal Mesothelioma
Pleural Mesothelioma
What is Mesothelioma

g. UK Cord Blood Terms

The use of cord blood storage to combat future disease is increasing in popularity. A decade ago the term cord blood, which is blood from a baby's umbilical cord or mother's placenta, was little used. Now it is a popular term among expectant mothers in the UK. Great strides in the medical profession have uncovered the value of stem cells taken from a baby's umbilical cord or mother's placenta. Cord blood is delivered from the hospital to a cord blood center that tests the blood and stores it. Private cord blood banks charge a few thousand dollars for collection and then ongoing storage fees that can last for decades if the blood continues to be stored. The number of highly valued cord blood terms is not limited in the United Kingdom. The terms below are important if you have content that will attract UK online users in search of cord blood research or a cord blood bank. The *average* CPC for the following terms range from $15 to $36 USD.

Cord Blood
Cord Blood Bank
Cord Blood Banking
Cord Blood Banks
Cord Blood Collection
Cord Blood Program
Cord Blood Registry
Cord Blood Stem Cell
Cord Blood Stem Cells
Cord Blood Storage
Cord Blood Transplant
Cord Blood Transplants
Cord Donation
Umbilical Cord Blood
Umbilical Cord Blood Bank
Umbilical Cord Blood Banking

h. UK Laser Hair Removal Terms

Permanent hair removal has become an obsession in many parts of the world. This applies to both men and women. The prime season for hair removal procedures is early spring. In the United Kingdom, laser hair removal is both popular and expensive, as in most countries. Patients are typically charged for each session of permanent hair removal, which can take numerous visits for just a small area. These ongoing hair removal treatments, which may address only a patch of skin at a time, are costly and typically not covered by medical insurance. Since permanent laser hair removal is expensive in the United Kingdom, doctors are willing to pay larger advertising sums to attract new clients and this is where you benefit. The terms below are important if you have content that will attract UK online users in search of laser hair removal procedures. Also keep in mind that hair removal equipment itself costs a lot of money and therefore attracting doctors and medical professionals who may purchase this equipment is desirable online. Note the different spellings of "Laser." The *average* CPC for the following terms range from $15 to $44 USD.

Back Hair Removal
Facial Hair Removal
Hair Removal
Hair Removal Berkshire
Hair Removal by Laser
Hair Removal Clinic
Hair Removal Equipment
Hair Removal in London
Hair Removal London
Hair Removal UK
Laser Hair Removal
Laser Hair Removal Birmingham
Laser Hair Removal Clinic
Laser Hair Removal Clinics
Laser Hair Removal Equipment
Laser Hair Removal London
Laser Hair Removal Machine
Laser Hair Removal Manchester
Laser Hair Removal Men
Laser Hair Removal Treatment
Lazer Hair Removal
Lazor Hair Removal
Permanent Facial Hair Removal
Permanent Hair Removal
Permanent Hair Removal UK
Permanent Hair Removal

i. UK Car Rental Terms

Car rentals are commonly termed car hire throughout Europe and the UK. This also includes the purchase of car driver services. Many of the terms below include top destination from the United Kingdom where people vacation and need a car and/or a driver for hire such as "Car Hire in Alicante" and "Car Rental Norway." Because of common travel within Europe on trains and planes, car rentals are needed in the destination country. The *average* CPC for the following terms range from \$15 to \$35 USD.

Budget Car Hire
Car Hire Alicante
Car Hire Alicante Spain
Car Hire in Alicante
Car Hire in Malaga Spain
Car Hire in Valencia
Car Hire Malaga
Car Rent
Car Renta
Car Rental Alicante
Car Rental Denmark
Car Rental Malaga
Car Rental Norway
Cheap Car Hire Alicante
Car Hire in Malaga
Spain Car Hire
Spanish Car Hire
One Way Car Rental

j. UK Secured Loan Terms

Secured loans are loans guaranteed by property that is used as collateral for the loan. If the purchaser should default on the loan, the lender for the property will receive the collateral, which is forfeited by the purchaser, which are typically consumers as opposed to businesses. There are many types of secured loans in the United Kingdom with personal debit consolidation loans—typically to pay off higher interest rate loans such as credit card and student debt—and mortgage loans being the most popular. Please see the mortgage term section for the best uses in this area. Use the secured loan terms below in your content to attract online Internet users in search of various types of secured loans in the United Kingdom. Both secured and non-secured loans are prominent in this industry. The *average* CPC for the following terms range from $15 to $64 USD.

Best Secured Loan
Cheap Secured Loan
Cheap Secured Loans
Debit Consolidation Secured Loan
Fast Secured Loan
Fast Secured Loans
Loans Unsecured
Non Secured Loan
Non Secured Loans
Secured Loan
Secured Loan Calculator
Secured Loan Company
Secured Loan Rates
Secured Loan UK
Secured Loans
Secured Personal Loan
UK Secured Loans
UK Secured Loan
UK Secured Loans
Unsecured Consolidation Loan
Unsecured Consolidation Loans
Unsecured Debt Consolidation Loan
Unsecured Debt Consolidation Loan
Secure Loans
Secured

Secured Finance

5. United States

a. US Domain Name Terms

Domain name interest was little abated by the dot com bust of 2001. It is as popular as ever. We are all familiar with Internet domain names. They are the unique URL names you register with a Top Level Domain ("TLD") extension such as www.BottleTreeBooks.com or a country level domain such as BottleTreeBooks.us. There are also regional domain extensions such as the relatively new .eu extension. American domain names, and many functions associated with US domain names, continue to be highly sought after by advertisers. What they are seeking in this instance is a yearly or monthly flow of income from domain registration or hosting that can last for years or decades. Some of the most lucrative businesses regarding US domain names relate to domain search, how to register a domain name, and domain hosting. The clusters of terms below are very telling in this regard and there are a lot of domain terms in the United States that are highly valued. All are important if you have content that will attract domain name searchers in the United States. The *average* CPC for following terms range from $15 to $30 USD.

Available Domain
Available Domain Name
Buy a Domain Name
Buy Domain Name
Buying Domain Names
Cheap Domain
Cheap Domain Hosting
Cheap Domain Names
Cheap Web Domains
DomainName
DomainNames
Domain Check

Domain Lookup
Domain Name Availability
Domain Name Registration Service
Domain Name Registrations
Domain Names
Domain Names Search
Domain Name Register
Domain Name Search
Domain Register
Domain Registers
Domain Registering
Domain Registrar
Domain Registration
Domain Registrations
Domain Search
Domain Searches
Get a Domain Name
Hosting
Hosting Domain Registration
How to Register a Domain Name
Inexpensive Domain
Info Domain
Low Cost Domain
Low Cost Domain Registration
Registering Domain Names
Register a Domain Name
Register Domain Names
Register Web Domain
Registering Domain Names
Registration Domain
Search Domain Name
Web Domain
Web Hosting Domains

b. US Mortgage Terms

Mortgage related terms are very popular in the United States, especially when interest rates are low. We are all familiar with most of them as consumers. The housing market continues to be hot. Both commercial and residential mortgages offer an ongoing revenue stream to the mortgagor and that is why the terms are so valued by advertisers. You will see below all the terms you would expect to see such as "Mortgage Application," "Mortgage Lenders," and "Refinancing a Mortgage." US mortgage and lending terms, and many functions associated with these US financing terms, continue to be highly sought after by advertisers. Again, what they are seeking in this instance is a yearly or monthly flow of income from a mortgage loan. The clusters of terms below are very telling in this regard. All are important if you have content that will attract mortgage and lending searchers in the United States. The *average* CPC for the following terms range from $15 to $36 USD.

Apply for Mortgage
Debt Consolidation Mortgage
Detroit Mortgage
Equity Mortgage
Indianapolis Mortgage
Kansas City Mortgage
Low Mortgage Rate
Mortgage Application
Mortgage Applications
Mortgage Broker Leads
Mortgage for People with Bad Credit
Mortgage Leads
Mortgage Loan
Mortgage Loans
Mortgage Payment Protection
Mortgage Rates
Mortgage Rate Quote
Mortgage Refinance

Mortgage Refinance Rate
No Closing Costs
No Down Payment
Pre Approval
Preapproval
Prequalify
RE Mortgage
Refi
Refinance
Refinancing
Refinancing a Mortgage
Refinancing Mortgage
Second Mortgages
Second Mortgage Rate
2nd Mortgage Loan
15 Year Mortgage Rates

c. US Online Degree Terms

Online degrees, where a student can learn over the Internet, are popular in the United States as in most countries. More and more universities are offering accredited degrees online. With online education, students benefit from learning in the comforts of their own home. They no longer have to commute or live on campus, which can substantially add to the cost of education. The rising cost of gas also makes university commuting more expensive. One of the best advantages to getting a degree over the Internet, such as a psychology degree online, is that students can attend online classes at some of the best universities in the country anywhere they have Internet access. Below is a list of the terms you would expect to see such as the general "Online Universities" to more specific areas of online education such as "Paralegal Degree Online" and "Psychology Degree Online." US online degree terms, and specific degrees associated with these US online degree terms, continue to be highly sought after by advertisers. New students provide a yearly or monthly flow of income. Classes can be much larger than traditional "presence" education where there are no building constraints. The clusters of terms below are telling in this regard. All are important if you have content that will attract online college searchers in the United States. The *average* CPC for the following terms range from $15 to $38 USD.

Accredited Online MBA
CFP Continuing Education
CFP Education
CFP Online
Colleges Online
Nurse Scholarship
Online Accounting Degree
Online College Degree
Online MBA Degree
Online Universities
Paralegal Degree Online
Psychology Degree Online
Teaching Degree Online
Universities Online

d. US Insurance Terms

The popularity of insurance products is no different in the United States than in other countries. The four main insurance categories continue to be best sellers: Auto Insurance, Health Insurance, Home Insurance, and Life Insurance. Comparative rates can be gathered quickly and easily on the Internet. Purchasers are no longer limited to their local insurance agent. Quotes are gotten free of charge from all over the United States using the Internet. Multinational companies also offer insurance quotes. While insurance products themselves are obviously popular, quotes on various insurance products are also used often. Below is a long list of popular terms in this content area such as the general “Auto Insurance Quotes” to more price specific insurance terms such as “Cheap House Insurance,” “Temporary Health Insurance,” and the life insurance product “Term Life Insurance quotes.” US insurance terms continue to be highly sought after by advertisers. Again, what they are seeking in this instance is a yearly or monthly flow of income from insurance policies in the four main categories listed above. All are important if you have content that will attract online insurance searchers in the United States. The *average* CPC for the following terms range from $15 to $50 USD.

Auto Insurance
Auto Insurance CA
Auto Insurance Quote
Auto Insurance Quotes
Best Insurance
Boat Insurance
Business Health Insurance
Car Insurance
Car Insurance California
Car Insurance Quote
Cheap Car Insurance
Cheap House Insurance
Classic Car Insurance
Discount Car Insurance
Discount Life Insurance
Group Health Insurance
Health Insurance Virginia
Health Insurance Quote
Homeowner Insurance
Homeowner's Insurance
Homeowner's Insurance
Homeowners Insurance quotes
IN Car Insurance
Instant Insurance Quote
Insurance Quotes
Insurance Young
International Health Insurance
Life Insurance

Life Insurance Leads
Life Insurance Quote
Life Insurance Quote Online
Low Cost Life Insurance
Medical Insurance
Medigap Insurance
Motorbike Insurance
Motorcycle Insurance
New York Auto Insurance
NJ Auto Insurance
Online Car Insurance
Online Insurance Quotes
Short Term Insurance
Short Term Medical Insurance
Temporary Health Insurance
Temporary Insurance
Term Life Insurance Quote
Term Life Insurance Quotes
Term Insurance
Texas Homeowners Insurance
Trip Insurance
Whole Life Insurance Quotes

e. US Legal Terms

Attorneys in the United States have a reputation for being litigious. As you may have guessed, the legal profession continues to offer some of the most lucrative content in the United States. We can bunch these into three main categories. The first is criminal defense and those terms associated with a defense attorney or criminal attorney. People accused of a crime (if they can afford it) will pay their attorneys a lot of money to stay out of jail. The second type of classification can be noticed by so called car accident attorneys or auto accident attorneys. The derogatory terms for these lawyers is "ambulance chasers." The third category of attorney related terms are focused on taxes and how to avoid them. Tax attorneys continue to be popular in the United States as in most countries. US personal injury lawyer terms continue to be highly sought after, too. Personal injury attorneys can get big fees (the percentage is usually in the range of twenty-five to fifty percent) or a share of large verdicts and they use advertising money to reflect the potential of getting new clients. All the terms below are important if you have content that will attract US online searchers in need of an attorney. The *average* CPC for the following terms range from $15 to $41 USD.

Accident Attorney
Accutane Class Action
Accutane Class Action Lawsuit
Arizona Lawyer
Attorney in Phoenix
Attorney Malpractice
Auto Accident Attorney
Auto Accident Lawyer
Benzene Lawyer
Birth Injury Lawyer
California Lawyer
Car accident Attorney
Car Accident Lawyer
Criminal Attorney
Criminal Defense Attorney
Defense Attorney
Drug Lawyer
DUI
Federal Criminal Attorney
Federal Lawyer
Florida Lawyer
Houston Lawyer
Injury Lawyer
Juvenile Lawyer
Lawyer Locator
Los Angeles Lawyer

Maryland DUI Lawyer
Medical Malpractice Lawyer
Mesothelioma Attorney
Milwaukee Lawyer
Motorcycle Accident Attorney
Orange County Lawyer
Personal Injury
Personal Injury Attorney
San Diego Lawyer
Securities Fraud Lawyer
Securities Lawyer
Slip and Fall
Tax Attorney
Vioxx Class Action
Workmans Comp Lawyer
Wrongful Death Attorney
Wrongful Death Attorneys

f. US Lemon Law Terms

Lemon law in the United States has nothing to do with fruit. Lemon laws are typically state laws that protect consumers who have purchased faulty vehicles (i.e., lemons). These lemon laws are mostly unique to the United States and may even extend to the purchase of used vehicles that are now outside the standard warranty period. You will notice that since lemon laws are state laws, many states names are listed along with the terms. Surprisingly, lemon law related terms are very lucrative so we have striped them out into a separate category. Ohio lemon law and Jersey lemon law are two of the best terms with Massachusetts Lemon Law being one of the lowest paying. Lemon law also extends to animals. The *average* CPC for the following terms range from $15 to $71 USD.

Arizona Lemon Law
Auto Lemon Law
Automobile Lemon Law

CA Lemon Law
California Lemon Laws
Car Lemon Law
Car Lemon Laws
Colorado Lemon Law
Georgia Lemon Law
Illinois Lemon Law
Indiana Lemon Law
Jersey Lemon Law
Lemmon Law
Lemon Law
Lemon Law attorney
Lemon Law attorneys
Lemon Law California
Lemon Law Florida
Lemon Law IN
Lemon Law Lawyer
Lemon Law Lawyers
Lemon Law Pennsylvania
Lemon Law Used Cars
Lemon Laws
Lemon Laws IN
Mass Lemon Law
Massachusetts Lemon Law
Michigan Lemon Law
Missouri Lemon Law
NC Lemon Law
New Jersey Lemon Law
NJ Lemon Law
North Carolina Lemon Law
Ohio Lemon Law
PA Lemon Law
Puppy Lemon Law
Tennessee Lemon Law

Texas Lemon Law
The Lemon Law
Used Car Lemon Law
Used Car Lemon Laws
Vehicle Lemon Law
Virginia Lemon Law
Wisconsin Lemon Law

g. US Mesothelioma Terms

Mesothelioma. The United States is no stranger to mesothelioma litigation. Mesothelioma is a big word for a big disease caused by asbestos exposure. The evidence of mesothelioma lung cancer does not appear for up to thirty years after the asbestos exposure. Pleural mesothelioma cancer is a type of malignant mesothelioma that affects the outer lining of the lungs. There apparently is no universal screening method for mesothelioma cancer. Driven by mesothelioma attorneys, mesothelioma terminology has become highly valued in the United States, which has a reputation for big lawsuits and big verdicts. Misspellings of the lengthy word are also popular. These include words such as “Mesotelioma,” “Mesotheloma,” and “Mesothilioma.” Mesothelioma attorneys can get big fees or a share of multimillion dollar verdicts from these types of suits, and they use advertising money to reflect the potential of getting new mesothelioma cancer clients. All the terms below are important if you have content that will attract online users in search of mesothelioma research or a mesothelioma attorney in the United States. The *average* CPC for the following terms range from $15 to $52 USD.

Asbestos Class Action
Malignant Mesothelioma
Malignant Pleural Mesothelioma
Mesothelioma
Mesothelioma Attorney
Mesothelioma Attorneys
Mesothelioma Information

Mesothelioma Lawyer
Mesothelioma lawyers
Mesothelioma Legal
Mesothelioma Prognosis
Mesothelioma Research
Mesothelioma Symptoms
Mesothelioma Treatment
Mesotelioma
Mesotheloma
Mesothilioma
Peritoneal
Peritoneal Mesothelioma
Pleural
Pleural Mesothelioma
What is Mesothelioma

h. US Cord Blood Terms

Cord blood is used to fight future and present diseases. A decade ago the term cord blood, which is blood from a baby's umbilical cord or mother's placenta, was little used. Great strides in the medical profession have uncovered the value of stem cells taken from a baby's umbilical cord or mother's placenta. Cord blood is delivered from the hospital to a cord blood center that tests the blood, reports on any diseases, and stores it to be used in the future if needed. Private cord blood banks charge a few thousand dollars for collection and then ongoing storage fees. The number of highly valued cord blood terms is not limited in the United States. The terms below are important if you have content that will attract US online users in search of cord blood research or a cord blood bank. Storage of cord blood can last for decades. It is interesting that there are no misspellings of the long word "umbilical." The *average* CPC for the following terms range from $15 to $46 USD.

Baby Cord Blood
Cell Cord Blood

Cord Blood
Cord Blood America
Cord Blood Bank
Cord Blood Banking
Cord Blood Banks
Cord Blood Cells
Cord Blood Collection
Cord Blood Donation
Cord Blood Donations
Cord Blood Preservation
Cord Blood Program
Cord Blood Registry
Cord Blood Research
Cord Blood Services
Cord Blood Stem Cell
Cord Blood Stem Cells
Cord Blood Storage
Cord Blood Transplant
Cord Blood Transplants
Cord Donation
Donate Cord Blood
Donating Cord Blood
New England Cord Blood
Public Cord Blood Bank
Saving Cord Blood
Umbilical Blood
Umbilical Cord Blood
Umbilical Cord Blood Bank
Umbilical Cord Blood Banking

i. US Laser Hair Removal Terms

Hair removal is increasingly popular. No one wants hair in unwanted areas and many are looking to rid the constant use of tweezers and razors. Permanent hair removal has become an obsession in many parts of the world. America is no exception and laser hair removal is the most popular. This is especially true in areas near the ocean. The prime season for hair removal procedures is early spring. In the United States, laser hair removal is both popular and expensive like other countries. Patients are typically charged for each session of permanent hair removal, which can take numerous visits for just a small area. These ongoing hair removal treatments, which may address only a patch of skin at a time, are costly and typically not covered by medical insurance. Since permanent laser hair removal is expensive and repetitive in the United States, doctors are willing to pay larger advertising sums to attract new clients and this is where you benefit. The terms below are important if you have content that will attract US online users in search of laser hair removal procedures. Note how many of them are linked to various states or large cities. Also keep in mind that hair removal equipment itself costs a lot of money and therefore attracting doctors and medical professionals who may purchase this equipment is desirable online. The *average* CPC for the following terms range from $15 to $49 USD.

Beverly Hills Plastic Surgeons
Cosmetic Surgery Birmingham
Cost of Laser Hair Removal
Facial Hair Removal
Hair Removal
Hair Removals
Hair Removal Atlanta
Hair Removal Boston
Hair Removal Chicago
Hair Removal Cost
Hair Removal Dallas
Hair Removal DC
Hair Removal Equipment
Hair Removal Houston
Hair Removal Los Angeles
Hair Removal Machine

Hair Removal NY
Hair Removal Michigan
Hair Removal New York City
Hair Removal Orlando
Hair Removal San Diego
Hair Removal San Francisco
Hair Removal Virginia
Laser Hair Removal
Laser Hair Removal Atlanta
Laser Hair Removal Boston
Laser Hair Removal Chicago
Laser Hair Removal Clinic
Laser Hair Removal Cost
Laser Hair Removal Costs
Laser Hair Removal Michigan
Laser Hair Removal New York
Laser Hair Removal NYC
Laser Hair Removal NJ
Laser Hair Removal Prices
Laser Hair Removal San Francisco
Lazer Hair Removal
Lasor Hair Removal
Permanent Hair Removal

j. US Secured Loan Terms

In the United States, as in most countries, secured loans are used often and are very popular in the consumer services industry. Secured loans are loans guaranteed by property that is used as collateral for the loan. If the purchaser should default on the loan, the lender for the property will receive the collateral, which is forfeited by the purchaser. There are many types of secured loans in the United States with personal debit consolidation loans—typically to pay off higher interest rate loans such as credit card and student debt—and mortgage loans being the most popular. Non-secured loans, which typically charge higher interest rates because the loan is unsecured, are popular in the consumer debt arena. Use the secured loan terms and non-secured loan terms below in your content to attract online Internet users in search of various types of secured loans in the United States. The *average* CPC for the following terms range from $15 to $42 USD.

Best Secured Loan
Cheap Secured Loan
Consolidate
Consolidate Debt
Consolidating
Consolidation
Debit Consolidation
Debit Consolidation Secured Loan
Debt Buster
Debt Consolidation
Debtbuster
Fast Secured Loans
Loans Unsecured
Low Interest Rate
Non Secured Loan
Non Secured Loans
Secured
Secured Lender
Secured Loan
Secured Loan Calculator
Secured Loan Rates
Secured Loan
Un Secured Loan
Un Secured Loans
Unsecured Consolidation Loan
Unsecured Consolidation Loans
Unsecured Debt Consolidation Loan
Unsecured Debt Consolidation Loans
Secured

CONTENT FIRST, ADSENSE SECOND

Content is king on AdSense and queen and prince and princess and . . . Do not create an AdSense site and try to add content around the adds. Instead, create a great "sticky" Website that has a targeted user base returning time and time again and then include your ads for much higher click rates.

C. Buy Generic Domain Names

We all remember the hay days of the Internet's infancy when domain names were hot properties and the top ones were fetching hundreds or even millions of dollars. Now, with the vast revenue potential of AdSense, registering domain names based upon the highest paying keywords can be very profitable. Why are domain names so hot when it is the content on the pages that trigger AdSense ads? The answer is simple: potential customers searching for content on a certain keyword are likely to type that keyword in as a URL first. For example, a person inquiring about the effects of Teflon may type in www.teflondangers.com. The owner can then display AdSense ads related to any adverse health effects Teflon may have and get click revenues.

PICK KEYWORD-RELEVANT DOMAIN NAMES

If you want to take AdSense publishing to the next level, register key domain names for top-paying keywords. Even if you are unable to obtain one, use the keyword in the extension of your domain such as: www.[website].com/[top-paying-keyword].htm

XI. AdSense Reports

Google has provided a number of free and powerful reporting tools to help you track nearly every aspect of your AdSense campaign. The Reports tab has three subsections.

A. Overview

Within the Overview section, you will be shown a snapshot of today's earnings covering AdSense for Content, AdSense for Search, and Referrals. This is the screen you are shown as soon as you log into your AdSense account. Google wants to prominently display how much you are earning through AdSense.

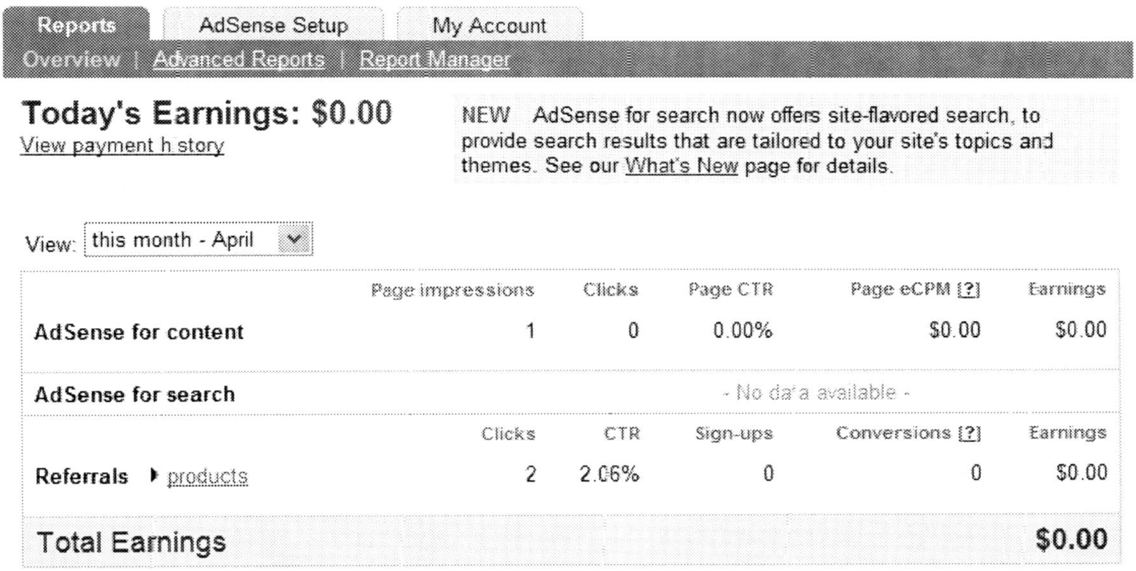

This is a great way to quickly view your earnings and it is the reports section you will likely visit the most. Also included are page impressions your Ad Units have received, effective CPM, and earnings for various time periods. The time period "Today" is preset and you cannot make another time period as the default in the Overview Report.

Overview Time Periods
Today Yesterday Last 7 Days This Month Last Month All Time/Since Last Payment

"SINCE LAST PAYMENT" DESIGNATION

If you have not received any click revenues from Google, you will see the "All Time" reporting option drop down. Once revenues are received, the "All Time" reporting option will be replaced with the "Since Last Payment" designation.

The Overview subsection of the Reports tab also enables you to expand AdSense for Content and AdSense for Search reports in include channel data.

CHANNEL REPORT DELAYS

Channel report data is delayed two days. So keep in mind that the Channel data you are receiving is from two days ago.

B. Quick Reports

Quick Reports are displayed directly beneath the Overview Reports and they provide a way to generate .CSV formatted files that can be imported into spreadsheet programs such as Microsoft Excel. You can view reports by "This month, by day" or "Last month, by day" by either AdSense for Content or Search.

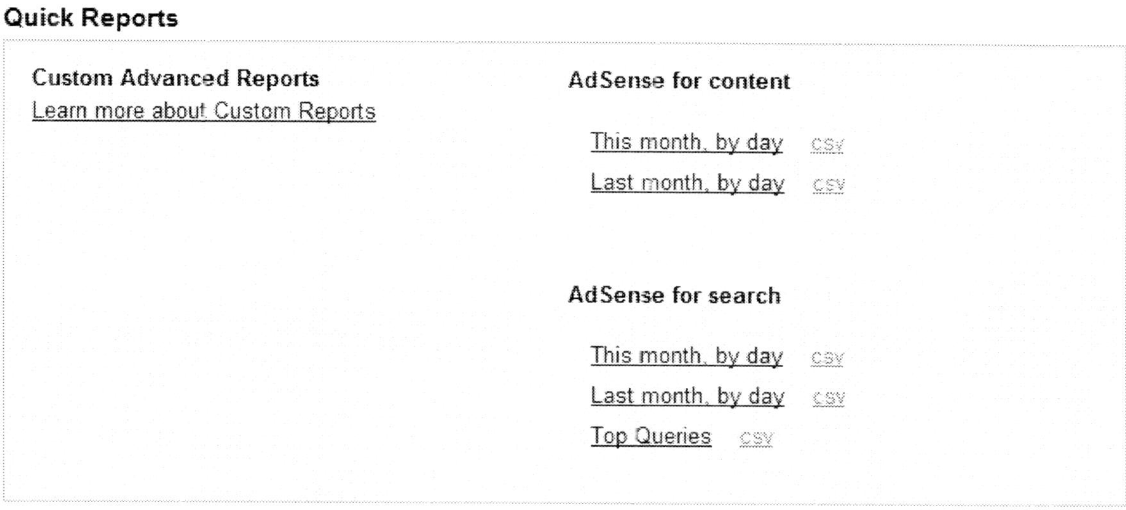

"TOP QUERIES" – ADSENSE FOR SEARCH

The AdSense for Search Quick Report provides an addition category of the "Top Queries" used on your site. It can also be created in the .CSV file format.

C. Advanced Reports

Advanced reports are very powerful. With them you can show data by Website page or by Ad Unit. With Advanced Reports you can also pick any date range, unlike the Overview Reports. You can also display aggregate ad data or Channel data by selecting the proper radio button on the advanced reports page.

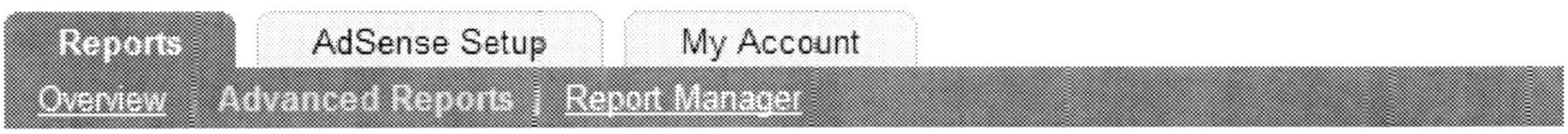

1. Advanced Content Network Reports

With Advanced Reports you can also find out if AdWord advertisers are using Site Targeting to focus on your Website by serving ads under the CPM model. Below you will see that to gather this information you simply "Show data by Individual Ad Unit" and then click the box next to "Show data by targeting type."

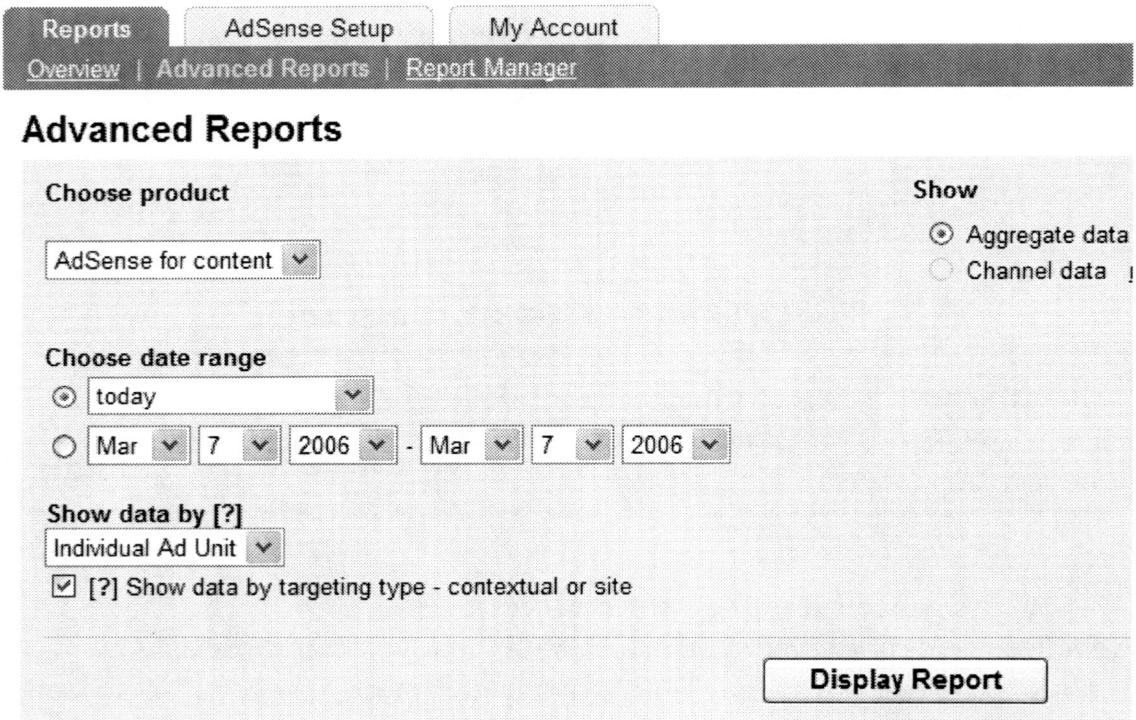

The displayed report will allow you to differentiate between which ads are on a Cost-Per-Click and which are on a Cost-Per-Impression model (i.e., general Content Network targeting versus Site Targeting).

We've established that if you have selected both Contextual Targeting and Site Targeting, Google will fill your Ad Units with ads paying the highest eCPM. If a Site Targeted ad wins out, its eCPM must be greater than the combined eCPM of the multiple ads it is replacing for that Ad Unit.

Sometimes you may see in your reports that a Site Targeted eCPM is lower than a CPC Ad Unit and wonder why since CPC ads are the default unless a CPM ad has a higher eCPM. The explanation for this anomaly is simple. One page of your site may have content where normal CPC ads will get you the highest eCPM (say $3) and the content on another page may get you the highest eCPM (say $2) with Site Targeted ads. You can always rest assured that Google's computer algorithms are working hard to make you the most money on AdSense. If you make the most money off AdSense, so does Google since it gets a cut of the revenues. That is how you *truly* know Google wants you to make the most money!

2. Advanced AdSense Search Reports

Like the other advanced reports, the advanced AdSense for Search report allows you to display general data for clicks or top queries that are inputted on your site. Knowing what your users are searching for is important to creating the product or services mix and also for adjusting the content mix on your site. You can also view Channel data if you have Channels enabled.

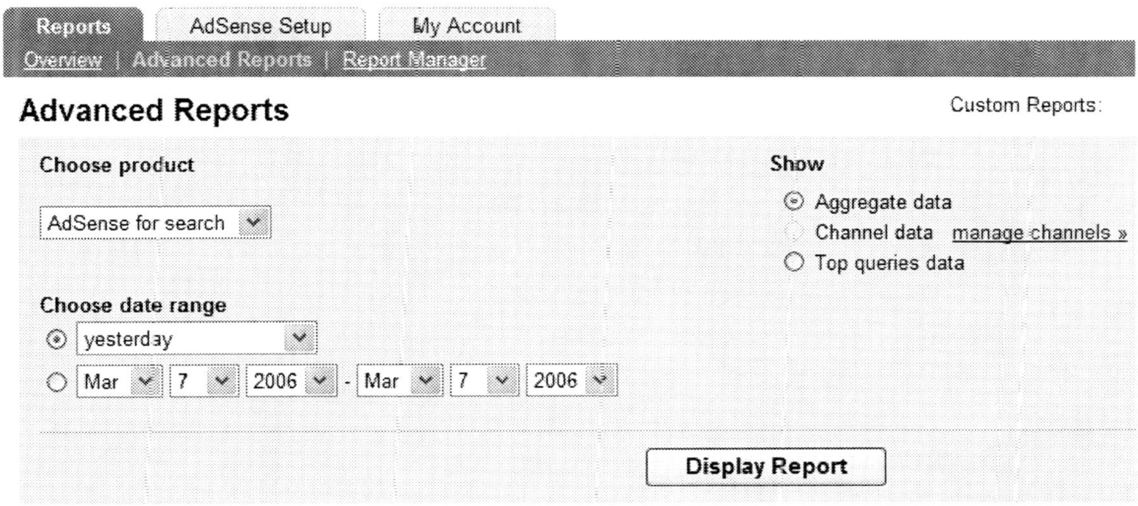

3. Advanced Referrals Reports

The Referrals Advanced Report will allow you to see a snapshot of earnings for the AdSense referrals button or text you have placed on your Website.

View conversions, earnings, referral clicks, and signups over a number of date ranges.

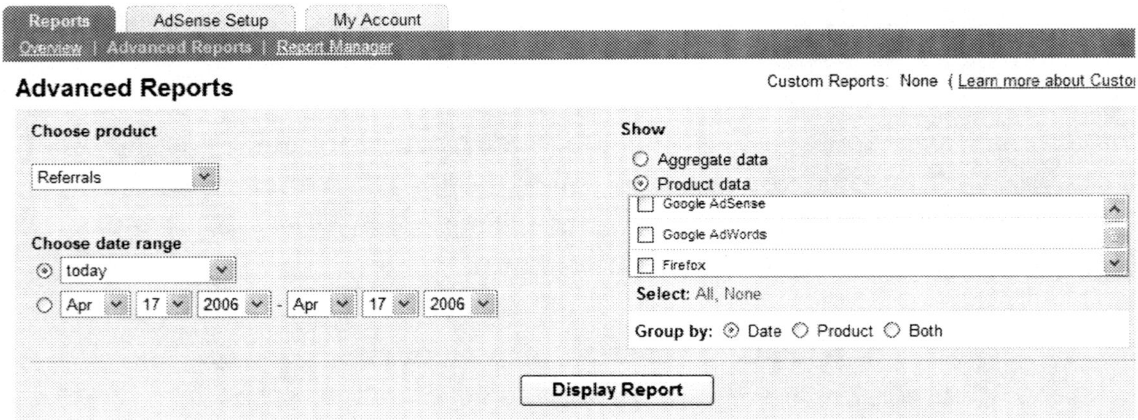

If you want to get specific, you can view data from the Google AdSense referral button(s), Google AdWords referral buttons, or the Firefox with Google Toolbar downloads by selecting "Product Data" as shown above. Your Website tracking software may register more impression than shown in your AdSense account. That is because Google only counts an impression when a user's browser activates the AdSense JavaScript.

When Google Will Not Count Ad Impressions
➢ Crawlers, Robots & Spiders from Non-Google Search Engines
➢ Browser Not JavaScript Enabled
➢ Browser Doesn't Support JavaScript
➢ Browser Doesn't Support iFrame HTML tag
➢ Script Written to Copy Website Content

D. Report Manager

This is where you can save your custom generated, advanced reports. Once saved, you can have these reports run automatically and be emailed to you on a periodic basis that you designate. It is a huge timesaver that will let you focus on building the content on your site.

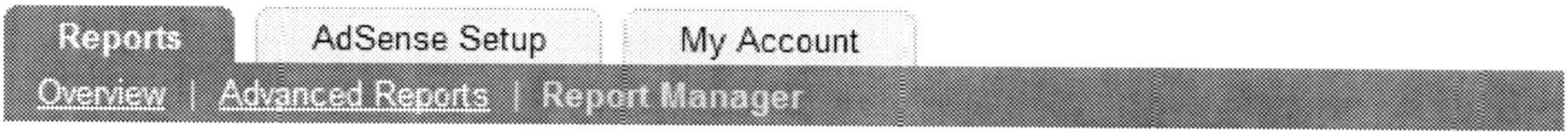

REPORTING DAYS

Google sends monthly reports on the first day of the month regardless of whether it is a weekday or holiday. Weekly reports are not sent on the first day of the week, but rather on Monday.

You can designate one or more email addresses that will receive your custom reports. This is beneficial if you have someone managing your AdSense account.

E. Payment History

Upon reaching your first $100 USD in click revenues, Google will display a Payment History subsection beneath the Reports tab that will let you track all data relating your payments, including the exchange rate on the day the check was cut or the EFT payment was wired. Google will break down the earnings by AdSense for Content, AdSense for Search, and AdSense for Referrals.

SAVE A FEW TREES

Instead of printing your AdSense reports periodically, use the date periods Google provides to run your reports. They will never disappear online and you can save a few trees in the process!

XII. The Google AdSense Intellectual Property

We all know that Google is a high tech company loaded with lots of smart employees. The foundation for any high tech company is its intellectual property portfolio. Intellectual property can best be described as intangible assets of a company such as ideas, know-how, patents, patent applications, trademarks, copyrights, and trade secrets. Google has a few of these up its sleeve and we will discuss its publicly disclosed AdSense patents and patent applications below, which provide great insight into the logic behind searching content on Websites and serving ads under the AdSense program.

A. The Google AdSense Patents

In 2003 Google acquired a company named Applied Semantics based in Los Angeles, California. Applied Semantics focused much of its efforts on "meaning-based" Internet searches. They have two U.S. patents in this area: US 6,816,857 entitled "Meaning-Based Advertising and Document Relevance Determination" and US 6,453,315 entitled "Meaning-Based Information Organization and Retrieval." Both patents disclose that "[I]nstead of simply indexing words that appear in target documents, and allowing users to find desired word instances within documents or an index, searches are instead conducted within the realm of 'semantic space', allowing users to locate information that is 'close in meaning' to the concepts they are interested in." In other words, this allows ads to be served to your Ad Units that are in the same subject category of the content on your page. If you would like to view the full text and methodology used in these patents, follow this link: www.uspto.gov and search for the patent numbers above. Here are links to the respective patents online: http://patft1.uspto.gov/netacgi/nph-Parser?Sect1=PTO2&Sect2=HITOFF&p=1&u=%2Fnetahtml%2FPTO%2Fsearch-bool.html&r=1&f=G&l=50&co1=AND&d=PTXT&s1=6,816,857.PN.&OS=PN/6,816,857&RS=PN/6,816,857 and http://patft1.uspto.gov/netacgi/nph-Parser?Sect1=PTO2&Sect2=HITOFF&p=1&u=%2Fnetahtml%2FPTO%2Fsearch-bool.html&r=1&f=G&l=50&co1=AND&d=PTXT&s1=6,453,315.PN.&OS=PN/6,453,315&RS=PN/6,453,315.

B. The Google AdSense Patent Application

At present, Google has a *pending* patent application that provides insight into the various ways it analyses the text on a publisher's Website to link it with ads. The first is by looking at the obvious, which is the text and title of the publisher's Website. Alternatively, Google can assign each term on the Website a relevance factor and the term must appear N times for it to be considered as relevant. Google may also weight terms. Those that do not appear very often may be given more weight than those appearing frequently such as the word "and" for example. It appears that Google is using a combination of these to serve its AdSense ads. You can read Google's pending patent application titled "Methods and Apparatus for Serving Relevant Advertisements" on file with the U.S. Patent Office under Application No. 20040059708 by following this link: www.uspto.gov and searching for patent application with this title or number. Here is a link to the patent application online: http://appft1.uspto.gov/netacgi/nph-Parser?Sect1=PTO2&Sect2=HITOFF&p=1&u=%2Fnetahtml%2FPTO%2Fsearch-bool.html&r=10&f=G&l=50&co1=AND&d=PG01&s1=google.AS.&OS=AN/google&RS=AN/google.

XIII. How to Keep Users Coming Back for More

The key to any successful AdSense Website is to keep the traffic flowing . . . not just with new users, but also with repeat users. If you do not protect your base of frequent users, you will not be able to maximize your click revenue. Here are two great ways to keep users coming back for more.

A. Keep Content Fresh

The content on a Website is like food, you can have the best in the world but if visitors to your Web restaurant always have to eat leftovers, they are going to stop visiting. Internet users want fresh, hot content that is tasty. That's why Blogs are so successful when done right. The content is constantly updated. So keep your content fresh, hot and tasty to get return users.

FLOW ARTICLES AROUND ADS

A great way to clicks on ads is to place them in the middle of an article such that that text flows around the ad. Only one ad per article is recommended to prevent ad overload.

B. Publish Free Articles

It is a little known fact that another great way to add relevant content to your Website is to publish *free* articles that are available on the Web. That's right, there are thousands of Web articles available for free on the Internet. Simply conduct a Google search on the terms "free articles" and "free content articles" to pull up a listing of sites offering these articles for free. Of course, you can always write your own articles.

FREE ARTICLE SITE

A great site with free content articles can be found at www.isnare.com.

By conducting a Google search you can also find Websites that are already developed with content. You merely have to purchase the site and set up your AdSense code.

C. Add Free Video Content

Gone are the days of static Web pages. Google now lets you, the AdSense publisher, embed Google Video content on *your* Website. Unless you are in the multimedia business, this at first may not seem of relevance. Consider, however, that Google Video has tens of thousands of videos in its digital archive on tons of topics.

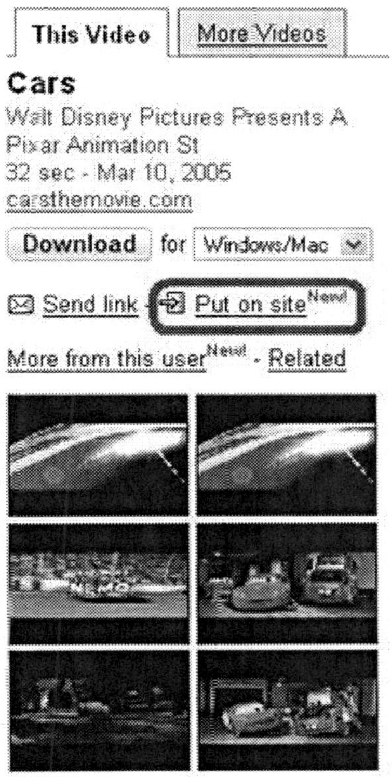

Simply visit www.video.google.com and search for the "Put on site" link on any video playback page. Once you have added the video HTML to your page, users can play the video directly without having to download any software.

IXV. More AdSense Tips & Tricks

A. Digital Millennium Copyright Act Infringement

If you believe that content has been copied from your Website, you may notify Google under the Digital Millennium Copyright Act ("DMCA") provisions at: http://www.google.com/adsense_dmca.html

DMCA NOTIFICATION MUST BE IN WRITING

Notice to Google of DMCA infringement must be in writing (email is not allowed).

B. How to Get Free AdSense Support

Google provides a couple of avenues where you can get free AdSense support. The email addresses are listed below.

FREE ADSENSE SUPPORT

If you have an issue, just send your question to adsense-support@google.com or adsense-tech@google.com. Google does not offer AdSense telephone support.

C. AdSense Tips at the AdSense Blog

A great way to learn the latest AdSense news is the AdSense Blog.

VISIT THE ENGLISH ADSENSE BLOG

Google has created a great AdSense Blog at http://adsense.blogspot.com/ that will keep you up to date on the latest strategies. You can even input your email address and Google will send you AdSense updates as they are created.

VISIT THE GERMAN ADSENSE BLOG

If you speak German, the AdSense group has created a sister Blog called "Inside AdSense: Das offizielle deutsche AdSense-Blog." You can subscribe by sending a blank email to inside-adsense-de@googlegroups.com.

D. Visit the AdSense Help Group

Google has started an AdSense help forum via Google Groups. Visit it for some of the latest help information.

VISIT THE ADSENSE BLOG

Subscribe to the AdSense Help Group by sending an email to: Inside-AdSense@googlegroups.com or visit http://groups.google.com/group/Inside-AdSense.

E. AdSense Help Button

Remember the AdSense Help Button that is located in the upper-right corner of your AdSense account.

USE THE ADSENSE HELP BUTTON

Any time you are logged into your AdSense account you can easily type a term into the "Search AdSense Help" box and click the button to be enlightened.

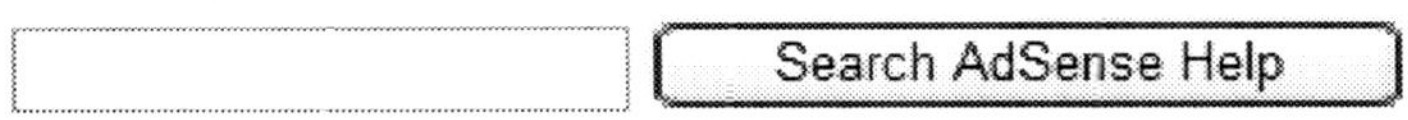

F. Get Expert Technical Help

If you are an SEO, Google's Webmaster Frequently Asked Questions site is for you.

VISIT GOOGLE'S WEBMASTER FAQ SITE

> You can often find great tips (they are on the technical side) on Google's Webmaster FAQ site: http://www.google.com/webmasters/seo.html.

G. Report an AdSense Violation

If you see a Website that is violating the AdSense Terms & Conditions, you can report it to Google by following the steps below.

Policy Violation Reporting Steps
1. Draft an email with "AdSense Policy Violation" as the heading. Preferably use the email address associated with your AdSense account, which is found under the "Account Preferences" tab. 2. Include the following details in the body of the email message: ➢ URL where you noticed the violation ➢ Description of the violation 3. Send email to: adsense-abuse@google.com

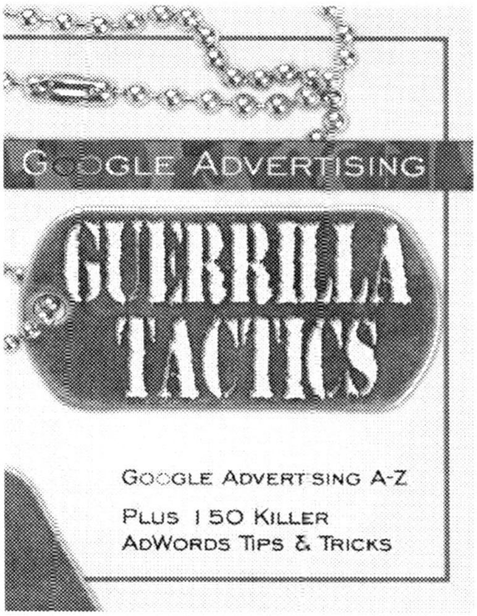

Google Advertising Guerrilla Tactics

Google Advertising A-Z Plus 150 Killer AdWords Tips & Tricks

"Google Advertising Guerrilla Tactics" is an extensive guide on all aspects of Google advertising and provides over 150 killer tips and tricks for getting the most clicks at the lowest cost. Stop wasting AdWords money and learn the guerrilla tactics you need to beat your competition. Here are but a few of the topics covered: How to Get Free AdWords Coupons - Breaking Down the Quality Score to Get More Clicks and Higher Ranking at Less Cost-Per-Click - Bid Traps: How to Prevent and Exploit Them - Vital Ad Stylization Techniques - Where to Find Keywords Your Competitors Will Not Think to Look - Ways to Use Abbreviations, Plurals and Misspellings - Most Popular Search Terms for Over 15 Holidays - Best Image Ad Sizes - Image Ad Colors that Will Wreck Your Campaign - Site Target Your Way to Quick Success - Search and Content Network Bid Strategies - How to Use Froogle, Google Base, Google Book Search, Google Catalogs, and Zeitgeist to Get Free Sales Conversions - The Key to Getting #1 Placement on Google - Industry Examples of Crucial Advertising Do's and Don'ts. If you want to beat your competition by getting more AdWords clicks at the lowest cost then "Google Advertising Guerrilla Tactics" is a must.

Book $13.98 | eBook $12.98
www.bottletreebooks.com/GuerrillaTactics.htm

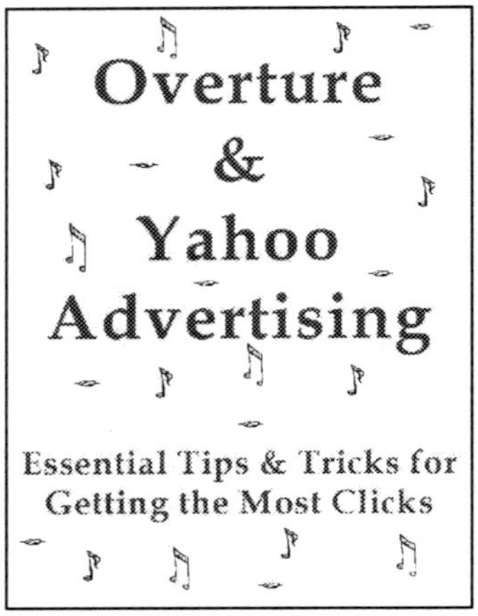

Overture & Yahoo Advertising

Plus 110 Tips & Tricks for Getting the Most Clicks

Do you want to learn the ins and outs of Overture and Yahoo advertising to make your products and services available for up to 275 million searches per day? Do you want to take advantage of 110 tips and tricks to dominate selling on Overture and Yahoo? Whether you are new to Pay-Per-Click advertising or a seasoned marketer, Overture and Yahoo Advertising will show you how in a quick and easy format loaded with charts, guides, hyperlinks to free Internet advertising tools, tables and 110 tips and tricks to maximizing your Return-on-Investment. See why Pay-Per-Click advertising is exploding on the Internet and why small businesses worldwide are adopting it as their primary sales tool. Here is but a sampling of the topics covered: Bid traps - How to exploit and avoid them - Get free Overture coupons worth up to $50 - How to get a Premium Listing without bidding in the top 3 spots - The Yahoo Premium Listing exception - Secrets of Content Match - The CNN Premium Listing exception - How to list your business for free on Yahoo's Local Match - Examples of great ad titles - The best keyword placement within the Bodylines - Definitive ad stylization - Tricks to keyword plurals and misspellings - Guide to Overture foreign countries and languages - 25 examples of ads that work on Yahoo and those that don't - Commonly overlooked Yahoo advertising programs - How to budget and control your monthly spending - And a whole lot more. . .

Book $14.98 | eBook $10.98

www.bottletreebooks.com/OvertureAdvertisingPages.htm

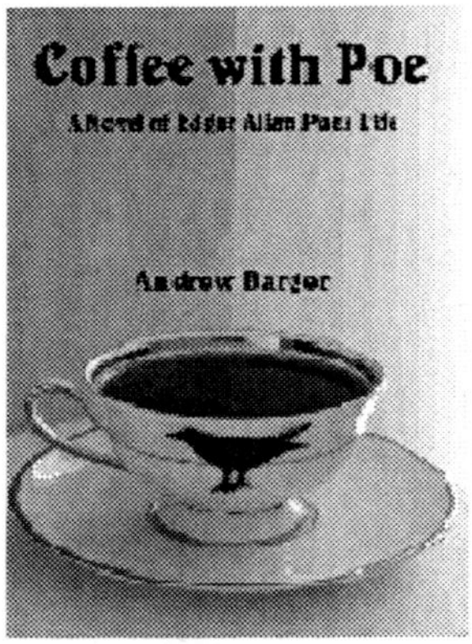
Coffee with Poe
Andrew Barger

Printed in the United States
121247LV00003B/14/A